COLLEGE MATHEMATICS
FOR BUSINESS

COLLEGE MATHEMATICS FOR BUSINESS

Elizabeth Bliss

Prentice Hall
Englewood Cliffs, New Jersey 07632

LIBRARY OF CONGRESS
Library of Congress Cataloging-in-Publication Data

Bliss, Elizabeth.
   College mathematics for business / Elizabeth Bliss.
      p.   cm.
   Includes index.
   ISBN 0-13-150186-0
   1. Business mathematics.   I. Title.
HF5691.B664 1989
512'.1--dc19   88-22479
                                                            CIP

Editorial/production supervision and
   interior design: Linda Zuk
Cover design: Ben Santora
Manufacturing buyer: Ed O'Dougherty

 © 1989 by Prentice-Hall, Inc.
A Division of Simon & Schuster
Englewood Cliffs, New Jersey 07632

Printed in the United States of America

10 9 8 7 6 5 4 3 2 1

ISBN 0-13-150186-0

Prentice-Hall International (UK) Limited, *London*
Prentice-Hall of Australia Pty. Limited, *Sydney*
Prentice-Hall Canada Inc., *Toronto*
Prentice-Hall Hispanoamericana, S.A., *Mexico*
Prentice-Hall of India Private Limited, *New Delhi*
Prentice-Hall of Japan, Inc., *Tokyo*
Simon & Schuster Asia Pte. Ltd., *Singapore*
Editora Prentice-Hall do Brasil, Ltda., *Rio de Janeiro*

CONTENTS

PREFACE   ix

Chapter 0
REVIEW OF ARITHMETIC AND ALGEBRA   1
0.1 Order of Operations 2
0.2 Arithmetic Operations on Signed Numbers 7
0.3 Distributive Property 14
0.4 Solving Equations 18
0.5 Ratio and Proportion 25
0.6 Percent 31
0.7 Exponents and Roots 38
0.8 Rounding and Significant Digits 42

Chapter 1
PERCENT   47
1.1 Percent Equation 48
1.2 Simple Interest 60
1.3 Bank Discount 69
1.4 Trade and Cash Discounts 76
1.5 Markup and Markdown 86
1.6 Payroll 97
1.7 Taxes 102
1.8 Financial Statement Analysis 108
1.9 Ratio and Proportion 121
      Summary 128
      Review Exercises 129

Chapter 2
COMPOUND INTEREST   133
2.1 Compound Amount   134
2.2 Present Value, Rate, and Time   142
2.3 Effective Interest Rate   151
2.4 Equations of Value   154
2.5 Economic Analysis   159
     Summary   165
     Review Exercises   166

Chapter 3
ANNUITIES   169
3.1 Ordinary Annuity   170
3.2 Present Value   178
3.3 Variations in Annuities   184
3.4 Periodic Payment   191
     Summary   198
     Review Exercises   198

Chapter 4
AMORTIZATION AND SINKING FUNDS   203
4.1 Finding Payment of Amortized Debt   204
4.2 Outstanding Principal   211
4.3 Sinking Funds   219
4.4 Bonds   223
4.5 Comparison of Debt and Repayment   230
     Summary   235
     Review Exercises   236

Chapter 5
ACCOUNTING COMPUTATIONS   239
5.1 Depreciation   240
5.2 Comparison of Depreciation Methods   250
5.3 Overhead   254
5.4 Inventory   260
5.5 Capitalized Cost   266
     Summary   269
     Review Exercises   271

Chapter 6
INSURANCE   277
6.1   Fire Insurance   278
6.2   Motor Vehicle Insurance   284
6.3   Life Insurance   290
6.4   Group Insurance   303
      Summary   304
      Review Exercises   305

Chapter 7
STATISTICAL METHODS   309
7.1   Frequency Distributions   310
7.2   Measures of Central Tendency   322
7.3   Measures of Dispersion   329
7.4   Normal Curve   338
7.5   Other Types of Graphs   347
      Summary   357
      Review Exercises   359

Chapter 8
STRAIGHT-LINE GRAPHS   367
8.1   Line Graphs   368
8.2   Linear Models   378
8.3   Slope   391
8.4   Best Line Fit for Data   407
      Summary   414
      Review Exercises   416

Chapter 9
PATTERNS, SEQUENCES, AND SERIES   423
9.1   Arithmetic Sequences   424
9.2   Geometric and Recursive Sequences   430
9.3   Series and Sigma Notation   439
9.4   Applications   445
      Summary   450
      Review Exercises   451

Chapter 10
MATRIX ALGEBRA   455
10.1   Matrix Arithmetic   456
10.2   Inverse Matrices   464
10.3   Solution of Linear Systems   472
10.4   Applications   479
       Summary   489
       Review Exercises   490

Chapter 11
LINEAR PROGRAMMING   495
11.1   Graphical Solution for Linear Inequalities   496
11.2   Graphical Solution to Linear Programming   501
11.3   Simplex Method   508
11.4   Solution of Minimization Problems   516
11.5   Transportation and Assignment Problems   522
       Review Exercises   534

Appendix
MATHEMATICAL TABLES   539
Table 1   The Number of Each Day of Year   540
Table 2   Compound Amounts And Values for Annuity Quantities   541
Table 3   Area Under Standard Normal Curve   562

INDEX   563

PREFACE

College Mathematics for Business is designed for students in business, accounting, and management programs. The text covers all precalculus topics required by business. The prerequisite skill is elementary algebra. For the student with a weak mathematics background, Chapter 0 provides a review of the concepts used in the text.

MAIN FEATURES

The development of the text is based on mathematical concepts. A concept is presented, and all applications of the developed concept follow. The student has the opportunity to use a concept in many different but similar settings. Terminology is emphasized throughout the text with important terms carefully introduced. Analogies among business applications are noted to provide the student with an understanding of the relationship among topics. Calculator usage is addressed throughout. Keystroke sequences are included in examples in most chapters. Traditional annuity tables are included in the appendix; the method of generating the values with the calculator is presented as well.

The chapters flow logically; each presentation builds on mastered techniques to new concepts. Examples are used to introduce concepts as well as to clarify and illustrate concepts previously presented. The style is informal and nonrigorous. Each chapter commences with an introduction giving an overview of the concepts in the chapter, a justification for the materials to the business student, and expected student outcomes after completion of the materials.

Each chapter includes a summary of formulas, applications, and vocabulary for easy reference. The chapter review exercises follow the summary; answers to all review exercises are provided. Each exercise set is numbered according to the section it follows. The even-numbered problems are generally equivalent to the odd-numbered problems; answers to the odd-numbered problems follow the exercises.

The organization of the book allows flexibility in chapter selection and sequencing. The first five chapters provide the background necessary for the remaining chapters. The chapters on insurance, statistical methods, straight line graphs, sequences, matrix algebra, and linear programming are independent presentations. Order and selection should be made to suit the needs of the students.

Supplementary materials include a student supplement with worked-out solutions and helpful study tips. An Instructor's Manual with answers to all exercises, chapter tests, commentaries and teaching tips is also available. Masters for transparencies showing solutions to some problems in each exercise set are included in the Instructor's Manual.

Acknowledgments

The author wishes to acknowledge the many helpful comments and suggestions provided during the preparation of the book. The students in my classes vocalized needs I have attempted to address, and my colleagues at Trident Technical College have given valuable direction. Comments from these reviewers shaped the final results: Charles F. Dye, York College of Pennsylvania; Paul C. Eberhardt, Vice President of Human Resources, Bryant and Stratton; David C. Frank, Corning Community College; Rex Bishop, Charles County Community College; Patricia Eyer, Northern Virginia Community College; and Charles W. Cooper, San Antonio College. The staff at Prentice Hall, especially Susan Jacobs, has provided guidance and encouragement. To all of these people and to many more unnamed individuals, thank you for your comments and suggestions, encouragement, and prodding. Finally, my husband Jay deserves special commendation for his encouragement, sacrifice, and suggestions throughout the writing of this text.

Chapter 0

REVIEW OF ARITHMETIC AND ALGEBRA

This chapter consists of a brief review of the operations involving numbers and algebraic expressions. The material in this book is based on the concepts of this chapter. A thorough understanding of the material presented in this chapter will prepare the student for the material covered in the following chapters. The organization of the material differs from many traditional texts. Arithmetic and algebraic operations are presented together—relating manipulative operations in arithmetic with like operations in algebra. The presentation should help the student in understanding and applying the mathematics needed for this course.

At the end of this chapter, the student will be able to:

1. Apply the order of operations to multioperation computations.

2. Perform addition, subtraction, multiplication, and division involving signed numbers, algebraic terms, fractions, and expressions within grouping symbols.

3. Apply the distributive property to monomials, binomials, and trinomials.

4. Solve linear equations for unknowns.

5. Determine ratios between quantities and solve proportions.

6. Solve problems involving percent.

7. Apply exponents and roots to numerical expressions.

8. Compare values of numbers and round answers to required accuracy.

0.1   ORDER OF OPERATIONS

One of the most powerful, and also frustrating, properties of arithmetic and algebra is uniqueness in correct answers. The answer can be written in a variety of ways—fraction, decimal, mixed number—but all represent the same quantity. To ensure uniqueness, a set of universally accepted rules dictate the order of operations performed in a calculation.

Example

$$8 - 4 \times 3 + 10 \div 5 = ?$$

The correct answer is -2.

The memory aid My Dear Aunt Sally (Multiply Divide Add Subtract) is a device for remembering the hierarchy of the four arithmetic operations.

Returning to the example, the multiplication and division operations are completed in the order the operations occur in the problem as one goes from left to right. Thus 12 replaces 4×3 and 2 replaces $10 \div 5$. The new problem is $8 - 12 + 2$.

Addition and subtraction are performed in the order the operations occur as one reads from left to right.

$$-4 + 2 = -2$$

The operations of percent, exponent, and root precede the arithmetic operations.

Example

$$3^2 \times 40\% + 20 \div 5 - 1$$

First, % means $\div 100$: $40 \div 100 = 0.40$. The second operation is an exponent: $3^2 = 9$. The problem can now be written as

$$9 \times 0.40 + 20 \div 5 - 1$$

Perform multiplications and divisions next and then the additions and subtractions.

$$3.6 + 4 - 1 = 6.6$$

The example contained only arithmetic operations; algebraic expressions obey the same rules.

$$4 + 2 \cdot x + y \div 3$$

$$2 \cdot x = 2x \qquad y \div 3 = \frac{y}{3}$$

Answer: $4 + 2x + y/3$.

The only override to the order-of-operations rule is a grouping symbol. Any grouping symbol indicates the operations within the set of parentheses are performed first, using the rules for the order of operations within the parentheses. Next the order-of-operations rule is applied to the expression without the parentheses.

Example

$$2 + 3(8 \div 2 + 6 \cdot 2) - 10 \cdot 5$$

First, determine the value within the parentheses.

$$8 \div 2 + 6 \cdot 2 = 4 + 12 = 16$$

Write the expression with the parentheses replaced by the value of 16.

$$2 + 3 \cdot 16 - 10 \cdot 5$$

Next, perform the multiplications and divisions and write the expression as:

$$2 + 48 - 50$$

Perform the additions and subtractions to obtain an answer of 0.

Example

$$1,000(1 + 20\% \cdot 7) + 5,000 \div 2$$

Replace the % by $\div 100$.

$$1,000(1 + 20 \div 100 \cdot 7) + 5,000 \div 2$$

Within parentheses, perform multiplications and divisions.

$$1{,}000(1 + 1.40) + 5{,}000 \div 2$$

The expression within parentheses is replaced by 2.40.

$$1{,}000 \cdot 2.40 + 5{,}000 \div 2$$

Multiply and divide. Then add.

$$2{,}400 + 2{,}500 = 4{,}900$$

Example

$$b - 3(b - 4) + 1$$

b and 4 cannot be subtracted and the expression is kept. Multiply the expression $b - 4$ by 3.

$$3 \cdot b - 3 \cdot 4 = 3b - 12$$

$3b - 12$ is subtracted from b. Subtraction in algebra means changing the sign of the quantity subtracted.

$$b - (3b - 12) = b - 3b + 12$$

Combine like terms.

$$b - 3b = -2b$$

Add 12.

$$-2b + 12$$

Add 1 as indicated in the original problem.

$$-2b + 12 + 1$$

Combine like terms $12 + 1$.

$$-2b + 13$$

Arithmetic problems can be keyed directly, left to right, into most calculators. Try some of the examples with your calculator to become familiar with the order of entry requirements of your calculator.

$$6 + 20\% \cdot 10 - 4 \div 2 \cdot 5$$

Some calculators will require $20\% \cdot 10$ to be performed first, whereas others will accept the entries from left to right.

Operator keys will be boxed in keystroke presentations. The calculator keystroke for the expression $20\% \cdot 10$ is

$$20 \boxed{\%} \boxed{\times} 10 \boxed{=}$$

The display should register 2. Keeping this number in the display, continue the calculation.

$$\boxed{+} \, 6 - (4 \boxed{\div} 2 \boxed{\times} 5)$$

The parentheses signal the calculator to perform the operations within first. The display should show -2.

An alternate calculator entry is

$$6 \boxed{+} 20 \boxed{\%} \boxed{\times} 10 \boxed{-} 4 \boxed{\div} 2 \boxed{\times} 5 \boxed{=}$$

If the display is -2, your calculator logically follows the order-of-operations rules.

Example

$$(8 + 4 + 3^2 - 19)(3 + 10 \div 7) \times 2^3$$

The expression in the left parentheses: 2.

The expression in the right parentheses: 4.428.

The exponent term: 8.

$$2 \div 4.428 \times 8$$

Answer: 3.6133. . .

Example

$$\frac{8 + 4 + 3^2 - 19}{(3 + 10 \div 7) \times 2^3}$$

The division bar is a grouping symbol and each part of the fraction must be calculated, then the division performed. If the expression is written as a line operation instead of a fraction the problem is written as:

$$[8 + 4 + 3^2 - 19] \div [(3 + 10 \div 7) \times 2^3]$$

$$[2] \div [(4.429) \times 8]$$

$$[2] \div [35.429] = 0.056$$

Practice the examples in the exercises to become familiar with the order of operations and the requirements of input for your calculator.

SECTION 1 EXERCISES

Indicate the order the following calculations are performed. Do the calculation with your calculator to become familiar with its order requirements.

1. $8 + 2 \div 4 \times 6 - 1.$ **Answer** 10

2. $3 - 2 \times 5 + 6 \div 4.$ **Answer** -5.5

3. $7 \times 5 - 12 \div 3 + 1.$ **Answer** 32

4. $7 + 20\% \times 25 - 6 \div 2.$ **Answer** 9

5. $1,000 \times 75\% - 25 \div 5\%.$ **Answer** 250

6. $2,000(20\% + 15\%) - 450 \div 90\%.$ **Answer** 200

7. $200 \times 2 - 120 \div 120\%.$ **Answer** 300

8. $4,000(1 + 5\% \times 8) - 100 \div 5\%.$ **Answer** 3,600

9. $3^2 \times 2^3 - 100 \div 5\%.$ **Answer** $-1,928$

10. $200(1 + 8\% \times 10).$ **Answer** 360

11. $5 + 12 \div 2 \times 8 \div 4 + 3.$ **Answer** 20

12. $\dfrac{3 + 4^2 - 2}{2 \times 3^2 - 7}.$ **Answer** 1.5454. . .

13. $\dfrac{4{,}000 \times 20\% - 5^2}{40 \div 20\% - 0.75 \times 10^2}.$ **Answer** 6.2

14. $25\%(10 + 5\% \times 200) + 25.$ **Answer** 30

15. $2{,}000(1 + 0.06 \div 4).$ **Answer** 2,030

16. $2 + 3(x + 6 \div 2).$ **Answer** $3x + 11$

17. $5 - 2(7 \cdot P - 6\% \times 25).$ **Answer** $8 - 14P$

18. $5 \div 2(7 \cdot P - 6\% \times 25).$ **Answer** $17.5P - 3.75$

19. $2P - 2(5\% \cdot P + 50).$ **Answer** $1.9P - 100$

20. $3x - 4 \div 10\% \cdot x + 3.$ **Answer** $-37x + 3$

0.2   ARITHMETIC OPERATIONS ON SIGNED NUMBERS

Positive numbers are used almost exclusively throughout school. The concepts and manipulations for negative numbers are often not understood or mastered.

Negative numbers represent concepts that exist in everyday life—temperatures below zero, debt, direction, feet below sea level, withdrawals, losses. A temperature of 5 degrees below zero is symbolized as $-5°$. A debt of \$5,000 is shown as $-\$5{,}000$, a depth of 200 feet below sea level is indicated as -200 feet, a withdrawal of \$4,000 is shown as $-\$4{,}000$ in a checkbook.

Because these concepts are meaningful in real-world situations, it is necessary to use negative numbers in numerical computations.

Rules for Addition

Addition involves two numbers at a time. The process continues until all numbers in the addition are used. If the two numbers have the same signs—$(+7) + (+4)$ or $(-3) + (-8)$—**add** the numbers and use the common sign.

$$(+7) + (+4) = +(7 + 4) = +11$$
$$(-3) + (-8) = -(3 + 8) = -11$$
$$(+250) + (+50) = +(250 + 50) = +300$$
$$(-21) + (-34) = -(21 + 34) = -55$$
$$(-2A) + (-15A) = -(2A + 15A) = -17A$$

In each of these examples, the numbers are added, the common sign affecting the sum.

If the two numbers have different signs, compare the numbers without the signs. Subtract the smaller from the larger and affix the sign of the larger to the remainder of the subtraction.

$$(+250) + (-150) = (+)(250 - 150) = +100$$

$$(+250) + (-400) = (-)(400 - 250) = -150$$

$$(+1.08P) + (-1.12P) = (-)(1.12P - 1.08P) = -0.04P$$

Usually problems look more like: $24 + (-18) + (-12) + (21)$.

If no sign accompanies a number, it is implied to be positive. The minus **must be written** if the quantity is negative.

If there are more than two numbers in the addition involving signed numbers, the most efficient method of totaling the numbers is to add the positive quantities, add the negative quantities, and then combine the positive and negative subtotals, using the rules for unlike signs.

In the previous example:

$$24 + (-18) + (-12) + 21$$

Total $24 + 21 = 45.$ $(+)$ implied.

Total $(-18) + (-12) = -30.$

Add:

$$(+45) + (-30) = (+)(45 - 30) = +15$$

To add signed numbers on a calculator, the number is entered followed by $\boxed{+/-}$ key to make the number negative. The entries are entered as listed in the problem.

Add:

$$(\$1,250) + (-\$425) + (-\$375) + (+\$560) + (-\$325)$$

By hand, add the positive entries:

$$(1,250 + 560) = +1,810$$

Add the negative entries:

$$(-)(425 + 375 + 325) = -1{,}125$$

Combine:

$$(+)(1{,}810 - 1{,}125) = +685$$

The calculator keystroke is

1,250 $\boxed{+}$ 425 $\boxed{+/-}$ $\boxed{+}$ 375 $\boxed{+/-}$ $\boxed{+}$ 560 $\boxed{+}$ 325 $\boxed{+/-}$ $\boxed{=}$

The $\boxed{+/-}$ following the number is the method used to enter negative numbers in a calculator.

Subtraction of Signed Numbers

Addition and subtraction of signed numbers are inverse operations. Inverse operations undo each other. For example, adding 5 and subtracting 5 undo each other and are inverse operations. For each subtraction problem, there is a corresponding addition statement.

Subtraction Statement	Addition Problem	Answer
$(-7) - (5)$	$(-7) + (-5)$	-12
$(+4) - (-11)$	$(+4) + (11)$	$+15$
$(+8) - (12)$	$(+8) + (-12)$	-4
$(-6) - (-8)$	$(-6) + (+8)$	$+2$

General Rule for Subtraction

Change the sign of the subtrahend (the number subtracted) and change the operation to addition. Perform the addition using the rules of addition for signed numbers.

Example

$$(1.11P) - (1.08P) = (1.11P) + (-1.08P) = (+)(1.11P - 1.08P)$$
$$= +0.03P$$

This problem is most easily done by subtraction rather than by changing to an addition problem. Changing to a corresponding addition problem is useful when either of the terms of the subtraction are negative but not necessary for traditional subtraction.

Example

$$(-11) - (5) = (-11) + (-5) = -16$$
$$(1.05P) - (-0.05P) = (1.05P) + (+0.05P) = +1.10P$$

Multiplication and Division of Signed Numbers

The numbers involved in multiplication and division are called factors. Perform the multiplication and division of the factors without signs and count the number of negative factors. If the number of negative factors is even, the final answer is positive. If the number of negative factors is odd, the answer is negative.

$$(-2) \times (-4) \div (+16) = (2 \times 4 \div 16) = 0.5$$

There are two negative factors, 2 is even, therefore the answer is $+0.5$.

$$(3) \times (1.05) \times (-0.02) = (3 \times 1.05 \times 0.02) = 0.063$$

There is one negative factor, 1 is odd, therefore the answer is -0.063.

Example

$$(-2a) \times (-3b) \times (-5)$$

The factors (without signs) (2), (3), (5), (a), and (b) multiply to $30ab$. There are three negative factors, 3 is odd the answer is $-30ab$.

This example demonstrates that unlike factors can be multiplied; they **cannot** be added!

Example

$$(-2,000)(1 + -6)/(-400)(2.05 + -5)$$

The operations within the parentheses must be performed first.

$$(1 + -6) = -5 \qquad (2.05 + -5) = (-)(5 - 2.05) = -2.95$$
$$(-2,000)(-5)/(-400)(-2.95)$$

Multiplication and division are performed from left to right.

$$10,000 \div 400 \times 2.95 = 73.75$$

There are four negative factors. The answer is positive. Answer: $+73.75$.

The operations within a set of parentheses must be completed before the number counts as a factor.

Example

$$(2,000)(1 + (-0.03)^2)/(1.12 - 1.85)$$

Do the exponent first.

$$(-0.03)^2 = (-0.03)(-0.03) = +0.0009$$

Complete the work in the parentheses.

$$1 + 0.0009 = 1.0009$$

Perform the subtraction in:

$$(1.12 - 1.85) = (1.12 + -1.85) = (-)(1.85 - 1.12) = -0.73$$
$$(2,000)(1.0009)/(-0.73)$$

The problem restated without parentheses is

$$2,000 \times 1.0009/-0.73 = 2,764.383562$$

One minus sign gives a negative answer. Answer: $-2,764.383562$.

Fractions usually send real panic into the student. Fractions, especially in business applications, can be replaced by decimal equivalents unless the decimal is nonterminating. To find the decimal equivalent using a calculator, enter the numerator, $\boxed{\div}$, denominator, $\boxed{=}$. If the display does not fill all the spaces, the fraction can be replaced by the decimal equivalent. If the display is filled with numbers, the fraction gives a nonterminating decimal. For the greatest accuracy the problem should be worked in fractions.

Example

$$\left(\frac{1}{4} - \frac{3}{8}\right) = 0.25 - 0.375 = (0.25) + (-0.375)$$

$$= (-)(0.375 - 0.25) = -0.125$$

Example

$$(-3)\Big/\left(\frac{1}{4}\right) = (3)/(0.25) = 12.$$

There is one minus sign and the answer is negative. Answer: -12.

Example

$$\left(\frac{1}{3} - \frac{1}{4}\right)\Big/\frac{1}{6}$$

$$\frac{1}{3} = 0.33333. . .$$

This is a nonterminating decimal, and the computation should be done using fractions to ensure the greatest accuracy.

To subtract fractions, a common denominator is needed. The common denominator is 12, the smallest number that 3 and 4 will divide into.

$$\frac{1}{3} = \frac{4}{12} \qquad \frac{1}{4} = \frac{3}{12} \qquad \frac{4}{12} - \frac{3}{12} = \frac{1}{12}$$

1/12 divided by 1/6. To divide by a fraction, invert the divisor and multiply. To multiply two fractions, multiply the numerator factors and place the product in the numerator of the answer. Multiply the factors of the denominator and place the product in the denominator of the answer.

$$\frac{1}{12} \div \frac{1}{6} = \frac{1}{12} \cdot \frac{6}{1}$$

Numerator product: $1 \cdot 6 = 6$.

Denominator product: $12 \cdot 1 = 12$.

Answer: $6/12 = 1/2 = 0.5$.

All of the factors were positive, the final answer is positive.

Parentheses must be used when entering fractional products or quotients into a calculator.

$$\left(\frac{1}{3} - \frac{1}{4}\right) \div \left(\frac{1}{6}\right)$$

$$(1 \div 3 - 1 \div 4) \div (1 \div 6) = 0.5$$

SECTION 2 EXERCISES

1. $(-5) + (+8)$.   **Answer** $+3$

2. $(+5) + (-8)$.   **Answer** -3

3. $(11) + (-14)$.   **Answer** -3

4. $(-8) + (14)$.   **Answer** 6

5. $(-2A) + (3B) + (-5A) + (-4B)$.   **Answer** $-7A - B$

6. $(0.3P) + (-1.1P) + (-0.2P) + (0.8P)$.   **Answer** $-0.2P$

7. $(+8) - (-5)$.   **Answer** 13

8. $(-8) - (5)$.   **Answer** -13

9. $(-2A) - (-11A)$.   **Answer** $9A$

10. $(0.6P) - (1.4P)$.   **Answer** $-0.8P$

11. $4A + (-11B) - (-5A) - (6B)$.   **Answer** $9A - 17B$

12. $8x + (-3y) - (2x) - (-5y)$.   **Answer** $6x + 2y$

13. $5{,}000 + (-560) + (230) - (470)$.   **Answer** 4,200

14. $\dfrac{(8)(-3)(-2)}{32}$.   **Answer** $\dfrac{3}{2}$

15. $(0.05P)(-0.8)(-4)(-0.2)$.   **Answer** $-0.032P$

16. $\dfrac{10}{(-4)(P)}$.   **Answer** $\dfrac{5}{-2P}$

17. $\dfrac{14a}{(-2)(7)}$.   **Answer** $-a$

18. $(-2r)(3t)(7)$.   **Answer** $-42rt$

19. $\dfrac{400(1 - 0.06^2)}{1.12 - (-1.3)}$.   **Answer** 164.69

20. $(6,000)(1.005)/(-0.005)$.   **Answer** $-1,206,000$

21. $\dfrac{\dfrac{3}{4} - \dfrac{1}{8}}{\dfrac{1}{5}}$.   **Answer** 3.125 or $3\dfrac{1}{8}$

22. $\left(\dfrac{1}{6} - \dfrac{1}{4}\right)\Big/\left(\dfrac{1}{2}\right)$.   **Answer** $-\dfrac{1}{6}$

23. $\dfrac{\left(\dfrac{2}{5} - \dfrac{1}{10}\right)}{\dfrac{1}{2}}$.   **Answer** $\dfrac{3}{5}$ or .6

24. $\dfrac{\dfrac{1}{12} - \dfrac{1}{6}}{\dfrac{1}{3} - \dfrac{1}{4}}$.   **Answer** -1

25. $\dfrac{1 - \dfrac{3}{50}}{1 + \dfrac{3}{50}}$.   **Answer** 0.8868

0.3 DISTRIBUTIVE PROPERTY

Multiplication of numbers is a process used to simplify repetitive addition. $17 + 17 + 17 + 17 + 17$ and 5×17 represent the same problem. Multiplication facts are required and the process of long multiplication is mastered. The calculator handles these facts accurately and quickly.

The numbers that are multiplied together are given the special name of **factors**—the elements involved in a multiplication or a division problem. The other name to keep in mind is **terms**—the elements involved in addition or subtraction processes.

The order in which **factors** are multiplied has no effect on the final answer. A factor is used only once unless there is an exponent present to indicate otherwise.

Example

$$2 \times 8 \times 5 = 16 \times 5 = 80 \quad \text{or} \quad 2 \times 40 = 80$$
$$2^3 \times 8 \times 5 = 2 \times 2 \times 2 \times 8 \times 5 = 320$$

The exponent of 3 indicates the factor 2 is used 3 times.

Multiplication of factors in algebra is indicated by placing the factors side by side without an operator between the factors.

Example

$2abc$ indicates the product of the factors 2, a, b, and c. The $\times$ is not used to indicate multiplication because x is frequently used as a variable. Other ways to indicate multiplication is by the raised dot between factors or by placing the factors in parentheses. The dot notation is usually used between numerical factors.

Example

$$5 \cdot 2 \cdot a \cdot a \cdot b \cdot b \cdot b = 10a^2b^3$$

The distributive property dictates the process for combining multiplication and addition. The property is especially useful for algebraic terms that cannot be added to a single term.

Example

$$2(3 + 4) = 2 \cdot 3 + 2 \cdot 4 \quad \text{or} \quad 2 \cdot 7 = 14$$
$$5(a + 2b) = 5 \cdot a + 5 \cdot 2b = 5a + 10b$$

The first problem can be simplified by adding $3 + 4$ for a sum of 7, then multiplying by 2 for a product of 14. An alternate method is multiplying 3 by 2 and 4 by 2, then adding the products of 6 and 8 for a sum of 14. When algebraic terms are involved, the actual addition cannot be performed; the distributive property is needed to complete the operations.

Example

$$2(a + b) = 2a + 2b$$

The multiplication problem involving the **factors** 2 and $a + b$ has been expressed an the sum of **terms** $2a$ and $2b$.

It is frequently necessary to go the opposite way—to express terms as factors. This skill in algebra is known as factoring and is used in solving equations and reducing fractions.

Example

$ab + ac$ is the sum of two terms, ab and ac. An equivalent expression for $ab + ac$ is $a(b + c)$. The original expression had two terms, the equivalent expression has two factors, a and $b + c$.

The most widely used technique in factoring is to look for the factor common to all of the terms.

Example

$$4b + 2bc - 6bd$$

All three terms $4b$, $2bc$, and $6bd$ has the common factors of 2 and b. 2 and b divide into each of the terms. The result from dividing each term by $2b$ is $2 + c - 3d$. $2 + c - 3d$ is one of the factors, $2b$ is the other factor.

$$4b + 2bc - 6bd = 2b(2 + c - 3d)$$

A check on the correctness of the result can be made by multiplying the factors, the product should be the original expression.

Example

$$B + PRB$$

B is a common factor to each of the terms B and PRB. The result of dividing B by B is 1 and the result of dividing PRB by B is PR.

$$B + PRB = B(1 + PR)$$

A check in the product

$$B \cdot 1 + B \cdot PR = B + BPR$$

There are many additional techniques available for factoring. The purpose of this review is to prepare for the material in the text. Factoring a common factor is sufficient for the material presented.

Example

$$\frac{p - prt}{d - drt}$$

Only **factors** can be cancelled in reducing fractions. p, prt, d, and drt are terms involved in subtractions.

Factor $p - prt$: $p(1 - rt)$.

Factor $d - drt$: $d(1 - rt)$.

Rewritten: $\dfrac{p(1 - rt)}{d(1 - rt)}$.

Now the numerator and denominator have a common factor of $1 - rt$. The fraction $(1 - rt)/(1 - rt)$ can be reduced to 1. The reduced value of the fraction is p/d.

SECTION 3 EXERCISES

Without using a calculator, factor, add, or multiply the following as indicated.

1. $(21 \cdot 14) + (21 \cdot 16)$.   **Answer** 630

2. $(17 \cdot 61) + (17 \cdot 39)$.   **Answer** 1,700

3. $(-24 \cdot 16) + (-24 \cdot 84)$.   **Answer** $-2,400$

Multiply and write as the sum of terms.

4. $3(y + 1)$.   **Answer** $3y + 3$

5. $-7(5 + a)$.   **Answer** $-35 - 7a$

6. $y(y - 6)$.   **Answer** $y^2 - 6y$

7. $2(6 - y)$.   **Answer** $12 - 2y$

8. $a(x - 3y)$.   **Answer** $ax - 3ay$

9. $3(x + y - z)$.   **Answer** $3x + 3y - 3z$

10. $b(a - b + c)$.   **Answer** $ab - b^2 + bc$

Factor and write the sum as a product.

11. $4x + 8$.   **Answer** $4(x + 2)$

12. $ac - ad$.   **Answer** $a(c - d)$

13. $ax + a$.   **Answer** $a(x + 1)$

14. $P + PRT$.   **Answer** $P(1 + RT)$

15. $D - DRT$.   **Answer** $D(1 - RT)$

Factor and reduce.

16. $(3x + 3)/3$.   **Answer** $3(x + 1)/3 = x + 1$

17. $(4 - 8y)/4$.   **Answer** $4(1 - 2y)/4 = 1 - 2y$

18. $(cx + bx)/x$.   **Answer** $x(c + b)/x = c + b$

19. $(b^2 + b)/b$.   **Answer** $b(b + 1)/b = b + 1$

20. $(ab + ac - a)/(b + c - 1)$.   **Answer** $a(b + c - 1)/(b + c - 1) = a$

0.4   SOLVING EQUATIONS

Reviewing computational skills has been preparatory for the task of solving problems. The problems addressed in this section are equations—a statement containing an equality between two quantities. In algebra, equations are identified as a statement containing an equal sign.

Example

$$\frac{a}{3} + \frac{2a}{5} \quad \text{is not an equation}$$

$$a + 2 = 5 \quad \text{is an equation}$$

$$a - 5 < 7 \quad \text{is not an equation}$$

The solution to an equation is a simplified statement of the original statement. The unknown is isolated on one side of the equal sign and the number or algebraic expression without the unknown is on the other side of the equal sign. We obtain the solution by following some manipulative rules of algebra. If the original statement represents an equality between two quantities and the same mathematical operation is applied to each side of the equation, the resulting statement is also an equation.

The process of performing the same operation on both sides of an equation will be called the **equal rights** of sides of an equation.

Equal-Rights Operations

If the unknown is affected by an addition, **subtraction** is applied to each side of the equation.

Example

$$x + 3 = 11$$

Because x is affected by an addition, subtraction of 3 is applied to each side of the equation.

$$x + 3 \boxed{-3} = 11 \boxed{-3} \quad \text{or} \quad x = 8$$

If the unknown is affected by a subtraction, **addition** is applied to each side of the equation.

Example

$$y - 4.2 = 11.8$$

Because y is affected by the subtraction of 4.2, addition of 4.2 is applied to each side of the equation.

$$y - 4.2 \boxed{+ 4.2} = 11.8 \boxed{+ 4.2} \quad \text{or} \quad y = 16.$$

If the unknown is affected by a multiplication, **division** is applied to each side of the equation.

Example

$$0.02\,T = 200$$

Because T is affected by a multiplication, division by 0.02 is applied to each side of the equation.

$$0.02\,T \boxed{/\ 0.02} = 200 \boxed{/\ 0.02} \quad \text{or} \quad T = 10{,}000$$

If the unknown is affected by a division, **multiplication** is applied to each side of the equation.

Example

$$\frac{x}{2} = 23$$

Because division affects x, multiplication by 2 is applied to each side of the equation.

$$(x/2)\boxed{\cdot 2} = (23)\boxed{\cdot 2} \quad \text{or} \quad x = 46$$

Just as the order-of-operations rule exists for computations, an order of operations is established in solving equations. This order gives a systematic and efficient procedure for solving equations. This is especially useful when more than one operation affects the variable in an equation.

To solve an equation:

1. Remove grouping symbols by using the distributive property.

2. Clear the equation of fractions by finding the common denominator of all fractions and multiplying each side of the equation by the common denominator.

3. If the unknown is on both sides of the equation, use addition or subtraction to isolate the unknown on one side.

4. If terms not containing the unknown are on both sides of the equation, use addition or subtraction to isolate the nonvariable terms on one side of the equation.

5. Combine like terms on each side of the equation.

6. If the unknown has a coefficient other than 1, divide both sides of the equation by the coefficient.

Example

$$2x + 3 = 9 - x \qquad \text{no grouping symbol, skip step 1}$$

$$\text{no denominator, skip step 2}$$

x is on both sides of the equation, add x to both sides to isolate x on the left-hand side of the equality.

$$2x + 3 \boxed{+ x} = 9 - x \boxed{+ x} \quad \text{or} \quad 2x + 3 + x = 9 \quad \text{or} \quad 3x + 3 = 9$$

Now 3 and 9 are on both sides of the equation but these terms must be on the right-hand side (away from x). Subtract 3 from each side of the equation.

$$3x + 3 \boxed{- 3} = 9 \boxed{- 3} \quad \text{or} \quad 3x = 6$$

Like terms have been combined in each step. Because x is multiplied by 3, both sides of the equation must be divided by 3.

$$3x \boxed{/ 3} = 6 \boxed{/ 3} \quad \text{or} \quad x = 2$$

The simplified equation, $x = 2$, is the solution of the original statement, $2x + 3 = 9 - x$. The simplified equation is the result of applying **equal rights** to the original statement.

Example

$$B - 0.05B + 5 = 80$$

The unknown terms are all on one side of the equation, the number terms of

5 and 80 are on opposite sides of the equation. Subtract 5 from each side to leave the unknown terms on one side and the number terms on the other.

$$B - 0.05B + 5 \boxed{-5} = 80 \boxed{-5}$$

Combine like terms (B represents $1B$).

$$1B - 0.05B = B(1 - 0.05) = B(0.95) \quad \text{or} \quad 0.95B$$

$$0.95B = 75$$

Now divide each side of the equation by 0.95.

$$0.95B \boxed{/\,0.95} = 75 \boxed{/\,0.95}$$

$$B = 78.947$$

Example

$$2(1 - 3x) = \frac{x}{3} + \frac{11}{2}$$

Remove grouping symbols.

$$2 - 6x = \frac{x}{3} + \frac{11}{2}$$

Clear of denominators. The common denominator is 6, multiply each side by 6.

$$6(2 - 6x) = 6\left(\frac{x}{3} + \frac{11}{2}\right)$$

Using the distributive property:

$$6 \cdot 2 - 6 \cdot 6x = 6 \cdot \frac{x}{3} + 6 \cdot \frac{11}{2}$$

$$12 - 36x = 2x + 33$$

Notice the equation is now free of fractions.

Isolate the variable on one side. Adding $36x$ to both sides will keep the variable term positive.

$$12 - 36x \boxed{+ 36x} = 2x + 33 \boxed{+ 36x}$$
$$12 = 38x + 33$$

There are number terms on both sides of the equation. Because x is on the right, the number term should be on the left. Subtract 33 from both sides of the equation.

$$12 \boxed{- 33} = 38x + 33 \boxed{- 33} \quad \text{or} \quad -21 = 38x$$

Divide both sides by 38.

$$-21 \boxed{/ 38} = 38x \boxed{/ 38} \quad \text{or} \quad x = -0.553$$

In business applications most answers are written in decimal form. The answers $-21/38$ and -0.553 are both correct.

There are equations containing more than one letter in the statement. Directions must indicate the variable to be solved for. The other letters are treated as numbers—isolated from the unknown—and are part of the solution.

Example

$$ax + 3 = b - 5$$

Solve for x.

Isolate the term containing x by subtracting 3 from each side of the equation.

$$ax + 3 \boxed{- 3} = b - 5 \boxed{- 3}$$

Combine like terms.

$$ax = b - 8$$

Divide both sides by a.

$$(ax) \boxed{/ a} = (b - 8) \boxed{/ a}$$

Simplified:

$$x = (b - 8)/a \quad \text{or} \quad b/a - 8/a$$

SECTION 4 EXERCISES

Find the solution for each of the equations.

1. $4x = 18$.   **Answer** $x = 4.5$

2. $6 = 4p/5$.   **Answer** $p = 7.5$

3. $72 = 8t$.   **Answer** $t = 9$

4. $x + 3 = 18$.   **Answer** $x = 15$

5. $7 = 4p - 5$.   **Answer** $p = 3$

6. $d/0.3 = 100$.   **Answer** $d = 30$

7. $2(p + 1)/3 = 9$.   **Answer** $p = 12.5$

8. $0.05p = 100$.   **Answer** $p = 2{,}000$

9. $5x + 2 = 17$.   **Answer** $x = 3$

10. $2y + 3 = 4y - 2$.   **Answer** $y = 2.5$

11. $(1/2)y - 9 = 4 - y$.   **Answer** $y = 26/3$

12. $4(x + 1) + 9 = 22 + x$.   **Answer** $x = 3$

13. $-3 = 12/x$.   **Answer** $x = -4$

14. $x/2 + x/3 = 5$.   **Answer** $x = 6$

15. $(x - 1)/2 + 3 = 17$.   **Answer** $x = 29$

16. $2p = 3p - 5$.   **Answer** $p = 5$

17. $9y - 23 + 5y = 3 + 6y - 18$.   **Answer** $y = 1$

18. $p - prt = 100$. Solve for r.   **Answer** $(p - 100)/pt$

19. $A = p + prt$. Solve for t.   **Answer** $t = (A - p)/pr$

20. $1/a + 1/2 = 4$.   **Answer** $a = 2/7$

0.5   RATIO AND PROPORTION

Ratio

Ratios are fractions used to compare two numbers or quantities. Ratios can be written as:

$$a : b \qquad a \text{ to } b \qquad a/b$$

In algebra a/b is the most common way of writing ratios, whereas business applications tend to use the $a : b$ notation. Ratios require units to be included unless the units are identical for each quantity.

Example
Write the ratio of 3 days to 8 hours.

3 days/8 hours is a ratio. If possible the units are made alike so the ratio reduces to a number.

3 days $= 3(24)$ hours or 72 hours, 3 days/8 hours can be written as 72 hours/8 hours.

72 hours/8 hours reduces to the ratio 9/1 or the number 9.

Write the ratio of $3.00 in cost to $6.00 in sales.

$$\frac{\$3.00}{\$6.00} = \frac{1}{2}$$

Because the dollar units are identical, the final answer is a number without units.

Write the ratio of $4.60 in cost for 5 gallons of gasoline.

$$\frac{\$4.60}{5 \text{ gallons}} = \$0.92/\text{gallon}$$

Because the units are different, the units must be included in the final answer.

Ratios are used in alloting parts or dividing a number into parts according to a ratio. The sum of the terms of the ratio are used as the unit of division when allocating parts. If profits of $2,000 are to be divided between two people in the ratio of 2 : 3, add the terms 2 and 3 to give 5, the unit of division. Divide the amount to be distributed by the sum of the terms. In this example, divide $2,000 by 5, giving the quotient $400. 2($400) is to be distributed to one person and 3($400) is to be distributed to the other. The $800 plus $1,200 equals the total to be distributed.

Example

An estate of $200,000 is to be divided among the heirs in the ratio of 1/2 : 1/3 : 1/6. Find the amount each heir receives.

The ratio 1/2 : 1/3 : 1/4 can be rewritten as 6 : 4 : 3. Parts of a ratio can be multiplied by the same number without changing the relationship among the parts. Multiply the ratios by 12 to give the alternate ratio of 6 : 4 : 3. Add 6, 4, 3 to obtain a total of 13. Divide $200,000 by 13 to obtain $15,384.62.

$$6(15,384.62) = \$92,307.69$$

$$4(15,384.62) = \$61,638.46$$

$$3(15,384.62) = \$46,153.85$$

Proportion

A proportion is a statement of equality between two ratios. For example, $7/19 = 21/57$ is a proportion. The statement equates the two ratios $7/19$ and $21/57$. The alternate notation for the proportion $a : b = c : d$ is $a/b = c/d$.

When the proportion is written as $a : b = c : d$, b and c are the middle elements of the proportion and are referred to as the "means," a and d are the "extremes" of the proportion. In a proportion, **the product of the means is equal to the product of the extremes.**

To show the product of the means equals the product of the extremes, look at the general proportion $\dfrac{a}{b} = \dfrac{c}{d}$. The common denominator is bd; multiply each side of the equation by bd.

$$bd\left(\frac{a}{b}\right) = bd\left(\frac{c}{d}\right)$$

The b in bd cancels with the b in the denominator. Similarly, the d in bd cancels with d in the denominator.

$$ad = bc$$

The arrows in the following proportion can help one to remember the products involved. The products are called **cross products**.

$$\frac{a}{b} \diagdown \diagup \frac{c}{d}$$

$$ad = bc$$

Example
Is the following statement a proportion?

$$\frac{\$3.75}{3} = \frac{\$6.25}{5}$$

Check to see if the product of the means equals the product of the extremes.

$$\text{Product of means} = 3 \cdot \$6.25 = \$18.75$$
$$\text{Product of extremes} = \$3.75 \cdot 5 = \$18.75$$

The products are equal, the statement is a proportion.

Four numbers are involved in a proportion. If any three of these numbers are known, the fourth can be determined.

Example
Find x if:

$$3 : 40 = x : 75 \quad \text{or} \quad \frac{3}{40} = \frac{x}{75}$$

The product of the means equals the product of the extremes.

$$40 \cdot x = 3 \cdot 75$$
$$40x = 225$$
$$x = 5.625$$

Example

Two business partners agree to split profits in the ratio of 3 : 7. The smaller profit distribution was $2,000. Find the larger distribution.

$$\frac{3}{7} = \frac{2,000}{x}$$

The smaller distribution, $2,000, is placed in the numerator to correspond to the position of the smaller number in the fraction 3/7. Multiply the means; multiply the extremes.

$$14,000 = 3x$$

Divide each side by 3.

$$x = \$4,666.67$$

Proportions are an efficient and easy way to solve a variety of problems.

Example

If 1 inch = 2.54 centimeters, how many centimeters equal 11.1 inches?

$$1 \text{ inch} : 2.54 \text{ centimeters} = 11.1 \text{ inches} : x \text{ centimeters}$$

$$\frac{1}{2.54} = \frac{11.1}{x}$$

$$x = 28.19 \text{ centimeters}$$

Example

130 bushels of wheat cost $540. Determine how many bushels are purchased for $800 if the same rate is paid.

$$\frac{130 \text{ bushels}}{\$540} = \frac{x \text{ bushels}}{\$800}$$

$$\$540x = \$104,000 \text{ bushels}$$

$$x = 192.59 \text{ bushels}$$

Example

The scale drawing on a house plan has the width of a room as 4.5 inches. The scale on the drawing is 1.25 inches for 8 feet. How many feet do the 4.5 inches represent?

$$\frac{1.25 \text{ inches}}{8 \text{ feet}} = \frac{4.5 \text{ inches}}{x \text{ feet}}$$

$$1.25x = 36$$

$$x = 28.8 \text{ feet}$$

Example
If 344 cubic feet of concrete cost $1,200, find the cost of 500 cubic feet.

$$\frac{344}{1,200} = \frac{500}{x}$$

$$344x = 600,000$$

$$x = \$1,744.19$$

SECTION 5 EXERCISES

Write the following as ratios.

1. 3 ounces to 3 pounds.

2. $0.40 to $2.00.

3. 12 hours to 2 days.

4. $5.50 for 5 minutes.

5. $8.45/7.2 gallons.

Divide the following numbers into parts.

6. Divide 8,000 into the ratio of 3 : 5.

7. Divide 4,500 into the ratio of 2 : 7.

8. Divide 500 into the ratio of 1 : 1 : 3.

9. Divide $10,000 into the ratio of $\frac{1}{3} : \frac{1}{4} : \frac{1}{5}$.

10. Divide $5,000 into the ratio of $\frac{1}{2} : 2 : 2\frac{1}{2}$.

Solve the following proportions.

11. $4 : 5$ as $3 : x$.

12. $2.1 : 8.36$ as $x : 11.56$.

13. $0.036 : x = 11 : 214$.

14. $x : 4,457 = 21.7 : 659$.

15. $0.97 : 47.95 \doteq x : 64.89$.

Write the following as proportions and solve for the unknown.

16. The ratio of men to women at Med University is $5 : 4$. If there are 4,580 men at Med University, how many women would you expect?

17. A new heat pump requires 75% as much electricity as the old model. The new model requires 960 watts. How much did the old model require?

18. A high-speed copier can print 180 copies in 3 minutes. How many copies can be made in 1 hour and 12 minutes?

19. The ratio of part-time instructors to full-time instructors is $5 : 3$. The college has 75 part-time instructors. How many full-time instructors are there?

20. A nurse counts 12 heartbeats in 10 seconds. What is the heartbeat per minute?

Answers

1. $\dfrac{3}{48} = \dfrac{1}{16}$

2. $0.40/2.00 = \dfrac{1}{5}$

3. $\dfrac{12}{48} = \dfrac{1}{4}$

4. \$5.50/5 minutes $=$ \$1.10/minute

5. \$8.45/7.2 gallons $=$ \$1.17/gallon

6. $3,000 : 5,000$

7. $1,000 : 3,500$

8. $100 : 100 : 300$

   9. $4,255.32 : 3,191.49 : 2,553.19

   10. $500 : 2,000 : 2,500

   11. $x = 3.75$

   12. $x = 2.90$

   13. $x = 0.7$

   14. $x = 146.76$

   15. $x = 1.31$

   16. $5/4 = 4,580/x.$ $x = 3,664$

   17. $75/100 = 960/x.$ $x = 1,280$

   18. $180/3 = x/72.$ $x = 4,320$

   19. $5/3 = 75/x.$ $x = 45$

   20. $12 : 10 = x : 60.$ $x = 72$

0.6   PERCENT

Percents are ratios or fractions—all percents are ratios with a denominator of 100. Percents are used in business activities because the units of percents (100) match the units of dollars (100 cents). Percent and hundredth are equivalent expressions, the symbol % and the denominator of 100 can be interchanged. Therefore 20% and 20/100 are the same quantities.

Changing a number to a percent is the same process as changing a dollar amount to cents. Changing $3.20, a dollar amount, to 320 cents is the same as changing the number 3.20 to 320%.

There are four types of conversions needed in working with percent.

Decimal number to percent.

Ratio to percent.

Percent to decimal number.

Percent to ratio.

Decimal Number to Percent

Using a proportion, decimal number = $x/100$, where x is the percent.

Example
2.05 is what percent?

$$2.05/1 = x/100$$

The cross product is

$$(1)(x) = (2.05)(100)$$
$$x = 205$$

Answer 2.05 is 205%.

Example
0.0075 is what percent?

$$0.0075/1 = x/100$$
$$x = 0.75$$

Answer: 0.0075 is 0.75%.

"To change a decimal number to a percent, move the decimal point two places to the right and add the percent sign" is a legitimate statement. Understanding the statement keeps accuracy in execution.

Percent means hundredths and proportion is a process that gives the denominator of 100.

Ratio to a Percent

Set up the ratio: $x/100$. The value of x is the percent.

Example
Write 5/9 as a percent.

$$\frac{5}{9} = \frac{x}{100}$$

The cross product gives

$$9x = 500$$

Divide both sides by 9.

$$x = 55.56$$

Answer: $\dfrac{5}{9} = 55.56\%$.

Example
Write 5/2 as a percent.

$$\frac{5}{2} = \frac{x}{100}$$

The cross product gives

$$2x = 500$$

Divide both sides by 2.

$$x = 250$$

Answer: 5/2 is 250%.

Percent as a Decimal

Write the percent as a number with a denominator of 100. Divide and write the quotient as a decimal. (Dividing by 100 results in the decimal point being moved two places to the left.)

Example
Write 4.5% as a number.

$$\frac{4.5}{100} = 0.045$$

The answer can be found on your calculator by entering 4.5 followed by the $\boxed{\%}$ key.

Example
Write 0.035% as a decimal number.

$$\frac{0.035}{100} = 0.00035$$

The calculator keystroke is $0.035\boxed{\%}$. The number 0.00035 shows in the display.

Percent as a Ratio

Write the percent as a ratio with a denominator of 100 replacing the percent sign. Reduce the ratio.

Example

$$26\% = \frac{26}{100}.$$

Both 26 and 100 are divisible by 2 so 26/100 can be reduced to the fraction 13/50.

Example
Convert 35% to a ratio.

$$35\% = \frac{35}{100}$$

Both parts of the fraction can be written as a product involving 5.

$$\frac{35}{100} = \frac{5 \cdot 7}{5 \cdot 20} = \frac{7}{20}$$

Computation Involving Percent

The formula involving percent is $P = RT$. P represents **percentage**. Percentage is a number, not a percent, resulting from a product where a percent is involved. Percentage is the product of the rate (expressed as a percent) and the base. B represents the **base**, the number regarded as the whole, the number the percent affects. R represents the **rate** and is meaningless without the base. By itself, 10% has no meaning but 10% of 200 has meaning.

To solve a percentage problem:

1. Identify the values as P, B, and R.

2. Substitute the values in the relationship, $P = RB$.

3. Solve for the unknown.

Example
What is 45% of 360?

45% is R (percent is always R).

360 is B (the number the percent is **of** is always B).

"What" represents P, the problem is asking what percentage is 45% of 360.

$$P = 45\% \cdot 360$$

Calculations require the percent to be changed to a number before multiplying.

$$45\% = \frac{45}{100} = 0.45$$

$$P = (0.45)(360) = 162$$

The calculator keystroke is

$$45 \; \boxed{\%} \; \boxed{\times} \; 360 \; \boxed{=}$$

Example
What percent of $459.50 is $23.50?

R is unknown and we use the notation $x/100$ or $x\%$.

$B = 459.50$ because it is the number associated with percent.

P is 23.50.

Substituting in $P = RB$:

$$23.50 = \frac{x}{100} \cdot 459.50$$

Multiply the equation by 100 to remove the denominator.

$$(100)(23.50) = (100)(x/100)(459.50)$$
$$2{,}350 = 459.50x$$

Divide both sides by 459.50.

$$x = 5.11$$

The setup of the problem made the value of x the percent and no further conversion is necessary.
    $23.50 is 5.11% of $459.50.

Example
$45.60 is 18% of what amount?

   $R = 18\%$ or $18/100$.

   $B =$ what amount of is the unknown.

   $P = 45.60$ for this is a part of the whole amount.

$$46.50 = \frac{18}{100}B$$

Multiply both sides of the equation by 100.

$$(100)(46.50) = (100)(18/100)B$$
$$4{,}650 = 18B$$

Divide both sides by 18.

$$B = \$258.33$$

SECTION 6 EXERCISES

Write the following as percents.

1. 0.64.   **Answer** 64%

2. 8.5.   **Answer** 850%

3. 0.0015.   **Answer** 0.15%

4. $\dfrac{5}{16}$.   **Answer** 31.25%

5. $1\dfrac{3}{5}$.   **Answer** 160%

6. $\dfrac{31}{100}$.   **Answer** 31%

Write the following as a decimal and a ratio in lowest terms.

7. 65%.   **Answer** 0.65 or $\dfrac{13}{20}$

8. 12.7%.   **Answer** 0.127 or $\dfrac{127}{1,000}$

9. 3/4%.   **Answer** 0.0075 or $\dfrac{3}{400}$

10. 125%   **Answer** 1.25 or $\dfrac{5}{4}$

11. 33 1/3%.   **Answer** 0.333 or $\dfrac{1}{3}$

12. 6 1/4%.   **Answer** 0.0625 or $\dfrac{1}{16}$

Use equations to solve the following.

13. 8% of 45 is what number?   **Answer** 3.6

14. 0.5% of 720 is what number?   **Answer** 3.6

15. 7.85 is what percent of 97?   **Answer** 8.1%

16. 642 is what percent of 600?   **Answer** 107%

17. 42 is 75% of what number?   **Answer** 56

18. 450 is 1/4% of what number?   **Answer** 180,000

19. What percent of 80 is 72?   **Answer** 90

20. 37 1/2% of 18 is what amount?   **Answer** 6.75

0.7   EXPONENTS AND ROOTS

Exponents

A power or exponent is a number written to the right and slightly above another number. In the expression y^x, x is the exponent, y is the base. y^x indicates that y multiplies itself x times. The exponent indicates the number of times the base is a factor.

The most common exponent is 2 and reads as "squared." Areas of circles and squares used the exponent 2 in their area formulas. Many calculators have an $\boxed{x^2}$ key. This key multiplies a base by itself. The key on the calculator performing any power is the $\boxed{y^x}$ key.

Example
1.075^3 is the notation (shorthand) for $1.075 \times 1.075 \times 1.075$.

The answer to this problem can be found by performing the two multiplications. This can be a tedious process with opportunities for error. The calculator can perform this problem in a variety of ways.

Using the $\boxed{y^x}$ key:

Enter the base, in this example, 1.075.

Press $\boxed{y^x}$.

Enter the power, in this example, 3.

Press $\boxed{=}$.

The display is 1.242 296 875.

If your calculator does not have a $\boxed{y^x}$ key, the following procedure will perform powers by entering the factor once.

Without the $\boxed{y^x}$ key:

Enter the base, 1.075.

Press $\boxed{\times}$.

Press $\boxed{=}$ as many times as the second factor should be entered. (This is one less than the exponent because the first factor has already been entered.)

The display is 1.242 296 875.

Example

$$1{,}000(1 + 0.06/12)^{60}$$

The operations within the parentheses must be performed first beginning with division, then addition.

$$0.06 \boxed{\div} 12 \boxed{+} 1 \boxed{=}$$

Now the exponent is applied, keeping the entry in the display.

$$\boxed{y^x}\ 60\ \boxed{=}$$

Finally, multiply by 1,000.

$$\boxed{\times}\ 1{,}000\ \boxed{=}$$

Answer: 1,348.850 153.

The process of rounding the answers is addressed in the next section. For the present, all digits will be used.

Roots

Roots are the opposite of exponents and undo powers just as division undoes multiplication and subtraction undoes addition. There are two notations used to indicate roots and the two notations can be interchanged. The notations $y^{1/x}$ or $\sqrt[x]{y}$ both indicate the xth root of y.

The process of taking roots by hand is a difficult and at times an impossible task. There are extensive tables and logarithms to help in finding roots if a calculator is not available. Calculators are used to find roots in this presentation.

Example

$$\sqrt[3]{350} \quad \text{or} \quad 350^{1/3}$$

Enter the base, 350.

Press $\boxed{INV}$ $\boxed{y^x}$ or $\boxed{2nd}$ $\boxed{y^x}$. (Calculators are not consistent in naming the undoing key, some calculators use $\boxed{2nd}$, some use $\boxed{INV}$.)

Enter the root, 3.

Press $\boxed{=}$.

The display is 7.047 298 732.

Example

$$\sqrt[4.5]{4{,}567} \quad \text{or} \quad 4{,}567^{1/4.5}$$

Enter the base 4,567.

Press $\boxed{INV}$ $\boxed{y^x}$ or $\boxed{2nd}$ $\boxed{y^x}$.

Enter the root, 4.5.

Press $\boxed{=}$.

The display is 6.505 060 438.

There are restrictions on the base for the $\boxed{y^x}$ function; the base must be a positive. Try finding the square root of -10.

$$10 \ \boxed{+/-} \ \boxed{2nd} \ \boxed{y^x} \ 2 \ \boxed{=}$$

The E in the display indicates an error. Some calculators actually print "error" in the display. The other unacceptable command is taking the "zeroth" root of a number. Once again, E is displayed.

Exponents include decimal and fractional numbers. The $\boxed{y^x}$ key works for decimal numbers. If the exponent is a fraction, use parentheses to group the exponent numbers.

> **Example**
>
> $$8^{2/3} = 8 \boxed{y^x} (2 \boxed{\div} 3) \boxed{=}$$

SECTION 7 EXERCISES

Use exponents to rewrite the following.

1. $2 \cdot 2 \cdot 2 \cdot 2 \cdot 2 \cdot 2 \cdot 2$.
2. $3 \cdot 3 \cdot 3 \cdot 3 \cdot 5 \cdot 5 \cdot 5 \cdot 5 \cdot 5$.
3. $2 \cdot x \cdot x \cdot x \cdot x \cdot y \cdot y \cdot y \cdot y \cdot y$.
4. $2 \cdot 3 \cdot 3 \cdot 5 \cdot 5 \cdot 5 \cdot 7 \cdot 7 \cdot 7 \cdot 7 \cdot 7$.

List the keystrokes and answer for each of the following.

5. $(1.05)^6$.
6. $500(1 - 0.06/12)^{36}$.
7. $350(1 + 0.10/12)^{48}$.
8. $2{,}500(1 + 0.09/12)^{30}$.
9. $46 \cdot 22.3^4$.
10. $89 \cdot (0.5)^6$.

List the keystrokes and find the answers for each of the following.

11. $\sqrt[3]{1.0234}$.
12. $\sqrt[4]{0.876}$.
13. $(350)^{1/5}$.
14. $\sqrt[4.1]{23.75}$.
15. $\sqrt{1.05}$.

Answers

1. 2^7
2. $3^4 \cdot 5^5$

3. $2x^4 \cdot y^5$

4. $2 \cdot 3^2 \cdot 5^3 \cdot 7^5$

5. 1.05 $\boxed{y^x}$ 6 $\boxed{=}$ 1.34

6. 0.06 $\boxed{\div}$ 12 $\boxed{=}\boxed{+/-}\boxed{+}$ 1 $\boxed{=}\boxed{y^x}$ 36 $\boxed{=}\boxed{\times}$ 500 $\boxed{=}$ 417.45

7. 0.10 $\boxed{\div}$ 12 $\boxed{=}\boxed{+}$ 1 $\boxed{=}\boxed{y^x}$ 48 $\boxed{=}\boxed{\times}$ 350 $\boxed{=}$ 521.27

8. 0.09 $\boxed{\div}$ 12 $\boxed{+}$ 1 $\boxed{=}\boxed{y^x}$ 30 $\boxed{=}\boxed{\times}$ 2,500 $\boxed{=}$ 3,128.18

9. 22.3 $\boxed{y^x}$ 4 $\boxed{=}\boxed{\times}$ 46 $\boxed{=}$ 11,375,677.83

10. 0.5 $\boxed{y^x}$ 6 $\boxed{=}\boxed{\times}$ 89 $\boxed{=}$ 1.390 625

11. 1.0234 $\boxed{2\text{nd}}\boxed{y^x}$ 3 $\boxed{=}$ 1.0077

12. 0.876 $\boxed{2\text{nd}}\boxed{y^x}$ 4 $\boxed{=}$ 0.967

13. 350 $\boxed{2\text{nd}}\boxed{y^x}$ 5 $\boxed{=}$ 3.227

14. 23.75 $\boxed{2\text{nd}}\boxed{y^x}$ 4.1 $\boxed{=}$ 2.165

15. 1.05 $\boxed{\text{INV}}\boxed{y^x}$ 2 $\boxed{=}$ 1.025

0.8   ROUNDING AND SIGNIFICANT DIGITS

Calculators and computers perform arithmetic operations quickly and give answers to accuracy far greater than is needed in most applications. Rules for rounding are needed for consistency. If the last decimal place desired is followed by the digits 0, 1, 2, 3, and 4, the number in question remains unchanged. If the last decimal place desired is followed by the digits 6, 7, 8, and 9, the number in question is increased by 1.

When the digit following the last decimal place desired is 5, however, it is necessary to look to the right of 5. If there are any digits other than 0, the number in question is increased by 1. If there are no other digits after 5 or all of them are 0, a procedure is developed to round up half of the time. The most common practice is to round up if the digit in question is odd, and to leave unchanged if the digit in question is even.

Example

$$19.453$$

1)9.453 rounded to tens. Because the digit following 1 is 9, 19 rounds to 20.

19.)453 rounded to units. Because the digit following 9 is 4, 19 remains unchanged.

19.4)53 rounded to tenths. Because the digit following 4 is 5, and the digit following 5 is 3, 19.4 rounds to 19.5.

19.45)3 rounded to hundredths. Because the digit following 5 is 3, 19.45 remains unchanged.

Example
67.45 rounded to tenths. Because 5 follows the tenth place and 4 is even, the number remains 67.4.
   67.35 rounded to tenths. Because 5 follows the tenth place and 3 is odd, the number is rounded to 67.4.

Calculators give answers with many decimal places; how many places should be used in answering a question? Computations never produce accuracy greater than the original information of the problem. In business applications because answers are in dollar and cent amounts, the accuracy is to the nearest cent. In some situations it is necessary to determine the number of significant digits to know what accuracy is appropriate.
   To determine the number of significant digits:

1. All nonzero digits and zeros between nonzero digits are significant. The following numbers have four significant digits.

$$3.001 \qquad 298.6 \qquad 420.3 \qquad 0.1111$$

2. Terminal zeros following the decimal point are considered significant. The following numbers have five significant digits.

$$2{,}345{,}600. \qquad 234.00 \qquad 3.0120 \qquad 500.00$$

3. In numbers less than 1, zeros between the decimal point and the first nonzero digit are not significant. The following numbers have three significant digits.

$$0.0203 \qquad 0.789 \qquad 0.000\ 00501 \qquad 0.0100$$

4. Terminal zeros on a whole number greater than 1 are usually not significant.

The amount $27,000 has two significant digits because it probably represents some amount between 26,500 and 27,499. If the amount were exactly $27,000, the number would be written as $27,000.00—there are seven significant digits in this number.

Suppose a compound interest problem requires that $1,000 be multiplied by 1.234 56789—a value from a compound interest table. To round the value from the table so our answer will have accuracy to the nearest cent, the number of digits in the approximate answer is needed. The approximate answer to the original problem is 1,250.00, a number with six significant digits. We must copy one more digit from the table than the number of significant digits in the answer to get this accuracy.

$$(1,000)(1.234\ 568) = \$1,234.57$$

The "one more" digit gives the extra digit to determine the rounding for the final answer.

Example
Multiply $256 by 0.987 65432.
The answer is approximately $250.00—an amount with five significant digits (250.00). Round 0.987 65432 to 6 (5 + 1) significant digits.

$$0.987\ 654 \times 256 = \$252.839\ 424$$

which rounds to $252.84.
Interpret the number in the display of your calculator and give an appropriate answer to the problem.

SECTION 8 EXERCISES

Round each to tens and hundredths accuracy.

1. 234.567.	**Answer** 230	234.57
2. 235.753.	**Answer** 240	235.75
3. 22,706.003.	**Answer** 22,710	22,706.00
4. 37.895.	**Answer** 40	37.90

5. 643.991.   **Answer** 640   643.99

Round the following amounts of money to the nearest cent.

6. $44.555.   **Answer** $44.56

7. $86.2349.   **Answer** $86.23

8. $89.995.   **Answer** $90.00

9. $2,340.536.   **Answer** $2,340.54

Round the following percents to the nearest whole number using the special rule for rounding.

10. 62.5%   **Answer** 62%

11. 37.5%   **Answer** 38%

12. 11.5%   **Answer** 12%

13. 88.5%   **Answer** 88%

14. 25.5%   **Answer** 26%

Find the number of significant digits in each of the following.

15. 0.650   **Answer** 3

16. 4,000,000   **Answer** 1

17. 4,000,000.0   **Answer** 8

18. 1,001   **Answer** 4

19. 4,130   **Answer** 3

20. 41.30   **Answer** 4

21. 0.0040   **Answer** 2

22. 7.003   **Answer** 4

Show the rounding done to give answers to the nearest cent.

23. ($86.45)(2.002 345 612).   **Answer** (86.45)(2.00235) = $173.10

24. ($20,000)(1.129 84576).   **Answer** (20,000)(1.129 8458) = $22,596.92

25. ($27.13)(1.04)^6.   **Answer** (27.13)(1.2653) = $34.33

Chapter 1

PERCENT

Percent is the heart of business analysis. Before specific applications of percent are studied, the basic relationship involving rate, base, and percentage is studied. Emphasis is made on understanding the meaning of the words, converting to mathematical notation, and using the basic equation-solving principles. Specific applications of percent are presented after an understanding of the basic relationship is mastered. The same principles are reinforced in various applications.

Business terminology is stressed throughout the chapter; interest, discounts, markups, and taxes are all special names for percentage. In each case, the specific name suggests the quantity representing the base and the appropriate procedure for solving the problem.

The presentation in this chapter is designed to be a unifying development of a basic mathematical relationship.

At the end of this chapter, the student will be able to:

1. Convert any percent to decimal or fractional notation.

2. Identify percentage, rate, and base in any business problem involving interest, discounts, markup, markdown, payroll taxes, property tax, and financial statement ratios.

3. Solve problems involving percentage, rate, and base.

4. Convert percent increase and percent decrease problems into a standard percent relationship.

5. Analyze financial statements for appropriate comparisons.

6. Solve ratio and proportion problems.

1.1   PERCENT EQUATION

Percent is one of the most valuable mathematical tools used in the business world. Before tackling problems involving the concept of percent, it may be helpful to look at a problem where the concept of percent is used to answer a question. Percent is translated as parts in 100. Suppose Sam brags he makes $19 on a $79 sale. Jose states his profits are $20.50 on $89. Does Sam or Jose have the better profit rate? The base of the profit differs (79 and 89). Therefore the profits of $19 and $20.50 cannot be compared. Percents share a common base of 100 and allow comparisons. To determine the percent of profit in each case, divide the profit by the selling price.

First, $19/79 = 0.24$, where 0.24 means $0.24 on $1 or $24 on $100. Second, $20.50/89 = 0.23$, where 0.23 means $0.23 on $1 or $23 on $100. The rate of profit is the amount of profit for each dollar amount. The rate per $100 is the percent. The rate of profit is multiplied by 100 and expressed as 24% or $24 for every $100. The second rate expressed as a percent is 23% or $23 for every $100. Percents allow us to compare two rates because the base of each number is 100. Twenty-four percent is a better rate of profit than 23%. Therefore Sam has the better profit rate.

The decimal number system is based on powers of 10; our money system is based on 100—a power of ten. Percents are parts in 100. Conversions among our monetary system, decimal numbers, and percents are easily made. A 5% tax converts to 5 cents on every 100 cents or $5 on every $100. Five percent can also be written as the decimal number 0.05. The English monetary measure of the pound and the Japanese money measure of the yen do not break down into subunits of $1/100$ and conversion to percent is not as easily made.

The basic relationship involving percent is

PERCENT OF BASE IS PERCENTAGE

In symbolized notation, this statement is

$$R \times B = P$$

P represents the percentage—part of the whole. *B* represents the base—the fundamental amount of the ingredient. *R* represents the rate—the quantitative measure of a part.

Rate is expressed as a percent; it never occurs alone but is associated with the base. **Of** means multiply; the number following **of** is the **base**. A percent must be converted to a decimal or fraction before performing the computation in the problem.

To convert a percent to a decimal:

1. Replace the percent sign (%) by a denominator of 100.

2. Divide—the quotient is the decimal replacement for the percent.

To convert a percent to a fraction:

1. Use the fraction (denominator 100) or reduce the fraction to an equivalent one.

To convert a percent on a calculator:

1. Enter the number associated with the percent sign.

2. Press $\boxed{\times}$, then $\boxed{\%}$.

3. The display is the decimal equivalent.

Example
Change 25% to an equivalent decimal and fraction.
    To obtain the decimal equivalent:

$$25\% = \frac{25}{100}$$

$$25 \div 100 = 0.25.$$

The fractional equivalent is $25/100$. To reduce the fraction $25/100$, divide the numerator and denominator by 25.

$$\frac{25}{100} = \frac{(25)(1)}{(25)(4)}$$

Cancel the common factor of 25. The reduced fraction is $1/4$.
    To convert 25% to a decimal equivalent, using a calculator:

$$25 \;\boxed{\times}\boxed{\%} = 0.25$$

Example
Change 0.8% to a decimal equivalent and fractional equivalent.

To obtain the fractional equivalent:

$$0.8\% = \frac{0.8}{100}$$

in fractional notation. Usually a decimal (0.8) is not included in a fraction, so multiply the numerator and denominator by 10.

$$\frac{(0.8)(10)}{(100)(10)} = \frac{8}{1,000}$$

$$\frac{8}{1,000} = \frac{(8)(1)}{(8)(125)}$$

Cancel the common factor of 8. The reduced fraction is 1/125.
    To obtain the decimal equivalent:

$$0.8 \div 100 = 0.008$$

Example
Change 0.05% to an equivalent decimal and fraction.

$$0.05 \div 100 = 0.0005$$

$$\frac{0.05}{100} = \frac{5}{10,000} = \frac{(5)(1)}{(5)(2,000)} = \frac{1}{2,000}$$

A **percent** equation involves three different quantities: rate, base, and percentage. If any two of these quantities are known, the third quantity can be found by substituting into the basic relationship and solving for the unknown. The first step involves matching the known quantities with the letters P, B, and R. R can always be identified by the word **percent** or the symbol %. B can be identified as the quantity following the statement "% of." P is defined as the part. The easiest way to identify P is to identify R and B; the remaining quantity is P. The equal sign in a mathematical equation translates as the verb **is** (or any form of the verb **to be**).

Example

42 is 30% of what number?

The number 30 is associated with the symbol % so it must be R. Because percent cannot be used in a mathematical equation, 30% must be written as either 0.30 or $^{30}/_{100}$. "What number" follows "% of," therefore the base is "what number." This can be named as B or x or any other symbol of your choice. By elimination, $42 = P$. These quantities are substituted in the basic percent relationship $P = B \times R$.

$$42 = (B)\left(\frac{30}{100}\right)$$

To solve this equation, multiply both sides by 100.

$$4,200 = 30B$$

Divide both sides by 30.

$$140 = B$$

The solution to the original statement is 140.

$$42 \text{ is } 30\% \text{ of } 140$$

If the concepts used in solving the equation, $42 = (B)(^{30}/_{100})$, are unfamiliar, refer to Chapter 0, Section 4, for a more detailed explanation.

Example

John Doe noted the tax deduction from his monthly check amounted to $836.56. He pays 26% of his income for taxes. Find his monthly income.

$R = 26\%$. The value used in the substitution is either 0.26 or $^{26}/_{100}$. "His income" follows "% of," so his income is the base. This is unknown; use either B or x for the base. By elimination, $836.56 must represent P. $836.56 is a part of the monthly income and percentage represents a part of. Substituting these quantities into the **percent** equation:

$$\$836.56 = (0.26)(x) \quad \text{usually written as } 0.26x$$

Divide each side of the equation by 0.26.

$$\$3,217.5384 = x$$

Because the answer is an amount of money, it should be rounded to the nearest cent. Therefore the monthly income is $3,217.54. Rounding is addressed in Chapter 0, Section 8.

Example

Susan Adams is self-employed. Her FICA obligations amounted to $2,534.80. The rate of social security withholdings for a self-employed person is 13.02% of the first $45,000 income. Find the income of Susan Adams.

$$R = 13.02\% = 0.1302 \quad \text{or} \quad \frac{13.02}{100}$$

$$B = \text{income (up to \$45,000)} = x$$

$$P = \text{tax} = \$2,534.80$$

Substituting into the basic formula:

$$2,534.80 = (0.1302)(x)$$

Solve this equation by dividing each side of the equation by 0.1302.

$$x = \$19,468.51$$

Two special types of percent occurring in business applications are percent **more** and percent **less**. These problems are also known as percent **increase** or percent **decrease** problems. **Percent** accompanied by the words more, less, increase, or decrease is the signal for a modified procedure to the basic percent equation.

Case 1 When R is unknown.

Example

What percent more than 60 is 75?

The base is 60. This is the number following the phrase "percent more." The rate is unknown. Therefore

$$R = x\% \text{ or } \frac{x}{100}$$

The percentage is **not** 75. The number 75 represents the base plus the increase. To determine the percentage, subtract the base 60 from the number 75.

$$75 - 60 = 15$$

The original question is restated as: What percent of 60 is 15? Substitute 15, 60, and $x/100$ in the percent equation.

$$15 = \left(\frac{x}{100}\right)(60)$$

Multiply each side of the equation by 100.

$$1{,}500 = 60x$$

Divide each side of the equation by 60.

$$x = 25$$

Recall that x represented percent in this problem. Because the word percent was included as a denominator of 100, the solution of the equation is the answer to the problem.

The solution states 15 is 25% of 60. The original problem asks what percent more than 60 is 75. The solution of 25% is also the solution to the original problem. 15 is 25% of 60 and 75 is 25% **more** than 60 say the same thing.

Determining the actual increase by subtracting the base from the percentage is the key to **percent more** problems. Restate the problem as a percent relationship.

Example
What percent **more than** 60 is 80?
"Percent more" signals us to subtract 60 from 80, giving 20. The question is now restated as: What percent of 60 is 20? Notice 60 was the base of the original problem—the number closest to the word percent. The base of

the restated problem remains the same. What percent of 60 is 20? $x/100$ is what percent? The base is 60 and the percentage is 20. Substitute into $P = R \times B$.

$$20 = \left(\frac{x}{100}\right)(60)$$

Multiply each side by 100.

$$2{,}000 = 60x$$

Divide each side by 60.

$$x = 33\frac{1}{3}$$

The original problem solution states 80 is $33^{1}/_{3}\%$ more than 60.

   Percent less problems are solved in a way similar to percent more problems. Determine the actual difference between the percentage and the base by subtracting the percentage amount from the base. Rewrite the problem as a percent problem.

Example
What percent **less than** 40 is 35?
   The base is 40 and the other quantity is 35. Subtract these quantities; the difference is 5.
   Restate the problem as: What percent of 40 is 5? $x/100$ is what percent? The base is 40 and the percentage is 5. Substitute into $P = B \times R$.

$$5 = (40)\left(\frac{x}{100}\right)$$

Multiply both sides of the equation by 100.

$$500 = 40x$$

Divide both sides of the equation by 40:

$$x = 12.5$$

| Thus 35 is 12.5% less than 40 or 5 is 12.5% of 40.

Case 2 When the base (B) or percentage (P) is unknown, and R is known.

An alternate procedure must be developed because subtraction cannot be performed when the base or percentage is unknown.

Example

This year's salary of $35,500 reflects a 10% increase over last year's salary. What was last year's salary?

$35,500 is P.

10% increase of B is $10\%B + B$. Replacing 10% by 0.10:

$$10\%B + 100\%B = 0.10B + 1B$$

$$0.10B + 1B = 1.10B$$

10% **increase over** last year's salary is written as 110% of last year's salary. If B represents last year's salary, $1.10B$ represents last year's salary $+$ the increase of last year's salary.

$$1.10B = 35,500$$

Divide by 1.10.

$$B = 32,272.727$$

Because this is a dollar amount, round the answer to the nearest cent.

$$B = \$32,272.73$$

If the words in the problem include **percent decrease**, a similar process will be used; subtraction from 100% is involved in restating the problem as a percent.

Example

Sales of $456,000 reflect a 15% **decrease** over last year's sales. Find last year's sales.

15% decrease over last year's sales is replaced by $(100\% - 15\%)$ of last year's sales

$$100\% - 15\% = 85\%$$

$$R = 85\% = 0.85$$

$$B = \text{last year's sales}$$

$$P = \$456{,}000$$

$$456{,}000 = 0.85B$$

Divide by 0.85 and round to the nearest cent.

$$B = \$536{,}470.59$$

The original problem can be restated as: $456,000 reflects a 15% decrease over last year's sales of $536,470.59

The procedure to follow to solve percent equations, using the basic relationship, $R \times B = P$, is outlined below.

1. Problem involving "percent of":
   a. Match quantities in the problem with R, B, and P.
   b. Write percent as a decimal or a fraction.
   c. Substitute quantities in $P = R \times B$ and solve.

2. Problem involving percent more than or percent less than, when the rate is unknown:
   a. Identify R as $x/100$.
   b. Subtract the two known quantities to determine P.
   c. Determine B as the quantity associated with percent more or percent less.
   d. Substitute in the basic relationship and solve.

3. Problem involving percent increase or percent decrease, when the base or percentage is unknown:
   a. Identify the number associated with the percent as R.
   b. Replace percent increase by $(100\% + R\%)$. Rewrite the problem as percent of, and solve.
   c. Replace percent decrease by $(100\% - R\%)$. Rewrite the problem as percent of, and solve.

SECTION 1 EXERCISES

1. Convert 2% to a decimal equivalent and a fractional equivalent reduced to lowest terms.

2. Convert 42% to a decimal equivalent and a fractional equivalent with a denominator of 100.

3. Convert 0.75% to a decimal equivalent and a fractional equivalent with a denominator of 10,000.

4. Convert 25% to a decimal equivalent and a fractional equivalent reduced to lowest terms.

5. 85% of $1,623.12 is what amount?

6. 23.1% of 217 is what number?

7. 120% of $456 is what amount?

8. What number is 135% of 5,280?

9. What is 62.5% of $823.15?

10. What is 0.02% of 745?

11. What percent of 86.2 is 37.1? Round answer to nearest percent.

12. What percent of 825 is 164? Round answer to nearest percent.

13. 431 is what percent of 218? Round answer to nearest percent.

14. $14.42 is what percent of $12.18? Round answer to nearest percent.

15. 82.5 is 15% of what number?

16. 32.2 is 18.5% of what number?

17. 8% of what amount is $40.30?

18. 140% of what amount is $60?

19. What percent more than 42 is 50?

20. What percent more than 520 is 700?

21. What percent less than 42 is 30?

22. What percent less than 520 is 480?

23. A 10% increase over what number is 520?

24. A 50% increase over what number is 2,000?

25. A 15% decrease over what amount is $20,500?

26. A 50% decrease over what amount is $3.25?

27. 5% of the cost of a stock is the dividend. If a stock cost $25.00, what is the dividend?

28. 20% of Carlos' take-home pay should be used for housing. If his monthly take-home pay is $1,726.45, how much should be used for housing?

29. Of 345 students enrolled in accounting, 268 received passing grades. What percent of the students passed?

30. A lawyer agrees to work for 33 1/3% of the award granted by the court. The court awarded a settlement of $500,000. How much did the lawyer collect?

31. The contractor estimated that the electrical work expense was 11% of the cost of the house. The electrical work expense amounted to $6,375. Find the cost of the house.

32. Pagota Restaurant has a monthly income of $45,280. The cost of food served was $24,589. What percent of the income is the cost of food?

33. Of the 68 employees of National Universe Corporation, 38 employees have never taken a sick day. What percent of the employees have never taken a sick day?

34. What percent increase in value has occurred in Nu Loc stock if the original value was $46.75 and the present value is $57.50?

35. What percent decrease in value has occurred in ARC stock if the original cost was $131.50 and the present value is $118?

36. What percent decrease in value of $47.75 is $34?

37. What percent increase in salary occurs when a salary of $34,000 increases to $38,500?

38. A 10% increase in cost gives a new cost of $45,000. What was the original cost?

39. A bill in the amount of $45.20 reflected a 20% decrease of the original bill. What was the original bill?

40. A 20% decrease of salary gave the president an annual salary of $450,000. What amount had he received before the decrease?

41. The cost of the bicycle increased by 25% over last year's price. If last year's price was $115, what is the increased cost?

42. A budget item of $4,800 is 40% less than last year's allotment. What was the allowance last year?

Answers to Odd-Numbered Exercises

1. 0.02. $^1/_{50}$.

3. 0.0075. 75/10,000.

5. $1,379.65.

7. $547.20.

9. $514.47.

11. 43%.

13. 198%.

15. 550.

17. $503.75.

19. 19%.

21. 28.6%.

23. 473.

25. $24,117.65.

27. $1.25.

29. 77.7%.

31. $57.954.55.

33. 56%.

35. 10%.

37. 13.2%.

39. $56.50.

41. $143.75.

1.2 SIMPLE INTEREST

An individual using something belonging to another person pays rent for this usage. When the item being used is money, the rent is called **interest** and is directly related to the amount used and the length of time it is used.

The basic relationship involving percent, base, and percentage works for simple interest. The terminology is specific to the world of finance.

The amount of money "rented" is the same as the **base** in the percent equation. This amount is given the special name of **principal** in an interest problem.

The rate of rent is a percent and is the same as the **rate** in the percent equation. Because the time involved in a transaction varies from problem to problem, rate in a simple interest problem always refers to the **annual rate** or the rate charged for rent for 1 year.

Percentage in the basic equation is renamed **interest** in an interest problem. The equation $P = R \times B$ becomes $I = R \times P$.

If the time of "rental" is other than 1 year it is necessary to add the additional factor of T. T is time expressed in years.

$$\textbf{Interest} = \textbf{principal} \times \textbf{rate} \times \textbf{time} \quad \text{or} \quad I = PRT$$

Example
A loan for $5,000 is granted at 6% for 10 months. How much interest is earned?

$$P = \$5,000 \qquad \text{amount of loan}$$

$$R = 6\% = 0.06 \qquad \text{rate of loan}$$

$$T = \frac{10}{12} \qquad \text{time in years}$$

$$I = (5,000)(0.06)\left(\frac{10}{12}\right) = \$250$$

The calculator keystroke is

$$5{,}000 \; \boxtimes \; 0.06 \; \boxtimes \; 10 \; \boxdiv \; 12 \; \boxminus$$

Both the borrower and the lender are also concerned with the **amount due** at the end of the period. **Maturity value** is another name for amount due and refers to the sum of the principal and the interest earned in the given time period. S is used to denote the maturity value.

$$S = P + I$$

In the preceding example, the **maturity value** of $5,000 loaned at 6% for 10 months is

$5,000 (principal) + $250 (computed interest) = $5,250 (maturity value)

To develop a single formula for the maturity value, the general relationship

maturity value = principal + interest

is used and then the formula for interest is substituted into this relationship. Replace interest by PRT in $S = P + I$.

$$S = P + PRT$$

Factor P from $P + PRT$.

$$S = P(1 + RT)$$

The maturity value can be found in one step, using $S = P(1 + RT)$.

$$S = 5,000\left(1 + (0.06)\left(\frac{10}{12}\right)\right)$$

The calculator keystroke is as follows. Do the calculations within the parentheses, starting with the multiplication.

0.06 $\boxed{\times}$ 10 $\boxed{\div}$ 12 $\boxed{+}$ 1 $\boxed{=}$$\boxed{\times}$ 5,000 $\boxed{=}$

$$S = 5,000(1.05) = \$5,250$$

Example
A loan for $800 is extended to Carlos Gonzalez for 18 months at an annual interest rate of 8%. What is the maturity value of the loan?

$$P = \$800 \qquad R = 0.08 \qquad T = \frac{18}{12}$$

$$S = 800\left(1 + (0.08)\left(\frac{18}{12}\right)\right)$$

The calculator keystroke is

$$0.08 \;\boxed{\times}\; 18 \;\boxed{\div}\; 12 \;\boxed{+}\; 1 \;\boxed{=}\boxed{\times}\; 800 \;\boxed{=}$$

$$S = \$896$$

The three formulas, $I = PRT$, $S = P(1 + RT)$, and $S = P + I$, can be solved for any one of the variables in terms of the other unknowns. In the percent equation, if two of the quantities are known, the third can be determined. In the first two interest formulas, if three of the four variables are known, the fourth can be determined. In the third relationship, if two of the variables are known, the third can be determined.

Example
What principal will have a maturity value of $1,498 after 9 months at a 15% interest rate?

$$P = ? \qquad S = 1,498 \qquad T = \frac{9}{12} \qquad R = 0.15$$

Substitute in $S = P(1 + RT)$.

$$1,498 = P\left(1 + (0.15)\left(\frac{9}{12}\right)\right)$$

$$= P(1.1125)$$

Divide 1,498 by 1.1125.

$$P = \$1,346.52$$

An alternate way of asking the question in the preceding example is: Find the present value of $1,498 after 9 months at 15% interest. The problem is asking: How much money must be invested today to amount to $1,498 in 9 months if money earns 15% interest?

Interest problems can have a time period calculated in days. The number of days is converted to a fractional part of a year either by approximating the number of days in a year as 360 or using the exact number of days (365 or 366).

Number of days/360 gives **ordinary interest**.

Number of days/(365 or 366) gives **exact interest**.

Example

Find the ordinary interest and exact interest on $50,000 for 100 days at 10% interest.

Ordinary interest:

$$I = (50{,}000)\left(\frac{100}{360}\right)(0.10) = \$1{,}388.89$$

The calculator keystroke is

$$50{,}000 \; \boxtimes \; 100 \; \boxdiv \; 360 \; \boxtimes \; 0.10 \; \boxminus$$

Exact interest:

$$I = (50{,}000)\left(\frac{100}{365}\right)(0.10) = \$1{,}369.86$$

The calculator keystroke is

$$50{,}000 \; \boxtimes \; 100 \; \boxdiv \; 365 \; \boxtimes \; 0.10 \; \boxminus$$

Notice ordinary interest is a larger amount. Lending institutions like the increased revenue and favor the 360-day year. Prior to calculators and computers, the use of 360-day years simplified computations. Today it is as easy to enter 365 as 360 in the formula.

Just as there are two types of interest when time is given in days, there are two ways to calculate the number of days when the beginning and end dates of a period are known.

Exact time calculates the exact number of days from the date of origin to the ending date of the loan. Using Table 1 in the Appendix is an easy way to find the exact number of days. The table associates a number with every date of the year. Identify the number associated with the beginning date and the number associated with the ending date, then subtract the two numbers. This is the exact time between the two dates. When the year is a leap year and February 29 falls within the loan period, add 1 to the remainder of the subtraction. Leap years occur when the year is exactly divisible by 4. The exception to this rule is on the turn of the century when the year must be divisible by 400 to be classified as a leap year.

Ordinary time is based on the assumption that all months contain 30 days. To calculate ordinary time, determine how many full months between the date of origin and the termination date, multiply by 30, and add the remaining number of days not included in the full months.

Example
Find the exact time and ordinary time between May 20 and December 7, using Table 1.

   Exact time:

   May 20 is day 140.

   December 7 is day 341.

$$\text{Exact time} = 341 - 140 = 201 \text{ days}$$

   Ordinary time:

   May 20 to November 20 = 6 months = 180 days.

   November 20 to December 7 = 17 days.

$$\text{Ordinary time} = 180 + 17 = 197 \text{ days}$$

Example
Find the exact time and ordinary time in the 8-month period beginning September 21, 1987.

   Exact time: Because these dates pass from one year to another, add 365 to the number associated with the end of the period.

   Eight months from September 21 is May 21.

   From Table 1, May 21 is 141.

   Add 365 to 141 because the time period spans December 31

$$141 + 365 = 506$$

From Table 1, September 21 is 264.

$$506 - 264 = 242 \text{ days}$$

Because 1988 is a leap year and the period includes February 29, add 1 day.

$$\text{Exact time} = 242 + 1 = 243 \text{ days}$$

ordinary time:

$$8 \text{ months} \times 30 \text{ days/month} = 240 \text{ days}$$

The amount of interest and maturity amount vary according to the selection of **exact** or **ordinary interest** over an **exact** or **ordinary time**. The variations necessitate that both parties involved in the loan agree on the type of interest and method for determining the number of days.

The four possible combinations are as follows.

1. **Ordinary time over ordinary interest.** $T =$ time calculated on 30-day months and is changed to years by dividing by 360.

2. **Exact time over ordinary interest (bankers' rule).** $T =$ exact number of days from date of origin to termination and is converted to years by dividing by 360.

3. **Ordinary time over exact interest.** $T =$ time calculated with 30-day months and is changed to years by dividing by 365 or 366.

4. **Exact time over exact interest (U.S. rule).** $T =$ exact number of days from date of origin to termination and is converted to years by dividing by 365 or 366.

The method used by most financial institutions is exact time over ordinary interest, the **bankers' rule**. The U.S. government and the Federal Reserve Bank use the method of exact interest over exact time, the **U.S. rule.**

Individuals usually elect ordinary time over ordinary interest because of the ease of calculations. For relatively small amounts of money, the difference in interest is negligible.

Example
Find the interest on $45,000 dated May 14, 1989 and terminating October

15, 1989, using the bankers' rule, the U.S. rule, and the ordinary time over ordinary interest method. The annual interest rate is 8%.

Solution:

Bankers' rule (Exact time/360):

May 14 is day 134.

October 15 is day 288.

Exact time = 288 − 134 = 154 days

$$T = \frac{154}{360}$$

$$I = (45,000)(0.08)\left(\frac{154}{360}\right) = \$1,540$$

U.S. rule (Exact time/365):

$$I = (45,000)(0.08)\left(\frac{154}{365}\right) = \$1,518.90$$

Individuals (ordinary time/360):

May 14 to October 15 = 5 months + 1 day

5(30) + 1 = 151 days

$$T = \frac{151}{360}$$

$$I = (45,000)(0.08)\left(\frac{151}{360}\right) = \$1,510$$

Interest calculations are summarized as follows.

Interest:

$$\text{Interest} = \text{principal} \times \text{rate} \times \text{time}$$

where the rate is an annual rate and time is given in years.

Maturity value:

$$S = P(1 + RT)$$

where P is the initial amount or the present value and S is the future amount or the maturity value.

Ordinary time counts as 30-day months without considering the month.

Exact time counts the days between the initial date and the ending date, making adjustments for leap years.

Ordinary interest uses 360 as the number of days in each year.

Exact interest uses 365 or 366 as the number of days in each year.

SECTION 2 EXERCISES

1. Find the amount of interest earned on $50,000 at 8% interest for 16 months.

2. Find the annual interest on $8,000 at 12% interest.

3. Find the rate that gives $400 annual interest on a principal of $6,000.

4. Find how long (in months) it will take for $12,000 to yield interest of $2,640 if the annual interest rate is 12%.

5. Find the present value of $20,000 that has been invested for 12 years at 10% interest.

6. Find the annual rate that gives $1,500 interest from a principal of $10,000.

7. How many years will it take for $10,000 to become $20,000 at an annual interest rate of 12.5%?

8. Find the amount of money to be deposited on the date of birth of your child to guarantee $5,000 on the child's eighteenth birthday. The money earns 10% simple interest.

9. Find the exact and ordinary time between March 17 and October 30.

10. Find the exact and ordinary time between June 4 and December 25.

11. Find the exact and ordinary time between September 14, 1988, and June 25, 1989.

12. Find the exact and ordinary time between September 1, 1987, and April 25, 1988.

13. Find the exact and ordinary time in an 8-month interval beginning on March 25.

14. Find the exact and ordinary time in a 9-month interval beginning April 15, 1988.

15. Find the amount of interest charged by a bank (use the bankers' rule) on $25,000 at 7% interest from April 14 to September 1.

16. Find the amount of interest paid under the U.S. rule on $25,000 at 7% interest from April 14 to September 1.

17. Find the interest paid by a U.S. reserve bank for the use of $100,000 at 12% interest for 3 months. The date of origin was February 20, 1989. All federal banks use the U.S. rule in interest calculations.

18. Find the amount due on $100,000 at 12% interest for 3 months. The date of origin was February 20, 1989, and the bankers' rule was used to determine the time.

19. A friendly loan between two individuals for $10,000 was made on March 15. The rate of interest charged was 8%. What amount was due to settle the loan and interest 3 months later?

20. Parents loaned their son $10,000 for a down payment on a home until his presently owned home is sold. The rate of interest charged was 6%, and the loan was paid back in four months. What amount was repaid?

Answers to Odd-Numbered Exercises

1. $5,333.33.

3. $6^{2}/_{3}\%$.

5. $9,090.91.

7. 8 years.

9. 227 days, 223 days.

11. 284 days, 281 days.

13. 245 days, 240 days.

15. $680.56.

17. $2,926.03.

19. $10,200.

1.3 BANK DISCOUNT

The interest charged for money is sometimes computed on the final amount (maturity value) of the loan rather than on the original amount (principal). When this process is used, the charge for the money is called the **bank discount** rather than interest.

The bank discount uses the basic percent formula (like interest does), along with the added time factor. The following chart compares percentage, interest, and discount.

Basic percentage	Simple Interest	Bank Discount
$P = R \times B$	$I = P \times r \times t$	$D = S \times d \times t$
$A = B + P$	$S = P + I$	$P = S - D$
$A = B(1 + R)$	$S = P(1 + rt)$	$P = S(1 - dt)$
$P =$ percentage	$I =$ interest	$D =$ discount
$R =$ rate	$r =$ interest rate	$d =$ discount rate
$B =$ base	$P =$ Present value	$S =$ maturity value
	$t =$ time (in year)	$t =$ time (in years)
$A =$ total amount	$S =$ maturity value	$P =$ present value

The bank discount is called interest in advance. The interest is paid in advance to receiving the money, and the interest is charged on the amount of money due at maturity. Let us look at an example to illustrate this point.

Example

An individual arranges to borrow $10,000 from a bank for 1 year at a rate of 12%. If the bank charges interest, the maturity value of this loan is

$$P = 10,000 \qquad r = 0.12 \qquad t = 1 \qquad S = ?$$

$$S = 10,000(1 + 0.12) = \$11,200$$

The amount due at maturity is $11,200.

If the bank discounts the note:

$$S = 10,000 \qquad d = 0.12 \qquad t = 1 \qquad P = ?$$

$$D = (10{,}000)(0.12)(1) = \$1{,}200$$

$$P = S - D$$

$$= 10{,}000 - 1{,}200$$

$$= \$8{,}800$$

The bank pays out \$8,800. The amount due at maturity is \$10,000.

If \$10,000 was needed, a larger amount is borrowed to ensure the required amount at the time of the loan. To find S:

$$P = 10{,}000 \qquad d = 0.12 \qquad t = 1$$

$$10{,}000 = S(1 - 0.12)$$

$$= S(0.88)$$

$$\$11{,}363.64 = S$$

Borrow \$11,364 now to get \$10,000 under the discounting process.

If a bank gives an individual the choice of a loan with interest charges added or a discounted note, the interest rate (r) should be compared with the discount rate (d) to determine the better deal. Take the two formulas $S = P(1 + rt)$ and $P = S(1 - dt)$. Replace S in the second formula by the $P(1 + rt)$ of the first formula.

$$P = P(1 + rt)(1 - dt)$$

Divide both sides of the equation by P.

$$1 = (1 + rt)(1 - dt)$$

Divide by $1 - dt$.

$$\frac{1}{(1 - dt)} = 1 + rt$$

Subtract 1 from each side.

$$\frac{1}{(1 - dt)} - 1 = rt$$

The common denominator on the left-hand side is

$$\frac{(1 - 1 + dt)}{(1 - dt)} = rt$$

$$\frac{dt}{(1 - dt)} = rt$$

Divide both sides by t.

$$\frac{d}{(1 - dt)} = r$$

An alternate solution in terms of d is

$$\frac{r}{(1 + rt)} = d$$

These two formulas provide a way to convert between interest and discount rates. Use $r = d/(1 - dt)$ if the discount rate is known and an equivalent interest rate is needed. Use $d = r/(1 + rt)$ if the interest rate is known and an equivalent discount rate is needed.

Example
A bank advertises an annual discount rate of 12%. What is the equivalent annual interest rate?

$$d = 0.12 \qquad t = 1 \qquad r = ?$$

$$r = \frac{0.12}{(1 - 0.12)} = \frac{0.12}{0.88} = 13.6\%$$

The calculator keystroke is

0.12 ÷ (1 − 0.12) =

Example
To earn 11% interest on a 6-month loan, what discount rate should the lender charge?

$$r = 0.11 \qquad d = ? \qquad t = \frac{6}{12}$$

$$d = \frac{0.11}{\left(1 + (0.11)\left(\frac{6}{12}\right)\right)}$$

$$= \frac{0.11}{1.055} = 0.104 = 10.4\%$$

The calculator keystroke is

$$0.11 \; \boxed{\div} \; \boxed{(} \boxed{(} 0.11 \; \boxed{\times} \; 6 \; \boxed{\div} \; 12 \; \boxed{+} \; 1 \boxed{)} \; \boxed{=}$$

Suppose the time factor is expressed as a number of days; how is t computed? Generally, the bankers' rule (exact number/360) is used, but the 365-day year is becoming more widespread with bank discounts. When commercial banks borrow funds from a federal reserve bank, exact days/365 or 366 days is used for the bank discount.

A promissory note is called a negotiable instrument, similar to a check or cash. The promissory note can be sold to a third party. The selling of a promissory note does not change the original obligation; it only changes the recipient of the obligation.

Example
On June 1 Ed Jones had extensive repair work done on his auto, and Big Heart Garage agreed to loan Ed the necessary amount of $1,500 for 3 months at 12% interest. On June 10 Big Heart Garage needed cash and took the loan agreement to the bank and sold the instrument to the bank. The bank discounted the note at 14%. How much did Big Heart Garage receive for the $1,500 loan?

A time-line chart is useful in this case. On the time line, enter the date of the loan, the date when the loan is due, and the date the loan was sold to the bank.

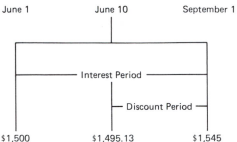

The computations are as follows.
Interest problem:

$$P = 1,500 \qquad r = 12\% \qquad t = \frac{3}{12}$$

$$S = 1,500\left(1 + (0.12)\left(\frac{3}{12}\right)\right)$$

$$= \$1,545$$

Discount problem:

$$S = 1,545 \qquad d = 0.14 \qquad t = \frac{83}{360}$$

(June 10 is day 161 and September 1 is day 244. 244 − 161 = 83.)

$$P = (1,545)\left(1 - (0.14)\left(\frac{83}{360}\right)\right)$$

$$= (1,545)(0.967\ 7222)$$

$$= \$1,495.13$$

Big Heart Garage is the loser—they received \$1,495.13 for work total-ing \$1,500. The difference was less than interest charges would have been to borrow \$1,500 for 83 days. Ed Jones will be notified to repay the loan to the bank.

To determine the proceeds of a discounted note:

1. Find the maturity value (S) of the simple interest loan.

2. Determine the term of the discount (t). The term is the number of days from discount date to date of maturity.

3. Find the proceeds, where S is the maturity value solved for in step 1. d is the discount rate, and t is the term of discount.

The selling of a loan can occur more than once. An individual might sell to a local bank, the local bank might sell to a regional bank, and so on. Each transaction involves a discounting process, but the maturity value is fixed from the original loan.

SECTION 3 EXERCISES

1. $S = \$5,000$, $d = 12.5\%$, and $t = 2$ years. Find P.

2. $S = \$4,000$, $d = 10.5\%$, and $t = 18$ months. Find P.

3. $P = \$10,000$, $d = 14\%$, and $t = 10$ months. Find S.

4. $P = \$6,500$, $d = 7.9\%$, and $t = 3$ years. Find S.

5. A bank agrees to make a loan of $7,500, discounted at 9%, for a period of 36 months. How much do you receive from the loan?

6. A bank makes a loan of $6,800, discounted at 10%, for 24 months. How much do you receive from the loan?

7. Find the annual discount rate equivalent to an annual interest rate of 13%.

8. Find the annual interest rate equivalent to a quoted annual discount rate of 10%.

9. Find the interest rate equivalent to a 9% discount rate for 4 months.

10. Find the discount rate equivalent to an interest rate of 10% for 6 months.

11. One bank offers a 6.9% discount rate for 24 months, and a competitive bank offers a loan with an interest rate of 7.5% for any given time period. Which is the better offer for the customer?

12. A bank discounts 2-year loans at 7%, and a loan company charges 8% interest for any 2-year loan. Does the bank or loan company offer the better deal?

13. To buy the automobile of your choice, you need $8,700 from the bank to complete the deal. The bank agrees to lend the money on a discounted note at 9.6% for 3 years. What is the maturity value of the loan?

14. You are buying a new home, and you need to borrow $50,000 for 3 months until the purchase of your existing home is completed. The bank agrees to loan you the money at a discount rate of 11%. Find the maturity value of the loan.

15. If you borrow $1,000 for 3 months and receive $975, find the discount rate.

16. If you receive $1,920 on a $2,000 discounted note and the term of the note is 6 months, find the discount rate.

17. A company sells a note to the bank. The note was for $780 at an interest rate of 12%, for 6 months. The note was dated July 1. On August 10 the company takes the note to the bank and the bank agrees to discount it at 12%. Find the amount the company receives for the note on August 10.

18. Sunrise Furniture Company extends credit to you for $2,500 for 1 year at 18% interest. One month later the bank discounts the note at 20%. Find how much Sunrise Furniture Company receives.

19. Seat's Furniture Company sold $12,000 worth of chairs and accepted a 120-day note at 12% interest. Twenty days later Seat's Furniture sold the note to Favorable Finance Company at a 16% discount rate. How much did Favorable Finance give Seat's Furniture for the note?

20. Mickey's Discount buys $15,000 worth of merchandise on May 15 and signs a 90-day promissory note with an interest rate of 12%. On June 12 the merchandiser sells the note to Farout Finance Company at a discount rate of 15%. What does Farout Finance pay for the note? What is Farout paid when the 90-day promissory note comes due?

21. Bob Sharp purchases a computer for $2,500. He signs a note on September 15 for the amount at an interest rate of 10%. The note is due on December 31. On October 11 the computer store discounts the note at Dollar Bank and Trust Company at 14%. Find the amount Dollar Bank and Trust Company pays for the note.

22. Green Lumber Company accepted a $4,000 note on June 14 for 90 days at 12% interest. On July 8 Green Lumber discounted the note at Central Bank and received $4,020. What was the rate of discount?

23. John Powell was the holder of a $750, 100-day note dated June 20. The interest rate was 10%. On September 1 he discounted the note at Broad Bank and received $760. What was the rate of discount at Broad Bank?

24. A company holds the following interest bearing notes. On June 15 the notes are discounted at a 10% discount rate. Find how much the company receives for the notes.

Date of Note	Time	Amount	Interest Rate
May 10	90 days	$4,200	8%
June 1	30 days	$5,000	9%

25. A company holds the following interest bearing notes. On September 1

the notes are discounted at a 12% discount rate. Find how much the company receives for the notes.

Date of Note	Time	Amount	Interest Rate
August 5	60 days	$1,200	10%
August 25	90 days	$2,000	11%

Answers to Odd-Numbered Exercises

1. $3,750.

3. $1,130.75.

5. $5,475.

7. 11.5%.

9. 9.3%.

11. 7.5%.

13. $12,219.

15. 10%.

17. $787.11.

19. $11,925.33.

21. $2,493.22.

23. 18.7%.

25. $3,204.74.

1.4 TRADE AND CASH DISCOUNTS

A **discount** is the amount of reduction in the selling price of an item. It is a percent of the selling price. Two types of discounts offered to the business community as incentives are trade discounts as incentives to buy and cash discounts as incentives to pay cash.

Trade Discount

Trade discounts are the amounts of reduction in the price of goods. The reduction is offered by the seller and is a percent of the list price.

$$\text{Trade discount} = \text{rate of discount} \times \text{list price}$$

$$\text{Net price} = \text{list price} - \text{discount}$$

$$= \text{list price} - (\text{list price} \times \text{rate of discount})$$

$$N = P(1 - d)$$

$$D = P \times d \qquad N = P - D \qquad N = P(1 - d)$$

where D is the amount of discount, d is the rate of discount, P is the list price, and N is the net price.

Trade discounts are used extensively in catalog sales. It is impractical to reprint a catalog for each price change. A catalog is printed, giving the list prices associated with each item. A separate flyer gives the discount rates for each category of items. This procedure allows different pricing structures for different categories of clients, special prices for seasonal items, and promotional sales.

Example

Handy Hardware Company has ordered $870 in merchandise from the catalog of a supplier. The trade discount offered is 27%. Find the amount of the discount and the net price of the merchandise.

$$P = 870 \qquad d = 0.27$$

$$D = P \times d = 870 \times 0.27 = \$234.90$$

$$N = P - D = 870 - 234.90 = \$635.10$$

Alternatively, using $N = P(1 - d)$:

$$N = 870(1 - 0.27)$$

$$= 870(0.73)$$

$$= \$635.10$$

The alternate method only gives the net price and does not give the actual discount received.

Example
Clear Swimmers, Inc., ordered pool chemicals from their supplier. The order amounted to $2,345. The company offers a 20% trade discount. Find the net amount of the order.

$$P = 2,345 \qquad d = 0.20$$

$$N = P(1 - d) = 2,345(1 - 0.20) = 2,345(0.8) = \$1,876.$$

Suppliers frequently offer additional incentives to promote sales. This is done by additional discounts. More than one discount is called a **chain discount.** The first discount is a percent of the list price. The second discount is a percent of the net price after the first discount. Each additional discount rate applies to the net price determined by the preceding discount rate.

Example
In September Circulating Fan Company sent a flyer to all customers offering the merchandise in their catalog at trade discounts of 20%, 15%, and 10%. Find the net price of a fan listed at $150.
    The first trade discount is 20% and is a percent of $150.

$$N_1 = 150(1 - 0.20) = 150(0.80) = \$120$$

The second trade discount is 15% and is a percent of $120.

$$N_2 = 120(1 - 0.15) = 120(0.85) = \$102$$

The third trade discount is 10% and is a percent of $102.

$$N_3 = 102(1 - 0.10) = 102(0.90) = \$91.80$$

The order in which the discounts are applied is irrelevant because the base changes in each successive operation. **Do not** add the discount rates and apply to the list price; each discount rate applies to a new net price.

Single Equivalent Discount

A single equivalent discount rate is a rate that gives the same net price as the application of successive discounts. To determine the single equivalent discount rate:

1. Subtract each of the chain discount rates (expressed as a decimal) from 1.
2. Multiply the remainders (obtained in step 1) together.
3. Subtract the product from 1.
4. Write the number as a percent to obtain the **single equivalent discount rate.**

Example

$$P = \$150 \qquad d = 20\%, \ 15\%, \ 10\%$$

Step 1:

$$1 - 0.20 = 0.80 \qquad 1 - 0.15 = 0.85 \qquad 1 - 0.10 = 0.90$$

Step 2:

$$(0.80)(0.85)(0.90) = 0.612$$

Step 3:

$$1 - 0.612 = 0.388$$

Step 4:

$$0.388 = 38.8\%$$

The single equivalent discount rate is 38.8%.

$$N = 150(1 - 0.388) = \$91.80$$

Conversion of a chain discount to a single equivalent discount rate simplifies computation and allows for comparison of incentives among competitors.

Example
Two competing companies wish to promote the sale of Christmas cards. One company offers trade discounts of 20%, 10%, and 5%. A second company has the same list prices on the merchandise but offers trade discounts of 25% and 8%. Which supplier offers the lowest net price?

For 20%, 10%, and 5%, the single equivalent trade discount is

$$1 - (0.8)(0.9)(0.95) = 0.316 = 31.6\%$$

because $(1 - 0.20) = 0.8$, $(1 - 0.10) = 0.9$, and $(1 - 0.05) = 0.95$.
For 25% and 8%, the single equivalent trade discount is

$$1 - (0.75)(0.92) = 31\%$$

because $(1 - 0.25) = 0.75$ and $(1 - 0.08) = 0.92$.

The supplier offering trade discounts of 20%, 10%, and 5% offers the larger rate of discount (31.6% versus 31%), and therefore the lower net price.

Cash Discount

The other type of discount offered to customers is the **cash** discount. The suppliers offer cash discounts to influence the date of payment. The cash discount rate is listed on the invoice. A typical cash discount might be 2% if the invoice is paid within 10 days from the invoice date with the net amount of the invoice to be paid within 30 days. A cash discount is indicated by 2/10, $n/30$. This notation reads as 2% discount if paid within 10 days, net amount of invoice due in 30 days.

To determine the cash discount, multiply the cash discount rate by the net price of the merchandise.

Example

A customer receives merchandise and an invoice indicating the net amount of the merchandise is $567. The terms of the invoice are 2/10, $n/30$. If the customer elects to pay the invoice within the first 10 days, find the cash discount and the net payment.

$$\text{Cash discount} = 567 \times 0.02 = \$11.34$$

$$\text{Net amount} = \$567 - \$11.34 = \$555.66$$

Alternatively, if only the net payment is required:

$$\text{Net amount} = 567(1 - 0.02) = 567(0.98) = \$555.66$$

If a discount of 2% is accepted, 98% of the invoice is paid.

There are a variety of methods for determining the period for a cash discount.

1. Ordinary dating method—the discount period begins with the date of the invoice.
2. Receipt of goods (ROG)—the discount period begins with the date the goods are received.
3. End of month (EOM)—the discount period begins at the end of the month of the invoice.

Example
Determine the last day the cash discount applies to an invoice dated May 23. Goods are received May 26 and the cash discount is 2/10, $n/30$. The period is to be determined as follows:

a. By the ordinary dating method.

b. By ROG.

c. By EOM.

(a) The 2% cash discount can be taken any time up to and including June 2 (10 days from May 23). June 2 is determined by referring to Table 1. May 23 is day 143; add 10 to find the date of the 153rd day—June 2. The net amount is due any time after June 2 but on or before June 22 (30 days from May 23).

(b) The 2% cash discount can be taken any time up to and including June 5 (10 days from May 26), the date of the receipt of merchandise. The net amount is due any time after June 5 but on or before June 25 (30 days from May 26).

(c) The 2% cash discount can be taken any time up to and including June 10 (10 days from the end of May). The net amount is due any time after June 10 but on or before June 30 (30 days from the end of May).

The cash discount applies only to the actual net price of merchandise purchased. Charges for shipping, credits for returned merchandise, and damaged merchandise credits must be subtracted from an invoice amount before cash discount rates are applied. The charges and credits are reapplied to the net amount.

If a partial payment is made on the invoice, a discount can be applied to the portion of the invoice paid within the cash discount period.

Example

You receive an invoice on April 2 with terms 2/10, $n/30$ ROG. The amount of the invoice is $4,397.24. The invoice included freight charges of $68.42. The merchandise arrived on April 4. You return $300 of the merchandise on April 10 and on April 13 you write a check to pay the bill. What is the correct amount of the check:

Invoice amount	$4,397.24
− Freight charges	−68.42
− Returned goods	−300.00
Cash discount amount	4,028.82
− Cash discount	−80.58
	3,948.24
+ Freight charges	+68.42
Amount paid	$4,016.66

(The cash discount applies because April 13 is within 10 days of April 4.)

The returned goods value must be subtracted from the invoice amount before the discount can be applied.

Example

Country Hardware receives a shipment of merchandise on June 10. The amount of the invoice is $546.35, including freight charges of $18. The terms of the invoice are 3/10, $n/30$ EOM. What payment must Country Hardware make on July 10 if the hardware store wishes to reduce the obligation to $400? What amount would be credited to the account if Country Hardware sent a check for $400 on July 10?

To reduce the obligation to $400 (the payment period is within the cash discount period):

$$\$546.35 - \$400 = \$146.35$$

(amount to be credited)

$$\$146.35 \times 0.03 = \$4.39$$

(amount of cash discount)

$$\$146.35 - \$4.39 = \$141.96$$

(amount of payment to reduce the obligation to $400).

A check for $400 is sent. Find the amount owed by Country Hardware.

$$400 = 0.97x$$

$$x = \$412.37$$

(amount credited to the account of Country Hardware).

$$\$546.35 - \$412.37 = \$133.98$$

is the amount owed by Country Hardware.

SECTION 4 EXERCISES

1. Find the amount of trade discount on an item with a list price of $459.95 and a rate of discount of 20%. Find the net price of the item.

2. Find the amount of trade discount on an item with a list price of $45.50 and a rate of discount of 15%. Find the net price of the item.

3. Find the net price of an article with a list price of $440 and a rate of discount of 30%.

4. Find the net price of an article with a list price of $79.95 and a rate of discount of 35%.

5. Find the single equivalent discount rate for chain discounts of 25%, 20%, and 15%.

6. Find the single equivalent discount rate for chain discounts of 30%, 10%, and 10%.

7. The catalog list price of a lawn mower is $239.95 with a listed trade discount of 15%. In October the firm offered an additional discount of 15%. Find the net price of the lawn mower after the additional discount.

8. Snow blowers had a list price of $399.95 and a trade discount of 20%. On March 15 the firm offered an additional discount of 15%. Find the net price of the snow blower after the additional discount.

9. Two competitive companies offer identical supplies. The first company offers trade discounts of 20%, 15%, and 10%, and the second company offers trade discounts of 15%, 10%, and 20%. Which company offers the better deal?

10. Two competitive companies offer identical supplies. One offers trade discounts of 25% and 15% and the other offers trade discounts of 25%, 10%, and 5%. Which company offers the more attractive deal?

11. The amount of an invoice dated January 12 is $468.92. The terms of the invoice are 1/10, n/30. What amount is due on January 22? What amount is due on January 23?

12. The amount of an invoice dated February 24, 1989 is $975.31. The terms of the invoice are 2/10, n/30. You wish to take advantage of the cash discount. What is the last date you can pay the invoice and still take advantage of the discount? Find the net amount due.

13. An invoice dated March 10 for the amount of $456.78 included freight charges of $42.39. The terms of the invoice are 2/10, n/30 EOM. Determine the last date possible to qualify for the cash discount. Find the cash discount. Find the amount of the check needed to settle the invoice.

14. An invoice dated April 15 for the amount of $654.75 included freight charges of $46.00. The terms of the invoice are 2/10, n/30 EOM. On April 20 goods valued at $23.90 were returned. Find the amount of the check needed to settle the account if the check was written on May 10. Find the amount of the check needed to settle the account if the check was written on May 15.

15. An invoice dated June 1 for the amount of $2,345 had terms of 3/10, n/30 ROM. The merchandise was received on June 17. The freight charges included on the invoice amounted to $93.65. The company was notified on June 17 of damaged goods amounting to $86. Find the last possible date allowed to write the check and to qualify for the cash discount. Determine the amount of the check.

16. An invoice dated August 10 for the amount of $25,697.85 included freight charges of $257. The terms of the invoice were 1/10, n/30 ROG. The goods were received on August 17. The company was notified of some damage to the shipment and an adjustment of $200 was made to the invoice to compensate for the damage. Find the final date for the cash discount and the amount of the check written to settle the invoice.

17. The catalog list price of an article was $569. The trade discount rates were 20% and 15%. The freight charges were $32.50. The terms of the invoice were 2/10, n/30 and the invoice was dated October 25.
    a. Find the amount of the invoice.
    b. Find the cash discount.

   c. Find the last date the cash discount can be taken.

   d. Find the amount of the check needed to settle the account.

18. The catalog list price of an item is $798.50. Trade discounts of 10% and 5% are given. The freight charges amount to $25. The terms of the invoice are 3/10, n/30, and the invoice is dated December 10.

   a. Find the amount of the invoice.

   b. Find the cash discount.

   c. Find the last date the cash discount can be taken.

   d. Find the amount of the check needed to settle the invoice.

19. What amount must be remitted if the following invoices are all paid on February 5? The terms of all of the invoices are 2/10, 1/20, n/30.

Invoice 1	dated January 15	$456.78
Invoice 2	dated January 22	234.75
Invoice 3	dated January 30	369.20

20. What amount must be remitted if the following invoices are paid in full on March 10? The terms of all of the invoices are 2/10, n/30 EOM.

Invoice 1	dated January 30	$678.00
Invoice 2	dated February 1	372.85
Invoice 3	dated February 15	579.20
Invoice 4	dated March 3	135.60

Answers to Odd-Numbered Exercises

  1. Discount, $91.99. Net price, $367.96.

  3. $308.

  5. 49%.

  7. $173.36.

  9. Same.

11. January 22, $464.23. January 23, $468.92.

13. April 10. Discount, $8.29. Net amount, $448.49.

15. June 27. $2,194.04.

17. (a) $419.42. (b) $7.74. (c) November 4. (d) $411.68.

19. $1,051.00.

1.5   MARKUP AND MARKDOWN

Profit is the primary reason for operating a business. Profit is the difference between the revenue received and the cost of the goods sold and the operating expense of the business.

profit = revenue − cost of goods − operating expenses

Markup

The difference between the cost and the selling price is **markup.** Markup is expressed as a percent of either the cost or the selling price. Therefore the basic percent equation is used to find markup.

Cost + (% markup based on cost)(cost) = selling price

Cost + (% markup based on selling price)(selling price) = selling price

Some definitions are presented to help clarify the terminology of merchandising.

Cost. The price paid for the merchandise plus all charges incurred in getting the merchandise to the store.

Selling price. The price received when the merchandise is sold.

Markup or **gross profit.** The difference between cost and selling price. Another term for this is **margin.**

Overhead and **net profit** are combined to generate the **markup.** Overhead includes such items as rent, lights, salaries, insurance, advertising, and taxes. Net profit is the actual profit after all expenses are taken.

The following diagram may help to illustrate the breakdown of selling price.

Cost	+	Markup	= Selling Price
Cost	+ Overhead + Net Profit		= Selling Price

These two equations are symbolized as

$$C + MP = SP \quad \text{and} \quad C + OH + NP = SP$$

where C is the cost, MP is the markup, SP is the selling price, OH is the overhead, and NP is the net profit.

Information from problems are substituted into these relationships to obtain additional information. The item usually involving some computation is markup. Markup is usually given as a percent. The amount of markup depends on the cost or selling price of the item. There are five possible combinations of information that allow for the generation of new information.

1. Given the cost and the rate of markup on cost, find the markup and the selling price.

Step 1. Determine the markup by:

$$MP = C \times \%MP$$

Step 2. Find the selling price by adding the cost and the markup.

If the amount of markup is not needed, the selling price can be found directly by:

$$SP = C(1 + \%MP)$$

Example

A radio cost $46.75 and there is a 40% markup based on cost. Find the selling price.

Substituting into $C \times \%C = MP$:

$$(46.75)(0.40) = \$18.70 \qquad \text{markup}$$

Substituting into $SP = C + MP$:

$$46.75 + 18.70 = \$65.45$$

Alternatively, using $C(1 + \%MP)$:

$$(46.75)(1 + 0.40) = 46.75(1.40) = \$65.45$$

The calculator keystroke is

$$46.75 \;\boxed{+}\; 0.40 \;\boxed{\times}\; 46.75 \;\boxed{=}$$

2. Given the cost and the rate of markup on selling price, find the markup and selling price.

Step 1. Substitute the givens in $C + MP = SP$:

$$C + \%(SP) = SP$$

Combine the two terms involving SP on one side of the equation.

$$C = SP - \% SP$$

Solve for SP by factoring SP from the left-hand side of the equation

$$C = SP(1 - \%)$$

Divide both sides by $(1 - \%)$

$$SP = \frac{C}{(1 - \%)}$$

Example

An item costs $54.60 and the markup is 25% of the selling price. Find the selling price.

Substituting into $C = SP(1 - \%)$:

$$54.60 = SP(1 - 0.25)$$

$$= 0.75SP$$

Divide both sides of the equation by 0.75.

$$\$72.80 = SP$$

If the only formula you remember is $C + MP = SP$, the example can be worked. Substituting:

$$54.60 + 25\% \ SP = SP$$

Put both terms containing selling price on the same side of the equation.

$$54.60 = SP - 25\% \ SP$$

Change 25% to 0.25 and factor out SP.

$$54.60 = SP(1 - 0.25) \quad \text{or} \quad 54.60 = SP(0.75)$$

Divide both sides by 0.75.

$$72.80 = SP$$

If the markup is needed, either subtract C and SP or apply 25% to $72.80.

3. Given the selling price and the rate of markup on cost, find the cost and the markup.
   Step 1. Substitute known and unknown quantities in $C + MP = SP$.

$$C + \%C = SP$$

Combine C terms

$$C(1 + \%) = SP$$

Solve for C

$$C = \frac{SP}{1 + \%}$$

Example
An item sells for $139.50 and the rate of markup is 35% of cost. Find the cost.
   Substituting into $C + \%MP(C) = SP$:

$$C + 0.35(C) = \$139.50$$

Combine $C + 0.35C$ by recalling C is $1C$. $1C + 0.35C = 1.35C$.

$$1.35C = \$139.50$$

Divide both sides of the equation by 1.35.

$$C = \$103.33$$

Markup can be determined by subtracting the cost and the selling price or applying 35% to $103.33.

$$MP = \$139.50 - \$103.33 = \$36.17$$

or

$$MP = 0.35(103.33) = \$36.17$$

4. Given the selling price and the rate of markup on selling price, find the markup and the cost.

Step 1. Determine the markup by the percent equation.

$$SP \times \% SP = MP$$

Step 2. Subtract MP from SP to determine C.

Example
A fan sells for $450 and the rate of markup is 20% of the selling price. Find the cost.

$$MP = \% MP(SP) = 20\% \times 450 = 0.20 \times 450 = \$90 \qquad \text{markup}$$

$$C = SP - MP = \$450 - \$90 = \$360 \qquad \text{cost}$$

5. Given the cost and the markup, the cost and the selling price, or the markup and the selling price, find the rate of markup on either cost or selling price.

Step 1. If the markup is not given, subtract the cost from the selling price to determine the markup.

Step 2. Divide the markup by the cost to give the rate of markup on cost, or divide the markup by the selling price to determine the rate of markup on selling price.

Step 3. Write the decimal as a percent by multiplying by 100.

Example
A tractor cost a dealer $12,450 and the dealer sold the tractor for $15,600. Find the rate of markup on cost and the rate of markup on selling price.

$$MP = SP - C = \$15,600 - \$12,450 = \$4,150$$

$$\% MP(C) = \frac{4{,}150}{12{,}450} = 0.3333 = 33\frac{1}{3}\%$$

$$\% MP(SP) = \frac{4{,}150}{15{,}600} = 0.266 = 26.6\%$$

Example

John Smith has determined that his overhead runs 30% of the cost of an item. He wants a net profit of 12% of the cost of an item. If an item costs $19.45, find the selling price.

Substituting into $C + OH + NP = SP$:

$$19.45 + (0.30)(19.45) + 0.12(19.45) = SP$$

The calculator keystroke is

$$19.45 + 0.30 \; \boxed{\times} \; 19.45 \; \boxed{+} \; 0.12 \; \boxed{\times} \; 19.45 \; \boxed{=}$$

Alternatively, add 30% and 12% to get $\% MP$.

$$30\% + 12\% = 42\%$$

Using $C + \% MP(C) = SP$:

$$19.45 + (0.42)(19.45) = \$27.62$$

If the question had asked the amount of overhead and net profit, the first method would be used.

Example

Determine the cost if an item is marked $69.95 and the markup is 35% of the cost.

Using $C + MP = SP$ and $MP = \% MP(C)$:

$$C + (0.35)C = \$69.95$$

Add $C + 0.35C$ to obtain $1.35C$.

$$1.35C = \$69.95$$

Divide both sides of the equation by 1.35.

$$C = \$51.81$$

Example

Too Low Company buys an item for $5.60 and sells that item for $6.95. Find the rate of markup based on cost.

Substituting into $C + MP = SP$:

$$5.60 + MP = 6.95$$

$$MP = 6.95 - 5.60 = 1.35$$

Using $(MP/C)(100) = \% MP(C)$:

$$\left(\frac{1.35}{5.60}\right)(100) = 24\%$$

Some justification should be offered for the two methods of determining markup: one based on cost and one based on selling price.

Markup based on cost. The cost figures are readily available for the item from the invoice of the goods.

Markup based on selling price. Many business expenses are calculated on sales—sales tax, commissions, inventory. For consistency and ease in calculations for key reports of company finances, markup is also calculated as a percent of sales. When markup is based on selling price, the gross profit for any day is easily approximated from the cash register tape.

Markdown

Markdown is the reduction in the selling price and may be caused by a variety of conditions.

1. Excess quantity in inventory.

2. Damaged merchandise.

3. Competition.

4. Newer models on market.

Markdown is the difference between the original selling price and the sale price.

$$MD = OSP - SP$$

The rate of markdown is a percent based on the original selling price and is calculated by dividing the markdown by the original selling price and multiplying by 100.

$$\%MD = \left(\frac{MD}{OSP}\right)(100)$$

There are three different groups of givens for markdown problems.

1. Given the original selling price and the rate of markdown, find the sale price and the markdown.

Step 1. $OSP \times \%OSP = MD.$
Step 2. $OSP - MD = SP.$

Example
Coats that originally sold for $190 were marked down 40%. Find the amount of markdown and the sale price.

$$OSP \times \%MD = (190) \times (0.40) = \$76 \qquad \text{markdown}$$

$$OSP - MD = SP = 190 - 76 = \$114 \qquad \text{sale price}$$

2. Given the original selling price and the sale price, find the markdown and the rate of markdown.

Step 1. $OSP - MD = SP.$ Solve for MD: $MD = OSP - SP.$
Step 2. $MD/OSP =$ Rate of $MD.$
Step 3. Rate of $MD \times 100 = \%MD.$

Example
An item originally marked $150 has a sale price of $110. Find the rate of markdown.

$$MD = OSP - SP = 150 - 110 = \$40$$

$$\%MD = \frac{40}{150} \times 100 = 26.67\%$$

3. Given the sale price and the rate of markdown, find the original selling price.

Step 1. Substitute knowns in $OSP - MD = SP$, $OSP - \%OSP = SP$, and solve for OSP.

Example

A mattress is on sale for $149.95 and the rate of markdown is 35%. Find the original selling price.

Substituting into $OSP - \%MD(OSP) = SP$:

$$OSP - 0.35OSP = \$149.95$$

Subtract $0.35OSP$ from $1OSP$.

$$0.65OSP = \$149.95$$

Divide both sides of the equation by 0.65.

$$OSP = \$230.69$$

SECTION 5 EXERCISES

Compute the unknowns in each of the following.

	Cost	Percent of Markup	Base of Markup	Markup	Selling Price
1.	$65.30	25%	Cost	16.33	81.33
2.	$99.95	33 1/3%	Cost	33.32	133.27
3.	$35.00	24%	Cost	$8.25	43.25
4.	$72.00	17%	Cost	$12.00	84.00
5.	$150.00	23%	Selling price	45.00	$195.00
6.	$225.00	31%	Selling price	100.00	$325.00

7. $24.95   25%   Selling price   6.24

8. $48.00   12%   Selling price

9. $76.00   Selling price $32.00

10. $234.00   Selling price $62.00

11.   18%   Cost $65.00

12.   25%   Cost $85.00

Compute the unknowns in each of the following.

	Original Selling Price	Percent of markdown	Markdown	Sale Price
13.	$249.95	40%		
14.	$178.00	25%		
15.	$450.00		$112.50	
16.	$950.00		$300.00	
17.		20%		$137.50
18.		35%		$120.00
19.	$450.00			$300.00
20.	$99.00			$55.00

21. The markup on an item is $4.50 and the cost of the item is $24.50. Find the rate of markup based on (a) cost and (b) selling price.

22. The rate of markup for a hardward store is 20% based on cost. The cash register tape for the day is $3,456.90. How much markup was realized that day?

23. Special Deal has a markup rate of 35% of the selling price. The cash register tape shows a total of $8,450.25 for the day. How much did the items cost that were sold that day? If the net profit is 20% of the markup, how much net profit was realized that day?

24. Daisy Discount has a markup rate of 30% of the selling price. The cash register receipts indicate total sales of $4,525 for the day. What was the markup realized by Daisy Discount that day? If the net profits are approximately 25% of the markup, how much net profit was realized that day?

25. Melanie's Merchandise has a markup policy of 25% on the cost. Find the selling price of an item that cost $47.50. Melanie reduced all items in her store by 40% to move last season's merchandise. Did she make a profit on an item that cost $47.50 after the markdown?

26. Brenda's Boutique has a markup policy of 20% on the selling price. Find the selling price of a dress that costs $175. Brenda reduces all merchandise by 15% to promote customer interest. How much markup did she make on the dress if she sold it during markdown?

27. As manager of two branch stores, you are deciding how to allocate hard to get items to each store. Store A charges a markup of 20% on the cost and store B has a markup policy of 25% on the selling price. Which store will receive the largest markup on the item?

28. A supplier is trying to convince you to carry a certain line of merchandise. The policy for the brand is to have a markup of 34% of the cost. Your store markup policy is 28% on selling price. Does the required markup of 34% of the cost represent an increase or decrease in markup for you?

29. A $200 watch marked down to $125 represents what rate of markdown?

30. A $550 fur coat marked down to $250 represents what rate of markdown?

Answers to Odd-Numbered Exercises

1. *M*, $16.33. *SP*, $81.63.

3. 23.57%. *SP*, $43.25.

5. *M*, $45. %*M*, 23%.

7. *SP*, $33.27. *M*, $8.32.

9. *SP*, $108. %*M*, 29.6%.

11. *C*, $55.08. *M*, $9.92.

13. *M*, $99.98. *SP*, $149.97.

15. 25%. *SP*, $337.50.

17. *OSP*, $171.88. *D*, $34.38.

19. 33.33%. *M*, $150.

21. (a) 18.4%. (b) 15.5%.

23. *C*, $5,492.66. *NP*, $591.52.

25. Lost $11.87.

27. Store B.

29. 37.5%.

1.6 PAYROLL

Percents are used in payroll calculations to find commissions and payroll deductions.

Commission is the payment to an individual based on the amount of net sales generated for the company. Commission is a percent of net sales.

$$C = R \times S$$

where *C* is the commission, *R* is the rate of commission, and *S* is the amount of net sales in a given time period.

Commission can take several forms:

Straight-line commission. A designated percent is paid on sales, regardless of the level of sales.

Graduated commission. A higher percent rate is paid for higher levels of sales.

Commissions combined with salary. A basic salary is paid, with a commission on all sales in excess of a stated amount called a **quota.** This method protects the employee from poor sales periods and acts as an incentive for outstanding sales.

Agents or **brokers** who sell consignments at the best possible price also earn commissions. These agents obtain **gross proceeds.** Commissions (percent of gross proceeds) and the **expenses** incurred in the transaction are deducted from the gross proceeds. The remainder is sent to the producer as **net proceeds.**

Example

George Strange sells annuities for Liberty Insurance Company. He is paid 1.5% commission on all sales. For the week ending June 10, his sales total $56,125. Find his commission.

$$R = 0.015 \qquad S = 56,125$$

$$C = R \times S = 0.015 \times 56,125 = \$841.88$$

Example

George Burns had net sales of $63,000 at Top Trader Autos. He receives 5% on the first $35,000, 6% on the next $25,000, and 7% on all sales over $60,000. Find the amount of his commission. It is necessary to determine the amount of sales in each category.

The $63,000 exceeds the first $35,000 by:

$$\$63,000 - \$35,000 = \$28,000$$

This amount exceeds the amount of sales in this category.

$$\$28,000 - \$25,000 = \$3,000.$$

This amount earns the commission in the category of exceeding $60,000.

$$R \times S = C$$

$$0.05 \times 35,000 = \$1,750 \qquad \text{first category}$$

$$0.06 \times 25,000 = \$1,500 \qquad \text{second category}$$

$$0.07 \times \ \ 3,000 = \$ \ \ 210 \qquad \text{third category}$$

Net sales of $63,000 produce

$$\$1,750 + \$1,500 + \$210 = \$3,460 \qquad \text{commission}$$

Example

George Sanders had net sales of $42,570. He receives a base salary of $400 with a 5% commission of all sales over $20,000. Find the amount due George Sanders.

Base salary	$ 400.00
Total sales	42,570.00
Less quota	20,000.00
Commission sales	22,570.00
Commission (0.05 × 22,570)	1,128.50
Amount due (commission + salary)	1,528.50

Example

2,500 bushels of tomatoes were sold by Fresh Vegies, Inc., for gross proceeds of $15,000. Fresh Vegies, Inc., incurred shipping charges of $250, insurance of $35, and a 5% commission on gross sales. Find the net proceeds due on the merchandise.

Gross proceeds	$15,000
− Shipping charges	−250
− Insurance costs	− 35
− Commission (0.05 × 15,000)	− 750
Net Proceeds	13,965

Payroll Deductions as a Percent

FICA or social security tax is a percent of gross wages. The rate used for Social Security tax is set by the Congress of the United States. At the present time the rate is 7.51% of gross wages. Wages in excess of $45,000 are not subject to FICA deductions. The yearly cap may be changed by Congress. Adjustments are made to ensure adequate revenues to provide benefits to retired and disabled workers as well as the surviving spouse and minor children of deceased workers.

All FICA deductions are matched by an equal contribution from the employer. The self-employed individual pays a FICA contribution of 13.02% of the first $45,000 earned.

Example

George Thomas earns $750 each week from Sam's Outlet. Find the FICA deductions.

$$750 \times 0.0751 = \$56.33$$

Example

A self-employed doctor has gross annual wages of $75,000. Find the amount of FICA deductions. Wages in excess of $45,000 are not subject to FICA deductions. The FICA rate for a self-employed person is 0.1302.

The yearly FICA deduction is

$$\$45,000 \times 0.1302 = \$5,859$$

Example

Jane Rich earns $8,000 a month. In what month will she fulfill her FICA tax obligation? How much FICA tax will be deducted in the last month?

$$\frac{45,000}{8,000} = 5.625 \text{ months}$$

Jane Rich will complete paying her FICA tax in June because 5.625 indicates that she pays five full months and part of the sixth month. Only $5,000 of her June paycheck will be subject to FICA tax because 5 months' salary (5 $\times$ 8,000 = 40,000) have been taxed and $45,000 − $40,000 = $5,000 left to be taxed. Therefore the amount deducted from the June paycheck for FICA tax is

$$5,000 \times 0.0751 = \$375.50$$

SECTION 6 EXERCISES

1. Arnold Palme works on a 5% straight-line commission selling mutual funds. Find his commission on sales amounting to $45,936.

2. Nancy Chen works on a 5% straight-line commission selling real estate. Find the commission she received for selling property amounting to $162.475.

3. Fair Deal Autos has a graduated commission for their salespeople. The rates are 3% for sales up to $25,000, 4% for sales between $25,000 and up to $50,000, and 5% for all sales in excess of $50,000 in a week. Joan is writing checks for the salespeople and is furnished with the following amounts of sales. Find the commission for each salesperson.

Joan Smith	$39,540
Tom Brown	23,200
Dick Baker	62,400

4. The appliance department at the local Seers store is on the system of graduated commissions for its sales personnel. The scale is 5% on all sales up to and including $5,000, 6% on sales over $5,000 but less than $8,000, and 7% on all sales in excess of $8,000. Find the weekly commissions for the following sales amounts.

Bob Jones	$9,250
Carol Cook	7,540
Alice Bean	3,200

5. Safe Investment Company pays each salesperson $100 per week and a commission of 5% on all sales in excess of $10,000. Find the weekly checks received by the following individuals.

Sally Neese	$18,675
John Lander	36,780
Cheryl Cook	86,450

6. Quick Turnover Company markets shrimp for the local fishermen. The gross proceeds on 2,000 pounds of shrimp is $7,550. The commission for handling the sale is 4% and the cost of shipping is $78.00. Find the net proceeds of the shrimp for the fishermen.

7. 5,000 bushels of oranges are consigned to Fast Move Company. The company is able to sell 3,500 bushels at $11.50 per bushel. The remainder of the oranges are sold at $10.50 per bushel. The shipping and handling charges are $535.00. Fast Move Company receives a 3.5% commission. Find the net proceeds.

In the following exercises, use 7.51% as the rate of FICA and $45,000 as the maximum amount to be taxed. The rate for self-employment is 13.02%.

8. Determine the FICA deduction from a payroll check amounting to $478.

9. Find the FICA taxes deducted from a weekly paycheck if the gross amount received is $520.

10. If the FICA deductions were $43.68, find the gross wages.

11. If the FICA deductions from a monthly paycheck were $260.74, find the gross wages.

12. Fred Smart earns $5,500 a month. Find the FICA deduction. In what month does Fred Smart complete his obligation to FICA? How much is deducted the last month?

13. Amy Levine earns $950 a week. Find the FICA deduction. In what week does Amy Levine complete her obligation to FICA? How much is deducted the final week?

14. A free-lance writer receives checks totaling $29,200 for articles published during a given year. How much must be paid for FICA contributions?

15. A talented musician received contributions of $64,000 for various performances during the year. Determine the FICA obligation.

16. Mildred Greene teaches school and earns $26,900. During the summer months, Ms. Greene performs as a folk dancer and receives contributions in the amount of $12,500. What are her FICA obligations on the $12,500?

17. Tom Knight teaches school and earns an annual income of $31,000. He receives royalty checks on a textbook he authored in the amount of $6,500. Find the FICA obligation on the royalties.

Answers to Odd-Numbered Exercises

1. $2,296.80.

3. Joan Smith, $1,331.60. Tom Brown, $696. Dick Baker, $2,370.

5. Sally Neese, $533.75. John Lander, $1,439. Cheryl Cook, $3,922.50.

7. Net proceeds, $53,505.

9. $39.05.

11. $3,471.90.

13. $71.35. Amy completes her obligation in the forty-eighth week. $26.29.

15. $5,859 FICA tax.

17. $846.30.

1.7 TAXES

Sales Tax

Most states and some cities levy a tax on retail sales to raise necessary revenue. The amount of the tax is a percent of retail sales and is collected at the time of the sale. The type of merchandise taxed varies from state to state. Businesses are required to remit the amount of the tax to the taxing authority at periodic intervals.

The amount of the tax is calculated as a percent problem.

$$P = R \times B$$

becomes

$$\text{Tax} = \text{rate} \times \text{total sales of taxable items}$$

Usually amounts less than $1.00 have the tax prescribed by the state to eliminate rounding discrepancies.

Example

Carolyn purchased a sweater for $19.95. Find the amount of sales tax and total amount of sales if the sales-tax rate is 4.5%.

$$B = 19.95 \qquad R = 0.045 \qquad \text{Tax} = 19.95 \times 0.045$$

$$\text{Sales tax} = 0.90 \qquad \text{(rounded to nearest cent)}$$

$$\text{Total amount} = 19.95 + 0.90 = \$20.85$$

Alternatively, to find the total amount, especially if a separate entry for the tax is not required:

$$\text{Sales price} + (\text{tax rate}) \times (\text{sale price}) = \text{total amount}$$

$$S + 0.045S = TA$$

$$1.045 \times 19.95 = \$20.85$$

Example

The total amount paid for a vacuum cleaner was $94.45. This amount included a 5% sales tax. What was the price of the vacuum cleaner?

The total amount equals the purchase price + the tax.

$$\text{Vacuum} + \text{sales tax} = \$94.45$$

The price of the vacuum cleaner is unknown and will be called x.

$$x + (0.05)x = \$94.45$$

$$x + 0.05x = 1x + 0.05x = 1.05x$$

$$1.05x = \$94.45$$

Divide each side of the equation by 1.05.

$$x = \$89.95$$

Every time sales tax is included in the price, the equation will be

$$(1 + \text{sales-tax rate}) \times \text{sale price} = \text{total price}$$

Property Tax

Another revenue dependent upon the value of the item is property tax. County and city governments derive most of their income from property taxes. Property has two classifications.

Real property—land, houses, and buildings.

Personal property—cars, furniture, jewelry, boats, and so on.

The amount of property tax is determined by two factors.

1. **Assessed value.** This is usually a percent of fair market value of the property. A person can challenge the assessed value of property. Each governmental authority has a Board of Assessors to arbitrate cases.

2. **Tax Rate.** This is the tax per $1.00 for the assessed value of the property. The tax rate varies from city to city. The tax rate is determined by dividing the total taxes needed by the total assessed value of property to be taxed.

The tax rate is expressed in a variety of ways.

1. **Percent.** When written as a decimal, this is the amount of tax for each dollar of assessed value. To find the total tax, multiply the decimal by the assessed value.

2. **Amount per $100.** This is the numerical value preceding the percent sign. Five percent and $5 per $100 are the same. Either write the rate per $1 by dividing by 100 or divide the assessed value by 100 before applying the rate.

3. **Mills.** This is the amount per $1,000. Divide mills by 1,000 to give the decimal rate, then multiply the decimal rate by the assessed valuation.

$$\textbf{Property tax} = \textbf{assessed value} \times \textbf{tax rate (per \$1)}$$

Example

Mr. Brown's home in Montgomery County has a fair market value of $145,000. The assessed value of the property is 65% of the fair market value. The tax rate in Montgomery County is 3.6%. Find the assessed value of the property and the amount of property tax.

$$\text{Assessed value} = 0.65 \times 145,000 = \$94,250$$

$$\text{Property tax} = 0.036 \times 94,250 = \$3,393$$

The property tax can be computed directly by:

$$\textbf{Tax} = \textbf{fair market value} \times \textbf{rate of assessment} \times \textbf{tax rate}$$

$$= 145,000 \times 0.65 \times 0.036 = \$3,393$$

Example

The taxes on a home were $805. The tax rate was 5.6% and the rate of assessment was 55% of the market value. Find the market value of the home.

$$\text{Tax} = \text{fair market value} \times \text{assessment rate} \times \text{tax rate}$$

Substitute the known values.

$$805 = FMV \times (0.55) \times (0.056)$$

Multiply 0.55 by 0.056 to give 0.0308.

$$805 = 0.0308 FMV$$

Divide both sides by 0.0308.

$$\$26,136.36 = FMV$$

Example
Find the property tax on property with an assessed value of $42,560 and tax rate of 40 mills.

Convert 40 mills to the decimal rate by dividing by 1,000.

$$\frac{40}{1,000} = 0.04$$

Property tax = assessed value × rate

Tax = 42,500 × 0.04 = $1,700

Example
Property taxes on a home assessed at $64,800 were $4,212. Find the tax rate expressed as a percent, expressed as value per $100, and expressed as mills.

Tax = tax rate × assessed value

Substitute the known values.

4,212 = tax rate × 64,800

Divide both sides by 64,800.

0.065 = tax rate

6.5% tax rate: Multiply the decimal rate by 100 and add %.

$6.50 per $100: Multiply the decimal rate by 100.

$65 mills: Multiply the decimal rate by 1,000.

SECTION 7 EXERCISES

1. An automobile was sold for $11,674. The rate of sales tax was 4.5%. Find the amount of sales tax. Find the total amount of the sale.

2. New appliances for a home totaled $2,810. The rate of sales tax was 4%. Find the amount of sales tax and the total amount of the sale.

3. The total amount paid for a bicycle, including a 5% sales tax, was $187.50. Find the price of the bicycle.

4. The total amount paid was $527.80, including a 4% sales tax. Find the cost of goods.

5. The final bill for a new automobile amounted to $13,750. This amount included the price of the vehicle, a 4.5% sales tax, and a service warranty for 3 years for $350. Find the actual price of the vehicle.

6. The final bill for a new lawn mower amounted to $1,273.72. This amount included a 3-year service warranty for $175.00 and a 5% sales tax. Find the actual price of the mower.

7. The gross sales, including sales tax, reported by Merchandise Stores for the third quarter was $456,896.34. The sales-tax rate for the state was 5%. How much was due to the state for tax?

8. Property in Pleasantville has an assessment rate of 90% and a tax rate of 6.7%. Find the assessed value of property that has a fair market value of $74,500. Find the property tax.

9. The assessment rate on property in Springfield is 85%. The tax rate is 3.8%. Find the assessed value of property valued at $62,750. Find the property tax.

10. The property tax amounted to $1,054.60. The tax rate is 62 mills. Find the assessed value of the property.

11. The property tax amounted to $892.27. The tax rate is 75 mills. Find the assessed value of the property.

12. The tax on property was $675.20. The tax rate listed on the bill was $4.80 per $100. Find the assessed value of the property.

13. A tax of $624.50 was charged on property. The tax rate listed on the bill was $6.10 per $100. Find the assessed value of the property.

14. The tax rate is 4.2% and the amount of tax is $674.20. Find the assessed value of the property. The assessment rate is 80%. Find the fair market value of the property.

15. The tax rate is 6.4% and the amount of tax on a given house is $742.40. Find the assessed value of the house. The assessment rate is listed as 85%. Find the fair market value of the property.

16. The assessed value is $72,000. The property tax is $872. Find the tax rate.

17. The fair market value of property at 25 Spring Street is $81,500. The assessment rate is 65%. The property tax is $815.00. Find the tax rate.

18. Property sold for $120,000. The assessment rate in the community is 65%. The taxes on the property are $1,428. Find the tax rate of the community.

Answers to Odd-Numbered Exercises

   1. $525.33. $12,199.33.

   3. $178.57.

   5. $12,822.97.

   7. $21,756.97.

   9. Assessed value, $53,337.50. Tax, $2,026.83.

 11. $11,896.93.

 13. $10,237.70.

 15. $13,647.06.

 17. 1.54%.

1.8 FINANCIAL STATEMENT ANALYSIS

The final application of the percent equation is financial ratios. A ratio is a fraction, a comparison of two quantities. In the business community, this comparison is expressed as a percent. The two financial reports that will be analyzed are the **balance sheet** and the **income statement.**

A **balance sheet** is the statement of the financial position of a company. It indicates all resources (**assets**) and all obligations (**liabilities**) and owners' equity. The balance sheet shows the current status of a company, the cumulative operation up to a year.

First, let us look at a typical balance sheet.

Deuce Company
Balance Sheet
March 31, 19XX

Assets	
Current assets	
Cash and short-term investment	$ 77,200
Accounts receivable	599,017
Inventories	601,709
Prepaid expenses	101,827
Total current assets	1,379,753
Noncurrent assets	
Property and equipment	4,069,155
Capital leases	54,757
Investments	673,058
Total assets	$6,176,723

Liabilities and Stockholders' Equity	
Current liabilities	
Current maturity of long-term debt	$ 8,443
Notes and accounts payable	253,294
Accrued liabilities	397,459
Total current liabilities	659,196
Long-term debt	1,366,063
Capital lease obligations	73,850
Other liabilities	733,873
Stockholders' equity	3,329,041
Total liabilities, and stockholders' equity	$6,176,723

In the analysis of assets, **total assets** are the base of all calculations. Some questions one might ask regarding total assets are:

1. Cash is what percent of total assets?

2. Accounts receivable are what percent of total assets?

3. Inventory is what percent of total assets?

To answer question 1, substitute the appropriate number for cash and total assets into the percent equation.

$$77,200 = x\%\,(6,176,723)$$

Replace $x\%$ by $x/100$.

$$77,200 = \frac{x}{100}(6,176,723)$$

Divide 6,176,723 by 100.

$$77,200 = 61,767.23x$$

Divide both sides of the equation by 61,767.23.

$$x = 1.25$$

Cash is 1.25% of assets.

To answer question 2, substitute the appropriate number for accounts receivable; the total assets remain fixed in every computation.

$$599,017 = \frac{x}{100}(6,176,723)$$

$$= 61,767.23x$$

Divide both sides of the equation by 61,767.23.

$$x = 9.7$$

Accounts receivable are 9.7% of assets.

To answer question 3:

$$601,709 = x\%(6,176,723) = \frac{x}{100}(6,176,723)$$

$$= 61,767.23x$$

$$x = 9.74$$

Inventories are 9.74% of assets.

This process can be used for each item of the balance sheet listed under Assets.

$$\text{Assets} = \text{liabilities} + \text{owner equity}$$

Total assets is used as the base for all asset ratios; liabilities + owner equity is the base of all liability and owner equity ratios. Notice the two amounts are identical, therefore 6,176,723 is the base of all ratios in this balance sheet.

We now have a balance sheet for Deuce Company showing a complete vertical analysis.

Deuce Company
Balance Sheet
March 31, 1987

Assets	*Amount*	*%*
Current assets		
Cash and short-term investment	$ 77,200	1.25
Accounts receivable	599,017	9.70
Inventories	601,709	9.74
Prepaid expenses	101,827	1.65
Total current assets	1,379,753	22.34
Noncurrent assets		
Property and equipment	4,069,155	65.88
Capital leases	54,757	0.88
Investments	673,058	10.90
Total assets	$6,176,723	100.00

Liabilities and Stockholders' Equity		
Current liabilities		
Current maturity of long-term debt	$ 8,443	0.14
Notes and accounts payable	253,294	4.10
Accrued liabilities	397,459	6.43
Total current liabilities	659,196	10.67
Long-term debt	1,366,063	22.13
Capital lease obligations	73,850	1.21
Other liabilities	733,873	11.89
Stockholders' equity	3,329,041	54.10
Total liabilities and stockholders' equity	$6,176,723	100.00

Vertical analysis allows management, investors, and potential investors some insight into the structure of the company for a single time period. Comparisons can be made with similar types of companies as to utilization of assets. Corrective action is taken if some item is out of line with known goals.

A much better picture can be obtained by comparing data over several time periods. This type of analysis is known as **horizontal analysis.** The earlier time period values are used as the base in percent calculations.

Deuce Company
Balance Sheet
March 31, 1987

Assets	1986	1987
Current assets		
Cash and short-term investment	$ 77,200	$ 79,800
Accounts receivable	599,017	585,972
Inventories	601,709	792,473
Prepaid expenses	101,827	96,346
Total current assets	1,379,753	1,554,591
Noncurrent assets		
Property and equipment	4,069,155	5,745,275
Capital leases	54,757	43,943
Investments	673,058	872,564
Total assets	$6,176,723	$8,216,373

Liabilities and Stockholders' Equity		
Current liabilities		
Current maturity of long-term debt	$ 8,443	$ 15,500
Notes and accounts payable	253,294	425,738
Accrued liabilities	397,459	637,580
Total current liabilities	669,196	1,078,818
Long-term debt	1,366,063	2,245,679
Capital lease obligations	73,850	62,750
Other liabilities	733,873	824,450
Stockholders' equity	3,329,041	2,925,858
Total liabilities and stockholders' equity	$6,176,723	$8,216,373

Certain accounting practices are utilized in horizontal analysis. The first new column to be generated will be a column denoting the change from 1986 to 1987. Decreases are shown as an amount enclosed in parentheses ( ) rather than with a minus sign. The next column will be percent change with the 1986 value the base of the percent. The results of the computations are indicated under each listing. A description of the computation is included in brackets for Assets.

Deuce Company
Balance Sheet
March 31, 1987

Assets	1986	1987	*Change*	%
Current assets				
Cash and short-term investment	$ 77,200	$ 79,800	$ 2,600	3.37

$$\left[79,800 - 77,200 = 2,600 \qquad \frac{2,600}{77,200} \times 100 = 3.37\% \right]$$

Accounts receivable	599,017	585,972	(13.045)	(2.18)

$$\left[585,972 - 599,017 = (13,045) \qquad \frac{13,045}{599,017} \times 100 = (2.18) \right]$$

Inventories	601,709	792,473	190,764	31.70

$$\left[792,473 - 601,709 = 190,764 \qquad \frac{190,764}{601,709} = 31.70 \right]$$

Prepaid expenses	101,827	96,346	(5,481)	(5.38)

$$\left[96,346 - 101,827 = (5,481) \qquad \frac{5,481}{101,827} = (5.38) \right]$$

Total current assets	1,379,753	1,634,391	254,638	18.46

$$\left[1,634,391 - 1,379,753 = 254,638 \qquad \frac{254,638}{1,379,753} \times 100 = 18.46 \right]$$

Noncurrent assets				
Property and equipment	4,069,155	5,745,275	1,676,120	41.20

$$\left[5,745,275 - 4,069,155 = 1,676,120 \qquad \frac{1,676,120}{4,069,155} \times 100 = 41.20 \right]$$

Capital leases	54,757	43,943	(10,814)	(19.75)

$$\left[43,943 - 54,757 = (10,814) \qquad \frac{10,814}{54,757} \times 100 = (19.75) \right]$$

Investments   673,058   872,564   199,506   29.60

$$\left[872,564 - 673,058 = 199,506 \quad \frac{199,506}{673,058} \times 100 = 29.60 \right]$$

Total assets $6,176,723 $8,296,173 $2,294,288   37.10

$$\left[8,296,173 - 6,176,723 = 2,294,173 \quad \frac{2,294,173}{6,176,723} \times 100 = 37.10 \right]$$

Liabilities and Stockholders' Equity				
Current liabilities				
Current maturity of long-term debt	8,443	15,500	7,057	83.58
Notes and accounts payable	253,294	425,738	172,444	68.10
Accrued liabilities	397,459	637,580	240,121	60.40
Total current liabilities	659,196	1,078,818	419,622	63.70
Long-term debt	1,366,063	2,245,679	879,616	64.40
Capital lease obligations	73,850	62,750	(11,106)	(15.00)
Other liabilities	733,873	824,450	90,577	12.30
Stockholders' equity	3,329,041	4,084,476	755,435	22.70
Total liabilities and stockholders' equity	$6,176,723	$8,296,173	$2,553,766	41.30

In horizontal analysis, all percents are obtained by dividing the change by the earlier year amount. From the horizontal analysis one can see that inventories increased 31.7% from 1986 to 1987, current liabilities increased by 63.7%, and shareholder's equity increased by 22.7%.

The **income statement** shows the results of operating a business for a given time period and shows the profit of the business. Vertical and horizontal analysis can be performed on an income statement. The results are used to monitor the balance and control within a company. Income statements vary in format. The following are some of the most widely used items.

Net sales: Gross sales — sales returned and allowances.

Cost of goods sold: Beginning inventory + purchases — returns and allowances — end inventory.

Gross profit on sales: Net sales — cost of goods sold.

Operating expense: Amounts for salaries, rent, utilities, administration, and/or depreciation.

Total operating expense: Sum of all operating expenses.

Operating income: Gross profit on sales — total operating expense.

Net income: operating income — taxes.

Deuce Company
Income Statement
Year Ending March 31
Current Year and Previous Year

	Current	Previous	Change	% Change	% Current	% Previous
Sales revenue						
Gross sales	$930,000	$924,000	$ 6,000	0.65	101.30	101.50
Sales allowances	(12,000)	(14,000)	(2,000)	(14.30)	1.30	1.50
Net sales	918,000	910,000	8,000	0.88	100.00	100.00
Cost of goods sold						
Beginning inventory	118,000	110,000	8,000	7.30	12.85	12.10
Purchases	824,000	730,000	94,000	12.90	89.80	80.20
Returns	(14,500)	(18,600)	(4,100)	(22.00)	1.60	2.00
End inventory	(105,000)	(98,000)	7,000	7.14	11.40	10.80
Cost of goods	822,500	723,400	99,100	13.70	89.60	79.50
Gross profit	95,500	186,600	(91,100)	(48.80)	10.40	20.50
Operating expenses						
Salaries	40,000	36,000	4,000	11.10	4.40	4.00
Rent	12,000	10,000	2,000	20.00	1.31	1.10
Utilities	6,000	6,500	(500)	(7.70)	0.65	0.71
Depreciation	8,000	7,500	500	0.07	0.87	0.82
Total	66,000	60,000	6,000	10.00	7.19	6.59
Operating income	29,500	126,600	(97,100)	(76.70)	3.21	13.91
Taxes	7,840	50,240	(42,400)	(84.00)	0.85	5.50
Net income	$ 21,660	$ 76,360	(54,700)	(71.63)	2.36	8.39

In the income statement, the column Change was found by subtracting column Previous from column Current

% change = change/current × 100

% current = current/current net sales × 100

% previous = previous/previous net sales × 100

All numbers written in ( ) indicate a decline or a loss. All vertical analyses use net sales as the base of the ratio. Horizontal analyses use the previous year's value as the base of the ratio. Many management decisions are made from the analysis of a comparative income statement. The comparative income statement is often referred to as the report card of management.

SECTION 8 EXERCISES

1. In the following balance sheet for two years, perform a vertical analysis for each year and a horizontal analysis for the two years.

Hard Sell, Inc.
Balance Sheet
December 31, 19XX

Assets	Current	Previous
Current assets		
Cash	$ 53,119	$ 37,236
Accounts and notes	467,124	431,406
Inventories	422,280	357,820
Total	942,523	826,462
Noncurrent assets		
Land	21,236	19,362
Buildings and equipment	884,795	773,951
Total investments	481,828	503,955
Other	58,107	51,443
Total assets	$2,388,489	$2,175,173

Liabilities and Stockholder's Equity		
Current liabilities		
Accounts payable	$ 149,030	$ 154,999
Short-term debt	97,716	59,716
Accrued expenses	152,094	170,581
Total	398,840	385,296
Long-term debt	421,015	350,494
Deferred taxes	157,861	129,464
Other liabilities	43,862	21,801
Stockholders' equity	1,366,911	1,288,118
Total liabilities and stockholders' equity	$2,388,489	$2,175,173

2. Given the following balance sheet for Flavorrite, Inc., perform the vertical analysis for each of the years listed. Perform a horizontal analysis for the two years.

FLAVORRITE, Inc.
Balance Sheet
March 31, 19XX

	Current	Previous
Assets	*(In Millions of Dollars)*	
Current assets		
Cash	$ 365.5	$ 820.5
Short-term investment	56.1	69.0
Accounts receivable	813.1	685.4
Inventories	801.4	736.7
Prepaid taxes	130.9	139.2
Total current assets	2,158.0	2,450.8
Noncurrent assets		
Long-term securities	788.8	179.4
Property and plant	1,268.3	1,161.7
Other	247.8	273.8
Total assets	$4,462.9	$4,065.7

Liabilities and Owner Equity		
Current liabilities		
Short-term loans	$ 185.9	$ 299.2
Accounts payable	270.5	221.6
Other	503.3	566.1
Total current liabilities	959.7	1,086.9
Long-term debt	323.5	341.7
Deferred taxes	170.0	68.7
Other liabilities	82.4	72.9
Total liabilities	1,535.6	1,570.2
Owner equity	2,927.3	2,495.5
Total liabilities and owner equity	$4,462.9	$4,065.7

3. Given the following income statement, complete where necessary and perform the vertical analysis for each year and the horizontal analysis for the two years.

	Current	*Previous*
Sales revenue		
Gross sales	$788,400	$799,800
Sales returns and allowances	(13,400)	(14,800)
Net sales	?	?
Cost of goods sold		
Beginning inventory	68,400	76,800
Purchases	640,400	649,750
Returns and allowances	(18,800)	(14,400)
Goods available	690,000	?
Ending inventory	(84,500)	(78,400)
Total cost of goods	?	633,750
Gross profits on sales	169,500	?
Operating expenses		
Salaries	37,300	44,600
Rent	8,100	7,000
Utilities	7,000	9,000
Advertising	13,700	13,100
Depreciation	11,200	11,800
Administrative	7,900	8,600
Total	85,200	94,100
Operating income	?	?
Taxes	76,600	44,500
Net income	$ 7,700	$12,650

4. Complete the following income statement. Perform a vertical analysis for each year and a horizontal analysis on the two years.

	Current	*Previous*
	(in Millions of Dollars)	
Net sales	$502.8	$503.9
Expenses		
Cost of Sales	370.1	370.1
Selling and administration	61.4	57.5
Depreciation	14.6	14.5
Total	446.1	442.1
Gross income	56.7	61.8
Other income	9.4	12.2
Income before taxes	66.1	74.0
Taxes	26.8	27.0
Net income	$39.3	$47.0

5. Analyze the following income statement, using a vertical analysis for each year and a horizontal analysis for the two years.

	Current	Previous
	(in Thousands of Dollars)	
Net sales	$5,205,579	$5,549,738
Real estate	111,914	86,935
Other income	30,419	(61,864)
Total	5,347,912	5,574,809
Operating costs	4,458,356	4,658,969
Selling expense	431,480	426,918
Research expense	44,141	45,648
Interest expense	116,453	124,603
Less interest capitalized	6,234	2,716
Total	5,044,196	5,253,422
Gross profits	303,716	321,387
Income taxes	103,600	95,200
Net profit	$ 200,116	$ 226,187

Answers to Odd-Numbered Exercises

1.

	Vertical Analysis		Horizontal Analysis	
Assets	*(%)*	*(%)*	*Change*	*%Change*
	2.22	1.71	$ 15,883	42.65
	19.56	19.83	35,718	8.28
	17.68	16.45	64,460	18.01
	39.46	37.99	116,061	14.04
	0.89	0.89	1.874	9.68
	37.04	35.58	110,844	14.32
	20.17	23.17	(22,127)	(4.39)
	2.43	2.37	6,664	12.95
Liabilities				
	6.24	7.13	(5,969)	(3.85)
	4.09	2.75	38,000	63.63
	6.37	7.84	(18,487)	(10.84)
	16.70	17.72	13,544	3.52
	17.63	16.11	70,521	20.12
	6.61	5.95	28,397	21.93
	1.84	1.00	22,061	101.19
	57.23	59.22	78,793	6.12
	100.00	100.00	213,316	9.81

3.

		Horizontal Analysis		Vertical Analysis	
			%	Current	Previous
?	?	Change	Change	%	%
		$(11,400)	(1.4)	101.7	101.9
		(1,400)	(9.5)	1.7	(1.9)
775,000	785,000	(10,000)	(1.3)	100.0	100.0
		(8,400)	(10.9)	8.8	9.8
		(9,350)	(1.4)	82.6	82.8
		4,400	30.6	2.4	1.8
	712,150	(22,150)	(3.1)	89.0	90.7
		6,100	7.8	10.9	10.0
605,500		(28,250)	(4.5)	78.0	80.7
	151,250	18,250	12.1	21.9	19.3
		(7,300)	(16.4)	4.8	5.7
		1,100	15.7	1.0	0.9
		(2,000)	(22.2)	0.9	1.1
		600	4.6	1.8	1.7
		(600)	(5.1)	1.4	1.5
		(700)	(8.1)	1.0	1.1
		(8,900)	(9.5)	11.0	12.0
84,300	57,150	27,150	47.5	10.9	7.3
		32,100	72.1	9.9	5.6
		(4,950)	(39.1)	1.0	1.6

5.

| Vertical Analysis | | Horizontal | |
%Current	%Previous	Change	%Change
100.0	100.0	$(344,159)	(6.2)
2.1	1.6	24,979	28.7
0.6	(1.1)	122,283	198.0
102.7	100.5	(226,897)	(4.1)
85.6	83.9	(200,613)	(4.3)
8.3	7.7	4,562	1.1
0.8	0.8	(1,507)	(3.3)
2.2	2.2	(8,150)	(6.5)
0.1	0.05	3,518	129.5
96.9	94.7	(209,226)	(4.0)
5.8	5.8	(17,671)	(5.5)
2.0	1.7	8,400	8.8
3.8	4.1	(26,071)	(11.5)

1.9   RATIO AND PROPORTION

Various types of problems including percents can be solved using ratios and proportion.

Ratio

Ratios are fractions—a ratio is the quotient of two numbers. The three forms for expressing a ratio involving a and b are

$$\frac{a}{b} \qquad a:b \qquad a \div b$$

Ratios are usually expressed in lowest terms. Because ratios are fractions, the rules used for reducing fractions are used in reducing ratios. For example, $15:5$ or $15/5$ can be reduced to $3:1$ or $3/1$ or 3.

   Fractions are made up of a numerator and a denominator. Ratios can involve more than two quantities. An example of a relationship involving three quantities is $2:3:5$. If the three quantities represent the assets of Adam, Bob, and Carla, the ratio of $2:3:5$ can give any of the given fractions:

$$\frac{\text{Adam}}{\text{Bob}} = \frac{2}{3} \qquad \frac{\text{Adam}}{\text{Carla}} = \frac{2}{5} \qquad \frac{\text{Bob}}{\text{Carla}} = \frac{3}{5}$$

The numbers can also be inverted as Carla/Adam $= 5/2$, and so on.

   To allocate or divide a quantity into parts according to a ratio, find the sum of the parts of the ratios to determine the unit of division.

Example
$75,000 is to be divided among three individuals in the ratio of $2:3:5$. Find the amount each individual receives.

   Sum the parts of the ratio:

$$2 + 3 + 5 = 10$$

To determine the amount for the first individual, multiply $75,000 by the fraction formed by the ratio part (2) and the sum of the ratios (10).

$$75,000 \times \frac{2}{10} = 15,000$$

The second distribution is determined by the multiplication of the fraction formed by the ratio part (3) and the sum of the ratios (10).

$$75,000 \times \frac{3}{10} = 22,500$$

Likewise, the third amount is determined by multiplying by the fraction 5/10

$$75,000 \times \frac{5}{10} = 37,500$$

Because ratios are fractions, the rules for manipulating fractions apply to ratios. The ratio of 2/5 : 3/4 : 1/20 can be rewritten as whole number ratios by multiplying each part by the common denominator. The common denominator of the fractions 2/5, 3/4, and 1/20 is 20. Multiply each part of the ratio by the common denominator.

$$\frac{2}{5} \times 20 = 8 \qquad \frac{3}{4} \times 20 = 15 \qquad \frac{1}{20} \times 20 = 1$$

$$\frac{2}{5} : \frac{3}{4} : \frac{1}{20} = 8:15:1$$

The whole number form is easier to use.

Example
Divide 480 into three numbers in the ratio of 2/5 : 3/4 : 1/20.
Rewrite the problem as: Divide 480 into three numbers in the ratio of 8 : 15 : 1 (8 : 15 : 1 are from the work before the example).
The sum of the ratios is

$$8 + 15 + 1 = 24$$

The first number is

$$480 \times \frac{8}{24} = 160$$

The second number is

$$480 \times \frac{15}{24} = 300$$

The third number is

$$480 \times \frac{1}{24} = 20$$

Example

Tom, Dick, Harry, and Joe are four partners in a business venture. They have agreed to split the profits in the ratio of $2:3:1/2:1/3$. How are the monthly profits of $4,320 divided among them?

6. Rewrite $2:3:1/2:1/3$ using the common denominator of

$$12:18:3:2$$

The sum of the ratios is

$$12 + 18 + 3 + 2 = 35$$

Tom's share:

$$4,320 \times \frac{12}{35} = \$1,481.14$$

Dick's share:

$$4,320 \times \frac{18}{35} = \$2,221.71$$

Harry's share:

$$4,320 \times \frac{3}{35} = \$370.29$$

Joe's share:

$$4,320 \times \frac{2}{35} = \$246.86$$

The total of the allocations should equal the original amount to be distributed.

$$\$1,481.14 + 2,221.71 + 370.29 + 246.86 = 4,320$$

Rounding error could make the total differ from the original by a cent or two.

Proportion

A statement equating two ratios is a proportion. Four quantities are involved in a proportion. The ratio of $3:4$ is equal to the ratio of $7:x$ denotes a proportion because two ratios are equated. The proportion is written as $3/4 = 7/x$.

Because a proportion is an equation, the rules for solving equations apply to proportions. The common denominator of the two fractions $3/4$ and $7/x$ is $4x$. Multiply both sides of the proportion by $4x$.

$$\left(\frac{3}{4}\right)4x = \left(\frac{7}{x}\right)4x \qquad 3x = 28 \quad \text{and} \quad x = \frac{28}{3}$$

An alternate method of solving a proportion is called the cross product.

$$\begin{array}{ccc} 3 & \nwarrow \nearrow & 7 \\ & \swarrow \searrow & \\ 4 & & x \end{array}$$

Multiply as indicated by the arrows. The products are $3x$ and 28. Notice these products are the same as the results obtained from clearing the equation of denominators. This technique of cross multiplication is used to solve any proportion.

Proportions can be used to solve many types of business problems.

Example
An auto can travel 210 miles on 6 gallons of gasoline. How far can the auto travel on 10 gallons of gasoline?

The proportion for this statement is

$$\frac{210 \text{ miles}}{6 \text{ gallons}} = \frac{x \text{ miles}}{10 \text{ gallons}}$$

Alternatively,

$$\frac{210 \text{ miles}}{x \text{ miles}} = \frac{6 \text{ gallons}}{10 \text{ gallons}}$$

The units must be in similar locations in the two ratios as in the first form or the units cancel out and the proportion involves only numbers as in the second form. The form used depends on the statement of the original problem.

Cross multiplication in either setup gives

$$6x = 2{,}100 \qquad x = 350 \text{ miles}$$

Example

A crew can bury 5 miles of cable in 3 days. How long will it take the crew to bury 22 miles of cable?

$$\frac{5 \text{ miles}}{3 \text{ days}} = \frac{22 \text{ miles}}{x \text{ days}}$$

or

$$\frac{5 \text{ miles}}{22 \text{ miles}} = \frac{3 \text{ days}}{x \text{ days}}$$

Cross multiplication gives

$$5x = 66 \qquad x = 13.2 \text{ days}$$

When proportion is used to solve a problem, the assumption of the same rate is built into the problem. If the rate of change is not constant, proportion cannot be used.

Example

If 800 bushels of wheat were produced on 2.4 acres of land, how many bushels of wheat could be produced on 7 acres?

$$\frac{800 \text{ bushels}}{2.4 \text{ acres}} = \frac{x \text{ bushels}}{7 \text{ acres}}$$

Cross multiplication gives

$$2.4x = 5{,}600 \qquad x = 2{,}333.3 \text{ bushels}$$

Proportion is useful in conversion problems, either within the English system or between the English and metric systems. For example, convert 100 feet to meters. Conversion factors from a chart are necessary to solve this problem. The conversion factor between meters and feet is: 1 meter = 3.2808 feet.

This conversion factor forms one ratio of the proportion; the given and unknown form the other ratio.

$$\frac{x \text{ meters}}{100 \text{ feet}} = \frac{1 \text{ meter}}{3.2808 \text{ feet}}$$

Cross multiplication gives

$$3.2808x = 100 \qquad x = 30.48 \text{ meters}$$

Proportions can be used to determine percents. Percents refer to parts in 100. Therefore expressing 3/5 as a percent can be solved by setting up the proportion $3/5 = x/100$. Cross multiplication produces the equation

$$5x = 300 \qquad x = 60$$

3/5 can be expressed as 60%.

Example

$456 represents a discount of 30%. What amount would represent a discount of 35%?

$$\frac{\$456}{0.30} = \frac{x}{0.35}$$

$$0.30x = 159.60$$

$$x = \$532$$

If a proportion were not used, the problem would involve two steps.
Step 1:

$$456 = \frac{30}{100} \times$$

$$x = 1,520$$

Step 2:

$$y = \frac{35}{100} (1,520)$$

$$= 532$$

SECTION 9 EXERCISES

1. Rewrite the ratio $2:1/2:1/3$, using whole numbers.

2. Rewrite the ratio $4:1/2:1/3$, using whole numbers.

3. Divide 288 into three numbers in the ratio of $2:3:7$.

4. Divide 856 into three numbers in the ratio of $1:4:7$.

5. Divide 1,000 among four numbers in the ratio of $1:2:2:5$.

6. Divide $50,000 among family members in the ratio of $5:2:2:3$.

7. Three partners are dividing the proceeds of a sale of $12,000 in the ratio of $1/2:1/3:1/4$. Find the division of the proceeds.

8. Three brothers realized profits of $460,000 from the sale of real estate. The ratio for the division of profits is $1/6:1/4:1/12$. Find the division of the profits.

9. 22 premiums amounted to $2,845. Find the value of 27 premiums.

10. 2,320 square feet of storage costs $840 a month rental. Find the number of square feet you could expect for a rental fee of $500.

11. A piece of equipment can move 42,000 cubic feet in 7 hours. How many cubic feet can be moved in 10 hours?

12. A 3.5-acre field can produce 2,200 bushels of corn. How many bushels can you expect from a 6.2-acre field?

13. The scale used on a map is 1 inch represents 75 miles. Find the number of miles represented by $3 1/2$ inches.

14. The scale drawing had a legend denoting $1/4$ inch represents 1 foot. Find the length representing $12 1/2$ feet.

15. If 1 kilogram is equivalent to 2.2046 pounds, find the weight of a person in kilograms if he weighs 172 pounds.

16. A gallon has 3.7853 liters. If your auto has a fuel tank that holds 15 gallons, what is the capacity in liters?

17. Convert $2/7$ to a percent.

18. Convert $37 1/2 \%$ to eighths.

19. A cash discount of 2% yields $45. What would be the discount for 3%?

20. A trade discount of 15% gave a reduction of $45.00 on a bill. If the discount had been 18%, what would have been the reduction?

Answers to Odd-Numbered Exercises

1. 12:3:2.

3. 48, 72, 168.

5. 100, 200, 200, 500.

7. $5,538.46, $3,692.31, $2,769.23.

9. 3,491.59.

11. 60,000.

13. 262.5 miles.

15. 78.02 kilograms.

17. 28.57%.

19. $67.50.

Summary

Basic Relationship in Percent

$$\text{Rate} \times \text{Base} = \text{Percentage}$$

$$(1 + R) \times \text{Base} = \text{Total Amount}$$

Applications and Vocabulary for Percent Relationship

rate	base	percentage	total amount
rate	principal	interest	maturity value
rate	maturity value	discount	present value
rate	list price	trade discount	net price
rate	net price	cash discount	net amount
rate	cost	markup	selling price
rate	selling price	markdown	sale price
rate	net sales	commission	
rate	gross wages	FICA tax	
rate	total sales	sales tax	total amount
rate	assessed value	property tax	

REVIEW EXERCISES

1. 345 is what percent of 563?

2. $35.24 is what percent more than $22.50?

3. $225 is what percent less than $300?

4. A commission of $550 is what percent of sales of $80,000?

5. A sales tax of $5.60 is what percent of sales of $140?

6. A markdown of $20 represents a markdown rate of what amount if the original price was $80?

7. The sale price of $80 included a markdown of $20. What was the markdown rate?

8. The property tax on an auto was $360.95. The fair market value of the automobile was $12,340 and the assessed value was at 65%. What was the tax rate per $100?

9. The list price of an article was $46.50. Trade discounts of 10% and 5% were given. A cash discount of 2% was realized because of prompt payment of the invoice. The selling price of the article was $49.95. What was the rate of markup based on cost?

10. The gross monthly wages of John Adams amounted to $2,150. Find the amount of wages after the FICA deduction of 7.51% is made.

11. The net sales of Capital Corporation for the present year are $56,347. The net sales for last year were $53,950. Find the rate of increase for net sales.

12. The cost of goods sold for ABC Corporation for the past year was $459,290. The net sales for the corporation was $675,290. Find the average rate of markup based on net sales.

13. Two banks are in direct competition to loan ABC Corporation money. One bank will make a loan at an annual interest rate of 8%. The other bank offers an annual discount rate of 7.5%. ABC needs $50,000. Which bank offers the better deal?

14. Find the amount of ordinary interest paid by Daniel Corporation for using $35,000 from May 21 to October 1 at an 8% interest.

15. Find the amount of tax due on a house with a fair market value of $120,000. The assessment rate is 90% and the tax rate is 12 mills.

16. Find the amount of commission paid on sales of $150,000 if the commis-

sion rate is 3% on the first $100,000 and 5% on all sales in excess of $100,000.

17. Find the amount of money received from a bank that discounted a 60-day note for $25,000 at a 7% discount rate.

18. Find the maturity value of $87,500 if exact interest is received at the rate of 9% from March 1 to December 1, using exact time.

19. Find the present value of $10,000 in 5 years invested at 7% simple interest.

20. A dealer offers trade discounts of 10%, 8%, and 5% on the list price of hardware. Find the equivalent single trade discount.

21. The administrative costs of Careless Corporation were $453,200. The total assets of the company were $5,235,750. The administrative costs for Small Enterprises were $20,250. The total assets of Small Enterprises were $253,000. Find the percent of each company's administrative costs. Which is the more favorable rate?

22. $450 represents an increase of 30% over the cost. Find the cost.

23. Find the principal if the maturity value of a loan is $2,650, the rate of interest is 6%, and the time is 65 days, using exact interest.

24. Find the proceeds from a discounted note. The maturity value of the note is $10,000, the term of the note is 100 days, and the discount rate is 7%.

25. The cash register tape from a business indicated gross sales of $45,678.24. The markup rate based on sales is 3%. Find the markup.

26. The cash register tape from a business indicated a gross sales amount of $25,450.89. The markup rate is 4.5% of cost. Find the amount of markup realized from the day's sales.

27. Commissions were paid by the following rates. 5% on the first $50,000, 6% on the next $50,000, and 8% on all sales over $100,000. Find the amount of sales made to receive commissions of $4,000.

28. Inventory amounts for the past 3 years for XYZ Corporation are as follows.

1986	$456,789
1987	543,987
1988	497,234

Determine the change and rate of change in inventories yearly.

29. A 10% increase in salary gives the amount of $678,000 for salaries. What was the amount of salary in the previous year's income statement?

30. After-Christmas sales listed an artificial tree with a regular price $60 and a markdown of 45%. The tree cost the seller $30 and selling expenses amounted to 25% of cost. Was there a profit or loss on the transaction?

31. Profits of $3,560 are to be distributed among three partners in the ratio of 2:3:7. Find the amount each partner receives.

32. A wealthy businessman died without a will. The courts determined that $1/3$ of his $750,000 estate would go to the widow and the remaining $2/3$ would be divided equally among his three children. What was the whole number ratio of the division of the estate? How much did the widow and each of the children receive?

33. If Store X made a profit of $8,456 on sales of $94,500, find the profits if the sales increased to $125,000.

34. If an 8% profit yields $4,500, determine the yield if the profit increased to 9%.

35. Convert 1,000 kilometers to miles if 1 kilometer is 0.6214 miles.

Answers to Review Exercises

  1. 61.3%.

  2. 56.6%.

  3. 25%.

  4. 0.69%.

  5. 4%.

  6. 25%.

  7. 20%.

  8. $4.50 per $100.

  9. 28.2%.

 10. $1,988.53.

 11. 4.4%.

 12. 32%.

 13. 8% interest by $54.

14. $1,034.44.

15. $1,296.

16. $5,500.

17. $24,711.70.

18. $93,433.22.

19. $7,407.41.

20. 21.3%.

21. 8% better rate.

22. $346.15.

23. $2,622.

24. $9,809.26.

25. $1,370.35.

26. $1,095.97.

27. $75,000.

28. $87,198 ($46,753). 19.9% (8.6%).

29. $616,363.64.

30. Loss of $4.50.

31. $593.33. $890. $2,076.67.

32. 3:2:2:2. $250,000, widow. $166,666.67, each child.

33. $11,185.19.

34. $5,062.50.

35. 621.4 miles.

Chapter 2

COMPOUND INTEREST

The application of percentage as interest was **simple interest.** Currently the business community uses the concept of compound interest to pay for the use of money or to accrue interest on money. **Compound interest** is accruing interest on any interest earned as well as on the principal.

Varying time periods as well as different interest rates affect the amount of interest earned in compound interest. The effective rate of interest is a way of comparing varying time periods and different interest rates.

The analysis of business growth is further complicated by the inflation change during the time period and the change in the value of the dollar during the time period. The consumer price index is a way of making comparisons during different time periods.

At the end of this chapter, the student will be able to:

1. Identify the quantities involved in a compound interest problem.

2. Identify the interest rate for a given period and the number of periods in a given time interval, use the information to substitute in the compound amount formula, and solve for the missing quantity.

3. Define the quantities associated with present-value problems, substitute accurately in the present-value formula, and solve for the unknown quantities.

4. Determine the effective interest rate for various rates and compound periods and use the concept of the effective interest rate in making rational business decisions.

5. Use the concept of compound interest to assist in understanding and generating economic indicators such as the value of the dollar, the consumer price index, and the gross national product.

6. Translate verbal problems involving the principles of compound interest into the formula for compound interest and use the result to solve the problem.

2.1   COMPOUND AMOUNT

There are two types of interest paid for the use of money: simple interest, where the principal remains constant throughout the problem, and compound interest, where the principal increases by the amount of interest for each period of the investment. For any given rate, compound interest exceeds simple interest for any time more than one period.

Simple interest is calculated by the formula $I = Prt$, and the total amount is calculated by the formula $S = P(1 + rt)$. These formulas are used to develop the compound interest formula. To keep the calculations as simple as possible in the development of the compound interest formula, a time period of 1 year will be used. The formula for simple interest is

$$\text{Amount after 1 year} = P(1 + rt) \quad \text{but} \quad t = 1 \text{ so } A = P(1 + r)$$

The $[P(1 + r)]$ becomes the principal in the next year's calculation.

$$\text{Amount after 2 years} = [P(1 + r)](1 + r) = P(1 + r)^2$$

The $[P(1 + r)^2]$ becomes the principal in the next year's calculation.

$$\text{Amount after 3 years} = [P(1 + r)^2](1 + r) = P(1 + r)^3$$

Once the pattern has been recognized, the formula can be generalized to:

$$A = P(1 + r)^t$$

This formula was generated for the time period of 1 year; the formula can be generalized for periods other than 1 year. The general compound amount formula is given by:

$$A = P(1 + i)^n$$

where i is the annual rate/number of compound periods per year, n is the number of years multiplied by the number of periods per year, P is the original amount invested, and A is the principal + compound interest earned.

To find the actual interest earned:

$$\text{Compound interest} = A - P$$

Example

Find the final amount on deposit if $10,000 is invested for 3 years at 5% interest, compounded semiannually. Find the amount of interest earned.

$$P = 10,000$$

$$i = \frac{0.05}{2} \quad \text{(semiannually means 2 periods/year)}$$

$$n = 3 \text{ years} \times 2 \text{ periods/year} = 6$$

Substituting:

$$A = 10,000(1 + 0.025)^6$$

$$= 10,000(1.025)^6 = 10,000(1.159\ 6934)$$

To find 1.025^6 on your calculator:

$$1.025 \boxed{y^x} \ 6 \ \boxed{=} \ \boxed{\times} \ 10,000 \ \boxed{=}$$

$$A = 11,596.93$$

To find the amount of interest earned, $I = A - P$:

$$I = \$11,596.93 - \$10,000 = \$1,596.93$$

To compare the compound amount with the amount the investment is worth using simple interest, calculate the simple interest on $10,000 for 3 years at 5% interest.

$$A = P(1 + rt) = 10,000(1 + (0.05)(3))$$

$$= 10,000(1.15) = \$11,500$$

The compound amount exceeds the simple interest amount by $96.93.

Calculations for the compound amount involve exponents. Either tables or a calculator are used to find the compound amount.

The procedure for using Table 2 in the Appendix is as follows. Determine i for the problem using the relationship $i = r/n$, where r is the annual rate of interest and n is the number of periods per year. The value of i determines the page of Table 2 to be used. Determine the column of the table by the column heading. The column heading needed is Compound Amount; therefore column 2 is used. The row of the table is determined by the number of periods (the number of years multiplied by the number of periods per year). The entry in column 2 for the required number of periods is the compound value of $1. To answer a specific problem, multiply P (the amount of the initial investment) by the entry from Table 2.

Example
An amount of $15,500 is invested at 6% interest, compounded quarterly, for 4 years. Find the compound amount.

$$i = \frac{6\%}{4} = 1.5\% = 0.015$$

$$\text{Periods} = 4 \times 4 = 16$$

The value from Table 2, rate 1.5%, column 2, line 16, is 1.268 985 5477.

$$A = (15,500)(1.268\ 985\ 5477) = \$19,669.28$$

To perform the computation on a calculator, your calculator must have a $\boxed{y^x}$ key.

Determine i by r/number of periods per year.

Add 1 to i and enter in calculator.

Press $\boxed{y^x}$.

Enter the number of periods (number of years $\times$ number of compound periods/year).

Press $\boxed{=}$. A number equal to the amount from Table 2 should be displayed.

Press $\boxed{\times}$.

Enter value for P.

Press $\boxed{=}$.

The number in the display is the compound amount. Write the amount rounded to the nearest cent.

The calculator keystroke for the compound amount for $15,500 invested at 6% interest, compounded quarterly, for 4 years is

$$0.06 \; \boxed{\div} \; 4 + 1 \; \boxed{=} \; \boxed{y^x} \; 16 \; \boxed{=}\boxed{\times} \; 15,500 \; \boxed{=}$$

Read compound amount of $15,500 from display: 19,669.276. Round to dollar amount: $19,699.28.

Note that occasionally, the compound amount calculated from Table 2 will vary by a cent from the amount generated by the calculator. The number of digits accepted by the calculator restricts the accuracy. If the table value 1.268 985 5477 is entered into a calculator, it becomes 1.268 9855 in a nine-bit display. If done by hand, the product is 19,669.275 989 3500. When rounded to dollars and cents, the amount becomes $19,669.28, which is identical to the result displayed in the calculator.

To illustrate the two methods of solution, several examples are given. Table 2 is a portion of a set of tables available to the financial community. Our examples are selected to guarantee appropriate entries from the tables in case a calculator is not available.

Example
Find the compound amount on the following at 8% interest, compounded monthly, for 5 years.

a. $500.

b. $5,000.

c. $25,000.

To determine (a), find the number of periods: $5 \times 12 = 60$ periods. The value from Table 2, rate $2/3$%, column 2, line 60, is 1.489 845 7083. Multiply:

$$1.489 \; 845 \; 7083 \times 500 = \$744.92285$$

Rounded to dollar and cents: $744.92.

The calculator keystroke is

$$0.08 \boxed{\div} 12 \boxed{+} 1 \boxed{=}\boxed{y^x} 60 \boxed{=}\boxed{\times} 500 \boxed{=}$$

To determine (b), use the same procedure as (a) until Multiply step. Multiply:

$$1.489\ 845\ 7083 \times 5,000 = \$7,449.2285$$

Rounded to dollars and cents: $7,449.23.
　　　To determine (c), use the same procedure as (a) until Multiply step. Multiply:

$$1.489\ 845\ 7083 \times 25,000 = \$37,246.143.$$

Rounded to dollar and cents: $37,246.14.

This example illustrates the importance of the rate per compound period and the number of compound periods per year. Generally, the more compound periods per year, the larger the compound amount for any given principal and rate.
　　　If this entire problem were done by calculator, the value in the calculator (not the rounded amount) after $\boxed{y^x}\boxed{=}$ needs to be retained for future use.

Press $\boxed{STO}$ [this stores the display value for use in parts (a), (b), and (c)].

Press $\boxed{\times}$. Enter 500. Press $\boxed{=}$ to obtain the answer to part (a).

Press $\boxed{RCL}$ to recall the display value. Press $\boxed{\times}$. Enter 5,000. Press $\boxed{=}$ to obtain the answer to part (b).

Press $\boxed{RCL}$. Press $\boxed{\times}$. Enter 25,000. Press $\boxed{=}$ to obtain the answer to part (c).

Example
Find the compound amount on $10,000 at an interest rate of 8% for 5 years, compounded:

　a. Semiannually

　b. Quarterly

　c. Monthly

Table method:

	(a)	(b)	(c)
Rate	$\dfrac{8\%}{2} = 4\%$	$\dfrac{8\%}{4} = 2\%$	$\dfrac{8\%}{12} = \dfrac{2}{3}\%$
Periods	$5 \times 2 = 10$	$5 \times 4 = 20$	$5 \times 12 = 60$
Value	1.480 244 2849	1.485 947 3960	1.489 845 7083
P × value	$14,802.44	$14,859.47	$14,898.46

Calculator Method:

Enter $r/n + 1$	1.04	1.02	1.006 6666
Press $\boxed{y^x}$			
Enter periods	10	20	60
Press $\boxed{=}$			
Press $\boxed{\times}$			
Enter 10,000	10,000	10,000	10,000
Press $\boxed{=}$	$14,802.44	$14,859.47	$14,898.46

The compound amount varies by almost $100 as the number of compound periods increase.

Many lending institutions advertise daily compounding or compounding continuously. To compound daily, the annual rate is divided by 360, the number of years is multiplied by 360. The advantage of daily compounding over monthly compounding is slight. An advantage to the consumer in daily compounding results from interest being paid from the day of deposit to the day of withdrawal. When a monthly period is used, the tenth of the month is the magic day—any deposits made on or before the tenth earned interest from the first, deposits made after the tenth earned no interest until the next month.

To perform continuous compounding, a formula generated in calculus is needed, $A = Pe^{rt}$. Actual calculations using this formula will be delayed until after a study of calculus.

SECTION 1 EXERCISES

1. From Table 2 find the value of $(1 + i)^n$ for each of the following:
   a. $r = 6\%$, $t = 4$ years, compounded quarterly.
   b. $r = 10\%$, $t = 3$ years, compounded monthly.
   c. $r = 7\%$, $t = 10$ years, compounded semiannually.
   d. $r = 8\%$, $t = 40$ years, compounded annually.

2. Find the compound amount of $51,000 at 9% interest, compounded monthly, for $3\frac{1}{2}$ years.

3. Find the compound amount of $20,000 at 8% interest, compounded monthly, for 4 1/2 years.

4. Find the compound amount of $5,000 at 8% interest, compounded quarterly, for 10 years.

5. Find the compound amount of $7,500 at 7% interest, compounded quarterly, for 7 years.

6. Find the compound amount of $60,000 at 5% interest, compounded semiannually, for 20 years.

7. Find the compound amount of $15,000 at 7% interest, compounded semiannually, for 15 years.

8. Find the compound amount of $350 at 7% interest, compounded quarterly, for 10 years.

9. Find the compound amount of $750 at 9% interest, compounded monthly, for 3 1/2 years.

10. Find the compound amount of $25,000 at 6% interest, compounded semiannually, for 21 years.

11. You invest $2,000 on April 1 in an investment earning 8% interest, compounded monthly. How much is the investment worth on December 1?

12. You invest $4,500 on March 15 at 7% interest, compounded quarterly. For any fractional part of a quarter, simple interest is used for the period less than the compound period. Find the value of the investment on December 31.

13. On May 1 $10,000 is invested at 8% interest, compounded monthly. Find the value of the investment on December 20. For a time period less than a month, simple interest is used.

14. Farmer Jones buys equipment for $10,000. He agrees to repay the compound amount in 2 1/2 years. The interest rate is 10%, compounded quarterly. How much money is necessary for repayment?

15. Mary Smith can invest $10,000 at 9% simple interest for the next 10 years or invest at 8% interest, compounded quarterly, for the next 10 years. What is the amount of the investment in 10 years (a) under simple interest and (b) under compound interest?

16. Mark Adams has two options for investment of $25,000.
    a. Simple interest at 7% for 12 years.
    b. Compound interest at 6% for 12 years, compounded quarterly.
    Find the value of each option at maturity.

17. A town's population is growing at 2% per year, compounded annually. Find the population in the year 2000 if the population in 1985 is 213,450.

18. An area in the Sunbelt is growing at the rate of 5% per year, compounded annually. Find the population in the year 2000 if the population in 1980 is 2,345,000.

19. You are bequeathed $2,000 which you can accept now, or you can receive $2,100 1 year from now. The best investment rate you can find is 10%, compounded monthly. Which offer will you accept?

20. An old passbook was found with $475 listed as the amount in the account on July 1, 1941. The bank has been paying 4.5% interest, compounded yearly. Find the value of the account in July 1, 1989.

21. An old passbook was found in an attic trunk with $234 in the account on July 1, 1935. The bank paid 3% interest, compounded semiannually, until 1946; raised the rate to 4%, compounded semiannually, on July 1, 1946; and continued at 4% until July 1, 1958. On July 1, 1958, the interest rate was raised to 5%, compounded semiannually, until January 1, 1974, when the rate was raised to 6%, compounded monthly. Find the value of the account on July 1, 1985.
Use a calculator to determine the following.

22. Find the compound amount of $4,000 invested at 5.5% interest, compounded daily, for 195 days.

23. Find the compound amount of $560 invested at 5.25% interest, compounded daily, for 300 days.

24. Find the year-end balance on an account valued at $456.75 on May 16, paying 5.5% interest, compounded daily.

25. Find the year-end balance on an account valued at $4,567 on April 15. The account earns 6.25% interest, compounded daily.

Answers to Odd-Numbered Exercises

1. (a) 1.268 985 5477. (b) 1.348 181 8424. (c) 1.989 788 8635. (d) 21.724 521 4968.

3. $28,632.36.

5. $12,190.60.

7. $42,101.90.

9. $1,026.49.

11. $2,109.19.

13. $10,520.33.

15. (a) $19,000. (b) $22,080.40.

17. 287,276.

19. Accept $2,000.

21. $2,223.07.

23. $585.04.

25. $4,777.85.

2.2   PRESENT VALUE, RATE, AND TIME

The compound amount formula has four variables, P, i, n, and A. All of the examples in the previous section solved for A, the **compound amount.** The compound amount is the value of the principal at some future date.

In this section we will solve for the other variables in $A = P(1 + i)^n$. P refers to the principal or the amount originally invested. When P is unknown, the problem becomes a present-value problem. When solving for P, the present value of an investment is needed, the future value is known. To solve for P, the compound or future amount formula is solved for P.

Solving $A = P(1 + i)^n$ for P

The compound amount formula is

$$A = P(1 + i)^n$$

Dividing by $(1 + i)^n$:

$$\frac{A}{(1 + i)^n} = P$$

This formula involves dividing by an entry from Table 2. This formula is more commonly written as a multiplication problem using a negative exponent for the $(1 + i)$ factor

$$P = A(1 + i)^{-n}$$

A negative exponent denotes the reciprocal of the factor the exponent affects.

$$x^{-1} = \frac{1}{x} \qquad (1+r)^{-3} = \frac{1}{(1+r)^3} \qquad (1+r)^{-8} = \frac{1}{(1+r)^8}$$

Therefore $P = A/(1+r)^n$ and $P = A(1+r)^{-n}$ are two forms of the same statement. To ease computation, values for $(1+r)^{-n}$ are listed in Table 2. The values in column 4 are the values for present value. The entries are the reciprocals of the corresponding entries in column 2. The values in this column are used when present value is the unknown.

Example
Find the present value of $18,500, compounded semiannually, at 8% interest for 4 years.

$$A = 18{,}500 \qquad i = \frac{8\%}{2} = 4\% = 10.04 \qquad n = 4 \times 2 = 8 \qquad P = ?$$

$$18{,}500(1.04)^{-8} = 18{,}500 \times 0.730\ 6902 = \$13{,}517.77$$

0.730 6902 is found in Table 2, rate 2%, column 4, line 8.
The calculator keystroke is

$$0.08\ \boxed{\div}\ 2\ \boxed{+}\ 1\ \boxed{=}\boxed{y^x}\ 8\ \boxed{+/-}\boxed{=}\boxed{\times}\ 18{,}500\ \boxed{=}$$

The display is rounded to the nearest cent to obtain the answer.

Example
A certificate of deposit has matured and has a value of $12,840. The interest rate of the certificate was 6%, compounded monthly. Find the purchase price of the certificate 4 years ago.

$$A = 12{,}840 \qquad i = 0.005 \qquad n = 48 \qquad P = ?$$

$$P = A(1+r)^{-n} = 12{,}840(1.005)^{-48}$$

Using Table 2, rate 0.5%, column 2, line 48:

$$12{,}840(0.787\ 098\ 4111) = \$10{,}106.34$$

The calculator keystroke is

0.06 $\boxed{\div}$ 12 $\boxed{+}$ 1 $\boxed{=}$$\boxed{y^x}$ 48 $\boxed{+/-}$$\boxed{=}$$\boxed{\times}$ 12,840 $\boxed{=}$

Solving $A = P(1 + i)^n$ for n

The compound amount formula has four variables. We have solved for two of the four using the formulas: $A = P(1 + i)^n$ and $P = A(1 + i)^{-n}$. If A, P, and i are known quantities, the unknown is n. If you are familiar with logarithms, n can be solved by using logarithms. The equation (without explanation) is

$$\frac{\log A - \log B}{\log(1 + r)} = n$$

If logarithms are not part of your expertise, Table 2 entries can give a close approximation for n. The following example outlines the procedure for using Table 2 to find a value for n.

Example
How long did it take $10,000 to become $15,000, compounded quarterly, at 8% interest?

$$P = 10,000 \qquad A = 15,000 \qquad i = 0.02 \qquad n = ?$$

Substitute these values in $A = P(1 + i)^n$.

$$15,000 = 10,000(1.02)^n$$

Divide both sides of the equation by 10,000.

$$1.5 = (1.02)^n$$

Using Table 2, rate 2%, column 2, go down the column until the entry is 1.5.

Period 20	1.485 947 3960
Period 21	1.515 666 3439

$10,000 will not become $15,000 until the twenty-first period. Because the periods are quarters, $21/4 = 5.25$ years. If a value closer than the approximate $5 1/4$ years is needed, linear interpolation must be used.

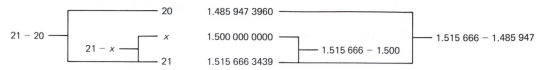

Linear interpolation from the entries in Table 2: Set up the following proportion.

$$\frac{(21 - 20)}{(21 - x)} = \frac{(1.515\ 666 - 1.485\ 947)}{(1.515\ 666 - 1.5)}$$

$$\frac{1}{(21 - x)} = \frac{0.029\ 719}{0.015\ 666}$$

Cross product:

$$0.015\ 666 = 0.624\ 099 - 0.029\ 719x$$

$$0.029\ 719x = 0.608\ 433$$

$$x = 20.47286$$

This answer tells us it took 20 quarters or 5 years and 0.47 of a quarter which is approximately 42 days (0.47×90 days). For the purposes of this book, approximate values of n will be accepted. Logarithms will give precise answers when needed. Calculators cannot give a solution to this problem without using logarithms.

Example
John Smith is given \$10,000. If he invests it in a certificate of deposit at 6% interest, compounded monthly, approximately how long before the value of the certificate is \$13,000?

$$P = 10,000 \qquad A = 13,000 \qquad i = 0.005$$

$$13,000 = 10,000(1.005)^n \qquad 1.3 = (1.005)^n$$

Using Table 2, rate 0.5%, column 2, go down until the value is 1.3. $n = 53$ periods. In this problem, this is 53 months or 4 years 5 months from the time of investment.

The generalized procedure to solve for n is as follows.

1. Identify A, P, and i.

2. Find the value of A/P.

3. Refer to Table 2, page determined by i.

4. Go down Compound Amount column (column 2) until the value in the column is equal to or exceeds the value of A/P.

5. Read off periods.

6. Convert periods to years by periods/compound periods per year.

Solving $A = P(1 + i)^n$ for i

The fourth variable of the formula is i. Given A, P, and n, the compound amount formula:

$$A = P(1 + i)^n$$

Divide by P.

$$\frac{A}{P} = (1 + i)^n$$

Take the nth root of each side.

$$\sqrt[n]{\frac{A}{P}} = (1 + i)$$

Subtract 1 from each side.

$$\sqrt[n]{\frac{A}{P}} - 1 = i$$

To find i utilizing Table 2:

1. Determine the value for A/P.

2. Determine n.

3. Refer to Table 2, n lines down column 2 until an entry closely approximating the $(1 + i)^n$ value.

4. Read i from Table 2.

5. Convert i to an annual rate by multiplying by periods/year.

To find i, using a calculator with the $\boxed{\sqrt[x]{y}}$ key:

1. Enter A, $\boxed{\div}$, enter P, $\boxed{=}$.

2. $\boxed{\sqrt[x]{y}}$, enter n, $\boxed{=}$.

3. $\boxed{-}$ 1 $\boxed{=}$. The value in the display is i.

4. $\boxed{\times}$ number of periods per year, $\boxed{=}$.

Example

At what compound rate must \$10,000 be invested to reach a value of \$12,500 in 3 years, compounded quarterly?

Using Table 2:

$$\frac{A}{P} = \frac{12,500}{10,000} = 1.25 \qquad n = 12$$

For 1.75%, twelfth line: 1.231 439
For 2%, twelfth line: 1.268 241

The quarterly rate of interest is between 1.75% and 2%. The annual rate of interest would be between $(1.75\%)(4) = 7\%$ and $(2\%)(4) = 8\%$.

The calculator solution is

$$12,500 = 10,000(1 + i)^{12}$$

12,500 $\boxed{\div}$ 10,000 $\boxed{=}$ $\boxed{\sqrt[x]{y}}$ $\boxed{12}$ $\boxed{=}$ $\boxed{-}$ 1 $\boxed{=}$ $\boxed{\times}$ 4 $\boxed{=}$

The display is 0.075 07706. The solution is 7.5%.

The calculator keystroke without the $\boxed{\sqrt[x]{y}}$ key is

1. Enter 1.25.

2. $\boxed{y^x}$.

3. Enter (1 $\boxed{\div}$ 12). Because the exponent $1/12$ is equivalent to $\sqrt[12]{}$, the $1/12$ must be enclosed in parentheses.

4. $\boxed{=}$.

5. The display shows 1.018 7693.

To complete the problem on the calculator:

6. $\boxed{-}$.

7. Enter 1.

8. $\boxed{=}$.

9. $\boxed{\times}$.

10. Enter 4.

11. $\boxed{=}$. The solution is 0.075 or 7.5%.

Example
At what rate of quarterly compound interest does $100 double in 5 years?

$$P = 100 \qquad A = 200 \text{ (double means } 100 \times 2) \qquad n = 20$$

Using Table 2:

$$\frac{A}{P} = 2 \text{ (double)} \qquad n = 5 \times 4 = 20$$

The answer is between 3.5% and 4% per quarter which is between 14% and 16% per year.
The calculator keystroke is

$$2 \; \boxed{y^x} \; 0.05 \; \boxed{=}\boxed{-} \; 1 \; \boxed{=}\boxed{\times} \; 4 \; \boxed{=}$$

Display (rounded) is .141 or 14.1%.

SECTION 2 EXERCISES

1. Find the present value of $20,000, compounded quarterly, at 8% interest for 8 years.

2. Find the present value of $3,500, compounded annually, at 5% interest for 25 years.

3. Find the present value of $8,000, compounded semiannually, at 6% interest for 15 years.

4. Find the present value of $5,000, compounded quarterly, at 10% interest for 5 years.

5. Find the present value of $50,000, compounded annually, at 6% interest for 40 years.

6. Find the present value of $32,000, compounded semiannually, at 8% interest for 16 years.

7. Approximately how long will it take for $3,000 to grow to $5,000 at 8% interest, compounded quarterly?

8. Approximately how long will it take $5,000 to become $7,500 at 9% interest, compounded monthly?

9. Approximately how long will it take $5,000 to become $12,000 at 7% interest, compounded annually?

10. At what rate must you invest $1,000 for the investment to be worth $1,500 in 3 years, compounded quarterly?

11. At what rate must you invest to triple your investment in 15 years?

12. At what rate must you invest to double your investment in 10 years?

13. What amount must you invest today to ensure your newborn grandchild will have $25,000 for college in 18 years. The rate of investment today is 9% interest, compounded semiannually.

14. You wish to invest an amount today that will ensure $50,000 upon your retirement in 15 years. The rate of return today is 8% interest, compounded quarterly. What investment should you make?

15. Telecom Company has declared bankruptcy and your company is given two options for your account.
    a. $10,000 today.
    b. A certificate of deposit due in 2 years with a maturity value of $12,000.
A call to your banker states you can earn 7% interest, compounded quarterly, on present investments. Which option is more attractive?

16. You are 18 years old and your grandfather calls and gives you two options as a gift:
    a. $21,000 today
    b. $25,000 when you turn 21
Your grandfather gives you the banker's quote of the day, 6% interest, compounded monthly. Which option would you select and why?

17. A friend is trying to interest you in an investment: $10,000 today, $20,000 in 5 years, compounded monthly. What rate of return is this investment yielding?

18. An advertisement reads: Invest $1,000 today, get $1,200 next year. What rate of return is this if the amount is compounded monthly? What rate of return is this, using simple interest?

19. How long will it take for $25,000 to become $100,000 if the money is invested at 6% interest, compounded semiannually?

20. How long will it take John White to become a millionaire if he inherited $250,000 and he has the money invested at 12% interest, compounded quarterly?

21. Jane Smith has $10,000 in the bank, invested at 8% interest, compounded monthly. She wishes to buy an automobile that has a sticker price of $12,000 today. The auto salesperson predicts prices on the auto will rise at 4% per year. In how many years will Jane Smith have sufficient funds to purchase the car in a cash transaction?

22. Sharon wishes to purchase a certificate of deposit which will have a value of $7,500 in 5 years. The investment yields 9% interest, compounded monthly. How much will the certificate cost today?

23. A stamp collection increases in value 5% per year. The appraised value of the collection today is $4,400. What was its value 4 years ago?

24. If the rate of inflation continues at the rate of 4% per year, what will be the value of a diamond in 10 years if the appraised value of the diamond today is $5,600?

25. An antiques dealer offered $6,500 for a painting. The owner wants $7,800. If the painting is appreciating 10% per year, how long will the owner have to wait to get the asking price?

Answers to Odd-Numbered Exercises

1. $10,612.67.

3. $3,295.89.

5. $4,861.11.

7. 6½ years.

9. 13 years.

11. 7.5%.

13. $5,125.70.

15. Option b is worth $10,444.94 today.

17. 13.9%.

19. 23 1/2 years.

21. 52 months.

23. $3,620.

25. 2 years.

2.3   EFFECTIVE INTEREST RATE

When we discussed bank discounts and simple interest in Chapter 1, it was necessary to have some way of comparing annual interest and discount rates. The two formulas, $r = d/(1 - d)$ and $d = r/(1 + r)$, were developed and used to compare different types of loan rates when simple interest was involved. In compound interest problems, there are three types of rates for each problem.

   Annual rate or **nominal rate** is the quoted rate; it is always accompanied by the frequency of compounding. The letter used to denote the annual rate is r.

   Rate per period, denoted as i, is the annual or nominal rate divided by the number of compound periods per year. The value of i determines the page used in Table 2.

   Effective rate is the annual rate that will produce the same amount of interest as the nominal rate over many compound periods. The effective rate allows rates with different compounding periods to be compared.

   To determine the **effective rate:**

Determine the value of $(1 + i)^m$, where m is the number of compound periods per year.

Subtract 1.

The remaining factor, written as a percent, is the effective rate.

Example

Find the effective rate for 6% interest, compounded monthly.

$$i = \frac{6\%}{12} = 0.5\% = 0.005$$

$m = 12$ the number of compound periods per year

$$(1 + 0.005)^{12} = (1.005)^{12} = 1.0617$$

$$1.0617 - 1 = 0.0617 = 6.17\%$$ effective rate

The value of the factor $(1 + i)^m$ can be obtained from Table 2 identifying the page by the value of i and looking down column 2 to the m entry. Subtract 1 to determine the effective rate.

The calculator keystroke is

$$1 + 0.005 \boxed{=} \boxed{y^x} \ 12 \boxed{=} \boxed{-} \ 1 \boxed{=}$$

Example
Determine which of the following is the higher rate, 6% interest, compounded monthly, or 7% interest, compounded quarterly.

6%, Compounded Monthly	*7%, Compounded Quarterly*
$i = \dfrac{6\%}{12} = 0.5\% = 0.005$	$i = \dfrac{7\%}{4} = 1.75\% = 0.0175$
$m = 12$	$m = 4$
$(1 + 0.005)^{12} = 1.0617$	$(1 + 0.0175)^4 = 1.0719$
Subtract 1	Subtract 1
$i = 0.0617 = 6.17\%$	$i = 0.0719 = 7.19\%$

Six percent interest, compounded monthly, is equivalent to a rate of 6.17%, compounded annually. Seven percent interest, compounded quarterly, is equivalent to 7.19%, compounded annually. The higher rate is 7% interest, compounded quarterly.

In the preceding example different rates over different compound periods were taken and an equivalent rate over an annual compound period was determined. When the compound periods are alike, the two rates can be compared without determining the effective rate.

Financial institutions use various advertising schemes to lure potential investors. Continuous compounding and compounding daily do not affect the compound amount substantially. When selecting a bank, consider the withdrawal policy as well as the frequency of compounding.

SECTION 3 EXERCISES

1. Find the effective rate of 7% interest, compounded monthly.

2. Find the effective rate of 12% interest, compounded quarterly.

3. Find the effective rate of 6% interest, compounded quarterly.

4. Find the effective rate of 8% interest, compounded semiannually.

5. Two competing institutions advertise the following interest rates.
   a. 7%, compounded monthly.
   b. 7.25%, compounded annually.
If all other considerations are equal, where would you place your money?

6. Two financial institutions compete for funds in the following ways.
   a. 5% interest, compounded quarterly.
   b. 5% interest, compounded semiannually.
Which is the higher effective rate and by how much?
   The remaining problems need a calculator for computation.
7. Find the effective rate of 8% interest, compounded daily.

8. Find the effective rate of 9% interest, compounded daily.

9. Find the higher effective rate for the following.
   a. 8.5% interest, compounded quarterly.
   b. 8% interest, compounded daily.

10. Find the higher effective rate for the following.
    a. 7.25% interest, compounded monthly.
    b. 7.125% interest, compounded daily.

11. Find the higher effective rate for the following.
    a. 6.25% interest, compounded monthly.
    b. 6.10% interest, compounded daily.

12. Find the higher effective rate for the following.
    a. 5.75% interest, compounded monthly.
    b. 5.67% interest, compounded daily.

Answers to Odd-Numbered Exercises

1. 7.23%.

3. 6.14%.

5. 7.23% versus 7.25%. 7.25% interest, compounded annually, is better.

7. 8.33%.

9. 8.5% versus 8.33%. 8.25% interest, compounded quarterly, is better.

11. 6.4% versus 6.3%. 6.25% interest, compounded monthly, is higher.

2.4   EQUATIONS OF VALUE

It is sometimes necessary to combine the concepts of compound amount and algebra to solve problems—the technique is called equations of value.

Suppose a grandfather dies, leaving $80,000 to be divided equally among his three grandchildren on each child's twenty-first birthday. The present ages of the grandchildren are 17, 19, and 20. How much will each child receive if the money is invested at 7% interest, compounded monthly, until distributed.

A time line will help to clarify the problem. On the time line, locate the present time, the time when each distribution is made, and the amount of each distribution (x).

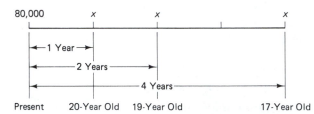

A method of solution for this problem is to relate each distribution to the present time when the value of the money is $80,000.

The present-value formula is

$$P = A(1 + r)^{-n}$$

where A is the amount distributed at age 21 and is the same for each of the grandchildren.

Present value of distributed amount to 20-year-old $= A(1 + 0.07/12)^{-12}$.

Present value of distributed amount to 19-year-old $= A(1 + 0.07/12)^{-24}$.

Present value of distributed amount to 17-year-old $= A(1 + 0.07/12)^{-48}$.

$$A(0.932\ 5835) + A(0.869\ 7119) + A(0.756\ 3988) = 80,000$$

$$2.559A = 80,000$$

$$A = \$31,265.95$$

Each grandchild will receive the amount of $31,265.95 on his or her twenty-first birthday.

An alternate solution is to determine the value of the $80,000 on the youngest child's twenty-first birthday, and then, using the compound amount, determine the amount of each distribution that would eventually have totaled $80,000(1 + $0.07/12)^{48}$.

To write an equation of value, a date must be selected and each distribution valued at that date. If the date precedes the distributions, the present value is used. If the date follows the distribution, the compound amount is used.

Determining Values for Balance Sheet

A company closes its books on June 30. Among the assets are $250,000 invested on January 30 at 6% interest, compounded quarterly, and a $300,000 note due on August 30, also compounded quarterly at 6% interest. Find the amounts of the assets for the June 30 balance sheet.

The first asset (January 30, $250,000 at 6% interest, compounded quarterly) only has 5 months at the time of the balance sheet, less than two compound periods. Find the compound amount at the end of one period.

$$250,000(1 + 0.015)^1 = \$253,750$$

For anything less than a period, simple interest is used to determine the amount. The principal for the simple interest is $253,750.

$$253,750\left(1 + (0.06)\left(\frac{2}{12}\right)\right) = \$256,287.50$$

$256,287.50 is the amount of the $250,000 asset shown on the balance sheet.

The $300,000 note requires finding the present value on June 30 of a note that is due on August 30. Again, the time is less than the quarterly period, and simple discounting is used.

$$300,000\left(1 - (0.06)\left(\frac{2}{12}\right)\right) = \$297,000$$

$297,000 is the amount listed on the balance sheet. All **assets** and **liabilities** must be valued on the date of the balance sheet.

Time Not Included in Tables

It is 1990, the amount of the investment is $48,000 at 6% interest, compounded monthly. You wish to find the compound amount in 1999.

$$P = 48,000 \qquad i = \frac{6\%}{12} = 0.005 \qquad n = (12)(9) = 108$$

$$A = 48,000(1.005)^{108}$$

Refer to Table 2, rate 0.5%, and look down column 2, Compound Amount. The table ends at 60 periods. To find 108 periods, some laws of exponents need to be used.

$$(x^2)(x^3) = x^5 \qquad (x^{12})(x^{24}) = x^{36} \qquad (x^{50})(x^{30}) = x^{80}$$

These examples show us exponents add in a multiplication problem. Turn this problem around to find the value of $(1.005)^{108}$.

$$(1.005)^{60}(1.005)^{48} = (1.005)^{108} \quad \text{or} \quad (1.005)^{50}(1.005)^{58} = (1.005)^{108}$$

There are a variety of ways to generate $(1.005)^{108}$ from Table 2. Let us use $(1.005)^{60}(1.005)^{48} = (1.005)^{108}$. From Table 2, substitute the value for $(1.005)^{60}$ and $(1.005)^{48}$:

$$(1.34885)(1.270\ 489) = 1.7137$$

To complete the problem:

$$A = 48,000(1.7137) = \$82,257.60$$

This is the value of $48,000 in 1999.

If the number of periods is not present in Table 2, write n as the sum of two or more numbers available in the tables. Find the compound amount for each of the terms selected. Multiply the compound amount entries to find the equivalent compound amount for the original n.

Example
Find $(1 + 0.005)^{110}$ $(110 = 50 + 60)$.

$$(1.005)^{50} = 1.283\ 225\ 8149$$

$$(1.005)^{60} = 1.348\ 850\ 1525$$

$$(1.005)^{110} = (1.283\ 226)(1.348\ 850) = 1.730\ 87939$$

SECTION 4 EXERCISES

1. A recently widowed woman receives a $100,000 insurance settlement. She invests the amount at 7% interest, compounded monthly. She wishes to receive equal amounts yearly over the next 5 years. Find the amount she receives annually.

2. A will divides an estate of $120,000 equally among the intermediate family. The wife is to receive her share immediately; the son, who is 14 years old, is to receive his share at age 19. Find the amount the wife receives. The money not distributed will be invested at 8% interest, compounded monthly.

3. A wealthy senior citizen sets up a trust for scholarships at Benefit College. His bequest is for $40,000 and the money is to be distributed in equal amounts over the next 4 years. The money is invested at 6% interest, compounded quarterly. How much is available for scholarships each year?

4. A $100,000 note is due in 5 years. The person to receive the $100,000 asks for five equal yearly payments. The note was earning 8% interest, compounded monthly. What yearly amount was distributed in lieu of the lump settlement of $100,000?

5. A $10,000 bequeath to a 12-year-old stipulates the child will receive the money in four equal annual payments, starting at age 18. The money is invested at 8% interest, compounded quarterly. How much is received each of the 4 years?

6. A $2,000 insurance settlement to an 8-year-old is invested at 8% interest, compounded quarterly. The distribution will be in three equal amounts on the child's eighteenth, nineteenth, and twentieth birthdays. Find the amount of the distribution.

7. A company wishes to consolidate its debts as of June 30. A $10,000 note dated February 28 carries 8% monthly compound interest. A second note has $20,000 due October 30 and carries 6% quarterly compound interest. Find the amount needed to consolidate the two notes.

8. An accountant is preparing a balance sheet for Gold, Inc., dated April 30. The assets include the following.
   a. $10,000 obligation due February 15, compounded monthly, at 8% interest.
   b. $10,000 obligation due March 30, compounded quarterly, at 8% interest.
   c. $15,000 obligation due June 30, compounded monthly, at 8% interest.

Find the total value on the balance sheet for these short-term assets.

9. A balance sheet is being prepared for September 30. Find the amount on the balance sheet for each of the following assets.

June 15	$4,500	8% interest, compounded quarterly
August 10	$8,000	8% interest, compounded quarterly
November 30	$10,000	8% interest, compounded monthly

Find the total value of these assets for the September 30 balance sheet.

10. A year-end balance sheet is being prepared and the following liabilities must be included.

November 15	$4,500	8% interest, compounded monthly
December 15	$5,000	8% interest, compounded quarterly
April 15	$8,000	8% interest, compounded monthly

Find the values of these liabilities at year's end.

11. From Table 2, determine the value of $10,000 in 10 years if invested at 8% interest, compounded monthly.

12. From Table 2, determine the value of $5,000 in 20 years if invested at 8% interest, compounded quarterly.

13. From Table 2, determine the value of $2,000 in 8 years if invested at 7% interest, compounded monthly.

14. From Table 2, determine the value of $100,000 in 9 years if invested at 9% interest, compounded monthly.

15. In 1976 at our nation's bicentennial, a committee member of the event contributed $100 to a fund for the tricentennial celebration. The money is invested at 6% interest, compounded annually. Find the value of the contribution in the year 2076.

16. A loyal college alumnus has an insurance policy of $25,000 with the college as the beneficiary. The will stipulates the money must be invested at 6% interest, compounded monthly, for 50 years, at which time the college

could use the money toward a library. How much will the college receive at the end of the 50-year period?

17. A loyal college alumnus wishes to give the college $25,000 in 10 years. How much money should be set aside today if the current rate of investment is 8% interest, compounded monthly?

18. How much must be invested today at 8% interest, compounded monthly, to amount to $40,000 in 18 years?

19. How much must be deposited today in an investment paying 6% interest, compounded quarterly, to amount to $250,000 in 25 years?

Answers to Odd-Numbered Exercises

1. $24,538.80 annually.

3. $11,580 yearly.

5. $4,510.76.

7. $29,874.30.

9. $4,605.30. $8,090.67. $9,867.99. Total, $22,563.96.

11. $(1.489\ 845)(1.489\ 845) = 2.219\ 638\ 124 \times 10,000 = \$22,196.40.$

13. $3,495.65.

15. $33,930.21.

17. $11,263.09.

19. $56,407.36.

2.5 ECONOMIC ANALYSIS

Inflation is one of the most common economic problems in the world today. Rapid rise in the cost of commodities precipitates the need for increases in salaries. The increase in salaries adds to the cost of goods, causing a price increase. This vicious cycle is a major economic problem.

The rate of inflation is determined by a number called the price index. The price index is used by unions, government, pensions, and social security to make adjustments in wages and benefits to reflect price increases.

In the United States, these important statistics are compiled by the government and published as consumer price indexes, known as CPIs. The CPI measures the average changes in the cost of goods and services. There are two published CPIs—CPI-W and CPI-U. The CPI-W reflects the buying habits of about 80% of the population. Think of it as the consumer price index for wage earners. The CPI-U reflects the buying habits of about 50% of the population. Think of it as the consumer price index of urban consumers. Both CPIs have a reference date of 1967 and a reference base of 100. Prices are collected from many different areas for about 250 different classes of items and services. The categories are weighted for the two published CPIs to reflect the buying habits of each of the populations.

CPIs are published annually by the U.S. government. Refer to the following table to see how the CPI has varied over a number of years; the general change is upward.

Value of CPI and the Dollar

Year	CPI 1967 = 100	Value of the Dollar
1940	42.0	2.38
1945	53.9	1.86
1950	72.1	1.39
1955	80.2	1.25
1960	88.7	1.13
1965	94.5	1.06
1970	116.3	0.86
1975	161.2	0.62
1979	217.4	0.47
1980	246.8	0.41
1981	272.4	0.37
1982	289.1	0.35
1983	298.4	0.34
1984	311.1	0.32
1985	318.5	0.31
1986	321.4	0.31

Source: Department of Labor, Bureau of Labor Statistics. Effective January 1987, the consumer price index was revised, with two indexes now being produced. A new index for All Urban Consumers covers 80% of the noninstitutional population; the other index, the Consumer Price Index for Urban Wage Earners and Clerical Workers, covers about half of those included in the new index and is a major revision of the one that had been published for many years.

Some uses of CPIs are as follows.

Value of dollar. To determine the value of the dollar from the CPI, substitute the current value of the CPI into the expression

$$\frac{1}{\text{CPI}} \times 100 = \text{value of dollar}$$

Example

The CPI in 1975 is 161.2. Find the value of $1 in 1975.

$$\frac{1}{161.2} \times 100 = \$0.62$$

This means that the purchasing power of $1 in 1967 is equivalent to the purchasing power of $0.62 in 1975.

Movements of price indexes. The changes in the price indexes are expressed as percentage changes rather than point increases or decreases. A change of 25 points when the base is 100 is quite different from a change of 25 points when the base is 250. The rate of change is determined by:

$$\frac{\text{Value of CPI at latest date} - \text{value of CPI for previous period}}{\text{value of CPI for previous period}}$$

The percentage rate of change is determined by multiplying the results by 100.

Example

Find the percentage change in the CPI if the CPI for October is 272 and the CPI for November is 282.

$$\frac{(282 - 272)}{272} \times 100 = 3.68\% \text{ increase}$$

Example

A drop in oil prices caused the CPI in October to be 249, whereas it was 268 in September. Find the percentage change in the CPI.

$$\frac{(249 - 268)}{268} \times 100 = -7.09\%$$

This is usually stated as a 7.09% decrease.

Long-Term Trends in Prices

To analyze long-term patterns in prices, the compound interest formula is used, substituting values of the CPIs. The value found is sometimes referred to as the rate of inflation.

Example
The CPI value in 1967 was 100 and in 1975 the CPI value was 161.2. Find the annual compound rate of change of the CPI and the value of the dollar in 1975.

$$A = 161.2 \qquad P = 100 \qquad n = 8$$

Substitute in $A = P(1 + i)^n$.

$$161.2 = 100(1 + i)^8$$

$$1.612 = (1 + i)^8$$

Using Table 2, look under $n = 8$ and find 1.612 in column 2, Compound Amount. i is between 6% and 7%. To find the value of the dollar in 1975:

$$\frac{1}{161.22} \times 100 = 0.62$$

The calculator keystroke is

$$1.612 \; \boxed{y^x} \; 8 \; \boxed{=}\boxed{-} \; 1 \; \boxed{\times} \; 100 \; \boxed{=} \; 6.15\%$$

Could a politician use the previous information to say: If this trend continues for 10 years, the value of the dollar will be less than 0.35?
If the CPI continues to grow at the annual compound rate of 6.15%:

$$\text{The CPI in 1985} = 161.2(1 + 0.0615)^{10}$$

$$= 161.2(1.81635)$$

$$\text{CPI} = 292.80$$

$$\text{Value of dollar in 1985} = \frac{1}{292.80} \times 100 = 0.34.$$

The politician has made a correct statement. However, the CPI does not usually continue as a constant rate of change. The gross national product (GNP) is a useful measure of the performance of the economy.

The GNP is the total value at current market prices of all final goods and services produced by a nation's economy in a year or at an annual rate. The GNP figures are deflated so year-to-year changes in constant dollars can be compared. To make the GNP a more meaningful number, per capita GNP is often used. In 1950 the per capita GNP in 1972 dollars was $3,504. The 1980 per capita GNP in 1972 dollars was $6,646. The numbers show a rising standard of living from 1950 to 1980. It was necessary to convert the GNP to a common year-dollar (1972) and to prorate the GNP to the population at the given date. Numbers by themselves can be misleading.

Example

If the money supply increased from 170.3 billion to 176.8 billion in 2 years, what was the annual compounded rate of increase?

$$176.8 = 170.3(1 + i)^2$$

$$1.03817 = (1 + i)^2 \qquad \text{(take square root of each side)}$$

$$1.019 = 1 + i$$

$$0.019 = i$$

The annual compound rate of increase is 1.9%.

SECTION 5 EXERCISES

1. Determine the value of the dollar in 1980 with respect to 1967 if the CPI in 1980 is 244.7.

2. Find the value of the dollar in 1979 with respect to 1967 if the CPI in 1979 is 217.4.

3. Find the value of the dollar in 1960 with respect to 1967 if the CPI in 1960 is 88.7.

4. Find the value of the dollar in 1955 with respect to 1967 if the CPI in 1955 is 80.2.

5. The CPI in 1979 was 217.4 and in 1980 it was 244.7. Find the percentage change in the CPI.

6. The energy CPI in 1980 was 347.0 and in 1981 it was 414.9. Find the percentage change in the CPI.

7. The CPI in 1954 was 80.5 and in 1955 the CPI was 80.2. Determine the percentage change in the CPI.

8. The transportation index of the CPI in 1954 was 78.3 and in 1956 the index was 77.4. Find the percentage change in the CPI.

9. The CPI in 1970 was 116.3 and in 1976 it was 170.5. Find the annual compound rate of change of the CPI. Find the value of the dollar for each year.

10. The CPI in 1972 was 125.3 and in 1979 it was 217.4. Find the annual compound rate of change of the CPI. Find the value of the dollar for each year.

11. Referring to the information in exercise 9, would the following political statement made in 1977 be classified as true or false: If the trend in the consumer price index continues the pattern established from 1970 to 1976, the dollar will be worth less than 0.40 in 1980.

12. Referring to the information in exercise 10, would the following political statement made in 1980 be classified as true or false: If the trend in the consumer price index continues the pattern established from 1972 to 1979, the dollar will be worth less than 0.25 in 1985.

13. The GNP in 1970 is 992.7 billion dollars. The GNP in 1979 is 2,413.9 billion dollars. Convert these numbers into a meaningful comparison. The population in 1970 was 185,784,000, the population in 1979 was 219,284,000, the CPI in 1970 was 116.3, and the CPI in 1979 was 217.4.

14. The GNP in 1965 is 691.1 billion dollars. The GNP in 1975 is 1,549.2 billion dollars. Convert these numbers into a meaningful comparison. The population in 1965 was 172,450,000, the population in 1975 was 206,850,000, the CPI in 1965 was 94.5, and the CPI in 1975 was 161.2.

Answers to Odd-Numbered Exercises

1. $0.41.

3. $1.13.

5. 12.55% increase.

7. −0.4% or 0.4% decrease.

9. $i = 6.6\%$.

11. Dollar value, $0.45. The statement is false.

13.

1970 GNP person, $5.34	1979 GNP/person, $11.00
1970 dollar value, 0.86	1979 dollar value, 0.46
1970 real GNP value, $4.59	1979 real GNP value, $5.06

Summary

- **Compound amount:**

$$A = P(1 + i)^n$$

where A is compound amount
  P is present amount or principal
  i is the interest rate per period
  n is the number of periods

- **Present value:**

$$P = A(1 + i)^{-n} \quad \text{or} \quad P = \frac{A}{(1 + i)^n}$$

- **Effective rate:**

$$\text{Effective Rate} = (1 + i)^m - 1$$

where m is the number of interest periods in one year

- **Compound amount** when time does not fall at end of period.
Find A, using n for number of complete periods.
Calculate final amount using simple interest for time less than one compound period.

- **Present value** when time does not fall at end of period.
Calculate P, using n for number of complete periods.
Calculate final present value using simple interest for time less than one period.

- **Value of dollar** for any year:

$$\text{Dollar Value (in cents)} = \frac{1}{\text{CPI}} \times 100$$

where CPI is number published annually by U.S. Dept. of Labor.

REVIEW EXERCISES

Determine the compound amount and the compound interest in each of the following.

1.

Present Value ($)	Rate (%)	Compound Period	Time (Years)
8,000	8	Quarterly	12
6,500	6	Monthly	5
7,500	9	Semiannually	20
10,000	7	Annually	50

2.

5,500	7	Monthly	4
9,500	5	Semiannually	14
12,000	9	Quarterly	12
20,000	6	Annually	21

Determine the present value for each of the following.

3.

Maturity Value ($)	Rate (%)	Compound Period	Time (Years)
20,000	6	Quarterly	10
15,000	5	Semiannually	12
40,000	8	Monthly	5
18,000	7	Annually	25

4.

4,500	7	Semiannually	20
8,000	8	Monthly	4
9,000	10	Quarterly	14
12,000	9	Annually	18

5. $12,000 grew to $14,500 in 3 years, compounded quarterly. What was the approximate rate of compound interest?

6. The maturity value was double the initial investment and the time was 6 years, compounded semiannually. Find the approximate rate of compound interest.

7. How long does it take for $12,000 to grow to $16,000 if invested at 6% interest, compounded monthly?

8. How long will it take for the value of an investment to triple if invested at 8% interest, compounded semiannually?

9. $20,000 is invested at 9% interest, compounded monthly, for 8 years. Using Table 2, find the maturity amount and the amount of compound interest.

10. Grandparents put an amount of money in a savings certificate at 6% interest, compounded monthly, so their newborn granddaughter will have $100,000 at age 18. Find the amount put into the savings certificate.

11. Find the effective rate of money invested at 7% interest, compounded monthly.

12. Find the effective rate of money invested at 9% interest, compounded quarterly.

13. Tom Jackson holds a 1-year note that can be cashed at any time for its face value of $10,000 or held until maturity to earn interest at 6%, compounded monthly. Six months prior to the maturity date, the holder needs $10,000. Would it be better to cash in the note or borrow the money for 6 months at 9% interest, compounded monthly?

14. Find the value on December 5 of a $3,500 note dated June 20 and earning interest at 9%, compounded monthly.

15. Three children, ages 10, 14, and 16, have parents who are killed in a car accident. The will stipulates that the estate, valued at $300,000, should be divided equally among the children, each receiving a share upon turning 18. The fund earns 8% interest, compounded monthly, until distributed. Find the amount each child receives.

16. Suppose the conditions of the will of exercise 15 were changed to read: The funds are divided equally and put into a trust fund of $100,000 for each. The trust fund earns 8% interest, compounded monthly. How much does each child receive upon turning 18?

17. If the consumer price index in 1978 is 195.4, find the value of the dollar in 1978 in terms of the 1967 dollar.

18. The annual rate of inflation is 5% and it is expected to continue at that rate. Present college costs average $25,000. Find the average cost of college you might expect in 15 years.

Answers to Review Exercises

1.

Compound Amount	Compound Interest
$ 20,696.56	$ 12,696.56
$ 8,767.53	$ 2,267.53
$ 43,622.73	$ 36,122.73
$294,570.25	$284,570.25

2.

$ 7,271.30	$ 1,771.30
$ 18,966.70	$ 9,466.70
$ 34,915.68	$ 22,915.68
$ 67,991.27	$ 47,991.27

3.
$ 11,025.25
$ 8,293.13
$ 26,848.42
$ 3,316.49

4.
$ 1,136.58
$ 5,815.36
$ 2,257.91
$ 2,543.92

5. 6.36%.

6. 12%.

7. 5 years.

8. 14 years.

9. $40,978.42, maturity value. $20,978.42, compound interest.

10. $34,051.06.

11. 7.23%.

12. 9.3%.

13. $10,616.78, maturity value. $10,458.52, cost of borrowing. $158.26, saved by borrowing.

14. $3,646.85.

15. $142,321.74.

16. 16-year old, $117,288.79. 14-year old, $137,566.66. 10-year old, $189,245.72.

17. $0.51.

18. $51,973.20.

Chapter 3

ANNUITIES

Simple interest involved an amount of money deposited, interest was paid periodically on the deposited amount, and the invested amount remained fixed.

Compound interest involved an amount of money deposited, interest was accrued on the amount deposited, and the new amount then earned interest. This procedure was continued; the amount on deposit changed by the amount of interest accrued at the end of each interest period.

Another type of savings plan involves an account that is empty at the beginning, periodic deposits are made to the amount, and interest is accrued on the amount in the account. The account builds by the periodic deposit as well as the accrued interest. Such an account is called an **annuity.**

This chapter will involve the mathematics of annuities.

At the end of this chapter, the student will be able to:

1. Define and identify the elements of an annuity and accurately substitute the identified values into the general formula of an annuity.

2. Calculate the value of an annuity, determine the time required to attain a value given the periodic investment and rate of interest, and approximate the rate of interest required to attain a value, given the periodic investment and time involved.

3. Define and identify the terms of the present value of an annuity and accurately substitute the identified values into the general formula for the present value of an annuity.

4. Differentiate among annuity due, deferred annuity, and forborne annuity and demonstrate an understanding of these types of annuities by using the basic annuity formula to calculate unknowns in the special types of annuity.

5. Demonstrate the ability to handle annuities where the interest period and the payment periods differ.

3.1   ORDINARY ANNUITY

In all of the compound interest problems, a single deposit remained invested for the entire time. The compound interest formula predicted how this amount would grow during a period of time at a given rate of interest and a prescribed compounding period. A more common event is the periodic investment of a prescribed amount of money with a guaranteed rate of return and a known compounding period. A periodic series of payments (usually of equal amount) is called an **annuity.**

Take an example of a monthly payment of $100 to an account paying 6% interest, compounded monthly. This event occurs at the end of each month. The value of the account at the end of 1 year is desired.

Date of Deposit	Amount	Compound Amount	Value
End month 1	$100	$100 (1 + 0.005)^{11}$	$ 105.64
End month 2	100	$100 (1 + 0.005)^{10}$	105.11
End month 3	100	$100 (1 + 0.005)^{9}$	104.59
End month 4	100	$100 (1 + 0.005)^{8}$	104.04
End month 5	100	$100 (1 + 0.005)^{7}$	103.55
End month 6	100	$100 (1 + 0.005)^{6}$	103.04
End month 7	100	$100 (1 + 0.005)^{5}$	102.53
End month 8	100	$100 (1 + 0.005)^{4}$	102.02
End month 9	100	$100 (1 + 0.005)^{3}$	101.51
End month 10	100	$100 (1 + 0.005)^{2}$	101.02
End month 11	100	$100 (1 + 0.005)^{1}$	100.50
End month 12	100	$100 (1 + 0.005)^{0}$	100.00
Total			$1,233.55

If the process is generalized, the sum is

$$P(1 + i)^{11} + P(1 + i)^{10} + P(1 + i)^{9} + \cdots + P(1 + i)^{2} + P(1 + i)^{1} + P$$

P is common to each term and represents the periodic payment.

$$(1 + i)^{11} + (1 + i)^{10} + (1 + i)^{9} + \cdots + (1 + i)^{1}$$

is a geometric series whose sum is equal to $((1 + i)^{12} - 1)/i$.

The general formula used for the annuity is

$$V = R \left[\frac{((1 + i)^n - 1)}{i} \right]$$

where V is the final value of the annuity, R is the regular periodic deposit, i is the rate of interest for each period, and n is the number of periods.

The expression in the brackets is often symbolized as $s_{\overline{n}|i}$ (read as s angle n at i).

$$s_{\overline{n}|i} = \frac{((1 + i)^n - 1)}{i}$$

Using the symbols as defined:

$$V = R \cdot s_{\overline{n}|i}$$

The values for $s_{\overline{n}|i}$ are given in Table 2 under column 3, Amount of Annuity. The column entries are the values of \$1 deposited periodically at rate i.

Using a financial function calculator, $V = R \cdot s_{\overline{n}|i}$ will be the most useful form as $s_{\overline{n}|i}$ values are available. Students using the $\boxed{y^x}$ key to compute the factor need to use the $R[(1 + i)^n - 1]/i$ form. Without a calculator, Table 2, column 3, must be used with i determining the page of Table 2 and n determining the line of column 3.

Analysis of column 3 of Table 2 will reveal that each entry in column 3 is the sum of the entries in column 1 up to and including that line. Generation of the formula indicates that annuities are the sums of compound amounts for a given number of time periods.

Ordinary annuity is an annuity involving payments at the end of the period, where the frequency of the payments is the same as the compound period. The value found by using $R[(1 + i)^n - 1]/i$ is the value of the annuity on the date of the final payment.

Example

Grandparents set up an annuity for their new granddaughter just before her first birthday. The periodic payment was \$1,000 per year, and the rate of interest was 8%, compounded annually. Find the value of the annuity on her eighteenth birthday.

$$R = 1,000 \qquad i = 0.08 \qquad n = 18$$

$$V = \frac{1,000\,[(1.08)^{18} - 1)]}{0.08}$$

$$= 1,000\ (37.45024)$$

$$= \$37,450.24$$

(37.45024 is from Table 2: rate 8%, column 3, line 18.)
The calculator keystroke is

1 $\boxed{+}$ 0.08 $\boxed{=}$ $\boxed{y^x}$ 18 $\boxed{=}$ $\boxed{-}$ 1 $\boxed{=}$ $\boxed{\div}$ 0.08 $\boxed{\times}$ 1,000 $\boxed{=}$ function

The financial function calculator keystroke is

0.08 $\boxed{s}$ 18 $\boxed{=}$ $\boxed{\times}$ 1,000 $\boxed{=}$

Example
Andrew White has $170 deducted from each monthly paycheck and invested in an annuity earning 9% interest, compounded monthly. How much is the value of the annuity at the end of 5 years?

$$R = 170 \qquad i = 0.0075 \qquad n = 60$$

$$V = \frac{170\,[(1.0075)^{60} - 1]}{0.0075} \qquad \text{or} \qquad V = 170\ s_{\overline{60}|\ 3/4\%}$$

$$= \frac{170\ (0.565\ 681)}{0.0075}$$

$$= \$12,822.10$$

If the amount of interest accrued in the annuity is needed, determine how much money has been deposited by multiplying the regular payment by the number of payments. In the preceding example:

$$\text{Total payments} = 170 \times 60 = \$10,200$$

$$\text{Interest} = \text{value of annuity} - \text{total payments}$$

$$= \$12,822 - \$10,200 = \$2,622$$

Example
High Profit Dan deposits $4,500 at the end of each quarter for 5 years. Find

the final amount on deposit if the interest rate is 6%, compounded quarterly.

$$R = 4{,}500 \qquad i = 0.015 \qquad n = 20$$

$$V = \frac{4{,}500\,[(1.015)^{20} - 1]}{0.015} = 4{,}500\,s_{\overline{20}|\,0.015}$$

$$= 4{,}500\,[23.123\ 667]$$

$$= \$104{,}056.50$$

If the investment could have been made at 8% interest, compounded quarterly, by how much would the final amount at 8% exceed the amount realized at 6%?

$$R = 4{,}500 \qquad i = 0.02 \qquad n = 20$$

$$V = \frac{4{,}500\,[(1.02)^{20} - 1]}{0.02} = 4{,}500\,s_{\overline{20}|\,0.02}$$

$$= 4{,}500\,[24.297\ 369]$$

$$= \$109{,}338.17$$

The 8% annuity exceeds the 6% annuity by $5,281.67.

Just as the compound interest formula was solved for its different variables, the annuity value formula can be solved for variables other than V.

Example

The Joneses plan to retire in 10 years and want the funds available to pay off the existing mortgage on their home. The mortgage will be $36,000 in 10 years. How much should be saved at the end of each year to ensure this amount if the annuity earns 8% interest, compounded annually?

$$V = 36{,}000 \qquad i = 0.08 \qquad n = 10 \qquad R = ?$$

$$36{,}000 = \frac{R[(1.08)^{10} - 1]}{0.08}$$

$$= R\,[45.761\ 964]$$

$$\$2{,}485.06 = R$$

Note that some tables include a column $1/s_{\overline{n}|i}$. Because most of the work is done on a calculator, no column $1/s_{\overline{n}|i}$ has been included in Table 2. To perform the preceding computation on the calculator, find the value of $[(1.08)^{10} - 1]$. This value is symbolized as $[\square]$.

Method 1:

$$[\square] \; \boxed{\div} \; 0.08 \; \boxed{=} \; \boxed{1/x} \; \boxed{\times} \; 36{,}000 \; \boxed{=}$$

Method 2:

$$[\square] \; \boxed{\div} \; 0.08 \; \boxed{=} \; \boxed{STO} \; \boxed{CLEAR} \; 36{,}000 \; \boxed{\div} \; \boxed{RCL} \; \boxed{=}$$

Example

Mary Adams needs \$8,000 in 5 years, and she can only afford to put aside \$100 a month in an annuity that is compounded monthly. What rate of interest does she need to attain her goal?

$$V = 8{,}000 \qquad R = 100 \qquad n = 60 \qquad i = ?$$

$$8{,}000 = \frac{100[(1 + i)^{60} - 1]}{i}$$

$$80 = \frac{[(1 + i)^{60} - 1]}{i}$$

Refer to Table 2, line 60, and look for a value in column 3 of 80.

5/6%	$n = 60$	77.437 072
x	$n = 60$	80.
1%	$n = 60$	81.669 669

The rate per compound period must be between 5/6% and 1%; the annual rate is between 10% and 12%—closer to 12%.

For a closer approximation, set up a proportion: The difference between x and 5/6 divided by the difference between 1 and 5/6 equals the difference between 80 and 77.437 divided by the difference between 81.6697 and 77.437

$$\frac{x - 5/6}{1 - 5/6} = \frac{2.563}{4.2327}$$

Solving this proportion:

$$4.23x - 3.527 = 0.4272$$

$$4.23x = 3.9542$$

$$x = 0.9350$$

$$12x = 11.2176 \quad \text{or annual rate of } 11.2\%$$

Example

Don Flutie, a talented quarterback, wishes to accumulate 1 million dollars in an annuity, and he plans to make annual payments of $40,000. The annuity pays 8% interest, compounded annually. How long must he participate in the plan to achieve his goal of 1 million dollars?

$$V = 1,000,000 \qquad R = 40,000 \qquad i = 0.08 \qquad n = ?$$

$$1,000,000 = \frac{40,000[(1.08)^n - 1]}{0.08}$$

$$25 = \frac{[(1.08)^n - 1]}{0.08}$$

Refer to Table 2, rate 8%, column 3, down until an entry of 25.

$$n = 14 \qquad 24.214\ 920$$
$$25.$$
$$n = 15 \qquad 27.152\ 114$$

The goal of 1 million dollars will be achieved in 15 years. The value of the annuity in 15 years will be

$$40,000\ (27.152\ 114) = \$1,086,084.60$$

SECTION 1 EXERCISES

1. At the end of each month $100 is deposited in an annuity with 6% interest, compounded monthly. Determine the amount of the annuity in 4 years. Find the amount of interest earned.

2. $150 is deducted from the monthly paycheck of Adam Smith and deposited in an annuity paying 8% interest, compounded monthly. Determine

the amount of the annuity in $3^1/_2$ years. Find the amount of interest earned in the account.

3. An annual bonus of $500 is deposited in an annuity at the end of each year. The annuity pays 9% interest, compounded annually. Find the amount of the annuity after 25 years. Find the amount of interest earned in the account.

4. A Christmas bonus of $750 is deposited at the end of each year in an annuity that pays 7% interest, compounded annually. Find the amount of the annuity after 15 years. Find the amount of interest earned in the account.

5. A real estate salesperson is paid monthly, with commissions distributed quarterly. At the end of each quarter $500 is deposited in an annuity earning 8% interest, compounded quarterly. Find the amount of the annuity at the end of 10 years. How much interest has accumulated in the account?

6. An auto sales representative is paid a base salary weekly; the remainder of the commission is paid quarterly. Tom Jordan, age 45, deposits $750 of his commission in an annuity that is compounded quarterly at an interest rate of 6%. Find the amount in the annuity at the time of his sixteenth birthday.

7. Parents are concerned with the college expense for their children. Twice a year $500 is deposited in an annuity to accumulate funds needed in 18 years. The annuity earns 8% interest, compounded semiannually. Find the amount in the annuity and the amount of interest earned.

8. A trip around the world is the dream of Mr. and Mrs. Albert Travel. To achieve this dream, $250 is deposited in an annuity twice a year for 10 years. The annuity earns 10% interest, compounded semiannually. How much money will be in the account after 10 years?

9. Safe Merchandising will need new facilities for its expanding business in 5 years. The company establishes an annuity for this purpose, depositing $1,000 a month in an annuity earning 8% interest, compounded monthly. Determine the amount available for the new facilities in 5 years.

10. Ronald McDavis wishes to retire from his own business in 25 years and does not have any pension plan. He establishes an annuity, depositing $600 every 6 months. The annuity earns 9% interest, compounded semiannually. Find the value of the annuity at his retirement time.

11. Rachel Cone needs $15,000 in 8 years. What amount should she deposit quarterly in an annuity paying 8% interest to guarantee this amount?

12. John Roberts wants $75,000 to pay off his remaining mortgage in 10 years. How much should he deposit quarterly in an annuity paying 6% interest to guarantee the necessary funds?

13. How much should Alice Lane have deducted from her monthly paycheck and deposited into an annuity paying 6% interest, compounded monthly, to ensure $10,000 in 5 years?

14. Find the annual deposit one must make to ensure $100,000 in 35 years. The annuity earns 8% interest, compounded annually.

15. Find how much should be deposited quarterly to ensure $250,000 in an annuity in 15 years. The annuity pays 8% interest, compounded quarterly.

16. How long will it take to accumulate $10,000 in an annuity if quarterly payments of $250 are made and the annuity pays 8% interest, compounded quarterly?

17. How long will it take to accumulate $30,000 if $1,000 is deposited semiannually in an annuity earning 6% interest, compounded semiannually.

18. Determine the length of time for an annuity to have a value of $4,500 if $100 is deposited monthly and the annuity earns 6% interest, compounded monthly.

19. How long will it take an annuity to reach the value of $50,000 if quarterly deposits of $500 are made and the annuity earns 7% interest, compounded quarterly?

20. Find the number of years needed for an annuity to reach a value of $100,000 if $1,000 is deposited every 6 months and the annuity earns 9% interest, compounded semiannually.

21. At what rate of interest will monthly deposits of $75 have a value of $5,000 in an annuity at the end of $4^{1}/_{2}$ years?

22. At what rate of interest will yearly deposits of $1,000 have a value of $50,000 if the annuity is invested for 25 years?

23. At what rate of compounding will quarterly deposits of $1,000 have a value of $50,000 if the annuity is invested for $7^{1}/_{2}$ years, compounded quarterly?

24. During 10 very productive years, Jack Cribbs deposited $1,000 in an annuity every quarter. The annuity earned 8% interest, compounded quarterly. Business conditions worsened and Jack was unable to make any more deposits but the amount continued to be invested. What was the value of the annuity after 25 years.?

25. Sarah Lincoln was on the LPGA tour for 10 years. She deposited $2,500 annually into an annuity that earned 8% interest, compounded annually, for her retirement. After she left the tour, she did not contribute to the annuity but left the money she had invested. The annuity continued to earn interest at 8%, compounded annually. How much was in the account after 40 years?

Answers to Odd-Numbered Exercises

1. $V = \$5,409.78.$ $I = \$609.78.$

3. $V = \$42,350.45.$ $I = \$29,850.45.$

5. $V = \$30,200.99.$ $I = \$10,200.99.$

7. $V = \$38,799.16.$ $I = \$20,799.16.$

9. $73,476.86.

11. $339.16.

13. $143.33.

15. $2,191.99.

17. 11 years.

19. 59 quarters or 14.75 years.

21. Between 9% and 10%.

23. About 14%.

25. $364,433.31.

3.2   PRESENT VALUE

In the preceding section, all annuities started with an empty account, periodic payments were made, and the amount in the account at a given time was determined. Present value of an annuity is the exact opposite. The largest amount is the initial amount, periodic payments are made, and the final amount is zero. The beginning balance of the account is the **present value.**

The example in the previous section involved periodic payments of $100 at the end of each month with interest of 6%, compounded monthly. Now we are interested in determining the **present value** of these 12 periodic payments.

Present Value	Amount	Periodic Payment	Time Period
$100 (1 + 0.005)^{-1}$	$ 99.50	$100	End month 1
$100 (1 + 0.005)^{-2}$	99.01	100	End month 2
$100 (1 + 0.005)^{-3}$	98.51	100	End month 3
$100 (1 + 0.005)^{-4}$	98.02	100	End month 4
$100 (1 + 0.005)^{-5}$	97.54	100	End month 5
$100 (1 + 0.005)^{-6}$	97.05	100	End month 6
$100 (1 + 0.005)^{-7}$	96.57	100	End month 7
$100 (1 + 0.005)^{-8}$	96.09	100	End month 8
$100 (1 + 0.005)^{-9}$	95.61	100	End month 9
$100 (1 + 0.005)^{-10}$	95.13	100	End month 10
$100 (1 + 0.005)^{-11}$	94.66	100	End month 11
$100 (1 + 0.005)^{-12}$	94.19	100	End month 12
Total	$1,161.88		

To generalize this procedure, the present value of each payment is added together:

$$R(1 + i)^{-1} + R(1 + i)^{-2} + R(1 + i)^{-3} + \cdots + R(1 + i)^{-10} + R(1 + i)^{-11} + R(1 + i)^{-12}$$

Each term contains the common factor R and the geometric series

$$(1 + i)^{-1} + (1 + i)^{-2} + (1 + i)^{-3} + \cdots + (1 + i)^{-11} + (1 + i)^{-12}$$

remains. The sum of these terms is $[1 - (1 + i)^{-n}]/i$. The present value of an annuity is

$$A = \frac{R[1 - (1 + i)^{-n}]}{i} = R \cdot a_{\overline{n}\,i}$$

where A is the present value of an ordinary annuity, R is the periodic payment, i is the rate of interest per period, and n is the number of periods.

The term $a_{\overline{n}\,i}$ represents the factor $[1 - (1 + i)^{-n}]/i$ and reads a angle n at i. This value is found in Table 2, column 5, Present Value of Partial Payment.

Example

George Good wishes to establish a fund that will pay his grandson $5,000 at the end of each year of successful college for 4 years. The annuity pays 8%

interest, compounded annually. How much should be deposited to provide these payments, starting in 1 year?

$$R = 5{,}000 \qquad i = 0.08 \qquad n = 4$$

$$A = \frac{5{,}000 \left[1 - (1.08)^{-4}\right]}{0.08} \qquad \text{or} \quad a_{\overline{4}|\,0.08}$$

$$= \$16{,}560.63$$

To perform this calculation, refer to Table 2, rate 8%, column 5, line 4, entry 3.312 12684. Multiply this entry by 5,000 to obtain an answer of $16,560.63. The financial function calculator keystroke is

$$0.08 \boxed{a} \; 4 \boxed{=} \boxed{\times} \; 5{,}000 \boxed{=}$$

The calculator keystroke is

$$1 \boxed{+} 0.08 \boxed{=} \boxed{y^x} \; 4 \boxed{+/-} \boxed{=} \boxed{+/-} \boxed{+} 1 \boxed{=} 0.08 \boxed{=} \boxed{\times} \; 5{,}000 \boxed{=}$$

Example
Find the present value of 20 semiannual payments of $5,000 if the annuity pays 9% interest, compounded semiannually.

$$R = 5{,}000 \qquad i = 0.045 \qquad n = 20$$

$$A = \frac{5{,}000 \left[1 - (1.045)^{-20}\right]}{0.045} = a_{\overline{20}|\,0.045}$$

$$= 5{,}000 \left[13.007 \; 936\right]$$

$$= \$65{,}039.68$$

(13.007 936 is from Table 2, rate 4.5%, column 5, line 20.)

Just as we solved the compound interest and ordinary annuity problem for its various parts, the present value of an annuity formula can be solved for variables other than A.

Example
David Down bought a $120,000 home. He paid $40,000 down, leaving a balance of $80,000 to be financed by a mortgage. The bank gives David a 9%

mortgage rate for 30 years. What payment must David make at the end of every 6 months to pay off the mortgage?

$$A = 80{,}000 \qquad i = 0.045 \qquad n = 60$$

$$80{,}000 = \frac{R[1 - (1.045)^{-60}]}{0.045}$$

$$= R[20.638]$$

$$\$3{,}876.34 = R$$

(20.638 is from Table 2, rate 4.5%, column 5, line 60.)
   The calculator keystroke is

$$1 \boxed{+} 0.045 \boxed{=} \boxed{y^x} 60 \boxed{+/-} \boxed{=} \boxed{+/-} \boxed{+} 1 \boxed{=} \boxed{\div} 0.045 \boxed{=} \boxed{1/x}$$
$$\boxed{\times} 30{,}000 \boxed{=}$$

Example
How many quarterly payments of $1,000 can be made from an annuity presently valued at $30,000 if the annuity earns 8% interest, compounded quarterly?

$$A = 30{,}000 \qquad R = 1{,}000 \qquad i = 0.02 \qquad n = ?$$

$$30{,}000 = 1{,}000\, a_{\overline{n}|\, 0.02}$$

$$30 = a_{\overline{n}|\, 0.02}$$

Refer to Table 2, rate 2%, column 5, n between 46 and 47. The answer to the question is 46 quarters with the forty-seventh quarter some amount less than $1,000.

SECTION 2 EXERCISES

Find the present value required to receive the following annuities, the value of each annuity, and the amount of interest included.

1. a. Payments of $200 quarterly at a compound interest rate of 7% for 6 years.
   b. Payments of $1,000 monthly at a compound interest rate of 6% for 4 years.
   c. Payments of $4,500 semiannually at a compound interest rate of 9% for 10 years.

    d. Payments of $8,000 annually at a compound interest rate of 7% for 25 years.

2. a. Payments of $250 monthly at a compound interest rate of 8% for 5 years.
b. Payments of $5,000 semiannually at a compound interest rate of 7% for 15 years.
c. Payments of $10,000 annually at a compound interest rate of 6% for 25 years.
d. Payments of $3,000 quarterly at a compound interest rate of 8% for 12 years.

3. A widow wishes to use her insurance settlement to purchase an annuity that will pay $4,000 a quarter for the next 12 years. The annuity pays 10% interest. Find the cost of the annuity.

4. A trust fund is established to provide periodic payments to a handicapped individual. The semiannual payments are for $10,000, the trust fund is for 15 years, and the compound interest rate is 9%. Find the amount needed to set up the trust fund.

5. A business deal on some real estate was $12,000 down and $1,000 a month for the next 5 years. What is the equivalent cash price if money earns 8% interest, compounded monthly?

6. The purchase agreement for the Joneses' house was $25,000 down and $2,000 a quarter for the next 10 years. If money is worth 12% interest, compounded quarterly, find the cash value of the real estate.

7. John Harrison is 55 years old and wants to retire at age 62. He wants an annuity that pays him $1,500 a quarter for 10 years after his retirement. The interest rate is 6%, compounded quarterly.
a. How much will the annuity cost him at age 62?
b. How much would the annuity cost if he purchased it today in anticipation of his retirement?

8. Ellen Perkins is 50 years old and wishes to retire at age 60. She wants an annuity that pays $2,500 semiannually for 15 years after her retirement. The compound interest rate is 9%.
a. Find the cost of the annuity at age 60.
b. Find the cost of the annuity at age 50.

9. A company writes a contract guaranteeing salary payments to an employee for the amount of $2,500 a month for the next 5 years. The current interest rate is 6%, compounded monthly. A competitor offers the same contract for $125,000. Which is the lower cost to the company?

10. A company writes a contract guaranteeing salary payments of $3,000 a month for the next 3 years. The current interest rate is 8%, compounded monthly. A competitor offers a lump sum contract of $100,000 for services for the next 3 years. Which is the more lucrative offer?

11. A family wishes to have scholarships of $4,000 awarded each year for the next 10 years in memory of the deceased patriarch of the family. Money earns 8% interest, compounded annually. How much money is required to establish the scholarships?

12. A woman wishes to establish a science scholarship for $4,000 to be awarded annually for the next 5 years. Money earns 7% interest, compounded annually. How much money is required to establish the scholarship?

13. The purchase price of an auto is advertised as $2,000 down and $150 a month for the next 3 years. Money earns 12% interest, compounded monthly. Find the equivalent cash price of the car.

14. An advertisement prices a refrigerator as $75 down and $40 a month for the next 24 months. What is the equivalent cash price if money earns 18% interest, compounded monthly?

Answers to Odd-Numbered Exercises

1. (a) $3,892.14, $5,902.20, $1,102.20
   (b) $42,580.32, $54,097.83, $6,097.83
   (c) $58,535.71, $141,171.40, $51,171.40
   (d) $93,228.67, $505,992.30, $305,992.30.

3. $111,092.61.

5. $61,318.43.

7. (a) $44,873.77. (b) $29,576.27.

9. $125,000 versus $129,313.90. $125,000 is the better offer.

11. $26,840.33.

13. $6,516.13.

3.3 VARIATIONS IN ANNUITIES

In Sections 1 and 2, the formulas and development were for ordinary annuities where payment was made at the end of each period, and the final payment was made on the same date as the calculated final amount. This section addresses three other types of annuities, defined as follows.

Annuity due is an annuity where the payments are made at the **beginning** of each interval, and the initial payment is due immediately. Insurance premiums and property rentals fall into this category.

Deferred annuity is an annuity where the first payment is not made at the beginning or end of the first interval, but at some later date. Trust funds and retirement annuities are sometimes deferred annuities.

Forborne annuity is an annuity that earns interest two or more periods after the final payment.

The computations involved for each of these three modifications of the ordinary annuity will be explained in the following discussion.

Annuity Due

If the annuity due is lined up with the ordinary annuity, justification can be made for the formulas used for determining the final amount and present value for an annuity due. A is present value, V is maturity value, and R_1, R_2, $R_3, \ldots, R_n$ are periodic payments.

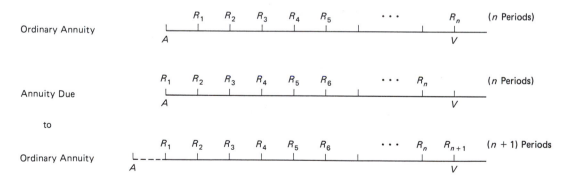

If an additional interval is added to the annuity due (dotted line), the number of intervals and payments are $n + 1$. Calculate the final amount of an ordinary annuity using the value of $n + 1$ for the number of payments.

$$V = \frac{R[(1 + i)^{n+1} - 1]}{i} \quad \text{or} \quad R \cdot s_{\overline{n+1}|\,i}$$

This amount exceeds the actual amount of the annuity by one payment so R must be subtracted from the calculated value.

The formula for determining the value of an annuity due is

$$V = R \cdot s_{\overline{n+1}|\,i} - R$$

or if R is factored out:

$$V = R[s_{\overline{n+1}|\,i} - 1]$$

Present Value of Annuity Due

Comparing the present value of the annuity due with the present value of an ordinary annuity, there will be one less payment than with the ordinary annuity. a_n is replaced by a_{n-1}.

$$A = R[a_{\overline{n-1}|\,i} + 1]$$

Example
The yearly premium of a 20-payment life insurance policy is $240, payable at the beginning of each year. Find the value of the insurance at the end of 20 years if the interest rate is 8%, compounded annually.

```
240   240   240   240    · · ·    240   240   240   V
 └─────┴─────┴─────┴───────────────┴─────┴─────┴─────┘
```

This is an **annuity due** because the payment is at the beginning of the period

$$R = 240 \qquad i = 0.08 \qquad n = 20 \qquad V = ?$$

$$V = R[s_{\overline{21}|\,0.08} - 1] \quad \text{where } n + 1 = 21$$

From Table 2, rate 8%, column 3, line 21, we obtain 50.4229. Substituting this into the equation:

$$V = 240[50.4229 - 1] = 240[49.4229]$$

$$= \$11,861.50$$

Example
Find the present value of the previous insurance policy.

```
240   240   240   240    · · ·    240   240   240
 └─────┴─────┴─────┴───────────────┴─────┴─────┘
 A
```

This is an **annuity due** and the problem is to find the present value of 20 years of premiums paid on the insurance policy.

$$R = 240 \qquad i = 0.08 \qquad n = 20 \qquad A = \,?$$

$$A = R[a_{\overline{19}|\,0.08} + 1]$$

$$n - 1 = 19$$

The value from Table 2, rate 8%, column 5, line 19, is 9.6036.

$$A = 240[9.6036 + 1] = 240[10.60336]$$

$$= \$2{,}544.86$$

Deferred Annuity

The following diagram shows a deferred annuity of n payments deferred for m payments.

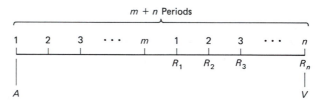

Annuity is deferred m periods; payments are for n periods.

The present value is determined as if the annuity has $m + n$ payments. Then the present value of the m payment is subtracted from the amount because no payments were made for m periods.

$$A = R \cdot a_{\overline{m+n}|\,i} - R \cdot a_{\overline{m}|\,i}$$

Factor out R.

$$A = R[a_{\overline{m+n}|\,i} - a_{\overline{m}|\,i}]$$

Determining the final value does not make any sense in a deferred annuity, because the annuity would not go into effect until the payments began.

Example
Find the present value of a deferred annuity of $1,000 every 6 months for 10 years that is deferred 5 years. Money is worth 8% interest.

$$R = 1,000 \qquad n = 20 \qquad m = 10 \qquad i = 0.04$$

$$A = 1,000[a_{\overline{30}|\,0.04} - a_{\overline{10}|\,0.04}] = 1,000[17.292 - 8.111]$$

$$= 1,000[9.181]$$

$$= \$9,181$$

The time line for this problem is

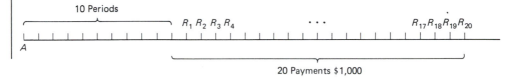

10 Periods

$R_1\,R_2\,R_3\,R_4$ $\cdots$ $R_{17}R_{18}R_{19}R_{20}$

A

20 Payments $1,000

Example

If the preceding example had stated $1,000 paid immediately after the 5-year deferment, consider the deferment $4\tfrac{1}{2}$ years. Use $m = 9$.

$$R = 1,000 \qquad n = 20 \qquad m = 9 \qquad i = 0.04$$

$$A = 1,000[a_{\overline{29}|\,0.04} - a_{\overline{9}|\,0.04}] = 1,000[16.984 - 8.111]$$

$$= 1,000[8.873]$$

$$= \$8,873$$

Forborne Annuity

The following diagram shows an annuity of n payments followed by p periods of no payments. Interest is earned during this period.

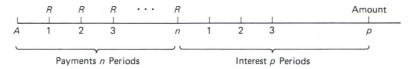

R R R $\cdots$ R Amount

A 1   2   3 n 1   2   3 p

Payments n Periods   Interest p Periods

The calculations consider an ordinary annuity for $n + p$ periods. Subtract off the value of the annuity when no payments were made. The earlier payments are still earning interest.

$$V = R \cdot s_{\overline{m+p}|\,i} - R \cdot s_{\overline{p}|\,i}$$

Factor out the regular payment, R.

$$V = R[s_{\overline{n+p}|\,i} - s_{\overline{p}|\,i}]$$

Example

Payments of \$500 are made semiannually for 20 years to an account paying 6% interest, compounded semiannually. Find the value of the account 4 years after the final payment.

$$R = 500 \qquad n = 40 \qquad i = 0.03 \qquad p = 8$$

$$V = R[s_{\overline{48}|\,0.03} - s_{\overline{8}|\,0.03}] = 500[104.4084 - 8.8923]$$

$$= 500[95.5161]$$

$$= \$47,758.05$$

How much interest did the account earn by leaving the money there 4 years after the final payment?

$$V = 500[s_{\overline{40}|\,0.03}] = 500[75.4013]$$

$$= \$37,700.65$$

the value of \$500 payments for 20 years. The difference between the two amounts is the amount of interest earned.

$$\$47,758.05 - \$37,700.65 = \$10,057.40$$

The interest could also be calculated by taking the value of the annuity after 20 years and applying compound interest semiannually for 4 years.

$$\text{Interest} = (37,700.65)[(1.03)^8 - 1]$$

$$= \$10,057.40$$

Summary

Note that in a and s notation, i is frequently omitted. In the summary, the interest rate i will be omitted in the notation.

   Ordinary annuity. Payments are made at the end of the interval, and the account is empty at the beginning.

$$\text{Final value} = \frac{R[(1 + i)^n - 1]}{i} = R \cdot s_{\overline{n}|}$$

$$\text{Present value} = \frac{R[1 - (1 + i)^{-n}]}{i} = R \cdot a_{\overline{n}|}$$

Annuity due. Payments are made at the beginning of the interval, and the account has R value at the beginning.

$$\text{Final value} = R\,[s_{\overline{n+1}|} + 1]$$
$$\text{Present value} = R\,[a_{\overline{n-1}|} + 1]$$

Deferred annuity. Payments are deferred for m intervals, and the account is empty until $m + 1$ intervals.

$$\text{Present value} = R\,[a_{\overline{m+n}|} - a_{\overline{m}|}]$$

Forborne annuity. Interest on the final value is earned p intervals after the final payment.

$$V = R\,[s_{\overline{n+p}|} - s_{\overline{p}|}]$$

SECTION 3 EXERCISES

In exercises 1 through 6, find the value of each of the annuities.

1. Ordinary annuity of $450 every 3 months at 6% interest, compounded quarterly, for 10 years.

2. Annuity due of $450 every 3 months at 6% interest, compounded quarterly, for 10 years.

3. Ordinary annuity of $1,000 every 6 months for 15 years at 8% interest, compounded semiannually. The account remains after the final payment for 4 years.

4. Ordinary annuity of $200 every month at 9% interest, compounded monthly, for 5 years.

5. Annuity due of $1,000 every 6 months at 10% interest, compounded semiannually, for 20 years.

6. Ordinary annuity of $300 every quarter at 8% interest, compounded quarterly, for 12 years. The account remains after the final payment for 3 more years to earn interest.

In exercises 7 through 12, find the present value of the annuities.

7. Annual payments of $5,000 at 5% interest, compounded annually, are made to an ordinary annuity for 20 years.

8. Quarterly payments of $250 at 6% interest, compounded quarterly, are made to an annuity due for 10 years.

9. A deferred annuity has quarterly payments of $500 for 10 years at an interest rate of 8%. The payments are deferred for 5 years, and the payments are made at the beginning of each period.

10. Semiannual payments of $625 are made to an ordinary annuity that earns 6% interest, compounded semiannually. Payments are made for 20 years.

11. Semiannual payments of $600 are made to an annuity due that earns 6% interest, compounded semiannually. Payments are made for 15 years.

12. Quarterly payments of $1,000 are deferred for 5 years. The payments are made at the end of each quarter for 10 years, and the interest rate is 8%, compounded quarterly.

13. Marsh Corporation bought 100 acres of land for $20,000 down, and $2,000 at the beginning of each month for the next 5 years. Current interest rates are 8%, compounded monthly. Find the cash value of the land.

14. George Green bought an apartment complex for $100,000 down and $10,000 a month for the next 4 years. Interest rates are 8%, compounded monthly. Find the cash value of the apartment complex.

15. Red Stone had an ordinary annuity of $5,000 a year for 20 years at 7% interest, compounded annually. His retirement is postponed for 5 years so the annuity is left intact to earn interest. Find the value of the annuity after the 5 years.

16. Evelyn Carter buys an annuity for her retirement in 3 years. Ms. Carter will receive semi-annual payments of $5,000 for 10 years, the first payment 6 months after her retirement. Find the cost of this annuity if the rate of interest is 8%.

17. Payments of $400 are made at the beginning of each quarter for 10 years. The annuity earns 8% interest, compounded quarterly. Find the present value of the annuity.

18. A 20-year endowment insurance policy had annual payments of $375. The annuity has 5% interest, compounded yearly. The money was left with the insurance company for another 10 years to earn interest. What is the value of the annuity at the end of the 10 years?

19. Sue Smith defers payments from her 10-year annuity for 2 years. She is to receive $1,000 at the end of every quarter. The annuity earns 6% interest, compounded quarterly. Find the present value.

20. Find the final value of an annuity due. Payments are $10,000 a year for 20 years at an interest rate of 7%, compounded yearly.

Answers to Odd-Numbered Exercises

1. $24,420.55.

3. $76,756.11.

5. $126,839.76.

7. $62,311.05.

9. $9,388.82.

11. $12,113.07.

13. $119,294.45.

15. $287,491.49.

17. $11,161.04.

19. $26,556.63.

3.4   PERIODIC PAYMENT

All annuities studied thus far have had the compound period and the payment period matched. This does not always happen, and it is necessary to find out how to handle yearly payments that have interest compounded quarterly, or quarterly payments in an annuity that is compounded semiannually.

One way to handle the problem is conversion of the interest rate into an equivalent rate for the payment period. The second method is the conversion of the original payments into equivalent payments that coincide with the interest period. The second method is usually the easier approach and will be the method we will use.

Payments Less Frequent than Interest Period

Consider a problem where payments of $1,000 are made at the end of each year, and the interest is computed at 8%, compounded quarterly. The $1,000 is one payment. We wish to divide this into four payments which are equivalent to $1,000 at the end of the year.

$$V = 1{,}000 \qquad i = 0.02 \qquad n = 4 \qquad R = \, ?$$

The amount of the annuity at the end of the year is $1,000. We need to find the equivalent periodic quarterly payment.

$$1,000 = R[s_{\overline{4}|\,0.02}] = R[4.121\ 608]$$

4.121 608 can be found from Table 2, rate 2%, column 3, line 4, or from $1,000/[(1.02)^4 - 1]/0.02$

$$R = \frac{1,000}{4.121\ 608}$$

$$= \$242.62$$

An equivalent amount to the $1,000 annual payment is four $242.62 payments made at the end of each quarter. The interest rate is 8%, compounded quarterly.

The general procedure is as follows.

1. Use the value of an ordinary annuity formula, $V = R \cdot s_{\overline{n}|\,i}$.
2. V is the payment whose period is larger than the interest period.
3. i is the interest rate/interest period.
4. n is the number of interest periods in a payment period.
5. Solve for R.

Example
Find the amount of an ordinary annuity of semiannual payments of $500 for 10 years if the annuity earns 8% interest, compounded quarterly.

To find the quarterly payment:

$$V = 500 \qquad i = 0.02 \qquad n = 2$$

$$500 = R \cdot s_{\overline{2}|\,0.02} = 2.02R$$

$$R = \$247.52$$

To find the amount of the annuity:

$$R = 247.52 \qquad i = 0.02 \qquad n = 40$$

$$V = 247.50 \cdot s_{\overline{40}|\,0.02}$$

$$= 247.52[60.401\ 983]$$

$$= \$14,950.70$$

Example
Find the present value of 10 semiannual payments of $1,000 if the interest rate is 6%, compounded monthly. The payment period is larger than the interest period.

$$V = 1,000 \qquad i = 0.005 \qquad n = 6$$

$$1,000 = R[s_{\overline{6}|\,0.005}] = R[6.075\ 502]$$

$$R = \$164.60$$

Therefore $1,000 every 6 months is equivalent to $164.60 monthly.

$$R = 164.60 \qquad i = 0.005 \qquad n = 60$$

$$V = 164.60[s_{\overline{60}|\,0.005}] = 164.60[51.72556]$$

$$= \$8,513.79$$

Payments More Frequent than Interest Period

When the payment period was longer than the interest period, the equivalent payment per interest period was found. When the payment period is shorter than the interest period, the amount of the payment is calculated for the interest period.

The periods for interest and payment **must match.** The interest period determines the period of the annuity, and the equivalent payment must be found for that period.

Suppose $170 is deducted from a monthly paycheck for an annuity that earns 8% interest, compounded semiannually. Find the value of the annuity after 12 years. The monthly deduction of $170 must be converted to an amount per 6 months. Banks and many commercial institutions pay simple interest on amounts earning interest for less than one interest period. A diagram will help determine the simple interest.

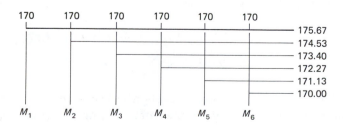

Deposit	t	r	P	$A = P(1 + rt)$
M_1	5/12	0.08	$170	$ \ \ 175.67
M_2	4/12	0.08	170	174.53
M_3	3/12	0.08	170	173.40
M_4	2/12	0.08	170	172.27
M_5	1/12	0.08	170	171.13
M_6	0/12			170.00
Total				$1,037.00

To find the value of the annuity:

$$R = 1,037.00 \qquad i = 0.04 \qquad n = 24$$

$$V = 1,037 s_{\overline{24}|\,0.04} = 1,037.03[39.0826]$$

$$= \$40,528.66$$

Compound interest for a part of a period is sometimes used in annuity problems. If the previous example of $170 a month for 12 years is an ordinary annuity earning 8% interest, compounded semiannually, the payments earn compound interest. Instead of finding simple interest, the compound amount for each payment is calculated.

The compound interest formula is

$$A = P(1 + i)^n$$

Deposit	i	n	Amount	$A = P(1 + i)^n$
M_1	0.04	5/6	$170 (1 + 0.04)^{5/6}$	$ \ \ 175.65
M_2	0.04	4/6	$170 (1 + 0.04)^{4/6}$	174.50
M_3	0.04	3/6	$170 (1 + 0.04)^{3/6}$	173.37
M_4	0.04	2/6	$170 (1 + 0.04)^{2/6}$	172.24
M_5	0.04	1/6	$170 (1 + 0.04)^{1/6}$	171.11
M_6	0.04	0/6	$170 (1.04)^{0/6}$	170.00
Total				$1,036.87

The value of the annuity is

$$V = 1,036.87 \, s_{\overline{24}|\,0.04} = 1,036.92[39.0826]$$

$$= \$40,523.58$$

The value of the annuity is slightly less when the payments earn compound interest instead of simple interest. For any time period less than the interest period, compound interest is slightly less than its corresponding simple interest. This is contrary to the popular belief that compound interest is always greater than simple interest. The key is the time interval. If the time interval of the interest is less than the compounding period, compound interest is less than simple interest for the equivalent period. If the time interval of the interest is greater than the compounding period, compound interest is more than simple interest for the equivalent period.

Each transaction where the interest period is longer than the payment period should indicate the type of interest used. For the purpose of the exercises in this book, simple interest will be used by the banks, and annuities will use compound interest.

Example
A bank pays 8% interest, compounded quarterly, on an account started by W. L. Cole & Sons. The company deposits $250 at the end of each month into the account. Find the value of the account in 5 years.

Step 1: Determine the amount $250 a month at 8% simple interest becomes in 3 months.

Deposit	r	t	P	A
M_1	0.08	2/12	$250	$253.38
M_2	0.08	1/12	250	251.67
M_3	0.08	0/12	250	250.00
Total				$755.05

Step 2: Use the generated quarterly payment in the ordinary annuity value formula.

$$R = 755.05 \qquad i = 0.02 \qquad n = 20$$

$$V = 755.05 \cdot s_{\overline{20}|\,0.02} = 755.05(24.29737)$$

$$= \$18{,}345.73$$

Example
Carol Capers has an annuity for retirement and has $150 a month deducted from her pay and deposited in an annuity fund that earns interest at the rate of 6%, compounded quarterly. Find the value of the annuity at the end of 10 years.

Step 1: Convert $150 a month to a quarterly payment. The payment earns compound interest because it is an annuity.

Deposit	i	n	P	A
M_1	0.015	2/3	$150	$151.50
M_2	0.015	1/3	150	150.75
M_3	0.015	0/3	150	150.00
Total				$452.25

Step 2: Determine the value of the annuity of payments of $452.25.

$$i = 0.015 \qquad n = 40$$

$$V = 452.25 \cdot s_{\overline{40}|\,0.015} = 425.25(54.26789)$$

$$= \$24{,}542.65$$

SECTION 4 EXERCISES

In exercises 1 through 6, determine the amount of payment over the indicated interest period.

1. Annual payments of $5,000, quarterly interest period, 8% annual rate.

2. Semiannual payments of $1,000, monthly interest period, 6% annual rate.

3. Quarterly payments of $500, monthly interest period, 8% annual rate.

4. Annual payments of $7,500, semiannual interest period, 10% annual rate.

5. Semiannual payments of $6,000, quarterly interest period, annual rate of 8%.

6. Quarterly payments of $450, monthly interest period, 9% annual rate.

In exercises 7 through 9, determine the amount of payment over the indicated interest period, using simple interest.

7. Quarterly payments of $450, annual interest period, annual rate of 8%.

8. Monthly payments of $100, semiannual interest period, annual rate of 6%.

9. Monthly payments of $150, quarterly interest period, annual rate of 6%.

In exercises 10 through 12, determine the amount of payment over the indicated interest period, using compound interest.

10. Quarterly payments of $600, annual interest period, annual rate of 7%.

11. Monthly payments of $125, semiannual interest period, annual rate of 6%.

12. Monthly payments of $1,000, quarterly interest period, annual rate of 9%.

13. Find the value in 10 years of an annuity paying 4% interest, compounded quarterly, if payments of $5,000 are made annually.

14. Find the value of an annuity paying 8% interest, compounded semiannually, if payments of $4,000 are made annually.

15. Find the present value of a 10-year annuity that makes semiannual payments of $10,000. The interest rate is 8%, compounded quarterly.

16. Find the present value of a 15-year annuity that makes quarterly payments of $3,000. The interest rate is 12%, compounded monthly.

17. Find the value in 3 years of a bank account where $5,000 is deposited monthly. The bank pays 8% interest, compounded quarterly.

18. Find the value of an account with First National Bank where $10,000 is deposited quarterly. The bank pays 10% interest, compounded semiannually.

19. An annuity is established where the monthly payment of $200 earns interest at a rate of 8%, compounded quarterly. Find the value of the annuity after 10 years.

20. A monthly annuity has payments of $120, and the annuity pays 9% interest, compounded quarterly. Find the value of the annuity in 12 years.

Answers to Odd-Numbered Exercises

1. Quarterly payment, $1,213.12.

3. Monthly payment, $165.54.

5. Quarterly payment, $2,970.30.

7. Annual payment, $1,854.

9. Quarterly payment, $452.25.

11. Semiannual payment, $759.44.

13. Quarterly payment, $1,231.40. $V = \$60,199.17$.

15. Quarterly payment, $4,950.50. $A = \$135,423.30$.

17. $A = \$202,522.55.$

19. Quarterly payment, $\$603.98.$ $V = \$36,481.59.$

Summary

- **Value of an ordinary annuity:**

$$V = \frac{R[(1 + i)^n - 1]}{i} = R \cdot s_{\overline{n}|\,i}$$

- **Present value of an ordinary annuity:**

$$A = \frac{R[1 - (1 + i)^{-n}]}{i} = R \cdot a_{\overline{n}|\,i}$$

- **Annuity due** (payments are made at the beginning of each period):

$$V = R[s_{\overline{n+1}|\,i} - 1]$$
$$A = R[a_{\overline{n-1}|\,i} + 1]$$

- **Deferred annuity** (first payment is made after m periods):

$$A = R[a_{\overline{n+m}|\,i} - a_{\overline{m}|\,i}]$$

- **Forborne annuity** (interest is earned for p periods after the final payment):

$$V = R[s_{\overline{n+p}|\,i} - s_{\overline{p}|\,i}]$$

REVIEW EXERCISES

Find the final values of each of the following deposits.

1. $1,000 at the end of every 3 months at 6% interest, compounded quarterly, for 8 years.

2. $500 at the end of every 6 months at 7% interest, compounded semiannually, for 15 years.

3. $350 at the end of each month at 6% interest, compounded monthly, for 5 years.

4. $1,000 at the beginning of every month at 6% interest, compounded monthly, for 4 years.

5. $5,000 at the beginning of each year at 8% interest, compounded annually, for 20 years.

6. $400 at the beginning of each quarter at 8% interest, compounded quarterly, for 10 years.

7. $1,000 at the end of every 6 months at 6% interest, compounded quarterly, for 5 years.

8. $500 at the end of every month at 9% interest, compounded quarterly, for 10 years, using simple interest.

9. $1,000 at the end of each month at 6% interest, compounded semiannually, for 15 years, using simple interest.

10. $4,000 at the end of each year at 6% interest, compounded quarterly, for 10 years.

11. $300 is deposited quarterly for 10 years at 10% interest, compounded quarterly. After the last payment, the money is left in the annuity for another 4 years. Find the value of the annuity at that time.

12. A retirement annuity required semiannual payments of $2,000 for 20 years. The annuity paid 10% interest, compounded semiannually. After the final payment, the money was left in the account for another 5 years. Find the value of the annuity.

In exercises 13 through 20, find the present value of each of the following annuities.

13. $1,500 annual payments at 6% interest, compounded annually, for 18 years, using ordinary annuity.

14. $2,000 semiannual payments at 10% interest, compounded every 6 months, for 25 years, using ordinary annuity.

15. $400 quarterly payments at 8% interest, compounded every quarter, for 10 years, using annuity due.

16. $5,000 semiannual payments at 9% interest, compounded semiannually, for 23 years, using annuity due.

17. $4,000 a quarter at 8% interest, compounded quarterly, for 10 years. The payment is deferred for 3 years.

18. $10,000 a year at 7% interest, compounded annually, for 30 years. The payment is deferred for 8 years.

19. $4,500 every 6 months at 6% interest, compounded quarterly, for 10 years.

20. $600 every month at 8% interest, compounded quarterly, for 12 years, using simple interest.

21. J. H. Rowe, Inc., borrows $200,000 from a bank to expand the business. The agreement is to repay the loan in equal payments at the end of each quarter for the next 5 years. Interest is earned at 8%, compounded quarterly. Find the amount of each payment.

22. Susan James borrows $15,000 from a bank to buy an automobile. The agreement calls for 36 equal monthly payments due at the end of each month. Interest is at 6%, compounded monthly. Find the amount of each payment.

23. Royalty checks for a publication amount to $5,000 at the end of every 6 months. The checks are deposited into an annuity that has an interest rate of 8%, compounded quarterly. Find the amount in the annuity in 10 years.

24. Find the present value of an annuity set up to give monthly payments of $400 for 10 years. The annuity earns 6% interest, compounded quarterly, and the payments are deferred for 4 years.

25. How long will it take an ordinary annuity of $5,000 annual payment paying 9% interest, compounded annually, to reach the value of $250,000?

Answers to Review Exercises

1. $40,688.29.

2. $25,811.34.

3. $24,419.51.

4. $54,368.32.

5. $247,114.61.

6. $24,644.01.

7. $11,475.81.

8. Quarterly payment, $1,511.25. $V = \$96,396.86$.

9. $R = \$6,075$. $V = \$289,020.65$.

10. $R = \$977.78$ quarterly. $V = \$53,062.06$.

11. $30,017.84.

12. $393,540.21.

13. $16,241.41.

14. $36,511.85.

15. $11,161.04.

16. $100,781.74.

17. $86,278.43.

18. $72,221.75.

19. $R = \$2,233.25$ quarterly. $A = \$66,809.60$.

20. $R = \$1,812$. $A = \$55,579.69$.

21. $12,231.34.

22. $456.33.

23. $R = \$2,475.25$. $V = \$149,510$.

24. $9,429.85.

25. 20 years.

Chapter 4

AMORTIZATION AND SINKING FUNDS

One of the uses of annuities is the repayment of loans. An amortized loan is a debt repaid by a series of periodic payments, usually equal in size. Each payment includes the interest due on the loan for the period plus some amount in excess of the interest due. This amount reduces the principal on each payment date. In an amortized loan, the amount of the loan decreases each period, the amount of interest due decreases, and the amount remaining that reduces the loan increases. Long-term loans are usually amortized.

If a major business expense such as building a new plant is anticipated, the company can establish a sinking fund to cover the anticipated expense. A sinking fund is an annuity with a specific purpose. The establishment of a sinking fund can be a tax advantage to the industry and saves great indebtedness when capital improvements are anticipated.

Another way of raising large amounts of money for an extended period of time is issuing bonds. The company is then obligated to the payment of interest to the holders of the bonds and the accumulation of funds to repay the bonds at maturity.

Comparisons are made between the cost of an amortized loan, a simple interest demand loan, and the establishment of a sinking fund. Changing interest rates influence decisions among the three options.

At the end of this chapter, the student will be able to:

1. Define the vocabulary associated with amortization, sinking funds, outstanding principal, and bonds.

2. Calculate the regular payment of an amortized loan.

3. Determine the outstanding principal of an amortized loan at any time in the term of the loan.

4. Calculate the payment required to establish a sinking fund.

5. Calculate the value of a bond, determine the yield rate, and calculate either the premium or discount due on a bond.

6. Make the necessary calculations for cost comparisons among the various types of loans.

7. Develop an understanding of how debts are amortized, how costs are affected by the factors of amortization, and how a wise selection of a lender and an amortization plan can be financially beneficial.

4.1   FINDING PAYMENT OF AMORTIZED DEBT

The word "amortized" means the repayment of a debt by equal payments at regular intervals. Most debts incurred by individuals are amortized. Examples of these are car loans, house mortgages, and installment buying. In each case, equal payments occur at regular intervals, usually monthly. The consumer is concerned with the amount of the payment and the number of payments.

Interest is accumulated in different ways in an amortized loan. The three principal ways of generating the interest are addressed.

Interest as an Add-On

When an item is purchased or money is borrowed, interest is determined for the amount borrowed for the entire length of the loan. The calculated interest is added to the principal, and that total is divided by the number of payments to determine the amount of each payment.

$$R = \frac{(P + I)}{n}$$

where R is the amount of payment, P is the principal (in dollars), I is the amount of interest on P dollars for time t, and n is the number of equal payments.

Example
$500 was borrowed for 2 years at 12% interest. The loan is to be repaid in equal quarterly payments. Find the amount of each payment.

$$P = 500 \qquad I = Prt = (500)(0.12)(2) = 120 \qquad t = 2 \qquad n = 8$$

$$R = \frac{(500 + 120)}{8} = \$77.50$$

The major advantage of this type of amortization is ease in computation. Disadvantages include the high cost. The consumer is paying as if the money is available to use for 2 years. The consumer pays back at regular intervals throughout the 2 years.

To emphasize the high cost of **add-on interest**, a formula for determining the effective rate of such an amortized loan is introduced.

$$\text{Effective rate} = \frac{(2)(K)(I)}{(P)(n + 1)}$$

where K is the number of payments per year, I is the amount of interest for the loan, P is the principal or amount borrowed, and n is the number of payments during the loan.

In the preceding example, to find the effective rate of interest the following values are substituted.

$$K = 4 \qquad I = 120 \qquad P = 500 \qquad n = 8$$

$$\text{Effective rate} = \frac{(2)(4)(120)}{(500)(9)}$$

$$= 0.213 = 21.3\%$$

The effective rate of 21.3% gives a different slant to the 12% rate advertised.

Interest per Payment

There are two ways of paying the interest and principal on an amortized loan. One method divides the interest evenly over the loan period. Each payment has the same amount for interest and the same amount credited against the principal. The second method has a larger part of the initial payments earmarked for interest than later payments. When the loan is half paid off, over 70% of the interest has been paid.

Example
Mac borrows $800, the balance due on a refrigerator after the down pay-

ment. The interest rate is 12%, and the loan is to be paid in 12 equal monthly payments.

$$P = 800 \qquad I = (800)(0.12)(1) = 96 \qquad n = 12$$

$$R = \frac{(800 + 96)}{12} = \$74.67$$

Rounding consistently can be a problem in loan payment calculations. Commercial practice is to round up any part of a cent. This ensures complete amortization in the specified time. The final payment is lowered to make the total repayment add up to the original loan.

In the preceding example, 11 equal payments of $74.67 and a final payment of 74.63 gives a total repayment of $896.

Level method. The interest and principal are divided equally among the payments. In the preceding example:

Payment Number	Fraction	Amount of Interest/Payment	Amount of Principal
1	1/12	$ 8.00	$ 66.67
2	1/12	8.00	66.67
3	1/12	8.00	66.67
⋮	⋮	⋮	⋮
12	1/12	8.00	66.63
Total	12/12	$96.00	$800.00

Rule of 78 method. The method gets its name from the fact that a loan of 12 payments uses a denominator of 78 (the sum of 1 through 12) to distribute the interest. If there were 18 payments, the denominator would be 171 (1 + 2 + 3 + 4 + ⋯ + 16 + 17 + 18); 24 payments would have a denominator of 300.

The numerator of the fraction is the payment number in reverse order. In a 12-payment loan, payment 1 has a numerator of 12, and payment 2 has a numerator of 11. Continuing this pattern, payment 12 has a numerator of 1. Each of the denominators is 78. The fraction formed is the part of the total interest charged in that particular payment.

To find the part of the interest charges applied to month 1, (12/78)(96) == $14.77. The balance of the payment of $66.67 is applied to the principal. To find this amount, subtract the interest charges from the total payment: $66.67 − $14.77 = $51.90. The $51.90 is applied to the debt of $800, leaving a balance of $748.10 after payment 1.

Payment 3 would have 10/78 of the $96 applied to the interest; the balance of the payment is applied to the principal.

Payment Number	Fraction	Amount of Interest	Amount of Principal/Payment
1	12/78	$14.77	$ 59.90
2	11/78	13.54	61.13
3	10/78	12.31	62.36
4	9/78	11.08	63.59
5	8/78	9.85	64.82
6	7/78	8.62	66.05
7	6/78	7.38	67.29
8	5/78	6.15	68.52
9	4/78	4.92	69.75
10	3/78	3.69	70.98
11	2/78	2.46	72.21
12	1/78	1.23	73.40
Total	78/78	$96.00	$800.00

If the loan is paid off at maturity, the two methods are identical in the amount of interest paid and the total amount of payments.

If an individual pays off the loan early, the two methods produce a different balance due.

Level method. After payment 3, Mac wishes to pay off the entire account. The amount of interest paid for the loan would have been $24. The amount required to pay off the loan is determined by:

$$\text{(Loan + interest for 3 months)} - 3 \text{ payments}$$

$$800 + 3(8) - 3(74.67) = \$599.99$$

Rule of 78. The amount of interest paid for the loan so far is $40.62, the sum of $14.77, $13.54, and $12.31. The amount needed to pay off the loan is

$$800 + 40.62 - 3(74.67) = \$616.61$$

The difference in the cost of the two loans is $16.62. The rule of 78 is more costly to the consumer.

The effective rate for each of the methods described is identical as long as the loan runs for the full term. The effective rate for the preceding example is

$$K = 12 \qquad I = 96 \qquad P = 800 \qquad n = 12$$

$$\text{Effective rate} = \frac{(2)(96)(12)}{(800)(13)} = 0.2215 = 22.15\%$$

Compound Interest Repaid in Equal Payments:
Ordinary Annuity

Amortizing a loan with compound interest is called the installment plan and is an ordinary annuity using the present-value formula to determine the periodic payment.

$$P = \frac{R[1 - (1 + i)^{-n}]}{i} \quad \text{or} \quad R \cdot a_{\overline{n}|i}$$

where P is the present value or original principal, R is the regular payment, i is the interest rate of the payment period, n is the number of payments, and $a_{\overline{n}|i}$ is the present value of $1 for n periods at rate i.

Most long-term loans use the present-value formula. Interest is only paid on the outstanding balance at each payment period. The types of interest discussed previously (add-on, level, and rule of 78) calculated the interest on the beginning principal for the entire term of the loan, even though the principal was decreasing throughout the period.

Example
An $80,000 home is purchased with a $20,000 down payment. The balance is amortized over 25 years at 9% annual interest. Find the monthly payment.

$$P = 80,000 - 20,000 \quad \text{or} \quad 60,000 \qquad i = 0.09/12 \quad \text{or} \quad 0.0075$$

$$n = (25)(12) \quad \text{or} \quad 300$$

$$60,000 = \frac{R[1 - (1.0075)^{-300}]}{0.0075} \quad \text{or} \quad 60,000 = R \cdot a_{\overline{300}|\,0.0075}$$

$$= R[119.16162]$$

This is easiest found by using a calculator.

$$1.0075 \;\boxed{y^x}\; 300 \;\boxed{+/-}\;\boxed{=}\;\boxed{+/-}\;\boxed{+}\; 1 \;\boxed{=}\;\boxed{\div}\; 0.0075 \;\boxed{=}\; 119.16162$$

$$R = \frac{60,000}{119.16162} = \$503.52$$

The formula for determining the effective interest rate can be used in this example also.

$$\text{Effective rate} = \frac{2KI}{(P)(n + 1)}$$

To find I, multiply the amount of each payment by the number of payments and subtract the initial amount borrowed.

$$I = (503.52)(300) - 60,000 = \$91,056$$

$$\text{Effective rate} = \frac{(2)(12)(91,056)}{(60,000)(301)}$$

The effective interest rate is 12.1%.

Notice the effective interest rate for the amortized loan under the present value of an annuity problem is lower than the effective interest rate was for add-on interest loans.

SECTION 1 EXERCISES

1. Determine the monthly payments of an add-on loan of $750 with an interest rate of 8% for 18 months. Find the effective rate of the loan.

2. Determine the monthly payments of an add-on loan of $3,000 with an interest rate of 7% for 30 months. Find the effective rate of the loan.

3. Determine the amount of interest paid in the monthly payments of a loan of $900 for 18 months at a 10% interest rate if interest is charged by the level method. Determine the effective rate of the loan.

4. Determine the amount of interest paid in each quarterly payment of a $2,000 loan that has an annual 9% interest rate for 2 years. The interest is charged by the level method. Determine the effective rate of the loan.

5. Determine the amount of interest paid in the first monthly payment of an $800 loan with an interest rate of 12% for 1 year. The interest is charged by the level method. Find the effective rate of the loan.

6. A loan is negotiated for $1,000 for 1 year at 8% interest. The interest is paid by the level method. The loan is repaid after the third monthly payment is made. Find the amount needed for repayment at that time.

7. Determine the amount of interest paid in the first monthly payment of an $800 loan with an interest rate of 12% for 1 year. The interest is paid by the rule of 78.

8. Determine the amount of interest paid in the third monthly payment of a $1,000 loan with an interest rate of 10% for 18 months. The interest is paid by the rule of 78.

9. A loan is negotiated for $1,000 for 1 year at 8% interest. The interest is paid by the rule of 78. The loan is repaid after the third monthly payment is made. Find the amount needed for repayment at that time.

10. A home is purchased for $95,000, and a down payment of $35,000 is made. The owner negotiated a 9% compound interest loan at the bank for 20 years with payments due at the end of each month. Find the amount of the monthly payment. Find the effective rate of the loan.

11. A business borrows $65,000 for expansion of facilities. The money was obtained from the local bank at 12% interest with payments due quarterly for 10 years. Find the amount of each quarterly payment. Find the effective rate of the loan.

12. A medical student borrows $20,000 for education expenses. The money was obtained from the local bank at 6% compound interest with annual payments due at the end of each year for 10 years. Find the amount of each payment. Find the effective rate of the loan.

13. John Powers borrows $1,200 at 12% for 6 months. Payments are due at the end of each month. He anticipates a windfall in 2 months and will pay the entire loan off at the time of the second payment. Find the amount due for repayment if the interest is charged by the
   a. Level method
   b. Rule of 78

14. Jane Sawyer won a sweepstakes and went to the bank with her winnings to pay off a 2-year loan of $8,000 with an interest rate of 9%. She had just paid her seventh monthly payment. Find the amount needed to repay the remainder of the loan if the interest is charged by the
   a. Level method
   b. Rule of 78

15. Shirley Carter negotiated a $20,000 loan with a 9% compound interest rate for 10 years. Find the amount of the monthly payment to repay the loan.

16. James Conner negotiated a $25,000 loan with 10% interest, compounded quarterly, for 8 years. Find the amount of the quarterly payment.

Answers to Odd-Numbered Exercises

1. $46.67, monthly payment. Effective rate, 15.16%.

3. $7.50, interest/month. Effective rate, 18.95%.

5. $8.00, interest/period. Effective rate, 22.15%.

7. $14.77, interest.

9. $763.85 to repay after three payments.

11. $2,812.05 quarterly. Effective rate 14.25%.

13. (a) $1,012.   (b) $1,025.71.

15. $253.35, monthly payment.

4.2   OUTSTANDING PRINCIPAL

Accounting practices, tax requirements, and good business procedures require an accurate and current balance for all loans. In the preceding section, three methods of determining interest on a loan were presented. The outstanding balance is determined differently for each of the methods.

Add-on Interest

For the add-on interest loan, all of the interest is added on at the origination of the loan. Early repayment does not affect the amount of interest. To determine the balance at any time, the total amount of the repayment is subtracted from the total of the principal and interest.

The following steps are involved in determining the balance of an add-on interest loan.

1. Determine I using the formula $I = Prt$, where P is the amount of the loan, r is the rate of interest charged, and t is the time of the loan in years.

2. Amount to be repaid $= P + I$.

3. Amount of each payment $= (P + I)/n$, where n is the number of payments.

4. Outstanding balance $= P + I - m(R)$, where m is the number of completed payments.

Example
$2,000 is borrowed at 8% interest for 2 years. After 6 monthly payments, the

consumer wishes to repay the balance. Find the balance due, using the add-on interest method.

$$I = (2{,}000)(0.08)(2) = 320$$

$$I + P = 2{,}320$$

$$R = \frac{(I + P)}{n} = 2{,}320/24$$

$$= \$96.67$$

$$\text{Balance} = 2{,}320 - 6(96.67)$$

$$= \$2{,}320 - \$580.02 = \$1{,}739.98$$

Level Method

The interest is divided among each of the regular payment periods. If the loan is paid off early, no interest is charged for the remainder of the loan.
    The following steps are used to calculate the balance on this type of loan.

1. Determine the amount of principal paid each payment period by P/n, where n is the number of payments for the full period of the loan.

2. Balance $= P - m(P/n)$, where m is the number of payments already made.

Example

Take the same problem used for the add-on interest example, $2,000 for 24 months at 8% interest. Calculate the balance due at the end of 6 months if the interest is charged by the level method.

$$\text{Principal paid each month} = \frac{2{,}000}{24} = \$83.34$$

$$\text{Balance} = 2{,}000 - 6(83.34) = \$1{,}499.96$$

Rule of 78

Different amounts of interest are charged at each payment. The rule of 78 states that part of the interest for any given month = (total number of payments $+ 1 -$ present payment number)/sum of digits of total number of payments. For 24 payments, the denominator is 300. The fractional part of the first payment credited to interest is $(24 + 1 - 1)/300$, the second is $(24 + 1 - 2)/300, \ldots$, the sixth payment is $(24 + 1 - 6)/300$. The part applied against the principal for any payment is the remainder of the payment after the interest has been deducted.

1. Calculate the interest by $I = Prt$.

2. Determine R, the regular monthly payment. $R = (P + I)/n$.

3. Determine the fractional parts of interest for each of the payments made and total these fractions. Multiply this fraction by I to find the total interest (TI) paid, in m payments.

4. Find the total amount of payments made, $m \cdot R$, where m is the number of payments completed.

5. Outstanding balance $= P - (m \cdot R - TI)$.

Example
Take the same problem as before, $2,000 for 24 months at 8% interest. Find the balance after 6 months, using the rule of 78.

$$I = (2,000)(0.08)(2) = \$320$$

$$R = \frac{2,320}{24} = \$96.67$$

$$\frac{24}{300} + \frac{23}{300} + \frac{22}{300} + \frac{21}{300} + \frac{20}{300} + \frac{19}{300}$$

$$\frac{(24 + 23 + 22 + 21 + 20 + 19)}{300} = \frac{129}{300}$$

$(129/300)(320) = \$137.60$ amount of interest paid in 6 months

$(6)(96.67) = \$580.02$ total payments in 6 months

$2,000 - (580.02 - 137.60) = \$1,557.58$ balance at end of 6 months

Note the difference in the balances due from the three methods of charging the same rate of interest. The add-on method had a balance of $1,740.00, the level method had a balance of $1,499.96, and the rule of 78 had a balance of $1,557.58. All three loans require the same amount of payment and the same number of payments, but the balance at any time, except at the final payment, differs. If early repayment is anticipated, try to negotiate the level method of charging interest. Most banks use the rule of 78 in short-term loans. Add-on interest is rarely beneficial to the customer.

Long-Term Loans

Long-term loans involve repayments by a set of regular equal payments determined by the present value of an annuity formula.

An **amortization schedule** needs to be made to completely describe the loan.

1. Determine the regular payment by $A = R \cdot a_{\overline{n}\,i}$.

2. Make column headings of:

   a. Number of payment.

   b. Outstanding balance at beginning of each period (outstanding balance of the previous period − part of R applied to principal).

   c. Interest due at end of period [Entry of column b $\times$ i (interest rate per period)].

   d. Payment due at the end of each period (calculated from $A = R \cdot a_{\overline{n}\,i}$).

   e. Amount of R to reduce outstanding balance [$(R - I)$ or entry in column d − column c].

Example
A $55,000 home was purchased with a down payment of $5,000 and monthly payments for 10 years. The interest rate was 10%, compounded monthly. (a) Find the size of the monthly payment. (b) Construct a partial amortization schedule to find the outstanding balance at the end of 12 months.
    To determine R:

$$50,000 = \frac{R[1 - (1.008\ 333)^{-120}]}{0.008\ 3333} = \$660.75$$

Next, make a schedule as described previously.

Payment Number	Principal Balance	Interest Due	Payment	Amount of Principal
n	*PB*	*I*	*R*	*R − I*
1	$50,000.00	$416.67	$660.75	$244.08
2	49,755.92	414.63	660.75	246.12
3	49,509.80	412.58	660.75	248.17
4	49,261.63	410.51	660.75	250.24
5	49,011.39	408.43	660.75	252.32
6	48,759.07	406.33	660.75	254.42
7	48,504.65	404.21	660.75	256.54
8	48,248.11	402.07	660.75	258.68
9	47,989.43	399.91	660.75	260.84
10	47,728.59	397.74	660.75	263.01
11	47,465.58	395.55	660.75	265.20
12	47,200.38	393.34	660.75	267.41
	46,932.97			

The explanation is as follows.
Line 1:

$$416.67 = 50,000(0.10/12) \qquad 660.75 - 416.67 = 244.08$$

Line 2:

$$50,000 - 244.08 = \$49,755.92$$

$$(49,755.92)(0.10/12) = \$414.63 \qquad \$660.75 - \$414.63 = \$246.12$$

The outstanding balance of the loan after 12 payments is $46,932.97. The amortization schedule can be continued for all 120 payments. The final balance after 120 payments is zero. The final payment might have a slight adjustment to compensate for rounding errors.

If a schedule of repayment is not needed, the amount of the outstanding principal can be obtained directly. First, determine the compound amount of the principal of the loan at the given rate after 12 payments. The formula is

$$A = P(1 + i)^{12}$$

For this example the compound amount is

$$(50,000)(1.008\ 3333)^{12} = \$55,235.63$$

Next, determine the value of an ordinary annuity for the number of payments with the periodic payment of the problem. Generally, the formula is

$$V = R \cdot s_{\overline{n}|} \quad \text{or} \quad \frac{R[(1 + i)^n - 1]}{i}$$

For this example the value of the annuity is

$$(660.75) \cdot s_{\overline{12}|\,0.0083} = 660.75(12.565\ 5681) = \$8{,}302.70$$

The outstanding principal is the difference of the two amounts.

$$OPB = P(1 + i)^n - R \cdot s_{\overline{n}|\,i}$$

For this example,

$$\$55{,}235.63 - \$8{,}302.70 = \$46{,}932.93$$

This procedure determined the compound amount of the principal for a given time period and the value of an annuity with the periodic investment of the loan payment for the given time period. The difference between the two gives the outstanding balance.

If all the problem requires is the outstanding principal after n payments, this procedure is much quicker and more direct than constructing an amortization schedule. Notice that in an amortized compound interest loan, the earlier payments contain a larger amount of interest than the later payments. This was also the case for the rule of 78.

The bank usually gives the consumer an **amortization schedule** at the time of the loan. The more recent variable-rate mortgages change the schedule and payments with every interest change.

A hand-held calculator or a short computer program will generate an amortization schedule.

The calculator keystroke for the amortization schedule described previously is

Interest rate $\div$ number of payments/year $=$ $\boxed{\text{STO}}$ $\boxed{C}$

Original balance $\boxed{\times}$ $\boxed{\text{RCL}}$ $=$ I [record in (c)] $\boxed{+/-}$ $\boxed{+}$ R

$=$ record in (e) $\boxed{+/-}$ $\boxed{+}$ original balance

$=$ record in (a) line 2 $\boxed{\times}$ $\boxed{\text{RCL}}$

$=$ I record in (c)

and so on. . . .

```
      COMPUTER PROGRAM (in Basic)
10    REM - AMORTIZATION SCHEDULE
20    INPUT "A":A [Amount of loan]
30    INPUT "I":I [Rate per payment period]
40    INPUT "N":N [Number of payments]
50    R = A*1/(1-(1+I)^(-N))
60    PRINT "(X)PERIOD","(B)O.B.","(C)INTEREST","(D)PAYMENT",
      "(E)R.A."
70    For X = 1 TO N
80    A = A
90    IT = A*I
100   RA = R - IT
110   PRINT X,A,IT,R,RA
120   A = A - RA
130   NEXT X
140   END
```

This program will only work on a fixed-rate mortgage.

SECTION 2 EXERCISES

1. Determine the outstanding balance on a loan of $5,000 after 11 monthly payments. The loan had an interest rate of 9% for 2 years. Use the add-on interest method.

2. Determine the outstanding balance on a loan of $4,000 after 5 quarterly payments. The loan had an interest rate of 10% for 3 years. Use the add-on interest method.

3. Determine the outstanding balance on a loan of $7,500 after 2 annual payments. The loan had an interest rate of 8% for 5 years. Use the add-on interest method.

4. Determine the outstanding balance on a loan of $5,800 after 18 months. Payments were due monthly and the interest rate of 12% was for 2 years. Use the add-on interest method.

5. Determine the outstanding balance on a loan of $5,000 after 11 monthly payments. The loan had an interest rate of 9% for 2 years. Use the level interest method.

6. Determine the outstanding balance on a loan of $4,000 after 5 quarterly payments. The loan had an interest rate of 10% for 3 years. Use the level interest method.

7. Determine the outstanding balance on a loan of $7,500 after 2 annual payments. The loan had an interest rate of 8% for 5 years. Use the level interest method.

8. Determine the outstanding balance on a loan of $5,800 after 18 months. Payments were due monthly and the interest rate of 12% was for 2 years. Use the level interest method.

9. Determine the outstanding balance on a loan of $5,000 after 11 monthly payments. The loan had an interest rate of 9% for 2 years. Use the rule of 78 method.

10. Determine the outstanding balance on a loan of $4,000 after 5 quarterly payments. The loan had an interest rate of 10% for 3 years. Use the rule of 78 method.

11. Determine the outstanding balance on a loan of $7,500 after 2 annual payments. The loan had an interest rate of 8% for 5 years. Use the rule of 78 method.

12. Determine the outstanding balance on a loan of $5,800 after 18 monthly payments. The loan had an interest rate of 12% for 2 years. Use the rule of 78 method.

13. Determine the outstanding balance on a loan of $5,000 after 11 monthly payments. The loan had a compound interest rate of 9% for 2 years.

14. Determine the outstanding balance on a loan of $4,000 after 5 quarterly payments. The loan had a compound interest rate of 10% for 3 years.

15. Determine the outstanding balance on a loan of $7,500 after 2 annual payments. The loan had a compound interest rate of 8% for 5 years.

16. Determine the outstanding balance on a loan of $5,800 after 18 monthly payments. The loan had a compound interest rate of 12% for 2 years.

17. Compare the size of payments in exercises 1, 5, 9, and 13. Compare the outstanding balance for exercises 1, 5, 9, and 13.

18. Compare the size of payments in exercises 2, 6, 10, and 14. Compare the outstanding balance for exercises 2, 6, 9, and 13.

19. Compare the size of payments in exercises 3, 7, 11, and 15. Compare the outstanding balance for exercises 3, 7, 11, and 15.

20. Compare the size of payments in exercises 4, 8, 12, and 16. Compare the outstanding balance for exercises 4, 8, 12, and 16.

21. If the terms of a loan, add-on interest, level interest, rule of 78, or compound interest for an amortized loan, were decided by you, the borrower, indicate and justify your decision. The rate and term of the loan is fixed.

Answers to Odd-Numbered Exercises

  1. $3,195.76.

  3. $6,300.

  5. $2,708.33.

  7. $4,500.

  9. $2,922.83.

 11. $5,100.

 13. $3,065.90.

 15. $4,840.89.

 17. Lowest balance by the level method. Lowest payment by the compound method.

 19. Lowest balance by the level method. Lowest payment by the compound method.

 21. If early repayment is anticipated, use the level interest method. Otherwise the compound interest method is superior for loans.

4.3 SINKING FUNDS

When the need for an amount of money is anticipated, and periodic amounts are saved in anticipation of this need, the account is called a **sinking fund**. A sinking fund is an ordinary annuity. Sinking funds are used by businesses as a means of acquiring funds needed to redeem bonds, to replace worn-out equipment, or to retire debts. A sinking fund is a savings account with a specific goal in a definite period of time, accrued by regular payments.

When sinking funds are used to accrue the cash to pay off a debt or bonds, the sinking fund does not include the funds to pay the required interest on the debt to be retired. A company must have two accounts, one to build an amount to retire the debt, and one to pay the current interest due on the debt.

Usually the dates coincide on payment on annuity and payment on interest due. In a sinking fund the final amount is known, the regular payment is determined, and the time period and rate of interest are known. The ordinary annuity value formula

$$V = R[(1 + i)^n - 1]/i \quad \text{or} \quad R \cdot s_{\overline{n}|i}$$

is used in a sinking fund to determine the amount of the regular payment.

Example

A company needs 2 million dollars in 10 years to redeem the bonds issued. What quarterly payment is necessary to a sinking fund if the interest rate is 8%, compounded quarterly, and the bonds carry a quarterly interest payment of 9%?

$$V = 2,000,000 \qquad n = 40 \qquad i = 0.02$$

$$2,000,000 = R[(1.02)^{40} - 1]/0.02 \quad \text{or} \quad R \cdot s_{\overline{40}|\,0.02}$$

$$= R(60.401\ 985)$$

$$R = \$33,111.50$$

$$\text{Interest on bonds} = Prt$$

$$= 2,000,000 \times 0.09 \times 3/12$$

$$= \$45,000$$

Quarterly payment $= \$33,111.50 + \$45,000 = \$78,111.50$

Example

DuBear Corporation borrows \$500,000 for 2 years. The loan has an interest rate of 9%, interest due quarterly. The principal must be repaid in a lump sum on the due date. DuBear Corporation wishes to set up a sinking fund to retire the loan. The corporation must also allocate funds to pay the quarterly interest on the loan. The sinking fund is set up at 8% interest, compounded quarterly. Find the total quarterly amount needed to be budgeted for the commitment.

$$\text{Quarterly interest} = 500,000 \times 0.09 \times 1/4 = \$11,250$$

Sinking fund payment:

$$500,000 = R[(1.02)^8 - 1]/0.02$$

$$= R(9.741\ 555)$$

$$R = \$58,254.90$$

Interest + sinking fund = $69,504.90   quarterly amount

Example

John Morris wishes to start a photography business and it is estimated he will need $15,000 to get started. If he can save $800 every quarter, how long will it take for the sinking fund to have a value of $15,000? The sinking fund is paying 6% interest, compounded quarterly.

$$15,000 = 800 \cdot s_{\overline{n}|\ 0.015}$$

$$18.75 = s_{\overline{n}|\ 0.015} \quad \text{From Table 2, rate } 1.5\%,$$

$$n = 16 \quad 17.9324$$

$$n = 17 \quad 19.2014$$

$$n = 17 \text{ quarters or } 4\frac{1}{4} \text{ years}$$

Sinking funds involve the same calculations as an ordinary annuity. Sinking fund is a business term, the account gets tax considerations, and the value of the fund is an asset of the business and is listed on the balance sheet.

SECTION 3 EXERCISES

1. Determine the periodic payment necessary to finance the following sinking funds. Calculate the total deposits of the sinking fund and the amount of interest earned by the periodic payments.

	Maturity Value	*Rate*	*Period*	*Time (Years)*
a.	$200,000	12%	Semiannual	10
b.	$ 75,000	10%	Quarterly	8
c.	$125,000	8%	Monthly	5

2. Follow the same instructions used in exercise 1.

	Maturity Value	Rate	Period	Time (Years)
a.	$100,000	9%	Semiannual	12
b.	$ 60,000	10%	Quarterly	15
c.	$150,000	6%	Monthly	5

3. R. B. Sawyer projects opening another store in 5 years. He wishes to establish a sinking fund to provide for some of the expense. He estimates he will need $250,000. How much should he deposit in the account monthly if the account can earn 8% interest, compounded monthly?

4. J. R. Adams wishes to plan for his daughter's education. He estimates he will need $35,000 in 10 years. He wants to make quarterly payments to a sinking fund. The bank has quoted 8% interest, compounded quarterly. How much is his quarterly deposit?

5. Frances Drake wishes to take a trip around the world the year she retires and she wants to establish a fund so the money will be available. How much should she deposit yearly if she will be eligible to retire in 25 years? The bank quotes 7% interest, compounded annually. She is planning on $25,000 to finance the trip.

6. George Oliver wants to set up his own health fitness center. The estimated cost of the equipment is $40,000. He plans to establish the business in 5 years. How much should be deposit monthly if the account earns 12% interest, compounded monthly?

7. Charge Electric Company has sold bonds to finance an expansion of its power plant. The company needs $2,000,000 in 25 years to redeem the bonds. How much should the company put into a sinking fund semiannually to provide for the anticipated expense? The sinking fund earns 6% interest, compounded semiannually.

8. John Perkins was given a new auto as a college graduation present. He wants to establish a sinking fund so the auto can be replaced in 5 years by a cash purchase. He anticipates he will need $8,000. The sinking fund pays 6% interest, compounded monthly. How much should he deposit monthly to meet his goal?

9. J. R. Gross Company estimates the plant will need a new roof in 15 years, a major expense for the company. A sinking fund is set up to provide $100,000 in 15 years. The fund earns 8% interest, compounded quarterly. How much should be put into the account quarterly to meet the goals of the fund?

10. Jane Turner borrowed $100,000 for the expansion of her restaurant. The lender wants interest on the loan quarterly at the rate of 8%. The face value of the loan must be repaid in 10 years. Ms. Turner establishes a sinking fund for the repayment of the loan, making quarterly payments in an account earning 6% interest. How much must she set aside quarterly to meet the obligation of the interest payment and the sinking fund?

11. Rusty of Rusty's Diner borrows $25,000 from a family member for renovation. He must make monthly interest payments on the 8% loan and repay the face value in 5 years. He establishes a sinking fund paying 6% interest for the repayment of the face value, making monthly deposits to the account. How much must he set aside each month for the interest payment and the sinking fund deposit?

12. A company borrows $100,000 for 6 years at 10% interest. To guarantee the necessary funds to repay the loan, a sinking fund is established where payments are made at the end of each year in an investment paying 8% interest, compounded annually. What is the total cost of the loan to the company?

Answers to Odd-Numbered Exercises

1. (a) $5,436.91 = R$. $108,738.23, total deposit. $91,261.77 = I$. (b) $1,557.62 = R$. $49,843.85, total deposit. $25,156.05 = I$. (c) $1,701.22 = R$. $102,072.96, total deposit. $22,927.04 = I$.

3. $3,402.43.

5. $395.26.

7. $17,730.99.

9. $876.80.

11. $358.32 = R$. Total, $524.99.

4.4   BONDS

Bonds are another way of raising money for an extended period of time, where the amount may be too large for a single lender or institution. Bonds are issued and sold by corporations in need of large sums of money; bonds are purchased by individuals or financial institutions such as life insurance companies or mutual funds. Bonds furnish the buyers with guaranteed income for an extended period of time.

Terminology of Bonds

Mortgage bonds. The debt is secured by a mortgage on the property of the issuing corporation.

Debenture bonds. No security is offered to the buyer except the reputation of the issuing corporation.

Municipal bond. A debt incurred by a state, county, or municipality. The rate of interest is lower than corporate bonds but the income is tax free from local and, in some cases, federal obligations.

Face value or par value. The redeemable amount of a bond at maturity, usually some figure like $100, $500, or $1,000.

Current yield. The rate of interest of a bond based on the amount actually paid on the bond (rather than its stated rate of interest paid on the par value of the bond).

Discount. The difference between the purchase price and the par value of the bond when the purchase price is below the par value.

Premium. The difference between the purchase price and the par value of the bond when the purchase price is above the par value.

Call provision. An option to the issuer of the bond to redeem the bond before the maturity date of the bond. Declining interest rates often cause companies to call bonds and replace them with lower interest rate bonds. A call provision must be included in the bond statement.

Bond Transactions for Issuer

Bonds are issued at a given face value, an announced rate of interest (based on the face value) and a maturity date, with the option of a call provision. The issuer either pays interest on established dates in the year or the bond document has coupons attached to it. Each coupon has a redeemable date and amount printed on it. The owner of the bond clips the coupon and presents it at a bank for redeeming. The coupon is legal tender; the bank is paid by the corporation on presentation of the coupon. The issuer must have established a sinking fund or made some financial arrangement to redeem the bond on the maturity date. The interest on bonds is paid prior to any dividends paid to stockholders. If a company goes through bankruptcy, the holder of the bond will lose both premiums and some part of the face value. The issuer may not receive the face value of the bond at the time of the sale, depending on market conditions and the financial integrity of the issuer.

Bond Transactions for Buyer

Bonds are traded on the various stock exchanges. Newspapers publish bond information. The quoted price is per $100 value.

Bond Valuation

Bonds are valued on a coupon or interest date of the bond. To find the value of a bond, the present value of the redemption price of the bond and the present value of the annuity formed by the coupons are combined. The basic formula for the value of a bond is

$$V = C(1 + i)^{-n} + Fra_{\overline{n}|r}$$

where C is the redemption value of the bond (same as face value unless stated otherwise), i is the investors rate per period, n is the number of periods from the given date to the redemption date, F is the face value of the bond, and r is the interest rate paid by bond per period.

Example
Find the value of a $1,000 bond that was issued as an 8% bond, payable twice a year for 20 years. Five years before the maturity date, an investor wishes interest of 5%, payable semiannually. Find the value of the bond.

$$C = \$1,000 \qquad i = 0.05 \qquad n = 10 \qquad F = \$1,000$$

$$r = 0.04 \qquad a_{\overline{10}|\,0.04} = 7.721\ 735$$

$$V = (1,000)(1.05)^{-10} + 1,000(0.04)(7.721\ 735)$$

$$= 613.91 + 308.87$$

$$= \$922.78$$

A buyer paying $922.78 is buying the bond at a discount (less than par value) because a yield rate higher than the interest rate on the bond is desired. The issuer of the bond will continue to pay $40 every 6 months regardless of who owns the bond or what the owner paid for the bond.

When an individual buys a callable bond, there is an uncertainty on the redemption date. The investor should determine the value of the bond, both at the maturity date and the callable date. The lower of the two values would be a safe amount to pay to ensure the desired yield.

Example

An Airtight Investment Company debenture bond of $1,000 pays 9% interest and is redeemable on April 1, 2005. Interest is paid April 1 and October 1. Find the value of the bond on October 1, 1990, to a buyer who wants a semi-annual return of 4% interest on his investment. Assume that the bond is (a) called at $104 on April 1, 2000, and (b) redeemed for $1,000 at its maturity date.

The solution to (a) is

$$C = \$1,040 \qquad \text{(callable price per \$100 value)}$$

$$i = 0.04$$

$$n = 19 \text{ semiannual payments}$$

$$F = \$1,000$$

$$r = 0.045$$

$$a_{\overline{19}|\,0.045} = 13.133\ 9394$$

$$V = 1,040(1.04)^{-19} + (1,000)(0.045)(13.133\ 9394)$$

$$= 493.63 + 591.03$$

$$= \$1,084.66$$

The solution to (b) is

$$C = \$1,000$$

$$i = 0.04$$

$$n = 29$$

$$F = 1,000$$

$$r = 0.045$$

$$a_{\overline{29}|\,0.045} = 16.983\ 7146$$

$$V = 1,000(1.04)^{-29} + (1,000)(0.045)(16.983\ 7146)$$

$$= 320.65 + 765.27$$

$$= \$1,084.92$$

A premium of $84.66 paid for the bond will still allow the buyer to realize his investment goal, whether the bond is called in the year 2000 or is allowed to run to its maturity in 2005.

Current Yield

The current yield of a bond differs from the stated rate of interest of a bond if an amount other than the maturity value of the bond is paid for the bond. Annual interest on a bond is determined by the simple interest formula $I = Prt$. For a bond, $P = F$, and t is the number of interest periods per year.

$$\text{Current yield} = \text{annual interest/purchase price}$$

Example
Two $1,000 bonds each pay 8% simple interest annually. The purchase price of one bond was quoted at $96, the other bond was quoted at $102. Find the current yield rate for each bond.

Solution:

The interest for each bond was $(1,000)(0.08)(1) = \$80$.

The purchase price of the first bond is $960.

The purchase price of the second bond is $1,020.

$$\text{Current yield of bond 1} = 80/960 = 8.34\%$$
$$\text{Current yield of bond 2} = 80/1020 = 7.8\%$$

Premium and Discount

Premiums are paid on bonds when the interest rate on the bond (r) is greater than the yield rate on the purchase price (i). The amount of premium one should pay is given by the formula:

$$P = (Fr - Fi) \cdot a_{\overline{m}\,i}$$

Discounts are charged on bonds when the yield rate on the bond is greater than the interest rate on the bond.

$$D = (Fi - Fr) \cdot a_{\overline{m}\,i}$$

Example
Find the value on May 1, 1989, of a $1,000, 6% bond maturing May 1, 2009, if it is to yield 8% interest, compounded semiannually.

Solution:
The yield rate is higher than the rate of the bond. Therefore there will be a discount involved.

$$a_{\overline{n}|\,i} = a_{\overline{40}|\,0.04} = 19.792\ 7739$$

$$D = [(1,000)(0.04) - (1,000)(0.03)][19.792\ 7739]$$

$$= \$197.93$$

$$V = \$1,000 - \$197.93 = \$802.07$$

Example
Find the value on April 1, 1991, of a $1,000, 8.5% bond maturing April 1, 2007, if it is to yield 7% interest, compounded semiannually.

Solution:

$$a_{\overline{n}|\,i} = a_{\overline{32}|\,0.0425}$$

$$P = [(1,000)(0.0425) - (1,000)(0.035)][17.318\ 19003]$$

$$= (7.50)(19.068\ 8655) = \$129.89$$

$$V = \$1,000 + \$129.89 = \$1,129.89$$

There is more to bond purchasing, determining the value of bonds, and calculating the yield rate than the introduction given in this section. Complete books are written on bond investments. This introduction is meant to give some of the terminology associated with bonds and a broad overview of bond trading.

SECTION 4 EXERCISES

1. Find the value of each of the following bonds.

	Face Value	Maturity Value/Date	Semiannual Rate	Yield Rate/Year
a.	$1,000	$1,000 in 9 years	4.5%	10%
b.	$1,000	$1,020 in 15 years	4%	8%
c.	$1,000	$1,000 in 12 years	7.5%	10%

2. Find the value of each of the following bonds.

	Face Value	Maturity Value/Date	Semiannual Rate	Yield Rate/Year
a.	$1,000	$1,000 in 20 years	4.5%	8%
b.	$1,000	$1,050 in 8 years	3%	7%
c.	$1,000	$1,000 in 15 years	5%	7.5%

3. A Strong Steel Company debenture bond of $1,000 pays 10% and is redeemable on October 1, 2008. Interest is paid on April 1 and October 1. Find the value of the bond on October 1, 1991, to a buyer who wants a semiannual return of 4% interest on his investment.
   a. Assume that the bond is redeemed at its maturity date for $1,000.
   b. Assume that Strong Steel Company uses the callable option to retire the bond on April 1, 2000, for the redeemable price of $104.

4. A Chancey Mining Company debenture bond of $1,000 pays 6% interest and is redeemable on July 1, 2000. Interest is paid on January 1 and July 1. Find the value of the bond on January 1, 1992, to a buyer who wants a semiannual return of 4% on his investment.
   a. Assume that the bond is redeemed at its maturity date for $1,000.
   b. Assume that Chancey Mining Company uses the callable option to retire the bond on July 1, 1995, for the redeemable price of par.

5. Find the current yield rate of a bond that has a maturity value of $1,000. The bond pays 5% interest twice a year. The purchase price of the bond is quoted at $108.

6. Find the current yield rate of a bond that has a maturity value of $1,000. The bond pays annual interest of 8%. The bond is quoted at the price of $86.

7. Two bonds are being considered for purchase. Both have a maturity value of $1,000. One has an annual yield of 6%; the other has a semiannual yield of 3.5%. The 6% bond is selling at $92; the other bond is selling at $95. Which bond has the higher current yield?

8. Two bonds are being considered for purchase. Both have a maturity value of $1,000. One has an annual yield of 10%; the other has a semiannual rate of 4.5%. The 10% bond is selling for $102; the 4.5% bond is selling at $96. Which bond has the higher current yield?

9. Find the discount on a $1,000, 7% bond maturing on November 1, 2001, if on May 1, 1992, we want a yield of 8%, compounded semiannually. Determine the value of the bond.

10. Find the discount on a $1,000, 6% bond maturing on July 1, 2010, if on

July 1, 1990, a yield of 8%, compounded semiannually, is desired. Determine the value of the bond on July 1, 1990.

11. Find the premium on a $1,000, 9% bond maturing April 1, 2005, if on October 1, 1998, the rate of yield required is 8%, compounded semiannually. Determine the value of the bond on October 1, 1998.

12. Find the premium on a $1,000, 9.5% bond maturing June 1, 2020, if on December 1, 1992, the rate of yield required is 8.5%, compounded semiannually. Determine the value of the bond on December 1, 1992.

Answers to Odd-Numbered Exercises

1. (a) $941.55. (b) $1,006.17. (c) $827.52.

3. (a) $1,184.11. (b) $1,142.19.

5. 9.26%.

7. 7.37% yield rate of 3.5%. Bond selling at $95.

9. Discount, $65.67. Value, $934.33.

11. Premium, $49.93. Value, $1,049.93.

4.5   COMPARISON OF DEBT AND REPAYMENT

After the presentation of the different methods of raising money and repaying obligations, amortization, sinking funds, and bonds, some analysis should be made of the various means of procuring needed finances.

For short-term loans, the only choice is how the interest for the loan will be accrued. The options include add-on interest, interest accumulated under the rule of 78, interest accrued by the level method, or payments determined by the present-value formula, interest being charged on the unpaid balance.

Anticipated early repayment favors the level method or paying interest on the unpaid balance. Complete understanding of the terms of the agreement are essential to a satisfactory loan arrangement.

Long-term loans and large loans have fewer options for obtaining funds. Amortized loans, sinking funds, and bonds are the options available. Sinking funds require anticipating the needs for capital; large amounts of money can only be raised by issuing bonds. Sinking funds are usually established to retire demand notes and bonds at maturity. Interest rates and availability of money influence loan decisions.

Example

$10,000 is borrowed for 5 years with payments to be made at the end of each month. Find the total monthly obligation under each of the following conditions.

a. The debt is amortized at 8% interest.

b. Interest is paid at 8% on the debt of $10,000 and a sinking fund is established at 7% interest.

c. Interest is paid at 8% on the $10,000 and a sinking fund is established at 9% interest.

d. Interest is paid at 8% on the $10,000 and a sinking fund is established at 8% interest.

(a) Monthly payment:

$$10,000 = R \cdot a_{\overline{60}|\, 8/12\%}$$
$$= R(49.318\ 4333)$$
$$R = \$202.76$$

(b) Monthly interest:

$$I = (10,000)(0.08)(1/12)$$
$$= 66.67$$

Sinking fund 7%:

$$10,000 = R \cdot s_{\overline{60}|\, 7/12\%}$$
$$= R(71.5929)$$
$$R = \$139.68$$
$$I + R = \$206.35$$

(c) Monthly interest:

$$I = (10,000)(0.08)(1/12)$$
$$= 66.67$$

Sinking fund 9%:

$$10,000 = R \cdot s_{\overline{60}|\ 9/12\%}$$

$$= R(75.424\ 136)$$

$$R = \$132.58$$

$$I + R = \$199.25$$

(d) Monthly interest:

$$I = (10,000)(0.08)(1/12)$$

$$= 66.67$$

Sinking fund 8%:

$$10,000 = R \cdot s_{\overline{60}|\ 8/12\%}$$

$$= R(73.476\ 856)$$

$$R = \$136.10$$

$$I + R = \$202.77$$

To condense the results from the example:

(a) Amortized loan, 8%	\$202.76
(b) Loan, 8%; Sinking fund, 7%	\$206.35
(c) Loan, 8%; Sinking fund, 9%	\$199.25
(d) Loan, 8%; Sinking fund, 8%	\$202.77

Conclusions

Although one example is not sufficient to draw conclusions, the results from the example will be generalized to assist in making comparisons.

If the rates of interest in an amortized loan, regular loan, and sinking fund are all the same under the same period, the costs are equal. These were the conditions of (a) and (d); the results differ by 1 cent, the result of rounding numbers.

If the amortized rate and regular loan rate are the same and the sinking fund rate is higher, the payment cost is less. These were the conditions of (c).

If the amortized rate and regular loan rate are the same and the sinking fund rate is lower, the payment cost is more. These are the conditions of (b).

SECTION 5 EXERCISES

1. $20,000 is borrowed for 4 years with payments to be made at the end of each month. Find the total monthly obligation under each of the following conditions.
a. The debt is amortized at 6% interest.
b. Interest is paid at 6.5% on the debt of $20,000 and a sinking fund is established at 7% interest.
c. Interest is paid at 6% on the debt of $20,000 and a sinking fund is established at 6% interest.
d. Interest is paid at 7% on the debt of $20,000 and a sinking fund is established at 7% interest.

2. $50,000 is borrowed for 15 years with payments to be made at the end of each quarter. Find the total quarterly obligation under each of the following conditions.
a. The debt is amortized at 8% interest.
b. Interest is paid at 8.5% on the debt of $50,000 and a sinking fund is established at 9% interest.
c. Interest is paid at 7.5% on the debt of $50,000 and a sinking fund is established at 8% interest.
d. Interest is paid at 8% on the debt of $50,000 and a sinking fund is established at 8% interest.

3. $200,000 is borrowed for 20 years with payments to be made at the end of every 6 months. Find the total quarterly obligation under each of the following conditions.
a. The debt is amortized at 6% interest.
b. Interest is paid at 7% on the debt of $200,000 and a sinking fund is established at 5% interest.
c. Interest is paid at 5% on the debt of $200,000 and a sinking fund is established at 7% interest.
d. Interest is paid at 6% on the debt of $200,000 and a sinking fund is established at 6% interest.

4. $25,000 is borrowed for 5 years with payments to be made monthly. Find the total monthly obligation under each of the following conditions.
a. The debt is amortized at 9% interest.
b. Interest is paid at 8% on the debt of $25,000 and a sinking fund is established at 9% interest.
c. Interest is paid at 9% on the debt of $25,000 and a sinking fund is established at 8% interest.

d. Interest is paid at 9% on the debt of $25,000 and a sinking fund is established at 9% interest.

5. $8,000 is borrowed for 10 years with payments to be made quarterly. Find the total monthly obligation under each of the following conditions.
   a. The debt is amortized at 10% interest.
   b. Interest is paid at 9% on the debt of $8,000 and a sinking fund is established at 10% interest.
   c. Interest is paid at 12% on the debt of $8,000 and a sinking fund is established at 12% interest.
   d. Interest is paid at 11% on the debt of $8,000 and a sinking fund is established at 10% interest.

6. $250,000 is borrowed for 20 years with payments to be made annually. Find the total monthly obligation under each of the following conditions.
   a. The debt is amortized at 7% interest.
   b. Interest is paid at 8% on the debt of $250,000 and a sinking fund is established at 8% interest.
   c. Interest is paid at 6% on the debt of $250,000 and a sinking fund is established at 6% interest.
   d. Interest is paid at 7% on the debt of $250,000 and a sinking fund is established at 7% interest.

7. Bonds were issued on April 1, 1990, by Broad Spectrum, Inc., for $100,000. Each bond was $1,000 in denomination with 8% payable interest on April 1 and October 1. The maturity date is April 1, 2005. Broad Spectrum, Inc., set up a sinking fund for 15 years with payments on April 1 and October 1 at 7% interest to retire the bonds. Find the semiannual amount needed to pay the interest and the payment to the sinking fund.

8. Bonds were issued on October 1, 1989, by Sword's Carpets. Each bond was $1,000 in denomination, and 10,000 bonds were sold. The bonds had an interest rate of 7% payable semiannually and a maturity date of October 1, 2009. A sinking fund at 9% was set up for 20 years, payments to coincide with bond interest payments. Find the amount needed to meet the interest payments and the regular payment to the sinking fund.

Answers to Odd-Numbered Exercises

1. (a) $469.70.
   (b) Interest, $108.33 + payment, $362.26. Total, $470.59.
   (c) Interest, $100 + payment, $369.70. Total, $469.70.
   (d) Interest, $116.67 + payment, $362.26. Total, $478.93.

3. (a) $8,652.48.
   (b) Interest, $7,000 + payment, $2,967.25. Total, $9,967.25.
   (c) Interest, $5,000 + payment, $2,365.46. Total, $7,365.46.
   (d) Interest, $6,000 + payment, $2,652.48. Total, $8,652.48.

5. (a) $318.69.
   (b) Interest, $180 + payment, $118.69. Total, $298.69.
   (c) Interest, $240 + payment, $106.10. Total, $346.10.
   (d) Interest, $220 + payment, $118.69. Total, $338.69.

7. Interest, $4,000 + payment, $1,937.13. Total, $5,937.13.

Summary

- **Amount of payment of loan**:

$$R = (P + I)/N$$

- **Methods of charging interest**:
  Level method: each payment includes same amount of interest
  Rule of 78: early payments include higher portion of interest

- **Outstanding principal**:
  Add-on interest: $OP = P + I - m(R)$
  Level method: $OP = P - m(P/n)$
  Rule of 78: $OP = P - (m \cdot R - TI)$
  m is number of payments made TI is total interest paid

- **Effective rate** $= 2(K)(I)/[(P)(n + 1)]$
  K is number of payments per year n is number of payments on loan

- **Amortized loan**: compound interest charged on loan, equal payments

$$A = R \cdot a_{\overline{n}|i}$$
$$OP = P(1 + i)^n - R \cdot s_{\overline{n}|i}$$

- **Sinking funds**

$$V = R \cdot s_{\overline{n}|i}$$

- **Bonds**
  Mortgage Bonds: debt is secured by property

Debenture Bonds: debt has no security
Municipal Bonds: debt is incurred by state, county, or municipality

REVIEW EXERCISES

1. Determine the monthly payment of an add-on loan of $4,500 if the rate of interest is 9% and the term of the loan is 36 months. Find the effective rate of the loan.

2. Determine the monthly payment of a $4,500 loan that has an interest rate of 9% for 36 months. The interest is charged by the level method. Determine the portion of the payment applied to interest and the effective rate of the loan.

3. Determine the monthly payment of a $4,500 loan that has an interest rate of 8% for 18 months. The interest is charged by the rule of 78. Determine what part of the monthly payment applies to the principal in the first payment. Determine the effective rate of interest in the loan.

4. Determine the monthly payment of an amortized loan of $5,000 for 4 years. The interest rate is 9%, compounded monthly. Determine the effective rate of the loan.

5. Determine the amount needed to repay a loan of $4,000 at 6% interest for 24 months, using add-on interest, after 12 months of payments.

6. Determine the amount needed to repay a loan of $4,000 at 6% interest for 24 months, using level interest, after 12 months of payments.

7. Determine the amount needed to repay a loan of $4,000 at 6% interest for 24 months, using the rule of 78, after 12 months of payments.

8. Determine the outstanding principal after 12 months on an amortized loan of $4,000 at 6% interest, compounded monthly, for 24 months.

9. Construct the first year in an amortization schedule for a loan of $10,000 at 8% interest, compounded quarterly. The loan is scheduled to run 5 years.

10. Determine the monthly charge to a company that borrows $100,000 at 6% interest for 10 years. The interest is payable monthly. The company sets up a sinking fund to accumulate the face value of the loan in 10 years. The sinking fund pays 8% interest, compounded monthly.

11. A family buys a home for $94,000. The cash payment was $24,000, the

remainder was a 20-year mortgage at 9% interest. After 4 years (48 payments), the family sells the house. What was the outstanding principal at the time of the sale?

12. Determine how many monthly payments of $250 it will take to accumulate $5,000 in a sinking fund that pays 6% interest.

13. Margaret Tanner anticipates a big rebate on her taxes. She needs $50,000 at the present time and is going to take a loan where the monthly payments are possible even if the rebate does not materialize. Her options for the loan are:

   a. Amortized loan at 8% interest for 5 years.

   b. Demand loan with add-on interest, 8% for 5 years.

   c. Demand loan with level interest, 8% for 5 years.

   d. Loan for 8% for 5 years, interest due monthly. A sinking fund for the face value of the loan at 6% interest.

   After 9 months, the tax rebate comes through. What is the cost of each loan if the loans can all be repaid without penalty at the time of the rebate?

14. Find the yield rate of a 9% bond with a face value of $1,000. The interest payment is semiannual, and the bond is quoted at $92.

15. Find the discount on a $1,000, 6% bond maturing on January 1, 2000, if on January 1, 1990, a yield of 7% interest, compounded semiannually, is desired. Find the value of the bond.

Answers to Review Exercises

1. Monthly payment, $158.75. Effective rate, 17.5%.

2. Monthly payment, $158.75. Effective rate, 17.5%. Interest/payment $33.75.

3. Monthly payment, $280. Principal, first payment, $223.16. Effective rate, 15.16%.

4. Monthly payment, $124.43. Effective rate, 9.5%.

5. $2,240, balance.

6. $1,999.96, balance.

7. $2,115.16, balance.

8. $2,059.86, balance.

9.
Payment Number	Balance Due	Interest	Payment	Amount to Principal
1	$10,000.00	$200.00	$611.57	$411.57
2	9,588.43	191.77	611.57	419.80
3	9,268.63	185.37	611.57	426.20
4	8,842.43	176.85	611.57	434.72
5	8,407.70			

10. Monthly payment, $1,046.61.

11. Balance, $63,971.25.

12. 19 payments gives $4,969.93. 20 payments gives $5,244.78.

13. (a) $2,835.70. (b) $20,000. (c) $3,000.00. (d) $2,869.49.

14. 9.8%.

15. Discount, $71.06. Value, $928.94.

Chapter 5

ACCOUNTING COMPUTATIONS

Many practices in business do not enhance the business or create new business, but are necessary to give a quantitative picture and description of the activity of the business. The federal government requires accountability in all areas. A prudent executive evaluates business activity by this type of accountability.

Depreciation, overhead expense, inventory, inventory turnover, and capitalized cost are items necessary to the accounting of a business. The way these items are costed to accounts determines the profitability and tax obligations of the business.

At the end of this chapter, the student will be able to:

1. Define the terminology and identify the elements of depreciation, overhead, inventory, inventory turnover, and capitalized cost.

2. Calculate depreciation by the ACRS, straight-line, declining-balance, and sum-of-the-digits methods.

3. Compare the different methods of depreciation by the amount allowed per year, present value of each depreciation method, and total depreciation charges allowed.

4. Calculate overhead distribution by area of floor space, net sales, and number of employees per department.

5. Determine inventory turnover based on average inventory value, FIFO inventory value, and LIFO inventory value.

6. Use calculated capitalized cost numbers in making business decisions advantageous to the company.

5.1   DEPRECIATION

The fixed assets of a business are its buildings, equipment, and properties expected to last more than 1 year but property that loses value yearly. A building deteriorates and will eventually have to be replaced. The land occupied by the building does not lose value and is not considered a fixed asset.

Depreciation is an expense allowed businesses to help in recovering capital. The expense is often called cost recovery instead of depreciation. The two terms mean the same thing. Depreciation is a tax-deductible expense for a business. Therefore the Internal Revenue Service regulates the method used in depreciating fixed assets when the calculated amount is used for tax purposes.

Prior to the 1981 tax revision, depreciation could be deducted at the rate the fixed asset decreased in value. No book value below the fair market value was allowed, book value indicating the value of the asset as shown on the balance sheet.

Under the Economic Recovery Act, items were categorized and cost recovery was allowed at a rate and time prescribed by the government. The book value under the accelerated-cost-recovery-system (ACRS) method of calculation often does not reflect the actual market value of the item. Accounting procedures employ other methods of calculating depreciation to determine a more realistic book value. Several terms are used in depreciation or cost recovery problems. These include:

Original cost of asset, denoted C.

Scrap value or the value of an asset of the end of its useful life, denoted S.

Useful life or the number of years of service expected, denoted n.

Periodic depreciation charge, which is usually yearly and not necessarily equal, denoted R_n, where n indicates the year of depreciation.

Total depreciation, or the sum of the yearly depreciations: $R_1 + R_2 + R_3 + \cdots$.

Book value, or the difference between the original cost and all periodic depreciation charges. $V = C - R_1 - R_2 \cdots$.

The main concern in this section is the calculation of the periodic depreciation charge. Four methods are presented.

Accelerated-Cost-Recovery-System Method

The accelerated-cost-recovery-system (ACRS) is the method prescribed in the 1981 legislation, and it is supposed to simplify and standardize depreciation. In 1987, new laws modified some accelerated writeoff advantages; the new laws are called the "modified ACRS" or MACRS.

There are five "useful life" periods—3-, 5-, 7-, 10-, and 15-class life—and items are grouped in categories by rules prescribed by the legislation. Some examples of items in each category are

3 years—experimental equipment, devices for the manufacture of food and beverages, and special tools

5 years—computers, copiers, cars, trailers, and cargo containers

7 years—office fixtures and furniture, railroad tracks, and agricultural structures

10 years—vessels and water transportation equipment and assets used in petroleum refining

15 years—municipal sewage treatment plants and telephone distribution plants.

The 1981 rate percentages are replaced with a double-declining method for business equipment in the three, five, seven, and ten year classes, and limits on depreciation of realty to straight line.

To calculate depreciation by the double declining method, follow this procedure:

1. Multiply 100% by 2.

2. Divide product by number of years to be depreciated.

3. Multiply the rate by yearly asset value to obtain depreciation. Asset value decreases by the amount of depreciation each year.

Exception: Under the half-year convention, all property acquired during a year, regardless of the acquisition date, is treated as acquired in the middle of the year and only one-half of the first-year depreciation is deductible.

Example
The 5-year category items have a cost of $15,000. Determine the book value,

the periodic depreciation charge, and the Modified Accelerated Cost Recovery using the double-declining balance method of calculation.

A table will help show the organization.

Year	C	%	R	MACR	V
0	15,000				$15,000
1	15,000	20	$3,000	$ 3,000	12,000
2	12,000	40	4,800	7,800	7,200
3	7,200	40	2,880	8,680	4,300
4	4,300	40	1,720	12,400	2,580
5	2,580	40	1,032	13,432	1,568
6	1,568		1,568	15,000	

Straight-Line Method

The method of depreciation that divides the amount evenly over the useful life of the asset is called the straight-line method of depreciation.

$$R = (C - S)/n$$

This periodic depreciation amount is found by subtracting the scrap value from the cost and dividing that amount by the number of years of useful life.

Example

A construction company buys a road grader for $150,000. The useful life of a grader is 12 years, and the scrap value of the equipment is $25,000. Find the periodic depreciation charge using the straight-line method.

$$R = \frac{(150,000 - 25,000)}{12} = \$10,416.67$$

Depreciation Schedule

Year	C − S	R	V
1	$125,000	$10,416.67	$139,583.33
2	125,000	10,416.67	129,166.66
3	125,000	10,416.67	118,749.99
⋮	⋮	⋮	⋮
12	125,000	10,416.67	25,000.00

The straight-line method is an acceptable accounting process but cannot be used for tax purposes. On the straight-line method, the asset must be given a scrap value. In the MACRS method all asset costs can be deducted and the final value is zero.

Declining-Balance Method

The key to the declining balance method is the use of the same rate (percent) each year. The rate is applied to the yearly book value of the asset. The book value is constantly decreasing. Therefore the periodic depreciation charge decreases as the years of use increase.

   If the scrap value exceeds the book value, no more depreciation can be taken on the item. Sometimes the declining balance method is changed to the straight line method of depreciation part way through the useful life of the item. The high initial depreciation charge is used as an accounting advantage; then the method of calculation is altered.

   The rate used in the declining-balance method is determined by taking the reciprocal of n, the years of useful life, multiplying by 2, and converting to a percent.

Example

The useful life is 8 years. Find the rate for the declining-balance method.

$$\text{Reciprocal of } 8 = \frac{1}{8}.$$

$$\text{Multiply by } 2 = 2\left(\frac{1}{8}\right) = \frac{1}{4}.$$

$$\text{Convert } \frac{1}{4} \text{ to percent} = \frac{1}{4} \times 100 = 25\%.$$

Example

A new automobile costing \$12,500 has an expected life of 4 years. Prepare a depreciation schedule by the declining-value method.

$$\text{Reciprocal of } 4 = \frac{1}{4}.$$

$$\text{Multiply by } 2 = 2\left(\frac{1}{4}\right) = \frac{1}{2}.$$

$$\text{Convert } \frac{1}{2} \text{ to percent} = \frac{1}{2} \times 100 = 50\%.$$

Year	Book Value	%	R
0	$12,500.00		
1	12,500.00	50	$6,250.00
2	6,250.00	50	3,125.00
3	3,125.00	50	1,562.50
4	1,562.50	50	781.25
	781.25		

The declining balance reflects a more realistic method of determining the book value. Machinery and equipment undergo the greatest depreciation in the early years. The book value under this method more closely resembles actual value and is useful in determining asset value. The method is not acceptable for determining depreciation as a business expense under the current tax laws because the first year depreciation is twice the allowable amount under MACRS.

Sum-of-the-Digits Method

The sum-of-the-digits method provides for large depreciation allowances at the early part of the useful life of an asset.

The steps involved in the sum-of-the-digits method are:

1. Add the digits of all of the useful years of the asset.

$$5 \text{ useful years:} \quad 1 + 2 + 3 + 4 + 5 = 15$$
$$10 \text{ useful years:} \quad 1 + 2 + 3 + \cdots + 9 + 10 = 55$$

2. The years' digits, taken in reverse order, is the numerator of a fraction; the sum of the digits is the denominator.

3. The fraction or equivalent percent multiplies the difference between the cost and scrap value of the item. The result is the periodic depreciation.

Example
The $12,500 automobile has an expected useful life of 4 years, and the value at the end of four years is $2,000. Prepare the depreciation schedule using the sum-of-the-digits method.

1. $1 + 2 + 3 + 4 = 10$

2. First year: $\dfrac{4}{10}$ or 40%

    Second year: $\dfrac{3}{10}$ or 30%

    Third year: $\dfrac{2}{10}$ or 20%

    Fourth year: $\dfrac{1}{10}$ or 10%

3. $12,500 - 2,000 = 10,500$

Year	B	%		R
1	$12,500	40	0.40 (10,500)	$4,200
2	8,300	30	0.30 (10,500)	3,150
3	5,150	20	0.20 (10,500)	2,100
4	3,050	10	0.10 (10,500)	1,050
Scrap value	$ 2,000			

In the declining balance method and MACRS, the base changed yearly, and the rate remained constant throughout. In the sum-of-the-digits method, the base stays constant, and the rate changes each year. Both methods give a large depreciation early in the useful life.

Depletion is a term meaning the reduction of a resource. It applies to resources such as timber, coal, or oil. The income from such resources should produce income that pays a return on investment and also recovers the cost of the exhausted resource.

Example

Suppose a track of timber is purchased for $60,000. An annual return of $10,000 over operating cost is expected for the next 10 years. At that time it is expected that the land can be sold for $15,000. The actual loss in the value of the track of timber is $45,000. This amount should be recovered by making periodic deposits to a sinking fund over the 10 years. For this example, assume the rate of the sinking fund is 6%.

$$\$45,000 = R \cdot s_{\overline{10}|\,6\%}$$
$$= R(13.181)$$
$$R = \$3,414$$

This amount should be deducted from the annual return of $10,000 to obtain the net return of the business venture.

$$\text{Net return} = \$10,000 - \$3,414 = \$6,586$$

The annual rate of return on the investment of $60,000 is

$$\text{Annual rate of return} = \$6,586/60,000 \times 100 = 10.97\% \text{ or about } 11\%.$$

This procedure is used to determine the purchase price of a natural resource so a predicted yield is realized.

SECTION 1 EXERCISES

1. A company has yearly expenses including experimental equipment costing $160,000. Using the MACRS method, determine the category this equipment falls into, the periodic depreciation charge, the accumulated cost recovery, and the book value for the entire life of the equipment.

2. Carolina Transportation Company just laid new railroad tracks this year at a cost of $5,000,000. The equipment is to be depreciated under the MACRS plan. Find the periodic depreciation charge, the accumulated cost recovery, and the book value for each year of the first 5 years.

3. Lem's Construction Company just bought grading machinery for $225,000. The projected life of the equipment is 15 years, and the anticipated scrap value is $50,000. Find the periodic depreciation charge using the straight-line method of depreciation. Find the book value after 3 years.

4. A textile firm replaces looms at a cost of $750,000. The projected life of the new equipment is 9 years with a scrap value of $50,000. Find the periodic depreciation charge using the straight line method of depreciation. Find the book value after 5 years.

5. Abis Car Rental Agency buys a new fleet of automobiles for $180,000. The useful life of the automobiles is 4 years, and the scrap value is projected to be $18,000. Prepare the depreciation schedule using the sum-of-the-digits method of depreciation.

6. A fleet of trucks for the highway department is purchased for $120,000. The useful life of the trucks is 5 years, and the scrap value is $6,000. Pre-

pare the depreciation schedule using the sum-of-the-digits method of depreciation.

7. The furniture of Parks Hospital cost $420,000. The useful life of the furnishings is projected to be 6 years. Prepare the depreciation schedule for the furniture by the declining-balance method. Find the book value after 3 years.

8. The lockers in a school building cost $52,000. The projected useful life of the lockers is 10 years. Prepare a depreciation schedule for the lockers by the declining-balance method. Find the book value after 5 years.

9. An apartment building cost $275,000. Compute the first 5 years' depreciation schedule under the MACRS method. The projected life of the building is 25 years with no scrap value. Determine the first 5 years' depreciation schedule under the straight-line method, the declining-value method, and the sum-of-the-digits method. Compare the book values at the end of 5 years under each method.

10. A mobile home was purchased and adapted to an office. The cost was $42,000. The projected useful life of the structure is 5 years, and the scrap value is $2,000. Prepare the first 2 years' depreciation schedule for the mobile home under the MACRS method, the straight-line method, the declining-balance method, and the sum-of-the-digits method. Compare the book value of the mobile home at the end of 2 years under each of the methods.

11. Copy Kat paid $11,500 for a high-speed copier that prints on both sides of the paper in two colors, collates, and staples the reports. The heavy demand will make the useful life of the equipment 5 years. The scrap value of the equipment after 5 years is $1,000. Find the amount of depreciation during the first year by all four methods and the book value of the equipment after 2 years.

12. Longer Processing buys computer equipment and software for $225,000. The equipment will be worth about $25,000 on a trade-in 5 years from now. Prepare a straight-line and a declining balance depreciation schedule for 2 years. If Longer Processing projects it will need a tax write-off 3 and 4 years from present, which method would provide the higher depreciation charge during that period?

13. A $24,000 automobile is depreciated over 4 years. The scrap value of the auto is $4,000. Determine the annual depreciation for each of the 4 years if the declining-balance method of depreciation is used.

14. A racing sailboat is purchased for $135,000. The useful life of the boat as a racer is 3 years. The scrap value of the boat at that time is $25,000. Determine the depreciation charge for each of the 3 years if the sum-of-digits method of depreciation is used.

15. An oil well is purchased for $150,000. It is estimated the annual income after expenses will be $20,000 and that the resource will last for 15 years. At that time the value of the well will be $5,000. A sinking fund is established at 8%; determine the net return on the investment and the annual rate of return.

16. A gold mine is purchased for $120,000. It is estimated the income from the mining operation will be $25,000 and that the resource will be exhausted in 10 years. At that time the value of the land will be $5,000. A sinking fund is established at an annual rate of 7% interest. Determine the net return on the investment and the annual rate of return on the investment.

Answers to Odd-Numbered Exercises

1. 3-year category.

Yr	Cost	Rate (%)	Depreciation	MACRS	Book Value
1	$160,000	33 1/3	$53,333	$ 53,333	$106,667
2	106,667	66 2/3	71,111	124,444	35,556
3	35,556	66 2/3	23,704	148,148	11,852
4	11,852		11,852	160,000	0

3. Depreciation charge = $(225,000 - 50,000)/15 = \$11,666.67$.
   Book value after 3 years = $225,000 - 3(11,667.67) = \$190,000$.

5. Sum of the digits = 10. $180,000 - $18,000 = $162,000, amount to be depreciated.

Year	Ratio	Amount to Depreciate	Depreciation	Book Value
1	4/10	$162,000	$64,800	$115,200
2	3/10	162,000	48,600	66,600
3	2/10	162,000	32,400	34,200
4	1/10	162,000	16,200	18,000

7. $(1/6)(2) = 1/3$, common ratio.

Year	Book Value	Ratio	Depreciation
1	$420,000	1/3	$140,000
2	280,000	1/3	93,333

Year	Book Value	Ratio	Depreciation
3	186,667	1/3	62,222
4	124,445	1/3	41,482
5	82,963	1/3	27,654
6	55,309	1/3	18,436
	36,873		

Book value after 5 years $55,309.

9. MACRS method: real estate cannot be depreciated.
   Straight line 275,000/25 = 11,000 annual depreciation

Year	Cost	Depreciation	Book Value
1	$275,000	11,000	$264,000
2	275,000	11,000	253,000
3	275,000	11,000	242,000
4	275,000	11,000	231,000
5	275,000	11,000	220,000

Declining-balance method [ratio, $(1/25)(2) = 8\%$]:

Year	Book Value	Ratio	Depreciation
1	$275,000.00	0.08	$22,000.00
2	253,000.00	0.08	20,240.00
3	232,760.00	0.08	18,620.80
4	214,139.20	0.08	17,131.14
5	197,008.06	0.08	15,760.65
	181,247.41		

Sum-of-the-digits method [$1 + 2 + 3 + \cdots + 25 = 325$]:

Year	Cost	Ratio	Depreciation	Book Value
1	$275,000	25/325	$21,153.85	$253,846.15
2	275,000	24/325	20,307.69	233,538.46
3	275,000	23/325	19,461.54	214,076.92
4	275,000	22/325	18,615.38	195,461.54
5	275,000	21/325	17,769.23	177,692.31

Book Values after 5 years: ACRS, $167,750; sum-of-the-digits, $177,692; declining balance, $181,247; straight-line, $220,000.

11. MACRS method:

Year	Cost	Rate (%)	Depreciation	MACRS	Book Value
1	$11,500	33$\frac{1}{3}$	$3,833.33	$3,833.33	$7,666.67
2	7,666.67	66$\frac{2}{3}$	5,111	8,944.44	2,555.55

straight-line method $[(11{,}500 - 1{,}000)/3 = \$3{,}500]$:

Year	Cost	Depreciation	Book Value
1	\$11,500	\$3,500	\$8,000
2	11,500	3,500	4,500

sum-of-the-digits method $[1 + 2 + 3 = 6 \; C - S = 10{,}500]$:

Year	Cost	Ratio	$C - S$	Depreciation	Book Value
1	\$11,500	3/6	\$10,500	\$5,250	\$6,250
2	11,500	2/6	10,500	3,500	2,750

declining-balance method [ratio, $(1/3)(2) = 2/3$]:

Year	Book Value	Ratio	Depreciation
1	\$11,500	2/3	\$7,666.67
2	3,833.33	2/3	2,555.56
3	1,277.77		

13. Ratio $(1/4)(2) = 1/2$

Year	Book Value	Ratio	Depreciation
1	\$24,000	1/2	\$12,000
2	12,000	1/2	6,000
3	6,000	1/2	3,000*

*Only \$2,000 can be taken because book value cannot be less than \$4,000 scrap value.

15. Depletion $\$150{,}000 - \$5{,}000 = \$145{,}000$.

$$145{,}000 = R \cdot s_{\overline{15}|\,8\%}$$

$$145{,}000 = R(27.152{,}114)$$

$$5{,}340.28 = R$$

$$20{,}000 - R = \$14{,}659.72$$

$$14{,}659.72/150{,}000 = 0.098 = 9.8\% \text{ rate of return}$$

5.2 COMPARISON OF DEPRECIATION METHODS

The objective of depreciation is the recovery of the initial investment. All the different methods eventually recover the entire asset. The rate of the recovery changes at different periods of the asset life.

To illustrate the different recovery rates, a problem is worked, using all four methods.

Example

An asset of $10,000 is to be depreciated over 5 years, and the scrap value is $1,000.

Year	ACRS	Straight Line	Declining Balance	Sum of the Digits
1	$ 2,000	$ 1,800	$4,000.00	$ 3,000
2	3,200	1,800	2,400.00	2,400
3	1,920	1,800	1,440.00	1,800
4	1,152	1,800	864.00	1,200
5	691	1,800	518.40	600
	1,036.80	1,000		1,000
Total	$10,000	$10,000	$9,233.40	$10,000

The preceding table can be explained as follows.

The amount to be depreciated is $10,000 - $1,000 = $9,000.

The rate under MACRS is 40% of the declining balance except for year 1 when the rate is 20%.

The rate under the straight-line method is $100\%/5 = 20\%$, which is applied to (cost - scrap value).

The rate under the declining-balance method is (1/5)(2) or 40%, applied to the asset value.

The rates under the sum-of-the-digits method are determined by the fractions 5/15, 4/15, 3/15, 2/15, and 1/15 and are applied to $(C - S)$.

Each year there is a different recovery rate, and the total of the recoveries (plus salvage value) is the initial asset except in the declining-balance method. To compare these different yearly amounts, the present value of each amount of depreciation is calculated, present value being the time of purchase. If the rate that money earns interest is 8%, apply the present value of the rate to each amount of depreciation to determine the present values of each of the entries in the depreciation table. The rates come from Table 2, rate 8%, column 4, Present Value. The numbers have been rounded to three decimal places, which gives sufficient accuracy for this example.

Year	Rate	MACRS	Straight Line	Declining Balance	Sum of the Digits
1	0.926	$1,852.00	$1,667	$3,704	$2,778
2	0.857	2,742.40	1,543	2,057	2,057
3	0.794	1,524.48	1,429	1,143	1,429
4	0.735	846.72	1,323	635	882
5	0.681	470.57	1,226	353	409
		706.06	681		681
Total		$8,142.23	$7,869	$7,892	$8,236

The total present values of each of the depreciation amounts differ. The sum-of-the-digits depreciation amounts have the greatest present value.

Income tax specialists should consider all methods of depreciation and determine the schedule most advantageous for the accounting practices of the business.

To compare the present value of the depreciation methods:

1. Determine the depreciation amount for each year using each method.

2. Determine the present value of money using the Present Value column of Table 2 for the annual rate of money.

3. Apply the yearly present-value rate to each of the entries of that year.

4. Apply the present-value rate to the scrap value of the asset under each method of calculation.

5. Total the present values under each method and make the comparisons.

SECTION 2 EXERCISES

1. A woman purchases a condominium and plans to rent the unit for several years. She buys furnishings at a cost of $15,000. At the end of 5 years, she plans to replace everything. There is no scrap value. Find the depreciation charge under each of the four methods. Find the present value at an 8% rate of depreciation under each of the four methods of computation.

2. A salesperson buys an automobile for $13,500. The salesperson plans to trade for a new vehicle in 3 years and anticipates the trade-in value of the present vehicle will be $4,500. Find the depreciation charges under each of the four methods and determine the total of the present values at a 7% rate under each method.

3. The city of Northville buys a fleet of 10 pickup trucks at a cost of $5,500 each. The city will run the trucks for 3 years and trade them. A trade-in of $1,000 per truck is anticipated. Find the depreciation charges under each of the four methods and determine the total present values under each method.

4. A doctor redecorates the waiting rooms of the office; the total cost of the new furnishings is $7,500. The doctor anticipates the furnishings will last 5 years and there will be no value of the furnishings at the end of 5 years. Find the depreciation charges under each of the four methods and determine the total present values at a 9% rate under each method.

Answers to Odd-Numbered Exercises

1. Depreciation:

Year	MACRS	Straight Line	Declining Balance	Sum of the Digits
1	$3,000	$3,000	$6,000	$5,000
2	4,800	3,000	3,600	4,000
3	2,880	3,000	2,160	3,000
4	1,728	3,000	1,296	2,000
5	1,037	3,000	777.60	1,000

Present value of depreciation:

Year	Factor	MACRS	Straight Line	Declining Balance	Sum of the Digits
1	.926	$ 2,778	$ 2,778	$ 5,556	$ 4,630
2	.857	4,113.60	2,571	3,085.20	3,428
3	.794	2,286.72	2,382	1,715.04	2,382
4	.735	1,270.08	2,205	952.56	1,470
5	.681	1,058.96	2,043	529.55	681
	Total	$11,507.36	$11,979	$11,838.35	$12,591

3. Depreciation $C = 55,000 \ S = 10,000$

Year	MACRS	Straight Line	Declining Balance	Sum of the Digits
1	$18,333	$15,000	$36,667	$22,500
2	24,444	15,000	8,333	15,000
3	2,223	15,000	0	7,500

Present value of depreciation:

Year	Factor	MACRS	Straight Line	Declining Balance	Sum of the Digits
1	.943	$17,288	$14,145	$34,577	$21,217.50
2	.890	21,755	13,350	7,416	13,350
3	.840	1,867	12,600	0	6,300
Scrap	.840	8,400	8,400	8,400	8,400
	Total	$49,310.56	$48,495	$50,393	$49,267.50

5.3 OVERHEAD

The previous sections have addressed how a capital expenditure is recovered over a number of years. Another expense that needs to be recovered by a business is **overhead** expense. **Overhead** expense is a collective term referring to the operating expenses of a business. Salaries, rent, utilities, taxes, depreciation, and insurance are all examples of expenses included in the general term of overhead.

Overhead is included in the total cost of the product, and each process or department is charged with a proportional part of the total. The three methods for distributing overhead charges to departments are:

1. According to floor space

2. According to total sales

3. According to the number of employees in the department

Example
The monthly overhead of $68,000 at Goldilock's Dress Company is distributed according to the floor space of each department. The floor space of each department is

Raw materials and cutting	4,000 square feet
Assembly and stitching	7,000 square feet
Finishing, packaging, and shipping	5,000 square feet
Administration	2,000 square feet

Find the distribution of the overhead among the departments.

Solution:
1. Total the department floor space—in this problem the total is 18,000 square feet.

2. Find the ratio of the floor space of each department to the total floor space.

$$\text{Cutting} \qquad \frac{4,000}{18,000} = \frac{4}{18}$$

$$\text{Assembly} \qquad \frac{7,000}{18,000} = \frac{7}{18}$$

$$\text{Finishing} \qquad \frac{5,000}{18,000} = \frac{5}{18}$$

$$\text{Administration} \qquad \frac{2,000}{18,000} = \frac{2}{18}$$

3. Apply the ratio to the total overhead charges to find the individual department charges or change the ratio to a percent and apply the percent to the total overhead charges.

$$\text{Cutting} \qquad (4/18)(68,000) = \$15,111.11$$

or

$$(4/18)(100) = 22.2\% \quad \text{of} \quad 68,000 = \$15,096$$

Assembly $(7/18)(68,000) = \$26,444.44$
Finishing $(5/18)(68,000) = \$18,888.89$
Administration $(2/18)(68,000) = \$ 7,555.56$

Example
The monthly overhead charges of $52,000 are distributed to departments according to net sales. Flavor Food Mart has monthly sales as follows.

Meats	$112,000
Produce	32,000
Frozen foods	74,000
Deli	56,000
Groceries	276,000

Distribute the overhead expense according to the total monthly sales.

Solution:
1. Total the department sales—$550,000.

2. Determine the ratio of the department sales to the total sales.

Meats $\dfrac{112,000}{550,000} = \dfrac{112}{550}$

Produce $\dfrac{32,000}{550,000} = \dfrac{32}{550}$

Frozen foods $\dfrac{74,000}{550,000} = \dfrac{74}{550}$

Deli $\dfrac{56,000}{550,000} = \dfrac{56}{550}$

Groceries $\dfrac{276,000}{550,000} = \dfrac{276}{550}$

3. Apply each ratio to the total overhead expense to determine the part of the overhead charge for each department.

Meats $\quad (112/550)(52,000) = \$10,589.09$
Produce $\quad (32/550)(52,000) = \$\ 3,025.45$
Frozen foods $\quad (74/550)(52,000) = \$\ 6,996.36$
Deli $\quad (56/550)(52,000) = \$\ 5,294.55$
Groceries $\quad (276/550)(52,000) = \$26,094.55$

Notice the sum of the department charges is equal to the total overhead expense. This is a quick check on the accuracy of the calculations.

Example
Albany Weave Company makes fabric used to cover the core of tennis balls. The monthly overhead charge of $74,000 is allocated to departments according to the number of employees in each department.

The number of employees by department is

Spinning $\quad$ 23 employees
Weaving $\quad$ 42 employees
Finishing $\quad$ 19 employees
Management $\quad$ 6 employees

1. Total the number of employees—90.

2. Form the ratio of the number of employees in a department to the total number of employees.

Spinning $\qquad \dfrac{23}{90}$

Weaving $\qquad \dfrac{42}{90}$

$$\text{Finishing} \quad \frac{19}{90}$$

$$\text{Management} \quad \frac{6}{90}$$

3. Apply each ratio to the total overhead charges.

Spinning   (23/90)(74,000) = $18,911.11
Weaving   (42/90)(74,000) = $34,533.34
Finishing   (19/90)(74,000) = $15,622.22
Management   (6/90)(74,000) = $ 4,933.34

Notice in all three methods of distributing overhead, a ratio is formed between the area, sales, and number of employees, and the total area, total sales, and total number of employees of the company. The allocation of overhead to any department is then determined by multiplying the determined ratio and the total overhead expense.

Instead of using a ratio, the percent for each department could be determined. Then use the percent to multiply the total overhead to determine the share of the overhead for each department.

Example

Dr. J, Dr. K, and Dr. M share an office building. They agree to distribute the overhead of the building by the number of square feet each doctor occupies. The overhead expense for October is $8,540. The floor space allocation for each doctor is

Dr. J   30,000 square feet
Dr. K   22,000 square feet
Dr. M   18,000 square feet

The total floor space is 70,000 square feet. The percentage used by each doctor is

Dr. J   (30,000/70,000) × 100 = 42.86%
Dr. K   (22,000/70,000) × 100 = 31.43%
Dr. M   (18,000/70,000) × 100 = 25.71%

The overhead allocations are

Dr. J = (0.4286)(8,540) = $3,660.24
Dr. K = (0.3143)(8,540) = $2,684.12
Dr. M = (0.2571)(8,540) = $2,195.64

SECTION 3 EXERCISES

1. Guarantee Auto Garage has monthly overhead charges of $4,860. The overhead charges are allocated according to the floor space of each department. The floor space used by each department is

Front-end alignments	3,100 square feet
Engine overhaul	1,800 square feet
Electrical service	1,200 square feet
Body repair and painting	3,900 square feet
Management and office	600 square feet

Determine the monthly overhead charges of each department.

2. Safe Drug Store has monthly overhead charges of $4,200. The overhead charges are allocated according to the floor space occupied by each department. The floor space used by each department is

Prescription drugs	600 square feet
Cosmetics	700 square feet
Generic drugs	550 square feet
Housewares	750 square feet

Determine the monthly overhead charges of each department.

3. Prompt Food Mart has monthly overhead charges of $3,800. The overhead charges are allocated according to the total sales of each department. The monthly sales are

Produce	$ 21,000
Meats	123,000
Frozen foods	36,000
Groceries	183,000
Deli	32,000

Determine the monthly overhead charges of each department.

4. Franklin's Department Store has a monthly overhead expense of $38,000. The overhead expense is allocated to departments according to total sales. The monthly sales are

Lingerie	$ 65,000
Ladies apparel	352,000
Men's shop	179,000
Shoe department	221,000
Housewares	33,000

Determine the monthly overhead charges of each department.

5. Jack's Machine Company charges off the monthly overhead expense according to the number of employees in each department. The monthly overhead expenses are $6,500. The number of employees in each department are

Grinding	2 employees
Tooling	3 employees
Polishing	1 employee
Management	1 employee

Allocate the monthly overhead charge to each of the departments.

6. Fast Print Company charges monthly overhead expenses of $23,000 according to the number of employees in each department. The number of employees are

Typesetting	8 employees
Printing	11 employees
Cutting and collating	6 employees
Management and office	2 employees

Allocate the monthly overhead charges to each of the departments.

7. As a department manager, you have an opportunity to recommend the method of allocating overhead. Your department occupies 3,500 square feet of a total of 250,000 square feet. Your sales are $415,000 of a total of $3,500,000. The number of employees in your department is 20 out of a total number of 157 employees. If you wish to have the smallest overhead charge, which method would you select?

8. A bakery has an overhead expense of $5,600 per month. As the department manager of baking, you would like to be charged the smallest possible overhead charge. Your department has 2 employees out of a total of 11, and the floor space occupied by the bakery department is 4,700 square feet out of a total of 25,000 square feet. The concept of net sales does not apply to this business. Which method of determining overhead expense would you choose?

Answers to Odd-Numbered Exercises

1. Total floor space, 10,600 square feet.

Front-end alignments	$1,421.32
Engine overhaul	825.28
Electrical service	550.19

Body repair and painting   1,788.11
Management and office   275.09

3. Total sales, $395,000.

Produce	$ 202.03
Meats	1,183.29
Frozen foods	346.33
Groceries	1,760.51
Deli	307.85

5. Total number of employees, 7.

Grinding	$1,857.14
Tooling	2,785.71
Polishing	928.57
Management	928.57

7. Area, 1.4%. Sales, 11.86%. Employees, 12.74%. Allocate by area.

5.4 INVENTORY

A key indicator of the activity of a business is the number of times the inventory is sold in a year—the number indicating the number of times inventory is sold is inventory turnover. The expected inventory turnover depends on the type of business—a florist would have a much higher inventory turnover than a furniture dealer.

To determine the inventory turnover, a value for inventory must be determined.

Perpetual inventory is kept by large companies through the use of a computer. As items are received, the quantity and cost are entered into the computer. At the time of a sale, the product code is entered into the computer (codes are automatically entered by an optical scanner). The computer alters the current inventory as well as displaying the price for sales.

Uniform product codes (UPC) are used by many retailers. These codes consist of a series of lines with printed numbers heading each line. Each product and product size has a unique code number. The scanner at the check-out counter records the code. The code is picked up by the computer, the price of the item is communicated, and the inventory is updated. The system provides more accurate inventory control, produces more accurate charges, especially for sale items, and results in lower labor costs at the store. The system is especially useful for retail establishments with more than one store.

Most businesses take a physical inventory (an actual count of items in stock) periodically. Even perpetual inventories must be checked occasionally for accuracy. If shoplifting is suspected in a store, the extent can be evaluated by taking a physical inventory and comparing the numbers with the perpetual inventory.

The quantity of an item is used to determine a value for the inventory. Inventory is more frequently computed at retail value than at cost. Many stores mark their items with only the retail price. It is impossible to take inventory at cost. Another reason for valuing inventory at retail prices is the consideration of reduced prices and the loss of goods (shoplifting). If merchandise is sold at regular prices, turnover is the same whether calculated on cost or retail prices. Generally, inventory turnover is smaller when figured on retail.

$$\text{Inventory turnover} = \text{net sales/average inventory value}$$

or

$$\text{Inventory turnover} = \text{cost of goods sold/average inventory value}$$

Average annual inventory is the average of the periodic inventories.

Example

Good Reading Bookstore had an inventory of $25,125 on January 31, an inventory of $36,850 on May 30, and an inventory of $28,450 on September 30. Find the average inventory and the rate of turnover for the year if the net sales for the year were $112,250. All inventories are based on retail prices.

$25,125   periodic inventories
 36,850
 28,450
─────────
$90,425 $90,425/3 = $30,141.66   average inventory

Inventory turnover = net sales inventory

$$\frac{112,250}{30,141.66} = 3.72$$

The inventory turnover of 3.72 indicates each book was sold an average of 3.72 times during the year. The inventory valuation was used without consideration of the process for determining the value of the inventory. If a perpetual inventory is kept, the new items received have a UPC code, subsequent sales are recorded, and the computer keeps an exact count and value of the inventory. The value of the inventory depends upon the inventory valuation method used.

The **average-cost method** involves finding the average cost of an item over the inventory period and multiplying the number of items by the average cost. The average cost is a weighted average. That is, the number of items purchased at each cost is considered as well as the price.

Example

In January, 25 refrigerators were purchased at $450 each; in April an additional 30 refrigerators were purchased at $470 each; and in September, 40 refrigerators were purchased at $460 each. To determine the average cost:

$$
\begin{array}{lll}
\text{January} & 25 \times 450 = \$11,250 \\
\text{April} & 30 \times 470 = \$14,100 \\
\text{September} & \underline{40} \times 460 = \underline{\$18,400} \\
\text{Total} & 95 & \$43,750
\end{array}
$$

The average cost per refrigerator is

$$\frac{43,750}{95} = \$460.53$$

If there were 18 refrigerators in inventory on December 31, the inventory value is

$$460.53 \times 18 = \$8,289.54$$

The inventory value by the average-cost method is $8,289.54.

The first-in, first-out (FIFO) method of inventory valuation assumes the first items in are the first items sold. Therefore the last items purchased are the items remaining at the time of inventory. The value of the items purchased most recently is used to determine the inventory valuation.

In the preceding example, there were 18 refrigerators at the time of inventory. Because 40 refrigerators were purchased in September, the FIFO method of valuation would consider all 18 in inventory were from the September purchase. Therefore the inventory value is

$$18 \times 460 = \$8,280$$

Notice this valuation is slightly less than the valuation under the average-cost method.

The last-in, first-out (LIFO) method of inventory valuation assumes the goods in inventory at the end of a period are the first items purchased during the period. Once again, if we look at the refrigerators purchased, the 18 in inventory would be considered the refrigerators purchased in January. Therefore the inventory valuation under the LIFO method is

$$18 \times 450 = \$8,100$$

This method appears to be contrary to most sales practices; however, the method can be justified from an accounting viewpoint.

The most popular method of determining the inventory valuation is FIFO. All reporting statements must specify the method used to evaluate the inventory.

Example

A carpet company takes inventory and has 2,540 square yards of carpet on December 31. The following purchases had been made during the year: 1,500 square yards in February at $9 per square yard, 2,400 square yards in May at $8.50 per square yard, 1,800 square yards in September at $9.25 per square yard, and 2,000 square yards in December at $8.75 per square yard. Find the inventory value by the following methods:

a. Weighted average

b. FIFO

c. LIFO

Weighted-average method:

February	1,500 @ $9.00 =	$13,500
May	2,400 @ $8.50 =	$20,400
September	1,800 @ $9.25 =	$16,650
December	2,000 @ $8.75 =	$17,500
Total	7,700	$68,050

$$\text{Average cost} = \frac{68,050}{7,700} = \$8.84$$

$$2,540 \times 8.84 = \$22,447.66 \qquad \text{inventory value at weighted average}$$

FIFO method:

> 2,520 remaining
> 2,000 @ $8.75 = $17,500
>   520 @ $9.25 = $ 4,810
>   Total $22,310   inventory value FIFO

LIFO method:

> 2,520 remaining
> 1,500 @ $9.00 = $13,500
> 1,020 @ $8.50 = $ 8,670
>   Total $21,170   inventory value LIFO

SECTION 4 EXERCISES

1. Safe Toy Store takes quarterly inventory. The cost of the toys in stock on January 31 was $4,570; on April 30 it was $6,830; on July 31 it was $5,930; and on October 31 it was $9,720. The cost of goods sold for the year was $2,124.780. Find the average inventory valuation and the turnover rate for the store.

2. The Irishman is a fast service store. The inventory was valued at $20,340 on January 31, $27,450 on April 30, $22,350 on July 31, and $25,420 on October 31. The net sales for the Irishman for the year were $623,780. Find the average inventory value and the turnover rate for the store.

3. Comfort Heating and Cooling has in stock 4 heat pumps valued at $2,600 each. During the past year, Comfort has net sales of $36,000. Determine the turnover rate.

4. Gentle Pet, Inc., has an inventory valued at $46,500. During the past year, Gentle Pet has net sales of $18,360. Determine the turnover rate.

5. Fashion Clothes has an inventory valued at $78,500 on January 31, $95,700 on May 30, and $82,300 on September 30. The annual net sales for Fashion Clothes is $380,200. Find the turnover rate.

6. The inventory at an appliance store consists of 14 refrigerators and 19 kitchen ranges. Inventory is valued by the average-cost method. Invoices for the year show 10 refrigerators purchased for $545 each and 7 kitchen ranges purchased for $469 each. A later invoice indicates 32 refrigerators purchased for $515 each and 35 kitchen ranges purchased for $440 each. The latest invoice indicates 35 refrigerators purchased for $525 each and

52 kitchen ranges purchased for $430 each. Find the value of the inventory.

7. A farm equipment sales office has an inventory of 4 tractors and 3 hay balers. During the year, 5 tractors were purchased for $6,300 each, 8 tractors were purchased for $6,650 each, and 10 tractors were purchased for $6,150 each. Only 6 hay balers were purchased, all of them for $3,850 each. Determine the value of the inventory if the farm equipment sales office determines inventory value by the average-cost method.

8. A furniture store takes inventory and finds it has 42 sofas in stock. Invoices for the year indicate the following purchases.

April 20	24 sofas @ $595
June 15	15 sofas @ $615
September 18	30 sofas @ $609
November 15	35 sofas @ $635

Determine the value of the inventory by FIFO and LIFO methods.

9. Use the FIFO method to determine the value of 30 items in inventory if the purchases were

April	25 units @ $52.00
May	42 units @ $49.50
July	20 units @ $48.00

10. Use the LIFO method to determine the value of the items as listed in exercise 9.

11. Computer Terminal has 15 printers in inventory at the end of the year. Purchases of printers during the year are as follows.

March	10 printers at $735.00
July	16 printers at $649.50
September	8 printers at $595.00

Determine the value of the inventory by the average-cost method, the FIFO method, and the LIFO method. Determine the turnover based on cost.

12. A bookstore made the following purchases of calenders, listed in order of purchase: 24 at $3.00 each, 60 at $2.50 each, 36 at $3.75 each, and 18 at $3.20 each. Inventory at the end of the year shows 27 remain. Determine the value of inventory by the average-cost method, the LIFO method, and the FIFO method. Determine the turnover by the FIFO method.

Answers to Odd-Numbered Exercises

1. Average inventory, $6,762.50. Turnover, 314.2 or 31,420%.

3. Inventory, $10,400. Turnover, 3.5 or 350%.

5. 4.45 or 445%.

7. Inventory, $36,976.08.

9. $1,455.

11. Inventory by average cost, $9,927.35. Inventory by FIFO, $9,306.50. Inventory by LIFO, $10,597.50. Turnover, 1.27 or 127%.

5.5 CAPITALIZED COST

An asset such as a building, equipment, or machinery requires renewal or replacement periodically. Depreciation is a way of recovering the cost of an asset over the life of the asset. It is an accounting procedure for keeping a current value of assets and determining the amount of loss in value of assets, which is a legitimate business expense.

Capitalized cost of an asset is the original cost of the asset plus the present value of future replacements. This suggests using an annuity value to determine capitalized cost. Capitalized costs are useful in comparing assets that have different costs, useful life, and cost replacements.

The formula for calculating capitalized cost is

$$K = C + (R/i)(1/s_{\overline{n}|\,i})$$

where K is the capitalized cost, C is the original cost, R is the renewal cost, n is the number of interest periods in useful life, and i is the interest rate per interest period.

Example

An airplane hangar cost $75,000. The hanger must be replaced every 25 years. Money can be invested at 8% interest, compounded semiannually. What is the capitalized cost if the replacement cost is $70,000?

$$C = 75,000 \qquad R = 70,000 \qquad i = 0.04 \qquad n = 50$$

$$s_{\overline{50}|\,0.04} = 152.66708$$

$$K = 75,000 + (70,000/0.04)(1/152.66708)$$
$$= 75,000 + 11,462.85$$
$$= \$86,462.85$$

Example
A machine costing $45,000 has an estimated life of 15 years and an estimated scrap value of $7,000. Find the capitalized cost of the machine if money is worth 6% interest, compounded quarterly, and the replacement cost of the machine is estimated to be the same as the cost today.

$$C = 45,000 \qquad R = 38,000 \ (45,000 - 7,000) \qquad n = 60 \qquad i = 0.015$$
$$K = 45,000 + (38,000/0.015)(1/s_{\overline{60}| \, 0.015})$$
$$= 45,000 + (38,000/0.015)(1/96.21465)$$
$$= 45,000 + 26,330$$
$$= \$71,330$$

Example
The cost of TV Gold is $730 with an estimated life of 8 years. The cost of TV Amber is $570 with an estimated life of 5 years. If money is worth 8% interest, compounded quarterly, which TV is comparatively lower in cost if their replacement costs are the same as the original costs?

TV Gold:

$$C = 730 \qquad R = 730 \qquad n = 32 \qquad i = 0.02$$
$$K = 730 + (730/0.02)(1/s_{\overline{32}| \, 0.02})$$
$$= 730 + (730/0.02)(1/44.22703)$$
$$= 730 + 825.29$$
$$= \$1,555.29$$

TV Amber:

$$C = 570 \qquad R = 570 \qquad n = 20 \qquad i = 0.02$$
$$K = 570 + (570/0.02)(1/s_{\overline{20}| \, 0.02})$$
$$= 570 + (570/0.02)(1/24.29373)$$
$$= 570 + 1,172.97$$
$$= \$1,742.97$$

TV Gold is more economical because the capitalized cost of TV Gold is lower.

SECTION 5 EXERCISES

1. The life of a swimming pool is estimated to be 25 years. The initial cost of the pool is $75,000 with the replacement cost estimated at $50,000. Money can be invested at 6% interest, compounded semiannually. Find the capitalized cost of the pool.

2. The air-conditioning unit for a multibuilding campus cost $100,000 with a replacement cost estimated at $60,000. The estimated life of the unit is 15 years. Money can be invested at 8% interest, compounded quarterly. Find the capitalized cost of the unit.

3. A memorial library is built at a cost of $250,000. The estimated life of the building is 60 years. If the replacement cost of the building is assumed to be $1^1/_2$ times the original cost, find the capitalized cost of the building. Money is worth 6% annual interest.

4. A memorial student center is built at a cost of $500,000, and the estimated life is 50 years. The replacement cost of the building is estimated to be $600,000. Money is currently worth 8% annual interest. Find the capitalized cost of the building.

5. A family wishes to leave as a memorial to their deceased father, a cancer-treatment wing at the existing hospital. The useful life of the wing is estimated to be 25 years. The family wishes to make a donation of the initial amount of $1,000,000 and to establish an account which will replace the unit. Find the capitalized cost if money has a semiannual value of 3.5%.

6. The original cost of a shelter for the band at the waterfront park is $40,000. The estimated life of the shelter is 15 years, and the replacement cost is estimated to be equal to the original cost. If money has a value of 2% quarterly interest, what is the capitalized cost of the shelter?

7. A company gets two bids for a roof for their main building. One bid is for $30,000 with a guarantee for 8 years. The other bid is for $50,000 with a guarantee of 15 years. If money is worth 6% interest, which is the most economical roof for the company?

8. One grade of vinyl for a floor in an industrial plant will cost $5,400 and have an estimated life of 12 years. A lower grade of vinyl will cost $3,800 with an estimated life of 8 years. The replacement costs are estimated to

be the same as the original cost. Money is worth 8% interest. Which is the more economical buy?

9. Two machines are available, and both perform adequately. One machine costs $95,000 with an estimated life of 20 years. The other machine costs $75,000 with an estimated life of 15 years. Money is worth 7% interest. Which machine is the most economical buy?

10. Two automobiles are available, and both have the same performance rating. Auto A costs $70,000 and has an estimated life of 20 years. Auto B costs $20,000 and has an estimated life of 5 years. Estimate the replacement cost to be the same as the original cost. Find the more economical buy if money is worth 6% interest.

Answers to Odd-Numbered Exercises

1. $K = \$89,775.81$.

3. $K = \$261,723.26$.

5. $K = \$1,218,106$.

7. The $30,000 roof has a capitalized cost of $80,517.96. The $50,000 roof has a capitalized cost of $85,802.30. The $30,000 roof is more economical.

9. The $75,000 machine is more economical.

Summary

- **Book value:**

$$V = C - R_1 - R_2 - \cdots - R_n$$

where R_n is the nth year depreciation charge

- **MACRS depreciation method:**

    Classify the asset as having a 3-, 5-, 7-, 10-, or 15-year life.

$$\text{Rate} = \frac{100\% \times 2}{n}$$

where n is number of years of life
Exception: Year 1, rate is $100\%/n$
$R = V \cdot \text{Rate}$, where V is current book value

- **Straight-line depreciation method:**

$$R = \frac{C - S}{n}$$

  where S is salvage value of asset

- **Declining-balance method:**

$$\text{Rate} = \frac{(2) \cdot (100\%)}{n}$$

$$R = V \cdot \text{Rate}$$

- **Sum-of-the-years-digits method:**

$$\text{Rate} = \frac{(\text{number of useful years of life remaining}) \cdot (100\%)}{(\text{sum of digits of years of life})}$$

$$R = (V) \cdot (\text{Rate})$$

- **Inventory turnover:**

$$\text{Turnover (based on sales)} = \frac{\text{Net Sales}}{\text{Average inventory value}}$$

$$\text{Turnover (based on cost)} = \frac{\text{Cost of Goods Sold}}{\text{Average Inventory Value}}$$

- **Inventory valuation:**

$$\text{Average Cost} = \frac{(n_1 C_1 + n_2 C_2 + \cdots + n_n C_n)}{(n_1 + n_2 + n_3 + \cdots + n_n)}$$

- **FIFO:** the cost of the most recently purchased items is used to determine inventory value

- **LIFO:** the cost of the items purchased at the beginning of the period is used to determine inventory value.

- **Capitalized cost:** the original cost of the asset plus the present value of the future replacements.

$$K = C + \left(\frac{R}{i}\right) \cdot \left(\frac{1}{s_{\overline{m}\,i}}\right)$$

where K is capitalized cost, C is original cost, R is renewal cost, n is the number of years of life

REVIEW EXERCISES

1. Calculate the first year's depreciation for a piece of equipment costing $12,500. The equipment has an estimated useful life of 5 years with an estimated salvage value of $1,250.
   a. Use the straight-line method.
   b. Use the declining-balance method.
   c. Use the sum-of-the-digits method.
   d. Use the MACRS method.

2. Calculate the first year's depreciation on a truck purchased at $35,800. The truck has an expected useful life of 8 years with an expected salvage value of $800.
   a. Use the straight-line method.
   b. Use the declining-balance method.
   c. Use the sum-of-the-digits method.
   d. Use the MACRS method (the allowable life under this method is 5 years).

3. A cable television installation company purchases a backhoe for $32,000. The estimated life of the backhoe is 8 years, and the salvage value is $2,000. Find the book value of the equipment at the end of 2 years if the sum-of-the-digits method is used for depreciation.

4. A small loom used by a hand weaver costs $46,000 and has a scrap value of $6,000. The estimated life of the loom is 12 years. Using the straight-line method of depreciation, find the book value at the end of 3 years.

5. A small computer is purchased for $56,000. The computer is expected to last 8 years and will have no scrap value. Prepare a depreciation schedule for the first 3 years, using the declining-balance method.

6. A jewelry store purchases a display case for $35,000. The useful life under the MACRS method of depreciation is 5 years. Prepare a depreciation schedule for the display case.

7. A newly formed company incurs a total cost of $74,500 for equipment that is to be depreciated over 5 years. Because of high start-up costs, the company wishes to delay as much of the depreciation expense as possible.

What method of depreciation should be used to ensure the largest amount of depreciation during the second year? Determine the amount of depreciation.

8. Sunrise Motel, Inc., has an annual overhead expense of $15,050 and allocates the expense by the allocation of floor space. Allocate the overhead expense among the following departments.

Department	Floor Space
Dining room	2,400 square feet
Motel rooms	74,000 square feet
Office space	1,800 square feet
Recreational	5,600 square feet

9. A wholesale lumber mill allocates its overhead of $25,600 by the sales value of its product. Allocate the overhead to the following products.

Product	Amount Produced	Value/Unit
Building 2 × 4's	846	$200
Plywood	1,250	350
Veneers	120	550
Wood chips	75	80
Furniture wood	365	150

10. Distribute an overhead expense of $80,000 by the number of employees in each department.

Department	Number of Employees
Carding	12
Spinning	88
Weaving	125
Finishing	60

11. Inventory value was recorded as $74,642 on March 1, $60,762 on June 1, $82,643 on September 1, and $98,692 on December 1. The sales of the year amounted to $496,692. Find the average inventory value and the turnover rate of the merchandise.

12. The regional retail beer distributors submitted the following monthly reports.

Store	Inventory	Sales
A	$41,875	$369,241
B	24,969	296,154
C	82,160	745,123

What was the average turnover rate for the distributor? Which store(s) should be commended for the activity of the month?

13. Comfy Furnishings purchased the following convertible sofas during the year.

February	25 @ $560 each
May	32 @ $526 each
August	17 @ $475 each
November	20 @ $602 each

On December 31 there were 29 sofas in stock. Find the inventory value if figured on:
a. Average cost
b. LIFO
c. FIFO

14. A branch manager notes that the price of carpet has declined steadily over the year. He is in a regional sales meeting and is asked which method of inventory valuation he favors: average cost, FIFO, or LIFO. His bonus for the year depends directly on the turnover rate of his branch business. Which method of inventory valuation should he favor and why?

15. Determine the turnover rate of Plush Carpet Company if the following purchases were made during the year and the net sales of carpet for the year were $318,672.

Date	Number of Square Yards	Price/Square Yard
February 15	235	$ 9.95
April 1	315	10.50
June 15	520	9.50
August 30	430	10.25
October 15	180	8.50
December 1	780	10.25

On December 31 Plush Carpets had an inventory of 500 square yards. Find the value of the inventory by:
a. Average cost
b. LIFO
c. FIFO
What is the highest turnover rate that can be claimed by Plush Carpets?

16. Find the capitalized cost of an auditorium. The original cost was $5,000,000. The replacement cost is estimated to be the same as the origi-

nal cost. The estimated life of the auditorium is 40 years. Money is worth 7% interest.

17. Find the capitalized cost of a piece of machinery purchased for $220,000. The replacement cost is estimated to be $250,000, and the estimated life of the machinery is 22 years. Money has a value of 8% interest.

18. Two grades of surface for a parking lot are available. The less expensive grade will have an initial cost of $180,000 with an estimated life of 10 years. The replacement cost is estimated to be the same as the original cost. The better surface has an initial cost of $250,000. The estimated life is 12 years, and the replacement cost is $110,000. Find the more economical purchase if money has a value of 9% interest.

19. A textile plant wishes to replace some equipment. Two grades of equipment are available. One is priced at $780,000 with an estimated useful life of 40 years. The other has a price of $610,000 with an estimated useful life of 30 years. The replacement cost for either is $700,000. The value of money is 6% interest. Find the more economical purchase.

20. A piece of equipment needs to be replaced. The original equipment was purchased for $1,500 with an estimated life of 8 years. The new equipment has an estimated life of 12 years. How much can the buyer afford to pay for the equipment in order to keep the capitalized cost the same or less than the capitalized cost of the original purchase? The value of money is 8% interest. Consider the replacement cost to be the same as the original cost in each situation.

Answers to Review Exercises

1. MACRS, $2,500. Straight line, $2,250. Declining balance, $5,000. Sum of the digits, $3,750.

2. MACRS, $7,160. Straight line, $4,375. Declining balance, $8,950. Sum of the digits, $7,778.

3. $20,407.40, book value.

4. $36,000, book value.

5.

Year	Depreciation	Book Value
1	$14,000	$42,000
2	10,500	31,500
3	7,875	23,625

6.

Year	Rate (%)	Depreciation	Book Value
1	0.20	$ 7,000	$28,000
2	0.40	11,200	16,800
3	0.40	6,720	10,080
4	0.40	4,032	6,048
5	0.40	2,419.20	3,628.80

7. MACRS gives $23,840 depreciation in year 2. This is higher than sum-of-the-digits method, $19,867; straight-line, $14,900; declining balance, $17,880.

8.

Dining room	$ 430.02
Motel rooms	13,259.07
Office space	322.52
Recreational	1,003.39

9.

Building 2 × 4's	$ 5,905.68
Plywood	15,270.30
Veneers	2,303.63
Wood chips	209.42
Furniture wood	1,910.97

10.

Carding	$ 3,368.42
Spinning	24,701.75
Weaving	35,087.72
Finishing	16,842.11

11. Average inventory, $79,184.75. Turnover rate, 6.27 or 627%.

12. Average turnover rate, 9.47 or 947%. Store B should be commended for exceeding average rate.

13. Inventory value by average cost, $15,717.69; by LIFO, $16,104; and by FIFO, $16,315.

14. FIFO because the lower-valued carpets would make a lower valuation for the inventory, a giving higher turnover rate.

15. Inventory value by average cost, $4,983.38; by LIFO, $5,120.75; and by FIFO, $5,125.00.

16. $K = \$5,357,795$.

17. $K = \$253,810.13$.

18. Most economical purchase is $250,000 original job.

19. Most economical equipment is $610,000.

20. Cost should be equal to or less than $1,967.

Chapter 6

INSURANCE

Insurance is a financial protection against losses resulting from an event. Businesses and individuals rely on insurance protection from catastrophic losses resulting from fire, theft, death, accident, or sickness. The key to insurance is the large number of policyholders; the contributions of many finance the claims of the few. The amount of assessment is determined from the application of the probability and statistics of an event occurring.

Mortality tables indicate 19 out of 10,000 males of age 20 will die during their twentieth year of life. A simplistic explanation of life insurance involves these 10,000 males of age 20. They take out life insurance in the amount of $10,000. The insurance company charges each $19.00 for the coverage. The total amount collected is $190,000. If the 19 die as predicted in the mortality table, the insurance company pays out $190,000.

At the end of this chapter, the student will be able to:

1. Define and identify correctly the terms associated with insurance.

2. Compute fire insurance premiums, determine the refund on cancelled policies, and find compensation for a loss under coinsurance and compensation when insured by more than one carrier.

3. Compute premiums for auto insurance; liability, collision, and comprehensive coverage.

4. Determine the extent of coverage in auto accidents with varying amounts of insurance coverage.

5. Determine the premiums for whole life, term, 20-payment life, and 20-year endowments.

6. Determine the benefits received under each of the types of life insurance.

7. Determine the amount of payments received under different types of settlements from life insurance.

8. Identify the types of insurance available under group coverage and the benefits from group coverage.

6.1   FIRE INSURANCE

Fire insurance provides financial protection against property damage resulting from fire or lightning. Basic fire insurance covers only the structure itself; additional insurance must be purchased to insure the contents of the building from fire. A third type of coverage is extended coverage providing protection against smoke, water, hurricane, wind, and hail damage. A comprehensive fire insurance policy includes all of the above plus protection against loss from theft and vandalism, as well as liability protection. Most homeowner insurance policies include comprehensive coverage.

Fire insurance premiums are the annual costs for the financial protection. Three basic factors affect the premiums in fire insurance.

1. The type of structure of the insured building. A wooden structure carries a higher rate than a brick structure; cedar shingles have a higher rate than asphalt shingles.

2. The geographic location of the building. Rural buildings remote from adequate water and fire-fighter protection carry higher rates than structures near fire hydrants and fire stations.

3. Class or use of building. Buildings used for making ammunition carry higher premiums than buildings used to manufacture computer chips.

A typical chart for fire insurance premiums for dwellings is as follows.

Class A Dwellings (1–2 Family)
Rates per $100

Type of Structure	Area				
	1	2	3	4	5
Brick	0.102	0.142	0.190	0.246	0.305
Brick veneer	0.135	0.180	0.233	0.294	0.358
Stucco, asbestos	0.174	0.223	0.283	0.349	0.416
Frame	0.229	0.272	0.341	0.403	0.472

Calculations for premiums can be made by multiplying the insurance rate from the table by the amount of coverage/100.

| **Example**
James Maynard wishes to insure his frame home for $75,000. His home is located in area 2. Find his yearly insurance premium.
| The rate from the table is 0.272. This is found under area 2, line labeled Frame.

$$\text{Premium} = 0.272 \times \left(\frac{75,000}{100} \right) = \$204$$

Insurance policies are usually written on an annual basis. Occasionally policies are written for 2-year or 3-year periods. The premiums are collected yearly. Fire insurance premiums are rounded to the nearest dollar.

Short-Term Insurance

Sometimes insurance is needed for an interval of less than 1 year. In business, merchandise may be brought in and sold within a period of less than 1 year. A transfer and sale of a home may cause cancellation of an insurance policy before the end of the term.

Each insurance company has a **short-rate cancellation schedule** for determining premiums for less than 1 year or rebates for policies canceled during an annual term.

A typical short-term cancellation schedule is as follows.

Months Coverage	Percent of Annual Premium	Months Coverage	Percent of Annual Premium
1	18	7	70
2	28	8	76
3	38	9	82
4	48	10	88
5	56	11	94
6	63	12	100

| **Example**
A brick veneer house valued at $43,000 is located in area 4. Five months after renewing the policy, the owner sells the house and cancels the policy. Find the annual premium. Find the refund received.

$$\text{Premium} = 0.294 \times \left(\frac{43,000}{100} \right) = \$126.42 = \$126$$

$$\text{Premium for 5-months coverage} = 0.56 \times 126.42 = \$71$$

$$\text{Refund} = \$126 - \$71 = \$55$$

Note that if the insurance company cancels the policy, the short-rate schedule does not apply. The cost of each month's premium is one twelfth of the annual premium.

Many businesses do not insure property for the full value of the property. Fires do not usually completely destroy a building. In such a situation, the fire insurance company is carrying most of the risk for less than the full premium. To protect the fire insurance company, a coinsurance clause is included in the policy. The clause states that if the insurance coverage is less than 80% of the value of the property, the insurance payment will be made only in the ratio of the actual coverage to the required coverage. The property owner is responsible for the remainder of the loss.

Example
Donald Smith owned a home valued at $85,000. He elected to provide fire insurance coverage of $50,000. The insured home burned with estimated damage of $40,000. How much will the insurance company pay if the policy had an 80% coinsurance clause?

$80\% \times 85,000 = \$68,000$ coverage required for 100% compensation

Because $50,000 is less than the required $68,000, the insurance company will pay only a ratio of the loss.

$$\frac{50,000 \text{ (coverage carried)}}{68,000 \text{ (coverage required)}} = 73.5\%$$

$40,000 \times 0.735 = \$29,400$ insurance compensation for the loss

Donald Smith's part of the loss is $10,600.

Multiple Carriers

There are times, especially for large manufacturing plants, when insurance coverage is provided by more than one insurance carrier. In such cases, when a loss occurs, each carrier pays damages determined by the percent coverage of his policy to the total insurance coverage. There is never a settlement exceeding the value of the property.

> **Example**
> TRA has fire insurance coverage with three companies as follows.
>
> | | |
> |---|---|
> | A Insurance Company | $ 500,000 |
> | B Insurance Company | 350,000 |
> | C Insurance Company | 150,000 |
> | Total | $1,000,000 |

TRA suffered fire damage amounting to $370,000. The total value of the TRA buildings was $1,200,000 so the coinsurance clause was not in effect. How much did each of the insurance companies pay?

$$A \text{ Insurance} = \frac{500,000}{1,000,000} = \frac{1}{2} \text{ of loss}$$

$$B \text{ Insurance} = \frac{350,000}{1,000,000} = \frac{35}{100} \text{ of loss}$$

$$C \text{ Insurance} = \frac{150,000}{1,000,000} = \frac{15}{100} \text{ of loss}$$

$$A \text{ pays} \left(\frac{1}{2}\right)(370,000) = \$185,000$$

$$B \text{ pays} \left(\frac{35}{100}\right)(370,000) = \$129,500$$

$$C \text{ pays} \left(\frac{15}{100}\right)(370,000) = \$55,500$$

$$\text{Total reimbursement} = \$370,000$$

SECTION 1 EXERCISES

1. Bette Birch wishes to insure her $80,000 home for $70,000. The house is brick and is located in area 5. Determine the annual premium for the insurance.

2. Tom Trouch has just purchased a stucco home and wants to insure the house for $57,000. The house is in an area 2 location. Determine the premium for the fire insurance.

3. Jane Jones has two homes and needs fire insurance for each. The value for each house is $65,000. She receives the policies with the bills for each. One bill is for $177, and the other bill is for $160. Determine the differences between the two homes.

4. Tom Brown and Ben Moore each purchased new homes for $68,000. They each bought their fire insurance policy from the same source. Tom's bill was $274, whereas Ben's premium was $69. What factors determined the difference in premiums?

5. Fran's Furs received their fall inventory during July and needed to store it for 3 months. The value of the furs was $500,000, and the quoted annual rate for the insurance was 0.682 per $100. Find the 3-month premium for the insurance.

6. Paramount Builders had some unsold finished homes and needed fire insurance coverage. The value of one of the brick veneer homes was $74,000 and it was located in area 4. Two months later Paramount Builders sold the home. What rebate did they receive on the fire insurance?

7. George Brent sold his $94,500 home. The house was a frame and located in area 1. His fire insurance had been in effect for 6 months at the time of the sale. What was the rebate on his premium?

8. Bonnie Carver sold her $82,000 stucco home 3 months after she had renewed her fire insurance policy. The house was located in area 3. Determine the rebate on the fire insurance premium.

9. A $120,000 home was insured for $85,000. A fire caused $68,000 damage. How much did the owner receive from the fire insurance policy if the policy had an 80% coinsurance clause? How much was the owner liable for?

10. A $100,000 home was insured for $80,000. A fire caused $60,000 damage. How much did the owner receive from the fire insurance company? How much of the $60,000 damage did the owner have to pay?

11. A $60,000 home was insured for $50,000. A kitchen fire caused $25,000 damage to the building. How much of the damage did the fire insurance company pay?

12. A couple owned their home for 30 years. They paid $25,000 for the house and carried insurance for that amount on the structure. The present value of the house is $82,000. Fire damage amounted to $19,000. How much did the fire insurance pay on the claim?

13. Time Shores was insured by three fire insurance carriers. Carrier A wrote a policy for $300,000, Carrier B had a fire insurance policy for $400,000, and Carrier C had written a policy for $550,000. The value of the property was $1,500,000. Fire damage to the building amounted to $725,000. How much did each carrier pay Time Shores?

14. Trace Mining Company had fire insurance policies with the following companies for the amounts indicated.

Wet Insurance	$450,000
Blue Insurance	750,000
Red Insurance	500,000

The total value of the building involved is $2,000,000. The fire damage from a recent fire was $820,000. Find the amount each of the insurance companies pays to Trace Mining.

15. Cosgrove Library had fire insurance policies with the following companies for the amounts indicated.

First Insurance	$170,000
Second Insurance	310,000
Third Insurance	220,000

The library building is valued at $1,000,000. Fire causes $400,000 damage to the building. Find the liability of each of the insurance companies to Cosgrove Library.

Answers to Odd-Numbered Exercises

1. $213.50.

3. $177 bill is for a frame house, area 2. $160 bill is for a brick house, area 4.

5. $1,295.80, 3-month premium.

7. $136, premium. $80, rebate.

9. $60,207 from insurance. $7,793 from owner.

11. $25,000.

13. A pays $174,000. B pays $232,000. C pays $319,000.

15. First pays $85,000. Second pays $155,000. Third pays $110,000. Total, $350,000.

6.2   MOTOR VEHICLE INSURANCE

Insurance is carried by individuals and businesses on motor vehicles to protect against financial losses due to accidents. Many states require evidence of liability insurance before registration of vehicles. Loan companies require collision insurance to protect their financial interest in the vehicle. There are three major types of motor vehicle insurance.

1. Liability insurance provides protection to the policyholder from suit by an injured party.

2. Collision insurance pays for repairs to the policyholder's own vehicle in case of an accident.

3. Comprehensive insurance pays for damages to the policyholder's vehicle from floods, wind, hail, and other nonaccident damages.

Liability Insurance

The face amount of liability insurance is given by three numbers. The first number represents the maximum amount (in thousands) paid for bodily injury to one person, the second number represents the maximum amount (in thousands) allowed in one accident for all persons suffering bodily injury, and the third number is the maximum amount (in thousands) paid for property damage in one accident. Liability insurance coverage is described as 10/25/20. The number 10 represents $10,000, the maximum amount paid to one person for bodily injury resulting from an accident. The number 25 represents $25,000, the maximum amount paid for bodily injury in one accident. The number 20 represents $20,000, the maximum amount of property damage coverage in one accident. Amounts in excess of the face value of the liability coverage are the responsibility of the policyholder.

The premiums for liability insurance depend upon the territory in which the vehicle is driven, the amount of liability coverage, and the classification of the driver (age, sex, driver record, and vehicle use). A typical schedule for determining premiums is as follows.

Liability—Bodily Injury

Territory	Annual Premiums		
	10/20	25/50	100/300
1	$156	$190	$235
2	94	135	160
3	236	270	315
4	165	198	248

Property Damage

Territory	Annual Premiums		
	$10,000	$20,000	$50,000
1	$62	$ 71	$105
2	45	54	75
3	87	112	130
4	74	83	117

Statistics indicate youthful male drivers are involved in a greater proportion of accidents. An additional premium is added to insurance for vehicles driven by youthful male drivers. Companies differ in the way the additional premiums are assessed. The following table is one type of assessment.

Male Youthful Operator Factor

Age	Driver's Training	Without Driver's Training	Honor Student
20 or less	1.60	1.75	1.50
21–25	1.20	1.30	1.15
Over 25		No additional premiums	

The premium for all the coverage desired is determined and this premium is then multiplied by the appropriate factor when youthful male drivers are involved.

Example

Using the preceding tables, determine the annual premium for liability insurance for Carl Burke, age 29, living in area 3, wanting 10/20/10 coverage. Because Carl Burke is over 25, no additional premium is assessed for him.

$10,000/$20,000 liability for area 3 = $236

$10,000 property damage for area 3 = $ 87

Total premium for Carl Burke = $323

Example

Using the preceding tables, determine the insurance premium for John Broke for liability insurance for 100/300/50. He is 42 years old and has a teenage honor student son driving the insured vehicle. The Broke family lives in area 4.

100/300 in area 4	$248
$50,000 property	117
Total	$365
Youthful operator factor	1.5
Premium	$547.50

Example

Determine the liability premium for a 24-year-old male high-school dropout who wishes to get the minimum amount of insurance allowed. He lives in area 2. The minimum coverage listed is 10/20/10.

$$\text{Premium} = 94 + 45 = 139$$

The youthful operator factor is 1.3.

$$\text{Total liability premium} = \$180.70$$

which would be billed as $181.

This insured driver is involved in an accident. The other car had three passengers and two of the passengers were critically injured. The legal settlements to the critically injured passengers were $10,000 and $18,000. The third received an award of $5,000. The Mercedes involved was totaled, a value of $27,000. Find the settlement of the insurance and the liability of the driver.

The insurance paid $10,000 to settle the first claim of $10,000.

$10,000 for the other two claims of $18,000 and $5,000.

$10,000 for the property damage of $27,000.

$30,000 total compensation from the insurance company.

The at fault driver pays

$13,000 ($8,000 to claimant 2, $5,000 to claimant 3).

$17,000 remainder of property damage.

$30,000 balance of claim to be paid by driver.

Collision insurance pays for damage to the vehicle of the policyholder in case of an accident. The premium for collision insurance depends on the territory in which the vehicle is driven, age of the vehicle, and cost or value of the vehicle. Collision insurance often includes a deductible, the amount the policyholder is liable for. The excess of the deductible is the amount the insurance company pays. The higher the deductible, the lower the premium because the owner is assuming more of the financial responsibility.

Comprehensive insurance pays for damage to the insured vehicle for non-accident damages. The amount of the premiums for comprehensive coverage depends on the same factors as collision insurance—age of vehicle, cost of vehicle, and amount of deductible.

Collision and comprehensive premiums are shown in the same table.

Passenger Cars
Territory 1, 2, 3, 4
Annual Premiums
$200 Deductible

Driver Class	Age of Vehicle	Vehicle Classification							
		1		2		3		4	
		Coll.	*Comp.*	*Coll.*	*Comp.*	*Coll.*	*Comp.*	*Coll.*	*Comp.*
A	1	52	20	63	22	74	25	86	28
	2	49	17	59	18	70	21	80	25
	3	46	15	55	16	67	19	76	22
	4 or more	42	14	50	15	63	16	70	20
B	1	64	20	75	22	86	25	98	28
	2	61	17	71	22	82	21	92	25
	3	58	15	67	16	79	19	88	22
	4 or more	54	14	62	16	75	16	82	20

Example
Mr. Small, a class B driver, had a 1-year-old class 3 vehicle. Determine the collision and comprehensive annual premiums with a $100 deductible.

Collision coverage	$ 86
Comprehensive coverage	25
Total	$111

Example

George Adams, a class A driver, wishes to insure his new class 4 vehicle. He wants liability coverage for 25/50/20 and collision insurance with a $200 deductible, territory 3. The vehicle will be driven by a 22-year-old male youth who has had driver's education. Find the amount of the annual premium.

Liability	$270 + $112
Collision	86
Comprehensive	28
Total	$496
Youthful operator factor	1.3
Premium	$644.80

If more than one vehicle is insured by the same insurance company, the premium for the second vehicle is reduced by a percent determined by the insurance company.

No-Fault Insurance

In no-fault insurance, the insurance company reimburses the insured for medical expenses and damages resulting from an accident, regardless of who caused the accident. When no-fault insurance was introduced (and in some states, legislated), it was believed it would lower insurance costs. Rising prices for property damage and repair to vehicles has offset any savings by the plan.

Uninsured motorist insurance is also available to cover an individual in the event of an accident with a vehicle driven by an individual with no liability insurance. An additional premium is added to include uninsured motorist insurance in a policy.

SECTION 2 EXERCISES

Find the annual motor vehicle insurance premium for liability, collision, and comprehensive for each of the following.

	Amount	Territory	Class	Vehicle Class	Age of Vehicle
1.	25/50/10	3	B	2	5
2.	100/300/50	2	A	1	2
3.	10/20/10	4	A	4	1
4.	25/50/0	1	B	3	3
5.	100/300/50	3	A	4	1

6. Ms. North is a class A driver. She has a two-year-old class 3 vehicle and lives in territory 4. She wishes to buy liability insurance for 100/300/50 coverage plus collision, no comprehensive coverage. Find the annual premium.

7. Jack West has a new class 2 vehicle. He is a class B driver and lives in territory 2. His 16-year-old son has just completed driver's training and will be driving the vehicle. Find the annual insurance premium if the deductible is $200 and he has 25/50/10 liability, collision and comprehensive.

8. John Sprague had liability insurance of 25/50/10, collision insurance ($200 deductible), and comprehensive insurance. He is involved in an accident and is determined to be at fault. The driver of the vehicle and his son were both injured, and the vehicle they were in was totaled. The court awarded damages of $30,000 to the driver, $15,000 to the son, and $15,000 property damage. Mr. Sprague claimed $22,000 damage to his vehicle. Determine the liability of the insurance company and the liability of Mr. Sprague.

9. Carla Adams falls asleep at the wheel of her vehicle and forces Ed Smith's vehicle off the road. Ms. Adams had 10/20/5 liability insurance, $100 deductible collision insurance, and no comprehensive coverage. Mr. Smith and his three children were awarded $10,000 each in damages. Mr. Smith's vehicle was valued at $6,500 and declared a total loss. Ms. Adams' vehicle did not suffer any damage. Find the amount Ms. Adams' insurance paid and the liability of Ms. Adams.

10. Calculate the annual premium for Mr. Brown.

Car 1 is 1 year old, classification 4, driver class B, liability insurance 100/300/50, territory 4.

Car 2 is 5 years old, classification 1, driver class B, liability insurance 100/300/50, territory 4.

Both cars will be driven by his 21-year-old son who is an honor student at college. The insurance company covers the second vehicle at 90% premium.

11. Calculate the annual premium for the following amount of insurance.

100/300/10 liability insurance coverage on all vehicles in territory 2.

Vehicle 1 is 2 years old, classification 2, driver class B.

Vehicle 2 is 4 years old, classification 4, driver class B.

There is no comprehensive coverage. Both vehicles will be driven by teen-age daughters who have had driver's education. The insurance company gives an incentive of 85% premium on the second vehicle.

Answers to Odd-Numbered Exercises

1. $435.

3. $353.

5. $559.

7. $443.20.

9. Insurance, $25,000. Ms. Adams, $21,500.

11. $541.95.

6.3   LIFE INSURANCE

Life insurance provides financial protection to the beneficiary of the insured at the time of the death of the insured. Individuals buy life insurance to provide financial security to the family, to pay off mortgages on homes, and to provide monies for college for children. Businesses are interested in life insurance for key personnel whose deaths would cause a severe loss to the business.

There are four major types of life insurance, each offering protection in the event of death, and some offering additional options.

Term Insurance

Term insurance provides protection for the term of the policy, usually 5, 10, or 15 years. Term insurance is the least expensive of the four types of insurance. Most policies have the option of renewal (at a higher rate) or conversion to another form of insurance. Term insurance is frequently used by heads of households during the periods when their responsibilities are greatest. Insurance taken out for a specific purpose such as an airplane trip or boat trip is term insurance. The duration of the trip is the term.

A decreasing term insurance is a modification of term insurance. The face value of the policy decreases throughout the term of the policy. A typical example of a decreasing term insurance is mortgage insurance. The face value of the insurance is the balance of the mortgage.

Ordinary Life

Ordinary life (also known as straight life or whole life) combines life insurance protection and a savings plan. The insured pays a fixed premium throughout his or her life. The premium is more than term insurance premiums for a young person but less than term insurance premiums as the age increases. Ordinary life insurance builds up a cash value, an amount that can be borrowed against at favorable rates and an amount of value retained by a policy even if payments are suspended.

Limited Payment Life

Limited payment life is similar to ordinary life except premiums are paid for a fixed number of years, such as 20 or 30 years. The premiums for limited payment life are larger than ordinary life. The premiums can be arranged for the more productive years of an individual, and the protection extends for life. The total amount paid in a limited payment life is approximately equivalent to the amount collected in an ordinary life policy during the average lifetime of the insured.

Endowment

Endowments guarantee protection to an individual for the face value of the policy for a specified number of years. If the policyholder is alive at the end of the period, the policyholder collects the face value of the policy, and the insurance protection ends. Endowments are the most expensive type of life insurance. They are often taken out by parents to guarantee a sum of money for college education costs.

Participating and Nonparticipating

Insurance policies are classified as participating and nonparticipating—so named to indicate whether the policyholder participates in the profits earned by the policy. Premium rates are determined by actuaries and require fairly involved mathematics. Rates must be adequate to cover the anticipated claims of the policyholders, the costs incurred by the insurance company, and the profits for insurance company shareholders. Participating policy premiums are higher. The insurance companies charge more than expected to pay the claims and operating expenses. The excess funds are refunded to the policyholders as **dividends.** Policyholders can use the dividends to reduce the following year's premium or to buy additional insurance coverage.

Most participating policies are sold by **mutual** life insurance companies. The companies are owned by the policyholders, not by the stockholders.

Premiums

Life insurance differs from other types of insurance. Fire and motor vehicle insurance premiums are determined by the probability of the occurrence of a fire or accident. Life insurance premiums are not determined by the probability of occurrence (100%) but by **when** the event will occur.

The officially approved table of the insurance industry is the Commissioners' Standard Ordinary Table of Mortality published periodically. The most recent table was published in 1980 and is reproduced to show the ex-

Commissioners 1980 Standard Ordinary Table of Mortality

Age	Male Mortality Rate Per 1,000	Male Expectancy, Years	Female Mortality Rate Per 1,000	Female Expectancy, Years	Age	Male Mortality Rate Per 1,000	Male Expectancy, Years	Female Mortality Rate Per 1,000	Female Expectancy, Years
0	4.18	70.83	2.89	75.83	50	6.71	25.36	4.96	29.53
1	1.07	70.13	.87	75.04	51	7.30	24.52	5.31	28.67
2	.99	69.20	.81	74.11	52	7.96	23.70	5.70	27.82
3	.98	68.27	.79	73.17	53	8.71	22.89	6.15	26.98
4	.95	67.34	.77	72.23	54	9.56	22.08	6.61	26.14
5	.90	66.40	.76	71.28	55	10.47	21.29	7.09	25.31
6	.85	65.46	.73	70.34	56	11.46	20.51	7.57	24.49
7	.80	64.52	.72	69.39	57	12.49	19.74	8.03	23.67
8	.76	63.57	.70	68.44	58	13.59	18.99	8.47	22.86
9	.74	62.62	.69	67.48	59	14.77	18.24	8.94	22.05
10	.73	61.66	.68	66.53	60	16.08	17.51	9.47	21.25
11	.77	60.71	.69	65.58	61	17.54	16.79	10.13	20.44
12	.85	59.75	.72	64.62	62	19.19	16.08	10.96	19.65
13	.99	58.80	.75	63.67	63	21.06	15.38	12.02	18.86
14	1.15	57.86	.80	62.71	64	23.14	14.70	13.25	18.08
15	1.33	56.93	.85	61.76	65	25.42	14.04	14.59	17.32
16	1.51	56.00	.90	60.82	66	27.85	13.39	16.00	16.57
17	1.67	55.09	.95	59.87	67	30.44	12.76	17.43	15.83
18	1.78	54.18	.98	58.93	68	33.19	12.14	18.84	15.10
19	1.86	53.27	1.02	57.98	69	36.17	11.54	20.36	14.38

Commissioners 1980 Standard Ordinary Table of Mortality

Age	Male Mortality Rate Per 1,000	Male Expectancy, Years	Female Mortality Rate Per 1,000	Female Expectancy, Years	Age	Male Mortality Rate Per 1,000	Male Expectancy, Years	Female Mortality Rate Per 1,000	Female Expectancy, Years
20	1.90	52.37	1.05	57.04	70	39.51	10.96	22.11	13.67
21	1.91	51.47	1.07	56.10	71	43.30	10.39	24.23	12.97
22	1.89	50.57	1.09	55.16	72	47.65	9.84	26.87	12.28
23	1.86	49.66	1.11	54.22	73	52.64	9.30	30.11	11.60
24	1.82	48.75	1.14	53.28	74	58.19	8.79	33.93	10.95
25	1.77	47.84	1.16	52.34	75	64.19	8.31	38.24	10.32
26	1.73	46.93	1.19	51.40	76	70.53	7.84	42.97	9.71
27	1.71	46.01	1.22	50.46	77	77.12	7.40	48.04	9.12
28	1.70	45.09	1.26	49.52	78	83.90	6.97	53.45	8.55
29	1.71	44.16	1.30	48.59	79	91.05	6.57	59.35	8.01
30	1.73	43.24	1.35	47.65	80	98.84	6.18	65.99	7.48
31	1.78	42.31	1.40	46.71	81	107.48	5.80	73.60	6.98
32	1.83	41.38	1.45	45.78	82	117.25	5.44	82.40	6.49
33	1.91	40.46	1.50	44.84	83	128.26	5.09	92.53	6.03
34	2.00	39.54	1.58	43.91	84	140.25	4.77	103.81	5.59
35	2.11	38.61	1.65	42.98	85	152.95	4.46	116.10	5.18
36	2.24	37.69	1.76	42.05	86	166.09	4.18	129.29	4.80
37	2.40	36.78	1.89	41.12	87	179.55	3.91	143.32	4.43
38	2.58	35.87	2.04	40.20	88	193.27	3.66	158.18	4.09
39	2.79	34.96	2.22	39.28	89	207.29	3.41	173.94	3.77
40	3.02	34.05	2.42	38.36	90	221.77	3.18	190.75	3.45
41	3.29	33.16	2.64	37.46	91	236.98	2.94	208.87	3.15
42	3.56	32.26	2.87	36.55	92	253.45	2.70	228.81	2.85
43	3.87	31.38	3.09	35.66	93	272.11	2.44	251.51	2.55
44	4.19	30.50	3.32	34.77	94	295.90	2.17	279.31	2.24
45	4.55	29.62	3.56	33.88	95	329.96	1.87	317.32	1.91
46	4.92	28.76	3.80	33.00	96	384.55	1.54	375.74	1.56
47	5.32	27.90	4.05	32.12	97	480.20	1.20	474.97	1.21
48	5.74	27.04	4.33	31.25	98	657.98	.84	655.85	.84
49	6.21	26.20	4.63	30.39	99	1000.00	.50	1000.00	.50

Based on experience of years 1970–1975.

pected mortality rate for males and females for every age from 0 to 99 years plus the life expectancy for both males and females for every age. This table is the basis for life insurance premium calculations. For any number of people of a given age taking out insurance during a given year, the mortality table predicts the number of claims from the group. The premiums paid by all policy-holders must be sufficient to pay all the claims.

Premiums and options costs vary from company to company. The following table is a representative table of premiums.

Life Insurance Premiums per $1,000 Face Value

	10-Year Term		Whole Life		20-Payment Life		20-Year Endowment	
Age	Male	Female	Male	Female	Male	Female	Male	Female
18	$6.75	$6.35	$14.55	$13.75	$24.55	$23.75	$42.85	$40.15
20	6.82	6.42	14.95	13.95	25.40	24.50	43.90	41.10
24	6.90	6.50	16.05	15.00	26.25	25.35	45.20	42.35
26	7.02	6.60	17.25	16.05	27.10	26.40	46.80	43.60
28	7.32	6.78	18.40	17.25	28.05	27.50	48.15	44.85
30	7.55	6.92	19.50	18.30	29.45	28.10	50.05	47.95
35	8.62	7.95	23.65	22.85	34.85	32.75	54.95	52.75
40	10.35	9.65	28.50	25.05	39.85	37.45	61.35	58.25
45	14.55	12.95	33.90	28.35	46.40	40.25	67.05	63.75
50	19.05	17.60	38.95	34.50	52.45	45.80	74.15	69.60
55	28.95	24.30	47.40	42.85	59.85	53.20	—	—
60	—	—	51.00	46.85	67.50	62.35	—	—

Example

Paul Scott is 30 years old and wishes to purchase $25,000 of life insurance. Determine the annual cost of (a) term, (b) ordinary life, and (c) 20-payment life.

From the preceding table, the three rates per $1,000 for a 30-year-old male are: term, $7.55; ordinary life, $19.50; 20-payment life, $29.45, per $25,000 (multiply by 25).

$$\text{Term:} \qquad 25(7.55) = \$188.75$$

$$\text{Ordinary life:} \qquad 25(19.50) = \$487.50$$

$$\text{20-payment life:} \qquad 25(29.45) = \$736.25$$

Example

Paul Scott (preceding example) continues the insurance until his death at age 59. Compute the total premiums paid under (a) term, (b) ordinary life, and (c) 20-payment life.

Term:

$$Age\ 30\text{–}40 = 10(188.75)\qquad = \$1,887.50$$

$$Age\ 40\text{–}50 = 10(10.35)\ (25) = \$2,587.50$$

$$Age\ 50\text{–}59 = 9(19.05)\ (25) = \$4,286.25$$

$$Total = \$8,761.25$$

Ordinary life:

$$29\ years\ at\ \$487.50 = \$14,137.50$$

20-payment life:

$$20\ payments\ at\ \$736.25 = \$14,725.00$$

The example shows that term insurance is the least expensive way to be covered. However, the example does not tell the whole story. We will cover nonforfeiture options to indicate a net-cost figure quite different from the premium costs.

Additional Options to Life Insurance Policies

Double indemnity benefit. The face value of the policy is doubled if death results from accidental causes (drowning, auto accident death, or fire).

Waiver of premium benefit. The annual premium is waivered or paid by the insurance company if the policyholder has total or permanent disability.

Nonforfeiture Options

Fire and motor vehicle insurance had value only if a fire or an accident occurred. Life insurance has value if the death of the policyholder occurs. It also accumulates value to the policyholder during the life of the policy. The exception to this is term insurance. The three forms of this accumulated value is cash value, paid-up insurance, and extended term insurance. A table describing the value of these options will be included in the life insurance policy.

Cash. The policyholder may receive the cash value of the amount of money stated in the policy. The insurance must be terminated to receive the cash. The cash value is available to the policyholder through borrowing, and the insurance policy remains in effect. If the loan has not been repaid at the time of death of the policyholder, the amount of the loan and interest will be deducted from the face value of the insurance.

Paid-up insurance. The cash value can be used to purchase life insurance that will remain in effect for the remainder of the policyholder's life.

Extended term insurance. The cash value can be used to purchase an amount of term insurance equal to the face value of the expiring policy. The term will depend upon the amount of cash value.

Nonforfeiture Options per $1,000

Policy Years	Ordinary Life			20-Payment Life			Endowment		
	Cash	Paid-Up	Term (Years)	Cash	Paid-Up	Term (Years)	Cash	Paid-Up	Term (Years)
5	$26.45	$102.50	7	$32.50	$122.00	12	$44.85	$140.00	15
10	78.45	295.00	19	108.20	294.00	26	114.50	289.00	25
15	134.20	415.00	23	173.50	545.00	30	195.45	530.00	22
20	187.20	775.00	18	285.00	820.00	30	345.00	750.00	22

Example

Carla Smith, age 24, is planning to buy a $20,000 ordinary life insurance policy. At age 39 she needs to borrow some money. Find the cash value of her insurance policy at that time. The insurance was in effect for 15 years. Therefore the cash value per $1,000 is $134.20.

$$(134.20) \, (20) = \$2,684.00$$

Net Cost of Insurance

Participating policy:

$$\text{Net cost} = \text{premiums} - \text{cash value} - \text{dividends}$$

Nonparticipating policy:

$$\text{Net cost} = \text{premiums} - \text{cash value}$$

Example

Robert Coats is planning to buy a 20-payment life insurance policy with a face value of $20,000. Mr. Coats is 26 years old. He can obtain insurance as quoted in the schedules in a participating policy. The dividends for the policy amounted to $1,163.00 for the 20 years. The nonparticipating premiums per $1,000 were $15.90. The cash values were the same for both policies. Determine the net cost for each of the policies.

Participating:

$$\text{Premiums} = (17.25)\,(20)\,(20\text{ years}) = \$6,900$$
$$\text{Cash value} = (285)\,(20) = \$5,700$$
$$\text{Dividends} = \$1,163$$
$$\text{Net cost} = \$6,900 - \$5,700 - \$1,163 = \$\quad 37$$

Nonparticipating:

$$\text{Premiums} = (15.90)\,(20)\,(20) = \$6,360$$
$$\text{Cash value} = (285)\,(20) = \$5,700$$
$$\text{Net cost} = \$6,360 - \$5,700 = \$\ 660$$

This example illustrates the need to compare more than the premium rates when choosing insurance coverage.

Interest-Adjusted Net Cost

When policies remain in effect for many years, the cash value and dividends often exceed the total premiums. This net cost does not consider the time value of money. The cash values and dividends need to be adjusted to the interest these funds have accumulated over the term of the policy.

The **interest-adjusted net cost** (IANC) method involves an interest-adjustment factor:

$$\text{Interest-adjustment factor} = \left[\frac{1}{s_{\overline{m}\,i} - 1}\right]n$$

$$\text{Interest-adjusted net cost} = \text{premiums} - (\text{dividends} + \text{cash value})$$
$$\times (\text{interest-adjustment factor})$$

If the preceding example were done by the interest-adjusted net-cost method:

$$= 6,900 - (5,700 + 1,163)\,(0.64580)$$

$$= 6,900 - 4,432.13$$

$$= \$2,467.87$$

This is a more realistic net cost of insurance than the $37 found without the interest-adjustment factor. The interest-adjustment factor is determined using 4% for 21 years.

$$\left[\frac{1}{s_{\overline{21}|\,0.04} - 1}\right](20) = 0.64580$$

Example

Maria Estes is considering a participating $10,000 whole life policy. The premiums are quoted at $19.25 per $1,000. After 15 years the cash value of the policy is $1,280 and the dividends amounted to $865. Find the interest-adjusted net cost of the policy if the interest rate is 5%.

$$\text{Interest-adjustment factor} - \left[\frac{1}{s_{\overline{15}|\,0.05} - 1}\right](15) = 0.6620$$

$$\text{Adjusted net cost} = 2,887.50 - (1,280 + 865)\,(0.6620)$$

$$\text{Adjusted net cost} = \$1,467.51$$

$$\text{Annual net cost} = \$97.83$$

$$\text{Annual cost per } \$1,000 = \$9.78$$

The $9.78 is the actual cost of the protection per $1,000; the remainder of the premium ($19.25 − $9.78 = $9.47) builds up cash value and dividends.

Settlement Options

At the death of a life insurance policyholder, there are several ways for the beneficiary to receive the death benefits. These are called settlement options.

1. **Lump-sum payment.** The beneficiary receives the face value in one lump-sum payment.

2. **An annuity.**

    a. Payment fixed—the fixed amount will be paid at equal intervals of time until the face value of the policy plus the accrued interest is depleted.

    b. Number of payments are fixed—the payments are determined so that the amount can be paid for the required number of payments.

    c. Annuity for life—payments depend on the age and sex of the beneficiary. Equal payments are made to the beneficiary for as long as the person lives. The insurance company pays only to the beneficiary. Upon the death of the beneficiary, all payments stop even if there is money left from the amount put into the annuity.

    d. Life annuity, guaranteed for a given number of years—similar to the annuity for life, but payments are smaller. The estate receives the payments for the guaranteed period even if the beneficiary should die.

All of these options except lump-sum payment involve an annuity problem.

    a. The amount of the annuity is the face value of the life insurance policy, the fixed payment is R, and i is known. Solve for n.

    b. The amount of the annuity is the face value of the life insurance policy, n is known, and i is known. Solve for R.

    c. The amount of the annuity is the face value of the life insurance policy. Mortality rates enter into the calculations of this type of annuity.

    d. The amount of the annuity is the face value of the life insurance policy. Mortality rates for the beneficiary enter into the calculations of the periodic payment.

Example
Joyce Weston, age 55 and the beneficiary of a $30,000 life insurance policy, has decided to receive the money in quarterly payments rather than a lump sum. Determine the quarterly amounts of the following options.

    a. Ms. Weston elects to receive payments for 15 years at an interest rate of 6%.

b. Ms. Weston elects an annuity for life and the insurance company quotes her $13.50 per $1,000 payment.

c. Ms. Weston elects a life annuity with 10 years guaranteed and the insurance company quotes $13.00 per $1,000 payment.

d. How long would payments continue if she needs quarterly payments of $900 per quarter and the interest rate of the annuity was 6%?

Option (a):

$$A = 30,000 \qquad i = 0.015 \qquad n = 60$$

$$30,000 = R \cdot a_{\overline{60}|\,0.015}$$

$$30,000 = R(39.380\ 268\ 8853)$$

$$R = \$761.80 \qquad \text{quarterly payment}$$

Option (b):

$$(13.50)\,(30) = \$405$$

Option (c):

$$(13.00)\,(30) = \$390$$

Option (d):

$$A = 30,000 \qquad i = 0.015 \qquad R = 900$$

$$30,000 = 900 \cdot a_{\overline{n}|\,0.015}$$

$$n = 46 \text{ or } 11^{1}/_{2} \text{ years}$$

SECTION 3 EXERCISES

Use the Life Insurance Premiums Table included in the text to determine the annual premiums of the following.

Face Value	Type	Sex	Age	Annual Premium
1. $5,000	Term	M	40	
2. $15,000	Limited payment	M	30	
3. $10,000	Ordinary	F	26	

4. $10,000   20-year endowment   F   20

5. $30,000   Limited payment   M   30

6. $100,000   Term   M   35

7. $25,000   20-year endowment   F   20

8. $50,000   Ordinary   M   18

9. Jane Bessey is 30 years old and wishes to purchase $20,000 life insurance. Determine the annual premiums for (a) term, (b) ordinary life, (c) 20-payment life, and (d) 20-year endowment. If Jane lives the expected life span as shown in the mortality tables, determine the premiums she will pay for each of the insurance types.

10. George Brown is 35 years old and wishes to purchase $30,000 life insurance. Determine the annual premiums for (a) term, (b) ordinary life, (c) 20-payment life, and (d) 20-year endowment. If George lives the expected life span as shown in the mortality tables, determine the total premiums he will pay for each of the insurance types.

11. At age 50 Henry Clark purchased a 20-payment life policy with a face value of $20,000. On his sixty-fifth birthday, he decided to cancel the policy. What were his options?

12. Mrs. Carter purchased a $10,000 ordinary life insurance policy at age 35. She is now 55 and is planning to cancel her policy. What options are available to her?

13. Calculate the net cost of a $25,000 ordinary life policy purchased by a male at age 45 and held to the age of 65 if the rate of interest is 6% and
   a. It was a nonparticipating policy.
   b. The policy had dividends of $2,286 during the period.

14. Calculate the net cost of a $50,000, 20-payment life policy purchased by a male at age 28 and held to the age of 65 if the rate of interest is 6% and
   a. It was a nonparticipating policy.
   b. The policy had dividends of $5,670 during the period.

15. Mrs. Jones' husband dies and leaves $30,000 in life insurance death benefits. If she elects to receive $2,000 a quarter and money is worth 8% annual interest, how many years will she receive benefits? If she elects instead to receive benefits for 15 years, how much are the quarterly benefits?

16. Mrs. Jones dies and leaves her daughter $50,000 in life insurance death benefits. If her daughter elects to receive $5,000 annually and the money

rate is 6% interest, how many years will she receive benefits? If she elects to receive benefits for 20 years, how much are her annual payments?

17. Mrs. Green has elected to receive monthly payments for life from her husband's $30,000 life insurance settlement. Mrs. Green is 53, the insurance company quotes $4.40 per $1,000 per month as her payment. What will be her monthly check? She dies at age 62. What settlement does the insurance make with her estate?

18. Barbara White has elected to take the death benefits of her husband's $25,000 insurance as a life annuity guaranteed for 100 months. She is 59 years old, the insurance company quotes her $4.90 per month per $1,000 as her monthly payment. She collects her monthly checks for 3 years and dies. What will the estate receive from the annuity?

Answers to Odd-Numbered Exercises

1. $51.75.

3. $160.50.

5. $883.

7. $1,027.50.

9.

	Annual Premium for 48 Years	
Term	$138.40	$6,834 for 30 years, none after 60
Ordinary life	366.00	$17,568.
20-payment life	562.00	$11,240.
20-year endowment	959.00	$19,180 received $20,000, age 50

11. Cash, $3,470 or paid-up insurance $10,900. Term insurance for 30 years.

13. (a) 16,950 − (4,680) (.55888) = $14,334.42   net cost
                                        716.70   annual cost
                                         28.67   annual per $1,000.
    (b) 16,950 − (6,974) (.55888) = $13,052.37   net cost
                                        652.62   annual cost
                                         26.10   annual per $1,000.

15. 18 periods or 4.5 years.

17. $132 monthly. 0 settlement.

6.4   GROUP INSURANCE

Most businesses and industries provide their employees some type of insurance option. Sometimes the premiums are paid by the employers, some insurance premiums are shared by employers and employee, and some are paid by the employees. The group rates are lower than those available to individuals.

Life Insurance

Life insurance provided by your employer is term insurance. All benefits are lost when employment is terminated. If the insurance is paid by the employee and employment is terminated, the employee may be offered the option of continuing the term insurance coverage at a higher premium. There is no requirement for a physical examination for group life insurance. However, the employer may require a physical examination for employment. Some professional organizations have options for life insurance for their members. The premiums are generally lower than the individual rate.

Health Insurance

Health insurance coverage is another benefit offered by many businesses and industries. The benefits from these policies differ, the premiums can be paid by the employer, the employee, or some combination of both. The insurance terminates when employment is terminated. Usually there is a grace period to provide time to the individual to become qualified under another plan. If health insurance is a benefit of employment, other family members can usually be included in the group insurance. Premiums are paid by the employee. The rates are usually lower than individual premiums.

Motor Vehicle Insurance

Vehicles owned by a business are insured by the business. If the individual owns the vehicle and is paid by the employer for the mileage used in business activity, the individual is liable for the insurance. The business will usually dictate the liability insurance coverage on the vehicle or will have a disclaimer for liability.

Summary

Fire Insurance

Factors affecting fire insurance rates

1. Type of structure

2. Geographic location

3. Building use

Motor Vehicle Insurance

Types

Liability—protects party injured by policyholder

Collision—protects property of policyholder

Comprehensive—protects policyholder against nonaccident damages

Factors affecting motor vehicle insurance rates

1. Amount of liability coverage

2. Territory in which vehicle is operated

3. Classification of driver

4. Age of vehicle

5. Value of vehicle

6. Amount of deductible

Life Insurance

Types

Term—protection for a specified term

Ordinary life—protection for life with a fixed premium

Limited Payment Life—fixed premium paid for a specified number of years

Endowment—protection for a specified number of years, face value paid to insured at the end of the period.

Additional Options

Double Indemnity—face value doubled if death results from accidental causes

Waiver of Premium benefit—premiums waived for disabled policyholder

Nonforfeiture option—face value of the policy increases each year the insurance remains in effect

Paid-up Insurance—dividends are used to buy additional insurance coverage

Interest-Adjusted Net Cost

$$\text{IANC} = \text{Total premiums paid} - [\text{Dividend} + \text{Cash value}] \\ \times [\text{Interest adjustment factor}]$$

$$\text{Interest adjustment factor} = \left[\frac{1}{s_{\overline{m}\,i} - 1}\right] n$$

REVIEW EXERCISES

In the following exercises, use values from the appropriate tables for rate information.

1. A business structure is valued at $625,000. The rate of fire insurance per $100 was 0.359. The business insured the structure for $400,000. During the term of the insurance, a fire caused $120,000 damage to the structure. The insurance policy carried an 80% coinsurance clause.
    a. Find the annual premium.
    b. Find the compensation received for the fire loss.

2. Casey Company had fire insurance coverage with three companies at the following rates per $1,000: $35,000 with A insurance @ $4.68; $26,000 with B Insurance @ $4.75; and $79,000 with C Insurance @ $4.70. The value of the building is $150,000. A fire extensively damaged the building, and the amount of damage was $96,000.
    a. Determine the annual premiums paid by each insurance company.

b. Determine the amount of compensation paid by each insurance company.

3. Determine the difference in premiums for two $75,000 homes. One is brick and located in area 1 and the other is wood (frame) and located in area 5.

4. Jane Andrews paid her annual insurance premium on her $62,500 brick veneer home in area 4. Four months later she sold the house. Find the amount of rebate she will receive from the fire insurance company when she cancels the coverage.

5. John Moore lives in territory 3 and owns an automobile that is 2 years old. He is a class B driver. He purchases insurance on his vehicle of the following type.

> Liability   25/50/10
> Collision $200 deductible
> No comprehensive coverage

John is 28 years old, and his wife, age 23, is also listed as a driver of the vehicle. Determine the annual premiums for the insurance coverage.

6. Carl Thompson lives in territory 2 and buys a new class 4 vehicle. He is a class A driver. One of the drivers listed on the insurance application is his 17-year-old son who has had driver training. Determine the amount of his premium if he elects the following coverage.

> Liability   100/300/20
> Collision $200 deductible
> Comprehensive

7. Carl Thompson's son was involved in an accident in a state where no-fault insurance is legal. Carl's son was severely injured and was hospitalized for 5 months. The medical bills were $86,000. The damage to the vehicle was $7,400. The other vehicle had damages of $3,400, but no one was injured. Find the settlement to Carl Thompson and to the other vehicle by the insurance company.

8. Tom Douglass purchased a new class 2 vehicle. He is a class A driver, age 22, and lives in territory 3. How much must he pay annually for 10/20/10 liability, comprehensive, and $200 deductible collision insurance? He did not take driver's training and is not a student. The first month he had an accident and was found at fault for $6,500 in damages to the other vehicle, $14,000 in bodily damage to the driver of the other vehicle, and $850

in damages to his car. What was the settlement of the insurance company and to whom was it paid?

9. Joyce Day purchased $10,000 ordinary life insurance at age 30. Find her annual premium. If Joyce lives exactly the years expected, find the total cost of the insurance if she continues the coverage throughout her life. If she decides at age 50 to cancel the insurance and take the paid-up insurance, how much insurance benefit does her estate receive when she dies at age 77?

10. Tom Smith took out a 20-payment life policy at age 26 for $25,000. Find his annual premium. Tom dies at age 40, and his widow elects to take the settlement in the form of an annuity. The insurance company quotes monthly payments of $36 per $1,000 for life. Find the amount of her monthly check.

11. Steve Armstrong purchased a 20-year endowment at age 18 for $50,000. Find the annual premiums for the coverage. At age 38, he collects the face value of the policy. What did he receive? How much of the amount that he received was capital gain—amount more than he had put into the policy?

12. Find the net annual cost per $1,000 of an ordinary life insurance policy of a female who purchased the insurance at age 28 and the insurance had been in effect for 15 years. The face value was $25,000, money is worth 6% annual interest, and
    a. The insurance was with a nonparticipating company.
    b. The insurance was with a mutual company, and the accumulated dividends amounted to $956.

13. Ms. Clarke is the beneficiary of her husband's $40,000 insurance policy. She elects to take the settlement as an annuity with quarterly payments of $1,250. Money earns 8% annual interest at the time she makes the settlement. How many years will she receive payments?

14. Tom Tanner purchased a $100,000 ordinary life insurance policy at age 30. Find his annual premiums. He dies at age 50, and his wife decides on an annuity as settlement. The mortality tables predict she will live another 30 years. What annual payment can she receive if money is worth 6% interest at the time she negotiates the annuity?

Answers to Review Exercises

1. (a) $1,436. (b) $96,000.

2.

Company	Premium	Compensation
A	$163.80	$24,000
B	123.50	17,829
C	317.30	54,171

3. Difference, $277.

4. Annual premium, $184. 4-month cost, $88. Rebate, $96.

5. $439.

6. $524.80.

7. $86,000 medical. $7,200 collision. Nothing to other vehicle as they would claim from their own insurance.

8. $530.40 premium. To owner of other vehicle, $6,500. To operator of other vehicle, $10,000. Tom Douglass, $650.

9. $183, annual premium. $8,601, total premiums. $7,750, insurance benefits if cancel at age 50.

10. $677.50, annual premium. $900 per month for remainder of her life.

11. $2,142.50, premium. $50,000, received. $7,150, capital gain.

12. (a) Net cost, $4,209.59 or net premium/1,000, $11.23. (b) Net cost, $3,565.85 or net premium/1,000, $9.51.

13. 12.75 years.

14. Annual payment, $7,265.

Chapter 7

STATISTICAL METHODS

In the present-day world large quantities of information are generated, accumulated, and preserved. Organized information provides meaning to past performance, predicts trends to future demands, and forms the basis for analysis and management of the business community. This chapter is concerned with the many tools available for ordering data and displaying the information in an attractive and meaningful array. A representative quantity can be more meaningful than a large array of items. These representative quantities are classified as measures of central tendency. It is important to select measures that best represent data. Measures of dispersion indicate how closely the measure of central tendency represents the original information.

The most common graphs used to represent data distribution are presented. These include the normal curve, the line graph, the bar graph, and the circle graph. Construction techniques and selection criteria are included for each of the types of graphs.

At the end of this chapter, the student will be able to:

1. Display data distribution by a frequency table, a histogram, a frequency polygon, and a cumulative frequency distribution.

2. Compute the measures of central tendency, the mean, median, and mode. Determine the appropriateness of each measure for the representation of the given data.

3. Compute the measures of dispersion, the range, mean deviation, standard deviation, and variance, and determine the distribution of data, given a measure of central tendency and a measure of dispersion.

4. Identify data that fit the pattern of a normal curve, construct a normal curve, determine the amount of data within one standard deviation from the mean, and predict the distribution of data if a normal curve represents the array.

5. Determine the standard score for any piece of data in a normal distribution and determine the percentage of data between two given values.

6. Present data by bar graphs, line graphs, stacked graphs, and component graphs, and select the graphs that best illustrate the data.

7.1   FREQUENCY DISTRIBUTIONS

Large quantities of raw data can be organized or arranged to clarify and give meaning to the array. Take as an example, a monthly printout of the number of customers served by order clerks in an 8-hour shift period at one of the fast food chains. The computer pulls the data from the cash registers automatically. An unorganized array of this information is

167	182	158	155	182	146	201	138	147	171
156	147	172	146	182	139	140	152	132	145
173	164	139	128	135	142	163	149	138	172
128	135	163	147	132	150	135	170	152	146
134	164	151	168	149	140	170	134	142	175
147	136	139	150	147	149	130	142	153	170

This printout of the data has little meaning or use. The collection of data that has not been systematically arranged is called **raw data**.

An **array** arranges the raw data in either ascending or descending order. The preceding information presented as an **array** is

128	128	130	132	132	134	134	135	135	135
136	138	138	139	139	139	140	140	142	142
142	145	146	146	146	147	147	147	147	147
149	149	149	150	150	151	152	152	153	155
156	158	163	163	164	164	167	168	170	170
170	171	172	172	173	175	182	182	182	201

The organization makes the highest and lowest scores readily available. An individual score can be compared with the scores of other employees. The relative standing of employees is readily available and is probably used as an evaluation tool by the employer.

A **frequency distribution table** is a tabular arrangement of raw data by classes or intervals. Each piece of raw data is tallied within an interval. The result of this tally is known as the **frequency**. A **frequency distribution table** indicates the size and frequency of each interval.

The steps to construct a frequency distribution table are as follows.

1. Identify the smallest and largest elements. Their difference is the **range**.

2. Determine the number of intervals or classes. This is usually some number between 5 and 15. The larger the range, the more intervals are needed to best represent the array.

3. Determine the size of each interval by dividing the range of the data by the number of intervals selected in step 2. Round the quotient up to the next whole number.

4. Determine the class boundaries. The lower boundary should be less than the smallest element, and the upper boundary should be larger than the largest element. Select boundaries so the location of elements is uniquely determined. If the raw data are in whole numbers, half units might determine boundaries so each whole number is uniquely placed. If the raw data are in tenths of units, select boundaries in hundredths.

5. Identify each element from the raw data with an interval. This process is usually accomplished by a tally mark in the proper location.

6. Determine the number of tallies in each interval. This is called the **class frequency**.

To illustrate each of these steps, the data presented previously as **raw data** and organized as an **array** are used.

Step 1. The smallest number is 128, the largest number is 201, and the range is 73 ($201 - 128 = 73$).

Step 2. The number of intervals is arbitrary. The range of 73 might suggest 8 intervals.

Step 3. The size of each class is range/number of intervals, rounded up. In this case $73/8 = 9.125$. Rounding up to the next largest integer gives an interval size of 10.

Step 4. Class boundaries must be selected so each piece of data is uniquely placed in an interval. If the first interval boundary is 125 to 135, the second interval boundary 135 to 145, and so on, the data element of 135 could be placed in either the first or second interval. Choosing boundaries in half units ensures a unique tally of each element in the array. The first interval is chosen as 125.5 to 135.5, the second 135.5 to 145.5, and so on, through 205.5.

Different boundary selections produce a slightly different frequency distribution table. Either is correct; it is important to indicate interval boundaries.

Step 5. Tally the data in the appropriate intervals. The following table shows the tally.

Step 6. Total each class tally to get the class frequency.

Step 7. Label the frequency distribution table.

**Number of Sales for Clerks at McDaniels
in an 8-Hour Interval**

Sales	Tally	Frequency
125.5–135.5	//////////	10
135.5–145.5	////////////	12
145.5–155.5	//////////////////	18
155.5–165.5	//////	6
165.5–175.5	//////////	10
175.5–185.5	///	3
185.5–195.5		0
195.5–205.5	/	1

Although the table has destroyed much of the original data, an "overall" picture has been obtained that makes pertinent facts more evident.

From the preceding frequency distribution table, the class with the greatest population has the boundary 145.5 to 155.5. The number used to categorize these 18 pieces of data is the **classmark**, the midpoint of the class. To obtain the classmark, add the endpoints together and divide by 2. The classmarks for the preceding table are

$$\text{Classmark 1} = 125.5 + 135.5 = 261 \qquad \frac{261}{2} = 130.5$$

$$\text{Classmark 2} = 135.5 + 145.5 = 281 \qquad \frac{281}{2} = 140.5$$

The remaining classmarks can be calculated by taking the average of the boundaries. Observe an increase of 10 in the classmarks so far and use the pattern to give the remaining classmarks of 150.5, 160.5, 170.5, 180.5, 190.5, and 200.5.

Another calculation possible from the frequency distribution table is the relative frequency of each class. To determine the **relative frequency**, divide the frequency of each class by the total number of data elements. The total number of data points in this example is 60. The relative frequencies for each of the eight classes is $10/60 = 0.17$, $12/60 = 0.2$, $18/60 = 0.3$, $6/60 = 0.10$, $10/60 = 0.17$, $3/60 = 0.05$, $0/60 = 0$, and $1/60 = 0.02$. The relative frequencies can be used to determine the percent of clerks with certain characteristics.

Example
The percent of clerks serving more than 155 customers can be determined by adding the relative frequencies of the top five intervals, giving a total of 0.34 or 34%.

A frequency table including all of this information is as follows.

Frequency Distribution Table
Number of Sales for Clerks in 8-Hours

Sales	Frequency	Classmark	Relative Frequency
125.5–135.5	10	130.5	0.17
135.5–145.5	12	140.5	0.20
145.5–155.5	18	150.5	0.30
155.5–165.5	6	160.5	0.10
165.5–175.5	10	170.5	0.17
175.5–185.5	3	180.5	0.05
185.5–195.5	0	190.5	0.00
195.5–205.5	1	200.5	0.02

Histograms and Frequency Polygons

Two graphical representations of frequency distributions are **histograms** and **frequency polygons**.

A **histogram** consists of a set of rectangles with the following characteristics.

1. Bases on the horizontal axis representing the interval boundaries, the center of the base labeled by the classmark.

2. If the class intervals are all of equal size, the heights of the rectangles are numerically equal to the class frequencies. If class intervals are not all of equal size, heights must be adjusted to compensate for the varying widths.

3. The areas of the rectangles are proportional to the class frequencies.

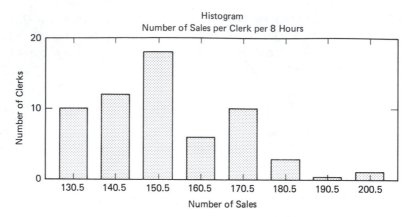

A **frequency polygon** is a line graph of class frequencies (vertical axis) plotted against the classmark (horizontal axis). The polygon can be obtained by connecting the midpoints of the tops of the rectangles in the histogram. It is customary to extend the horizontal axis to include a classmark above and below the classmarks in the frequency distribution chart. The frequency associated with these marks is zero. The completed polygon has a closed area, and the total area of the polygon is equal to the total area of the histogram representing the distribution.

Be sure to label a histogram or frequency polygon with a title, and identify the quantity and units of each axis.

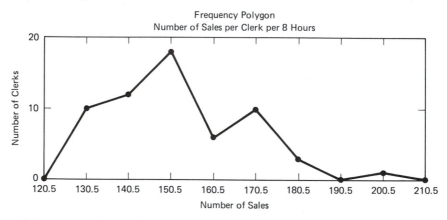

Other variations of pictorial representations of frequency distributions include the following.

1. In a relative frequency polygon the horizontal axis remains the same as the frequency polygon. The vertical axis scale is relative frequency values expressed as a percent. The diagram resembles the frequency polygon, but the markings on the vertical axis are relative frequency rather than frequency.

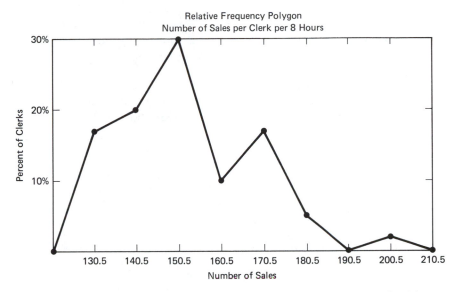

2. Relative frequency histograms change the vertical scales of a histogram from frequency to relative frequency.

3. The cumulative frequency polygon retains the same horizontal axis. The vertical axis represents the population frequency up to and including that class interval. Cumulative frequency polygons are also called ogives. In

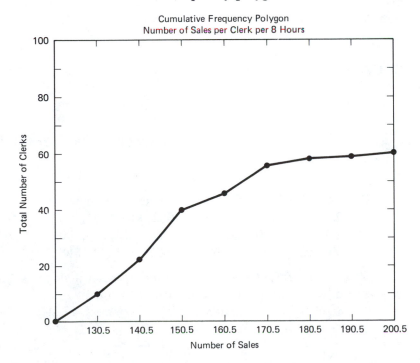

the preceding frequency distribution chart, the cumulative frequencies (from top to bottom) are 10, 22, 40, 46, 56, 59, 59, and 60. These are plotted against each corresponding classmark.

4. If a frequency polygon represents a large population and each class interval is small, a frequency polygon is made up of so many small broken line segments that the broken lines approximate curves. These smoothed-out lines formed into a curve produce a graph called a **frequency curve**.

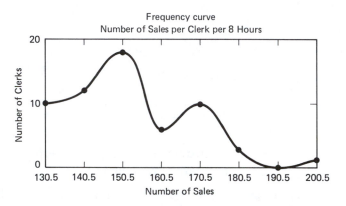

Frequency distribution charts, the histogram, the frequency polygon, the relative frequency polygon or histogram, and the cumulative frequency polygon or histogram are all pictorial representations of the distribution of data.

SECTION 1 EXERCISES

Use the following four sets of raw data throughout the exercises.

Raw data A: Measured widths (in centimeters) of woolen fabric
112.4, 115.6, 109.2, 110.0, 115.2, 116.0, 108.5, 108.5, 111.7, 112.2, 116.4, 114.7, 113.9, 117.1, 116.7, 109.7, 111.1, 111.5, 112.6, 112.9

Raw data B: Real estate transactions at Econoworld
$52,250, $74,200, $69,900, $62,000, $84,500, $49,900, $87,500, $62,250, $75,500, $57,700, $87,700, $64,400, $76,700, $67,700, $82,000, $55,500, $67,100, $79,500, $82,200, $68,200

Raw data C: Recorded high temperatures (in degrees Fahrenheit) at Presque Isle, Maine for the month of October
58, 70, 67, 62, 56, 54, 50, 59, 65, 63, 58, 60, 52, 47, 47, 55, 58, 60, 61, 67, 67, 65, 68, 66, 59, 62, 64, 61, 54, 50, 51

Raw data D: Recorded high temperatures (in degrees Fahrenheit) at Miami, Florida for the month of July
82, 98, 96, 92, 88, 90, 86, 95, 101, 96, 94, 88, 87, 85, 89, 92, 91, 94, 92, 84, 86, 86, 92, 91, 90, 87, 89, 90, 92, 91, 90

1. Make an array of raw data A. Describe the position of entry 116.0 from the array.

2. Make an array for raw data B. Describe the $75,500 sale in comparison to the other sales at Econoworld.

3. Make a frequency distribution table for raw data A. Group the data using 108.05 to 109.55 as the first interval.

4. Make a frequency distribution table for raw data B. Group the data using $49,000 to $54,000 as the first interval.

5. Make a frequency distribution table for raw data C. Group the data using 45.5 to 49.5 as the first interval.

6. Make a frequency distribution table for raw data D. Group the data using 81.5 to 84.5 as the first interval.

7. Determine the range of raw data A.

8. Determine the range of raw data B.

9. Determine the classmarks of raw data C.

10. Determine the classmarks of raw data D.

11. Determine the relative frequencies of raw data A.

12. Determine the relative frequencies of raw data B.

13. Determine the cumulative frequencies of raw data C.

14. Determine the cumulative frequencies of raw data D.

15. Draw a histogram to represent raw data A.

16. Draw a histogram to represent raw data B.

17. Draw a histogram to represent raw data C.

18. Draw a histogram to represent raw data D.

19. Draw a frequency polygon for raw data A.

20. Draw a frequency polygon for raw data B.

21. Draw a frequency polygon for raw data C.

22. Draw a frequency polygon for raw data D.

23. Draw a relative frequency polygon for raw data A.

24. Draw a relative frequency polygon for raw data B.

25. Draw a relative frequency histogram for raw data C.

26. Draw a relative frequency histogram for raw data D.

27. Draw a cumulative frequency polygon for raw data A.

28. Draw a cumulative frequency polygon for raw data B.

29. Draw a frequency curve for raw data C.

30. Draw a frequency curve for raw data D.

31. Do a second workup (frequency distribution, histogram, cumulative frequency), using an interval size of 3 for raw data C. Compare the result with the results of exercises 5, 9, 13, 17, 21, and 25.

32. Do a second workup (frequency distribution, histogram, cumulative frequency), using an interval size of 2 for raw data D. Compare the result with the results of exercises 6, 10, 14, 18, 22, and 26.

Answers to Odd-Numbered Exercises

1.
108.5   108.5   109.2   109.7   110.0   111.1   111.5
111.7   112.2   112.4   112.6   112.9   113.9   114.7
115.2   115.6   116.0   116.4   116.7   117.1

116.0 is in the top quarter of widths.

3.

108.05–109.55	///	3
109.55–111.05	//	2
111.05–112.55	/////	5
112.55–114.05	///	3
114.05–115.55	//	2
115.55–117.05	////	4
117.05–118.55	/	1

5.

45.5–49.5	//	2
49.5–53.5	////	4
53.5–57.5	////	4
57.5–61.5	////////	9

61.5–65.5	//////	6
65.5–69.5	/////	5
69.5–73.5	/	1

7. Range, 8.6.

9. Classmarks, 47.5, 51.5, 55.5, 59.5, 63.5, 67.5, and 71.5.

11. 0.15, 0.10, 0.25, 0.15, 0.10, 0.20, and 0.05.

13. 2, 6, 10, 19, 25, 30, and 31.

15.

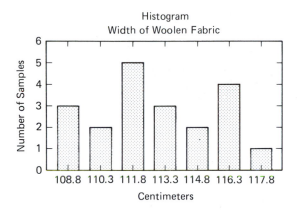

17.

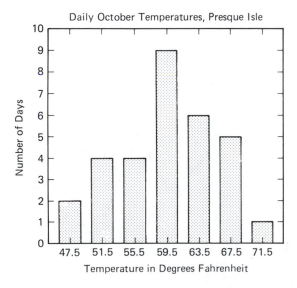

19.

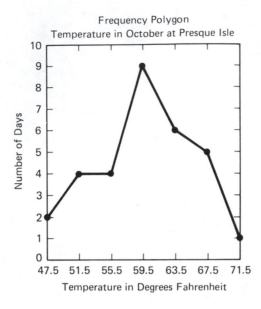

Frequency Polygon
Temperature in October at Presque Isle

21.

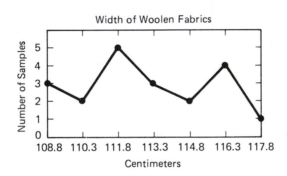

23.

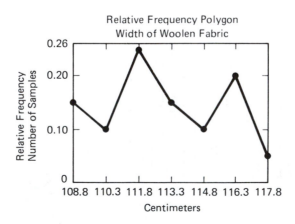

25.

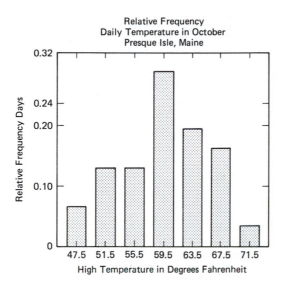

Relative Frequency
Daily Temperature in October
Presque Isle, Maine

27.

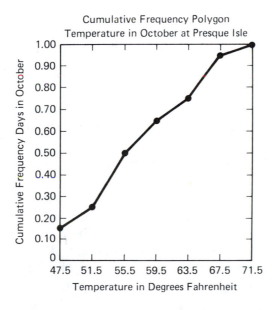

Cumulative Frequency Polygon
Temperature in October at Presque Isle

29.

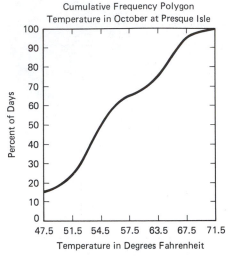

Cumulative Frequency Polygon
Temperature in October at Presque Isle

31.

Interval	Frequency	Classmark	Cumulative Frequency
45.5–48.5	2	47	2
48.5–51.5	3	50	5
51.5–54.5	3	53	8
54.5–57.5	2	56	10
57.5–60.5	7	59	17
60.5–63.5	5	62	22
63.5–66.5	4	65	26
66.5–69.5	4	68	30
69.5–72.5	1	71	31

With smaller intervals, the data is more spread out.

7.2 MEASURES OF CENTRAL TENDENCY

More data are available to businesses than can reasonably be handled or absorbed. It is desirable to quantify large amounts of information by a single numerical representation. This number can be chosen from three available measures of central tendency, the **mean, mode**, and **median**. To explore measures of central tendency, the following two sets of information will be used to illustrate the differences.

Set A	Set B
28.5	20
28.5	25
28.5	27
28.5	28

Set A	*Set B*
28.5	28
28.5	30
29.0	32
32.0	33
	38

The **average** or **mean** is the middle of all the values. The average is not the same as the physical middle. The mean does not have to be any of the elements of the set. The symbol used to denote average or mean is $\bar{x}$.

The average or mean is found by adding all of the elements of the set and dividing by the number of elements of the set.

$$\bar{x} = \Sigma\, x/n$$

where Σ is the symbol for "sum of," x represents the individual elements, and n is the number of elements.

$\bar{x}$ of set A:

$$\frac{(28.5 + 28.5 + 28.5 + 28.5 + 28.5 + 28.5 + 29 + 32)}{8} = 29$$

$\bar{x}$ of set B:

$$\frac{(20 + 25 + 27 + 28 + 28 + 30 + 32 + 33 + 38)}{9} = 29$$

The **mean** of each set is 29. The mean of 29 can represent different arrays of values. Representation of a set of elements by its mean introduces some inaccuracy but is more convenient than listing all of the elements.

Mean from a Frequency Distribution Table

The mean can be calculated from data presented in a frequency distribution table. The mean will be similar to, but not precisely equal to, the mathematical mean of the raw data.

We will use the frequency diagram from the last section to illustrate the procedure for finding the mean from grouped data.

Sales	Classmark	Frequency
125.5–135.5	130.5	10
135.5–145.5	140.5	12
145.5–155.5	150.5	18
155.5–165.5	160.5	6
165.5–175.5	170.5	10
175.5–185.5	180.5	3
185.5–195.5	190.5	0
195.5–205.5	200.5	1

The classmark is identified for each interval in the table. Multiply the classmark by the frequency for each interval and record the product. The heading of the column is $f \cdot x$ or fx. Total the entries in column fx and divide by the total of the class frequencies (this is the total number of entries). The quotient is the frequency distribution table mean.

Sales	Classmark	Frequency	fx
125.5–135.5	130.5	10	1,305.0
135.5–145.5	140.5	12	1,686.0
145.5–155.5	150.5	18	2,709.0
155.5–165.5	160.5	6	963.0
165.5–175.5	170.5	10	1,705.0
175.5–185.5	180.5	3	541.5
185.5–195.5	190.5	0	0.0
195.5–205.5	200.5	1	200.5
		$\Sigma f = 60$	$\Sigma fx = 9,110.0$

$$\text{Mean} = \frac{9,110}{60} = 151.83$$

The mean from the original data is 148.73. The difference is small and when the number of observations is large, the convenience of grouped data outweighs the loss in accuracy.

The formula used for finding the mean from a frequency table is

$$\text{Sample mean} = \bar{x} = \frac{\Sigma fx}{\Sigma f}$$

The mean, as a single number representing a whole data set, has important advantages. First, the concept of mean or average is familiar to most people. Second, every set of data has one and only one mean. Finally, a mean is a number that allows comparison of several data sets.

Mode

The element occurring most frequently in a set is called the **mode**. A set can have more than one mode, or no mode. Set A has a mode of 28.5 because the element 28.5 occurs 6 times. Set B has a mode of 28 because the element 28 occurs 2 times. All other elements occur only once.

The **mode** is the measure used to answer the question: Which element occurred most frequently? The mode is always an element in the set because the definition states the mode is the element occurring most often.

To determine the mode from the data presented in a frequency distribution table, identify the interval with the greatest frequency and use the classmark of that interval as the mode. In the preceding frequency distribution table, the largest frequency is 18, and the classmark of the interval is 150.5. This is the mode for the information presented in tabular form. The mode from the raw data presented in Section 1 is 147.

The mode is not affected by extreme values in the data and is the tool that shows preference. Modes are not always unique, and some sets have no mode. Modes are not used as frequently as means for representing a set of data.

Median

The **median** is the physical middle of the set of elements arranged as an array. If the number of elements in the set is even, the median is found by averaging the two middle elements. In set A, the median is $(28.5 + 28.5)/2 = 28.5$. If the number of elements is odd, the middle element of the array is the median of the set. In set B the number of elements is odd, therefore the median is the middle element, 28. This array has four elements above 28, and four elements below 28.

To determine the median from tabular data:

1. Identify the total frequency.

2. Divide the total frequency by 2.

3. Starting from either the top or the bottom of the table, add frequencies until the total frequency/2 is reached. The classmark of the interval is the median.

In the frequency distribution table used in illustrating the mean, the total frequency/2 is 30. Adding frequencies from the top, $10 + 12 = 22$, $22 + 18 = 40$. Thirty is less than 40 but larger than 22. The median falls in this interval and the classmark of 150.5 is used as the median. The array has a median of 148.

Advantages of the median include the small effect of extreme values. The median is uniquely determined and can be found for descriptive words as well as numerical entries. The data must be put into an array before the median can be determined. This is a disadvantage for a large number of elements.

Example
The weight of 10 basketball players was not known. However, statistics revealed the mean weight was 178 pounds, and the median weight was 176.5. What deductions can be made from this information?

Because half of the weights lie above 176.5 and half below 176.5 and have a mean weight of 178, it would be reasonable to deduce that at least one player is quite a bit heavier than the average 178 pounds.

Example
Rounds of cheese vary in weight. A company assumes an average weight of 82 pounds. When the order arrives, the median weight is listed as 85 pounds. What conclusions can be made concerning the weights of the cheeses ordered?

Because the median weight is higher than the mean weight, at least one of the cheeses is quite a bit lighter than the mean weight of 82 pounds.

SECTION 2 EXERCISES

Use the following arrays of data as referred to in the exercises.

Array A	Array B	Array C	Array D
108.5	49,900	47	82
108.5	52,250	47	84
109.2	55,500	50	85
109.7	57,700	50	86
110.0	62,000	51	86
111.1	62,250	52	86
111.5	64,400	54	87
111.7	67,000	54	87
112.2	67,700	55	88
112.4	68,200	56	88
112.6	69,900	58	89
112.9	74,200	58	89
113.9	75,500	58	90

Array A	Array B	Array C	Array D
114.7	76,600	59	90
115.2	79,500	59	90
115.6	82,000	60	90
116.0	82,200	60	91
116.4	84,500	61	91
116.7	87,500	61	91
117.1	87,700	62	92
		62	92
		63	92
		64	92
		65	92
		65	94
		66	94
		67	95
		67	96
		67	96
		68	98
		70	101

1. Determine the median for array A.

2. Determine the median for array B.

3. Determine the median for array C.

4. Determine the median for array D.

5. Determine the mean for array A.

6. Determine the mean for array B.

7. Determine the mean for array C.

8. Determine the mean for array D.

9. Determine the mode for array A.

10. Determine the mode for array B.

11. Determine the mode for array C.

12. Determine the mode for array D.

13. Determine the mean from a frequency distribution table for array A. Compare this answer with the answer to exercise 5. This array has the same data as in the exercises following Section 1. The distribution table constructed in exercise 3 may be used.

14. Determine the mean from a frequency distribution table for array *B* (exercise 4, Section 1). Compare this answer with the answer to exercise 6.

15. Determine the mean from a frequency distribution table for array *C* (exercise 5, Section 1). Compare this answer with the answer to exercise 7.

16. Determine the mean from a frequency distribution table for array *D* (exercise 6, Section 1). Compare this answer with the answer to exercise 8.

17. The class mean on a final examination was 82. The median was 78. The mode was 88. Describe the type of distribution of the grades.

18. Test scores on a mathematics test had a mean of 77.8, a median of 79, and a mode of 75. Describe the scores of the class.

19. You are to be hanged on the village oak tree. Two lots of rope are available for the hanging and you have the privilege of choosing the lot to be used. Your weight is 185 pounds. Weight tests before breaking:

| Lot *A* | Mean 188 | Mode 189 | Median 186 |
| Lot *B* | Mean 188 | Mode 184 | Median 189 |

Which lot would you choose and why?

20. You are betting $100 on a basketball team. The only statistics available concern height.

| Team *A* | Mean 80 inches | Median 80 inches | Mode 80 inches |
| Team *B* | Mean 79 inches | Median 81 inches | Mode 80 inches |

Which team would you bet on and why?

Answers to Odd-Numbered Exercises

1. 112.5.

3. 60.

5. 112.8.

7. 59.2.

9. 108.5.

11. 58 and 67.

13. 112.925—this is slightly higher than the mean calculated from the raw data.

15. 59.63—this is higher by 0.43 degrees.

17. The number of grades above and below 78 were equal. The grades above 78 were further above than the grades below. More than 1 student received 88.

19. Lot *B*. Maybe a rope of test weight below 185 pounds will be selected, the rope will break, and your life will be spared.

7.3 MEASURES OF DISPERSION

The way data spread out about the mean is called the **variation** or **dispersion** of the data. Various measures of variation are available. This section will address range, mean deviation, and standard deviation.

Range

The range of a set of numbers is the difference between the smallest and largest elements of the set. Set *A* represents 28.5, 28.5, 28.5, 28.5, 28.5, 28.5, 29, 32 and the range is $32 - 28.5 = 3.5$. The range is indicated either as the actual difference 3.5 or by the statement $28.5 - 32$. Set *B* represents 20, 25, 27, 28, 28, 30, 33, 38 and the range of set *B* is $38 - 20 = 18$ or $20 - 38$.

Reviewing the measures of central tendency along with the ranges for set *A* and set *B* gives some meaning to **range**.

Set *A*:			Set *B*:		
	Mean	29.0		Mean	29
	Mode	28.5		Mode	28
	Median	28.5		Median	28
	Range	3.5		Range	18

The range is the first measure that suggests two really different sets of data. The means of set *A* and set *B* are identical, the modes are close, 28.5 and 28, and the medians are close, 28.5 and 28. The ranges vary dramatically; one is 3.5 and the other is 18. Generally, the smaller the range, the closer the measures of central tendency approximate the original information. The small range represents a packed set of elements; none differ much from the measure of central tendency.

The range for grouped data is the difference between the upper limit of the largest interval and the lower limit of the smallest interval.

The range is greatly influenced by the extreme elements and does not consider the number or location of "middle" elements. Range is likely to change dramatically from one sample to another even when the samples are quite similar.

Referring to set A and set B as described previously, if set A and set B represent the test strength of two different brands of fishing line, set A would have the more desirable statistics because of greater consistency in the test strength.

If set A and set B represent the scoring statistics of two potential basketball recruits, set B might be more attractive because of the potential for a really high-scoring game. Notice one of the elements in set B is 38.

Mean or Average Deviation

The mean or average deviation of a set of numbers is the average amount each element deviates from the mean. The concept of absolute value is needed in this definition. The symbol for absolute value is two vertical lines. The absolute value of a quantity is the value without the sign associated with the quantity.

Example

$$|8| = 8 \qquad |-8| = 8 \qquad |2 - 5| = 3 \qquad |5 - 2| = 3$$

Whenever mean deviation is to be computed, the first quantity needed is the mean.

To determine the mean deviation:

1. Calculate the mean.

2. Subtract each element of the set from the mean.

3. Apply absolute value to each of the differences.

4. Total the absolute values.

5. Divide the total found in step 4 by the number of elements in the set.

$$\text{Mean deviation} = \frac{\Sigma\ |\bar{x} - x|}{n}$$

Example
Determine the mean deviation using the data set: 20, 25, 27, 28, 28, 30, 32, 33, 38.

1. The mean, symbolized as $\bar{x}$, is 29.

2. Subtract each element from the mean and apply the absolute value to each difference.

3. The absolute value of a number relates to its magnitude. It is the number without the sign. Absolute value is commonly indicated by a vertical line on each side of the expression. Absolute value signs act like a set of parentheses. Perform the operations indicated, then disregard the sign.

$\bar{x} - x$	$|\bar{x} - x|$
$29 - 20 = 9$	$|9| = 9$
$29 - 25 = 4$	$|4| = 4$
$29 - 27 = 2$	$|2| = 2$
$29 - 28 = 1$	$|1| = 1$
$29 - 28 = 1$	$|1| = 1$
$29 - 30 = -1$	$|-1| = 1$
$29 - 32 = -3$	$|-3| = 3$
$29 - 33 = -4$	$|-4| = 4$
$29 - 38 = -9$	$|-9| = 9$

4. Total the absolute values.

$$(9 + 4 + 2 + 1 + 1 + 1 + 3 + 4 + 9) = 34$$

5. Divide 34 by 9, the number of elements in the set. $34/9 = 3.8$. 3.8 is the mean deviation of the raw data.

Mean Deviation from Grouped Data

The grouped data must list the interval, classmark, frequency, and the column fx to allow for calculation of the mean. Additional columns headed $\bar{x} - x$ and $|\bar{x} - x|$ and $f|\bar{x} - x|$ are needed.

Sales	Classmark	Frequency	fx	$\bar{x} - x$	$|\bar{x} - x|$	$f(|\bar{x} - x|)$
125.5–135.5	130.5	10	1,305.0	151.8 − 130.5	21.3	213.0
135.5–145.5	140.5	12	1,686.0	151.8 − 140.5	11.3	135.6
145.5–155.5	150.5	18	2,709.0	151.8 − 150.5	1.3	23.4
155.5–165.5	160.5	6	963.0	151.8 − 160.5	8.7	52.2
165.5–175.5	170.5	10	1,705.0	151.8 − 170.5	18.7	187.0
175.5–185.5	180.5	3	541.5	151.8 − 180.5	28.7	86.1
185.5–195.5	190.5	0	0.0	151.8 − 190.5	38.7	0.0
195.5–205.5	200.5	1	200.5	151.8 − 200.5	48.7	48.7
		60	9,110.0			746.0

$$\text{Mean} = \frac{\Sigma fx}{n} = \bar{x} = 151.8$$

$$\text{Average deviation} = \frac{\Sigma f(|\bar{x} - x|)}{n} = \frac{746}{60} = 12.4$$

The **average deviation** is a better measure of dispersion than the range. It takes each element into consideration and weighs it equally with every other element. The number indicates, on average, how far each element deviates from the mean. For technical reasons, average or mean deviation is seldom used as a measure of deviation.

Standard Deviation

The measure of deviation most frequently used to describe data is the **standard deviation** and the symbol used to represent standard deviation is σ. To compute the standard deviation, many of the same steps used for mean deviation are used. Instead of using absolute value to delete minus signs, the standard deviation squares each difference. The square of either a positive or a negative number is a positive number. The final step of standard deviation is to take the square root of the number.

To determine the standard deviation:

1. Find the mean.

2. Subtract each element from the mean of the set.

3. Square each of the differences.

4. Total the square of the differences.

5. Divide the total by the number of elements in the set.

6. Take the square root of the quotient.

Because of the operations involved, standard deviation is referred to as the root mean square deviation.

$$\text{Standard deviation} = \sigma = \sqrt{\Sigma f(\bar{x} - x)^2 / n}$$

where $\sqrt{}$ indicates the square root, Σ is the symbol for sum, $\bar{x}$ is the symbol for the mean, and the exponent 2 indicates square.

Example

Take the data from the previous example; the mean has been determined as 29.

$\bar{x}$	x	$\bar{x} - x$	$(\bar{x} - x)^2$
29	20	9	81
29	25	4	16
29	27	2	4
29	28	1	1
29	28	1	1
29	30	−1	1
29	32	−3	9
29	33	−4	16
29	38	−9	81
		$\Sigma\,(\bar{x} - x)^2 =$	210

$$\frac{210}{9} = 23.33$$

$$\sqrt{23.33} = 4.8$$

These calculations can be done on a hand-held calculator. The $\boxed{x^2}$ key gives the square of a number, and the $\boxed{\sqrt{}}$ key gives the square root. If you have a statistical calculator, the keystrokes for standard deviation are: $\boxed{2\text{nd}}\,\boxed{\text{CSR}}$ to put the calculator in statistical mode.

$20\,\boxed{\Sigma+}$ $25\,\boxed{\Sigma+}$ $27\,\boxed{\Sigma+}$ $28\,\boxed{\Sigma+}$ $28\,\boxed{\Sigma+}$ $30\,\boxed{\Sigma+}$ $32\,\boxed{\Sigma+}$ $33\,\boxed{\Sigma+}$
$38\,\boxed{\Sigma+}$ $\boxed{2\text{nd}}\,\boxed{\bar{x}}$

(display should show 29, the mean) $\boxed{2\text{nd}}\,\boxed{\sigma}$ (4.8 in display).

To calculate the standard deviation for data in tabular form, columns headed Interval, Classmark, Frequency, fx, $\bar{x} - x$, $(\bar{x} - x)^2$, and $f(\bar{x} - x)^2$ are needed.

Interval	Classmark	f	fx	$\bar{x} - x$	$(\bar{x} - x)^2$	$f(\bar{x} - x)^2$
125.5–135.5	130.5	10	1,305.0	151.8 − 130.5	453.69	4,536.90
135.5–145.5	140.5	12	1,686.0	151.8 − 140.5	127.69	1.532.28
145.5–155.5	150.5	18	2,709.0	151.8 − 159.5	1.69	30.42
155.5–165.5	160.5	6	963.0	151.8 − 160.5	75.69	454.14
165.5–175.5	170.5	10	1,705.0	151.8 − 179.5	349.69	3,496.90

Interval	Classmark	f	fx	$\bar{x} - x$	$(\bar{x} - x)^2$	$f(\bar{x} - x)^2$
175.5–185.5	180.5	3	541.5	151.8 − 180.5	823.69	2,471.07
185.5–195.5	190.5	0	0.0	151.8 − 190.5	1,497.69	0.00
195.5–205.5	200.5	1	200.5	151.8 − 200.5	2,371.69	2,371.69

$$x = 151.8$$

$$f(\bar{x} - x)^2 = 14{,}893.40$$
$$f(\bar{x} - x)^2/n = 248.22$$
$$\sqrt{248.22} = 15.76$$

The standard deviation is a number that helps predict the location of elements of a set in relation to the mean. The percentage of items of a set within intervals can be predicted for normal distributions. This material will be addressed in Section 7.4.

Sometimes a denominator of $n - 1$ is used instead of n in computing standard deviation. $n - 1$ is used whenever a sample of a population is used instead of the whole population. On a statistical calculator, two keys are available, $\boxed{\sigma_n}$ and $\boxed{\sigma_n - 1}$. For large values of n (when $n > 30$), there is little difference between the two generated values.

Example
The grades from the insurance test administered to 25 students were recorded as:

$$78 \quad 93 \quad 67 \quad 89 \quad 75 \quad 95 \quad 77 \quad 83 \quad 84 \quad 89 \quad 70 \quad 75 \quad 79$$
$$87 \quad 80 \quad 95 \quad 63 \quad 84 \quad 90 \quad 86 \quad 72 \quad 76 \quad 97 \quad 82 \quad 81$$

a. Working with the raw data, determine the range, average deviation, and standard deviation.

b. Working from a frequency distribution table, determine the range, average deviation, and standard deviation.

(a) The highest grade is 97, the lowest grade is 63, and the range is 97 − 63 or 34.

$$\text{Mean} = \frac{\text{sum of grades}}{25} = 82$$

$$\text{Average deviation} = \Sigma f\,|(\bar{x} - x)|/25 = 7.16$$
$$\text{Standard deviation} = \sqrt{\Sigma f\,(\bar{x} - x)^2/25} = 8.8$$

(b)

Interval	f	x	fx	$(\bar{x} - x)$	$(\bar{x} - x)^2$	$f(\bar{x} - x)^2$
62.5–66.5	1	64.5	64.5	−17.6	309.76	309.76
66.5–70.5	2	68.5	129.0	−13.6	184.96	369.92
70.5–74.5	1	72.5	72.5	− 9.6	92.16	92.16
74.5–78.5	5	76.5	382.5	− 5.6	31.36	156.8
78.5–82.5	4	80.5	322.0	− 1.6	2.56	10.24
82.5–86.5	4	84.5	338.0	2.4	5.76	23.04
86.5–90.5	4	88.5	354.0	6.4	40.96	163.84
90.5–94.5	1	92.5	92.5	10.4	108.16	108.16
94.5–98.5	3	96.5	289.5	14.4	207.36	622.08
	25		2,057.5			1,856.00

Mean 82.1
Standard deviation 8.6
Range 36
Average deviation 7.1

SECTION 3 EXERCISES

Use the following four arrays of data to perform the computations of the exercises.

Array A	Array B	Array C	Array D
108.5	49,900	47	82
108.5	52,250	47	84
109.2	55,500	50	85
109.7	57,700	50	86
110.0	62,000	51	86
111.1	62,250	52	86
111.5	64,400	54	87
111.7	67,000	54	87
112.2	67,700	55	88
112.4	68,200	56	88
112.6	69,900	58	89
112.9	74,200	58	89
113.9	75,500	58	90
114.7	76,600	59	90
115.2	79,500	59	90
115.6	82,000	60	90
116.0	82,200	60	91

Array A	Array B	Array C	Array D
116.4	84,500	61	91
116.7	87,500	61	91
117.1	87,700	62	92
		62	92
		63	92
		64	92
		65	92
		65	94
		66	94
		67	95
		67	96
		67	96
		68	98
		70	101

1. Determine the range for array A.

2. Determine the range for array B.

3. Determine the range for array C.

4. Determine the range for array D.

5. Determine the mean deviation for array A, using the raw data.

6. Determine the mean deviation for array B.

7. Determine the mean deviation for array C, using a distribution table. There are nine intervals of size 3, and the first interval is 45.5 to 48.5.

8. Determine the mean deviation for array D, using a distribution table. The first interval is 81.5 to 83.5.

9. Determine the standard deviation for array A.

10. Determine the standard deviation for array B.

11. Determine the standard deviation for array C, using a distribution table as described in exercise 7.

12. Determine the standard deviation for array D, using a distribution table as described in exercise 8.

13. The class mean on a final examination was 82. The standard deviation in one section is 6 and the standard deviation in another section is 4. If you are known as the "brain," in which section would you prefer to be a member? Justify your answer.

14. The class mean on a final examination is 79. The two sections tested had standard deviations of 4.9 and 7.0. If you are a typical average student, which section would you prefer to be associated with if your exam performance was average? Justify your answer.

15. The actual weights of bags of grass seed were recorded as packed. Pellinton Seed Company guarantees the actual weight of each bag is 5 pounds +0.5%. The mean weight was 5.05 with a standard deviation of 0.05 in the Plainville plant. The Watertown plant had a mean weight of 5.01 with a standard deviation of 0.06. As general manager of the total operation, which results would you consider the best for the company and why?

16. The mean wage of Factory A is $7.50 an hour with an average deviation of 0.50, and the mean wage of Factory B is $7.70 an hour with an average deviation of 0.25. If you are entering the work force at the lower end of the wage scale, which factory would you ask to be assigned to? Give reasons for your answer.

17. City A advertises an average monthly high temperature of 92 degrees with a standard deviation of 5 degrees. City B advertises an average high temperature of 90 degrees with a standard deviation of 7 degrees. You are an avid golfer, and you do not go on the course when the temperature exceeds 90 degrees. Which city would allow you more days of golf during the month?

18. The relative humidity is an important factor in the manufacture of woolen fabrics. You are making a recommendation on a new plant site. Site A has a mean relative humidity of 59% with an average deviation of 3%. Site B has a mean relative humidity of 60% with an average deviation of 7%. Consistency of relative humidity is important. Which site would you recommend on the basis of relative humidity and why?

Answers to Odd-Numbered Exercises

1. 8.6.

3. 23.

5. 2.335.

7. 5.26.

9. 2.7.

11. 6.5.

13. The one with a standard deviation of 6. The distribution has higher grades.

15. The Plainville plant. The weights vary from 5 to 5.1 pounds, within the guaranteed weight. The Watertown plant has weight variations ranging from 4.95 to 5.07. 4.95 is below the guaranteed content.

17. City *B* has half of the days of the month with temperatures less than or equal to 90 degrees.

7.4 NORMAL CURVE

Frequency curves representing distribution of data take on certain characteristic shapes. One such shape represents a heavy concentration of values in the middle and a tapering-off of data symmetrically on both sides of the mean. Many characteristics of individual and business data form this type of graph.

A **normal curve** (or **bell curve**) is a mathematical model determined by the mean and the standard deviation of the observations. The distribution is reasonably symmetrical. The Russian mathematician P. L. Chebyshev (1821–1894) predicted distribution regardless of the shape of the distribution. If the curve is a symmetrical bell-shaped curve as in the following diagram, the distribution can be predicted with even more precision.

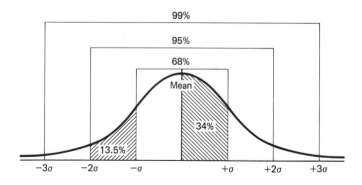

About 68% of the values in a population will fall within $^+/_-$ 1 standard deviation of the mean.

About 95% of the values in a population will fall within $^+/_-$ 2 standard deviations of the mean.

About 99% of the values in a population will fall within $^+/_-$ 3 standard deviations of the mean.

Human characteristics such as height, weight, IQ, and outputs from physical processes (industry) can be approximated by the normal curve. This distribution is useful in ordering sizes for sale in a retail center or for manufacturing clothing items. Tolerance categories in manufacturing can be predicted and monitored using the normal curve characteristics.

Some characteristics of the normal curve are

1. The curve has a single peak—one mode.

2. The mean lies in the center.

3. The median and mode are also at the center.

4. The tails extend indefinitely.

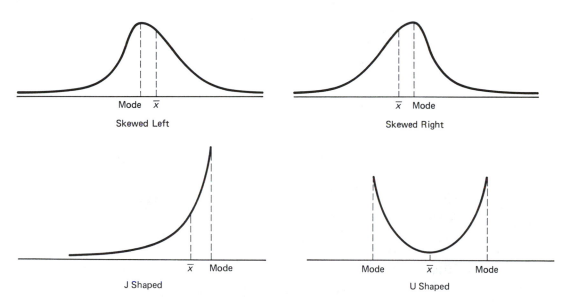

If the mean and mode do not coincide, the distribution is **skewed** from the normal distribution. A distribution **skewed left** has the mode to the left of the mean, and a distribution **skewed right** has the mode to the right of the mean. A J-shaped or reverse J-shaped distribution indicates a maximum number of elements occur at one of the ends. The mode is at the maximum value, and the mean is between the mode and the tail. A U-shaped distribution has a mode at both ends. The mean and median occur at the low point of the U.

Bimodal curves have two modes with the mean and median between them.

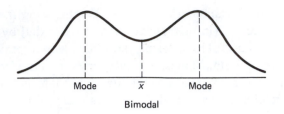

Bimodal

Example

The mean of a set of data is 125 and the distribution curve of the data is a normal curve. The standard deviation is 10. Find the range of 99.73% of the data.

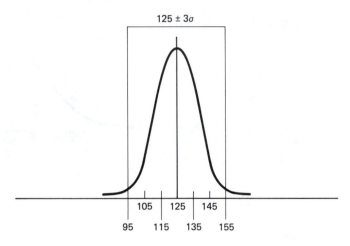

Low:

$$125 - 3(10) = 125 - 30 = 95$$

High:

$$125 + 3(10) = 125 + 30 = 155$$

$$\text{Range} = 155 - 95 = 60 \quad \text{or} \quad 6\sigma$$

Example

The mean size of women's belts is 27 with a standard deviation of 2. If the distribution of sizes resembles a normal distribution:

a. What percent of the belts are size 27 or larger?

b. What percent of the belts are smaller than size 25?

c. What percent of the belts are larger than size 23?

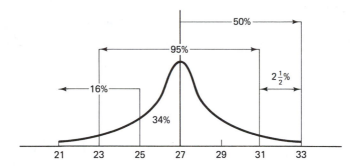

Solution:

a. Because the mean is 27, 50% of the belts are size 27 or larger.

b. Sixty-eight percent are between 25 and 29 or 34% are between 25 and 27. Fifty percent are below 27. Therefore 16% are smaller than 25.

c. Because 23 is 2 standard deviations below the mean of 27, 95% of the belts are between 23 and 31. Another 2.5% are above 31. The percent of belts larger than 23 is 95% + 2.5% or 97.5%.

Standard Scores

The variable z is used to denote a standard score and is found by

$$z = \frac{(x - \bar{x})}{\sigma}$$

The standard score is the number of standard deviations an element from a set of data is above (or below) the mean. Standard score has meaning only in a normal distribution.

Example
A student receives a grade of 82 on a final exam. The mean grade of the exam is 77 and the standard deviation is 11. Find the standard score.

$$z = \frac{(82 - 77)}{11} = \frac{5}{11} = 0.45$$

The standard score of 0.45 denotes a grade 0.45 of a standard deviation above the mean.

Example

A standardized test is given and a student scores 82 when the mean score is 100. The standard deviation of the scores on the test is 20. Find the standard score.

$$z = \frac{(82 - 100)}{20} = \frac{-18}{20} = -0.9$$

The student has a standard score of -0.9, indicating a score 0.9 of a standard deviation below the mean.

The use of standard score eliminates the need for expressing the mean or the size of the standard deviation. It is a standard way of expressing a result with respect to the other scores.

Percentile Ranking or Percent of Population

A frequent method of expressing an individual's achievement is percentile ranking. In a normal curve, percentile ranking can be determined by the standard score or z value. Statistical tables are available for finding the numerical values. Table 3 (Area Under the Standard Normal Curve) in the Appendix is an example of one such statistical table. The method of using Table 3 is presented in the following discussion.

A normal curve is symmetrical about the mean, and has 50% of its population above the mean and 50% below the mean.

To determine the percentile ranking:

1. Determine z by the formula

$$z = \frac{(x - \bar{x})}{\sigma}$$

   Round to 2 decimal places.

2. Take the absolute value of z.

3. Match the number in the left-hand column of the table with the first two digits of the z value.

4. Match the column heading and the third digit of the z score.

5. The intersection of the row and column in the table is the value needed.

6. If $z > 0$ from step 1, add the table value to 0.50 to obtain the decimal value and convert to a percent to obtain the percentile ranking.

7. If $z < 0$ from step 1, subtract the table value from 0.50 to obtain the decimal value and convert to a percent to obtain the percentile ranking.

In the preceding example of a score of 82 when the mean score was 100, the standard deviation was 20. The standard score was found to be -0.9. To obtain the percentile ranking:

1. $z = -0.9$.

2. $|-0.9| = 0.9$.

3. From Table 3, 0.9 is 0.90 and the value is 0.3159.

Because z is negative, subtract 0.3159 from 0.5 to obtain 0.1839 or 18.39%. Therefore 18.39% of the population scored below 82 and 100% − 18.39% or 81.61% of the population scored 82 or above.

Example

Find the percent of the population with a standard score between 0.5 and 1.8.

1. $z_1 = 0.5$. $z_2 = 1.8$.

2. The decimal value for 0.5 from Table 3 is 0.1915. The decimal value for 1.8 from Table 3 is 0.4641.

3. These are both positive, so 0.50 is added to each, giving 0.6915 and 0.9641.

4. The percentiles are 69 and 96.

5. The percent of the population between the standard scores of 0.5 and 1.8 is found by subtracting the two percentiles.

$$95\% - 69\% = 26\% \text{ of the population}$$

Example

A bag of potato chips must contain 16 ounces. The machine that fills the chip bags is set so that, on the average, a bag contains 16.4 ounces. The weights of filled bags closely approximate a normal curve. What percent of the bags are between 16 and 16.6 ounces if the standard deviation is 0.3 ounces?

1. $z_1 = (16 - 16.4)/0.3 = -1.33$. $z_2 = (16.6 - 16.4)/0.3 = 0.67$.

2. The absolute value of $z_1 = 1.33$. The absolute value of $z_2 = 0.67$.

3. From Table 3, $1.33 = 0.4082$ and $0.67 = 0.2486$. Because 1.33 is negative, 0.4082 is subtracted from 0.50, giving 0.0918 or 9%. Because 0.67 is positive, 0.2486 is added to 0.50, giving 0.7486 or 75%.

4. To find the percent of bags between 16 and 16.6 ounces, subtract the two percents:

$$75\% - 9\% = 66\%$$

Other terms found in these types of problems are "at least," "less than," and "more than." "At least" means anything more or equal to. Find the percentile of the number and subtract it from 100 to give the percent "at least." "Less than" is the percentile of the number as calculated in the previous example. "More than" is the same as at least except it does not include equal to. Find the percentile of the number and subtract it from 100 to give the percent "more than."

Example
A student is informed he scored in the ninetieth percentile on a competitive exam. If the mean score was 80 and one standard deviation is 7, determine the actual score of the student.

Ninetieth percentile means fortieth percentile above the mean. Fortieth percentile means 0.40 in the table which corresponds to $z = 1.29$. $z = 1.29$ corresponds to 1.29 standard deviations or

$$(1.29)(7) = 9.03$$

$$9.03 + 80 = 89.03 \qquad \text{score}$$

SECTION 4 EXERCISES

1. Sketch the distributions described as follows.
   a. The mode is 50, the extreme right value; the mean is 45, and the range is 50.
   b. The mean is 50, the mode is 52, and the range is 25.
   c. Two modes are 70 and 90, the mean is 80, and the range is 40.

2. Sketch the distributions described as follows.
   a. The mean, median, and mode coincide at 40, and the range is 20.

    b. The modes are at the ends at 70 and 90, and the mean is halfway between the modes.

    c. The mean is 50, the mode is 45, and the range is 40.

3. For a normal curve, the mean is 85 and $\sigma = 5$. Determine the range of 95% of the data.

4. For a normal curve, find the percent of data included between $x - \sigma$ and $x + 2\sigma$.

5. For a normal curve, find the percent of data included between $x - 2\sigma$ and $x + \sigma$.

6. For a normal curve, find the percent of data included between $x - \sigma$ and $x + 3\sigma$.

7. If the mean is 47.24 and $\sigma = 4.5$, the distribution resembles a normal curve. Find the range of 99.73% of the data.

8. If the mean is \$47,000 and $\sigma = \$4,500$, the distribution resembles a normal curve. Find the range of 95.45% of the data.

9. If the mean is 2.38 and $\sigma = 0.03$, find the range of 68.27% of the data.

10. If the distribution of data can be represented by a normal curve and 99.73% of the data occurs between 610 and 840, determine the mean and standard deviation of the distribution.

11. Find the standard score for 48 if the data can be represented by a normal curve. The mean is 51.35 and the standard deviation is 1.78.

12. Find the standard score for 75 if the data can be represented by a normal curve. The mean is 72.3 and the standard deviation is 1.96.

13. Find the standard score for 560 hours if the mean is 500 hours and the standard deviation is 100 hours. The length of life resembles the normal curve.

14. Find the standard score for 1,300 miles if the average number of miles driven per month is 1,200 and the standard deviation is 125 miles. Assume that the number of miles is closely approximated by a normal curve.

15. The average weight of freshman female students at a small college is 118 pounds with a standard deviation of 4.5 pounds. Find the percentile rating of students who weigh at least 125 pounds if the data closely resemble a normal curve.

    a. Find the percent of students who weigh between 110 and 120 pounds.

   b. Find the percent of students who weigh at least 110 pounds.
   c. Find the percent of students who weigh at most 120 pounds.

16. A machine tool company produces bolts with an average diameter of 0.28
    inches and a standard deviation of 0.015 inches. The diameter of the bolts
    is approximated closely by a normal curve.
    a. Find the percentile rating of a bolt with a diameter of 0.27 inches.
    b. What percent of the bolts has a diameter between 0.26 and 0.32
    inches?
    c. What percent of the bolts has a diameter less than 0.315 inches?

17. The lengths of nails produced by a nail-making machine are normally dis-
    tributed with a mean of 5.08 centimeters and a standard deviation of 0.03
    centimeters. Draw the normal curve representing the information and
    find the approximate percent of nails having length:
    a. Between 5.05 and 5.11 centimeters
    b. More than 5.02 centimeters
    c. Less than 5.11 centimeters
    d. At least 5.08 centimeters
    e. Between 5.02 and 5.05 centimeters

18. The lifetime of watch batteries is normally distributed with a mean life of
    400 days and a standard deviation of 40 days. Draw the normal curve rep-
    resenting the information and find the approximate percent of batteries
    having a lifetime
    a. Between 320 and 440 days
    b. More than 360 days
    c. Less than 400 days
    d. At least 320 days
    e. Between 360 and 520 days

19. The time customers wait in line to check out at the grocery store is nor-
    mally distributed with a mean time of 8.2 minutes and a standard devia-
    tion of 1.1 minute. Determine the following.
    a. The percent of customers who wait in line 10 minutes.
    b. The percent of customers who wait in line less than 5 minutes.
    c. The percent of customers who wait in line at least 5 minutes.

20. The average weight of newborn babies is 7.3 pounds with a standard devi-
    ation of 0.5 pounds. The weight of newborns is normally distributed.
    Find:
    a. The percent of babies that weigh at least 6.5 pounds.
    b. The percent of babies that weigh over 8 pounds.
    c. The percent of babies that weigh between 7 and 8 pounds.

Answers to Odd-Numbered Exercises

1.

(a)
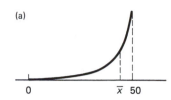

(b)
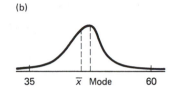

(c)
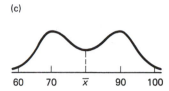

3. 75–95.

5. 81.5%.

7. 33.74–60.74.

9. 2.35–2.41.

11. −1.9.

13. +0.6.

15. 94% weigh at least 125 pounds. (a) 63%. (b) 96%. (c) 67%.

17. (a) 68%. (b) 97.5%. (c) 84%. (d) 13.5%.

19. (a) 5%. (b) 1%. (c) 99%.

7.5   OTHER TYPES OF GRAPHS

Information is often presented in a graphical manner to emphasize a trend as well as to illustrate facts. One of the most frequent uses of graphs is the representation of a variable as a function of time or what is happening to a quantity over a period of time. This type of representation is called a **time series table** or **graph**.

In a time series graph, **time** is usually shown on the horizontal axis. The horizontal axis does not necessarily start at zero. The vertical axis represents the variable quantity. It is not often practical to start the vertical axis at zero. To avoid erroneous conclusions from the visual representation, either a zigzag line on the bottom of the vertical axis or a jagged line across the bottom of the graph is used to emphasize the fact that the axis does not start at zero.

Always give the graph a heading, label each axis with quantity and units, and include a legend where needed. A legend is the explanation and identification of different colors, types of lines, and other special features of the graph.

There are three different types of time series graphs.

Line Graph

Points are located for each value of the variable at each time interval. These points are connected by a series of straight lines. The first point is located on the vertical axis. Line graphs are especially appropriate for continuous data. If a graph were made of sales per month, the increase or decrease would be a gradual change, not a jump. Therefore a line graph is appropriate because the line passes through all values from one point to the next.

More than one variable can be shown on line graphs; different colored or types of lines are used to indicate the variables. Use a legend to identify these.

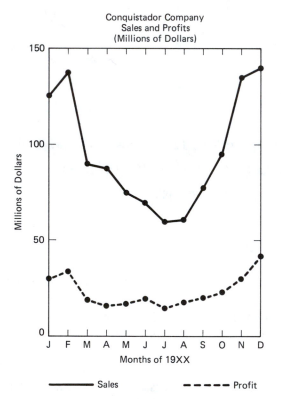

Example

Conquistador Company wishes to represent data related to sales and net profits for the months January through December in 19XX. The data to be represented are

Month	Jan	Feb	Mar	Apr	May	Jun	Jul	Aug	Sep	Oct	Nov	Dec
Sales	126	138	90	87	80	75	60	62	78	96	136	140
Profits	30	34	18	16	17	20	14	18	20	23	30	42

Sales and profits are expressed in millions of dollars. The horizontal axis will have 12 equally spaced marks representing the months. January will be the vertical axis (Label: Months of 19XX).

The vertical axis must represent values from 14 to 140. Determine 15 equal spaces, starting at 0. Each space will represent 10. (Label: Sales and Profits in Millions of Dollars) (Label the graph: Monthly Sales and Net Profits for Conquistador Company 19XX).

Bar Graph

Rectangles of equal widths are drawn. The height represents the quantity of the variable. Empty spaces occur between the bars. There is usually an empty space between the vertical axis and the first rectangle. Bar graphs can have horizontal bars as well as vertical bars. More than one variable can be pictured on a bar graph; the rectangles are shown in a different color or hue, and adjacent to each other for a given time.

Example

Year	1980	1981	1982	1983	1984
Capital expenditures	238	330	360	123	115
Research	122	151	164	145	136

(Label: Capital Expenditures and Research in Millions of Dollars).

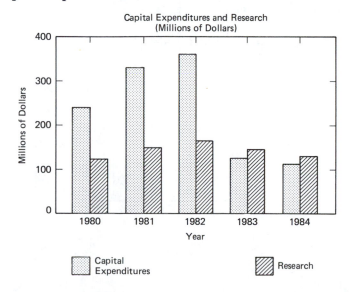

Stacked Bar Graph

Stacked bar graphs are used for information with more than one variable and where the total of the variables has some meaning. If a graph were drawn to represent the total monthly assets of a bank, and these assets are made up of deposits, loans, and stockholders' equity, stacked rectangles of equal widths are used. The first variable is drawn as in a bar graph, the second variable rectangle is stacked on top of the first with a height appropriate to the value of the variable, and so on. The total height represents the total quantity of the variables. A stacked bar graph is useful in representing components as well as totals of a quantity.

Example
Using the same information as demonstrated in the bar graph, a stacked bar graph is constructed.

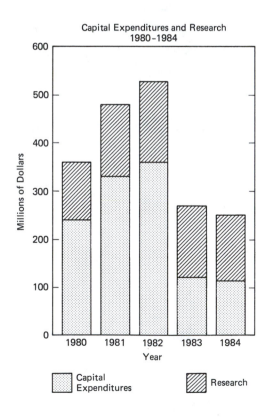

The actual amounts could be distorted in this graph if the vertical axis starts at 100. Shortening the rectangles expressing capital, the rectangles denoting research are represented according to scale. The graph is not incorrect; the viewer must read the scales with care and not be fooled by the relative heights in the picture. An individual requesting more capital might use such a graph to distort the historical amount of capital expenditure.

Pie Graph

Another type of graph that is useful to show how a total amount is broken up into components is a **pie graph**. The areas of the sectors of the circle are in the same ratio to the whole circle as the components are to the total. To construct a pie graph, draw a circle and indicate the center. The size of any component divided by the total of all of the components times 360 degrees gives the size of the central angle of the sector representing the component.

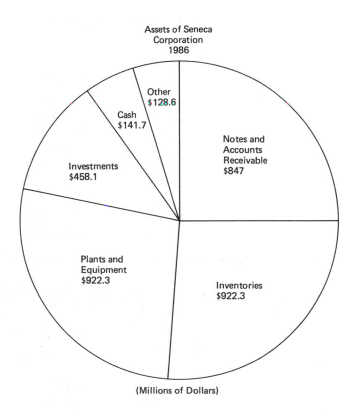

Assets of Seneca
Corporation
1986

Other
$128.6

Cash
$141.7

Notes and
Accounts
Receivable
$847

Investments
$458.1

Plants and
Equipment
$922.3

Inventories
$922.3

(Millions of Dollars)

Example

Assets of Seneca Corporation, 1986
(in Millions of Dollars)

		Degrees
Cash and short-term investments	$ 141.7	15
Notes and accounts receivable	847.0	89
Inventories	922.3	97
Other current assets	128.6	14
Investments	458.1	48
Plants and equipment	922.3	97
Total	$3,420.0	360

SECTION 5 EXERCISES

1. Draw a time series line graph to illustrate the following information.

Net Sales for Adam Corporation
(Dollars in Thousands)

1976	$241,061
1977	320,701
1978	298,651
1979	392,872
1980	350,180
1981	400,086
1982	392,100
1983	420,152
1984	435,550
1985	470,156
1986	450,680

2. Draw a time series line graph to illustrate the following information.

Capital Expenditures for Adam Corporation
(Dollars in Thousands)

1976	$ 5,725
1977	12,207
1978	11,736
1979	20,320
1980	21,923

1981	16,560
1982	17,209
1983	10,984
1984	17,742
1985	16,969
1986	15,800

3. Draw a vertical bar graph to illustrate the following information.

**Sales for Crazy Carl's Car Corporation, 1987
(in Thousands of Dollars)**

January	$115
February	98
March	125
April	165
May	130
June	98
July	90
August	120
September	170
October	150
November	140
December	165

4. Draw a vertical bar graph to illustrate the following information.

Paramount Corporation

Year	Number of Employees	Number of Stockholders
1976	5,700	9,341
1977	6,100	9,195
1978	6,600	8,952
1979	7,300	8,048
1980	6,700	9,779
1981	7,000	9,801
1982	5,600	9,216
1983	5,900	9,299
1984	6,100	9,535
1985	6,600	9,140
1986	7,100	9,540

(Numbers in Thousands)

5. Draw a stacked bar graph to represent the following information.

Consolidated Company Sales
(Dollars in Thousands)

Year	Europe	Asia	Canada	Africa
1980	$535	$356	$287	$127
1981	480	280	320	105
1982	420	250	310	120
1983	540	260	290	150
1984	600	300	280	180
1985	500	240	220	140
1986	620	290	320	220
1987	550	290	280	160

6. Draw a stacked bar graph to represent the following information.

Operating Cost and Expenses
Southern Fan Company

Year	Cost of Goods Sold	Marketing Expense	Research Expense
1983	$1,548	$1,227	$229
1984	1,528	1,252	254
1985	1,545	1,312	286
1986	1,650	1,250	250

7. Draw a pie graph to represent the following information.

Assets for Peter Paul Construction Company, 1986
(Dollars in Thousands)

Land, including quarries	$ 67.3
Buildings	542.2
Machinery and equipment	1,297.0
Construction in progress	83.0
Other	314.0

8. Draw a pie graph to represent the following information.

Assets for Able Automated Associates, 1987

Cash and due from banks	$ 440,800
Short-term investments	273,650
Investment securities	916,000
Loans	2,611,000

Premises and equipment	71,000
Due from customers on acceptances	3,742
Other assets	103,000

9. Represent the following information by two different diagrams. Discuss which diagram is the more effective representation of the data and why.

Operation Optimal Sales, Inc.
(Dollars in Millions)

	1982	1983	1984
Net sales	550	556	619
Profits from operations	52	52	67
Identifiable assets	271	303	358
Capital expenditures	32	29	41
Depreciation and amortization	20	21	22

10. Represent the following information by two different diagrams. Discuss which diagram is the most effective representation of the data and why.

Selected Financial Data
Sensible Select Corporation

	1980	1981	1982	1983	1984
Net sales	$3,295	$3,262	$2,820	$2,740	$2,571
Income	154	108	41	77	44
Dividends per share	1.51	1.44	1.42	1.44	1.48
Net assets	1,998	1,835	1,826	1,758	1,772

Answers to Odd-Numbered Exercises

1.

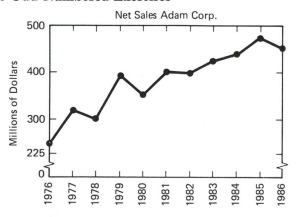

3.

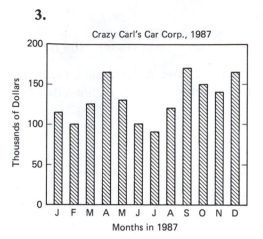

Crazy Carl's Car Corp., 1987

5.

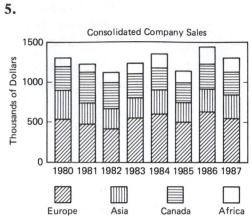

Consolidated Company Sales

7.

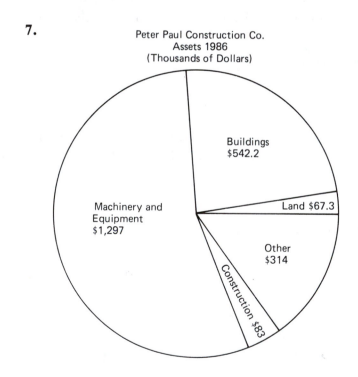

Peter Paul Construction Co.
Assets 1986
(Thousands of Dollars)

9.

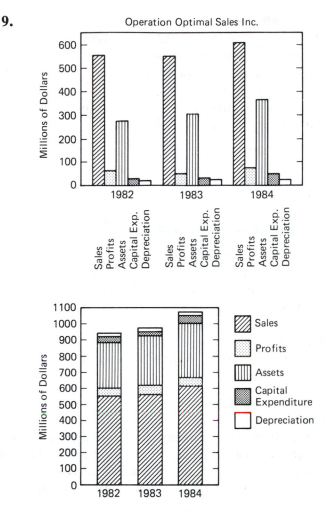

Operation Optimal Sales Inc.

Total as well as components can be compared

Summary

- **Array:** data arranged in ascending or descending order
- **Frequency distribution table:** tabular arrangement of raw data by classes or intervals
- **Classmark:** midpoint of class or interval
- **Relative frequency:** frequency in class/total frequency

- **Graphical representation of data**
  Histogram: rectangles whose width represents the interval size, and whose height represents the frequency
  Frequency polygon: line graph connecting points determined by class mark, frequency
  Pie graph: circle representing a total amount; divisions within the circle represent components of the total

- **Measures of central tendency**
  Mean: average

  Array: $\bar{x} = \dfrac{\Sigma x}{n}$

  Frequency distribution table: $\bar{x} = \dfrac{\Sigma fx}{\Sigma f}$

  Mode: element occurring most frequently
  Array: element(s) occurring most frequently
  Frequency distribution table: classmark of interval with greatest frequency

  Median: element in the middle of array
  Array: count $n/2$ elements from top
  Frequency distribution table: classmark of interval where cumulative frequency $\geq 1/2 f$

- **Measures of variation or dispersion**
  - **Range**
    Array: difference between largest and smallest element
    Frequency distribution table: difference between upper limit of largest and lower limit of smallest interval
  - **Mean deviation:** average deviation from the mean

    Array: $\dfrac{\Sigma |\bar{x} - x|}{n}$

    Frequency distribution table: $\dfrac{\Sigma f|\bar{x} - x|}{n}$

  - **Standard deviation**

    Array: $\sigma = \sqrt{\dfrac{\Sigma (\bar{x} - x)^2}{n}}$

    Frequency distribution table: $\sqrt{\dfrac{\Sigma f(\bar{x} - x)^2}{n}}$

  - **Normal curve:** a mathematical model where

$$x \pm 1\sigma \qquad 68\% \text{ population}$$

$$x \pm 2\sigma \qquad 95\% \text{ population}$$

$$x \pm 3\sigma \qquad 99\% \text{ population}$$

- **Standard score:** number of standard deviations an element is above or below the mean

$$z = \frac{x - \bar{x}}{\sigma}$$

- **Time series graph:** the horizontal axis represents time; the vertical axis represents quantity

REVIEW EXERCISES

Use the following arrays of data as referred to in the exercises.

Array A: Top 27 batting averages

.381	.340	.333	.327	.319	.317	.316	.310	.302
.298	.295	.292	.291	.281	.280	.278	.278	.277
.274	.270	.270	.263	.263	.250	.247	.247	.241

Array B: Top golf scores after 72 holes

204	206	209	209	210	210	210	211	211	211
212	212	213	214	215	215	215	215	215	217
218	220	221	221	225	226	226	230	232	235

1. Make a frequency diagram for array A, using intervals of size 0.02 and starting at 0.2355.

2. Make a frequency diagram for array B, using intervals of 4 using 202.5 as a starting value.

3. Determine the range of array A.

4. Determine the range of array B.

5. Determine the classmarks for each of the intervals of frequency diagram A.

6. Determine the classmarks for each of the intervals of frequency diagram B.

7. Determine the relative frequency of each interval of frequency diagram A.

8. Determine the cumulative frequency of each interval of frequency diagram B.

9. Draw a histogram to represent array A.

10. Draw a frequency polygon to represent array B.

11. Draw a cumulative frequency polygon for array A.

12. Determine the median for array A.

13. Determine the median for array B.

14. Determine the mode for array A.

15. Determine the mode for array B.

16. Determine the mean for array A.

17. Determine the mean for array B.

18. Determine the mean deviation for array A using the distribution table.

19. Determine the standard deviation for array A using the distribution table.

20. Determine the standard deviation for array B using the distribution table.

21. Can array A be categorized as a normal distribution? Justify your answer.

22. Can array B be categorized as a normal distribution? Justify your answer.

23. The results of an IQ test can be represented by a normal curve. The test has a mean of 100 and a standard deviation of 10.
    a. Find the standard score represented by the score 115.
    b. Find the percent of the population scoring above 95.
    c. Find the percent of the population scoring at least 120.

24. The results of SAT scores form a normal distribution with a mean total score of 800. The standard deviation is 100.
    a. Find the standard score for the score of 1,050.
    b. Find the percent of the population scoring below 950.
    c. Find the percent of the population scoring between 750 and 1,000.

25. Draw a time series graph to determine the average high temperatures in the two locations listed in 1990.

	Paradise	*Mooreville*
January	68	85
February	62	89
March	69	93

	Paradise	Mooreville
April	73	85
May	80	78
June	87	72
July	91	62
August	83	55
September	88	58
October	79	65
November	82	74
December	72	82

26. Draw a vertical bar graph to represent the following concerning M Corporation.

Year	Value/Share	Dividend/Share
1981	$12.50	$1.00
1982	14.75	0.80
1983	12.80	1.20
1984	16.50	1.90
1985	22.80	4.50
1986	10.40	1.75
1987	17.50	3.25
1988	27.90	5.20

27. Draw a pie graph to represent the following information.

Total income	$36,000
Taxes	7,000
Housing	9,500
Food	5,000
Automobiles	4,000
Clothing	2,500
Recreation	1,500
Education, savings	4,000
Medical expense	2,500

Answers to Review Exercises

1.

Interval	f	Classmark	$|\bar{x} - x|$	$f(|\bar{x} - x|)^2$
0.2355–0.2555	4	0.2455	0.0455	0.00828
0.2555–0.2755	5	0.2655	0.0255	0.00325
0.2755–0.2955	8	0.2855	0.0055	0.0002
0.2955–0.3155	3	0.3055	0.0145	0.0006
0.3155–0.3355	5	0.3255	0.0345	0.0060

1.

Interval	f	Classmark	$\lvert \bar{x} - x \rvert$	$f(\lvert \bar{x} - x \rvert)^2$
0.3355–0.3555	1	0.3455	0.0545	0.0030
0.3555–0.3755	0	0.3655	0.0745	0.0000
0.3755–0.3955	1	0.3855	0.0945	0.0089
	27	7.8685		

2.

Interval	f	Classmark	$\lvert \bar{x} - x \rvert^2$	$f(\lvert \bar{x} - x \rvert)^2$
202.5–206.5	2	204.5	136.89	273.78
206.5–210.5	5	208.5	59.29	296.45
210.5–214.5	7	212.5	13.69	95.83
214.5–218.5	7	216.5	0.09	0.63
218.5–222.5	3	220.5	18.49	55.47
222.5–226.5	3	224.5	68.89	206.67
226.5–230.5	1	228.5	151.29	151.29
230.5–234.5	1	232.5	265.69	265.69
234.5–238.5	1	236.5	412.09	412.09
	30	6,487.0		1,757.90

3. 0.140.

4. 31.

5. Shown in exercise 1.

6. Shown in exercise 2.

7. 0.15, 0.18, 0.30, 0.11, 0.18, 0.04, 0, 0.04.

8. 0.07, 0.23, 0.47, 0.70, 0.80, 0.90, 0.93, 0.97, 1.00.

9.

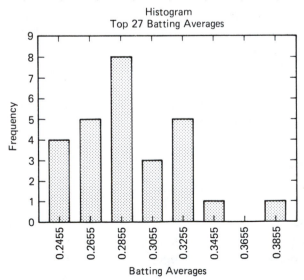

Histogram
Top 27 Batting Averages

10.

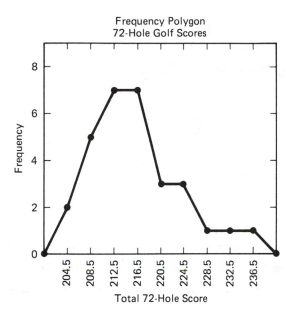

Frequency Polygon
72-Hole Golf Scores

11.

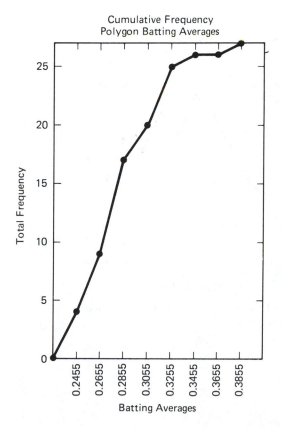

Cumulative Frequency
Polygon Batting Averages

12. 0.281.

13. 215.

14. 0.278, 0.270, 0.263, 0.247.

15. 215.

16. 0.291.

17. 216.2.

18. 0.027.

19. 0.033.

20. 7.65.

21. Median, 0.281. Mode, 0.278, 0.270, 0.263, 0.247. Mean, 0.291. No, too much variation in three measures of central tendency.

22. Median, 215. Mode, 215. Mean, 216. Yes, central tendencies are almost equal.

23. (a) 1.5. (b) 69.15%. (c) 2.28%.

24. (a) 2.5. (b) 93.32%. (c) 66.87%.

25.

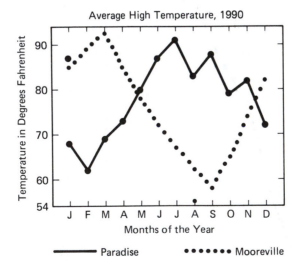

26.

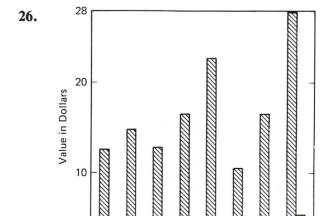

27.

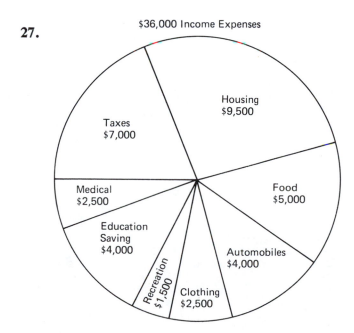

Chapter 8

STRAIGHT-LINE GRAPHS

In order to study and understand real-world problems, **models** are constructed. These models are then used to predict outcomes from untried actions and to determine the reliability of untested hypotheses. A mathematical model is a description of a real-world problem. To construct a mathematical model, a broad understanding of mathematics and the situation to be modeled is required.

The straight-line model is the simplest of mathematical models. It is also the most used model. This chapter provides the opportunity for a good understanding of straight lines, the characteristics, equations, and graphs for any linear equation.

Slope or rate of change is defined and the concept is used in interpreting graphs as well as in writing the mathematical model for a given situation.

Many sets of data do not graph precisely as a straight line, but a straight line can approximate the data. The method for determining the best approximation of a straight line is presented.

At the end of this chapter, the student will be able to:

1. Name and locate points on the xy coordinate axis, plot points satisfying a given relationship, and connect these points with a straight line or a series of straight lines.

2. Determine the x and y intercepts for a linear equation, plot the intercepts, and draw a line through the two points. Recognition of graphs with positive, negative, and zero rates of change from given data is practiced. Recognition of data most accurately modeled by step graphs and interpretation of step graphs is presented and practiced.

3. Use the definition of slope to determine the slope of lines passing through two known points, determine the slope of a line from the graph, and write the equation of a line if the y intercept and slope are known.

4. Determine the "best" fit for a set of data approximating a straight line and use the generated equation to predict other data points. Determine the reliability of the linear equation generated by finding the coefficient of correlation for the set of data.

8.1   LINE GRAPHS

Defining the relationship between two quantities promotes a better understanding of the behavior of these quantities. Graphing is one way relationships can be analyzed and compared. Any two quantities are generally labeled as X and Y unless more appropriate variables are available. The graph of the relationship between two variables is accomplished on the XY coordinate axis. A horizontal line is drawn to represent X, and a vertical intersecting line is drawn to represent Y. These two lines are called the **axes** and are labeled by the appropriate variable. The four sections created from these two intersecting lines are called **quadrants**, and are numbered I through IV, starting with the upper right-hand quarter as I and moving counterclockwise through II, III, and IV.

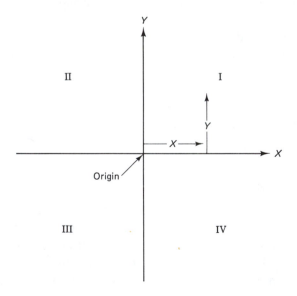

The intersection of the two axes is called the **origin** and all points are named with respect to this location. Any point on this XY coordinate plane can be named by an ordered pair. The first number refers to the X component, and the second number refers to the Y component. The first number in the ordered pair describes the amount of displacement left or right from the origin, and the second number of the ordered pair is the amount of displacement up or down from the origin. Right and up is denoted by a $+$ and left and down is indicated by a $-$. Therefore the ordered pair 2,3 denotes a point 2 units to the right of the origin and 3 units up from the origin. Likewise, the point $-4,5$ is a point 4 units to the left of the origin and 5 units up. The point $4, -5$ is a point four units to the right of the origin and 5 units down. These numbers are referred to as **ordered pairs**. The pairs 2,3 and 3,2 denote two different locations on the graph; the order in which the numbers appear makes a difference in the location. An ordered pair is enclosed in parentheses with a comma separating the two numbers. The ordered pair (x,y) uniquely determines any point on the XY coordinate plane.

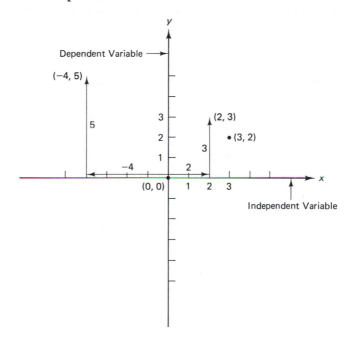

When graphing two quantities, each axis must be labeled to indicate the quantities represented on each axis. The horizontal axis is reserved for the independent variable, and the vertical axis is identified with the dependent quantity. In all relationships, one quantity depends on the other. The vertical axis represents the dependent quantity. If time is one of the variables, time is usually put on the horizontal axis. A scale is shown on each axis (the scales do not have to be the same but they should be clearly marked). The origin is denoted by the ordered pair (0,0).

Example

Draw a graph for the following information.

Number of hours	1	2	3
Miles	55	110	165

The horizontal axis represents time (in hours), and the vertical axis represents distance (in miles). This choice is made because distance depends upon time. The horizontal scale has three markings to the right of the origin, labeled 1, 2, and 3. The vertical axis might start at 50. Each mark denotes a change of 10, and the last mark is labeled as 175.

Each of the entries is positive, meaning they are right and up from the origin. Therefore only quadrant I is needed to graph this relationship. An alternate scale could be used for the vertical axis for greater accuracy of the graph. Use a jagged line between the origin and the first mark to denote that the remaining scale is different from that between the origin and the first mark.

The information from the first column of the table can be written as the ordered pair (1,55). This point is located 1 unit to the right and up halfway between the markings of 50 and 60. The second column (2,110) is located two units right and 7 units up from the 50 mark. The third column represents the

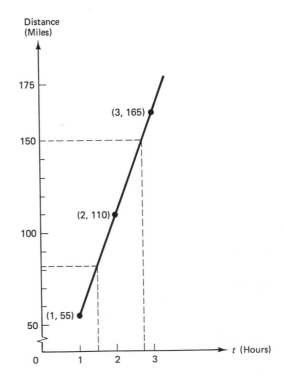

point (3,165) and is located three units to the right of the origin and 11 units up from the 50 mark. These three points lie on a straight line. The points are connected by the straight line and are extended to the right. The graph can be used to approximate the distance when the time is 1.5 hours (about 83 miles) or the time when the distance is 150 miles (about 2.8 hours).

Graphing can involve all four quadrants. In most business applications, the first quadrant is the only one used because most data are positive.

Example
The following table shows the relationship between disposable income and consumption expenditure.

Disposable income	$4,000	$6,000	$9,000
Consumption expenditure	4,100	5,900	8,600

Draw a graph representing the data.

Let the X axis represent disposable income and each square represent $2,000. Let the Y axis represent consumption expenditure and each square represent $2,000. This choice was made because expenditures depend upon income.

The tabulated data can be translated into the ordered pairs (4,000,4,100), (6,000,5,900), and (9,000,8,600). If these points are plotted and connected by the smoothest curve possible, the graph is a straight line. If the line is extended, it passes through (0,0)—no disposable income, no capital expenditure.

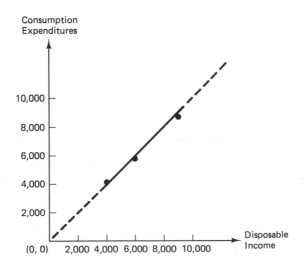

The relationship between two variables can be expressed by an equation rather than in tabular form. It is necessary to determine ordered pairs that satisfy the relationship in order to graph the relationship.

Example

$$A = 1.06P$$

relates the variables P and A. Because A depends upon P, the ordered pairs are (P, A). If $P = 0, A = 0$, giving the ordered pair $(0,0)$. If $P = 100, A = 106$, giving $(100,106)$. If $P = 500, A = 530$, producing the ordered pair $(500,530)$. Graphing these three ordered pairs and connecting them by a straight line produces the picture of the relationship between P and A.

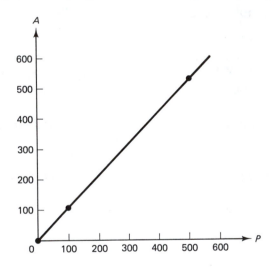

SECTION 1 EXERCISES

In exercises 1 through 4, use the accompanying graph to obtain the answers.

1. Locate the following points on the xy coordinate axis.

(5,2)	(2,5)	(−1,3)	(3,−1)	(−4,−3)	(−4,0)
(2,2)	(2,−2)	(0,4)	(0,−3)	(−3,−5)	(5,0)

2. Locate the following points on the xy coordinate axis.

(2,6)	(6,2)	(−3,5)	(5,−3)	(1,1)	(−3,−4)
(0,0)	(0,2)	(2,0)	(0,−2)	(−4,3)	(5,5)

3. Name points A, B, C, D, E, F, G, H as ordered pairs.

4. Name points J, K, L, M, N, P, R, S as ordered pairs.

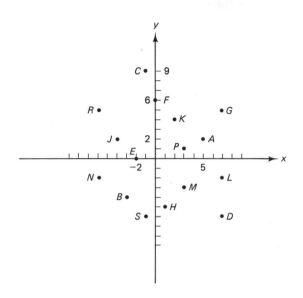

5. Plot the following points and connect the points with a straight line.

Hours	3	6	7
Miles	150	300	350

Approximate the mileage for 4.5 hours.

6. Plot the following points and connect the points with a straight line.

Hours	20	30	35
Pay	$47	$70.50	$82.25

Approximate how many hours are necessary for pay to equal $100.

7. Draw a graph of the following information.

Debt (in millions)	4	5	9
Equity (in millions)	2.4	3	5.4

Approximate the debt when the equity is 4.5 million.

8. Draw a graph of the following information.

Cost of goods sold (in millions)	15	24	40
Average inventory (in millions)	3	4.8	8

9. Draw a graph of the following information.

Assessed value (in thousands)	40	100	150
Property tax (in dollars)	140	350	525

Approximate the assessed value if the property tax is $400.

10. Draw a graph of the following information.

Current assets (in millions)	125	430	710
Current liabilities (in millions)	87.5	301	497

If the current assets are 200 million, what are the current liabilities?

11. Draw a graph of the following information.

Income (in thousands)	45	62	81
Federal tax (in dollars)	1,800	2,480	3,240

What income has 0 federal tax?

12. Draw a graph of the following information.

Present value (in thousands)	6	14	21.5
Future value (in thousands)	7.8	18.2	27.95

Use the graph to predict the future value of $25,000.

13. Draw a graph representing the following information.

Relative humidity	0.30	0.40	0.50
Defects/yard	7	5	3

Does the data point (0.70,9) appear to belong to the information?

14. Draw a graph representing the following information.

Temperature (degrees Celsius)	10	20	30
Temperature (degrees Fahrenheit)	50	68	86

Use the graph to predict the Celsius reading when the Fahrenheit reading is 32 degrees.

15. Given the relationship $A = 1.1P$, find three ordered pairs that satisfy the relationship. Graph the relationship. From the graph, predict the value of P when $A = 100$.

16. Draw a graph representing the relationship: Depreciation $= 0.125$ value. From the graph predict the value that gives $100 depreciation.

17. FICA deduction $= 0.0715$ gross pay. Draw a graph representing the relationship. Why should the graph terminate at 42,000 for gross pay? What is the largest FICA amount needed on the graph?

18. Monthly commission = 0.20 sales + 200. Draw a graph to represent this relationship between sales and commission.

19. Sales tax = 0.05 gross sales. Draw a graph to represent this relationship and use the graph to determine the gross sales that will have a sales tax of $9.25.

20. Annual interest = principal × rate. Graph the relationship between annual interest and rate when the principal is $500.

Answers to Odd-Numbered Exercises

1.

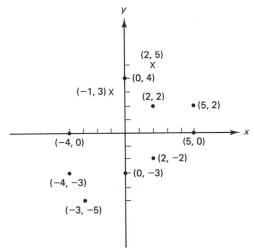

3. A (5,2), B (−3,−4), C (−1,9), D (7,−6), E (−2,0), F (0,6), G (7,5), H (1,−5).

5.

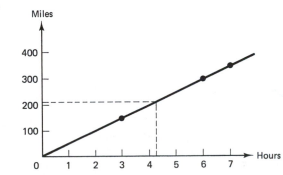

7.

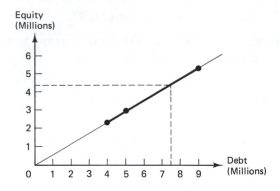

(b) $7.5 million

9.

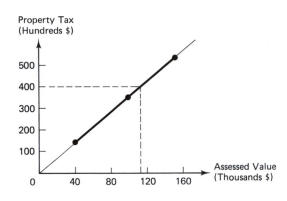

(b) $110 million

11.

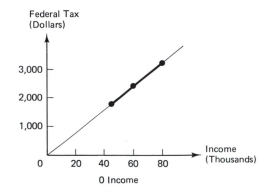

0 Income

13.

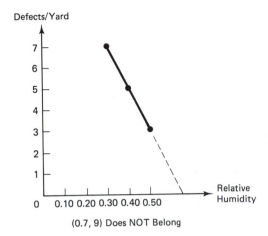

(0.7, 9) Does NOT Belong

15.

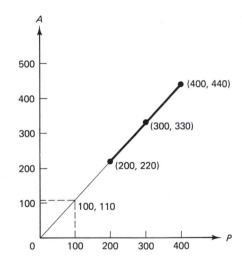

17.

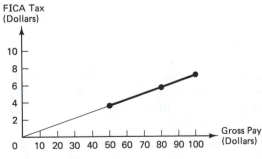

$42,000 is maximum pay affected by 0.0715.
FICA ≤ $3,003.

19.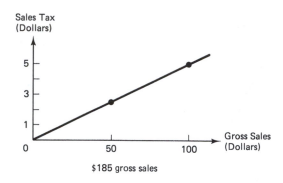

$185 gross sales

8.2 LINEAR MODELS

A model is a mathematical description of a real-world situation. In this chapter, linear models are discussed, the graphs of linear models are presented, and the relationships producing line graphs are predicted.

Linear models represent data whose graph is approximated by a straight line. Straight lines come from relationships of the form:

$$ax + by = c$$

This indicates the equation contains an x term (ax), a y term (by), and a number term (c). The a and b are needed to allow for different multiples of x and y. Some examples of equations that graph to straight lines are

$$2x + 3y = 7$$
$$x - 5y = 15$$
$$3x \quad\quad = 20 \quad\text{or}\quad 3x + 0y = 20$$
$$\quad + 4y = -10 \quad\text{or}\quad 0x + 4y = -10$$
$$7x + 3y = 0$$

All of these equations have an x and a y variable (even if there are zero of them). The variable has an exponent of 1, and the third term is a number term. These are the characteristics of a linear equation. "Line"ar equations graph to straight lines.

To find a table of values satisfying a linear equation, the relationship is rewritten, solving for y.

Example

$$2x + 3y = 7$$

Subtract $2x$ from each side

$$2x - 2x + 3y = 7 - 2x$$
$$3y = 7 - 2x$$

Divide each side by 3

$$\frac{3y}{3} = \frac{7}{3} - \frac{2}{3}x$$

$$y = \frac{7}{3} - \frac{2}{3}x$$

Assign values for x and find the corresponding values of y (select x values divisible by 3 to avoid fractions).

x	0	3	6	-3	$3^{1/2}$
y	$7/3$	$1/3$	$-5/3$	$4^{1/3}$	0

If these values are plotted on an xy coordinate axis and the points are connected, a straight line results. This straight line is the graph of the linear relationship $2x + 3y = 7$. Regardless of the artist, the scale chosen, or the values selected for x, all results resemble the line shown.

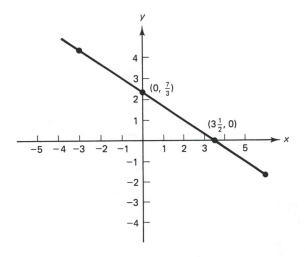

Two points uniquely determine a line. This means only two of the points selected previously were necessary to graph the line. The two points frequently chosen are $(0, 7/3)$ and $(3 1/2, 0)$. Each of these ordered pairs has the special characteristic of a 0 in one of the parts of the ordered pair and each is designed as an "intercept."

By definition, the x intercept is the point the graph intersects the x axis. $(3 1/2, 0)$ is the x intercept in the preceding example. All x intercepts have a 0 in the y component. The y intercept is the point the graph crosses the y axis. It is the ordered pair with 0 as the x component. In the preceding example, $(0, 7/3)$ is the y intercept.

The x and y intercepts can be found without solving the equation for y. Take the equation:

$$2x + 3y = 7$$

To find the x intercept, substitute 0 for y and solve for x.

$$2x + 3(0) = 7 \qquad 2x = 7 \qquad x = 7/2 \qquad (7/2, 0) \quad \text{or} \quad (3 1/2, 0)$$

To find the y intercept, substitute 0 for x and solve for y.

$$2(0) + 3y = 7 \qquad 3y = 7 \qquad y = 7/3 \qquad (0, 7/3) \quad \text{or} \quad (0, 2 1/3)$$

Graph these two points. The line is identical to the line generated by the method in the preceding example and is called graphing by intercepts.

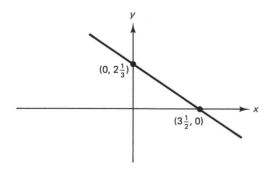

There are four special types of line graphs that should be recognized and understood.

The first graph is a horizontal line. In this type of graph the y variable remains the same and the x variable changes. The graph represents a variable with a **zero rate of change**. The equation representing a horizontal line contains a y term, a number term, but no x term. An example of the equation of a horizontal line is

$$3y - 2 = 0$$

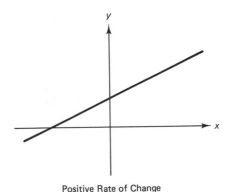

Zero Rate of Change

The second graph is a straight line rising from left to right across the graph. The graph represents two increasing variables. Because the graph is a straight line, the rate of increase is constant. The two variables are directly related. This type of graph represents a **constant positive rate of change**.

Positive Rate of Change

The third graph is a falling straight line as the line moves from left to right. This graph represents a dependent (y) variable decreasing (falling) as the independent variable (x) increases (moves right). Because the graph is a straight line, the decrease is at a constant rate. This type of graph represents a **constant negative rate of change**.

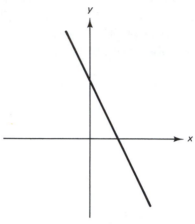

Negative Rate of Change

The fourth graph is a vertical line and is a picture of the y variable being any value for a given x value. This graph is not useful in the business world. If you purchase 5 gallons of gasoline, your charge could be any value—not a common situation in the business world.

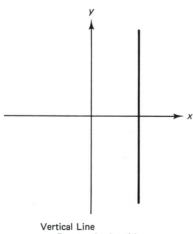

Vertical Line
$x = 5$, y can be Anything

Example

Given the following graphs, describe each of the situations.

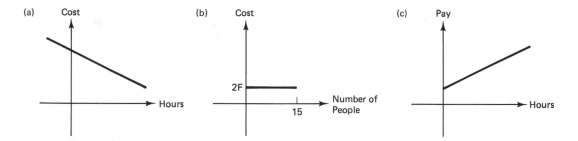

a. As the number of hours increases, the cost decreases at a constant rate.

b. As the number of people increases up to 15, the cost remains constant at 2*F*.

c. As the number of hours increases, the pay increases at a constant rate.

A Series of Straight Lines

A **broken-line graph** is a graph made up of a series of connected lines. The graph can be analyzed in parts—where a positive rate of change exists, where there is a zero rate of change, or where a negative rate of change exists—and also as a whole. The graph can give an overall impression of increasing, with fluctuations within the increase.

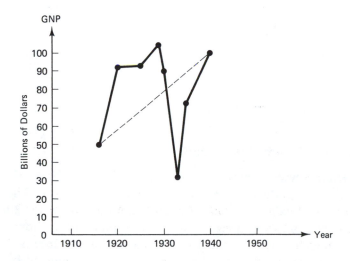

Example
In economics a study is being made of the gross national product and the following data are available from 1916 to 1940 (in billions of dollars)

Year	1916	1920	1925	1929	1930	1933	1935	1940
GNP	48.3	91.5	93.1	103.4	90.4	55.8	72.2	100.0

Draw a broken-line graph to represent the data.

    The graph certainly illustrates a general increase in the gross national product from 1916 to 1940. However, negative fluctuations occur in this increase in the period from 1929 to 1933.

Step Graphs

Another type of graph made up of a series of straight lines is the **step graph**. This graph does not connect the various straight lines as in the broken-line graph. The **step graph** is used when jumps occur and intervening values are never realized. If the charges of a parking garage are $1.00 for the first hour and $0.50 for each additional hour and these charges are graphed on a time series graph, the graph would be as follows.

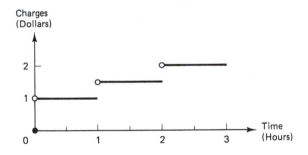

The tabular information is

t (in hours)	0	$1/4$	$1/2$	$3/4$	1	$1\frac{1}{2}$	2	$2\frac{1}{2}$
Charges (in dollars)	0	1.00	1.00	1.00	1.00	1.50	1.50	2.00

A step graph is necessary to indicate a jump from $1.00 to $1.50. A broken-line graph would indicate a gradual increase in the charge. The empty dots at the beginning of each horizontal line indicate the charge for 2 hours is $1.50, not $2.00. A step graph does not have to be made up of horizontal lines but might be modeled by increasing or decreasing discontinuous lines. If curves are used to represent changes, linear equations are replaced by other types of equations. Curves are often the most realistic representation of changes. This presentation does not include the study of curves.

SECTION 2 EXERCISES

1. Describe the graphical representation of salary with respect to years of experience if:
   a. The salary stays fixed, regardless of years of experience.
   b. The salary increases at 5% each additional year of experience.
   c. The salary decreases by 10% for every year of experience in the job.

2. Describe the graphical representation of commission received with respect to total sales when:
   a. The commission increases by 0.20 as sales increase.
   b. The commission stays constant as sales increase.
   c. The total sales increase and the commission decreases.

3. Given the following graphical representation of hours and wages, describe the relationship.

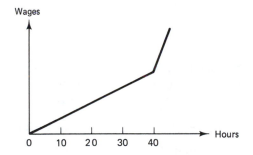

4. Given the following graphical representation of cost and sale price, describe the relationship.

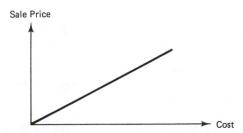

5. Given the following graphical representation of cost of goods and turn-over, describe the relationship.

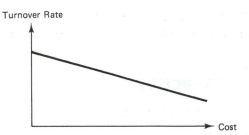

Turnover Rate

Cost

6. Given the following graphical representation of balance (in dollars) and carrying charges, describe the relationship.

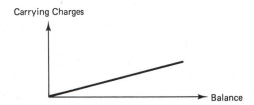

Carrying Charges

Balance

7. Draw a graph of the following time series graph representing the average cost of 4 years at a private college.

Year	1960	1965	1970	1975	1980	1985
Cost (in dollars)	10,000	14,000	14,000	19,000	24,000	23,000

a. Where does the graph have a positive rate of change?
b. Where does the graph have a zero rate of change?
c. Where does the graph have a negative rate of change?
d. From 1960 to 1985, what is the overall effect on the cost of college?

8. Draw a graph representing the rate of inflation over the time indicated.

Year	1960	1965	1970	1975	1980	1985
Rate (%)	6	8	8	7	13	5

a. Where does the graph have a positive rate of change?
b. Where does the graph have a zero rate of change?
c. Where does the graph have a negative rate of change?
d. From 1960 to 1985, what is the overall effect on inflation?

9. Draw a graph to represent taxi charges in a city. The rate is $1.50 for any amount up to 1 mile with a $0.35 increase for every additional mile or part of a mile thereafter.

10. Draw a graph to represent the charges for mailing a package. The charges are $0.70 for any amount up to 1 pound with an additional $0.20 increase for each additional 1/2 pound.

11. Draw a graph to show the balance on a $1,000 account. Simple interest was accumulated at the rate of 12%, paid semiannually, for a 3-year period.

12. Draw a graph to show the balance on a $1,000 account. Compound interest was accumulated at the rate of 12%, compounded daily, for a 3-year period.

13. Draw a graph of the balance on a loan of $1,000 with interest charged at 12% on the unpaid balance if payments of $100 are made monthly.

14. Draw a graph to represent the following information. Connect the points by broken lines and by curve. Which graph best represents the information?

Unemployment rate	0.11	0.095	0.08	0.075	0.08	0.06
Inflation rate	0.14	0.10	0.08	0.065	0.05	0.04

15. Given $4x - 2y = 10$, why is this a linear relationship? Find the x and y intercepts of the equation. Plot the intercepts and then draw the graph of $4x - 2y = 10$. Describe the rate of change of the relationship.

16. Given tax $= 0.28$ gross pay $- 350$, is this a linear relationship? What is the independent variable? Find the intercepts and graph the relationship. Describe the rate of change of tax with respect to gross pay.

17. A poll tax is a flat tax, and regardless of income, the tax is $15. Is there a linear relationship between income and tax? Determine the intercepts. Graph the relationship. Describe the relationship.

18. Graph the following set of data and connect the points by a series of broken lines.

Year	1967	1969	1971	1973	1975	1977	1979	1981
Value	1.00	0.95	1.05	1.34	1.61	1.75	1.63	1.63

   a. Determine the intervals where there is a positive rate of change.
   b. Determine the intervals having no rate of change.
   c. Describe the overall change from 1967 to 1981.

19. Graph the following set of data and connect the points by a series of broken lines.

Year	1967	1969	1971	1973	1975	1977	1979	1981
Inflation	6.6	4.5	5.8	6.1	9.2	11.5	9.4	6.6

   a. Determine the intervals where there is no rate of change.
   b. Determine the intervals where there is a negative rate of change.

c. Describe the overall change in the inflation rate from 1967 to 1981.

20. Draw a graph to show the amount of depreciation allowed under the accelerated cost recovery system on a piece of equipment valued at $15,000.

Year	1	2	3	4	5
Depreciation	$2,250	3,300	3,150	3,150	3,150

a. Determine the years where there is a positive rate of change of depreciation.

b. Determine the years where there is a zero rate of change of depreciation.

c. Determine the years where there is a negative rate of change of depreciation.

Answers to Odd-Numbered Exercises

1. (a) Horizontal line, year is independent variable, salary is dependent. (b) Line rises as you move from left to right on the graph. (c) Line falls as you move from left to right on the graph.

3. Increase up to 40 hours. Sharp increase above 40 hours.

5. As the cost of goods increases, the turnover decreases.

7.

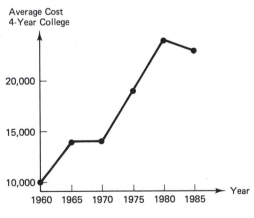

(a) 1960–1965, 1970–1980
(b) 1965–1970
(c) 1980–1985
(d) Increase

9.

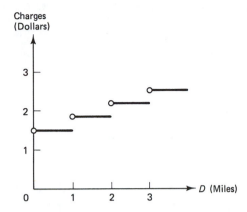

11.

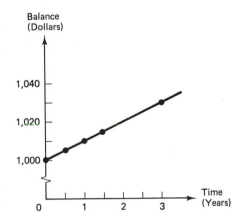

13.

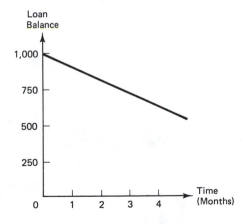

15. Contains an x term, a y term, a number term. x intercept, 2.5; y intercept −5.

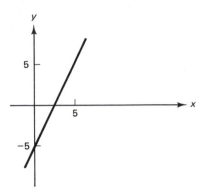

Positive rate of change.

17. Yes. Only a y intercept of 15.

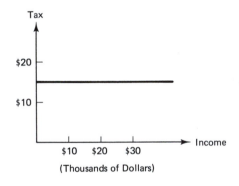

No change in tax as income increases.

19.

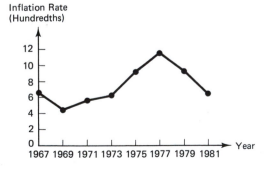

1967 to 1981, zero change. 1967 to 1969 and 1977 to 1981, negative changes. Zero change.

8.3 SLOPE

One of the more useful descriptions in a linear model is slope. Outside the world of mathematics, slope has a meaning of steepness or inclination to the horizontal. The land has a steep slope gives a picture of hilly or mountainous terrain. In mathematics, the term slope refers to the amount of inclination a line has to the horizontal. If a line rises as the x component increases, the line has a positive rate of change or a positive slope. On the other hand, if the line falls as x increases, the line has a negative rate of change or a negative slope. It is possible to determine a numerical value for the slope. The larger the number, the steeper the slope.

By definition, the slope is the ratio of the change in the y values of two ordered pairs divided by the difference of the x values. An alternate definition of slope is the ratio of the vertical change to the horizontal change.

To illustrate this definition, let us take two points on the XY plane—(2,5) and (4,8). The words "change in" involve the operation of subtraction. The slope is

$$\frac{(5-8)}{(2-4)} = \frac{-3}{-2} = \frac{3}{2}$$

or

$$\frac{(8-5)}{(4-2)} = \frac{3}{2}$$

Either of these calculations will give a slope of $3/2$ or 1.5. If the points are plotted on the XY coordinate axis, the line connecting the two points has a slope of $3/2$ or 1.5. That the slope is positive means the line rises as x becomes larger or moves to the right.

Example

Determine the slope of the line connecting the points $(1,4)$ and $(3,-1)$. Using the definition of slope as the change in y values divided by the change in x values, the calculation of the slope is

$$\frac{(4-(-1))}{(1-3)} = \frac{5}{-2}$$

An alternate approach to calculating the slope is to graph the two points. Since the change in y is another way of saying vertical change, mark off the vertical change between the points. The change in x is the horizontal change between the two points. Mark off this quantity on the graph. Since slope is the ratio of the vertical change over the horizontal change, the numerical value of $-5/2$ or -2.5 can be determined from the graph.

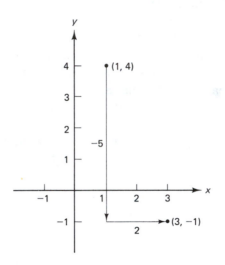

$$\text{Slope} = (y_2 - y_1)/(x_2 - x_1)$$

$$= \text{vertical change/horizontal change}$$

$$= \text{rise/run}$$

x_1 and y_1 refer to the components of one ordered pair, and x_2 and y_2 are the components of the second ordered pair. Most errors in finding slope are caused by errors in manipulating the signed numbers and inconsistency in the order of subtraction. The y value used first in the numerator designates the x value that must be used first in the denominator. To further emphasize the concept of slope and the meaning of constant slope, the following two sets of data are analyzed.

Set I:

Quantity	0	2	5	10	13
Price	20	90	195	370	475

Set II:

Quantity	0	2	5	10	13
Price	0	80	500	2,000	3,360

In set I, the data points can be written as (quantity, price): (0,20), (2,90), (5,195), (10,370), (13,475).

Example

$$\text{Slope} = \frac{(90 - 20)}{(2 - 0)} = \frac{70}{2} = 35$$

if the first and second ordered pairs are used.

$$\text{Slope} = \frac{(370 - 90)}{(10 - 2)} = \frac{280}{8} = 35$$

if the fourth and second ordered pairs are chosen. The same slope of 35 is obtained regardless of the pairs selected for the calculation. Thus the expression: constant positive rate of change.

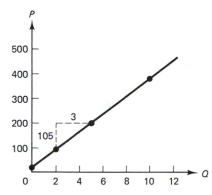

In set II, the data points can be written as (quantity, price): (0,0), (2,80), (5,500), (10,2,000), (13,3,360).

Example

$$\text{Slope} = \frac{(80 - 0)}{(2 - 0)} = \frac{80}{2} = 40$$

if the first and second ordered pairs are used.

$$\text{Slope} = \frac{(2{,}000 - 80)}{(10 - 2)} = \frac{1{,}920}{8} = 240$$

if the second and fourth ordered pairs are used. The slope between the points is not a constant. Therefore the second set of data does not graph to a straight line.

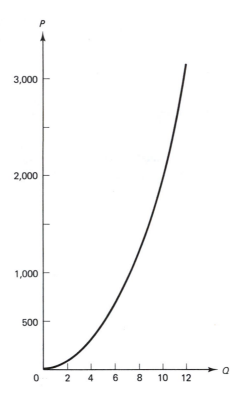

A constant slope or rate of change graphs to a straight line. If the data do not have a constant slope, a curve or a series of broken lines is used to graph the relationship. If a graph of a straight line is given, the rate of change or slope can be determined.

Method 1: Name two points on the graph by ordered pairs. Using the definition of slope, determine the ratio using the two points as values.

Method 2: Locate two points on the graph. Mark off the vertical and

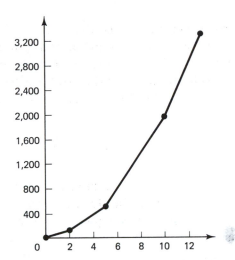

horizontal changes between the two points. Using the units on each axis, determine the numerical value for each change.

$$\text{Slope} = \text{vertical change/horizontal change}$$

Example

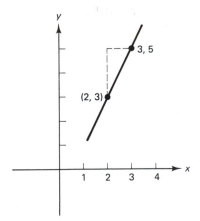

Given the graph shown above, identify two points on the line (2,3) and (3,5). Calculate the slope.

$$\frac{(3-5)}{(2-3)} = \frac{-2}{-1} = 2$$

Example

Suppose an economist has studied the relationship between the demand for electricity and the price per kilowatt hour and presented the graph to show the result of his study. Find the rate of change between demand and price.

The vertical change between the two identified points is -200. The horizontal change is 0.01. The slope or rate of change is

$$\frac{-200}{0.01} = -20,000$$

Slope gives a line a unique characteristic. If a line is known to have a slope of 2 or $^2/_1$, regardless of the starting point, the next point can be determined as 2 units up, and 1 unit right. Different lines have different starting points. The easiest starting point to select is the y intercept. Every linear equation (except a vertical line) has a y intercept. Locate the y intercept and from that point count off the value of the slope.

Example

Draw a line with a y intercept of 3 and a slope of $^2/_3$. Locate the point on the y axis with the value of 3. From that point, count up 2 units and to the right 3 units. This gives the second point on the line. This point has a y value of 5 and an x value of 3 or the ordered pair (3,5).

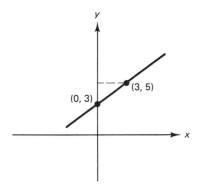

Example

Draw a line with a y intercept of 1 and a slope of -3 ($-3/1$). Locate the point 1 on the y axis. From that point, count down ($-$) 3 units and to the right 1 unit. The ordered pair is (1,-2).

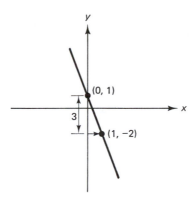

If any linear equation in two variables is given, the line can be graphed using the concept of the *y* intercept and slope.

The slope-intercept procedure is as follows.

1. Solve the equation for the *y* variable.

2. The number associated with the *x* variable is the slope.

3. The number term is the *y* intercept.

4. Locate the point on the *y* axis associated with the *y* intercept.

5. From that point, count up or down the numerator of the ratio denoting slope and count right or left the denominator of the ratio.

6. Draw the line through the *y* intercept and the point determined from the slope.

Example
Graph the line representing $2x - 5y = 15$ using the slope-intercept procedure.

Subtract $2x$ from both sides.

$$-5y = 15 - 2x$$

Divide each term by -5.

$$y = -3 + \tfrac{2}{5}x$$

The *y* intercept is -3. Locate -3 on the *y* axis. The slope of $\tfrac{2}{5}$ means to count up 2 and to the right 5. Draw the line through the points.

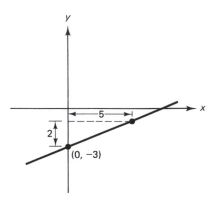

There are exceptions to the general procedure outlined previously. These will be demonstrated in the examples that follow.

Example
The x term is missing. $y = 4$. In mathematics, this statement is equivalent to $y = 0x + 4$. The statement is shortened by not writing $0x$. The graph of $y = 4$ is a **horizontal** line with a y intercept of 4. Horizontal lines have a slope of 0. The form $y = 0x + 4$ states a zero slope with a y intercept of 4. This equation has a zero rate of change between successive x values.

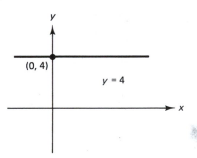

Example
The y term is missing. $0 = x - 4$. This is the equation of a vertical line passing through the x intercept of 4.

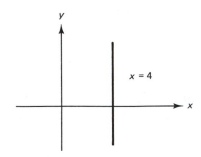

Example

The number term is missing. $3y = 2x$. The number 0 can always be included in an equation without changing it.

$$3y = 2x + 0$$

Divide by 3.

$$y = 2/3x + \frac{0}{3} \quad \text{or} \quad y = 2/3x + 0$$

The slope is $2/3$ and the y intercept is 0. Start at the origin as the y intercept, count up 2 units, and count right 3 units. Draw the line through (0,0) and (3,2).

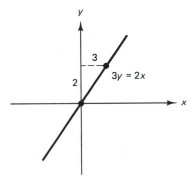

Knowing the form $y = (\text{slope})x + (y \text{ intercept})$, it is possible to write the equation for a line from the graph.

Example

Write the equation of the following graphs.

a. The y intercept is 4. The slope is $1/2$ (or $2/4$). The equation relating x and y is

$$y = 1/2x + 4$$

b. The cost intercept is 20. The slope is $10/3$. The equation relating quantity and cost is

$$\text{Cost} = 10/3 \text{ Quantity} + 20$$

(a)

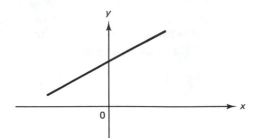

(b)

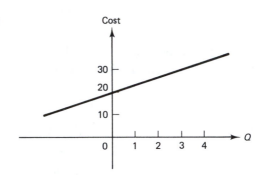

(c)

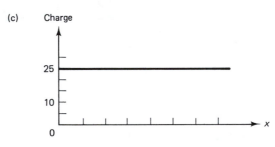

(d)

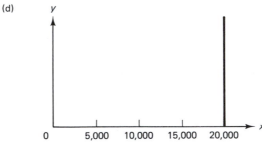

c. The vertical intercept is 25. The line is horizontal, and therefore there is no x term in the equation. The equation relating x and charge is

$$\text{Charge} = 25$$

d. The graph is a vertical line. The form of the equation of a vertical line is $x = \cdots$. On the graph, the line crossed the horizontal axis at 20,000. The equation relating x and y is

$$x = 20,000$$

SECTION 3 EXERCISES

1. Graph the following pairs of points and draw a line through the points. Determine the slope from the graph and from the computation.
   a. (4,1) and (5,8).
   b. (5,2) and (2,3).
   c. (0,3) and (5,1).
   d. (1,3) and (4,3).

2. Graph the following pairs of points and draw a line through the points. Determine the slope from the graph and from the computation.
   a. (2,7) and (4,5).
   b. (1,4) and (4,5).
   c. (3,0) and (1,5).
   d. (0,4) and (4,4).

3. Graph the following pairs of points and draw a line through the points. Determine the slope from the graph and from the computation.
   a. (−3,4) and (1,−2).
   b. (0,−2) and (4,2).
   c. (−3,0) and (5,0).
   d. (−6,1) and (2,3).

4. Graph the following pairs of points and draw a line through the points. Determine the slope from the graph and from the computation.
   a. (3,−4) and (−1,2).
   b. (0,2) and (4,−2).
   c. (3,0) and (−5,0).
   d. (6,−1) and (2,3).

5. Given the following set of data, is the slope constant in the set?

Quantity	0	3	5	9	15
Price	0	12	20	36	60

   Do the data graph to a straight line?

6. Given the following set of data, is the slope constant in the set?

Hours	0	8	12	25	60
Wages	0	25.60	38.40	80	224

Do the data graph to a line?

7. Given the following set of data, is the slope constant in the set?

Hours	0	2	5	9
Miles	0	100	240	432

Do the data graph to a line?

8. Given the following set of data, is the slope constant in the set?

Quantity	115	380	650	810
Price	9.20	30.40	52	64.80

Do the data graph to a line?

9. Given the following graph, determine the slope of the line.

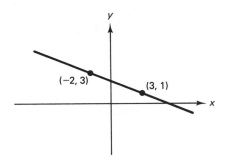

10. Given the following graph, determine the slope of the line.

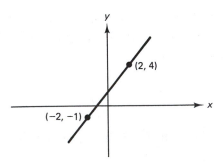

11. Determine the slope and y intercept of $4x - 3y = 9$.

12. Determine the slope and y intercept of $3x + 2y = 4$.

13. Determine the slope and y intercept of $x - 3y = 6$.

14. Determine the slope and y intercept of $4x - 2y = 7$.

15. Graph $4x - 3y = 9$ (exercise 11) using the slope and y intercept.

16. Graph $3x + 2y = 4$ (exercise 12) using the slope and y intercept.

17. Graph $x + 3y = 6$ (exercise 13) using the slope and y intercept.

18. Graph $4x + 2y = 7$ (exercise 14) using the slope and y intercept.

19. Graph $4y = 8$. Identify the slope and y intercept.

20. Graph $3y - 9 = 0$. Identify the slope and y intercept.

21. Graph $5x - 15 = 0$. Identify the slope and y intercept.

22. Graph $3x - 12 = 0$. Identify the slope and y intercept.

23. The rate of change (slope) is 4 and the y intercept is 10. Write the linear equation that represents the information.

24. The slope of the line is $5/2$ and the point $(0,4)$ is on the line. Write the linear equation that represents the information.

25. Given the following graph, identify the slope and intercept. Write the linear equation.

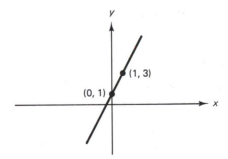

26. Given the following graph, identify the slope and intercept. Write the linear equation.

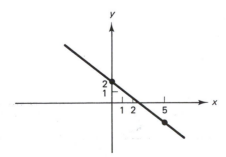

27. Given the two points of data (0,25) and (15,30), write the linear equation to represent the data.

28. Given the two points of data (0,60) and (15,30), write the linear equation to represent the data.

29. Given the following information:

Population	0	5,000	8,000	11,000
Unemployed	0	325	520	715

Do the data represent a constant rate of change? Find the linear equation to represent the data. What is the rate of unemployment? Predict the number of unemployed in a population of 21,500.

30. Given the following information:

Credit hours	0	5	8	9	10
Tuition charge	0	60	96	108	120

Do the data represent a constant rate of change? Write the linear equation to represent the data. What is the charge per credit hour?

Answers to Odd-Numbered Exercises

1. (a) 7. (b) $-1/3$. (c) $-2/5$. (d) 0.

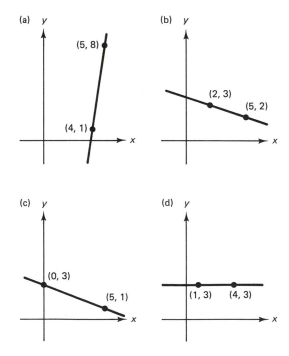

3. (a) $-6/4$. (b) 1. (c) 0. (d) $-2/-8 = 1/4$.

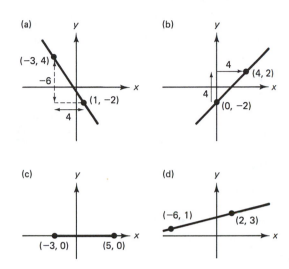

5. Slope, $12/3$, $8/2$, $16/4$, $24/6$. Yes, graphs to a line.

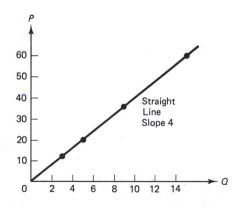

7. Slope, 50, 140/3, 48. No, does not graph to a line.

9. $-2/5$.

11. Slope, $4/3$. y intercept, -3.

13. Slope, $1/3$. y intercept, -2.

15.

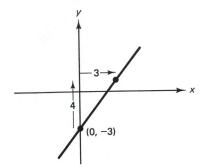

17.

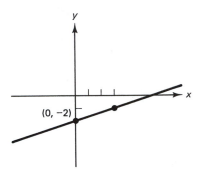

19.

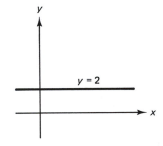

$m = 0, b = 2$

21.

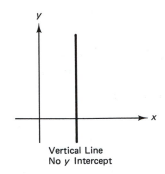

Vertical Line
No y Intercept

23. $y = 4x + 10$.

25. $y = 2x + 1$.

27. Slope, $1/3$. y intercept, 25. $y = 1/3x + 25$.

29. Constant rate of change of $195/3{,}000$.
Unemployment $= 195/3{,}000$ (population).
Rate of unemployment $= 195/3{,}000$.
1,398 unemployed in a population of 21,500.

8.4   BEST LINE FIT FOR DATA

In the previous section, we graphed straight lines from linear equations and from ordered pairs that lie on a line. Sometimes given data do not lie on a line, but a line could be a close approximation for the relationship. A set of data that represents this situation is

Number of items	25	100	500
Defective items	1	2	9

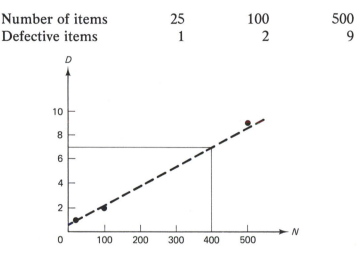

The data points $(25,1)$, $(100,2)$, and $(500,9)$ do not lie on a line but a close approximation to the relationship is shown by the dotted line. The approximating line can be used to predict other points in the relationship. For example, given 400 items, about 7 of them would be defective.

The question is how to find the "best" fitting line. One of the methods used to find the "best" fitting line minimizes the sum of the squares of the distances from the given points to the line. The diagram will show what we are describing.

P_1, P_2, P_3, P_4, P_5, and P_6 are the data points. d_1, d_2, d_3, d_4, d_5, and d_6 are the distances to the proposed line. Mathematics determine the line where $(d_1)^2 + (d_2)^2 + (d_3)^2 + (d_4)^2 + (d_5)^2 + (d_6)^2$ is minimized. Using higher

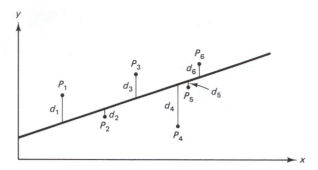

mathematics, we can obtain formulas to determine the slope and y intercept of the "best fit" line.

$$m = \frac{n(\Sigma\, xy) - (\Sigma\, x)(\Sigma\, y)}{n(\Sigma\, x^2) - (\Sigma\, x)^2}$$

$$b = \frac{\Sigma\, y - m(\Sigma\, x)}{n}$$

The "best" fit line is given by the linear equation $y = mx + b$, where m and b are determined by the two formulas given previously.

The two formulas were used in the previous example relating number of items and the corresponding number of defects.

$x(N)$	25	100	500
$y(D)$	1	2	9

Set up the following columns.

x	y	xy	x^2	y^2
25	1	25	625	1
100	2	200	10,000	4
500	9	4,500	250,000	81
Sum 625	12	4,725	260,625	86

Identify $n = 3$, $\Sigma\, x = 625$, $\Sigma\, y = 12$, $\Sigma\, xy = 4{,}725$, $\Sigma\, x^2 = 260{,}625$, $\Sigma\, y^2 = 86$.

$$m = \frac{(3)(4{,}725) - (625)(12)}{(3)(260{,}625) - (625)^2} = 0.017\ 0607$$

$$b = \frac{(12) - (0.017\ 0607)(625)}{3} = 0.446$$

The equation is

$$\text{Defects} = 0.017(\text{number of items}) + 0.446$$

The equation can be used to generate other ordered pairs of items and defects.

$$\text{Defects} = (0.017)(400) + 0.446 = 7.246$$

when there are 400 items. Remember that the visual approximation from the graph for 400 items was about 7.

If the points appear to fit the line quite closely, future points can be predicted with some accuracy. If the points are so widely scattered that a line is not a good approximation of the points, predictions made from the "best" line are not reliable.

A coefficient-of-correlation formula is available to predict the reliability of the "best" line. The formula uses values already determined for the generation of m and b.

$$\text{Coefficient of correlation} = \frac{n(\Sigma\, xy) - (\Sigma\, x)(\Sigma\, y)}{\sqrt{n(\Sigma\, x^2) - (\Sigma\, x)^2} \cdot \sqrt{n(\Sigma\, y^2) - (\Sigma\, y)^2}}$$

The value of the coefficient of correlation will be between -1 and 1. If the slope of the "best" line is negative, the coefficient of correlation will be negative. If the slope of the "best" fit line is positive, the coefficient of correlation will be positive. The closer the value is to -1 or 1, the better the fit of the line. A value close to 0 means there is no "best" line for the data points.

For the previous example relating items and defects, the coefficient of correlation is

$$r = \frac{6{,}675}{\sqrt{(391{,}250)} \cdot \sqrt{(114)}} = 0.999\ 4759$$

(Note that the number 6,675 is the same as the numerator of the fraction for m.)

This is an indication that the linear equation $y = 0.017x + 0.25$ is a close approximation of the relationship given in the original data.

Example
A college is trying to find a predictable relationship between high school stu-

dent GPA and college student GPA. The registrar provided the following data for a determination of a predictable relationship.

| H.S.GPA (x) | 2.5 | 3.6 | 3.0 | 2.8 | 3.4 | 3.3 | 2.9 | 3.1 | 3.9 | 4.0 |
| Col. GPA (y) | 2.2 | 3.6 | 2.6 | 2.4 | 3.5 | 3.1 | 2.5 | 3.0 | 4.0 | 3.7 |

1. Find the "best" fit line.

2. Use the results to predict the college GPA for a student with a high school GPA of 2.0.

3. Find the coefficient of correlation.

Solution:

1. Make columns for x, y, xy, x^2, and y^2.

x	y	xy	x^2	y^2
2.5	2.2	5.5	6.25	4.84
3.6	3.6	12.96	12.96	12.96
3.0	2.6	7.8	9.0	6.76
2.8	2.4	6.72	7.84	5.76
3.4	3.5	11.9	11.56	12.25
3.3	3.1	10.23	10.89	9.61
2.9	2.5	7.25	8.41	6.25
3.1	3.0	9.3	9.61	9.0
3.9	4.0	15.6	15.21	16.0
4.0	3.7	14.8	16.0	13.69
32.5	30.6	102.06	107.73	97.12

2. $n = 10$ and each of the required sums are

$$\Sigma x = 32.5 \qquad \Sigma y = 30.6 \qquad \Sigma xy = 102.06$$
$$\Sigma x^2 = 107.73 \qquad \Sigma y^2 = 97.12$$

3. Determine m.

$$m = \frac{10(102.06) - (32.5)(30.6)}{10(107.73) - (32.5)^2} = \frac{26.1}{21.05} = 1.24$$

4. Use the value for $m = 1.24$ to solve for b.

$$b = \frac{30.6 - (1.24)(32.5)}{10} = -0.97$$

This gives the "best" fit line as

$$y = 1.24x - 0.97.$$

Substituting 2.0 for x:

$$y = 1.24(2.0) - 0.97 \qquad y = 1.51$$

5. Substituting into the coefficient-of-correlation formula:

$$r = \frac{(10)(102.06) - (32.5)(30.6)}{\sqrt{10(107.73) - (32.5)^2} \cdot \sqrt{10(97.12) - (30.6)^2}}$$

$$= \frac{26.1}{\sqrt{21.05}\sqrt{34.84}} = 0.96$$

This indicates a high level of correlation between high school GPA and college GPA for the 10 students. A much larger sample would be needed for a firm conclusion of the relationship.

If m, b, and r are determined by hand, it is essential to set the data up in an organized way and to use your calculator efficiently in the generation of data. In the x^2 columns, enter x, press the $\boxed{x^2}$ key, $\boxed{+}$, next x, $\boxed{x^2}$ (record in table), $\boxed{+}$, for the entire column.

Whenever many calculations are involved in a problem, a computer program is in order. The following is a program in basic to generate the values for m, b, and r.

```
10      REM: DETERMINING SLOPE, INTERCEPT, AND
             COEFFICIENT OF CORRELATION.
15      LET N=1
20      PSUM = 0
21      QSUM = 0
22      XSUM = 0
23      YSUM = 0
24      RSUM = 0
30      PRINT "X VALUE": Input X
40      PRINT "Y VALUE": Input Y
50      XSUM = X + XSUM
60      YSUM = Y + YSUM
70      XY = X*Y: PSUM = PSUM + XY
80      XQ = X*X: PSUM = PSUM + XQ
90      YQ = Y*Y: RSUM = RSUM + YQ
100     N = N + 1
```

```
110        IF N<=A GOTO 30
120        M = (A*PSUM - XSUM*YSUM)/(A*QSUM-XSUM*XSUM)
130        B = (YSUM - M*XSUM)/A
140        PRINT "M=":M
150        PRINT "B=":B
160        C=(A*PSUM-XSUM*YSUM)/(SQR(A-
           QSUM-XSUM*XSUM)*SQR(A*RSUM-YSUM*YSUM))
170        PRINT "C=":C
180        END
```

SECTION 4 EXERCISES

1. Given the following speeds a machine can be operated and the number of recorded defective items turned out at each speed, find the equation for the least-squares line.

Speed (rpm)	88	100	120	160
Defects	4	5	7	9

Find the coefficient of correlation. If the speed was 150 revolutions per minute, how many defects are predictable?

2. Given the following SAT scores and college freshman GPA, find the equation for the least-squares line.

SAT	700	800	900	1,000	1,100	1,200
GPA	1.8	2.4	2.7	3.5	3.6	3.7

Find the coefficient of correlation. What GPA would you predict for an SAT score of 950?

3. Given the following information relating height in inches and weight in pounds for 10 adult women, find the equation of the least-squares line.

Height	58	60	62	63	63	65	68
Weight	92	105	110	110	125	130	140

Find the coefficient of correlation. Find the predicted height of an adult woman weighing 120 pounds.

4. Given the following information relating the cost of maintenance per mile for average number of miles driven daily, find the equation of the least-squares line.

Miles	25	100	200	300	400
Maintenance	3	4	3.5	4.5	3.7

Find the coefficient of correlation. Find the predicted cost per mile for 500 miles per day.

5. Given the following information relating blood-pressure level and cholesterol level, find the equation of the least-squares line.

Blood pressure	90	120	140	160	190
Cholesterol	170	160	200	240	300

Find the coefficient of correlation. Find the predicted blood-pressure level of an individual with a cholesterol reading of 250.

6. Given the following data relating the weight in ounces of an infant and the number of weeks of gestation, write the equation of the least-squares line.

Weeks	30	32	34	36	38	40
Weight	62	70	78	85	109	118

Find the coefficient of correlation. Find the predicted weight of a 39-week-old baby.

7. Given the following data recorded in the laboratory using a Fahrenheit thermometer and a Celsius thermometer, find the least-squares line equation relating the two readings.

Celsius	5	10	12	15	18	20
Fahrenheit	40	51	55	60	65	70

Find the coefficient of correlation. Find the predicted Fahrenheit reading when the Celsius reading is 23.

8. Given the following data relating the number of pages of a book and the weight of the book in ounces, find the equation of the least-squares line relating number of pages and weight of book.

Number of pages	375	470	675	790	1,048
Weight	24	30	40	50	75

Find the coefficient of correlation. Find the predicted weight of a book that has 900 pages.

9. Given the following data relating the number of days of absence from class and the GPA of the student for the same period, write the least-squares line equation relating absences and GPA.

Days absent	0	2	3	5	7	10
GPA	2.8	3.0	2.7	2.4	2.0	1.2

10. Given the following data relating the number of employees and the average number of days of sick time recorded, find the least-squares line equation relating the number of days and the number of employees.

Number of employees	2	5	7	12	26	57
Sick days	2.5	3.1	3.0	5.0	5.0	6.5

Find the coefficient of correlation. Find the predicted average number of sick days where there are 45 employees.

Answers to Odd-Numbered Exercises

1. $m = 0.07$, $b = -2$, $r = 0.99$.
   Defects $= 0.07$(speed) $- 2$. Speed $= 150$. Defects $= 8.5$.

3. $m = 4.8$, $b = -187.5$, $r = 0.96$.
   Weight $= 4.8$(height) $- 187.5$. Weight $= 120$. Height $= 63.5$.

5. $m = 1.4$, $b = 18$, $r = 0.52$.
   Cholesterol $= 1.4$(blood pressure) $+ 18$. Blood pressure $= 165$.

7. $m = 1.94$, $b = 31$, $r = 0.998$.
   $F = 1.94C + 31$. $F = 76$.

9. $m = -0.17$, $b = 3$, $r = -0.95$.
   GPR $= -0.17$(absences) $+ 3$.

Summary

A graph on a coordinate axis shows a unique location for each pair of numbers given. The intersection of the two axes is called the origin. Each location is named in relationship to the origin. The first number of the ordered pair denotes the amount to the right or left of the origin. The second number indicates the amount above or below the horizontal axis. The intersection of these two distances is the unique location represented by the ordered pair.

Linear model: the graph is approximated by a straight line.

Equation of a linear model most generally has both an x and y term.

$ax + by = c$ is the general relationship.

x intercept, or point where the line crosses the x axis, is $(c/a, 0)$

y intercept, or point where the line crosses the y axis, is $(0, c/b)$

Slope of a line describes the slant or steepness of the line:

$$\text{Slope} = \frac{\text{Horizontal change}}{\text{Vertical change}} = \frac{y_2 - y_1}{x_2 - x_1} = \frac{\text{Rise}}{\text{Run}}$$

Special Linear Relationships

Horizontal line—equation contains only y variable: $3y = 5$
   ZERO rate of change
   Slope is 0

Line rises—equation has both an x and a y variable.
   CONSTANT positive rate of change
   Slope is positive
   Direct relationship

Line falls—equation has both an x and a y variable
   Constant negative rate of change
   Slope is negative
   Direct relationship

Vertical line—equation has only an x variable: $5x - 2 = 0$
   Slope is undefined (too steep to talk about!)

Broken line graph—a series of straight lines, each line defined by a slope.

Step graph—a series of horizontal lines modeling jumps in values.

Approximating Data by Linear Model

$$y = mx + b,$$

where

$$m = \frac{n(\Sigma\, xy) - (\Sigma\, x)(\Sigma\, y)}{n(\Sigma\, x^2) - (\Sigma\, x)^2}$$

$$b = \frac{(\Sigma\, y) - m(\Sigma\, x)}{n}$$

Coefficient of Correlation predicts reliability of the linear model.

$$r = \frac{n(\Sigma\, xy) - (\Sigma\, x)(\Sigma\, y)}{\sqrt{n(\Sigma\, x^2) - (\Sigma\, x)^2} \cdot \sqrt{n(\Sigma\, y^2) - (\Sigma\, y)^2}}$$

REVIEW EXERCISES

1. Given the following x and y values

x	0	2	3	7
y	3	7	9	17

   a. Plot these points in quadrant I of the xy coordinate axis.
   b. Determine the slope between (0,3) and (2,7), between (0,3) and (3,9), and between (0,3) and (7,17).

   c. Is there a line that passes through the four points?

   d. Write the equation of the line.

2. Given the following graph, identify two points on line. Determine the slope. Write the equation of the line. Describe the graph.

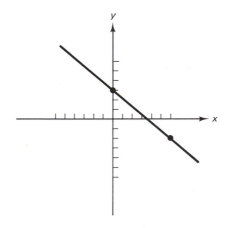

3. Plot the following data on a graph.

Assets (in millions)	165	180	202	220	250
Liabilities (in millions)	80	92	100	120	122

   Connect the points by a series of straight lines. Determine the least-squares line equation for the data. Draw the graph of the least-squares line on the same graph as the original data were plotted.

4. The charges for renting a copying machine are listed as $100 a month plus $25 per hundred for any copies made over 1,000. Draw a graph to show the monthly charges for up to 1,500 copies.

5. Write the linear equation that represents the following relationship.

Number of cars sold	0	5	10	18	32
Commission paid	750	3,250	5,750	9,750	16,750

Find the commission paid for 25 cars sold.

6. Identify the slope and y intercept of the linear equation: $y = 2,000x + 16,000$, where x represents the number of years and y represents the dollars of sales. Is the rate of sales increasing or decreasing?

7. The cost of producing vacuum cleaners is approximated by the linear equation

$$C = 21n + 100$$

If no vacuum cleaners are produced, what is the cost? What expense makes up the $100? What is the additional cost per vacuum cleaner? Find the cost of producing 100 vacuum cleaners.

8. The results of using an antibacterial spray in the environment are recorded as

Time (in hours)	0	1	3	8	24
Number of bacteria	100	90	70	20	0

What is the hourly rate of change of bacteria? Write an equation representing the first four pieces of data. Does the point (24,0) satisfy the equation?

9. A chain saw rental firm advertises a $15 charge plus $2 per hour or any fractional part of an hour for the time the chain saw is checked out. Write a set of 5 values that satisfy the description of the charges. Will there ever be a charge of exactly $20? Graph the relationship.

10. Draw a graph to represent the average noon temperature each month of the year.

J	F	M	A	M	J	J	A	S	O	N	D
43	37	45	58	65	72	89	92	83	76	59	43

a. Where is there a positive rate of change?
b. Where is there a zero rate of change?
c. Where is the rate of change negative?
d. From January to December, how does the temperature change?

11. The pricing policy for a jewelry store is $SP = 2C + 10$. Is there a linear relationship between the cost and the selling price?
a. At what rate does the cost change?

b. What is the flat charge added onto each rate times cost?

c. Graph the relationship.

12. A company states that overhead remains fixed regardless of sales. If the overhead is listed at $45,000 per month, draw a graph of the relationship between sales and overhead.

13. Given the points (0,2) and (5,17), determine the slope and write the equation representing the line through the two points.

14. Determine the slope and y intercept of $7x - 3y = 9$.

15. Graph the following points.

$$(1.1,2), \quad (0.8,1.5), \quad (1.4,2.3), \quad (1.7,3.0), \quad (1.5,2.5), \quad (1.3,2.4)$$

Determine if these points lie on a line by comparing slopes. Determine the least-squares line that best represents the relationship. Graph the line on the same graph as the points are graphed. Determine the coefficient of correlation for the line.

Answers to Review Exercises

1. (a)

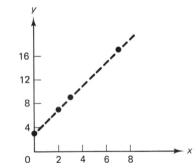

(b) All slopes, 2. (c) Yes. (d) $y = 2x + 3$.

2. (0,3) (6,-2). Slope, $-5/6$. $y = -5/6x + 3$. Negative rate of change.

3. (a)

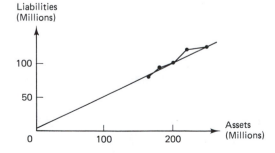

(b) $m = 1/2$, $b = 1.1$.
Liabilities $= 1/2$(assets) $+ 1$.

4.

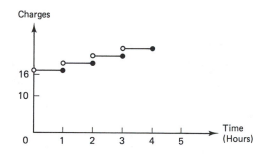

5. Slope, 500.
Commission $= 500$(Sales) $+ 750$.
Selling 25 cars. Commission, $13,250.

6. Slope, 2,000. y intercept, 16,000. Rate of sales increasing.

7. Cost, $100. This is overhead. Each additional vacuum, $21. Cost to produce 100 vacuums, $2,200.

8. -10 bacteria/hour. $N = -10t + 100$. 24,0 does not satisfy relationship.

9.

t	0	1	2	3	4
C	15	17	19	21	23

No charge of exactly $20.

10. (a) February to August. (b) None. (c) August to February. (d) No change.

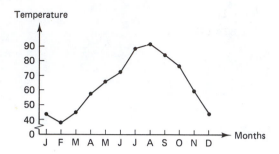

11. Linear relationship. 2 times cost. 10.

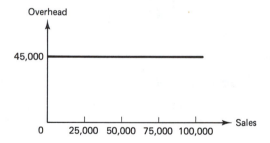

12.

13. Slope $= 3$. $y = 3x + 2$.

14. $m = 7/3$, $b = -3$.

15. Slopes are unequal. $y = 1.56x + 0.25.$ $r = 0.98.$

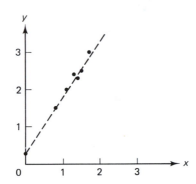

Chapter 9

PATTERNS, SEQUENCES, AND SERIES

Observing patterns can make events predictable. Early civilizations observed patterns of the sun and moon, using the observations to predict and plan their everyday routines. After a pattern is observed, some scientific explanation is made for the phenomenon. The theory is tested and the observation accepted or rejected.

Numbers frequently occur in patterns. Mathematicians study numerical patterns, determine a relationship among the numbers, and predict future numbers of the sequence. This chapter is an introduction to the most common categories of sequences of numbers.

At the end of this chapter, the student will be able to:

1. Identify arithmetic, geometric, and recursive sequences and predict future terms of the sequence.

2. Define and use standard notation for terms of a sequence.

3. Write the general relationship of an arithmetic, geometric, and recursive sequence, given three terms of the sequence.

4. Given the general relationship of the terms of a sequence, generate the first three terms and any term of an arithmetic or geometric sequence.

5. Use the sum formulas for arithmetic and geometric series to find the sum of any number of terms.

6. Use the difference equation to find any term for a recursive formula where the general relationship involves the preceding term.

7. Use series and sequences to assist in finding solutions to business applications.

9.1   ARITHMETIC SEQUENCES

A sequence of numbers is a functional relationship between a set of numbers and the set of natural numbers. The word functional in mathematics can be replaced by the word unique. Natural numbers are the counting numbers 1, 2, 3. . . . The notation 1, 2, 3 . . . is the notation for the natural numbers that start at 1 and continue on forever, each number exceeding the preceding one by 1. If the notation had been 1, 2, 3, . . . , 25, the same numbers are generated but this sequence stops at 25. The three dots are used to indicate that the numerical sequence continues in the same pattern as the first three. At least three numbers of the sequence must be listed to uniquely determine additional terms.

The notation for numbers in a sequence is closely related to the definition of a sequence. The small letter a is used to denote terms of a sequence. The a is followed by a natural number subscript. A subscript is a number or letter immediately following a character and written below the character. The combination of a and some counting number subscript denotes a particular term of a sequence.

a_1 symbolizes the first term.

a_2 symbolizes the second term.

a_3 symbolizes the third term.

a_{10} symbolizes the tenth term.

a_{241} symbolizes the 241st term.

a_n symbolizes the nth term and denotes the general term of a sequence.

When several terms of a sequence are known, an algebraic expression in terms of n is useful to accurately predict subsequent terms of the sequence.

Example
2, 4, 6, 8, ...

$$a_1 = 2 \qquad a_2 = 4 \qquad a_3 = 6 \qquad a_4 = 8$$

The value of the term is twice the n value or the subscript of the term. The algebraic statement of this relationship is $a_n = 2n$. Once this relationship has been established, finding the 231st term is a matter of substituting 231 for n.

$$a_n = 2n \qquad a_{231} = 2(231) = 462$$

The two types of problems concerning sequences are

1. Given a defined relationship, generate a particular term.

2. Find the general relationship if at least three terms of the sequence are given.

Example
The general relationship of a particular sequence is given by:

$$a_n = 3n - 2$$

Find the first five terms, the twentieth term, and the 427th term.
    The solution to this example involves substituting 1, 2, 3, 4, 5, 20, and 427 for n in the general relationship formula.

$$a_1 = 3(1) - 2 = 1$$
$$a_2 = 3(2) - 2 = 4$$
$$a_3 = 3(3) - 2 = 7$$
$$a_4 = 3(4) - 2 = 10$$
$$a_5 = 3(5) - 2 = 13$$
$$a_{20} = 3(20) - 2 = 58$$
$$a_{427} = 3(427) - 2 = 1{,}279$$

Example
Given the sequence $3, 5, 7, \ldots$, determine the general relationship and predict the 159th term.

$$a_1 = 3 \qquad a_2 = 5 \qquad a_3 = 7$$

A relationship is needed between

$$
\begin{array}{ccc}
n & & a_n \\
1 & \longrightarrow & 3 \\
2 & \longrightarrow & 5 \\
3 & \longrightarrow & 7
\end{array}
$$

A common difference of 2 exists between successive terms. When a common difference is observed, the sequence can be categorized as arithmetic and the formula

$$a_n = a_1 + (n - 1)d$$

can be used to generate the general relationship formula. a_1 refers to the first term, and d is the common difference. In this example, $a_1 = 3$ and $d = 2$.

$$
\begin{aligned}
a_n &= (3) + (n - 1)(2) \\
&= 3 + 2n - 2 \\
&= 2n + 1
\end{aligned}
$$

This is the general relationship that generates any term of the sequence. To determine the 159th term, substitute 159 for n in the general formula.

$$a_{159} = 2(159) + 1 = 319$$

Business applications produce sequences. Suppose \$1,000 is invested at a simple interest rate of 8%, accumulated quarterly. The amount of the \$1,000 (principal + interest) over time is 1,020, 1,040, 1,060, 1,080, ... To determine the general relationship between the number of the term and the value of the term:

n	a_n	d
1	1,020	
2	1,040	$1,040 - 1,020 = 20$
3	1,060	$1,060 - 1,040 = 20$
4	1,080	$1,080 - 1,060 = 20$

$$a_n = a_1 + (n - 1)d \qquad a_n = 1,020 + (n - 1)(20) \qquad a_n = 1,000 + 20n$$

If $a_n = 1,000 + 20n$ is compared to the formula $A = P + PRT$, the two expressions are similar. The product of $(1,000)(0.02)$ is 20, and n and T both refer to the number of intervals at which interest is computed. Sometimes it is not possible to devise a relationship involving the number of the term. These types of sequences will be discussed in the next section.

If the terms of a sequence have a common difference the sequence is described as arithmetic.

1, 2, 3, . . . is an arithmetic sequence with a common difference of 1.

2, 4, 6, . . . is an arithmetic sequence with a common difference of 2.

1, 3, 5, . . . is an arithmetic sequence with a common difference of 2.

1, 3, 9, 27, . . . has differences of 2, 6, and 18 and therefore is not an arithmetic sequence.

If a sequence is arithmetic, $a_n = a_1 + (n - 1)d$ is used to generate the general term where a_1 is the first term and d is the common difference between successive terms. In the sequence 1, 3, 5, . . . , $a_1 = 1$ and $d = 2$.

$$a_n = (1) + (n - 1)(2)$$
$$= 1 + 2n - 2 = 2n - 1$$

Example
Given 10, 7, 4, 1, . . ., find the general relationship and the 171st term.

The common difference is -3. Note that when the value of the terms is decreasing in an arithmetic sequence, the difference is negative.

$$a_1 = 10 \qquad d = -3$$

Substituting in $a_n = a_1 + (n - 1)d$:

$$a_n = 10 + (n - 1)(-3)$$
$$= 10 - 3n + 3$$
$$= 13 - 3n$$

The general rule for the sequence 10, 7, 4, 1 is $a_n = 13 - 3n$. To determine the 171st term, substitute 171 in the general rule.

$$a_{171} = 13 - 3(171) = 13 - 521 = -508$$

Generating the general relationship and substituting 171 for n is far better than writing out all 171 terms.

SECTION 1 EXERCISES

In exercises 1 through 20, the rule is given for generating a sequence. Determine the first five terms, the tenth term, and the 241st term.

1. $a_n = 3n - 2$.

2. $a_n = 5n + 7$.

3. $a_n = (n + 3)/4$.

4. $a_n = n + 1/2$.

5. $a_n = n^2$.

6. $a_n = -n^2$.

7. $a_n = 2^n$.

8. $a_n = 3(2^n) + 1$.

9. $a_n = n^2 - 2n + 3$.

10. $a_n = n^2 + n + 1$.

11. $a_n = 14 - 5n$.

12. $a_n = 100 - n$.

13. $a_n = (2n - 1)/(n + 3)$.

14. $a_n = 1/n$.

15. $a_n = 1/(n + 1)$.

16. $a_n = 1,500 + 30n$.

17. $a_n = 500 + 50n$.

18. $a_n = 5,000 + 100n$.

19. $a_n = 7,000 + 560n$.

20. $a_n = 10,000 + 100n$.

21. Determine the rate of interest in exercise 17 if n represents annual increments.

22. Determine the rate of interest in exercise 16 if n represents quarterly increments.

23. Predict the interest period in exercise 19 if the sequence represents the amount at the end of each period.

24. Determine the rate of interest in exercise 18 if n represents semiannual interest periods.

25. Predict the interest period in exercise 20 if the current interest rate is between 8% and 13%.

26. For the even-numbered exercises between 1 and 20, determine those that generate arithmetic sequences.

27. For the odd-numbered exercises between 1 and 20, determine those that generate arithmetic sequences.

Generate the general relationship for the following arithmetic sequences.

28. 7, 6, 5, 4, ...

29. 32, 33, 34, ...

30. 12, 14, 16, ...

31. 14, 11, 8, 5, ...

32. 5,000, 5,100, 5,200, ...

33. 0.09, 0.08, 0.07, ...

Answers to Odd-Numbered Exercises

1. 1, 4, 7, 10, 13. $a_{10} = 28$. $a_{241} = 721$.

3. 1, $5/4$, $6/4$, $7/4$, $8/4$. $a_{10} = 13/4$. $a_{241} = 244/4$.

5. 1, 4, 9, 16, 25. $a_{10} = 100$. $a_{241} = 241^2$.

7. 2, 4, 8, 16, 32. $a_{10} = 2^{10}$. $a_{241} = 2^{241}$.

9. 2, 3, 6, 11, 18. $a_{10} = 83$. $a_{241} = 57{,}602$.

11. 9, 4, -1, -6, -11. $a_{10} = -36$. $a_{241} = -1{,}191$.

13. $1/4$, $3/5$, $5/6$, $7/7$, $9/8$. $a_{10} = 19/13$. $a_{241} = 481/244$.

15. $1/2$, $1/3$, $1/4$, $1/5$, $1/6$. $a_{10} = 1/11$. $a_{241} = 1/242$.

17. 550, 600, 650, 700, 750. $a_{10} = 1{,}000$. $a_{241} = 12{,}550$.

19. 7,560, 8,120, 8,680, 9,240, 9,800. $a_{10} = 12{,}600$. $a_{241} = 141{,}960$.

21. 10%.

23. Annual.

25. 1%, period is monthly.

27. 1, 3, 11, 17, 19.

29. $a_n = 31 + n$.

31. $a_n = 17 - 3n$.

33. $a_n = 0.10 - 0.01n$.

9.2 GEOMETRIC AND RECURSIVE SEQUENCES

Not all sequences of numbers qualify as arithmetic sequences. For example, in the sequence 2, 4, 8, 16, . . . , the differences are

$$4 - 2 = 2$$
$$8 - 4 = 4$$
$$16 - 8 = 8$$

No common difference exists.

We use the same type of notation for all sequences, $a_1, a_2, a_3, \ldots , a_n$.

$$a_1 = 2 \qquad a_2 = 4 \qquad a_3 = 8 \qquad a_4 = 16$$

Associating the number and value of the term, the following pairs of values are generated.

n	a_n
1	2
2	4
3	8
4	16

Successive a values have a common ratio. The ratios are 4/2, 8/4, and 16/8, and all reduce to the number 2. The number 2 is the common ratio of the sequence and the letter r is used to represent the common ratio. Each successive term can be generated by multiplying the preceding term by r.

$$a_2 = a_1(2) \quad \text{or} \quad a_2 = a_1r$$
$$a_3 = a_2(2) \quad \text{or} \quad a_3 = a_2r = (a_1r)(r) = a_1r^2$$
$$a_4 = a_3(2) \quad \text{or} \quad a_4 = a_3r = (a_1r^2)r = a_1r^3$$

This pattern suggests the relationship for all sequences with a common ratio.

$$a_n = a_1 r^{n-1}$$

Sequences where successive terms have a common ratio are called geometric sequences.

Example

$$a_n = 3(2)^{n-1}$$

Generate the first five terms and the forty-second term.

$$a_1 = 3(2)^0 = 3$$

(recall that any number raised to the zero power is 1).

$$a_2 = 3(2)^1 = 6$$
$$a_3 = 3(2)^2 = 12$$
$$a_4 = 3(2)^3 = 24$$
$$a_5 = 3(2)^4 = 48$$

The formula does not have to be used once the pattern is obvious—simply write the successive terms by multiplying the preceding term by 2.

To generate the forty-second term in the geometric sequence, a calculator is desirable if the actual value of the term is needed.

$$a_{42} = 3(2)^{41}$$

To find the numerical value of this term on the calculator, use the $\boxed{y^x}$ key.

$$2 \;\boxed{y^x}\; 41 \;\boxed{=}$$

The display will show 2.199 12. This is a large number written in scientific notation. The number of digits in the number exceeds the number of places in the display of the instrument. To complete the example:

$$\boxed{\times} \; 3 \; \boxed{=}$$

The display shows 6.5971 12. This is the scientific notation for a number with the decimal point moved 12 places to the right, 6,597,100,000,000. This is a close approximation to the actual number.

Geometric sequences get very large when r is 2 or greater. Rather than multiplying everything out, the answer can be written in exponential form as $3(2)^{41}$.

When using the calculator to determine values, the exponent part of the problem must be performed first, then any multiplication or division, and finally any addition or subtraction. This is an application of the order of operations used in arithmetic and algebra.

Example
Determine the general relationship for the sequence 4, 6, 9, 13.5, . . . and find the tenth term.

$$a_1 = 4 \qquad \text{associate } 1\text{–}4$$
$$a_2 = 6 \qquad\qquad\quad 2\text{–}6$$
$$a_3 = 9 \qquad\qquad\quad 3\text{–}9$$
$$a_4 = 13.5 \qquad\qquad 4\text{–}13.5$$

4, 6, 9, and 13.5 have differences of 2, 3, and 4.5. The sequence is not arithmetic. 4, 6, 9, and 13.5 have ratios of 6/4, 9/6, and 13.5/9. All of these ratios have a value of 1.5. Therefore 4, 6, 9, 13.5, . . . is a geometric sequence with $a_1 = 4$ and $r = 1.5$. Substituting in the general formula

$$a_n = a_1 r^{n-1}$$

the relationship

$$a_n = 4(1.5)^{n-1}$$

is generated. The tenth term is

$$a_{10} = 4(1.5)^9 = 153.77344$$

Arithmetic and geometric sequences can represent the growth pattern of a company. If a company has an annual growth of $50,000, the yearly value of the company has a common difference of 50,000; this is an arithmetic sequence. Use the general relationship for the arithmetic sequence

$$a_n = a_1 + (n - 1)(50,000)$$

to find the value at a given time. If the company started with a value in total assets of $250,000 (the value of a_1), the corresponding amount of assets after 1, 2, and 3 years is $300,000, $350,000, and $400,000, respectively. The general relationship is expressed as

$$250,000 + (n - 1)(50,000) \quad \text{or} \quad 50,000n + 200,000$$

This is a linear relationship and the graph of the equation is a straight line. The y intercept is 200,000 and the slope of the graph is 50,000. An asset amount is available for any number of years in the future. In 10 years:

$$a_{10} = (50,000)(10) + 200,000 = 700,000$$

A more realistic growth pattern might be described as 10% per year. The change would increase as the assets of the company increase. The ratio of total assets for any 2 years is a constant. In the preceding example, the company started with assets of $250,000. If the growth rate was 10% per year the following amounts would represent the assets.

Beginning:	a_1:	$250,000
After 1 year:	a_2:	$250,000 + (0.10)(250,000) = $275,000
After 2 years:	a_3:	$275,000 + (0.10)(275,000) = $302,500
After 3 years:	a_4:	$302,500 + (0.10)(302,500) = $332,750

This produces the sequence 250,000, 275,000, 302,500, 332,750, ... This sequence has differences of 25,000, 27,500, and 30,250, indicating the sequence is not arithmetic. The sequence has ratios of 332,750/302,500, 302,500/275,000, and 275,000/250,000. Each of these fractions reduces to 1.1. The sequence is geometric with the r value equal to 1.1. The 1.1 can be generated from the original statement of the problem. An increase of 10% means the original +10% of the original, giving 1.10 of the original. The value of the company at any time can be determined by the general relationship $(250,000)(1.1)^{n-1}$. The value of the company after 9 years or the value of the company the tenth year is

$$a_{10} = (250,000)(1.1)^9 = \$589,486.92$$

Geometric sequences can also represent decreasing sequences, the value of r is less than 1. Suppose the value of a piece of equipment depreciates 10% per year. If the original equipment was valued at $25,000, the depreciation for the first year is $2,500. The new value is $22,500. The following year depreciation is $(22,500)(0.10) = \$2,250$. The book value is now $20,250. This same process can be done using geometric sequences. The original value, a_1, is $25,000. The ratio is 0.9 (the original minus 0.10 of the original). The general relationship is $25,000(0.9)^{n-1}$. The value of the equipment after 9 years (a_{10}) is

$$25,000(0.9)^9 = \$9,685.51$$

There is a strong analogy between the formula for geometric sequences and the formula for finding the compound amount.

Compound Amount	Geometric Sequence
$A = P(1 + i)^n$	$a_n = a_1 r^{n-1}$
A, compound amount	a_n, nth term of sequence
P, principal	a_1, original amount
i, interest rate/period	r, common ratio
n, number of periods	$n - 1$, one less than number of terms

Example

Find the compound amount of $10,000 invested at 8% interest, compounded quarterly, for 7 years.

Compound Amount	Geometric Sequence
$A = 10,000(1.02)^{28}$	$a_{29} = (10,000)(1.02)^{28}$
$= \$17,410.24$	$= \$17,410.24$

In a sequence, the first term is the original amount. Therefore n is 1 more than the number of periods. Some sequences have neither a common difference nor a common ratio. Another classification of sequences is **recursive**— each term is determined by applying a formula to the preceding term or terms. 2, 3, 5, 8, 13, 21, . . . is a recursive sequence. The third term is determined by adding the first and second terms, and the fourth term is determined by adding the two preceding terms. To generate such a sequence, the first two terms must be known.

To generalize naming terms of a sequence $a_1, a_2, a_3, \ldots , a_n$:

The term preceding a_n is $a_{n(-1)} = a_{n-1}$.

The term preceding a_{n-1} is $a_{n-1-1} = a_{n-2}$.

The term following a_n is $a_{n(+1)} = a_{n+1}$.

The term following a_{n+1} is $a_{n+1+1} = a_{n+2}$.

The terms of a sequence can be written as $a_1, a_2, a_3, \ldots, a_{n-2}, a_{n-1}, a_n, a_{n+1}, a_{n+2}, \ldots$.

If a sequence is described as numbers generated by adding the two preceding terms together, the general notation is

$$a_n = a_{n-1} + a_{n-2}$$

An alternative way of writing this same relationship is

$$a_{n+2} = a_n + a_{n+1} \quad \text{or} \quad a_{n+1} = a_n + a_{n-1}$$

The arithmetic sequence formula solved in terms of a_n is

$$a_n = a_1 + (n-1)d$$

The geometric sequence formula solved in terms of a_n is

$$a_n = a_1 r^{n-1}$$

Therefore the recursive rule will also solve in terms of a_n and the notation for any term equal to the sum of the two preceding terms will be written as:

$$a_n = a_{n-1} + a_{n+2} \qquad a_1 = 2 \qquad a_2 = 3$$

It is necessary to identify the first terms in order to generate the remaining terms.

Example

$$a_n = 2a_{n-2} + 3a_{n-1} \qquad a_1 = 1 \qquad a_2 = 2$$

Determine the first five terms.

$a_1 = 1$ (given)

$a_2 = 2$ (given)

$$a_3 = 2a_{3-2} + 3a_{3-1} = 2a_1 + 3a_2 = 2(1) + 3(2) = 8$$
$$a_4 = 2a_{4-2} + 3a_{4-1} = 2a_2 + 3a_3 = 2(2) + 3(8) = 28$$
$$a_5 = 2a_{5-2} + 3a_{5-1} = 2a_3 + 3a_4 = 2(8) + 3(28) = 100$$

The first five terms of the sequence are 1, 2, 8, 28, 100, ...

Example

$$1, 1, 2, 3, 5, 8, \ldots$$

It appears the third term is the sum of the first two terms, the fourth term (3) is the sum of the second and third terms, and so on. To write this relationship in general form:

$$a_n = a_{n-2} + a_{n-1} \qquad a_1 = 1 \qquad a_1 = 1$$

Example
Generate the first five terms of the sequence described by:

$$a_n = \frac{\left(\dfrac{16}{a_{n-1}}\right) + a_{n-1}}{2} \qquad a_1 = 1$$

Solution:

$$a_1 = 1 \quad \text{(given)}$$

$$a_2 = \frac{\left(\dfrac{16}{1}\right) + 1}{2} = 8.5$$

$$a_3 = \frac{\left(\dfrac{16}{8.5}\right) + 8.5}{2} = 5.2$$

$$a_4 = \frac{\left(\dfrac{16}{5.2}\right) + 5.2}{2} = 4.1$$

$$a_5 = \frac{\left(\dfrac{16}{4.1}\right) + 4.1}{2} = 4.0$$

The first five terms of the sequence are 1, 8.5, 5.2, 4.1, 4, ...

If this sequence were continued, every term generated would be 4. The general rule is a way of finding the square root of any number—in this case 16—by generating a few terms of the sequence.

SECTION 2 EXERCISES

Determine the first five terms of each of the sequences defined by the given formulas.

1. $a_n = 2(1.5)^{n-1}$.

2. $a_n = 5(2)^{n-1}$.

3. $a_n = 1.5(1.75)^{n-1}$.

4. $a_n = 8(0.75)^{n-1}$.

5. $a_n = 2{,}000(1.1)^{n-1}$.

6. $a_n = 4{,}000(0.85)^{n-1}$.

7. $a_n = 2(0.5)^{n-1}$.

8. $a_n = 2(1/n)$.

9. $a_n = a_{n-2} + 2a_{n-1}$; $a_1 = 1$, $a_2 = 2$.

10. $a_n = 3a_{n-1} + a_{n-2}$; $a_1 = 1$, $a_2 = 1$.

11. $a_n = 3a_{n-2} + 2a_{n-1}$; $a_1 = 2$, $a_2 = 3$.

12. $a_n = (9/a_{n-1} + a_{n-1})/2$; $a_1 = 1$.

13. $a_n = (9/a_{n-1} + a_{n-1})/2$; $a_1 = 2$.

14. $a_n = (9/a_{n-1} + a_{n-1})/2$; $a_1 = 3$.

15. $a_n = (9/a_{n-1} + a_{n-1})/2$; $a_1 = 4$.

16. How are the sequences in exercises 12 through 15 related? Predict the sixth term of the sequence $a_n = (16/a_{n-1} + a_{n-1})/2$; $a_1 = 3$, without substitution.

17. Give the formula for the recursive rule that generates the square root of 30.

18. Determine the general formula for predicting the compound amount at the end of any quarter on $8,500, compounded quarterly, at an annual rate of 9% interest.

19. Determine the general formula to predict the compound amount of $10,000 at an annual rate of 6% interest, compounded monthly.

20. Determine the general formula to predict the compound amount of $5,000 at an annual rate of 8% interest, compounded quarterly.

Determine the general formula for each of the following.

21. 8, 4, 2, 1, ...

22. 100, 110, 121, 133.1, ...

23. 2, 3, 4.5, 6.75, ...

24. 1, 0.1, 0.01, 0.001, ...

25. 1/2, 5/2, 3, 11/2, ...

26. 5, 6, 17, 40, 97, ...

27. 17, 15, 13, 11, ...

28. 1, −1, −3, −5, ...

29. 10,000, 9,500, 9,000, 8,500, ...

30. 10,000, 9,500, 9,025, 8,573.75, ...

Answers to Odd-Numbered Exercises

1. 2, 3, 4.5, 6.75, 10.125.

3. 1.5, 2.625, 4.6, 8.04, 14.07.

5. 2,000, 2,200, 2,420, 2,662, 2,928.

7. 2, 1, 0.5, 0.25, 0.125.

9. 1, 2, 5, 12, 29.

11. 2, 3, 12, 33, 102.

13. $[(9/2) + 2]/2 = 3.25$. $[(9/3.25) + 3.25]/2 = 3$. 3.25, 3, 3, 3, 3.

15. $[(9/4) + 4]/2 = 3.125$. $[(9/3.125) + 3.125]/2 = 3.125$, 3, 3, 3, 3.

17. $[(30/a_{n-1}) + a_{n-1}]/2; a_1 = 5.$

19. $a_n = 10,000(1.005)^n$ where n is the number of quarters.

21. $a_n = 8(0.5)^{n-1}.$

23. $a_n = 2(1.5)^{n-1}.$

25. $a_n = a_{n-1} + a_{n-2}; a_1 = 1/2, a_2 = 5/2.$

27. $a_n = 17 + (n - 1)(-2); a_n = 19 - 2n.$

29. $a_n = 10,000 + (n - 1)(-500) = 10,500 - 500n.$

9.3   SERIES AND SIGMA NOTATION

If $a_1, a_2, a_3, a_4, \ldots, a_n$ are the elements of a sequence, then $a_1 + a_2 + a_3 + a_4 + \cdots + a_n$ is a series. The sum can be symbolized as $\sum_{n=1}^{n} a_n$. This notation reads as the sum of (Σ) a_n as n varies from 1 to n. Adding the integers from 1 to 100 is a time-consuming, tedious, and error-prone operation. The sum of the integers from 1 to 100 can be written as $\sum_{n=1}^{100} n$. The terms of the series form an arithmetic sequence, and the sum is called an arithmetic series.

If the terms of the series are paired as follows:

First	+ last	$1 + 100 = 101$
Second	+ next to last	$2 + 99 = 101$
Third	+ third to last	$3 + 98 = 101$
a_{49}	+ a_{52}	$49 + 52 = 101$
a_{50}	+ a_{51}	$50 + 51 = 101$

The sum of each pair of numbers is 101. There are $n/2$ pairs of numbers, $100/2 = 50$. There are 50 pairs of numbers, each pair summing to 101, which gives a total of $50(101) = 5,050$.

The general formula for the sum of the terms of an arithmetic series is

$$S = \frac{n}{2}(a_1 + a_n)$$

An alternate form of the formula where d is used instead of a_n is

$$S = a_1 n + \left[\frac{n(n-1)}{2} \right] d$$

In the preceding example:

$$a_1 = 1 \qquad a_{100} = 100 \qquad n = 100 \qquad d = 1$$

Using the general formula:

$$S = \frac{n}{2} [a_1 + a_n] = \frac{100}{2} [1 + 100] = 50(101) = 5{,}050$$

Using the alternate formula:

$$S = a_1 n + \left[\frac{n(n-1)}{2} \right] d = (1)(100) + \left[\frac{100(99)}{2} \right](1) = 5{,}050$$

Example
Find the sum of the first 100 even integers. The series we are interested in is $2 + 4 + 6 + \cdots + 196 + 198 + 200$. If the stopping place is not readily known, generate it using the formula $a_n = a_1 + (n-1)d$.

$$S_{100} = 2(100) + \left[\frac{(100)(99)}{2} \right](2) = 200 + 9{,}900 = 10{,}100$$

The sigma notation for this problem is $\sum\limits_{n=1}^{100} (2n)$, where $2n$ is the general notation for the sequence of even numbers.

Example
Tom Swift earned \$18,500 the first year of his employment and was given a \$2,000 raise each year. Find Tom's total earnings after 25 years.

$$n = 26$$

(notice the wording of "after 25 years," meaning one must be added to 25 to find n)

$$a_1 = 18{,}500 \qquad d = 2{,}000$$

$$S_{26} = 18{,}500(26) + \left[\frac{26(25)}{2}\right](2{,}000)$$

$$= 481{,}000 + 650{,}000$$

$$= \$1{,}131{,}000$$

An alternate method of computation is

$$a_{26} = 18{,}500 + 25(2{,}000) = 68{,}500$$

$$S_{26} = \left(\frac{26}{2}\right)[18{,}500 + 68{,}500]$$

$$= \$1{,}131{,}000$$

The sigma notation is $\sum\limits_{n=1}^{26} 16{,}500 + 2{,}000n$.

A geometric series is the sum of the terms of a geometric sequence

$$S = a_1 + a_1 r + a_1 r^2 + a_1 r^3 + \cdots + a_1 r^{n-1}$$

To find a formula that gives the sum of the terms of a geometric sequence, multiply each term of the previous series by r.

$$rS = a_1 r + a_1 r^2 + a_1 r^3 + a_1 r^4 + \cdots + a_1 r^{n-1} + a_1 r^n$$

Subtract the original series.

$$-[S = a_1 + a_1 r + a_1 r^2 + a_1 r^3 + a_1 r^4 + \cdots + a_1 r^{n-1}]$$

$$rS - S = a_1 r^n - a_1$$

$$(r - 1)S = a_1 r^n - a_1 = a_1(r^n - 1)$$

$$S = \frac{a_1(r^n - 1)}{(r - 1)} \qquad r \neq 1$$

Example
Find the sum of the first six terms of the geometric series 4, 12, 36, ...

$$a_1 = 4 \qquad r = 3 \qquad n = 6$$

$$S = \frac{(4)(3^6 - 1)}{(3 - 1)} = \frac{(4)(728)}{(2)} = 1{,}456$$

The order-of-operations rule dictates the order of exponents, parentheses, multiplication, and division.

Example
Find the sum of the depreciation charged against a piece of equipment valued originally at $25,000 if the depreciation rate is 20% of the declining value in the first six years.

$$5{,}000 + 4{,}000 + 3{,}200 + 2{,}560 + \cdots$$

$$a_1 = 5{,}000 \qquad n = 6 \qquad r = 0.8$$

$$S = (5{,}000)\,\frac{(0.8^6 - 1)}{(0.8 - 1)}$$

$$= (5{,}000)\,\frac{(-0.737\ 856)}{(-0.2)}$$

$$= \$18{,}446.40$$

The problem can be expressed in sigma notation as:

$$S = \sum_{n=1}^{6} (5{,}000)(0.8)^{n-1}$$

Many mathematical quantities are determined by the use of series—trigonometric function values, logarithm values, and the value for pi are some examples.

If a function is neither arithmetic nor geometric, other techniques are needed to determine the sum. For the purpose of this text, adding the required terms will be the way to arrive at a sum.

To summarize:

1. Determine if the terms form an arithmetic or geometric sequence.

2. If arithmetic, find the sum by:

$$S_n = \frac{n}{2}\,[a_1 + a_n] \quad \text{or} \quad a_1 n + \left[\frac{(n)(n-1)}{2}\right] d$$

If geometric, find the sum by:

$$S_n = a_1\,\frac{(r^n - 1)}{(r - 1)}$$

3. If sigma notation is used to describe the terms, the series is arithmetic. If the expression is represented by a linear expression, the series is geometric if an exponent of n or $n - 1$ is involved.

SECTION 3 EXERCISES

Calculate the sum of each of the following.

1. $3 + 5 + 7 + \cdots$ (6 terms).

2. $7 + 9 + 11 + \cdots + 73$.

3. $11 + 8 + 5 + \cdots + -19$.

4. $4 + 4 + 0 + \cdots$ (22 terms).

5. $3/2 + 5/2 + 7/2 + \cdots$ (15 terms).

6. $0.3 + 0.4 + 0.5 + \cdots$ (17 terms).

7. $-5 + 0 + 5 + \cdots + 60$.

8. $1/2 + 7/16 + 3/8 + \cdots$ (20 terms).

9. $3 + 0.3 + 0.03 + \cdots$ (6 terms).

10. $7 + (-7) + 7 + (-7) + \cdots$ (1,471 terms).

11. $1 + 1/2 + 1/4 + \cdots$ (20 terms).

12. $27 - 9 + 3 - 1 + \cdots$ (10 terms).

13. $1 + 1/2 + 1/3 + 1/4 + \cdots$ (10 terms).

14. $1 + 1 + 2 + 3 + 5 + 8 + \cdots$ (10 terms).

15. A piece of equipment had an initial value of $20,000 and it was depreciated yearly for 7 years. The depreciated amounts were 2,000, 1,800, 1,620, ... Find the total depreciated amount after 7 years of depreciation.

16. Jane Smith noted that the amount of her yearly income tax formed the sequence 1,640, 1,740, 1,840, ... Find the total tax paid over the past 10 years if the tax paid this year was $2,040.

17. A basketball is dropped from the top of a 100-foot building. Each time the ball strikes the ground, it rebounds 30% of the height it falls. Find the total distance the ball travels when it strikes the ground the sixth time.

18. A grandfather clock strikes the hour on the hour and once on the half

hour. Find the number of strikes in a 12-hour period. Find the number of strikes in a 24-hour period.

19. Mr. Smith borrows $1,200 and agrees to repay the loan in 12 installments of $100 plus the interest of 2% on the unpaid balance. Find the total amount repaid.

20. $1,000 is invested at 12% interest, compounded annually, so the annual interest is $120, 134.40, 150.53, ... Find the total interest earned and the total amount of the investment after 7 years.

21. Write the summation notation for exercise 1.

22. Write the summation notation for exercise 2.

23. Write the summation notation for exercise 3.

24. Write the summation notation for exercise 4.

25. Write the summation notation for exercise 5.

26. Write the summation notation for exercise 8.

27. Write the summation notation for exercise 9.

28. Write the summation notation for exercise 10.

29. Write the summation notation for exercise 11.

30. Write the summation notation for exercise 12.

Answers to Odd-Numbered Exercises

1. 48.

3. −44.

5. 127.5

7. 385.

9. 3.33333.

11. 2.

13. 2.93.

15. $10.434.

17. 185.50.

19. $1,356.

21. $\sum\limits_{n=1}^{6} (2n + 1)$.

23. $\sum\limits_{n=1}^{11} (14 - 3n)$.

25. $\sum\limits_{n=1}^{15} (n + 1/2)$.

27. $\sum\limits_{n=1}^{6} 3(0.1)^{n-1}$.

29. $\sum\limits_{n=1}^{20} (1/2)^{n-1}$.

9.4   APPLICATIONS

Many businesses and finance problems can be solved using the concepts presented in sequences and series. It is important to compute the first few terms to model the problem and analyze the pattern.

Example

Suppose \$100 is the initial investment in a savings account that earns 6% interest, compounded annually. Determine a formula which describes how to compute the yearly balance from the previous year's balance.

Year	Balance	Interest (%)
0	\$100.00	6.00
1	106.00	6.36
2	112.36	6.74
3	119.10	

The question is how to compute a balance from the previous year's balance. The sequence is 100, 106, 112.36, 119.08, ... Test the sequence to see if the sequence is arithmetic or geometric. The differences are 6, 6.36, and 6.74. The sequence is not arithmetic. The ratios are 1.06, 1.06, and 1.06. The sequence is geometric. Therefore

$$a_n = a_1 r^{n-1}$$

and

$$S = \frac{a_1(r^n - 1)}{(r - 1)}$$

are the appropriate formulas.

$$a_n = a_{n-1}(1.06) \quad \text{or} \quad a_{n+1} = 1.06 a_n$$

Given any balance, multiply by 1.06 to get the next balance. Compound amounts form a geometric sequence.

Example

$100 is invested in an account where interest is compounded at a rate of 6%. At the end of each year $10 is withdrawn. Determine the amount in the account at the end of the tenth year.

Year	Balance	Interest (%)	Withdrawal
0	$100.00	6.00	$10.00
1	94.00	5.64	10.00
2	91.76	5.38	10.00
3	87.27		

Balance 3 = (balance 2) + interest − withdrawal

= (balance 2) + 1.06(balance 2) − withdrawal

= 1.06(balance 2) − 10

Balance 4 = 1.06(balance 3) − 10

Balance 5 = 1.06(balance 4) − 10

In general:

$$Y_{N+1} = (1.06)Y_N - 10$$

This is a recursive rule formula where any balance is generated from the preceding balance. The difference equation generates individual recursive terms without having to generate all of the terms of the sequence. In this example, the balance in the account after 10 years is needed. The general notation is $Y_{n+1} = (1.06)Y_n - 10$. The coefficient of Y_n is 1.06 and this is denoted as a in the difference equation ($a = 1.06$). B_1 is the original amount in the problem ($B_1 = 100$). The numerical term in the general notation is -10. This is denoted as b in the difference equation ($b = -10$). The difference equation formula is

$$B_n = \frac{b}{1-a} + \left[B_1 - \frac{b}{1-a} \right] a^{n-1}$$

First, generate $b/(1 - a)$, using the values identified previously.

$$\frac{b}{1 - a} = \frac{-10}{(1 - 1.06)} = \frac{-10}{-0.06} = 166.67$$

Substituting 166.67 for $b/(1 - a)$ into the difference equation formula along with the other substitutions:

$$B_n = 166.67 + [100 - 166.67](1.06)^{10}$$

$$B = 47.27$$

The difference equation can be derived by using successive substitutions and the knowledge that

$$1 + a + a^2 + \cdots + a^{n-1} = \frac{(a^n - 1)}{(a - 1)}$$

The difference equation is useful for generating specific terms of a recursive formula without having to generate all of the terms preceding it. Any term of a sequence can be determined from the preceding term or can be determined by the difference equation formula.

The steps required for using the difference equation formula are as follows.

1. Generate the first few terms of the sequence to predict how successive terms are determined.

2. Identify the values of a, b, and B_1 from the formula

$$B_{n+1} = a \cdot B_n - b$$

where a is the ratio affecting the preceding term, and b is the amount added to or subtracted from the product.

3. Determine the value of $b/(1 - a)$ and the initial value $(B_1) - b/(1 - a)$.

4. Substitute the generated values into the difference equation formula.

$$Y_n = \left[\frac{b}{(1 - a)}\right] + \left[B_1 - \frac{b}{(1 - a)}\right]a^{n-1}$$

5. Solve for Y_n.

Example

Suppose a mortgage of $20,000 carries an annual interest rate of 12%, compounded annually, and a payment of $3,000 is made each year. Using the difference equation, determine the balance of the mortgage at the end of 10 years.

Year	Balance	Interest	Payment
0	$20,000	$2,400	$3,000
1	19,400	2,328	3,000
2	18,728		

New balance = old balance + interest − payment

$$Y_{n+1} = Y_n + 0.12\,Y_n - 3,000$$

$$Y_{n+1} = 1.12\,Y_n - 3,000$$

$$a = 1.12 \qquad b = 3,000 \qquad B_1 = 20,000$$

$$\frac{b}{(1-a)} = \frac{-3,000}{-0.12} = 25,000$$

$$\left[B_1 - \frac{b}{(1-a)} \right] = 20,000 - 25,000 = -5,000$$

$$Y_{11} = 20,000 + (-5,000)(1.12)^{10}$$

$$= \$4,470.76$$

Periodic values for annuities, compound interest, and mortgages can all be determined by using the difference equation. Variable rate mortgages cannot use the difference equation.

SECTION 4 EXERCISES

1. A savings account was started with $500 and the interest rate was 6%, compounded monthly. The last balance recorded in the account was $674.43. What entry should you expect at the end of the next month?

2. The original deposit in a savings account was $750. The interest earned was 8%, compounded quarterly. The account remained inactive for 10 years. The balance of the account was updated to $1,656.03. Find the amount at the end of the next quarter.

3. The depreciation schedule for a piece of equipment originally valued at $15,000 was 10% on the declining balance. Last year's depreciation

claimed on the income tax form was $885.74. Find the amount of depreciation for this year.

4. The depreciation schedule for an automobile originally valued at $12,500 was 25% on the declining balance. The balance indicated the present value of the automobile is $3,955.08. Find the value of the automobile on the books for next year.

5. Find the predicted value of property in 1995 if in 1980 the property is valued at $57,000 and the prediction is that the property value will increase $800 each year.

6. Find the value of a diamond in 1990 if the purchase price in 1950 was $32,000 and the diamond appreciated $850 each year.

7. The divorce court awarded Jane a settlement of $25,000 (her share of the house) plus $900 a month for living expenses. She puts the $25,000 into a savings and loan that pays 6% annual interest, payable monthly. The $900 is deposited into the account and she withdraws $750 a month from the account for living expenses. Find the amount in the account at the end of 5 years.

8. A child support settlement awarded a cash amount of $10,000 plus $500 a month. The $10,000 was put into an account at the local savings bank, and the $500 was deposited monthly to the account. The interest rate at the bank was 6%, compounded monthly. $600 was withdrawn monthly to meet current expenses. Find the balance in the account after 5 years.

9. The paid-up annuity of $10,000 earns interest at 8%, compounded monthly. No additional payments are made. Find the balance at the end of 3 years.

10. An initial amount of $25,000 was used to establish an annuity for Sarah. The interest rate was 6%, compounded quarterly. Each quarter, an additional $500 was added to the account. Find the value of the annuity after 8 years.

11. A $50,000 mortgage had an interest rate of 9%, compounded monthly. Monthly payments of $600 are made against the mortgage. Find the balance of the mortgage after 5 years.

12. A bankruptcy court determined that a balance of $250,000 would earn interest at the rate of 1% per month. A monthly payment of $7,500 was assessed against the account to meet creditor obligations. Find the balance at the end of 2 years if $4,000 is added to the account monthly.

Answers to Odd-Numbered Exercises

1. $677.80.

3. $797.17.

5. $69,000.

7. $44,186.76.

9. $12,702.36.

11. $33,029.57.

Summary

- **Arithmetic** common difference between terms:

$$a_n = a_1 + (n - 1)d$$

$$S = \frac{n}{2}(a_1 + a_n) = 2a + a_1 n + \left[\frac{n(n-1)}{2}\right]d$$

where a_n = general term
a_1 = first term
n = number of terms
d = common difference

- **Geometric** common ratio between terms:

$$a_n = a_1 r^{n-1}$$

$$S = \frac{a_1(r^n - 1)}{r - 1}, \quad r \neq 1$$

where r = common ratio

- **Recursive** terms generated from preceding term(s):

$$a_n = a_{n-1} + a_{n-2}$$

an example of term generated from sum of two preceding terms.

- Difference Equation for generating any term in a repayment problem:

$$Y_n = \frac{b}{1-a} + \left(B_1 - \frac{b}{1-a}\right)a^{n-1}$$

where Y_n = outstanding balance
b = periodic payment (a negative quantity if balance is decreasing)
$a = 1 + i$
B_1 = original balance

- **Sigma notation**

$$S = \sum_{n=1}^{n} a_n$$

where a_n represents the general term in any sequence

REVIEW EXERCISES

Write the general notation for exercises 1 through 10. If the sequence is arithmetic, find the sum of the first 12 terms. If the sequence is geometric, find the sum of the first 7 terms. If the sequence is neither arithmetic nor geometric, write the sum of the first 10 terms in sigma notation.

1. 3, 5, 7, 9, ...

2. 2, 4, 8, ...

3. 1, 2, 3, 5, 8, ...

4. 49, 46, 43, ...

5. 36, 18, 9, ...

6. 1, 2, 6, 24, 120, 720, ...

7. 0.8, 0.96, 1.152, ...

8. 2,000, 2,040, 2,080, ...

9. 1, $1/2$, $1/3$, $1/4$, ...

10. 100, 104, 108.16, ...

Write the first five terms of the following sequences.

11. $a_n = 2n + 1$.

12. $a_n = (-1/2)^n$.

13. $a_n = 3a_{n-1} - 1; a_1 = 2$.

14. $a_n = n^2$.

15. $a_n = n/(n + 1)$.

16. $a_n = 2a_{n-1} + 1; a_1 = -1$.

17. $a_n = (-1)^n 2^n$.

18. $a_n = 5 - 2n$.

19. $a_n = (n + 1)/(n + 2)$.

20. $a_n = (-1)^{2n} (1.5)^n$.

21. The salary policy of an office firm is to start each employee at $10,000 with an increase of $500 each year. Is the sequence arithmetic or geometric? Express the relationship as an equation. How much will the employee be earning after 10 years? What are the total earnings after 10 years?

22. Another employer starts employees at $10,000 and gives an increase of 5% each year. Is the relationship arithmetic or geometric? Express the relationship as an equation. How much will the employee be earning after 10 years? What are the total earnings after 10 years?

23. A store holds a sale. A given item is priced at $100 and will be reduced by 5% each day until the item is sold. What will the discount be on the eighth day? What will be the price of the item on the eighth day?

24. The contract for a building had the clause that if the building is not finished by the contract date, a penalty of $100 is assessed the first day, $150 the second day, $200 the third day, and so on. The contract was completed the eighth day after the contract date. What was the total penalty assessed against the contractor?

25. The number of bacteria in a culture triples every 3 hours. If 500 bacteria are present initially, how many bacteria are there after 24 hours?

26. A piece of equipment has an initial value of $8,000. It loses 30% of its value at the beginning of each year. Find the value of the equipment at the end of the fifth year.

27. In chemistry, the half-life of a radioactive material is the time required for

$1/2$ of the material to decay. If the half-life of an element is 5 years, $1/2$ of the element decays the first 5 years, $1/2$ of the remaining ($1/4$ of the original) decays the second 5 years, and so on. Express the amount that decays for each 5 years for 7 intervals. Find the amount of the original remaining after the 7 intervals.

28. The amount of glucose in the blood is affected by two factors. It is increased by the steady infusion of glucose from an intravenous infusion; each minute the amount is increased by 80 milligrams. On the other hand, 3% of the original amount is absorbed into the body. Write the difference equation to represent the relationship if the initial amount of glucose was 2,000 milligrams. Find the amount after intravenous infusion for 30 minutes.

29. In a certain country with a current population of 200 million, each year the number of births is 3% of the current population and the number of deaths is 2 million. Find the difference equation for the population and determine the population after 10 years.

30. The monthly payment of a $30,000 mortgage is $350. The mortgage carries an interest rate of 12%, compounded monthly. Determine the balance after 5 years.

Answers to Review Exercises

1. $a_n = 2n + 1.$ $S_{12} = 168.$

2. $a_n = 2^n.$ $S_7 = 254.$

3. $a_n = a_{n-2} + a_{n-1}; a_1 = 1, a_2 = 2.$ $\sum_{n=3}^{10} a_{n-2} + a_{n-1}; a_1 = 1, a_2 = 2.$

4. $a_n = 52 - 3n.$ $S_{12} = 390.$

5. $a_n = 36(1/2)^{n-1}.$ $S_7 = 71.44.$

6. $a_n = na_{n-1}; a_1 = 1.$ $\sum_{2}^{10} na_{n-1}; a_1 = 1.$

7. $a_n = 0.8(1.2)^{n-1}.$ $S_7 = 10.333.$

8. $a_n = 1,960 + 40n.$ $S_{12} = 26,400.$

9. $a_n = 1/n.$ $\sum_{n=1}^{10} 1/n.$

10. $a_n = 100(1.04)^{n-1}.$ $S_7 = 789.83.$

11. 3, 5, 7, 9, 11.

12. $-1/2, 1/4, -1/8, 1/16, -1/32.$

13. 2, 5, 14, 41, 122.

14. 1, 4, 9, 16, 25.

15. $1/2$, $2/3$, $3/4$, $4/5$, $5/6$.

16. -1, -1, -1, -1, -1.

17. -2, 4, -8, 16, -32.

18. 3, 1, -1, -3, -5.

19. $2/3$, $3/4$, $4/5$, $5/6$, $6/7$.

20. 1.5, 2.25, 3.375, 5.0625, 7.59375.

21. Arithmetic.

$a_n = 500n + 9{,}500$

$a_{11} = \$15{,}000$

$S_{11} = \$137{,}500$

22. Geometric.

$a_n = 10{,}000(1.05)^{n-1}$

$a_{11} = \$16{,}288.95$

$S_{11} = \$142{,}067.87$

23. Discount, \$3.68. Price, \$69.83.

24. \$2,200.

25. 3,280,500.

26. \$1,920.80.

27. $1/2$, $1/4$, $1/8$, $1/16$, $1/32$, $1/64$, $1/128$. Amount remaining, 0.007 8125.

28. $Y = 2{,}666.67 + (B_0 - 2{,}666.67)(0.97)^{30}$

$= 2{,}399$ milligrams.

29. $Y_{n+1} = 66.67 + (B_0 - 66.67)(1.03)^n$.

245.85 million.

30. \$25,916.52.

Chapter 10

MATRIX ALGEBRA

Matrix algebra was developed and introduced by Arthur Cayley in the mid 1800's. Like many mathematical concepts, the theory was developed before the need for the mathematics existed. In the 1930's, matrix algebra was used in quantum mechanics. Subsequently, it has found uses in both the physical and social sciences.

The use of matrix algebra has expanded greatly since the advent of the computer. It is a natural and efficient way to organize data. Matrix algebra allows modeling and solution of many types of problems from inventory control to economic forecasting.

At the end of this chapter, the student will be able to:

1. Define the terminology of matrices, use and interpret the standard notation of matrices, and perform the arithmetic operations on appropriate matrices.

2. Generate the inverse of a square matrix if one exists.

3. Set up the solution for systems of linear equations in matrix notation and solve systems up to a 3×3 matrix.

4. Provide the notation and concepts necessary to generate computer solutions involving matrices.

10.1   MATRIX ARITHMETIC

A matrix is a rectangular array of numbers written in rows and columns and enclosed by parentheses or brackets. Capital letters are used to denote a matrix, and the corresponding lowercase letters with subscripts represent individual elements in the matrix.

$$A = \begin{pmatrix} 4 & 5 & 6 \\ 7 & 8 & 9 \end{pmatrix} = \begin{pmatrix} a_{11} & a_{12} & a_{13} \\ a_{21} & a_{22} & a_{23} \end{pmatrix}$$

$$a_{11} = 4 \qquad a_{12} = 5 \qquad a_{13} = 6$$

$$a_{21} = 7 \qquad a_{22} = 8 \qquad a_{23} = 9$$

Matrix A has dimension 2×3 (two rows, three columns). The subscripts of the elements define the location of the element in the matrix. a_{12} is the element of matrix A in the first row, second column. $a_{R,C}$ is the element notation, where R is the row of the element and C is the column of the element. a_{23} has a value of 9 in matrix A.

The general element of any matrix has the subscript ij. In the following B matrix, b_{ij} is the element in the ith row, jth column in the matrix with dimension $m \times n$.

$$B = \begin{pmatrix} b_{11} & b_{12} & \vdots & b_{1n} & & & j\text{th column} \\ b_{21} & b_{22} & & b_{2n} & & \\ \vdots & \vdots & & \vdots & & \\ b_{i1} & b_{i2} & b_{ij} & b_{in} & \cdots & \cdots i\text{th row} \\ \vdots & \vdots & & \vdots & & \\ b_{m1} & b_{m2} & & b_{mn} & & \end{pmatrix}$$

There are m rows and n columns. i represents any row in the matrix, $i \le m$. j represents any column in the matrix, $j \le n$. b_{ij} represents any element of matrix B.

Equal Matrices

Two matrices are equal if they have the same dimensions and each element of the first matrix is identical to the corresponding element of the second matrix.

$$A = \begin{pmatrix} -1 & 5 & 0 \\ 7 & -3 & 2 \end{pmatrix}$$

$$B = \begin{pmatrix} -1 & 5 & 0 \\ 7 & -3 & 2 \end{pmatrix}$$

$A = B$

$$C = \begin{pmatrix} 1 & x \\ 3 & 5 \end{pmatrix}$$

$$D = \begin{pmatrix} x+y & 7 \\ 3 & 5 \end{pmatrix}$$

If $C = D$, find x and y

$x = 7$ because the matrices are equal and the corresponding elements are equal. $x + y = 1$ for the same reason. Substitute

$$7 + y = 1$$

Solve for y

$$y = -6$$

Zero Matrix

Every element of the matrix is 0.

Square Matrix

If the number of rows is equal to the number of columns, the matrix is classified as a square matrix. $A_{2\times2}$, $B_{3\times3}$, and $C_{5\times5}$ represent square matrices.

Main Diagonal

Elements whose row and column subscripts are equal in a square matrix are the diagonal elements of the matrix. a_{11}, a_{22}, a_{33}, a_{44} are diagonal elements of square matrix A.

Identity Matrix or Unit Matrix

An identity matrix is a square matrix whose diagonal elements are 1; all other elements have a value of 0. I is used to symbolize any identity matrix.

$$\begin{pmatrix} 1 & 0 & 0 \\ 0 & 1 & 0 \\ 0 & 0 & 1 \end{pmatrix} \quad \text{is a } 3 \times 3 \text{ identity matrix}$$

Row Matrix

A matrix with one row, A_{1n} is a row matrix.

$$(1 \quad 2 \quad 3 \quad 4 \quad 5 \quad 6) \quad \text{is a row matrix of dimension } 1 \times 6$$

Column Matrix

A matrix that has only one column, A_{n1} is a column matrix.

$$\begin{pmatrix} 1 \\ 2 \\ 3 \end{pmatrix} \quad \text{is a } 3 \times 1 \text{ column matrix}$$

Transpose of a Matrix

Given a matrix, the transpose of that matrix can be written by interchanging the elements of the rows and columns. If A has dimensions $m \times n$, the transpose of A, symbolized as A^T, has dimensions $n \times m$. Given

$$A = \begin{pmatrix} 1 & -3 \\ -1 & 2 \\ 6 & 4 \end{pmatrix} \quad A^T = \begin{pmatrix} 1 & -1 & 6 \\ -3 & 2 & 4 \end{pmatrix}$$

Addition and Subtraction of Matrices

To add or subtract matrices, the dimensions of the matrices must be equal. The sum or difference of the matrices is the sum or difference of the corresponding elements of the two matrices.

$$A = \begin{pmatrix} 1 & 2 & 3 \\ 4 & 5 & 6 \end{pmatrix} \quad B = \begin{pmatrix} -2 & 3 & -5 \\ 4 & -6 & 7 \end{pmatrix}$$

1. Determine the dimensions of matrix A and matrix B.

$$A \text{ has 2 rows, 3 columns} \qquad A \quad 2 \times 3$$
$$B \text{ has 2 rows, 3 columns} \qquad B \quad 2 \times 3$$

2. Because the dimensions are the same, corresponding elements can be added.

$$A + B = \begin{pmatrix} 1 + -2 & 2 + 3 & 3 + -5 \\ 4 + 4 & 5 + -6 & 6 + 7 \end{pmatrix}$$

3. The total matrix has the same dimension as the components.

$$A + B = \begin{pmatrix} -1 & 5 & -2 \\ 8 & -1 & 13 \end{pmatrix}$$

Matrix addition is commutative: $A + B = B + A$. Matrix subtraction is not commutative: $A - B \neq B - A$.

Scalar Multiplication

A factor preceding a matrix is called a scalar factor. In matrix arithmetic, a scalar product involves multiplication of each element of the matrix by the scalar.

$$2A = 2\begin{pmatrix} 1 & 2 & 3 \\ 4 & 5 & 6 \end{pmatrix} = \begin{pmatrix} 4 & 5 & 6 \\ 8 & 10 & 12 \end{pmatrix}$$

Matrix Multiplication

Two matrices can be multiplied only if the number of columns of the first matrix equals the number of rows of the second matrix. $A_{2\times3} \cdot B_{3\times1}$ can be multiplied; the product matrix has dimension 2×1. $B_{3\times1} \cdot A_{2\times3}$ cannot be multiplied because the columns of B do not equal the rows of A. This example illustrates that matrix multiplication is not commutative. The dimension of the product matrix is the rows of the first matrix multiplied by the columns of the second matrix.

$$A_{2\times3} \cdot B_{3\times1} = (AB)_{2\times1}$$

Example

$$A = \begin{pmatrix} 1 & 2 & 3 \\ 4 & 5 & 6 \end{pmatrix}_{2 \times 3} \qquad B = \begin{pmatrix} 7 & 5 \\ 4 & 8 \\ 9 & 3 \end{pmatrix}_{3 \times 2}$$

Find AB.

     The number of columns of A equals the number of rows of B. The dimension of the product is 2×2.

$$AB = \begin{pmatrix} (ab)_{11} & (ab)_{12} \\ (ab)_{21} & (ab)_{22} \end{pmatrix}$$

To generate ab_{11}, multiply the elements of row 1 of matrix A with the elements of column 1 of matrix B.

The sum of the three products is the element ab.

$$1 \cdot 7 + 2 \cdot 4 + 3 \cdot 9 = 7 + 8 + 27 = 42$$

To generate ab_{12}: multiply the elements of row 1 of matrix A with the elements of column 2 of matrix B.

$$1 \cdot 5 + 2 \cdot 8 + 3 \cdot 3 = 5 + 16 + 9 = 30$$

To generate ab_{21}:

$$(4 \quad 5 \quad 6)\begin{pmatrix} 7 \\ 4 \\ 9 \end{pmatrix} = 4 \cdot 7 + 5 \cdot 4 + 6 \cdot 9$$
$$= 28 + 20 + 54 = 102$$

To generate ab_{22}:

$$(4 \quad 5 \quad 6)\begin{pmatrix} 5 \\ 8 \\ 3 \end{pmatrix} = 4 \cdot 5 + 5 \cdot 8 + 6 \cdot 3$$
$$= 20 + 40 + 18 = 78$$

$$AB = \begin{pmatrix} 42 & 30 \\ 102 & 78 \end{pmatrix}$$

In general, to generate an element of a product matrix from the two matrices A and B:

$$C_{11} = a_{11}b_{11} + a_{12}b_{21} + a_{13}b_{31} + \cdots$$

until all the elements of column 1 of matrix A are matched to the corresponding elements of row 1 of matrix B. This can be written in summation notation as follows.

A is a matrix of dimension $n \times t$.

B is a matrix of dimension $t \times m$.

$C = A \cdot B$.

$$c_{ij} = \sum_{t=1}^{t} a_{it}b_{tj} \quad \text{where } i \leq n, j \leq m$$

Example

Write the summation notation for c_{34} if $A_{34}B_{44} = C_{34}$

$$c_{34} = \sum_{n=1}^{4} a_{3n}b_{n4}$$

Special Properties of the Zero and Identity Matrix

The zero matrix in a product of appropriate dimensions gives a product of the zero matrix.

$$\begin{pmatrix} 0 & 0 \\ 0 & 0 \end{pmatrix} \cdot \begin{pmatrix} 1 & 2 & 5 \\ 3 & 4 & 6 \end{pmatrix} = \begin{pmatrix} 0 & 0 & 0 \\ 0 & 0 & 0 \end{pmatrix}$$

The identity matrix in a product of appropriate dimensions gives a matrix identical to the original nonidentity matrix.

$$\begin{pmatrix} 1 & 0 & 0 \\ 0 & 1 & 0 \\ 0 & 0 & 1 \end{pmatrix} \cdot \begin{pmatrix} 7 & 1 \\ 4 & 3 \\ 6 & 2 \end{pmatrix} = \begin{pmatrix} 7 & 1 \\ 4 & 3 \\ 6 & 2 \end{pmatrix}$$

SECTION 1 EXERCISES

Use the following matrices for the exercises.

$$A = \begin{pmatrix} 5 & -2 \\ -1 & 4 \\ 3 & 0 \end{pmatrix} \qquad B = \begin{pmatrix} 1 & 0 & 0 \\ 0 & 1 & 0 \\ 0 & 0 & 1 \end{pmatrix} \qquad C = \begin{pmatrix} 4 & 3 & 2 \\ 1 & 2 & 3 \end{pmatrix}$$

$$D = (7 \quad 6 \quad 5) \qquad E = \begin{pmatrix} a & b \\ c & d \\ e & f \end{pmatrix} \qquad F = \begin{pmatrix} x & y & z \\ 1 & 2 & 3 \end{pmatrix}$$

1. Give the dimensions of matrices A, C, and E.

2. Give the dimensions of matrices B, D, and F.

3. Identify a_{32}, c_{12}, and e_{22}.

4. Identify b_{23}, d_{13}, and f_{21}.

5. If matrix $C = $ matrix F, find the value of x, y, and z.

6. If matrix $A = $ matrix E, find the value of a, c, and e.

7. Find $A + E$.

8. Find $C - F$.

9. What products are available for matrix A involving matrices B, C, D, E, and F?

10. What products are available for matrix C involving matrices A, B, D, E, and F?

11. Determine $4C$.

12. Determine $3F$.

13. Find $A \cdot B$.

14. Find $B \cdot E$.

15. Find $A \cdot C$.

16. Find $E \cdot F$.

17. Find $C \cdot A$.

18. Find $F \cdot E$.

19. Find $C \cdot D$.

20. Find $F \cdot D$.

21. If A has dimension 20×25 and B has dimension 25×30, write $c_{10,15}$ in summation notation if $C = A \cdot B$.

22. If A has dimension 10×15 and B has dimension 15×18, write c in summation notation if $C = A \cdot B$.

23. Write the general form for finding $c_{3,8}$ if $C = A + B$ and A and B are matrices of dimension 12×15.

24. Write the general form for finding $c_{6,3}$ if $C = A + B$ and A and B are matrices of dimension 8×12.

Answers to Odd-Numbered Exercises

1. A, 3×2. C, 2×3. E, 3×2.

3. $a_{32} = 0$. $c_{12} = 3$. $e_{22} = d$.

5. $x = 4$. $y = 3$. $z = 2$.

7.
$$\begin{pmatrix} 5 + a & -2 + b \\ -1 + c & 4 + d \\ 3 + e & 0 + f \end{pmatrix}.$$

9. $A \cdot C$, $A \cdot F$, $B \cdot A$, $C \cdot A$, $D \cdot A$, $F \cdot A$.

11.
$$\begin{pmatrix} 16 & 12 & 8 \\ 4 & 8 & 12 \end{pmatrix}.$$

13. Impossible.

15.
$$\begin{pmatrix} 18 & 11 & 4 \\ 0 & 5 & 10 \\ 12 & 9 & 6 \end{pmatrix}.$$

17.
$$\begin{pmatrix} 23 & 4 \\ 12 & 6 \end{pmatrix}.$$

19. Impossible.

21. $c_{10,15} = \sum\limits_{n=1}^{25} a_{10,n} \cdot b_{n,15}.$

23. $c_{3,8} = a_{3,8} + b_{3,8}.$

10.2 INVERSE MATRICES

Before an inverse matrix is defined, it might be wise to define the word inverse. Inverse is defined as reversed in order or effect. There are two inverses in numbers. The reciprocal of a designated quantity is the multiplicative inverse. The negative of a designated quantity is the additive inverse.

For example,

$1/3$ is the multiplicative inverse of 3 because $(1/3)(3) = 1$. $1/3$ is also the reciprocal of 3.

$2/5$ is the multiplicative inverse of $5/2$ because $(2/5)(5/2) = 1$. $2/5$ is also the reciprocal of $5/2$.

-2 is the additive inverse of 2 because $-2 + 2 = 0$.

7 is the additive inverse of -7 because $7 + (-7) = 0$.

The inverse matrix is the matrix that has the effect of multiplying a designated matrix and giving the identity matrix. The inverse matrix of matrix A is denoted as A^{-1}. $A \cdot A^{-1} = I$ or $A^{-1} \cdot A = I$. The inverse is only available for square matrices and the value of the determinant of the matrix cannot equal zero.

If

$$A = \begin{pmatrix} 2 & 5 \\ 1 & 3 \end{pmatrix}$$

is

$$\begin{pmatrix} 3 & -5 \\ -1 & 2 \end{pmatrix} = A^{-1}$$

If $A \cdot A^{-1} = I$, then it is the inverse.

$$\begin{pmatrix} 2 & 5 \\ 1 & 3 \end{pmatrix} \cdot \begin{pmatrix} 3 & -5 \\ -1 & 2 \end{pmatrix} = \begin{pmatrix} 1 & 0 \\ 0 & 1 \end{pmatrix}$$

Likewise

$$\begin{pmatrix} 3 & -5 \\ -1 & 2 \end{pmatrix} \cdot \begin{pmatrix} 2 & 5 \\ 1 & 3 \end{pmatrix} = \begin{pmatrix} 1 & 0 \\ 0 & 1 \end{pmatrix}$$

Notice that

$$\begin{pmatrix} 3 & -5 \\ -1 & 2 \end{pmatrix} \text{ is } A^{-1} \text{ if } A = \begin{pmatrix} 2 & 5 \\ 1 & 3 \end{pmatrix}.$$

Before a procedure to generate the inverse of a matrix can be outlined, the concept of a determinant must be presented. A determinant is a real number value associated with a square matrix. If A represents a square matrix, $|A|$ represents the determinant of A. The determinant of a 2×2 determinant is the product of the elements on the main diagonal **minus** the product of the other two elements. If

$$A = \begin{pmatrix} 2 & 3 \\ 4 & 5 \end{pmatrix} \qquad |A| = (2) \cdot (5) - (3) \cdot (4) = 10 - 12 = -2$$

If

$$B = \begin{pmatrix} b_{11} & b_{12} \\ b_{21} & b_{22} \end{pmatrix} \qquad |B| = b_{11} \cdot b_{22} - b_{12} \cdot b_{21}$$

The **minor** of an element of a square matrix is the determinant resulting when the row and column of the element are deleted.

Example

Given

$$A = \begin{pmatrix} -3 - 5 - -1 - \\ 4 & -2 & 7 \\ 1 & 6 & 8 \end{pmatrix}$$

the minor of 5 is

$$\begin{vmatrix} 4 & 7 \\ 1 & 8 \end{vmatrix} = 32 - 7 = 25$$

Given

$$\begin{pmatrix} b_{11} & b_{12} & b_{13} \\ b_{21} & b_{22} & b_{23} \\ b_{31} - b_{32} - b_{33} \end{pmatrix}$$

the minor of b_{33} is

$$\begin{vmatrix} b_{11} & b_{12} \\ b_{21} & b_{22} \end{vmatrix} = b_{11} \cdot b_{22} - b_{21} \cdot b_{12}$$

The minor of a 4 × 4 matrix is a determinant with three rows and three columns.

The cofactor of any element of a matrix, a_{ij}, is the product of $(-1)^{i+j}$ and the minor of a_{ij}. The sign of the product is determined by the position of the element. If the element has position ij, add i and j. The sum $i + j$ is the exponent of a factor of -1. The sign is positive if $(i + j)$ is even, and the sign is negative if $(i + j)$ is odd.

To find the determinant value of a 3 × 3 matrix:

1. Choose any row or column of the matrix. If any row or column contains zero elements, this row or column should be chosen.

2. Each element of the row or column chosen is multiplied by its cofactor; the sum of the products is the value of the determinant of the 3 × 3 matrix.

Example

Given

$$A = \begin{pmatrix} 1 & -2 & 3 \\ -3 & 1 & 2 \\ 4 & -3 & -2 \end{pmatrix}$$

Find $|A|$.

Select $(1 \quad -2 \quad 3)$ (row 1)

Cofactor of 1:

$$a_{11}: \quad (-1)^2 \begin{vmatrix} 1 & 2 \\ -3 & -2 \end{vmatrix} = (1)[(-2) - (-6)] = 4$$

Cofactor of -2:

$$a_{12}: \quad (-1)^3 \begin{vmatrix} -3 & 2 \\ 4 & -2 \end{vmatrix} = (-1)[6 - 8] = 2$$

Cofactor of 3:

$$a_{13}: \quad (-1)^4 \begin{vmatrix} -3 & 1 \\ 4 & -3 \end{vmatrix} = (1)[9 - 4] = 5$$

Total:

$$1 \cdot 4 + -2 \cdot 2 + 3 \cdot 5 = 15 \qquad |A| = 15$$

If the value of the determinant is zero, the matrix does not have an inverse. Determinants are needed for generating the inverse of any matrix.

To generate the inverse of a matrix:

1. Find the value of the determinant of the matrix.

2. Find the cofactor of each element of the matrix.

3. Replace each element by its cofactor.

4. Find the transpose of the new matrix. (Interchange the rows and columns—write column 1 as row 1, column 2 as row 2, and so on.)

5. Multiply each element by $1/|A|$.

Example
Find the inverse of:

$$\begin{pmatrix} -3 & 1 & 2 \\ 10 & -5 & 0 \\ -11 & 7 & -1 \end{pmatrix}$$

Find the value of the determinant. Choose column 3 because of entry 0.

$$\text{Cofactor of } 2 = (-1)^4(15) = 15$$
$$\text{Cofactor of } 0 = (-1)^5(-10) = 10$$
$$\text{Cofactor of } -1 = (-1)^6(5) = 5$$
$$\text{Determinant} = (2) \cdot (15) + (0) \cdot (10) + (-1) \cdot (5) = 25$$

(The computation illustrates why columns or rows with zero elements are chosen. There is no need to even generate the cofactor because the product will always have a value of zero).
    Replace each element by its cofactors.

$$\begin{pmatrix} 5 & 10 & 15 \\ 15 & 25 & 10 \\ 10 & 20 & 5 \end{pmatrix}$$

Determine the transpose.

$$\begin{pmatrix} 5 & 15 & 10 \\ 10 & 25 & 20 \\ 15 & 10 & 5 \end{pmatrix}$$

Multiply by $^1/_{25}$.

$$\frac{1}{25}\begin{pmatrix} 5 & 15 & 10 \\ 10 & 25 & 20 \\ 15 & 10 & 5 \end{pmatrix} = \begin{pmatrix} 0.2 & 0.6 & 0.4 \\ 0.4 & 1 & 0.8 \\ 0.6 & 0.4 & 0.2 \end{pmatrix}$$

Check.

$$\begin{pmatrix} 0.2 & 0.6 & 0.4 \\ 0.4 & 1 & 0.8 \\ 0.6 & 0.4 & 0.2 \end{pmatrix} \cdot \begin{pmatrix} -3 & 1 & 2 \\ 10 & -5 & 0 \\ -11 & 7 & -1 \end{pmatrix} = \begin{pmatrix} 1 & 0 & 0 \\ 0 & 1 & 0 \\ 0 & 0 & 1 \end{pmatrix}$$

Because the product produces the identity matrix, the matrix generated is the inverse of the original matrix.

SECTION 2 EXERCISES

1. $A = \begin{pmatrix} 2 & 5 \\ 1 & 3 \end{pmatrix}$ $B = \begin{pmatrix} 3 & -5 \\ -1 & 2 \end{pmatrix}$.

Does $B = A^{-1}$?

2. $A = \begin{pmatrix} 1 & 1 \\ 3 & 4 \end{pmatrix}$ $B = \begin{pmatrix} 4 & -1 \\ -3 & 1 \end{pmatrix}$.

Does $A = B^{-1}$?

3. $A = \begin{pmatrix} 7 & -4 \\ 3 & 1 \end{pmatrix}$.

Find $|A|$. Find the minor of 3.

4. $A = \begin{pmatrix} 2 & 4 \\ 3 & -5 \end{pmatrix}$.

Find $|A|$. Find the minor of -5.

5. $A = \begin{pmatrix} a & b \\ c & d \end{pmatrix}$.

Find $|A|$. Find the minor of b.

6. $A = \begin{pmatrix} e & g \\ f & h \end{pmatrix}.$

Find $|A|$. Find the minor of e.

7. $A = \begin{pmatrix} 3 & 2 \\ 6 & 4 \end{pmatrix}.$

Find $|A|$. Does A^{-1} exist?

8. $A = \begin{pmatrix} 2 & 6 \\ -1 & -3 \end{pmatrix}.$

Find $|A^{-1}|$. Does A^{-1} exist?

Use the following matrix in exercises 9 through 14.

$$A = \begin{pmatrix} 7 & 3 & 1 \\ 6 & 0 & -3 \\ -2 & 5 & 4 \end{pmatrix}$$

9. Find the minor of 3.

10. Find the minor of 5.

11. Find the cofactor of 5.

12. Find the cofactor of 3.

13. Find $|A|$.

14. Find A^{-1}.

15. $A = \begin{pmatrix} 4 & 2 \\ -3 & 1 \end{pmatrix}.$

Find A^{-1}.

16. $A = \begin{pmatrix} 7 & -1 \\ -4 & 2 \end{pmatrix}.$

Find A^{-1}.

17. $A = \begin{pmatrix} 3 & -3 \\ -3 & 3 \end{pmatrix}$.

Find A^{-1}.

18. $A = \begin{pmatrix} 6 & -12 \\ 1 & -2 \end{pmatrix}$.

Find A^{-1}.

19. Find the inverse of:

$$\begin{pmatrix} 1 & 0 & 3 \\ 1 & 1 & 3 \\ 0 & 2 & 2 \end{pmatrix}$$

20. Find the inverse of:

$$\begin{pmatrix} 2 & 2 & -3 \\ -2 & -3 & 3 \\ 1 & 2 & -2 \end{pmatrix}$$

21. Find the inverse of:

$$\begin{pmatrix} 3 & -1 & 2 \\ 1 & 1 & 0 \\ 2 & 0 & 1 \end{pmatrix}$$

22. Find the inverse of:

$$\begin{pmatrix} -3 & 1 & 2 \\ 10 & -5 & 0 \\ -11 & 7 & -1 \end{pmatrix}$$

Answers to Odd-Numbered Exercises

1. Yes.

3. $A = 19. -4.$

5. $ad - bc. c.$

7. $A = 0. A^{-1}$ does not exist.

9. 18.

11. 27.

13. 81.

15. $\begin{pmatrix} 0.1 & -0.2 \\ 0.3 & 0.4 \end{pmatrix}.$

17. Does not exist.

19. $\begin{pmatrix} -2 & 3 & -1.5 \\ -1 & 1 & 0 \\ 1 & -1 & 0.5 \end{pmatrix}.$

21. Does not exist.

10.3   SOLUTION OF LINEAR SYSTEMS

Many models of business activities are represented by a large number of linear equations or inequalities having many variables. The set of equations is called a linear system of equations. The solution of a linear system of equations is the set of values satisfying all of the equations.

There are several methods of solution for linear systems of equations. This section introduces solution by matrix algebra. The computer is useful in the solution of large systems. The concepts learned in this section are representative of the theory involved in a computer solution.

To obtain a unique solution to a linear system, there must be as many equations as there are unknowns. Systems are usually categorized as a 2 × 2 system, a 3 × 3 system, or a 10 × 10 system. A 2 × 2 system, for example, has 2 equations and 2 unknowns.

Example

Specific Problem	*General Notation*

$$2x + \ \ y = \ \ 9 \qquad\qquad a_1x + b_1y = c_1$$

$$x - 3y = 10 \qquad\qquad a_2x + b_2y = c_2$$

This system can be written in matrix notation as:

$$\text{Specific: } \begin{pmatrix} 2 & 1 \\ 1 & -3 \end{pmatrix} \cdot \begin{pmatrix} x \\ y \end{pmatrix} = \begin{pmatrix} 9 \\ 10 \end{pmatrix}$$

$$\text{General: } \begin{pmatrix} a_1 & b_1 \\ a_2 & b_2 \end{pmatrix} \cdot \begin{pmatrix} x \\ y \end{pmatrix} = \begin{pmatrix} c_1 \\ c_2 \end{pmatrix}$$

The coefficient matrix is called A, the variable matrix X, and the right-hand numbers are written as a matrix called C.

$$A \cdot X = C$$

The concepts involved in the solution of a linear equation hold for matrix algebra—multiply both sides by the inverse of A to isolate the variable.

$$A^{-1} \cdot A \cdot X = A^{-1} \cdot C$$

$$A^{-1} \cdot A = I \ \ \text{ so } \ \ I \cdot X = A^{-1} \cdot C$$

$$I \cdot X = X \qquad\qquad X = A^{-1} \cdot C$$

In the specific problem:

$$2x + 5y = \ \ 9$$

$$x - 3y = 10$$

$$\begin{pmatrix} 2 & 5 \\ 1 & -3 \end{pmatrix} \cdot \begin{pmatrix} x \\ y \end{pmatrix} = \begin{pmatrix} 9 \\ 10 \end{pmatrix}$$

Find A^{-1}

$$|A| = -11.$$

$$A^{-1} = \frac{-1}{11}\begin{pmatrix} -3 & -5 \\ -1 & 2 \end{pmatrix}$$

$$\frac{-1}{11}\begin{pmatrix} -3 & -5 \\ -1 & 2 \end{pmatrix} \cdot \begin{pmatrix} 2 & 5 \\ 1 & -3 \end{pmatrix}\begin{pmatrix} x \\ y \end{pmatrix} = \frac{-1}{11}\begin{pmatrix} -3 & -5 \\ -1 & 2 \end{pmatrix} \cdot \begin{pmatrix} 9 \\ 10 \end{pmatrix}$$

$$\begin{pmatrix} 1 & 0 \\ 0 & 1 \end{pmatrix}\begin{pmatrix} x \\ y \end{pmatrix} = \frac{-1}{11}\begin{pmatrix} -77 \\ 11 \end{pmatrix}$$

$$\begin{pmatrix} x \\ y \end{pmatrix} = \begin{pmatrix} 7 \\ -1 \end{pmatrix}$$

$x = 7$ and $y = -1$ is the solution to the system.

All systems can be solved by the matrix method, but generating the inverse is time consuming and tedious. The computer can be programmed to create inverses. The matrix method is an efficient way to solve many problems because the coefficient matrix often remains constant, and the numerical values change under different cost and profit conditions. There is only one inverse matrix needed for the changing situations.

The matrix solution to linear systems is as follows.

1. Write the system in matrix form.

2. Find the determinant of the coefficient matrix. If $|A| = 0$, there is no solution.

3. Find the inverse of the coefficient matrix.

4. Multiply both sides of the matrix equation by the generated inverse.

5. Set the variables equal to the corresponding values in the product matrix.

Example
Solve

$$\begin{aligned} x + y - 2z &= 6 \\ x + 3y &= 8 \\ -3x - 3y + 5z &= -20 \end{aligned}$$

by matrix algebra.

In matrix form:

$$\begin{pmatrix} 1 & 1 & -2 \\ 1 & 3 & 0 \\ -3 & -3 & 5 \end{pmatrix} \cdot \begin{pmatrix} x \\ y \\ z \end{pmatrix} = \begin{pmatrix} 6 \\ 8 \\ -20 \end{pmatrix}$$

Notice that the z term is missing in the second equation; an entry of 0 is the indication for a missing variable.

The value of the determinant using column 3 is

$$(+)(-2)(+6) + (+)(5)(2) = -2$$

Find the inverse of the coefficient matrix.

Cofactors:

$$\begin{array}{ccc} 15 & -5 & 6 \\ +1 & -1 & 0 \\ 6 & -2 & 2 \end{array}$$

Transpose and multiply by $-1/2$.

$$A^{-1} = \begin{pmatrix} -15/2 & -1/2 & -3 \\ 5/2 & 1/2 & +1 \\ -3 & 0 & -1 \end{pmatrix}$$

Multiply both sides by the inverse.

$$\begin{pmatrix} -15/2 & -1/2 & -3 \\ 5/2 & 1/2 & +1 \\ -3 & 0 & -1 \end{pmatrix} \cdot \begin{pmatrix} 1 & 1 & -2 \\ 1 & 3 & 0 \\ -3 & -3 & 5 \end{pmatrix} \cdot \begin{pmatrix} x \\ y \\ z \end{pmatrix}$$

$$= \begin{pmatrix} -15/2 & -1/2 & -3 \\ 5/2 & 1/2 & 1 \\ -3 & 0 & -1 \end{pmatrix} \cdot \begin{pmatrix} 6 \\ 8 \\ -20 \end{pmatrix}$$

$$\begin{pmatrix} x \\ y \\ z \end{pmatrix} = \begin{pmatrix} 11 \\ -1 \\ 2 \end{pmatrix}$$

$$x = 11 \qquad y = -1 \qquad z = 2$$

It is wise to check these answers in the original system as a way of validating the computations.

$$
\begin{aligned}
x + y - 2z &= 6 & 11 + (-1) - 2(2) &= 6 \\
x + 3y &= 8 & 11 + 3(-1) &= 8 \\
-3x - 3y + 5z &= -20 & -3(11) - 3(-1) + 5(2) &= -20
\end{aligned}
$$

This system works for any size linear system of equations. Without the benefit of the computer to find the inverse, a 3×3 system provides the necessary practice.

SECTION 3 EXERCISES

Solve the following linear systems using matrix algebra.

1. $2x + 3y = 2$
$8x - 15y = -1$

2. $x + 8y = 9$
$3x - 2y = 14$

3. $0.8x - 0.3y = 3$
$1.1x + 0.1y = 40$

4. $0.1x + 0.7y = 12$
$x - 4y = 10$

5. Use the inverse of exercise 1.
$2x + 3y = 5$
$8x - 15y = -3$

6. Use the inverse of exercise 2.
$x + 8y = 11$
$3x - 2y = 15$

7. Use the inverse of exercise 3.
$0.8x - 0.3y = 4$
$1.1x + 0.1y = 34$

8. Use the inverse of exercise 4.
$0.1x + 0.7y = 15$
$x - 4y = 8$

9. $2x - 3y + z = 1$
$x - y + z = 5$
$3x + 4y + 5z = 10$

10. $5x + 2y + 3z = 4$
$x + y + z = 1$
$2x - y - z = 3$

11. $0.5x - 0.4y + 0.8z = 3$
$0.1x + 0.3y - 0.1z = 5$
$0.2x + 0.4y - z = 3$

12. $x + y + z = -17$
$x + 2y + 2z = 3$
$z - y = 16$

13. Use the inverse of exercise 9.
$2x - 3y + z = 2$
$x - y + z = 4$
$3x + 4y + 5z = 11$

14. Use the inverse of exercise 10.
$5x + 2y + 3z = 5$
$x + y + z = 0$
$2x - y - z = 4$

15. Use the inverse of exercise 11.
$0.5x - 0.4y + 0.8z = 3.1$
$0.1x + 0.3y - 0.1z = 4.9$
$0.2x + 0.4y - z = 3.5$

16. Use the inverse of exercise 12.
$x + y + z = -18$
$x + 2y + 2z = 2$
$z - y = 15$

17. The price of admission to a football game was \$14 for the sidelines and \$10 for the endzones. A total of 80,000 tickets were sold with a resulting revenue of \$1,104,800. How many sideline and endzone tickets were sold?

18. The price of admission to a rock concert was \$16 for orchestra seats and \$12 for balcony seats. A total of 10,000 tickets were sold and the receipts from the rock concert totaled \$154,400. How many orchestra tickets were sold?

19.

Suit Brand	Original Price	Sale Price
Cordet	$ 190	$ 150
Saxet	225	190
Valit	150	125
Total	$17,115	$14,355

How many suits of each brand were sold if the total number involved is 90?

20.

Dress Brand	Original Price	Sale Price
Dotch	$ 80	$ 65
Manec	110	80
Terec	135	98
Total	$7,325	$5,397

If 63 dresses were involved, how many of each brand were sold at the sale price?

21. The total investment was $50,000, some of the investment earned 8.5% and the remainder earned 9% interest. The annual interest from the investments is $4,460. Find the amount invested at each rate.

22. The total investment was $68,000. Some of the money is invested at 6.7% and the remainder at 7.5%. The annual interest from the investments is $4,660. Find the amount invested at each rate.

Answers to Odd-Numbered Exercises

1. $x = 1/2, y = 1/3$.

3. $x = 30, y = 70$.

5. $x = 1.22, y = 0.85$.

7. $x = 25.85, y = 55.6$.

9. $x = -13.2, y = -4.6, z = 13.6$.

11. $x = 10, y = 15, z = 5$.

13. $x = -7.2, y = -2.6, z = 8.6$.

15. $x = 10.7, y = 14.2, z = 4.32$.

17. Sideline, 76,200. Endzone, 3,800.

19. Cordet, 28. Saxet, 37. Valit, 25.

21. $8,000 at 8.5% and $42,000 at 9%.

10.4 APPLICATIONS

The solution of systems of linear equations is one of the greatest uses of matrix algebra. However, other applications have developed, especially since the availability of computers to generate inverses. Matrices are a convenient and orderly way to store information. Inventories and value of inventories are two examples of using matrices to store information in an orderly way. The two applications presented in this section are codes and input-output analysis.

Codes

A matrix and its inverse can be used to code and decode messages. To ensure security, several matrices and their inverses may be involved in the process with matrices of dimensions up to 20×20. The example used in this section will be much simpler but will give the essentials of the process. The letters of the alphabet are assigned unique numerical values. The simplest assignment will be used here. $a = 1$, $b = 2$, $c = 3$, . . . , $z = 26$, and a space $= 27$.

A coding matrix is selected. A good selection would have the determinant value equal to 1 to avoid fractions. For our example, the coding matrix will be

$$A = \begin{pmatrix} 1 & 2 & 0 \\ 0 & 0 & 1 \\ 3 & 5 & 4 \end{pmatrix}$$

Because the coding matrix is 3×3, the message must be broken up into groups of 3 numbers and listed as a 1×3 matrix or a 3×1 matrix. The receiver must have the inverse of A available for decoding.

$$A^{-1} = \begin{pmatrix} -5 & -8 & 2 \\ 3 & 4 & -1 \\ 0 & 1 & 0 \end{pmatrix}$$

The message to be coded is

HUMPTY DUMPTY WAS PUSHED

Using the numerical assignments for the letters and a / to group numbers by three, the message becomes

8 21 13/16 20 25/27 4 21/13 16 20/25 27 23/1 19 27/6 21 19/8 5 4

The message has been grouped into 1 × 3 matrices.

$$(8 \quad 21 \quad 13) \cdot A = (47 \quad 81 \quad 73)$$
$$(16 \quad 20 \quad 25) \cdot A = (91 \quad 157 \quad 120)$$
$$(27 \quad 4 \quad 21) \cdot A = (90 \quad 159 \quad 88)$$
$$(13 \quad 16 \quad 20) \cdot A = (73 \quad 126 \quad 96)$$
$$(25 \quad 27 \quad 23) \cdot A = (94 \quad 165 \quad 119)$$
$$(1 \quad 19 \quad 27) \cdot A = (82 \quad 137 \quad 127)$$
$$(16 \quad 21 \quad 19) \cdot A = (73 \quad 127 \quad 97)$$
$$(8 \quad 5 \quad 4) \cdot A = (20 \quad 36 \quad 21)$$

The numbers are then changed back to letters to send the message. Subtract multiples of 27 to change back to a number with a letter assignment. Eighty-one represents a space.

T S J V L I X G S R O M C K A B S S S P T I U

The message is received and changed back to numbers and grouped by three.

24 27 19/10 22 12/9 20 7/19 18 15/13 3 11/1 2 19/19 19 16/20 9 21

The numbers are grouped into 1 × 3 matrices and multiplied by A^{-1}.

$$(20 \quad 27 \quad 19) \cdot A^{-1} = (-19 \quad -33 \quad 13) = (8 \quad 21 \quad 13)$$
$$(10 \quad 22 \quad 12) \cdot A^{-1} = (16 \quad 20 \quad -25) = (16 \quad 20 \quad 25)$$
$$(9 \quad 24 \quad 7) \cdot A^{-1} = (27 \quad -23 \quad -6) = (27 \quad 4 \quad 21)$$
$$(19 \quad 18 \quad 15) \cdot A^{-1} = (-41 \quad -65 \quad 20) = (13 \quad 16 \quad 20)$$
$$(13 \quad 3 \quad 11) \cdot A^{-1} = (-56 \quad -81 \quad 23) = (25 \quad 27 \quad 23)$$
$$(1 \quad 2 \quad 19) \cdot A^{-1} = (1 \quad 19 \quad 0) = (1 \quad 19 \quad 27)$$
$$(19 \quad 19 \quad 16) \cdot A^{-1} = (16 \quad -60 \quad 19) = (16 \quad 21 \quad 19)$$
$$(20 \quad 9 \quad 21) \cdot A^{-1} = (-73 \quad -103 \quad 31) = (8 \quad 5 \quad 4)$$

H U M P T Y D U M P T Y W A S P U S H E D

Example

Send a coded message for H E L P. The message translated into numbers is
8 5 12 16. The coding matrix is

$$\begin{pmatrix} 2 & 5 \\ 1 & 3 \end{pmatrix}$$

The decoding matrix is

$$\begin{pmatrix} 3 & -5 \\ -1 & 2 \end{pmatrix}$$

The message is put into 1×2 matrices.

$$(8 \quad 5) \cdot \begin{pmatrix} 2 & 5 \\ 1 & 3 \end{pmatrix} = (21 \quad 55)$$

$$(12 \quad 16) \cdot \begin{pmatrix} 2 & 5 \\ 1 & 3 \end{pmatrix} = (40 \quad 108)$$

Subtracting off multiples of 27: 21 1 13 27. The coded message is

$$U \; A \; M \; -$$

(The dash at the end of the previous message denotes a space—represented
by the number 27.) The message is received and translated back to numbers:
21 1 13 27.

$$\text{Multiply (21 1) and (13 27) times} \begin{pmatrix} 3 & -5 \\ -1 & 2 \end{pmatrix} \text{to give}$$

$$(62 \; -103) \text{ and } (12 \; -11).$$

$$8 \; 5 \; 12 \; 16$$

$$H \; E \; L \; P$$

This entire process occurs on the computer. In secret government messages, the code may involve 5 products. The coding matrix changes daily.

Input-Output Analysis

Input-output analysis is concerned with the interrelationships among industries. Matrix theory provides the mathematics needed for the analysis. The input-output theory was developed by W. W. Leontief, who was awarded the Nobel Prize in 1973 for this development. The production of any commodity requires some or all of the other commodities in the economy. For example, a loaf of bread requires wheat, milk, and electricity. The amounts of each commodity used in the production of 1 unit of each commodity is written as a matrix, called a technological matrix. For a simplified version of a technological matrix, use the wheat, milk, and electricity commodities required in a loaf of bread.

$$
\begin{array}{c}
\begin{array}{ccc}
\text{Wheat} & \text{Milk} & \text{Electricity}
\end{array} \\
\begin{array}{c}
\text{Wheat} \\
\text{Milk} \\
\text{Electricity}
\end{array}
\begin{pmatrix}
0 & 0.10 & 0.20 \\
0.10 & 0 & 0.10 \\
0.05 & 0.20 & 0
\end{pmatrix}
\end{array}
$$

The top row represents the amount of each of the three commodities consumed in the production of 1 unit of wheat. The second row represents the amount of each commodity consumed in the production of 1 unit of milk. The third row represents the amount of each commodity consumed in the production of one unit of electricity. The matrix will be labeled A.

A row matrix represents the number of units of each commodity produced. It is called the production matrix and is labeled X.

$$X = (x_1, x_2, x_3, \ldots, x_n)$$

In this example,

$$X = (50 \quad 80 \quad 45)$$

The X matrix states that 50 units of wheat, 80 units of milk, and 45 units of electricity are produced. XA (the product of matrix X and matrix A) gives the amount of each commodity used up in the production process.

$$
XA = (50 \quad 80 \quad 45) \cdot
\begin{pmatrix}
0 & 0.10 & 0.20 \\
0.10 & 0 & 0.10 \\
0.05 & 0.20 & 0
\end{pmatrix}
= (10.25 \quad 14 \quad 18)
$$

10.25 units of wheat, 14 units of milk, and 18 units of electricity are used up to produce 50 units of wheat, 80 units of milk, and 45 units of electricity.

The differences between gross production and the amount used up in the production process is the net production, shown as the Y matrix.

$$Y = X - XA$$

In the preceding example:

$$Y = (50 \quad 80 \quad 45) - (10.25 \quad 14 \quad 18)$$

$$= (39.75 \quad 66 \quad 27)$$

In most problems, Y, the net production, and A, the technological matrix, are known and it is necessary to solve for X, the gross production.

$$Y = X - XA$$

can be written as:

$$Y = XI - XA$$

By the distributive property:

$$Y = X(I - A)$$

To solve the matrix equation for X, multiply both sides by $(I - A)^{-1}$.

$$X = Y(I - A)^{-1}$$

In our example, suppose we want a net production of 320 units of wheat, 220 units of milk, and 140 units of electricity.

$$Y = (320 \quad 220 \quad 140)$$

$$I - A = \begin{pmatrix} 1 & 0 & 0 \\ 0 & 1 & 0 \\ 0 & 0 & 1 \end{pmatrix} - \begin{pmatrix} 0 & 0.10 & 0.20 \\ 0.10 & 0 & 0.10 \\ 0.05 & 0.20 & 0 \end{pmatrix} = \begin{pmatrix} 1 & -0.10 & -0.20 \\ -0.10 & 1 & -0.10 \\ -0.05 & -0.20 & 1 \end{pmatrix}$$

Find the inverse of matrix $(I - A)$.

$$(I - A)^{-1} = \begin{pmatrix} 1.026 & 0.146 & 0.220 \\ 0.110 & 1.040 & 0.146 \\ 0.073 & 0.215 & 1.040 \end{pmatrix}$$

$$X = (320 \quad 220 \quad 140) \cdot \begin{pmatrix} 1.026 & 0.146 & -0.220 \\ -1.100 & 0.942 & 0.126 \\ 0.073 & 0.215 & 1.040 \end{pmatrix}$$

$$= (363.6 \quad 291 \quad 248.1)$$

This last product indicates it will be necessary to produce the gross amount of 363.3 units of wheat, 291 units of milk, and 248 units of electricity to obtain the net amounts of 320 units of wheat, 220 units of milk, and 140 units of electricity.

Input-output analysis is usually applied to entire economies—hundreds of industries are involved. The relationships among the industries do not change much, and the net amounts can change periodically. The use of matrix algebra is especially appropriate in this situation.

To determine the gross production matrix:

1. Write the technological matrix X for the described situation.

2. Find $I - A$.

3. Find $(I - A)^{-1}$.

4. Find the gross production, X, by multiplying the net production, Y, by $(I - A)^{-1}$.

Example

Suppose it takes $1/3$ unit of water and $1/2$ unit of electricity to produce 1 unit of electricity; to produce 1 unit of water, it takes $3/4$ unit of water and $1/4$ unit of electricity. Write the 2×2 technological matrix A.

$$\begin{array}{c} \\ \text{Water} \\ \text{Electricity} \end{array} \begin{array}{cc} \text{Water} & \text{Electricity} \\ \begin{pmatrix} 3/4 & 1/4 \\ 1/3 & 1/2 \end{pmatrix} \end{array}$$

Write the 1×2 matrix Y to represent 5,000 units of water and 8,000 units of electricity.

$$Y = (5{,}000 \quad 8{,}000)$$

Find $(I - A)$.

$$\begin{pmatrix} 1 & 0 \\ 0 & 1 \end{pmatrix} - \begin{pmatrix} 3/4 & 1/4 \\ 1/3 & 1/2 \end{pmatrix} = \begin{pmatrix} 1/4 & -1/4 \\ -1/3 & 1/2 \end{pmatrix}$$

Find $(I - A)^{-1}$.

$$\begin{pmatrix} 12 & 6 \\ 8 & 6 \end{pmatrix}$$

The gross production is

$$X = (5{,}000 \quad 8{,}000) \cdot \begin{pmatrix} 12 & 6 \\ 8 & 6 \end{pmatrix} = (124{,}000 \quad 78{,}000)$$

Therefore 124,000 units of water and 78,000 units of electricity are needed to obtain a net production of 5,000 units of water and 8,000 units of electricity.

SECTION 4 EXERCISES

1. A company has three apartment complexes in a city. Complex A has 15 one-bedroom, 25 two-bedroom, and 10 three-bedroom apartments. Complex B has 20 one-bedroom, 20 two-bedroom, and 10 three-bedroom apartments. Complex C has 10 one-bedroom, 25 two-bedroom, and 15 three-bedroom apartments. Rentals gross $275 for one-bedroom, $375 for two-bedroom, and $450 for three-bedroom apartments. Set up the information in matrix form. Determine the gross income from one-bedroom, two-bedroom, and three-bedroom apartments. Complex A has 80% occupancy, complex B has 95% occupancy, and complex C has 65% occupancy. Determine the income from each complex.

2. Economical Car Rentals has three types of automobiles available for rent. The economy auto rents for $20 per day, the standard model rents for $28

per day, and the sports model rents for \$35 per day. The company has rental business in four cities with the following inventory.

Dolton: 35 economy, 55 standard, 8 sports

Molton: 50 economy, 75 standard, 15 sports

Solton: 25 economy, 55 standard, 30 sports

Wolton: 40 economy, 35 standard, 0 sports

Set up the information in matrix form. Determine the daily proceeds from each city if the company averages 75% rentals daily.

3. Cooper, Ashley, and Northwoods area stores all handle stereos, televisions, and videocameras. The inventories reported by each store are as follows.

Cooper: 42 stereos, 75 televisions, 12 videocameras

Ashley: 23 stereos, 52 televisions, 7 videocameras

Northwoods: 47 stereos, 62 televisions, 19 videocameras

The average cost of each of the items is \$275 for televisions, \$320 for stereos, and \$450 for videocameras. Find the value of inventory for each of the three stores.

For exercises 4 through 10, use matrices A, A^{-1}, B, and B^{-1}.

$$A = \begin{pmatrix} 1 & 2 & 0 \\ 0 & 0 & 1 \\ 3 & 5 & 4 \end{pmatrix} \qquad A^{-1} = \begin{pmatrix} -5 & -8 & 2 \\ 3 & 4 & -1 \\ 0 & 1 & 0 \end{pmatrix}$$

$$B = \begin{pmatrix} 2 & 5 \\ 1 & 3 \end{pmatrix} \qquad B^{-1} = \begin{pmatrix} 3 & -5 \\ -1 & 2 \end{pmatrix}$$

4. Send the following message, using the 3×3 matrix.

DELAY DEPARTURE

5. Send the following message, using the 3×3 matrix.

PREPARE FOR RETREAT

6. Send the following message, using the 2 × 2 matrix.

ELIMINATE ENEMY

7. Send the following message, using the 2 × 2 matrix.

CONFIRM POSITION

8. The following message has just been received. The decoding device is the 2 × 2 inverse matrix. Determine the message sent.

DSWQFWQNII NAI

9. The message of A L E R T is so sensitive the coding is first multiplied by A, then B. Determine the message sent.

10. The following message has just been received. The decoding device is the 3 × 3 inverse matrix. Determine the message sent.

FKLR UKTHFTZTEQOSTEJDHK LXL

11. An economy depends on two basic products, coal and oil. To produce 1 unit of coal it takes 3/4 unit of coal and 1/4 unit of oil. To produce 1 unit of oil, it takes 1/2 unit of coal and 1/4 unit of oil. Find the gross production necessary for a net production of 1,000 units of coal and 8,000 units of oil.

12. An economy depends on two basic products, coffee and transportation. To produce 1 unit of coffee it takes 3/4 unit of coffee and 1/2 unit of transportation. To produce 1 unit of transportation it takes 0 coffee and 1 unit of transportation. Find the gross production of 5,000 units of coffee and 2,000 units of transportation.

13. A technological matrix relating grain, fertilizer, and fuel is given as

	Grain	Fertilizer	Fuel
Grain	0	1/4	1/3
Fertilizer	1/2	0	1/4
Fuel	1/4	1/4	0

The net production is given by:

$$(100 \quad 120 \quad 80)$$

Find the gross production.

14. A technological matrix relating a three-sector economy is

$$
\begin{array}{cc}
& \begin{array}{ccc} A & B & C \end{array} \\
\begin{array}{c} A \\ B \\ C \end{array} &
\begin{pmatrix}
0.20 & 0.30 & 0.10 \\
0.10 & 0 & 0.50 \\
0.10 & 0.20 & 0.20
\end{pmatrix}
\end{array}
$$

The net production matrix is

$$(50 \quad 80 \quad 120)$$

Find the gross production matrix.

Answers to Odd-Numbered Exercises

1. 1 bedroom: $12,375.
   2 bedroom: $26,250.
   3 bedroom: $15,750.

3.
$$
\begin{array}{c}
\begin{array}{ccc} S & TV & VC \end{array} \\
\begin{array}{c} C \\ A \\ N \end{array}
\begin{pmatrix}
42 & 75 & 12 \\
23 & 52 & 7 \\
47 & 62 & 19
\end{pmatrix}
\cdot
\begin{pmatrix}
320 \\
275 \\
450
\end{pmatrix}
=
\begin{array}{c} C \\ A \\ N \end{array}
\begin{pmatrix}
39,465 \\
24,810 \\
40,640
\end{pmatrix}
\end{array}
$$

Cooper $39,465; Ashley $24,810; Northwoods $40,640

5. D C K P N S W M X O C R X A D U N I T M–.

7. U F G G I R Z K T Q T N V S Q I.

9. E Z A Y K X.

11. 76,000 units of coal and 36,000 units of oil.

13. 285 units of grain, 250 units of fertilizer, and 238 units of fuel.

Summary

$$A = \begin{pmatrix} a_{11} & a_{12} & a_{13} \\ a_{21} & a_{22} & a_{23} \end{pmatrix} \qquad B = \begin{pmatrix} b_{11} & b_{12} \\ b_{21} & b_{22} \end{pmatrix} \qquad C = \begin{pmatrix} 1 & 0 \\ 0 & 1 \end{pmatrix}$$

Dimensions of A are 2×3

$$B + C = \begin{pmatrix} b_{11} + 1 & b_{12} \\ b_{21} & b_{22} + 1 \end{pmatrix}$$

$A \cdot B$ is not possible

$$B \cdot A = \begin{pmatrix} b_{11} \cdot a_{11} + b_{12} \cdot a_{21} & b_{11} \cdot a_{12} + b_{12} \cdot a_{22} & b_{11} \cdot a_{13} + b_{12} \cdot a_{23} \\ b_{21} \cdot a_{11} + b_{22} \cdot a_{21} & b_{21} \cdot a_{12} + b_{22} \cdot a_{22} & b_{21} \cdot a_{13} + b_{22} \cdot a_{23} \end{pmatrix}$$

$$B \cdot A = \begin{pmatrix} \sum\limits_{k=1}^{2} b_{1k} a_{k1} & \sum\limits_{k=1}^{2} b_{1k} a_{k2} & \sum\limits_{k=1}^{2} b_{1k} a_{k3} \\ \sum\limits_{k=1}^{2} b_{2k} a_{k1} & \sum\limits_{k=1}^{2} b_{2k} a_{k22} & \sum\limits_{k=1}^{2} b_{2k} a_{k3} \end{pmatrix}$$

C is the identity matrix for 2×2.

$$B^{-1} = \frac{1}{|B|} \begin{pmatrix} b_{22} & -b_{12} \\ -b_{21} & b_{11} \end{pmatrix}$$

$$A^{\mathrm{T}} = \begin{pmatrix} a_{11} & a_{21} \\ a_{12} & a_{22} \\ a_{13} & a_{23} \end{pmatrix}$$

Inverse of any square matrix A

1. Find $|A|$.

2. Replace each element of A by its cofactor.

3. Write the transpose of the new matrix.

4. Multiply each element of the transpose by $1/|A|$.

Solution of a linear system of equations by matrix algebra:

$$ax + by = c$$
$$dx + ey = f$$

1. Write the system in matrix form

$$\begin{pmatrix} a & b \\ d & e \end{pmatrix} \cdot \begin{pmatrix} x \\ y \end{pmatrix} = \begin{pmatrix} c \\ f \end{pmatrix}$$

2. Find the inverse of

$$\begin{pmatrix} a & b \\ d & e \end{pmatrix}$$

3. Multiply each side of the matrix equation by the generated inverse matrix.

4. Solution

$$\begin{pmatrix} x \\ y \end{pmatrix} = \begin{pmatrix} \text{Inverse} \\ \text{matrix} \end{pmatrix} \begin{pmatrix} c \\ f \end{pmatrix} = \begin{pmatrix} g \\ h \end{pmatrix}$$

$$x = g \qquad y = h$$

REVIEW EXERCISES

Given

$$A = \begin{pmatrix} 3 & -1 & 7 \\ 5 & 2 & -4 \\ 0 & 6 & 9 \end{pmatrix} \qquad B = \begin{pmatrix} -6 & 5 \\ 1 & 4 \\ -9 & -3 \end{pmatrix}$$

$$C = \begin{pmatrix} 1 & 2 \\ 3 & 4 \end{pmatrix} \qquad D = \begin{pmatrix} 2 & 7 & -1 \\ -3 & 5 & 16 \end{pmatrix}$$

$$E = \begin{pmatrix} x+1 & a \\ 1 & 4 \\ y-7 & b \end{pmatrix} \qquad F = \begin{pmatrix} -2 & 1 \\ 3/2 & -1/2 \end{pmatrix}$$

$$G = \begin{pmatrix} 4 & 4 & -6 \\ -4 & -6 & 6 \\ 2 & 4 & -4 \end{pmatrix} \qquad H = \begin{pmatrix} 0 & -1 & -3/2 \\ -1/2 & -1/2 & 0 \\ -1/2 & -1 & -1 \end{pmatrix}$$

1. Determine the dimensions of E and F.

2. Find the values of x, y, a, and b in matrix E if $E = B$.

3. Determine the additions possible in the given matrices. (Do not do the additions.)

4. Determine the possible products involving matrices A, B, C, and D.

5. Write the transpose of E.

6. Identify two matrices that multiply to the 2×2 identity matrix.

7. If $A \cdot B = R$, find r_{32}.

8. If $F \cdot D = S$, find s_{21}.

9. Find $|A|$.

10. Find the cofactor of a_{13}.

11. Find the inverse of A.

12. Solve the system of equations.

$$\begin{aligned} 3x - y + 7z &= 12 \\ 5x + 2y - 4z &= 23 \\ 6y + 9z &= 17 \end{aligned}$$

13. Solve the system of equations.

$$\begin{aligned} -2A + B &= 0.08 \\ 1.5A - 0.5B &= 0.42 \end{aligned}$$

14. Code the message R E D   A L E R T using the matrix

$$\begin{pmatrix} 3 & 4 \\ 2 & 3 \end{pmatrix}$$

15. Happy Hour, Inc., sells three types of drinks, each requiring the following amounts of basic ingredients.

Types of drinks

	A	B	C
Whiskey	1	0	0.5
Vodka	0	1	0.5
Tonic	0	1	0
Ginger	1	0	0
Ice	1	1	2

The number of drinks sold were 123,248,85. Put this information into an appropriate matrix to find the amount of each ingredient used. If the charges for each of the drinks are $1.50, $1.25, and $2.00, find the gross revenues from the sales.

16. An economy depends on two commodities, potatoes and peat. It takes $1/4$ unit of potatoes and 1 unit of peat to produce 1 unit of potatoes; it takes $1/2$ unit of potatoes and $2/3$ unit of peat to produce 1 unit of peat. Write the technological matrix. What gross production is required to produce 500 units of potatoes and 800 units of peat?

Answers to Review Exercises

1. E, (3×2). F, (2×2).

2. $x = -7, y = -2, a = 5, b = -3$.

3. $A + G, A + H, H + G, B + E, C + F$.

4. $A \cdot B, B \cdot C, B \cdot D, C \cdot D, D \cdot A, D \cdot B$.

5. $\begin{pmatrix} x+1 & 1 & y-7 \\ a & 4 & b \end{pmatrix}.$

6. $C \cdot F$.

7.
$$(0 \quad 6 \quad 9) \cdot \begin{pmatrix} 5 \\ 4 \\ -3 \end{pmatrix} = -3.$$

8.
$$(^3/_2 \quad -^1/_2) \cdot \begin{pmatrix} 2 \\ -3 \end{pmatrix} = ^9/_2.$$

9. 381.

10. $+30$.

11.
$$\frac{1}{381} \begin{pmatrix} 42 & 51 & -10 \\ -45 & 27 & 47 \\ 30 & -18 & 11 \end{pmatrix}.$$

12. $x = 3.96$, $y = 2.31$, $z = 0.35$.

13. $A = 0.92$. $B = 1.92$.

14. J F L P   M X T F Z

15.
Whiskey	165.5
Vodka	290.5
Tonic	248.0
Ginger	123.0
Ice	541.0

$\begin{pmatrix} \end{pmatrix}$

$664.50.

16.

	Potatoes	Peat
Potatoes	$^1/_4$	1
Peat	$^1/_2$	$^2/_3$

Gross production: potatoes, 66.7; peat, 1,400.

Chapter 11

Linear Programming

Linear programming is a relatively recent development in mathematics. This development was promoted by the urgent need to handle many variables during World War II. An American mathematician, George Dantzig, is credited with the theory of linear programming, and the computer was the vehicle that allowed the theory to be used to assist in supplying and transporting troops throughout the world in an efficient and economical manner.

In Chapter 10, matrix algebra was used to solve linear systems of equations. Linear programming techniques are used to produce the best solutions to systems of linear inequalities. In order to give some insight into the nature of linear programming, the graphical representation of the system of inequalities is presented first. The nature of graphing dictates that only two variables can be involved. The simplex method is the algebraic approach to the solution. The simplex method provides solutions for large systems of inequalities involving many variables. Computers are essential in solving large systems of linear inequalities.

At the end of this chapter, the student will be able to:

1. Provide the graphical representation for two-variable problems. Interpretation of the graphical solution provides the solution to the problem.
2. Use the simplex method of solution for maximization to give an algebraic solution to a linear programming problem.
3. Utilize the duality theorem to give a method of solution for minimization problems.
4. Use the available algorithms for minimizing transportation or workload problems.

11.1 GRAPHICAL SOLUTION FOR LINEAR INEQUALITIES

Linear inequalities look much like linear equations, but the $=$ is replaced by one of the following signs:

$>$	greater than
$<$	less than
$\geq$	greater than or equal to
$\leq$	less than or equal to

Examples of linear inequalities are

$$3x + 2y \leq 6$$

$$2x - 5y \geq 10$$

Recall that the graphing of a linear equation is a straight line. The most common method of graphing a linear equation is the intercept method or the slope-intercept method.

To graph a linear inequality, first graph the expression written as an equation. Graph $3x + 2y = 6$. The intercepts are $(0, 3)$ and $(2, 0)$. Locate these points on the x and y axis.

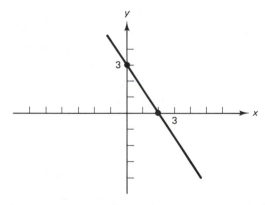

The graph of the linear inequality $3x + 2y \leq 6$ has $3x + 2y = 6$ as a boundary. Either the area above the line or below the line is the region representing the inequality. It is an area, not a line.

To determine if the region representing the inequality is above or below the line, take any point not on the line. An example might be $(1, 1)$. Substitute $(1, 1)$ into $3x + 2y < 6$. $3 + 2 <(?) 6$. 5 is less than 6. Therefore the area containing $(1, 1)$ is shaded and the area under the line is the graph of the inequality.

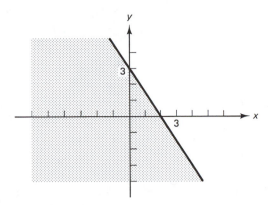

As a second example, graph $2x - 5y \geq 10$. Write the expression as an equation.

$$2x - 5y = 10$$

Determine the intercepts: $(0,\ \ )(\ ,0)$. If $x = 0$, $y = -2$ and if $y = 0$, $x = 5$. The intercepts are $(0, -2)$ and $(5, 0)$. Graph these points and draw a line through them.

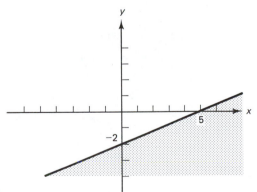

Try a point definitely not on the line such as $(2, 1)$. Substitute that point into the inequality. $2(2) - 5(1) >(?)$ 10. This is incorrect. Therefore this point is not part of the shaded area. Shade the part of the graph below the line that does not include $(2, 1)$. If the inequality contains $<$ or $>$ without the equal, the line is drawn in by dashes to indicate the region satisfying the inequality does not include the line but all points up to the line.

To graph a system of inequalities, each inequality is graphed on the same graph. The intersection of the shaded regions is the area representing the system.

Example

$$x + 4y < 8;$$

$$3x + 2y < 9$$

Graph $x + 4y = 8$. The intercepts are $(0, 2)$ and $(8, 0)$. Connect these points by a dashed line. Check the point $(1, 1)$ to see if the region containing the point satisfies the inequality. $(1) + 4(1) <(?) 8$. Yes. Therefore the region including $(1, 1)$ is shaded.

Graph $3x + 2y = 9$. The intercepts are $(0, 4.5)$ and $(3, 0)$. Connect these points by a dashed line. Check the point $(1, 1)$ to see if the region containing the point satisfies the inequality. $3(1) + 2(1) <(?) 9$. The inequality is satisfied so the region containing $(1, 1)$ is shaded.

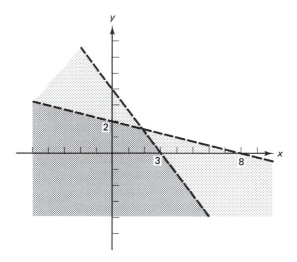

The graphical solution to the system of linear inequalities is the intersection of the two shaded areas (shown darker) in the diagram. Because the inequalities do not contain "or equal to," the boundary lines are dotted lines. Any point in the shaded area satisfies both of the inequalities.

If graphs extend indefinitely in some direction, the regions are called unbounded. All of the examples in this section are unbounded. If a region is cut off in every direction by line segments, the region is called bounded.

Corner points, intersection points of lines, are called vertices of the system. The vertex of the preceding example is approximately $(2, 1.5)$.

SECTION 1 EXERCISES

Sketch the graph of each inequality.

1. $2x - 3y > 6.$

2. $3x + y - 3 < 0.$

3. $2x + 7y \leq 14.$

4. $5x - 15 \geq 3y.$

5. $x \geq 0.$

6. $y \geq 0.$

7. $y < 0.$

8. $x < 0.$

Sketch the graph of the system of linear inequalities. Determine if the system is bounded or unbounded. Name the vertices of the corner points.

9. $3x - 4y \geq 12$
   $2x + 5y \leq 10.$

10. $2x + 7y < 14$
    $x - 3y < 6.$

11. $x + 2y > 8$
    $3x - y < 6.$

12. $3x + 4y \leq 18$
    $2x + y \leq 4.$

13. $x + 2y \leq 10$
    $3x + 4y \leq 12$
    $x \geq 0, y \geq 0.$

14. $4x - 5y < 20$
    $2x + 3y < 6$
    $x \leq 0, y \leq 0.$

Answers to Odd-Numbered Exercises

1.

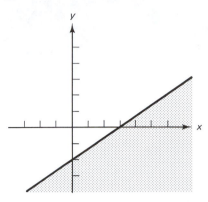

3.

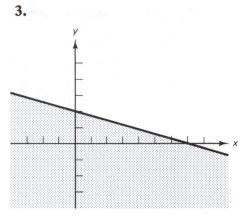

5.

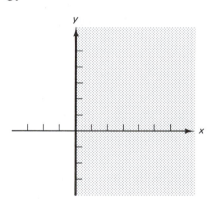

7.

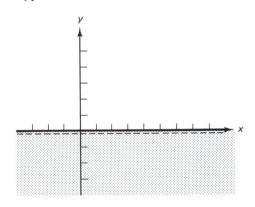

9.

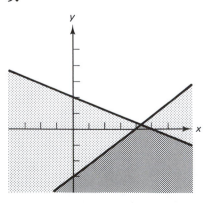

11.

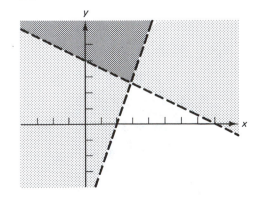

13.

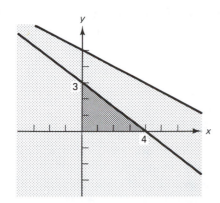

11.2 GRAPHICAL SOLUTION TO LINEAR PROGRAMMING

Linear programming problems consist of a system of inequalities that has many solutions and an objective for the system that allows a unique solution. The objective is either to maximize or minimize a quantity and is called the objective function. An example is considered to illustrate the concepts.

> **Example**
> ABC Manufacturing Company manufactures products A and B. Three machines are used in the production of these products. Product A requires 3 hours on machine I, 7 hours on machine II, and 10 hours on machine III. Product B requires 4 hours on machine I, 5 hours on machine II, and 4 hours on machine III. Machine I has at most 120 production hours per week. Machine II has at most 144 production hours per week. Machine III has at most 168 production hours per week. Business is good and any number of products A and B can be sold. The profit for product A is \$5 per item and the profit for product B is \$3 per item. Find the production product mix to maximize profits.
>
>   All of the preceding information can be organized into a table.
>
> | | A | B | Maximum Time Available |
> |-------------|-----|-----|------------------------|
> | Machine I | 3 | 4 | 120 |
> | Machine II | 7 | 5 | 144 |
> | Machine III | 10 | 4 | 168 |
> | Profit | 5 | 3 | |
>
> The variables A and B represent the number of items produced. The

preceding information written as algebraic inequalities is

$$3A + 4B \leq 120$$

$$7A + 5B \leq 144$$

$$10A + 4B \leq 168$$

$$5A + 3B \qquad \text{profit to be maximized}$$

Graph the three inequalities. Two additional constraints are inherent to the problem, $A \geq 0$ and $B \geq 0$. Negative quantities cannot be produced; no production is possible. These constraints put the graph into quadrant I. The intercepts are (0, 30) and (40, 0) for (1), (0, 29) and (20, 5, 0) for (2), and (0, 42) and (16.8, 0) for (3).

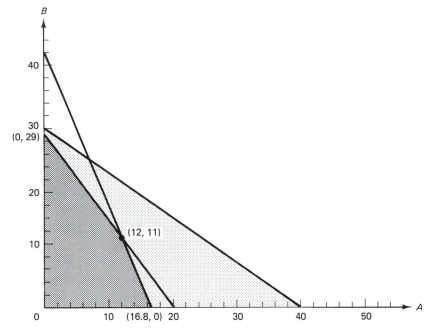

The area bounded by $7A + 5B = 144$ (machine II) and $10A + 4B = 168$ (Machine III) forms the solution to the linear programming problem. The vertices of the bounded area are (0, 0), (16.8, 0), (12, 11), and (0, 29).

The maximum and minimum values for the objective function (profit) **must** occur at one of the vertices. This is basic to obtaining a solution.

This theorem is stated without proof: *Every linear function defined over the set of points of a convex polygon reaches its maximum value at one vertex of the polygon and its minimum value at another vertex of the polygon.*

The theorem applies to convex polygons: the area must be bounded by a closed figure.

The profit is dependent on the number of each product (A and B) produced.

$$5A + 3B \quad \text{is the profit statement}$$

Substitute the vertex values into the profit statement expression.

$$5(0) + 3(0) = \quad 0 \quad \text{minimum}$$

$$5(16.8) + 3(0) = 84$$

$$\boxed{5(12) + 3(11) = 93 \quad \text{maximum}}$$

$$5(0) + 3(29.5) = 88.5$$

The numbers indicate the greatest profit is realized when 12 of product A and 11 of product B are manufactured. The least profit is realized when none of either product is manufactured. In finding the quantity, a rounded integer answer is usually more meaningful than fractional answers.

Linear programming problems are usually verbal problems.

1. Organize the information in tabular form.

2. Write each of the constraints as a linear inequality and the objective function as an algebraic expression.

3. Graph each of the linear inequalities on a single graph (usually quadrant I), shading the area representing the solution set. If the solution is a closed polygon, the linear programming theorem holds and the intersection of the shaded areas is the solution area.

4. Identify the vertices of the solution set.

5. Substitute the values of the vertices into the objective function. The vertex giving the largest value is the required solution for a maximum objective; the vertex giving the smallest value is the required solution for a minimum objective.

Example

Two gems—sapphires and diamonds—are cut and polished. Sapphires require 3 hours of cutting time and 7 hours for polishing. Diamonds require 5 hours cutting time and 3 hours for polishing. The operation has at most 300 hours available for cutting and 300 hours available for polishing. What mixture of gems should be processed to maximize profit which is $200 for each sapphire and $275 for each diamond?

In tabular form:

	Sapphire	Diamond	Maximum
Cutting	3	5	300
Polishing	7	3	300
Profit	200	275	

As linear inequalities:

$$3S + 5D \leq 300$$

$$7S + 3D \leq 300$$

$$200S + 275D$$

$$S \geq 0 \quad \text{and} \quad D \geq 0$$

Intercepts

$$(100, 0) \text{ and } (0, 60)$$

$$(43, 0) \text{ and } (0, 100).$$

The graph

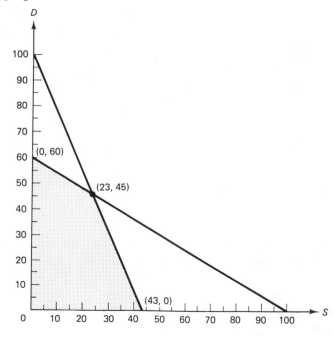

The solution is a bounded region with vertices at (0, 0), (43, 0), (23, 45), and (0, 60).

The value of the profit at each vertex is

$$200(0) + 275(0) = \quad 0 \quad \text{minimum}$$

$$200(43) + 275(0) = \quad 8{,}600$$

$$200(23) + 275(45) = 12{,}375$$

$$\boxed{200(0) + 275(60) = 16{,}500 \quad \text{maximum}}$$

The strategy for the greatest profit is to cut and polish 60 diamonds and no sapphires.

If the profit function changed to $275 for either sapphires or diamonds, the strategy would change. The optimal strategy would then be cutting and polishing 23 sapphires and 45 diamonds for a profit of $18,700.

SECTION 2 EXERCISES

In exercises 1–4, the solution regions are given with the vertices marked. Use these regions to find the maximum and minimum values of each of the objective functions.

1. $7x + 4y$

2. $x + 2y$

3. $1.25x + 0.60y$

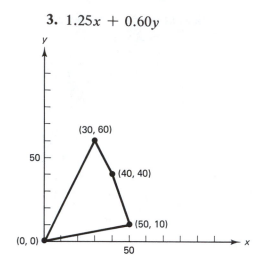

4. $0.45x + 0.90y$

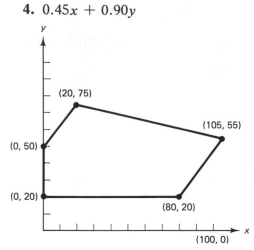

Use the graphical method to solve each of the problems for the maximum and minimum values.

5. $x + 3y \leq 12$

$2x + y \leq 6$

$x \leq 2.$

Objective function, $x + 7y$.

6. $x + y \leq 8$

$5x + y \leq 15$

$2x + y \leq 9$

Objective function, $3x + y$.

7. $7x + 6y \leq 17$

$x + 4y \leq 8$

$9x + 4y \leq 18.$

Objective function, $5x + 4y$.

8. $2x + y \leq 7$

$2x + 3y \leq 9$

$x \geq 1.$

Objective function, $3x + 4y$.

9. $x + 3y \leq 340$

$3x + 4y \leq 600$

$x + y \leq 180.$

Objective function, $7x + 7y.$

10. $6x + 7y \leq 21.$

$2x + 5y \leq 12$

$3x + 2y \leq 9.$

Objective function, $5x + 4y.$

11. A manufacturer of televisions and radios must produce at most 350 televisions and 700 radios each week. 24 worker-hours are required to assemble a television. 5 worker-hours are required to assemble a radio. The company has at most 10,000 worker-hours available each week. The profit for each television is $25 and for each radio $10. Find the production of televisions and radios that will maximize profits.

12. A wood craftsperson makes tables and beds. The production time for each table is 3 hours on the lathe and 5 hours on a joiner. Each bed requires 14 hours on the lathe and 3 hours on the joiner. There are 80 hours available on the lathe and 60 hours on the joiner. The product is unique and all merchandise can be sold with a profit of $60 on each table and $90 on each bed. Determine the production output to maximize profits.

13. Two plants manufacture products A and B for the same firm. Plant 1 can make product A in 10 hours and product B in 8 hours. Plant 2 can make product A in 7 hours and product B in 9 hours. The maximum number of hours available in plant 1 is 1,200 hours, and the maximum number of hours available in plant 2 is 1,000 hours. Contracts dictate at least 80 units of product A be produced. The profit from product A is $15. The profit from product B is $18. How would you schedule production in the two plants to maximize profit?

14. A man has $100,000 to invest in stocks and bonds. Stocks average a return of 10% and bonds yield 12%. The stockbroker advises the man to invest not more than $90,000, leaving $10,000 in a savings account for emergencies. The stockbroker also advises at least twice as much should be invested in the stock market than in the bond market as a hedge against inflation. Find the most profitable investment mix.

Answers to Odd-Numbered Exercises

1. (1, 2) minimum of 15. (8, 6) maximum of 80.

3. (0, 0) minimum of 0. (40, 40) maximum of 74.

5. (0, 0) minimum of 0. (0, 4) maximum of 28.

7. (0, 0) minimum of 0. (1.5, 1.1) maximum of 11.9.

9. (0, 0) minimum of 0. (120, 60) maximum of 1,260.

11. 350 televisions and 340 radios for a profit of $12,150.

13. Make 80 units of product A and 48 units of product B in plants 1 and 2 for a profit of $4,128 ($2,064 in each plant).

11.3   SIMPLEX METHOD

The graphical solution to linear programming problems is limited to two variables and all solutions are approximate. The algebraic method, known as the simplex method, can be used for many variables and the answers are precise. To introduce the simplex method, the same example solved graphically in the previous section will be solved by the simplex method. The verbal problem and tabular form are omitted, and the process starts with the algebraic inequalities.

$$3A + 4B \leq 120$$

$$7A + 5B \leq 144$$

$$10A + 4B \leq 168$$

$$P = 5A + 3B \qquad \text{profit to be maximized}$$

Linear inequalities have many solutions. Our problem is to find the best solution. Each inequality is changed to an equation. This is achieved by adding a positive quantity to the left-hand side of the inequality. Because the quantity added to each statement is different, these different amounts are denoted as s_1, s_2, and s_3.

The inequalities are rewritten as equations.

$$3A + 4B + s_1 \qquad\qquad = 120$$

$$7A + 5B \qquad + s_2 \qquad = 144$$

$$10A + 4B \qquad\qquad + s_3 = 168$$

$$P = 5A + 3B$$

Once the information is in equation form, a matrix array can be used to represent the information.

A	B	s_1	s_2	s_3	
3	4	1	0	0	120
7	5	0	1	0	144
10	4	0	0	1	168
−5	−3	0	0	0	0

The array should be self-explanatory except for the last line, the objective function. The profit is 0 when $A = 0$ and $B = 0$, the starting place of the problem. When the numerical value is 0, the A and B variables must be algebraically moved to the left-hand side of the $=$. This format is necessary for the implementation of the simplex method.

The initial tableau reads as follows.

s_1 has a value of 120 because of the 1   0   0   0 in the s_1 column.

s_2 has a value of 144 because of the 0   1   0   0 in the s_2 column.

s_3 has a value of 168 because of the 0   0   1   0 in the s_3 column.

A and B are both 0 as is the profit.

The objective of the problem is to find the values of A and B that maximize profit. The last row is the profit statement. The initial selection is the product generating the largest profit. -5 indicates the larger profit; column 1 is our first selection. The goal in column 1 is one entry of 1 and the other entries 0. To determine which element should be 1, use the ratio test. The ratio test involves taking the right entry of each row and dividing it by each column entry. In this case, $120/3$, $144/7$, and $168/10$. The smallest resulting quotient determines the entry called the **pivot** point. Since $168/10$ is the smallest ratio, 10 is the pivot point.

Important considerations in finding a pivot point are

The entry cannot be negative.

The entry cannot be zero.

If two entries have the same ratio, either may be selected.

The pivot point is made 1 by dividing every entry in the row by the value of the pivot point.

The values of the row were

$$10 \quad 4 \quad 0 \quad 0 \quad 1 \quad 168$$

Divide each entry by 10.

$$1 \quad 0.4 \quad 0 \quad 0 \quad 0.1 \quad 16.8 \text{ New Row 3}$$

This is now classified as the working row. This row will be multiplied and added to the other rows of the tableau to produce a 0 in all other entries of the column. The process of multiplying and adding rows is referred to as elementary row operations.

Row 1	3	4	1	0	0	120	
(−3)Working Row	−3	−1.2	0	0	−.3	−50.4	
Row 1 + (−3) WR	0	2.8	1	0	−.3	69.6	New Row 1

Row 2	7	5	0	1	0	144	
(−7)Working Row	−7	−2.8	0	0	−.7	−117.6	
Row 2 + (−7) WR	0	2.2	1	0	−.7	26.4	New Row 2

Bottom Row	−5	−3	0	0	0	0	
(5) Working Row	5	2	0	0	.5	84	
Bottom + (5) WR	0	−1	0	0	.5	84	New Bottom Row

The new tableau created by these operations is

A	B	s_1	s_2	s_3	
0	2.8	1	0	−0.3	69.3
0	2.2	0	1	−0.7	26.4
1	0.4	0	0	0.1	16.8
0	−1	0	0	0.5	84

This array can be interpreted as

$$A = 16.8 \quad B = 0 \quad s_1 = 69.3 \quad s_2 = 26.4 \quad s_3 = 0 \quad P = 84$$

A negative in the bottom row indicates that the problem is not finished. The profit can be improved.

Return to the graphical solution to this problem. The vertex values were substituted into the profit statement expression to find the maximum profit. One of the choices was $A = 16.8$, $B = 0$, profit $= 84$. This was not the maximum. The simplex method is picking up the vertices of the polygon formed by graphing.

The simplex process is repeated for the new tableau. No choice exists for column selection; there is only one negative entry. By the ratio test we obtain the ratios 69.3/2.8, 26.4/2.2, and 16.8/.4. Because 26.4/2.2 gives the smallest quantity, 2.2 is the entry used as the pivot. Make the pivot entry 1 by dividing each entry of the row by 2.2. The new row 2 is the working row for producing a new tableau and is arrived at by dividing each entry by 2.2.

New working row   0   1   0   0.45 -0.32 12

To produce a 0 where there is 2.8, multiply the working row by -2.8 and add the result to row 1.

(-2.8) working row	0	-2.8	0	-1.26	$+0.9$	-33.6
Row 1	0	2.8	1	0	-0.3	69.3
New row 1	0	0	1	-1.26	$+0.6$	35.7

To produce a 0 where 0.4 is in row 3:

(-0.4) working row	0	-0.4	0	-0.18	$+0.13$	-4.8
Row 3	1	0.4	0	0	0.1	16.8
New row 3:	1	0	0	-0.18	$+0.23$	12

To produce a 0 in the bottom row, add the working row and bottom row.

Working row	0	1	0	0.45	-0.32	12
Bottom row	0	-1	0	0.45	0.5	84
New row	0	0	0	0.45	0.18	96

The new tableau is completed as:

	A	B	s_1	s_2	s_3		
0	0	1	-1.26	0.6	35.7
0	1	0	0.45	-0.32	12
1	0	0	-0.18	0.23	12
0	0	0	0.45	0.18	96	profit

All entries in the bottom row are nonnegative. The problem is complete.
The solution is

$$A = 12, \quad B = 12, \quad s_1 = 35.7 \quad \text{profit} = \$96$$

The graphical solution was

$$A = 12, \quad B = 11 \quad \text{profit} = \$93$$

The s_1 value is an indicator the first inequality had some unused capacity. In this problem, machine I will be unused for 35.7 hours. Management might be able to add another product to use machine I and add to the profit.

The steps involved in the simplex method of solution are as follows.

1. Write each linear inequality as an equation, introducing slack variables $s_1, s_2, s_3, \ldots, s_n$ for n inequalities.

2. Set up the initial tableau based on the coefficients of the variables of the constraints written as equations. The objective function is the bottom row of the tableau, the coefficients are negated, and all other entries are zero.

3. Determine the column by selecting the most negative entry in the bottom row.

4. Apply the ratio test—right entry of each row divided by entries of selected column. The smallest ratio value determines the pivot entry.

5. Divide each element of the row containing the pivot entry by the pivot entry. This makes the pivot entry value 1.

6. Using the row containing the pivot entry of 1 as the working row, use elementary row operations to produce a new array. All entries of the selected column are zero except the pivot entry of 1.

7. Repeat steps 3 through 6 until all elements in the bottom row are nonnegative.

8. Interpret the results. The lower right entry is the maximum value, the columns containing 1 and the remaining entries 0 give the values to the variables heading the column.

SECTION 3 EXERCISES

1. Maximize $5x + 4y$

   Subject to: $7x + 6y \leq 19$

   $\qquad\qquad\quad x + 4y \leq 10$

   $\qquad\qquad\; 3x + 5y \leq 13$

   Set up the initial tableau for this problem.

2. Maximize $4x + 5y$

   Subject to: $x + 6y \leq 300$

   $2x + 3y \leq 280$

   $5x + y \leq 440$

   Set up the initial tableau for this problem.

3. Write the algebraic inequalities and objective function for the following tableau.

A	B	s_1	s_2	s_3	
8	7	1	0	0	182
3	5	0	1	0	136
5	2	0	0	1	147
-6	-10	0	0	0	0

4. Write the algebraic inequalities and objective function for the following tableau.

x	y	s_1	s_2	s_3	
13	12	1	0	0	72
5	6	0	1	0	8
2	3	0	0	1	12
-3	-1	0	0	0	0

5. Select the pivot element of exercise 3.

6. Select the pivot element of exercise 4.

7. Find the first new tableau for the given problem and interpret the results.

A	B	s_1	s_2	
4	5	1	0	36
1	2	0	1	11
-2	-3	0	0	0

8. Find the first new tableau for the given problem and interpret the results.

x	y	s_1	s_2	s_3	
4	1	1	0	0	47
1	6	0	1	0	50
3	2	0	0	1	39
-3	-8	0	0	0	0

9. Solve, using the simplex method.

$$x + 3y \leq 12$$

$$2x + y \leq 6.$$

Maximize $x + 7y$.

10. $A + B \leq 8$

$5A + B \leq 15$

$2A + B \leq 9.$

Maximize $3A + B$.

11. $7x + 6y \leq 17$

$x + 4y \leq 8$

$9x + 2y \leq 18.$

Maximize $5x + 4y$.

12. $x + 3y \leq 340$

$3x + 4y \leq 600$

$2x + y \leq 180.$

Maximize $7x + 5y$.

13. A firm manufactures two lawn mowers, Cut Easy and Cut Well. Cut Easy requires 6 hours in processing and 12 hours in assembly. Cut Well requires 10 hours in processing and 6 hours in assembly. There are 90 hours of processing and 120 hours of assembly available each day. The profit for each Cut Easy is $15 and for each Cut Well the profit is $12. The company would like to produce the combination of items which would maximize profit.
    a. Prepare the linear inequalities to represent the constraints.
    b. Set up the initial tableau.
    c. Pivot until the optimal solution is attained.
    d. Explain the information from the final tableau.

14. A jacket company has an unlimited market for jackets for professional football team fans. The profit for each unlined jacket is $10, and for each lined jacket the profit is $15. Each jacket requires varying times for cutting and sewing. Each unlined jacket requires 1 hour of cutting, and each lined jacket requires 2 hours of cutting. A total of 80 cutting hours are available each day. The unlined jacket requires 4 sewing hours, and the

lined jacket requires 6 sewing hours. A total of 144 sewing hours are available each day. Use the simplex method to find the best production strategy to maximize profit.

15. The Quick Calculate Company produces two different products, P_1 and P_2. The hourly machine requirements for each product are as follows:

	M_1	M_2	M_3
P_1	0.6	0.5	0.7
P_2	0.4	0.7	0.5

M_1 is available 200 hours, M_2 is available 140 hours, M_3 is available 100 hours. The profit contribution for product 1 is \$10 and for product 2 the profit contribution is \$8. The company would like to schedule production to maximize profit. The sales department can sell all products produced. Solve the problem using the simplex method.

Answers to Odd-Numbered Exercises

1.

x	y	s_1	s_2	s_3	
7	6	1	0	0	19
1	4	0	1	0	10
3	5	0	0	1	13
−5	−4	0	0	0	0

3. $8A + 7B \leq 182$
   $3A + 5B \leq 136$
   $5A + 2B \leq 147$
   Maximize $6A + 10B$.

5. Pivot element, 7.

7.

A	B	s_1	s_2	
1.5	0	1	−2.5	8.5
.5	1	0	0.5	5.5
−.5	0	0	1.5	16.5

The profit can be further improved. Present solution: $B = 5.5$ and $s_1 = 8.5$. Profit, 16.5

9. $y = 4$, $s_2 = 2$. Profit, 28.

11. $x = 1.85$, $y = .67$. Profit, 12.

13. Cut Well $= 4$, Cut Easy $= 8$. Profit, \$169.35.

15. $P_1 = 5.8$, $P_2 = 196$. Profit, \$1,626.

11.4   SOLUTION OF MINIMIZATION PROBLEMS

In the previous section, the simplex method of solution was applied to maximization problems with less than or equal to inequalities. In this section, the simplex method will be applied to minimization problems with greater than or equal to relationships.

A typical minimization problem might involve nutrients needed for feeding an animal. Arrow feed contains 8 units of iron and 12 units of zinc. Dart feed contains 6 units of iron and 5 units of zinc. The vet has prescribed at least 80 units of iron and 105 units of zinc for the ailing cow.

Arrow feed costs $5 per bag, and Dart feed costs $3 per bag. Find the least expensive way to feed the animal to ensure the proper amounts of nutrients.

The words "at least" are symbolized by $>$.

$$8A + 6D \geq 80$$

is the relationship concerning iron.

$$12A + 5D \geq 105$$

is the relationship concerning zinc.

$$5A + 3D$$

is the cost to be minimized.

To determine the graphical solution to this problem, the intercepts for each relationship are found. $8A + 6D = 80$ has intercepts $(10, 0)$ and $(0, 13.3)$. $12A + 5D = 105$ has intercepts $(8.75, 0)$ and $(0, 21)$. The problem suggests $A \geq 0$ and $D \geq 0$. Quadrant 1 is appropriate in the graphical representation.

To determine the shading, try the point $(1, 1)$ in each inequality. Since neither inequality is satisfied, shade the area of the graph not including $(1, 1)$. The corner points of the shaded area are approximately $(10, 0)$, $(7, 4)$, and $(0, 21)$.

The minimum value of the objective function $5A + 3B$ is determined by naming the corner points of the shaded area and evaluating $5A + 3B$ at those points.

$$5(10) + 3(0) = 50$$

$$5(7) + 3(4) = 47$$

$$5(0) + 3(21) = 63$$

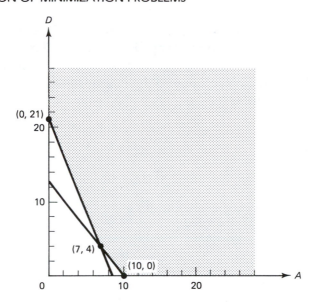

The graphical solution to the problem is 7 bags of Arrow and 4 bags of Dart at a cost of $47.

The simplex solution to the same problem follows. Without going to slave variable, make a matrix of the coefficients and objective function.

A	D	
8	6	80
12	5	105
5	3	0

A **dual** problem to this array is formed by taking the transpose of the matrix. The transpose is the array with the columns written as rows.

X	Y	
8	12	5
6	5	3
80	105	0

The solution to the minimization problem depends upon the solution to the dual maximization problem.

The following theorem states the validity of solving a minimizing problem by solving the dual maximization problem.

Theorem. *The objective function z of a maximizing linear programming problem takes on a maximizing value if and only if the objective function of the corresponding dual problem takes on a minimum value, the maximum value of the maximizing problem is equal to the minimum value of the minimizing problem.*

The dual problem is written with slack variables in the initial tableau array, the bottom row becoming negative entries. Different variables are used as a reminder that our solution is to the dual problem. The final array must be interpreted to provide a solution to the minimization problem.

The initial tableau is

X	Y	s_1	s_2	
8	12	1	0	5
6	5	0	1	3
-80	-105	0	0	0

The pivot point is 12 (row 1, column 2).

X	Y	s_1	s_2	
$2/3$	1	$1/12$	0	$42/100$
$8/3$	0	$-5/12$	1	1
-10	0	$8 3/4$	0	44

The second pivot point is $8/3$.

X	Y	s_1	s_2	
0	1	$-2/96$	$1/4$	$17/100$
1	0	$-5/32$	$3/8$	$3/8$
0	0	$7 6/32$	$30/8$	$47 3/4$

This final tableau indicates the minimum cost is $47.75 (the same value as the maximization value of the dual). The desired nutrients will be achieved by using $7 6/32$ bags of A and $3 6/8$ bags of D. These values are found in the bottom row under the columns headed by the slack variables. The X, Y variables are reminders not to read the solution for A and D under these headings.

Suppose we rounded this to 7 units of A and 4 units of D. The cost would be $5(7) + 3(4) = \$47$.

$$\text{Iron} \qquad 7(8) + 4(6) = 80 \text{ units}$$

$$\text{Zinc} \qquad 7(12) + 4(5) = 104 \text{ units}$$

The number 104 is 1 less than the prescribed amount. The fractional answers would have produced the required amounts.

The steps for solving a minimization problem using the simplex method are as follows.

1. Form the dual maximization problem by transporting the original array and adding slack variables.

2. Solve the maximization problem using the simplex method.

3. The minimum value of the original problem is the maximum of the dual problem.

4. The solution variable values are given in the bottom row, the entries in the columns headed by the slack variables.

Other special cases of linear programming problems exist—problems containing some relationships with equality and some problems with a mixture of greater than and less than relationships. Special rules exist for each of these situations. The presentation in this chapter is meant to be an introduction to linear programming and the types of problems that can be solved. Special situations will not be considered.

Linear programming problems solved today contain hundreds of variables and constraints. The computer is programmed to carry out the simplex method of solution. Writing accurate and meaningful constraints is the difficult part of linear programming. The usefulness of the results is dependent on the accuracy and completeness of the constraints.

SECTION 4 EXERCISES

1. Minimize $5x + 4y$

   Subject to: $7x + 6y \geq 19$

   $$x + 4y \geq 10$$

   $$3x + 5y \geq 13$$

   Set up the tableau for solving the problem as a maximization problem.

2. Minimize $4x + 5y$

   Subject to: $x + 6y \geq 300$

   $$2x + 3y \geq 280$$

   $$5x + y \geq 440$$

3. The following represents the initial maximization tableau.

A	B	s_1	s_2	s_3	
8	7	1	0	0	182
3	5	0	1	0	136
5	2	0	0	1	147
-6	-10	0	0	0	0

Write the algebraic inequalities and objective function for the minimization problem involving the variables x, y, and z.

4. The following represents the initial maximization tableau.

x	y	s_1	s_2	
13	12	1	0	72
5	6	0	1	8
−3	−1	0	0	0

Write the algebraic inequalities and objective function for the minimization problem involving the variables A and B.

5. Solve the following.

$$2x + y \geq 20$$

$$x + y \geq 14$$

$$x + 3y \geq 18.$$

Minimize $10x + 6y$.

$$x \geq 0, y \geq 0.$$

6. Solve the following.

$$x + y \geq 5$$

$$2x + y \geq 6.$$

Minimize $6x + 2y$.

7. Given the following constraints:

$$2x + 5y \geq 20$$

$$3x + 2y \geq 12$$

$$x \quad\quad \geq 0$$

$$y \geq 2.$$

Minimize $3x + 4y$.

8. Given the following constraints:

$$2A + 5B \geq 7$$

$$A + 2B \geq 6$$

$$A \geq 0 \quad B \geq 0.$$

Minimize $5A + 3B$.

9. A farmer discovers his crops need at least 15 units of nitrogen and 8 units of phosphate per acre to be fertilized properly. Two products, Viga and Pro, are available. The content of the two products are as follows. Viga has 4 units of nitrogen and 1 unit of phosphate per bag. The cost of Viga is $4 per bag. Pro has 3 units of nitrogen and 3 units of phosphate per bag. The cost of Pro is $6 per bag. Find the least expensive mixture satisfying the requirements for his crops.

10. Accommodations for 600 athletes must be provided. Buildings are of two types, A and B. Building A requires 180 units of wood, 50 units of concrete, has a capacity of 18 athletes, and the cost for each building is $65,000. Building B uses 75 units of wood, 300 units of concrete, has a capacity of 24 athletes, and the cost for each building is $100,000. At least 1,200 units of wood must be used, at least 4,000 units of concrete are available. How many of each type of building should be constructed if the objective is to keep the cost at a minimum?

11. In a water treatment plant, there are three ingredients necessary for successful treatment. The minimum hourly requirement of each item is listed in the table, along with the two commercial preparations available as a supply for the three items, and the cost of each preparation.

Product	Item A	Item B	Item C	Cost
Clere	8	6	1	$0.80
Pur	4	10	3	0.65
Minimum requirement	24	30	15	

Subject to the listed requirements, find the minimum cost for the ingredients.

12. Two vitamin companies have offered tablets for undernourished children. The two products available are Pep and Fire. Analysis of each of the tablets gives the following information.

Product	Vitamin 1	Vitamin 2	Vitamin 3	Cost
Pep	4	3	5	$0.06
Fire	5	6	3	0.08
Minimum requirement	30	28	25	

Find the minimum daily cost for each child and determine what blend of the two tablets would supply the minimum daily requirements of vitamins 1, 2, and 3.

Answers to Odd-Numbered Exercises

1.

	A	B	C	s_1	s_2	
	7	1	3	1	0	5
	6	4	5	0	1	4
	-19	-10	-13	0	0	0

3.
$$8x + 3y + 5z \geq 6$$
$$7x + 5y + 2z \geq 10$$
$$182x + 136y + 147z \quad \text{minimize.}$$

5. $x = 6$, $y = 8$. Minimum value, 108.

7. $x = 1.8$, $y = 3.28$. Minimum value, 18.56.

9. $V = 2.35$, $P = 1.87$. Minimum cost, $20.65.

11. Clere, 0.62; Pur, 4.75. Minimum cost, $3.56.

11.5   TRANSPORTATION AND ASSIGNMENT PROBLEMS

Problems exist that resemble linear programming problems, needing special computational techniques.

Transportation Problem

The transportation problem refers to a minimum cost plan for shipping a product from a number of supply locations to a number of points of demand. The number of the resource must equal or exceed the demand. To present the method of solution for transportation problems, a specific problem will be used to demonstrate the techniques needed for solution.

General Manufacturing has three plants where product A is manufactured. There are four destination points for the product. The following table indicates the capacities and requirements for each of the sources and destinations.

Capacity	Source	Destination	Requirement
250	Factory 1	Center A	80
125	Factory 2	Center B	185
210	Factory 3	Center C	190
		Center D	100
585 units available			555 units required

The problem is to move product A from the factories to the destination centers at a minimum transportation cost. The cost of shipping one unit from each of the factories to each of the destinations is as follows.

Source	Destination			
	A	B	C	D
1	3.50	3.20	4.20	3.70
2	2.80	3.90	3.20	3.35
3	2.20	4.20	3.70	3.00

To solve a problem by the transportation method, the cost of shipping does not vary for any amount shipped. If 10 items cost $32, 100 items would cost $320.

Step 1. Set up the initial tableau. This involves taking all of the information given and putting it in one array. Each source will be represented by a row, each destination by a column, the capacities will be the right-hand column, and the requirements will be the bottom row.

Source	Destination				S	Capacity
	A	B	C	D		
1	3.50	3.20	4.20	3.70		250
2	2.80	3.90	3.20	3.35		125
3	2.20	4.20	3.70	3.00		210
	80	185	190	100	30	585

The bottom row and right column are the capacity and requirement constraints of the problem. The cost information is contained inside the tableau. Notice an extra column headed S for destinations—this is a "slack" destination because there are more items produced than required at the destinations. If the number produced is exactly equal to the number required, no slack destination is needed.

Step 2. Develop an initial solution. After the initial tableau, the next step is to find a better solution that satisfies all of the constraints. The initial solution can be arrived at in a variety of ways. The northeast corner rule is a logical, systematic procedure for determining the initial tableau.

Using the northeast corner rule, begin in the upper left-hand corner of the tableau and assign quantities to the locations until the destination requirement and source capacity of column A and row 1 is utilized. Then move to the next row or column and assign quantities until the requirements are met. The rim numbers are the key. They must be met before moving to the next column. Continue in this manner throughout the tableau. Check the constraints to be sure all sources are used and requirements met.

In our example, 80 is assigned to 1-A. This fulfills the requirements of destination A; it leaves 170 units from factory 1 to be distributed to B. Destination B requires an additional 15 units. Enter 15 in 2-B.

Row 1 has been satisfied; Columns A and B are complete. Continue the process throughout the tableau to obtain the resulting tableau.

	A	B	C	D	S	
1	3.50 / 80	3.20 / 170	4.20	3.70	0	250
2	2.80	3.90 / 15	3.20 / 110	3.35	0	125
3	2.20	4.20	3.70 / 80	3.00 / 100	0 / 30	210
	80	185	190	100	30	585

This is the initial solution using the northeast corner rule.

Notice there are unused squares in the tableau. For any solution, the number of used squares must equal the number of rim requirements minus 1. For this problem, the number of used squares is 7. The number of rim requirements is 8.

$$7 = 8 - 1$$

If this rule is not satisfied, additional techniques are required to solve the problem. An imaginary tiny quantity, shown as Δ is used to fill one square. The source and destination quantities are unaffected. Δ does not appear in the final solution.

The objective of the problem was to minimize shipping cost. The cost of the initial solution must be computed. For each occupied square, the number of units is multiplied by the shipping cost.

A-1	80 × 3.50 =	$ 280.00
B-1	170 × 3.20 =	$ 544.00
B-2	15 × 3.90 =	$ 58.50
C-2	110 × 3.20 =	$ 352.00
C-3	80 × 3.70 =	$ 296.00
D-3	100 × 3.00 =	$ 300.00
S-3	30 × 0 =	$ 0.00
Total		$1,830.50

The next step is to determine if the initial solution is the best solution. To determine if a better solution is possible, each unused square is evaluated. The process involves moving 1 unit. The result of the move is called the improvement index. Start at any empty square. Horizontal and vertical moves are made to used squares until the return to the starting point has been realized. The route may skip over unused squares and corners can occur only at used squares. There is only one path for each unused square.

A-2 is unused. The path for A-2 is $A\text{-}1 \to B\text{-}1 \to B\text{-}2 \to A\text{-}2$. This path forms a closed path with one empty square. The remaining squares are filled. Beginning with a plus sign and the cost associated with A-2, a minus sign and the cost associated with A-1, assign alternating plus and minus signs to the costs of the squares involved in the closed path. The improvement index of A-2 is

$$+2.80 - 3.50 + 3.20 - 3.90 = -1.40$$

A-3 is unused. The path is $A\text{-}3 - A\text{-}1 \to B\text{-}1 \to B\text{-}2 \to C\text{-}2 \to C\text{-}3 \to A\text{-}3$. The improvement index of A-3 is

$$+2.20 - 3.50 + 3.20 - 3.90 + 3.20 - 3.70 = -2.50$$

B-3 is unused. The path is $B\text{-}3 \to B\text{-}2 \to C\text{-}2 \to C\text{-}3 \to B\text{-}3$. The improvement index of B-3 is

$$+4.20 - 3.90 + 3.20 - 3.70 = -0.20$$

C-1 is unused. The path is $C\text{-}1 \to C\text{-}2 \to B\text{-}2 \to B\text{-}1 \to C\text{-}1$. The improvement index of B-3 is

$$+4.20 - 3.20 + 3.90 - 3.20 = +1.70$$

D-1 is unused. The path is D-1 $\rightarrow$ D-3 $\rightarrow$ C-3 $\rightarrow$ C-2 $\rightarrow$ B-2 $\rightarrow$ B-1 $\rightarrow$ D-1. The improvement index for $D = 1$ is

$$+3.70 - 3.00 + 3.70 - 3.20 + 3.90 - 3.20 = +1.90$$

S-1 is unused. The path is S-1 $\rightarrow$ S-3 $\rightarrow$ C-3 $\rightarrow$ C-2 $\rightarrow$ B-2 $\rightarrow$ B-1 $\rightarrow$ S-1. The improvement index for S-1 is

$$+0 - 0 + 3.70 - 3.20 + 3.90 - 3.20 = +1.20$$

S-2 is unused. The path is S-2 $\rightarrow$ S-3 $\rightarrow$ C-3 $\rightarrow$ C-2 $\rightarrow$ S-2. The improvement index of S-2 is

$$+0 - 0 + 3.70 - 3.20 = +0.50$$

The improvement index is the cost change of moving one unit into the unused square. Because the objective is to minimize cost, negative improvement index values indicate where improvement to the initial solution can be made. If all improvement indexes are positive, the optimal solution has been found. If negative values exist for any improvement index, a lower transportation cost can be attained.

Squares A-2, A-3, and B-3 have negative indexes. A new solution must be developed. A-3 has the most negative improvement index. Retrace the closed path for A-3. The most units that can be moved in this closed path is 15 (the smallest number of units in a subtract square). Therefore 15 is moved to A-3. Subtract 15 from A-1, add 15 to B-1, subtract 15 from B-2, add 15 to C-2, and subtract 15 from C-3. Notice the rim requirements are still fulfilled and the cost has been lowered by $15(2.50) = \$37.50$. The closed path originating at A-2 has a zero cell; no product can be moved. Finally, because one of the cells in B-3 contains a 0, none can be moved.

	A	B	C	D	S	
	3.50	3.20	4.20	3.70	0	
1	65	185				250
	2.80	3.90	3.20	3.35	0	
2		0	125			125
	2.20	4.20	3.70	3.00	0	
3	15		65	100	30	210
	80	185	190	100	30	585

This is the second solution.

The total cost of the second solution can now be computed.

$$A\text{-}1 \qquad 65 \times 3.50 = \$\ \ 227.50$$
$$B\text{-}1 \qquad 185 \times 3.20 = \quad \$592.00$$
$$C\text{-}2 \qquad 125 \times 3.20 = \quad \$400.00$$
$$A\text{-}3 \qquad 15 \times 2.20 = \quad \$\ 33.00$$
$$C\text{-}3 \qquad 65 \times 3.70 = \quad \$240.50$$
$$D\text{-}3 \qquad 100 \times 3.00 = \quad \$300.00$$
$$S\text{-}3 \qquad 30 \times 0 \quad = \quad \underline{\$\ \ 0.00}$$
$$\text{Total} \qquad\qquad\qquad\quad \$1{,}793.00$$

All unused squares must be reevaluated to determine their improvement index.

$$C\text{-}1 \qquad +4.20 - 3.70 + 2.20 - 3.50 = -0.80$$
$$D\text{-}1 \qquad +3.70 - 3.00 + 2.20 - 3.50 = -0.60$$
$$S\text{-}1 \qquad +0 - 0 + 2.20 - 3.50 = -1.30$$
$$A\text{-}2 \qquad +2.80 - 3.20 + 3.70 - 2.20 = +0.10$$
$$B\text{-}2 \qquad +3.90 - 3.20 + 3.70 - 2.20 + 3.50 - 3.20 = +2.50$$
$$D\text{-}2 \qquad +3.35 - 3.00 + 3.70 - 3.20 = +0.85$$
$$S\text{-}2 \qquad 0 - 0 + 3.70 - 3.20 = +0.50$$
$$B\text{-}3 \qquad +4.20 - 2.20 + 3.50 - 3.20 = +2.30$$

The second solution is altered because of negative indexes in C-1, D-1, and S-1. C-1 gets 35 units and S-1 gets 30 units, A-3 gets 80, C-3 decreases to 30, and S-3 goes to 0.

	A	B	C	D	S	
	3.50	3.20	4.20	3.70	0	
1	0	185	35		30	240
	2.80	3.90	3.20	3.35	0	
2			125			125
	2.20	4.20	3.70	3.00	0	
3	80		30	100		210
	80	185	190	100	30	585

This is a better solution.

The total cost of transportation for this solution is

B-1	$185 \times 3.20 =$	$ 592
C-1	$35 \times 4.20 =$	147
S-1		0
C-2	$125 \times 3.20 =$	400
A-3	$80 \times 2.20 =$	176
C-3	$30 \times 3.70 =$	111
D-3	$100 \times 3.00 =$	300
Total		$1,726

The improvement indexes are checked again and they are all nonnegative. Therefore this solution is the optimal solution. The minimum transportation cost for this problem is $1,726.

Assignment Problem

The assignment problem involves the task of assigning a number of jobs to operators. Any of the operators could handle the job but at different rates of performance. The assignment problem is solved by modifying the transportation problem solution technique.

The assignment method matches tasks and facilities so as to optimize the given measure of effectiveness. A simple problem will be used to demonstrate the procedure for the assignment method.

A customizing company has three jobs to accomplish. There are three different work stations where these jobs can be accomplished but available tools and expertise give different time estimates (in hours) for each of the work stations.

		Job	
Work Station	*1*	*2*	*3*
A	12	25	32
B	20	20	28
C	26	24	40

The assignments are made to minimize the time needed to complete the job. The number of rows must equal the number of jobs. If this is not the case, slack variables must be used to equalize the number of jobs and work stations. There is only one assignment in a given row or column in the optimal solution.

There are basically three steps in solving an assignment problem.

First, subtract the lowest entry in each column from every entry in the column. Column 1 has entries 12, 20, and 26. Because 12 is the lowest, subtract 12 from each entry. The new column 1 is 0, 8, 14. Do the same for each column. The new array is

	Job		
Work Station	*1*	*2*	*3*
A	0	5	4
B	8	0	0
C	14	4	12

This is the job opportunity–cost array.

It is necessary to consider work-station costs as well as job opportunity versus cost. Subtract the lowest row entry from the elements of the job opportunity–cost array. Subtract the smallest row entry from each entry in the array. Subtract 0 from row 1, subtract 0 from row 2, and 4 from row 3.

	Job		
Work Station	*1*	*2*	*3*
A	0	5	4
B	8	0	0
C	10	0	8

This is the total opportunity–cost matrix.

Second, determine if an optimal assignment can be made. Straight lines are drawn (either vertically or horizontally) through the total opportunity–cost matrix to cover all zero entries. Use the minimum number of lines possible. If the number of lines required to cover the zero entries is equal to the number of columns in the array, an optimal assignment can be made. To determine the optimal assignments:

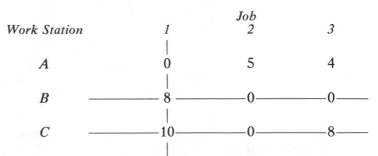

The minimum number of lines needed to cover the zero entries is 3. There is an optimal solution because $3 = 3$.

The assignment for this problem is

Station A does job 1.

Station B can do either job 2 or job 3 but is assigned job 3.

Station C does job 2; job 1 and job 3 are too costly.

Finally, to revise the total opportunity–cost array if no solution is found, select the smallest number in the matrix not covered by straight lines. Subtract this number from all entries not covered by lines and add this same number to the numbers at the intersection of lines. Take the following array that does not have an initial solution.

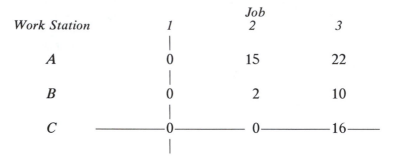

		Job	
Work Station	1	2	3
A	0	15	22
B	0	2	10
C	0	0	16

This array can have the zero entries covered by two lines, $2 < 3$; no solution. The smallest number not covered in the matrix is 2. The number 2 is subtracted from 15, 2, 22, 10 and 16 and added to the entry 0 at C-1, the intersection of the two lines covering the zero entries.

The revised matrix is

		Job	
Work Station	1	2	3
A	0	13	20
B	0	0	8
C	2	0	14

The zero in the revised matrix can be covered by two vertical lines so no optimal solution exists yet.

Do another revision. 8 is the smallest uncovered entry.

Work Station	1	Job 2	3
A	0	13	12
B	0	0	0
C	2	0	6

It now takes three lines to cover the zeros. An optimal solution has been achieved. The solution is

Work station B gets job 3.

Work station A gets job 1.

Work station C gets job 2.

Returning to the original information permits an analysis of total assignment time according to the assignments determined by the optimal solution.

SECTION 5 EXERCISES

1. Given the following matrix for a transportation problem, find the initial solution to the problem.

Source	Destination A	B	C	S	Capacity
1	1.75	1.65	1.20		300
2	2.10	1.85	2.00		250
3	2.30	1.50	1.90		350
	400	250	200	50	900

2. Given the following matrix for a transportation problem, find the initial solution to the problem.

Source	A	B	C	S	Capacity
	Destination				
1	0.95	0.85	1.05		1,200
2	0.65	0.80	0.85		1,000
3	0.80	0.95	0.70		1,100
	1,500	1,200	500	100	3,300

3. Evaluate each of the empty cells in the initial solution of exercise 1.

4. Evaluate each of the empty cells in the initial solution of exercise 2.

5. Find the optimal solution to exercise 1.

6. Find the optimal solution to exercise 2.

7. Comfortable Chair Corporation has three plants where recliner chairs are manufactured. There are four destination points for the chairs, Chicago, Atlanta, Dallas, and San Francisco. The following table indicates the capacities and requirements for each of the sources and destinations.

Capacity	Source	Destination	Requirement
900	Factory 1	Chicago	1,200
1,800	Factory 2	Atlanta	1,000
1,400	Factory 3	Dallas	700
		San Francisco	900
4,100	chairs available		3,800 chairs needed

The cost of shipping 1 chair from each of the factories to each of the destinations is as follows.

Source	C	A	D	SF
	Destination			
1	3.20	2.80	4.05	5.50
2	4.20	3.90	2.45	3.20
3	5.00	3.40	2.10	3.80

Determine the minimum cost transportation for the 3,800 chairs.

8. Quick Microwave Company has four factories manufacturing the basic unit with five destination points of distributions. The following table shows the production capacity and the distribution requirements.

Capacity	Source	Destination	Requirement
1,900	Factory 1	Center A	1,500
2,000	Factory 2	Center B	1,200
1,750	Factory 3	Center C	1,400
2,400	Factory 4	Center D	1,800
		Center E	1,600
8,050			7,500

The transportation costs from the factories to the destinations is shown in the following table.

	Destination				
Source	A	B	C	D	E
1	2.30	2.50	3.20	2.90	3.50
2	3.10	2.90	2.40	2.75	2.80
3	3.50	3.00	2.80	1.90	2.20
4	1.90	4.10	3.30	3.50	2.50

Determine the minimum transportation costs for delivering 7,500 microwave ovens to the required destinations.

9. An assembly plant has three jobs to accomplish. There are three work stations available where these jobs can be done. Time studies give the following information on the length of time (in minutes) required for each of the jobs at each of the work stations.

	Job		
Work Station	1	2	3
A	43	39	50
B	40	42	46
C	39	44	52

Determine the job assignments made to minimize the time needed to complete the jobs.

10. A repair garage has four all purpose mechanics who handle different jobs and relatively accurate time requirements for each mechanic have been established.

			Job	
Mechanic	*1*	*2*	*3*	*4*
A	75	110	160	220
B	90	125	150	210
C	80	130	175	225
D	95	115	170	200

Determine the job assignments made to minimize the time required to complete the jobs.

Answers to Odd-Numbered Exercises

1.

	A	*B*	*C*	*S*	
1	300				300
2	100	150			250
3		100	200	50	350
	400	250	200	50	900

3. *B*-1, $+0.15$. *C*-1, -0.70. *S*-1, 0. *C*-2, -0.25. *S*-2, $+0.35$. *A*-3, $+0.55$.

5.

	A	*B*	*C*	*S*	
1	100		200		300
2	250				250
3	50	250		50	350
	400	250	200	50	900

Total transportation cost, $1,430.

7.

	C	*A*	*D*	*SF*	*S*	
1	600	300				900
2	600		300	900		1,800
3		700	400		300	1,400
	1,200	1,000	700	900	300	4,100

Total transportation cost, $12,115.

9. Assign job 2 to *A*, job 3 to *B*, and job 1 to *C*. Total time, 124 minutes.

REVIEW EXERCISES

1. Lemonade and Lemon Surprise are sold at a neighborhood stand. The ingredients per quart are as follows.

Lemonade	*Lemon Surprise*
1 cup sugar	$1/2$ cup sugar
2 lemons	3 lemons
1 quart water	1 quart ginger ale

There are only 10 cups of sugar, 34 lemons, and 8 quarts of ginger ale. The profit for each quart of lemonade is $0.35 and for each quart of Lemon Surprise, $0.50. Draw the graph for the constraints and determine the maximum profit that can be made using the results of the graph.

2. A public accounting firm wants to maximize the revenue from work completed in a week in their office for the month of March. There are 240 staff hours available, and 60 review hours available. Audits require 8 hours of staff time and 2 hours of review time and contribute $200 in revenue. Tax returns require 2 hours of staff time and 1.5 hour of review time and contribute $80 in revenue. Draw the graphs of the constraints and determine the strategy for the public accounting firm to maximize profits. (During March the number of audits and tax returns are without limit.)

3. Solve exercise 1 using the simplex method.

4. Solve exercise 2 using the simplex method.

5. ABC Manufacturing Company is limited in warehouse space, amount in accounts receivable, and amount in the cash outflow account. ABC Manufacturing Company has three products: A, B, and C. Product A requires 25 square feet of warehouse space, $1,500 in accounts receivable, and $800 in cash outflow. Product B requires 40 square feet of warehouse space, $1,000 in accounts receivable, and $1,200 in cash outflow. Product C requires 30 square feet of warehouse space, $1,500 in accounts receivable, and $900 in cash outflow. The maximum amount of warehouse space is 235,000, the maximum amount of the accounts receivable is $250,000, and the maximum amount for the cash outflow is $175,000. The profit for Product A is $150, product B is $225, and product C is $180. Find the strategy of production that maximizes the profit of ABC Company.

6. A review of past records indicates that Watertight Company can sell no more than 36,000 sleeping bags, 10,000 full-sized tents, and 20,000 pup tents per month. It has two production lines. The first assembly line can produce 5,000 sleeping bags, 1,000 full-sized tents, and 3,000 pup tents per day. The second assembly line can produce 3,000 sleeping bags, 1,000 full-sized tents, and 1,000 pup tents per day. The board has decided to produce no more than they know they can sell in a month. How many days

per month should each of the two assembly lines work on manufacturing these three products? Watertight Company wishes to maximize profits. The profit on each sleeping bag is $5, on each full sized tent $14, and on each pup tent $10. What assembly schedule should be used to satisfy the constraints and maximize the profits?

7. A company knows that they have to produce at least 25,000 gears and 14,500 axles. They have two machines that they can use to fill these orders. The first costs $2,000 per hour to operate and can produce 1,000 gears and 300 axles per hour. The second costs $2,400 per hour to operate and can produce 600 gears and 600 axles per hour. How many hours should each machine operate and what is the minimum cost?

8. An appliance company has a contract to supply at least 1,000,000 trash compactors and at least 1,000,000 garbage disposals to a mobile-home manufacturer. The company has two assembly lines to use to fill this particular order. Line 1 can produce 1,000 trash compactors and 500 garbage disposals in an hour. Line 2 can produce 750 trash compactors and 1,000 garbage disposals in an hour. It costs $12,000 per hour to operate line 1 and $15,000 per hour to operate line 2. How many hours should each line operate to minimize production costs? What is the minimum production cost?

9. Eastline Air Transport Company needs to procure fuel for its fleet of planes. The planes are operated out of four different bases. Base 1 requires 9,000 gallons daily, base 2 requires 7,500 gallons daily, base 3 requires 9,500 gallons daily, and base 4 requires 8,500 gallons daily. Three suppliers have submitted bids to furnish the fuel. Supplier A can supply 12,000 gallons daily, supplier B can supply 15,000 gallons daily, and supplier C can supply 13,000 gallons daily. The delivered, per gallon, price (in cents) from each of the suppliers to each of the bases is set forth in the following table.

	\multicolumn{4}{c}{Base}
	1	2	3	4
A	52	43	57	48
B	48	47	53	54
C	58	52	49	50

What quantities of fuel should be obtained from each of the suppliers for each of the bases?

10. A road construction company has to move four pieces of heavy machinery from a completed job to a new job. The distance (in miles) between the old locations and the new locations are given in the following matrix.

	N_1	N_2	N_3	N_4
O_1	25	37	17	42
O_2	22	29	34	45
O_3	42	32	18	26
O_4	21	33	28	32

Any equipment can be used at any site. Determine the plan for moving the equipment that will minimize the total distance involved in the move.

Answers to Review

1.   **2.**

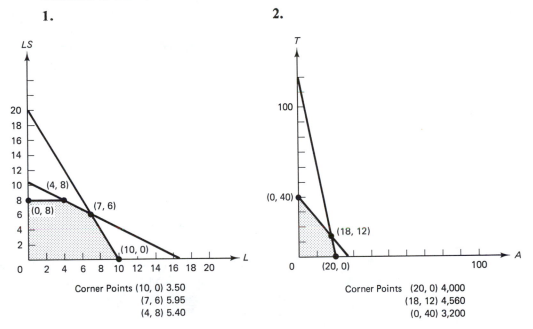

Corner Points (10, 0) 3.50
(7, 6) 5.95
(4, 8) 5.40

Corner Points (20, 0) 4,000
(18, 12) 4,560
(0, 40) 3,200

3. 6.5 quarts of lemonade and 7 Lemon Surprise. Profit, $5.78.

4. 17 tax returns and 17 audits. Profit, $4,793.

5. 41.6 B and 139 C. Profit, $34,375.

6. $A = 6$ hours and $B = 2$ hours. Profit, $11,400.

7. $A = 15$ hours and $B = 16\frac{2}{3}$ hours. Cost, $70,000.

8. Line 1, 400. Line 2, 800. Cost, $16,800,000.

9. A-2, 7,500. A-4, 4,500. B-1, 9,000. B-3, 6,000. C-3, 3,500. C-4, 4,000. C-S, 5,500. Total cost, $16,600.

10. N_1 to 4, N_2 to 2, N_3 to 1, and N_4 to 3 for 93 miles.

Appendix

MATHEMATICAL TABLES

Table 1   The Number of Each Day of the Year   540

Table 2   Compound Amount and Annuity Values   541

Table 3   Area Under Standard Normal Curve   562

Table 1   The Number of Each Day of the Year

Day of Month	January	February	March	April	May	June	July	August	September	October	November	December	Day of Month
1	1	32	60	91	121	152	182	213	244	274	305	335	1
2	2	33	61	92	122	153	183	214	245	275	306	336	2
3	3	34	62	93	123	154	184	215	246	276	307	337	3
4	4	35	63	94	124	155	185	216	247	277	308	338	4
5	5	36	64	95	125	156	186	217	248	278	309	339	5
6	6	37	65	96	126	157	187	218	249	279	310	340	6
7	7	38	66	97	127	158	188	219	250	280	311	341	7
8	8	39	67	98	128	159	189	220	251	281	312	342	8
9	9	40	68	99	129	160	190	221	252	282	313	343	9
10	10	41	69	100	130	161	191	222	253	283	314	344	10
11	11	42	70	101	131	162	192	223	254	284	315	345	11
12	12	43	71	102	132	163	193	224	255	285	316	346	12
13	13	44	72	103	133	164	194	225	256	286	317	347	13
14	14	45	73	104	134	165	195	226	257	287	318	348	14
15	15	46	74	105	135	166	196	227	258	288	319	349	15
16	16	47	75	106	136	167	197	228	259	289	320	350	16
17	17	48	76	107	137	168	198	229	260	290	321	351	17
18	18	49	77	108	138	169	199	230	261	291	322	352	18
19	19	50	78	109	139	170	200	231	262	292	323	353	19
20	20	51	79	110	140	171	201	232	263	293	324	354	20
21	21	52	80	111	141	172	202	233	264	294	325	355	21
22	22	53	81	112	142	173	203	234	265	295	326	356	22
23	23	54	82	113	143	174	204	235	266	296	327	357	23
24	24	55	83	114	144	175	205	236	267	297	328	358	24
25	25	56	84	115	145	176	206	237	268	298	329	359	25
26	26	57	85	116	146	177	207	238	269	299	330	360	26
27	27	58	86	117	147	178	208	239	270	300	331	361	27
28	28	59	87	118	148	179	209	240	271	301	332	362	28
29	29		88	119	149	180	210	241	272	302	333	363	29
30	30		89	120	150	181	211	242	273	303	334	364	30
31	31		90		151		212	243		304		365	31

For leap years, add 1 to each number after February 28.

Table 2   Compound Amounts and Values for Annuity Quantities: Rate ½%, 0.005 per period

Period	Compound Amount	Amount of Annuity	Present Value	Present Value of Future $1 Payments
1	1.005 000 0000	1.000 000 0000	0.995 024 8756	0.995 024 8756
2	1.010 025 0000	2.005 000 0000	0.990 074 5031	1.985 099 3787
3	1.015 075 1250	3.015 025 0000	0.985 148 7593	2.970 248 1380
4	1.020 150 5006	4.030 100 1250	0.980 247 5217	3.950 495 6597
5	1.025 251 2531	5.050 250 6256	0.975 370 6684	4.925 866 3281
6	1.030 377 5094	6.075 501 8788	0.970 518 0780	5.896 384 4061
7	1.035 529 3969	7.105 879 3881	0.965 689 6298	6.862 074 0359
8	1.040 707 0439	8.141 408 7851	0.960 885 2038	7.822 959 2397
9	1.045 910 5791	9.182 115 8290	0.956 104 6804	8.779 063 9201
10	1.051 140 1320	10.228 026 4082	0.951 347 9407	9.730 411 8608
11	1.056 395 8327	11.279 166 5402	0.946 614 8664	10.677 026 7272
12	1.061 677 8119	12.335 562 3729	0.941 905 3397	11.618 932 0668
13	1.066 986 2009	13.397 240 1848	0.937 219 2434	12.556 151 3103
14	1.072 321 1319	14.464 226 3857	0.932 556 4611	13.488 707 7714
15	1.077 682 7376	15.536 547 5176	0.927 916 8768	14.416 624 6482
16	1.083 071 1513	16.614 230 2552	0.923 300 3749	15.339 925 0231
17	1.088 486 5070	17.697 301 4065	0.918 706 8407	16.258 631 8637
18	1.093 928 9396	18.785 787 9135	0.914 136 1599	17.172 768 0236
19	1.099 398 5843	19.879 716 8531	0.909 588 2188	18.082 356 2424
20	1.104 895 5772	20.979 115 4373	0.905 062 9043	18.987 419 1467
21	1.110 420 0551	22.084 011 0145	0.900 560 1037	19.887 979 2504
22	1.115 972 1553	23.194 431 0696	0.896 079 7052	20.784 058 9556
23	1.121.552 0161	24.310 403 2250	0.891 621 5972	21.675 680 5529
24	1.127 159 7762	25.431 955 2411	0.887 185 6689	22.562 866 2218
25	1.132 795 5751	26.559 115 0173	0.882 771 8098	23.445 638 0316
26	1.138 459 5530	27.691 910 5924	0.878 379 9103	24.324 017 9419
27	1.144 151 8507	28.830 370 1453	0.874 009 8610	25.198 027 8029
28	1.149 872 6100	29.974 521 9961	0.869 661 5532	26.067 689 3561
29	1.155 621 9730	31.124 394 6060	0.865 334 8788	26.933 024 2349
30	1.161 400 0829	32.280 016 5791	0.861 029 7302	27.794 053 9651
31	1.167 207 0833	33.441 416 6620	0.856 746 0002	28.650 799 9653
32	1.173 043 1187	34.608 623 7453	0.852 483 5823	29.503 283 5475
33	1.178 908 3343	35.781 666 8640	0.848 242 3704	30.351 525 9179
34	1.184 802 8760	36.960 575 1983	0.844 022 2591	31.195 548 1771
35	1.190 726 8904	38.145 378 0743	0.839 823 1434	32.035 371 3205
36	1.196 680 5248	39.336 104 9647	0.835 644 9188	32.871 016 2393
37	1.202 663 9274	40.532 785 4895	0.831 487 4814	33.702 503 7207
38	1.208 677 2471	41.735 449 4170	0.827 350 7278	34.529 854 4484
39	1.214 720 6333	42.944 126 6640	0.823 234 5550	35.353 089 0034
40	1.220 794 2365	44.158 847 2974	0.819 138 8607	36.172 227 8641
41	1.226 898 2077	45.379 641 5338	0.815 063 5430	36.987 291 4070
42	1.233 032 6987	46.606 539 7415	0.811 008 5005	37.798 299 9075
43	1.239 197 8622	47.839 572 4402	0.806 973 6323	38.605 273 5398
44	1.245 393 8515	49.078 770 3024	0.802 958 8381	39.408 232 3779
45	1.251 620 8208	50.324 164 1539	0.798 964 0180	40.207 196 3959
46	1.257 878 9249	51.575 784 9747	0.794 989 0727	41.002 185 4686
47	1.264 168 3195	52.833 663 8996	0.791 033 9031	41.793 219 3717
48	1.270 489 1611	54.097 832 2191	0.787 098 4111	42.580 317 7828
49	1.276 841 6069	55.368 321 3802	0.783 182 4986	43.363 500 2814
50	1.283 225 8149	56.645 162 9871	0.779 286 0683	44.142 786 3497
51	1.289 641 9440	57.928 388 8020	0.775 409 0231	44.918 195 3728
52	1.296 090 1537	59.218 030 7460	0.771 551 2668	45.689 746 6396
53	1.302 570 6045	60.514 120 8997	0.767 712 7033	46.457 459 3429
54	1.309 083 4575	61.816 691 5042	0.763 893 2371	47.221 352 5800
55	1.315 628 8748	63.125 774 9618	0.760 092 7732	47.981 445 3532
56	1.322 207 0192	64.441 403 8366	0.756 311 2171	48.737 756 5704
57	1.328 818 0543	65.763 610 8558	0.752 548 4748	49.490 305 0452
58	1.335 462 1446	67.092 428 9100	0.748 804 4525	50.239 109 4977
59	1.342 139 4553	68.427 891 0546	0.745 079 0572	50.984 188 5549
60	1.348 850 1525	69.770 030 5099	0.741 372 1962	51.725 560 7511

Table 2 Compound Amounts and Values for Annuity Quantities: Rate 7/12%, 0.0058333 per period

Period	Compound Amount	Amount of Annuity	Present Value	Present Value of Future $1 Payments
1	1.005 833 3333	1.000 000 0000	0.994 200 4971	0.994 200 4971
2	1.011 700 6944	2.005 833 3333	0.988 434 6284	1.982 635 1255
3	1.017 602 2818	3.017 534 0278	0.982 702 1989	2.965 337 3245
4	1.023 538 2951	4.035 136 3096	0.977 003 0147	3.942 340 3392
5	1.029 508 9352	5.058 674 6047	0.971 336 8829	4.913 677 2220
6	1.035 514 4040	6.088 183 5399	0.965 703 6118	5.879 380 8338
7	1.041 554 9047	7.123 697 9439	0.960 103 0109	6.839 483 8447
8	1.047 630 6416	8.165 252 8486	0.954 534 8907	7.794 018 7355
9	1.053 741 8204	9.212 883 4902	0.948 999 0628	8.743 017 7983
10	1.059 888 6476	10.266 625 3106	0.943 495 3400	9.686 513 1383
11	1.066 071 3314	11.326 513 9582	0.938 023 5361	10.624 536 6744
12	1.072 290 0809	12.392 585 2896	0.932 583 4658	11.557 120 1402
13	1.078 545 1063	13.464 875 3705	0.927 174 9453	12.484 295 0856
14	1.084 836 6194	14.543 420 4768	0.921 797 7916	13.406 092 8771
15	1.091 164 8331	15.628 257 0963	0.916 451 8226	14.322 544 6997
16	1.097 529 9613	16.719 421 9293	0.911 136 8576	15.233 681 5573
17	1.103 932 2194	17.816 951 8906	0.905 852 7167	16.139 534 2740
18	1.110 371 8240	18.920 884 1100	0.900 599 2213	17.040 133 4953
19	1.116 848 9929	20.031 255 9339	0.895 376 1935	17.935 509 6888
20	1.123 363 9454	21.148 104 9269	0.890 183 4567	18.825 693 1454
21	1.129 916 9018	22.271 468 8723	0.885 020 8351	19.710 713 9805
22	1.136 508 0837	23.401 385 7740	0.879 888 1542	20.590 602 1348
23	1.143 137 7142	24.537 893 8577	0.874 785 2403	21.465 387 3751
24	1.149 806 0175	25.681 031 5719	0.869 711 9208	22.335 099 2958
25	1.156 513 2193	26.830 837 5894	0.864 668 0240	23.199 767 3198
26	1.163 259 5464	27.987 350 8087	0.859 653 3793	24.059 420 6991
27	1.170 045 2271	29.150 610 3550	0.854 667 8170	24.914 088 5161
28	1.176 870 4909	30.320 655 5821	0.849 711 1685	25.763 799 6846
29	1.183 735 5688	31.497 526 0730	0.844 783 2661	26.608 582 9507
30	1.190 640 6929	32.681 261 6418	0.839 883 9431	27.448 466 8938
31	1.197 586 0970	33.871 902 3347	0.835 013 0338	28.283 479 9276
32	1.204 572 0159	35.069 488 4316	0.830 170 3732	29.113 650 3008
33	1.211 598 6859	36.274 060 4475	0.825 355 7978	29.939 006 0986
34	1.218 666 3449	37.485 659 1334	0.820 569 1444	30.759 575 2430
35	1.225 775 2320	38.704 325 4784	0.815 810 2513	31.575 385 4943
36	1.232 925 5875	39.930 100 7103	0.811 078 9574	32.386 464 4516
37	1.240 117 6534	41.163 026 2978	0.806 375 1026	33.192 839 5542
38	1.247 351 6730	42.403 143 9512	0.801 698 5279	33.994 538 0821
39	1.254 627 8911	43.650 495 6243	0.797 049 0749	34.791 587 1570
40	1.261 946 5538	44.905 123 5154	0.792 426 5865	35.584 013 7435
41	1.269 307 9087	46.167 070 0692	0.787 830 9062	36.371 844 6497
42	1.276 712 2049	47.436 377 9780	0.783 261 8786	37.155 106 5283
43	1.284 159 6927	48.713 090 1829	0.778 719 3490	37.933 825 8773
44	1.291 650 6243	49.997 249 8756	0.774 203 1639	38.708 029 0413
45	1.299 185 2529	51.288 900 4999	0.769 713 1704	39.477 742 2117
46	1.306 763 8336	52.588 085 7528	0.765 249 2167	40.242 991 4284
47	1.314 386 6226	53.894 849 5863	0.760 811 1516	41.003 802 5800
48	1.322 053 8779	55.209 236 2089	0.756 398 8251	41.760 201 4051
49	1.329 765 8588	56.531 290 0868	0.752 012 0880	42.512 213 4931
50	1.337 522 8263	57.861 055 9456	0.747 650 7917	43.259 864 2848
51	1.345 325 0428	59.198 578 7720	0.743 314 7887	44.003 179 0735
52	1.353 172 7723	60.543 903 8148	0.739 003 9325	44.742 183 0060
53	1.361 066 2801	61.897 076 5871	0.734 718 0770	45.476 901 0830
54	1.369 005 8334	63.258 142 8672	0.730 457 0774	46.207 358 1604
55	1.376 991 7008	64.627 148 7006	0.726 220 7895	46.933 578 9498
56	1.385 024 1523	66.004 140 4013	0.722 009 0699	47.655 588 0197
57	1.393 103 4599	67.389 164 5537	0.717 821 7762	48.373 409 7959
58	1.401 229 8967	68.782 268 0136	0.713 658 7667	49.087 068 5626
59	1.409 403 7378	70.183 497 9103	0.709 519 9006	49.796 588 4633
60	1.417 625 2596	71.592 901 6481	0.705 405 0379	50.501 993 5012

542

Table 2 Compound Amounts and Values for Annuity Quantities: Rate ⅔%, 0.00666666 per period

Period	Compound Amount	Amount of Annuity	Present Value	Present Value of Future $1 Payments
1	1.006 666 6667	1.000 000 0000	0.993 377 4834	0.993 377 4834
2	1.013 377 7778	2.006 666 6667	0.986 798 8246	1.980 176 3081
3	1.020 133 6296	3.020 044 4444	0.980 263 7331	2.960 440 0411
4	1.026 934 5205	4.040 178 0741	0.973 771 9203	3.934 211 9614
5	1.033 780 7506	5.067 112 5946	0.967 323 0996	4.901 535 0610
6	1.040 672 6223	6.100 893 3452	0.960 916 9864	5.862 452 0473
7	1.047 610 4398	7.141 565 9675	0.954 553 2977	6.817 005 3450
8	1.054 594 5094	8.189 176 4073	0.948 231 7527	7.765 237 0977
9	1.061 625 1394	9.243 770 9167	0.941 952 0722	8.707 189 1699
10	1.068 702 6404	10.305 396 0561	0.935 713 9790	9.642 903 1489
11	1.075 827 3246	11.374 098 6965	0.929 517 1977	10.572 420 3466
12	1.082 999 5068	12.449 926 0211	0.923 361 4547	11.495 781 8013
13	1.090 219 5035	13.532 925 5279	0.917 246 4781	12.413 028 2794
14	1.097 487 6335	14.623 145 0315	0.911 171 9981	13.324 200 2775
15	1.104 804 2178	15.720 632 6650	0.905 137 7465	14.229 338 0240
16	1.112 169 5792	16.825 436 8828	0.899 143 4568	15.128 481 4808
17	1.119 584 0431	17.937 606 4620	0.893 188 8644	16.021 670 3452
18	1.127 047 9367	19.057 190 5051	0.887 273 7063	16.908 944 0515
19	1.134 561 5896	20.184 238 4418	0.881 397 7215	17.790 341 7730
20	1.142 125 3335	21.318 800 0314	0.875 560 6505	18.665 902 4236
21	1.149 739 5024	22.460 925 3649	0.869 762 2356	19.535 664 6592
22	1.157 404 4324	23.610 664 8673	0.864 002 2208	20.399 666 8800
23	1.165 120 4620	24.768 069 2998	0.858 280 3518	21.257 947 2317
24	1.172 887 9317	25.933 189 7618	0.852 596 3759	22.110 543 6077
25	1.180 707 1846	27.106 077 6935	0.846 950 0423	22.957 493 6500
26	1.188 578 5659	28.286 784 8782	0.841 341 1017	23.798 834 7517
27	1.196 502 4230	29.475 363 4440	0.835 769 3063	24.634 604 0580
28	1.204 479 1058	30.671 865 8670	0.830 234 4102	25.464 838 4682
29	1.212 508 9665	31.876 344 9728	0.824 736 1691	26.289 574 6373
30	1.220 592 3596	33.088 853 9392	0.819 274 3402	27.108 848 9774
31	1.228 729 6420	34.309 446 2988	0.813 848 6823	27.922 697 6597
32	1.236 921 1729	35.538 175 9408	0.808 458 9559	28.731 156 6156
33	1.245 167 3141	36.775 097 1138	0.803 104 9231	29.534 261 5387
34	1.253 468 4295	38.020 264 4279	0.797 786 3474	30.332 047 8861
35	1.261 824 8857	39.273 732 8574	0.792 502 9941	31.124 550 8802
36	1.270 237 0516	40.535 557 7431	0.787 254 6299	31.911 805 5101
37	1.278 705 2986	41.805 794 7947	0.782 041 0231	32.693 846 5333
38	1.287 230 0006	43.084 500 0934	0.776 861 9435	33.470 708 4767
39	1.295 811 5340	44.371 730 0940	0.771 717 1624	34.242 425 6392
40	1.304 450 2775	45.667 541 6279	0.766 606 4527	35.009 032 0919
41	1.313 146 6127	46.971 991 9055	0.761 529 5888	35.770 561 6807
42	1.321 900 9235	48.285 138 5182	0.756 486 3465	36.527 048 0272
43	1.330 713 5963	49.607 039 4416	0.751 476 5031	37.278 524 5303
44	1.339 585 0203	50.937 753 0379	0.746 499 8375	38.025 024 3678
45	1.348 515 5871	52.277 338 0581	0.741 556 1300	38.766 580 4978
46	1.357 505 6910	53.625 853 6452	0.736 645 1623	39.503 225 6601
47	1.366 555 7289	54.983 359 3362	0.731 766 7175	40.234 992 3776
48	1.375 666 1004	56.349 915 0651	0.726 920 5803	40.961 912 9579
49	1.384 837 2078	57.725 581 1655	0.722 106 5367	41.684 019 4946
50	1.394 069 4558	59.110 418 3733	0.717 324 3742	42.401 343 8688
51	1.403 363 2522	60.504 487 8291	0.712 573 8817	43.113 917 7505
52	1.412 719 0072	61.907 851 0813	0.707 854 8493	43.821 772 5998
53	1.422 137 1339	63.320 570 0885	0.703 167 0689	44.524 939 6687
54	1.431 618 0481	64.742 707 2224	0.698 510 3333	45.223 450 0020
55	1.441 162 1685	66.174 325 2706	0.693 884 4371	45.917 334 4391
56	1.450 769 9163	67.615 487 4390	0.689 289 1759	46.606 623 6150
57	1.460 441 7157	69.066 257 3553	0.684 724 3469	47.291 347 9619
58	1.470 177 9938	70.526 699 0710	0.680 189 7486	47.971 537 7105
59	1.479 979 1804	71.996 877 0648	0.675 685 1807	48.647 222 8912
60	1.489 845 7083	73.476 856 2452	0.671 210 4444	49.318 433 3356

Table 2 Compound Amounts and Values for Annuity Quantities: Rate ¾%, 0.0075 per period

Period	Compound Amount	Amount of Annuity	Present Value	Present Value of Future $1 Payments
1	1.007 500 0000	1.000 000 0000	0.992 555 8313	0.992 555 8313
2	1.015 056 2500	2.007 500 0000	0.985 167 0782	1.977 722 9094
3	1.022 669 1719	3.022 556 2500	0.977 833 3282	2.955 556 2377
4	1.030 339 1907	4.045 225 4219	0.970 554 1719	3.926 110 4096
5	1.038 066 7346	5.075 564 6125	0.963 329 2029	4.889 439 6125
6	1.045 852 2351	6.113 631 3471	0.956 158 0178	5.845 597 6303
7	1.053 696 1269	7.159 483 5822	0.949 040 2162	6.794 637 8464
8	1.061 598 8478	8.213 179 7091	0.941 975 4006	7.736 613 2471
9	1.069 560 8392	9.274 778 5569	0.934 963 1768	8.671 576 4239
10	1.077 582 5455	10.344 339 3961	0.928 003 1532	9.599 579 5771
11	1.085 664 4146	11.421 921 9416	0.921 094 9411	10.520 674 5182
12	1.093 806 8977	12.507 586 3561	0.914 238 1550	11.434 912 6731
13	1.102 010 4494	13.601 393 2538	0.907 432 4119	12.342 345 0850
14	1.110 275 5278	14.703 403 7032	0.900 677 3319	13.243 022 4169
15	1.118 602 5942	15.813 679 2310	0.893 972 5378	14.136 994 9547
16	1.126 992 1137	16.932 281 8252	0.887 317 6554	15.024 312 6101
17	1.135 444 5545	18.059 273 9389	0.880 712 3131	15.905 024 9232
18	1.143 960 3887	19.194 718 4934	0.874 156 1420	16.779 181 0652
19	1.152 540 0916	20.338 678 8821	0.867 648 7762	17.646 829 8414
20	1.161 184 1423	21.491 218 9738	0.861 189 8523	18.508 019 6937
21	1.169 893 0234	22.652 403 1161	0.854 779 0097	19.362 798 7034
22	1.178 667 2210	23.822 296 1394	0.848 415 8905	20.211 214 5940
23	1.187 507 2252	25.000 963 3605	0.842 100 1395	21.053 314 7335
24	1.196 413 5294	26.188 470 5857	0.835 831 4040	21.889 146 1374
25	1.205 386 6309	27.384 884 1151	0.829 609 3340	22.718 755 4714
26	1.214 427 0306	28.590 270 7459	0.823 433 5821	23.542 189 0535
27	1.223 535 2333	29.804 697 7765	0.817 303 8036	24.359 492 8571
28	1.232 711 7476	31.028 233 0099	0.811 219 6562	25.170 712 5132
29	1.241 957 0857	32.260 944 7574	0.805 180 8001	25.975 893 3134
30	1.251 271 7638	33.502 901 8431	0.799 186 8984	26.775 080 2118
31	1.260 656 3021	34.754 173 6069	0.793 237 6163	27.568 317 8281
32	1.270 111 2243	36.014 829 9090	0.787 332 6216	28.355 650 4497
33	1.279 637 0585	37.284 941 1333	0.781 471 5847	29.137 122 0344
34	1.289 234 3364	38.564 578 1918	0.775 654 1784	29.912 776 2128
35	1.298 903 5940	39.853 812 5282	0.769 880 0778	30.682 656 2907
36	1.308 645 3709	41.152 716 1222	0.764 148 9606	31.446 805 2513
37	1.318 460 2112	42.461 361 4931	0.758 460 5068	32.205 265 7581
38	1.328 348 6628	43.779 821 7043	0.752 814 3988	32.958 080 1569
39	1.338 311 2778	45.108 170 3671	0.747 210 3214	33.705 290 4783
40	1.348 348 6123	46.446 481 6449	0.741 647 9617	34.446 938 4400
41	1.358 461 2269	47.794 830 2572	0.736 127 0091	35.183 065 4492
42	1.368 649 6861	49.153 291 4841	0.730 647 1555	35.913 712 6046
43	1.378 914 5588	50.521 941 1703	0.725 208 0948	36.638 920 6994
44	1.389 256 4180	51.900 855 7290	0.719 809 5233	37.358 730 2227
45	1.399 675 8411	53.290 112 1470	0.714 451 1398	38.073 181 3625
46	1.410 173 4099	54.689 787 9881	0.709 132 6449	38.782 314 0074
47	1.420 749 7105	56.099 961 3980	0.703 853 7419	39.486 167 7493
48	1.431 405 3333	57.520 711 1085	0.698 614 1359	40.184 781 8852
49	1.442 140 8733	58.952 116 4418	0.693 413 5344	40.878 195 4195
50	1.452 956 9299	60.394 257 3151	0.688 251 6470	41.566 447 0665
51	1.463 854 1068	61.847 214 2450	0.683 128 1856	42.249 575 2521
52	1.474 833 0126	63.311 068 3518	0.678 042 8641	42.927 618 1163
53	1.485 894 2602	64.785 901 3645	0.672 995 3986	43.600 613 5149
54	1.497 038 4672	66.271 795 6247	0.667 985 5073	44.268 599 0222
55	1.508 266 2557	67.768 834 0919	0.663 012 9105	44.931 611 9327
56	1.519 578 2526	69.277 100 3476	0.658 077 3305	45.589 689 2633
57	1.530 975 0895	70.796 678 6002	0.653 178 4918	46.242 867 7551
58	1.542 457 4027	72.327 653 6897	0.648 316 1209	46.891 183 8760
59	1.554 025 8332	73.870 111 0923	0.643 489 9463	47.534 673 8224
60	1.565 681 0269	75.424 136 9255	0.638 699 6986	48.173 373 5210

Table 2   Compound Amounts and Values for Annuity Quantities: Rate ⅚%, 0.00833333 per period

Period	Compound Amount	Amount of Annuity	Present Value	Present Value of Future $1 Payments
1	1.008 333 3333	1.000 000 0000	0.991 735 5372	0.991 735 5372
2	1.016 736 1111	2.008 333 3333	0.983 539 3757	1.975 274 9129
3	1.025 208 9120	3.025 069 4444	0.975 410 9511	2.950 685 8640
4	1.033 752 3196	4.050 278 3565	0.967 349 7036	3.918 035 5677
5	1.042 366 9223	5.084 030 6761	0.959 355 0780	4.877 390 6456
6	1.051 053 3133	6.126 397 5984	0.951 426 5236	5.828 817 1692
7	1.059 812 0909	7.177 450 9117	0.943 563 4945	6.772 380 6637
8	1.068 643 8584	8.237 263 0027	0.935 765 4491	7.708 146 1127
9	1.077 549 2238	9.305 906 8610	0.928 031 8503	8.636 177 9630
10	1.086 528 8007	10.383 456 0849	0.920 362 1656	9.556 540 1286
11	1.095 583 2074	11.469 984 8856	0.912 755 8667	10.469 295 9953
12	1.104 713 0674	12.565 568 0930	0.905 212 4298	11.374 508 4251
13	1.113 919 0097	13.670 281 1604	0.897 731 3353	12.272 239 7605
14	1.123 201 6681	14.784 200 1701	0.890 312 0681	13.162 551 8285
15	1.132 561 6820	15.907 401 8382	0.882 954 1171	14.045 505 9457
16	1.141 999 6960	17.039 963 5201	0.875 656 9757	14.921 162 9213
17	1.151 516 3601	18.181 963 2161	0.868 420 1411	15.789 583 0625
18	1.161 112 3298	19.333 479 5763	0.861 243 1152	16.650 826 1777
19	1.170 788 2659	20.494 591 9061	0.854 125 4035	17.504 951 5811
20	1.180 544 8348	21.665 380 1720	0.847 066 5159	18.352 018 0970
21	1.190 382 7084	22.845 925 0067	0.840 065 9661	19.192 084 0631
22	1.200 302 5643	24.036 307 7151	0.833 123 2722	20.025 207 3354
23	1.210 305 0857	25.236 610 2794	0.826 237 9559	20.851 445 2913
24	1.220 390 9614	26.446 915 3651	0.819 409 5430	21.670 854 8343
25	1.230 560 8861	27.667 306 3264	0.812 637 5634	22.483 492 3977
26	1.240 815 5601	28.897 867 2125	0.805 921 5504	23.289 413 9481
27	1.251 155 6898	30.138 682 7726	0.799 261 0418	24.088 674 9898
28	1.261 581 9872	31.389 838 4624	0.792 655 5786	24.881 330 5684
29	1.272 095 1704	32.651 420 4496	0.786 104 7060	25.667 435 2745
30	1.282 695 9635	33.923 515 6200	0.779 607 9729	26.447 043 2474
31	1.293 385 0965	35.206 211 5835	0.773 164 9318	27.220 208 1793
32	1.304 163 3057	36.499 596 6800	0.766 775 1390	27.986 983 3183
33	1.315 031 3332	37.803 759 9857	0.760 438 1544	28.747 421 4727
34	1.325 989 9277	39.118 791 3189	0.754 153 5415	29.501 575 0142
35	1.337 039 8437	40.444 781 2465	0.747 920 8677	30.249 495 8819
36	1.348 181 8424	41.781 821 0903	0.741 739 7035	30.991 235 5853
37	1.359 416 6911	43.130 002 9327	0.735 609 6233	31.726 845 2086
38	1.370 745 1635	44.489 419 6238	0.729 530 2049	32.456 375 4135
39	1.382 168 0399	45.860 164 7873	0.723 501 0296	33.179 876 4431
40	1.393 686 1069	47.242 332 8272	0.717 521 6823	33.897 398 1254
41	1.405 300 1578	48.636 018 9341	0.711 591 7510	34.608 989 8764
42	1.417 010 9924	50.041 319 0919	0.705 710 8275	35.314 700 7039
43	1.428 819 4174	51.458 330 0843	0.699 878 5066	36.014 579 2105
44	1.440 726 2458	52.887 149 5017	0.694 094 3867	36.708 673 5972
45	1.452 732 2979	54.327 875 7475	0.688 358 0694	37.397 031 6666
46	1.464 838 4004	55.780 608 0454	0.682 669 1598	38.079 700 8264
47	1.477 045 3870	57.245 446 4458	0.677 027 2659	38.756 728 0923
48	1.489 354 0986	58.722 491 8329	0.671 431 9992	39.428 160 0915
49	1.501 765 3828	60.211 845 9315	0.665 882 9745	40.094 043 0660
50	1.514 280 0943	61.713 611 3142	0.660 379 8094	40.754 422 8754
51	1.526 899 0951	63.227 891 4085	0.654 922 1250	41.409 345 0003
52	1.539 623 2542	64.754 790 5036	0.649 509 5455	42.058 854 5458
53	1.552 453 4480	66.294 413 7578	0.644 141 6980	42.702 996 2438
54	1.565 390 5600	67.846 867 2058	0.638 818 2129	43.341 814 4566
55	1.578 435 4814	69.412 257 7658	0.633 538 7235	43.975 353 1801
56	1.591 589 1104	70.990 693 2472	0.628 302 8663	44.603 656 0464
57	1.604 852 3530	72.582 282 3576	0.623 110 2806	45.226 766 3270
58	1.618 226 1226	74.187 134 7106	0.617 960 6089	45.844 726 9359
59	1.631 711 3403	75.805 360 8832	0.612 853 4964	46.457 580 4323
60	1.645 308 9348	77.437 072 1734	0.607 788 5915	47.065 369 0238

Table 2 Compound Amounts and Values for Annuity Quantities: Rate 1%, 0.01 per period

Period	Compound Amount	Amount of Annuity	Present Value	Present Value of Future $1 Payments
1	1.010 000 0000	1.000 000 0000	0.990 099 0099	0.990 099 0099
2	1.020 100 0000	2.010 000 0000	0.980 296 0494	1.970 395 0593
3	1.030 301 0000	3.030 100 0000	0.970 590 1479	2.940 985 2072
4	1.040 604 0100	4.060 401 0000	0.960 980 3445	3.901 965 5517
5	1.051 010 0501	5.101 005 0100	0.951 465 6876	4.853 431 2393
6	1.061 520 1506	6.152 015 0601	0.942 045 2353	5.795 476 4746
7	1.072 135 3521	7.213 535 2107	0.932 718 0547	6.728 194 5293
8	1.082 856 7056	8.285 670 5628	0.923 483 2225	7.651 677 7518
9	1.093 685 2727	9.368 527 2684	0.914 339 8242	8.566 017 5760
10	1.104 622 1254	10.462 212 5411	0.905 286 9547	9.471 304 5307
11	1.115 668 3467	11.566 834 6665	0.896 323 7175	10.367 628 2482
12	1.126 825 0301	12.682 503 0132	0.887 449 2253	11.255 077 4735
13	1.138 093 2804	13.809 328 0433	0.878 662 5993	12.133 740 0728
14	1.149 474 2132	14.947 421 3238	0.869 962 9696	13.003 703 0423
15	1.160 968 9554	16.096 895 5370	0.861 349 4748	13.865 052 5172
16	1.172 578 6449	17.257 864 4924	0.852 821 2622	14.717 873 7794
17	1.184 304 4314	18.430 443 1373	0.844 377 4873	15.562 251 2667
18	1.196 147 4757	19.614 747 5687	0.836 017 3142	16.398 268 5809
19	1.208 108 9504	20.810 895 0444	0.827 739 9150	17.226 008 4959
20	1.220 190 0399	22.019 003 9948	0.819 544 4703	18.045 552 9663
21	1.232 391 9403	23.239 194 0347	0.811 430 1687	18.856 983 1349
22	1.244 715 8598	24.471 585 9751	0.803 396 2066	19.660 379 3415
23	1.257 163 0183	25.716 301 8348	0.795 441 7887	20.455 821 1302
24	1.269 734 6485	26.973 464 8532	0.787 566 1274	21.243 387 2576
25	1.282 431 9950	28.243 199 5017	0.779 768 4430	22.023 155 7006
26	1.295 256 3150	29.525 631 4967	0.772 047 9634	22.795 203 6640
27	1.308 208 8781	30.820 887 8117	0.764 403 9241	23.559 607 5881
28	1.321 290 9669	32.129 096 6898	0.756 835 5684	24.316 443 1565
29	1.334 503 8766	33.450 387 6567	0.749 342 1470	25.065 785 3035
30	1.347 848 9153	34.784 891 5333	0.741 922 9178	25.807 708 2213
31	1.361 327 4045	36.132 740 4486	0.734 577 1463	26.542 285 3676
32	1.374 940 6785	37.494 067 8531	0.727 304 1053	27.269 589 4729
33	1.388 690 0853	38.869 008 5316	0.720 103 0745	27.989 692 5474
34	1.402 576 9862	40.257 698 6170	0.712 973 3411	28.702 665 8885
35	1.416 602 7560	41.660 275 6031	0.705 914 1991	29.408 580 0876
36	1.430 768 7836	43.076 878 3592	0.698 924 9496	30.107 505 0373
37	1.445 076 4714	44.507 647 1427	0.692 004 9006	30.799 509 9379
38	1.459 527 2361	45.952 723 6142	0.685 153 3670	31.484 663 3048
39	1.474 122 5085	47.412 250 8503	0.678 369 6702	32.163 032 9751
40	1.488 863 7336	48.886 373 3588	0.671 653 1389	32.834 686 1140
41	1.503 752 3709	50.375 237 0924	0.665 003 1078	33.499 689 2217
42	1.518 789 8946	51.878 989 4633	0.658 418 9186	34.158 108 1403
43	1.533 977 7936	53.397 779 3580	0.651 899 9194	34.810 008 0597
44	1.549 317 5715	54.931 757 1515	0.645 445 4648	35.455 453 5245
45	1.564 810 7472	56.481 074 7231	0.639 054 9156	36.094 508 4401
46	1.580 458 8547	58.045 885 4703	0.632 727 6392	36.727 236 0793
47	1.596 263 4432	59.626 344 3250	0.626 463 0091	37.353 699 0884
48	1.612 226 0777	61.222 607 7682	0.620 260 4051	37.973 959 4935
49	1.628 348 3385	62.834 833 8459	0.614 119 2129	38.588 078 7064
50	1.644 631 8218	64.463 182 1844	0.608 038 8247	39.196 117 5311
51	1.661 078 1401	66.107 814 0062	0.602 018 6383	39.798 136 1694
52	1.677 688 9215	67.768 892 1463	0.596 058 0577	40.394 194 2271
53	1.694 465 8107	69.446 581 0678	0.590 156 4928	40.984 350 7199
54	1.711 410 4688	71.141 046 8784	0.584 313 3592	41.568 664 0791
55	1.728 524 5735	72.852 457 3472	0.578 528 0784	42.147 192 1576
56	1.745 809 8192	74.580 981 9207	0.572 800 0776	42.719 992 2352
57	1.763 267 9174	76.326 791 7399	0.567 128 7898	43.287 121 0250
58	1.780 900 5966	78.090 059 6573	0.561 513 6532	43.848 634 6782
59	1.798 709 6025	79.870 960 2539	0.555 954 1121	44.404 588 7903
60	1.816 696 6986	81.669 669 8564	0.550 449 6159	44.955 038 4062

Table 2 Compound Amounts and Values for Annuity Quantities:
Rate 1¼%, 0.0125 per period

Period	Compound Amount	Amount of Annuity	Present Value	Present Value of Future $1 Payments
1	1.012 500 0000	1.000 000 0000	0.987 654 3210	0.987 654 3210
2	1.025 156 2500	2.012 500 0000	0.975 461 0578	1.963 115 3788
3	1.037 970 7031	3.037 656 2500	0.963 418 3287	2.926 533 7074
4	1.050 945 3369	4.075 626 9531	0.951 524 2752	3.878 057 9826
5	1.064 082 1536	5.126 572 2900	0.939 777 0619	4.817 835 0446
6	1.077 383 1805	6.190 654 4437	0.928 174 8760	5.746 009 9206
7	1.090 850 4703	7.268 037 6242	0.916 715 9269	6.662 725 8475
8	1.104 486 1012	8.358 888 0945	0.905 398 4463	7.568 124 2938
9	1.118 292 1774	9.463 374 1957	0.894 220 6877	8.462 344 9815
10	1.132 270 8297	10.581 666 3731	0.883 180 9262	9.345 525 9077
11	1.146 424 2150	11.713 937 2028	0.872 277 4579	10.217 803 3656
12	1.160 754 5177	12.860 361 4178	0.861 508 6004	11.079 311 9660
13	1.175 263 9492	14.021 115 9356	0.850 872 6918	11.930 184 6578
14	1.189 954 7486	15.196 379 8848	0.840 368 0906	12.770 552 7485
15	1.204 829 1829	16.386 334 6333	0.829 993 1759	13.600 545 9244
16	1.219 889 5477	17.591 163 8162	0.819 746 3466	14.420 292 2710
17	1.235 138 1670	18.811 053 3639	0.809 626 0213	15.229 918 2924
18	1.250 577 3941	20.046 191 5310	0.799 630 6384	16.029 548 9307
19	1.266 209 6116	21.296 768 9251	0.789 758 6552	16.819 307 5859
20	1.282 037 2317	22.562 978 5367	0.780 008 5483	17.599 316 1342
21	1.298 062 6971	23.845 015 7684	0.770 378 8132	18.369 694 9474
22	1.314 288 4808	25.143 078 4655	0.760 867 9636	19.130 562 9110
23	1.330 717 0868	26.457 366 9463	0.751 474 5320	19.882 037 4430
24	1.347 351 0504	27.788 084 0331	0.742 197 0686	20.624 234 5116
25	1.364 192 9385	29.135 435 0836	0.733 034 1418	21.357 268 6534
26	1.381 245 3503	30.499 628 0221	0.723 984 3376	22.081 252 9910
27	1.398 510 9172	31.880 873 3724	0.715 046 2594	22.796 299 2504
28	1.415 992 3036	33.279 384 2895	0.706 218 5278	23.502 517 7782
29	1.433 692 2074	34.695 376 5932	0.697 499 7805	24.200 017 5587
30	1.451 613 3600	36.129 068 8006	0.688 888 6721	24.888 906 2308
31	1.469 758 5270	37.580 682 1606	0.680 383 8737	25.569 290 1045
32	1.488 130 5086	39.050 440 6876	0.671 984 0728	26.241 274 1773
33	1.506 732 1400	40.538 571 1962	0.663 687 9731	26.904 962 1504
34	1.525 566 2917	42.045 303 3361	0.655 494 2944	27.560 456 4448
35	1.544 635 8703	43.570 869 6278	0.647 401 7723	28.207 858 2171
36	1.563 943 8187	45.115 505 4982	0.639 409 1578	28.847 267 3749
37	1.583 493 1165	46.679 449 3169	0.631 515 2176	29.478 782 5925
38	1.603 286 7804	48.262 942 4334	0.623 718 7334	30.102 501 3259
39	1.623 327 8652	49.866 229 2138	0.616 018 5021	30.718 519 8281
40	1.643 619 4635	51.489 557 0790	0.608 413 3355	31.326 933 1635
41	1.664 164 7068	53.133 176 5424	0.600 902 0597	31.927 835 2233
42	1.684 966 7656	54.797 341 2492	0.593 483 5158	32.521 318 7390
43	1.706 028 8502	56.482 308 0148	0.586 156 5588	33.107 475 2978
44	1.727 354 2108	58.188 336 8650	0.578 920 0581	33.686 395 3558
45	1.748 946 1384	59.915 691 0758	0.571 772 8968	34.258 168 2527
46	1.770 807 9652	61.664 637 2143	0.564 713 9722	34.822 882 2249
47	1.792 943 0647	63.435 445 1795	0.557 742 1948	35.380 624 4196
48	1.815 354 8531	65.228 388 2442	0.550 856 4886	35.931 480 9083
49	1.838 046 7887	67.043 743 0973	0.544 055 7913	36.475 536 6995
50	1.861 022 3736	68.881 789 8860	0.537 339 0531	37.012 875 7526
51	1.884 285 1532	70.742 812 2596	0.530 705 2376	37.543 580 9902
52	1.907 838 7177	72.627 097 4128	0.524 153 3211	38.067 734 3114
53	1.931 686 7016	74.534 936 1304	0.517 682 2925	38.585 416 6038
54	1.955 832 7854	76.466 622 8321	0.511 291 1530	39.096 707 7568
55	1.980 280 6952	78.422 455 6175	0.504 978 9166	39.601 686 6734
56	2.005 034 2049	80.402 736 3127	0.498 744 6090	40.100 431 2824
57	2.030 097 1315	82.407 770 5166	0.492 587 2681	40.593 018 5505
58	2.055 473 3456	84.437 867 6481	0.486 505 9438	41.079 524 4943
59	2.081 166 7624	86.493 340 9937	0.480 499 6976	41.560 024 1919
60	2.107 181 3470	88.574 507 7561	0.474 567 6026	42.034 591 7945

Table 2 Compound Amounts and Values for Annuity Quantities: Rate 1½%, 0.015 per period

Period	Compound Amount	Amount of Annuity	Present Value	Present Value of Future $1 Payments
1	1.015 000 0000	1.000 000 0000	0.985 221 6749	0.985 221 6749
2	1.030 225 0000	2.015 000 0000	0.970 661 7486	1.955 883 4235
3	1.045 678 3750	3.045 225 0000	0.956 316 9937	2.912 200 4173
4	1.061 363 5506	4.090 903 3750	0.942 184 2303	3.854 384 6476
5	1.077 284 0039	5.152 266 9256	0.928 260 3254	4.782 644 9730
6	1.093 443 2639	6.229 550 9295	0.914 542 1925	5.697 187 1655
7	1.109 844 9129	7.322 994 1935	0.901 026 7907	6.598 213 9561
8	1.126 492 5866	8.432 839 1064	0.887 711 1238	7.485 925 0799
9	1.143 389 9754	9.559 331 6929	0.874 592 2402	8.360 517 3201
10	1.160 540 8250	10.702 721 6683	0.861 667 2317	9.222 184 5519
11	1.177 948 9374	11.863 262 4934	0.848 933 2332	10.071 117 7851
12	1.195 618 1715	13.041 211 4308	0.836 387 4219	10.907 505 2070
13	1.213 552 4440	14.236 829 6022	0.824 027 0166	11.731 532 2236
14	1.231 755 7307	15.450 382 0463	0.811 849 2775	12.543 381 5011
15	1.250 232 0667	16.682 137 7770	0.799 851 5049	13.343 233 0060
16	1.268 985 5477	17.932 369 8436	0.788 031 0393	14.131 264 0453
17	1.288 020 3309	19.201 355 3913	0.776 385 2604	14.907 649 3057
18	1.307 340 6358	20.489 375 7221	0.764 911 5866	15.672 560 8924
19	1.326 950 7454	21.796 716 3580	0.753 607 4745	16.426 168 3669
20	1.346 855 0066	23.123 667 1033	0.742 470 4182	17.168 638 7851
21	1.367 057 8316	24.470 522 1099	0.731 497 9490	17.900 136 7341
22	1.387 563 6991	25.837 579 9415	0.720 687 6345	18.620 824 3685
23	1.408 377 1546	27.225 143 6407	0.710 037 0783	19.330 861 4468
24	1.429 502 8119	28.633 520 7953	0.699 543 9195	20.030 405 3663
25	1.450 945 3541	30.063 023 6072	0.689 205 8320	20.719 611 1984
26	1.472 709 5344	31.513 968 9613	0.679 020 5242	21.398 631 7225
27	1.494 800 1774	32.986 678 4957	0.668 985 7381	22.067 617 4606
28	1.517 222 1801	34.481 478 6732	0.659 099 2494	22.726 716 7100
29	1.539 980 5128	35.998 700 8533	0.649 358 8664	23.376 075 5763
30	1.563 080 2205	37.538 681 3661	0.639 762 4299	24.015 838 0062
31	1.586 526 4238	39.101 761 5865	0.630 307 8127	24.646 145 8189
32	1.610 324 3202	40.688 288 0103	0.620 992 9189	25.267 138 7379
33	1.634 479 1850	42.298 612 3305	0.611 815 6837	25.878 954 4216
34	1.658 996 3727	43.933 091 5155	0.602 774 0726	26.481 728 4941
35	1.683 881 3183	45.592 087 8882	0.593 866 0814	27.075 594 5755
36	1.709 139 5381	47.275 969 2065	0.585 089 7353	27.660 684 3109
37	1.734 776 6312	48.985 108 7446	0.576 443 0890	28.237 127 3999
38	1.760 798 2806	50.719 885 3758	0.567 924 2256	28.805 051 6255
39	1.787 210 2548	52.480 683 6564	0.559 531 2568	29.364 582 8822
40	1.814 018 4087	54.267 893 9113	0.551 262 3219	29.915 845 2042
41	1.841 228 6848	56.081 912 3199	0.543 115 5881	30.458 960 7923
42	1.868 847 1151	57.923 141 0047	0.535 089 2494	30.994 050 0417
43	1.896 879 8218	59.791 988 1198	0.527 181 5265	31.521 231 5681
44	1.925 333 0191	61.688 867 9416	0.519 390 6665	32.040 622 2346
45	1.954 213 0144	63.614 200 9607	0.511 714 9423	32.552 337 1770
46	1.983 526 2096	65.568 413 9751	0.504 152 6526	33.056 489 8295
47	2.013 279 1028	67.551 940 1848	0.496 702 1207	33.553 191 9503
48	2.043 478 2893	69.565 219 2875	0.489 361 6953	34.042 553 6456
49	2.074 130 4637	71.608 697 5768	0.482 129 7491	34.524 683 3947
50	2.105 242 4206	73.682 828 0405	0.475 004 6789	34.999 688 0736
51	2.136 821 0569	75.788 070 4611	0.467 984 9053	35.467 672 9789
52	2.168 873 3728	77.924 891 5180	0.461 068 8722	35.928 741 8511
53	2.201 406 4734	80.093 764 8908	0.454 255 0465	36.382 996 8977
54	2.234 427 5705	82.295 171 3642	0.447 541 9178	36.830 538 8154
55	2.267 943 9840	84.529 598 9346	0.440 927 9978	37.271 466 8132
56	2.301 963 1438	86.797 542 9186	0.434 411 8205	37.705 878 6337
57	2.336 492 5909	89.099 506 0624	0.427 991 9414	38.133 870 5751
58	2.371 539 9798	91.435 998 6534	0.421 666 9373	38.555 537 5124
59	2.407 113 0795	93.807 538 6332	0.415 435 4062	38.970 972 9186
60	2.443 219 7757	96.214 651 7126	0.409 295 9667	39.380 268 8853

Table 2   Compound Amounts and Values for Annuity Quantities:
Rate 1¾%, 0.0175 per period

Period	Compound Amount	Amount of Annuity	Present Value	Present Value of Future $1 Payments
1	1.017 500 0000	1.000 000 0000	0.982 800 9828	0.982 800 9828
2	1.035 306 2500	2.107 500 0000	0.965 897 7718	1.948 698 7546
3	1.053 424 1094	3.052 806 2500	0.949 285 2794	2.897 984 0340
4	1.071 859 0313	4.106 230 3594	0.932 958 5056	3.830 942 5396
5	1.090 616 5643	5.178 089 3907	0.916 912 5362	4.747 855 0757
6	1.109 702 3542	6.268 705 9550	0.901 142 5417	5.648 997 6174
7	1.129 122 1454	7.378 408 3092	0.885 643 7756	6.534 641 3930
8	1.148 881 7830	8.507 530 4546	0.870 411 5731	7.405 052 9661
9	1.168 987 2142	9.656 412 2376	0.855 441 3495	8.260 494 3156
10	1.189 444 4904	10.825 399 4517	0.840 728 5990	9.101 222 9146
11	1.210 259 7690	12.014 843 9421	0.826 268 8934	9.927 491 8080
12	1.231 439 3149	13.225 103 7111	0.812 057 8805	10.739 549 6884
13	1.252 989 5030	14.456 543 0261	0.798 091 2830	11.537 640 9714
14	1.274 916 8193	15.709 532 5290	0.784 364 8973	12.322 005 8687
15	1.297 227 8636	16.984 449 3483	0.770 874 5919	13.092 880 4607
16	1.319 929 3512	18.281 677 2119	0.757 616 3066	13.850 496 7672
17	1.343 028 1149	19.601 606 5631	0.744 586 0507	14.595 082 8179
18	1.366 531 1069	20.944 634 6779	0.731 779 9024	15.326 862 7203
19	1.390 445 4012	22.311 165 7848	0.719 194 0073	16.046 056 7276
20	1.414 778 1958	23.701 611 1860	0.706 824 5772	16.752 881 3048
21	1.439 536 8142	25.116 389 3818	0.694 667 8891	17.447 549 1939
22	1.464 728 7084	26.555 926 1960	0.682 720 2841	18.130 269 4780
23	1.490 361 4608	28.020 654 9044	0.670 978 1662	18.801 247 6442
24	1.516 442 7864	29.511 016 3652	0.659 438 0012	19.460 685 6454
25	1.542 980 5352	31.027 459 1516	0.648 096 3157	20.108 781 9611
26	1.569 982 6945	32.570 439 6868	0.636 949 6960	20.745 731 6571
27	1.597 457 3917	34.140 422 3813	0.625 994 7872	21.371 726 4443
28	1.625 412 8960	35.737 879 7730	0.615 228 2921	21.986 954 7364
29	1.653 857 6217	37.363 292 6690	0.604 646 9701	22.591 601 7066
30	1.682 800 1301	39.017 150 2907	0.594 247 6365	23.185 849 3431
31	1.712 249 1324	40.699 950 4208	0.584 027 1612	23.769 876 5042
32	1.742 213 4922	42.412 199 5532	0.573 982 4680	24.343 858 9722
33	1.772 702 2283	44.154 413 0453	0.564 110 5336	24.907 969 5059
34	1.803 724 5173	45.927 115 2736	0.554 408 3869	25.462 377 8928
35	1.835 289 6963	47.730 839 7909	0.544 873 1075	26.007 251 0003
36	1.867 407 2660	49.566 129 4873	0.535 501 8255	26.542 752 8258
37	1.900 086 8932	51.433 536 7533	0.526 291 7204	27.069 044 5462
38	1.933 338 4138	53.333 623 6465	0.517 240 0201	27.586 284 5663
39	1.967 171 8361	55.266 962 0603	0.508 344 0001	28.094 628 5664
40	2.001 597 3432	57.234 133 8963	0.499 600 9829	28.594 229 5493
41	2.036 625 2967	59.235 731 2395	0.491 008 3370	29.085 237 8863
42	2.072 266 2394	61.272 356 5362	0.482 563 4762	29.567 801 3625
43	2.108 530 8986	63.344 622 7756	0.474 263 8586	30.042 065 2211
44	2.145 430 1893	65.453 153 6742	0.466 106 9864	30.508 172 2075
45	2.182 975 2176	67.598 583 8635	0.458 090 4043	30.966 262 6117
46	2.221 177 2839	69.781 559 0811	0.450 211 6996	31.416 474 3113
47	2.260 047 8864	72.002 736 3650	0.442 468 5008	31.858 942 8121
48	2.299 598 7244	74.262 784 2514	0.434 858 4774	32.293 801 2895
49	2.339 841 7021	76.562 382 9758	0.427 379 3390	32.721 180 6285
50	2.380 788 9319	78.902 224 6779	0.420 028 8344	33.141 209 4629
51	2.422 452 7382	81.283 013 6097	0.412 804 7513	33.554 014 2142
52	2.464 845 6611	83.705 466 3479	0.405 704 9152	33.959 719 1294
53	2.507 980 4602	86.170 312 0090	0.398 727 1894	34.358 446 3188
54	2.551 870 1182	88.678 292 4691	0.391 869 4736	34.750 315 7925
55	2.596 527 8453	91.230 162 5874	0.385 129 7038	35.135 445 4963
56	2.641 967 0826	93.826 690 4326	0.378 505 8514	35.513 951 3477
57	2.688 201 5065	96.468 657 5152	0.371 995 9228	35.885 947 2705
58	2.735 245 0329	99.156 859 0217	0.365 597 9585	36.251 545 2290
59	2.783 111 8210	101.892 104 0546	0.359 310 0329	36.610 855 2619
60	2.831 816 2778	104.675 215 8756	0.353 130 2535	36.963 985 5154

Table 2 Compound Amounts and Values for Annuity Quantities: Rate 2%, 0.02 per period

Period	Compound Amount	Amount of Annuity	Present Value	Present Value of Future $1 Payments
1	1.020 000 0000	1.000 000 0000	0.980 392 1569	0.980 392 1569
2	1.040 400 0000	2.020 000 0000	0.961 168 7812	1.941 560 9381
3	1.061 208 0000	3.060 400 0000	0.942 322 3345	2.883 883 2726
4	1.082 432 1600	4.121 608 0000	0.923 845 4260	3.807 728 6987
5	1.104 080 8032	5.204 040 1600	0.905 730 8098	4.713 459 5085
6	1.126 162 4193	6.308 120 9632	0.887 971 3822	5.601 430 8907
7	1.148 685 6676	7.434 283 3825	0.870 560 1786	6.471 991 0693
8	1.171 659 3810	8.582 969 0501	0.853 490 3712	7.325 481 4405
9	1.195 092 5686	9.754 628 4311	0.836 755 2659	8.162 236 7064
10	1.218 994 4200	10.949 720 9997	0.820 348 2999	8.982 585 0062
11	1.243 374 3084	12.168 715 4197	0.804 263 0391	9.786 848 0453
12	1.268 241 7946	13.412 089 7281	0.788 493 1756	10.575 341 2209
13	1.293 606 6305	14.680 331 5227	0.773 032 5251	11.348 373 7460
14	1.319 478 7631	15.973 938 1531	0.757 875 0246	12.106 248 7706
15	1.345 868 3383	17.293 416 9162	0.743 014 7300	12.849 263 5006
16	1.372 785 7051	18.639 285 2545	0.728 445 8137	13.577 709 3143
17	1.400 241 4192	20.012 070 9596	0.714 162 5625	14.291 871 8768
18	1.428 246 2476	21.412 312 3788	0.700 159 3750	14.992 031 2517
19	1.456 811 1725	22.840 558 6264	0.686 430 7598	15.678 462 0115
20	1.485 947 3960	24.297 369 7989	0.672 971 3331	16.351 433 3446
21	1.515 666 3439	25.783 317 1949	0.659 775 8168	17.011 209 1614
22	1.545 979 6708	27.298 983 5388	0.646 839 0361	17.658 048 1974
23	1.576 899 2642	28.844 963 2096	0.634 155 9177	18.292 204 1151
24	1.608 437 2495	30.421 862 4738	0.621 721 4879	18.913 925 6031
25	1.640 605 9945	32.030 299 7232	0.609 530 8705	19.523 456 4736
26	1.673 418 1144	33.670 905 7177	0.597 579 2848	20.121 035 7584
27	1.706 886 4766	35.344 323 8321	0.585 862 0440	20.706 897 8024
28	1.741 024 2062	37.051 210 3087	0.574 374 5529	21.281 272 3553
29	1.775 844 6903	38.792 234 5149	0.563 112 3068	21.844 384 6620
30	1.811 361 5841	40.568 079 2052	0.552 070 8890	22.396 455 5510
31	1.847 588 8158	42.379 440 7893	0.541 245 9696	22.937 701 5206
32	1.884 540 5921	44.227 029 6051	0.530 633 3035	23.468 334 8241
33	1.922 231 4039	46.111 570 1972	0.520 228 7289	23.988 563 5530
34	1.960 676 0320	48.033 801 6011	0.510 028 1656	24.498 591 7187
35	1.999 889 5527	49.994 477 6331	0.500 027 6134	24.998 619 3320
36	2.039 887 3437	51.994 367 1858	0.490 223 1504	25.448 842 4824
37	2.080 685 0906	54.034 254 5295	0.480 610 9317	25.969 453 4141
38	2.122 298 7924	56.114 939 6201	0.471 187 1880	26.440 640 6021
39	2.164 744 7682	58.237 238 4125	0.461 948 2235	26.902 538 8256
40	2.208 039 6636	60.401 983 1807	0.452 890 4152	27.355 479 2407
41	2.252 200 4569	62.610 022 8444	0.444 010 2110	27.799 489 4517
42	2.297 244 4660	64.862 223 3012	0.435 304 1284	28.234 793 5801
43	2.343 189 3553	67.159 467 7673	0.426 768 7533	28.661 562 3334
44	2.390 053 1425	69.502 657 1226	0.418 400 7386	28.079 963 0720
45	2.437 854 2053	71.892 710 2651	0.410 196 8025	29.490 159 8745
46	2.486 611 2894	74.330 564 4704	0.402 153 7280	29.892 313 6025
47	2.536 343 5152	76.817 175 7598	0.394 268 3607	30.286 581 9632
48	2.587 070 3855	79.353 519 2750	0.386 537 6086	30.673 119 5718
49	2.638 811 7932	81.940 589 6605	0.378 958 4398	31.052 078 0115
50	2.691 588 0291	84.579 401 4537	0.371 527 6821	31.423 605 8937
51	2.745 419 7897	87.270 989 4828	0.364 243 0217	31.787 848 9153
52	2.800 328 1854	90.016 409 2724	0.357 101 0017	32.144 949 9170
53	2.856 334 7492	92.816 737 4579	0.350 099 0212	32.495 048 9382
54	2.913 461 4441	95.673 072 2070	0.343 234 3345	32.838 283 2728
55	2.971 730 6730	98.586 533 6512	0.336 504 2496	33.174 787 5223
56	3.031 165 2865	101.558 264 3242	0.329 906 1270	33.504 693 6494
57	3.091 788 5922	104.589 429 6107	0.323 437 3794	33.828 131 0288
58	3.153 624 3641	107.681 218 2029	0.317 095 4700	34.145 226 4988
59	3.216 696 8513	110.834 842 5669	0.310 877 9118	34.456 104 4106
60	3.281 030 7884	114.051 539 4183	0.304 782 2665	34.760 886 6770

Table 2 Compound Amounts and Values for Annuity Quantities: Rate 2¼%, 0.0225 per period

Period	Compound Amount	Amount of Annuity	Present Value	Present Value of Future $1 Payments
1	1.022 500 0000	1.000 000 0000	0.977 995 1100	0.977 995 1100
2	1.045 506 2500	2.022 500 0000	0.956 474 4352	1.934 469 5453
3	1.069 030 1406	3.068 006 2500	0.935 427 3205	2.869 896 8658
4	1.093 083 3188	4.137 036 3906	0.914 843 3453	3.784 740 2110
5	1.117 677 6935	5.230 119 7094	0.894 712 3181	4.679 452 5291
6	1.142 825 4416	6.347 797 4029	0.875 024 2720	5.554 476 8011
7	1.168 539 0140	7.490 622 8444	0.855 769 4591	6.410 246 2602
8	1.194 831 1418	8.659 161 8584	0.836 938 3464	7.247 184 6066
9	1.221 714 8425	9.853 993 0003	0.818 521 6101	8.065 706 2167
10	1.249 203 4265	11.075 707 8428	0.800 510 1322	8.866 216 3489
11	1.277 310 5036	12.324 911 2692	0.782 894 9948	9.649 111 3436
12	1.306 049 9899	13.602 221 7728	0.765 667 4765	10.414 778 8202
13	1.335 436 1147	14.908 271 7627	0.748 819 0480	11.163 597 8681
14	1.365 483 4272	16.243 707 8773	0.732 341 3672	11.895 939 2354
15	1.396 206 8044	17.609 191 3046	0.716 226 2760	12.612 165 5113
16	1.427 621 4575	19.005 398 1089	0.700 465 7956	13.312 631 3069
17	1.459 742 9402	20.433 019 5664	0.685 052 1228	13.997 683 4298
18	1.492 587 1564	21.892 762 5066	0.669 977 6262	14.667 661 0560
19	1.526 170 3674	23.385 349 6630	0.655 234 8423	15.322 895 8983
20	1.560 509 2007	24.911 520 0304	0.640 816 4717	15.963 712 3700
21	1.595 620 6577	26.472 029 2311	0.626 715 3757	16.590 427 7457
22	1.631 522 1225	28.067 649 8888	0.612 924 5728	17.203 352 3185
23	1.668 231 3703	29.699 172 0113	0.599 437 2350	17.802 789 5536
24	1.705 766 5761	31.367 403 3816	0.586 246 6846	18.389 036 2382
25	1.744 146 3240	33.073 169 9577	0.573 346 3908	18.962 382 6291
26	1.783 389 6163	34.817 316 2817	0.560 729 9666	19.523 112 5957
27	1.823 515 8827	36.600 705 8980	0.548 391 1654	20.071 503 7610
28	1.864 544 9901	38.424 221 7807	0.536 323 8781	20.607 827 6392
29	1.906 497 2523	40.288 766 7708	0.524 522 1302	21.132 349 7693
30	1.949 393 4405	42.195 264 0232	0.512 980 0784	21.645 329 8478
31	1.993 254 7929	44.144 657 4637	0.501 692 0082	22.147 021 8560
32	2.038 103 0258	46.137 912 2566	0.490 652 3308	22.637 674 1868
33	2.083 960 3439	48.176 015 2824	0.479 855 5802	23.117 529 7670
34	2.130 849 4516	50.259 975 6562	0.469 296 4110	23.586 826 1780
35	2.178 793 5643	52.390 825 0778	0.458 969 5951	24.045 795 7731
36	2.227 816 4194	54.569 618 6421	0.448 870 0197	24.494 665 7928
37	2.277 942 3889	56.797 435 0615	0.438 992 6843	24.933 658 4771
38	2.329 195 9904	59.075 377 3504	0.429 332 6985	25.362 991 1756
39	2.381 602 9002	61.404 573 3408	0.419 885 2798	25.782 876 4554
40	2.435 188 9654	63.786 176 2410	0.410 645 7504	26.193 522 2057
41	2.489 980 7171	66.221 365 2064	0.401 609 5358	26.595 131 7416
42	2.546 005 2833	68.711 345 9235	0.392 772 1622	26.987 903 9037
43	2.603 290 4022	71.257 351 2068	0.384 129 2540	27.372 033 1577
44	2.661 864 4362	73.860 641 6090	0.375 676 5320	27.747 709 6897
45	2.721 756 3860	76.522 506 0452	0.367 409 8112	28.115 119 5009
46	2.782 995 9047	79.244 262 4312	0.359 324 9988	28.474 444 4997
47	2.845 613 3126	82.027 258 3359	0.351 418 0917	28.825 862 5913
48	2.909 639 6121	84.872 871 6484	0.343 685 1753	29.169 547 7666
49	2.975 106 5034	87.782 511 2605	0.336 122 4208	29.505 670 1874
50	3.042 046 3997	90.757 617 7639	0.328 726 0839	29.834 396 2713
51	2.110 492 4437	93.799 664 1636	0.321 492 5026	30.155 888 7739
52	3.180 478 5237	96.910 156 6073	0.314 418 0954	30.470 306 8693
53	3.252 039 2904	100.090 635 1309	0.307 499 3598	30.777 806 2291
54	3.325 210 1745	103.342 674 4214	0.300 732 8703	31.078 539 0994
55	3.400 027 4034	106.667 884 5958	0.294 115 1765	31.372 654 3760
56	3.476 528 0200	110.067 911 9993	0.287 643 3022	31.660 297 6782
57	3.554 749 9004	113.544 440 0192	0.281 313 7430	31.941 611 4212
58	3.634 731 7732	117.099 189 9197	0.275 123 4651	32.216 734 8863
59	3.716 513 2381	120.733 921 6929	0.269 069 4035	32.485 804 2898
60	3.800 134 7859	124.450 434 9310	0.263 148 5609	32.748 952 8506

Table 2 Compound Amounts and Values for Annuity Quantities: Rate 2½%, 0.025 per period

Period	Compound Amount	Amount of Annuity	Present Value	Present Value of Future $1 Payments
1	1.025 000 0000	1.000 000 0000	0.975 609 7561	0.975 609 7561
2	1.050 625 0000	2.025 000 0000	0.951 814 3962	1.927 424 1523
3	1.076 890 6250	3.075 625 0000	0.928 599 4109	2.856 023 5632
4	1.103 812 8906	4.152 515 6250	0.905 950 6448	3.761 974 2080
5	1.131 408 2129	5.256 328 5156	0.883 854 2876	4.645 828 4956
6	1.159 693 4182	6.387 736 7285	0.862 296 8660	5.508 125 3616
7	1.188 685 7537	7.547 430 1467	0.841 265 2351	6.349 390 5967
8	1.218 402 8975	8.736 115 9004	0.820 746 5708	7.170 137 1675
9	1.248 862 9699	9.954 518 7979	0.800 728 3618	7.970 865 5292
10	1.280 084 5442	11.203 381 7679	0.781 198 4017	8.752 063 9310
11	1.312 086 6578	12.483 466 3121	0.762 144 7822	9.514 208 7131
12	1.344 888 8242	13.795 552 9699	0.743 555 8850	10.257 764 5982
13	1.378 511 0449	15.140 441 7941	0.725 420 3757	10.983 184 9738
14	1.412 973 8210	16.518 952 8390	0.707 727 1958	11.690 912 1696
15	1.448 298 1665	17.931 926 6599	0.690 465 5568	12.381 377 7264
16	1.484 505 6207	19.380 224 8264	0.673 624 9335	13.055 002 6599
17	1.521 618 2612	20.864 730 4471	0.657 195 0571	13.712 197 7170
18	1.559 658 7177	22.386 348 7083	0.641 165 9093	14.353 363 6264
19	1.598 650 1856	23.946 007 4260	0.625 527 7164	14.978 891 3428
20	1.638 616 4403	25.544 657 6116	0.610 270 9429	15.589 162 2856
21	1.679 581 8513	27.183 274 0519	0.595 386 2857	16.184 548 5714
22	1.721 571 3976	28.862 855 9032	0.580 864 6690	16.765 413 2404
23	1.764 610 6825	30.584 427 3008	0.566 697 2380	17.332 110 4784
24	1.808 725 9496	32.349 037 9833	0.552 875 3542	17.884 985 8326
25	1.853 944 0983	34.157 763 9328	0.539 390 5894	18.424 376 4220
26	1.900 292 7008	36.011 708 0312	0.526 234 7214	18.950 611 1434
27	1.947 800 0183	37.912 000 7320	0.513 339 7282	19.464 010 8717
28	1.996 495 0188	39.859 800 7503	0.500 877 7836	19.964 888 6553
29	2.046 407 3942	41.856 295 7690	0.488 661 2523	20.453 549 9076
30	2.097 567 5791	43.902 703 1633	0.476 742 6852	20.930 292 5928
31	2.150 006 7686	46.000 270 7424	0.465 114 8148	21.395 407 4076
32	2.203 756 9378	48.150 277 5109	0.453 770 5510	21.849 177 9586
33	2.258 850 8612	50.354 034 4487	0.442 702 9766	22.291 880 9352
34	2.315 322 1327	52.612 885 3099	0.431 905 3430	22.723 786 2783
35	2.373 205 1861	54.928 207 4426	0.421 371 0664	23.145 157 3447
36	2.432 535 3157	57.301 412 6287	0.411 093 7233	23.556 251 0680
37	2.493 348 6986	59.733 947 9444	0.401 067 0471	23.957 318 1151
38	2.555 682 4161	62.227 296 6430	0.391 284 9240	24.348 603 0391
39	2.619 574 4765	64.782 979 0591	0.381 741 3893	24.730 344 4284
40	2.685 063 8384	67.402 553 5356	0.372 430 6237	25.102 775 0521
41	2.752 190 4343	70.087 617 3740	0.363 346 9499	25.466 122 0020
42	2.820 995 1952	72.839 807 8083	0.354 484 8292	25.820 606 8313
43	2.891 520 0751	75.660 803 0035	0.345 838 8578	26.166 445 6890
44	2.963 808 0770	78.552 323 0786	0.337 403 7637	26.503 849 4527
45	3.037 903 2789	81.516 131 1556	0.329 174 4036	26.833 023 8563
46	3.113 850 8609	84.554 034 4345	0.321 145 7596	27.154 169 6159
47	3.191 697 1324	87.667 385 2954	0.313 312 9362	27.467 482 5521
48	3.271 489 5607	90.859 082 4277	0.305 671 1573	27.773 153 7094
49	3.353 276 7997	94.131 071 9884	0.298 215 7632	28.071 369 4726
50	3.437 108 7197	97.484 348 7881	0.290 942 2080	28.362 311 6805
51	3.523 036 4377	100.921 457 5078	0.283 846 0566	28.646 157 7371
52	3.611 112 3486	104.444 493 9455	0.276 922 9820	28.923 080 7191
53	3.701 390 1574	108.055 606 2942	0.270 168 7629	29.193 249 4821
54	3.793 924 9113	111.756 996 4515	0.263 579 2809	29.456 828 7630
55	3.888 773 0341	115.550 921 3628	0.257 150 5180	29.713 979 2810
56	3.985 992 3599	119.439 694 3969	0.250 878 5541	29.964 857 8351
57	4.085 642 1689	123.425 686 7568	0.244 759 5650	30.209 617 4001
58	4.187 783 2231	127.511 328 9257	0.238 789 8195	30.448 407 2196
59	4.292 477 8037	131.699 112 1489	0.232 965 6776	30.681 372 8972
60	4.399 789 7488	135.991 589 9526	0.227 283 5879	30.908 656 4851

Table 2 Compound Amounts and Values for Annuity Quantities: Rate 3%, 0.03 per period

Period	Compound Amount	Amount of Annuity	Present Value	Present Value of Future $1 Payments
1	1.030 000 0000	1.000 000 0000	0.970 873 7864	0.970 873 7864
2	1.060 900 0000	2.030 000 0000	0.942 595 9091	1.913 469 6955
3	1.092 727 0000	3.090 900 0000	0.915 141 6594	2.828 611 3549
4	1.125 508 8100	4.183 627 0000	0.888 487 0479	3.717 098 4028
5	1.159 274 0743	5.309 135 8100	0.862 608 7844	4.579 707 1872
6	1.194 052 2965	6.468 409 8843	0.837 484 2567	5.417 191 4439
7	1.229 873 8654	7.662 462 1808	0.813 091 5113	6.230 282 9552
8	1.266 770 0814	8.892 336 0463	0.789 409 2343	7.019 692 1895
9	1.304 773 1838	10.159 106 1276	0.766 416 7323	7.786 108 9219
10	1.343 916 3793	11.463 879 3115	0.744 093 9149	8.530 202 8368
11	1.384 233 8707	12.807 795 6908	0.722 421 2766	9.252 624 1134
12	1.425 760 8868	14.192 029 5615	0.701 379 8802	9.954 003 9936
13	1.468 533 7135	15.617 790 4484	0.680 951 3400	10.634 955 3336
14	1.512 589 7249	17.086 324 1618	0.661 117 8058	11.296 073 1394
15	1.557 967 4166	18.598 913 8867	0.641 861 9474	11.937 935 0868
16	1.604 706 4391	20.156 881 3033	0.623 166 9392	12.561 102 0260
17	1.652 847 6323	21.761 587 7424	0.605 016 4458	13.166 118 4718
18	1.702 433 0612	23.414 435 3747	0.587 394 6076	13.753 513 0795
19	1.753 506 0531	25.116 868 4359	0.570 286 0268	14.323 799 1063
20	1.806 111 2347	26.870 374 4890	0.553 675 7542	14.877 474 8605
21	1.860 294 5717	28.676 485 7236	0.537 549 2759	15.415 024 1364
22	1.916 103 4089	30.536 780 2954	0.521 892 5009	15.936 916 6372
23	1.973 586 5111	32.452 883 7042	0.506 691 7484	16.443 608 3857
24	2.032 794 1065	34.426 470 2153	0.491 933 7363	16.935 542 1220
25	2.093 777 9297	36.459 264 3218	0.477 605 5693	17.413 147 6913
26	2.156 591 2675	38.553 042 2515	0.463 694 7274	17.876 842 4187
27	2.221 289 0056	40.709 633 5190	0.450 189 0558	18.327 031 4745
28	2.287 927 6757	42.930 922 5246	0.437 076 7532	18.764 108 2277
29	2.356 565 5060	45.218 850 2003	0.424 346 3623	19.188 454 5900
30	2.427 262 4712	47.575 415 7063	0.411 986 7595	19.600 441 3495
31	2.500 080 3453	50.002 678 1775	0.399 987 1452	20.000 428 4946
32	2.575 082 7557	52.502 758 5228	0.388 337 0341	20.388 765 5288
33	2.652 335 2384	55.077 841 2785	0.377 026 2467	20.765 791 7755
34	2.731 905 2955	57.730 176 5169	0.366 044 8997	21.131 836 6752
35	2.813 862 4544	60.462 081 8124	0.355 383 3978	21.487 220 0731
36	2.898 278 3280	63.275 944 2668	0.345 032 4251	21.832 252 4981
37	2.985 226 6778	66.174 222 5948	0.334 982 9369	22.167 235 4351
38	3.074 783 4782	69.159 449 2726	0.325 226 1524	22.492 461 5874
39	3.167 026 9825	72.234 232 7508	0.315 753 5460	22.808 215 1334
40	3.262 037 7920	75.401 259 7333	0.306 556 8408	23.114 771 9742
41	3.359 898 9258	78.663 297 5253	0.297 628 0008	23.412 399 9750
42	3.460 695 8935	82.023 196 4511	0.288 959 2240	23.701 359 1990
43	3.564 516 7703	85.483 892 3446	0.280 542 9360	23.981 902 1349
44	3.671 452 2734	89.048 409 1149	0.272 371 7825	24.254 273 9174
45	3.781 595 8417	92.719 861 3884	0.264 438 6238	24.518 712 5412
46	3.895 043 7169	96.501 457 2300	0.256 736 5279	24.775 449 0691
47	4.011 895 0284	100.396 500 9469	0.249 258 7650	25.024 707 8341
48	4.132 251 8793	104.408 395 9753	0.241 998 8009	25.266 706 6350
49	4.256 219 4356	108.540 647 8546	0.234 950 2922	25.501 656 9272
50	4.383 906 0187	112.796 867 2902	0.228 107 0798	25.729 764 0070
51	4.515 423 1993	117.180 773 3089	0.221 463 1843	25.951 227 1913
52	4.650 885 8952	121.696 196 5082	0.215 012 8003	26.166 239 9915
53	4.790 412 4721	126.347 082 4035	0.208 750 2915	26.374 990 2830
54	4.934 124 8463	131.137 494 8756	0.202 670 1859	26.577 660 4690
55	5.082 148 5917	136.071 619 7218	0.196 767 1708	26.774 427 6398
56	5.234 613 0494	141.153 768 3135	0.191 036 0882	26.965 463 7279
57	5.391 651 4409	146.388 381 3629	0.185 471 9303	27.150 935 6582
58	5.553 400 9841	151.780 032 8038	0.180 069 8352	27.331 005 4934
59	5.720 003 0136	157.333 433 7879	0.174 825 0827	27.505 830 5761
60	5.891 603 1040	163.053 436 8015	0.169 733 0900	27.675 563 6661

Table 2 Compound Amounts and Values for Annuity Quantities: Rate 3½%, 0.035 per period

Period	Compound Amount	Amount of Annuity	Present Value	Present Value of Future $1 Payments
1	1.035 000 0000	1.000 000 0000	0.966 183 5749	0.966 183 5749
2	1.071 225 0000	2.035 000 0000	0.933 510 7004	1.899 694 2752
3	1.108 717 8750	3.106 225 0000	0.901 942 7057	2.801 636 9809
4	1.147 523 0006	4.214 942 8750	0.871 442 2277	3.673 079 2086
5	1.187 686 3056	5.362 465 8756	0.841 973 1669	4.515 052 3755
6	1.229 255 3263	6.550 152 1813	0.813 500 6443	5.328 553 0198
7	1.272 279 2628	7.779 407 5076	0.785 990 9607	6.114 543 9805
8	1.316 809 0370	9.051 686 7704	0.759 411 5562	6.873 955 5367
9	1.362 897 3533	10.368 495 8073	0.733 730 9722	7.607 686 5089
10	1.410 598 7606	11.731 393 1606	0.708 918 8137	8.316 605 3226
11	1.459 969 7172	13.141 991 9212	0.684 945 7137	9.001 551 0363
12	1.511 068 6573	14.601 961 6385	0.661 783 2983	9.663 334 3346
13	1.563 956 0604	16.113 030 2958	0.639 404 1529	10.302 738 4875
14	1.618 694 5225	17.676 986 3562	0.617 781 7903	10.920 520 2778
15	1.675 348 8308	19.295 680 8786	0.596 890 6186	11.517 410 8964
16	1.733 986 0398	20.971 029 7094	0.576 705 9117	12.094 116 8081
17	1.794 675 5512	22.705 015 7492	0.557 203 7794	12.651 320 5876
18	1.857 489 1955	24.499 691 3004	0.538 361 1396	13.189 681 7271
19	1.922 501 3174	26.357 180 4960	0.520 155 6904	13.709 837 4175
20	1.989 788 8635	28.279 681 8133	0.502 565 8844	14.212 403 3020
21	2.059 431 4737	30.269 470 6768	0.485 570 9028	14.697 974 2048
22	2.131 511 5753	32.328 902 1505	0.469 150 6308	15.167 124 8355
23	2.206 114 4804	34.460 413 7257	0.453 285 6336	15.620 410 4691
24	2.283 328 4872	36.666 528 2061	0.437 957 1339	16.058 367 6030
25	2.363 244 9843	38.949 856 6933	0.423 146 9893	16.481 514 5923
26	2.445 958 5587	41.313 101 6776	0.408 837 6708	16.890 352 2631
27	2.531 567 1083	43.759 060 2363	0.395 012 2423	17.285 364 5054
28	2.620 171 9571	46.290 627 3446	0.381 654 3404	17.667 018 8458
29	2.711 877 9756	48.910 799 3017	0.368 748 1550	18.035 767 0008
30	2.806 793 7047	51.622 677 2772	0.356 278 4106	18.392 045 4114
31	2.905 031 4844	54.429 470 9819	0.344 230 3484	18.736 275 7598
32	3.006 707 5863	57.334 502 4663	0.332 589 7086	19.068 865 4684
33	3.111 942 3518	60.341 210 0526	0.321 342 7136	19.390 208 1820
34	3.220 860 3342	63.453 152 4044	0.310 476 0518	19.700 684 2338
35	3.333 590 4459	66.674 012 7386	0.299 976 8617	20.000 661 0955
36	3.450 266 1115	70.007 603 1845	0.289 832 7166	20.290 493 8121
37	3.571 025 4254	73.457 869 2959	0.280 031 6102	20.570 525 4223
38	3.696 011 3152	77.028 894 7213	0.270 561 9422	20.841 087 3645
39	3.825 371 7113	80.724 906 0365	0.261 412 5046	21.102 499 8691
40	3.959 259 7212	84.550 277 7478	0.252 572 4682	21.355 072 3373
41	4.097 833 8114	88.509 537 4690	0.244 031 3702	21.599 103 7075
42	4.241 157 9948	92.607 371 2804	0.235 779 1017	21.834 882 8092
43	4.389 702 0246	96.848 629 2752	0.227 805 8953	22.062 688 7046
44	4.543 341 5955	101.238 331 2998	0.220 102 3143	22.282 791 0189
45	4.702 358 5513	105.781 672 8953	0.212 659 2409	22.495 450 2598
46	4.866 941 1006	110.484 031 4467	0.205 467 8656	22.700 918 1254
47	5.037 284 0392	115.350 972 5473	0.198 519 6769	22.899 437 8023
48	5.213 588 9805	120.388 256 5864	0.191 806 4511	23.091 244 2535
49	5.396 064 5948	125.601 845 5670	0.185 320 2426	23.276 564 4961
50	5.584 926 8557	130 997 910 1618	0.179 053 3745	23.455 617 8706
51	5.780 399 2956	136 582 837 0175	0.172 998 4295	23.628 616 3001
52	5.982 713 2710	142.363 236 3131	0.167 148 2411	23.795 764 5412
53	6.192 108 2354	148.345 949 5840	0.161 495 8851	23.957 260 4263
54	6.408 832 0237	154.538 057 8195	0.156 034 6716	24.113 295 0978
55	6.633 141 1445	160.946 889 8432	0.150 758 1368	24.264 053 2346
56	6.865 301 0846	167.580 030 9877	0.145 660 0355	24.409 713 2702
57	7.105 586 6225	174.445 332 0722	0.140 734 3339	24.550 447 6040
58	7.354 282 1543	181.550 918 6948	0.135 975 2018	24.686 422 8058
59	7.611 682 0297	188.905 200 8491	0.131 377 0066	24.817 799 8124
60	7.878 090 9008	196.516 882 8788	0.126 934 3059	24.944 734 1182

Table 2 Compound Amounts and Values for Annuity Quantities: Rate 4%, 0.04 per period

Period	Compound Amount	Amount of Annuity	Present Value	Present Value of Future $1 Payments
1	1.040 000 0000	1.000 000 0000	0.961 538 4615	0.961 538 4615
2	1.081 600 0000	2.040 000 0000	0.924 556 2130	1.886 094 6746
3	1.124 864 0000	3.121 600 0000	0.888 996 3587	2.775 091 0332
4	1.169 858 5600	4.246 464 0000	0.854 804 1910	3.629 895 2243
5	1.216 652 9024	5.416 322 5600	0.821 927 1068	4.451 822 3310
6	1.265 319 0185	6.632 975 4624	0.790 314 5257	5.242 136 8567
7	1.315 931 7792	7.898 294 4809	0.759 917 8132	6.002 054 6699
8	1.368 569 0504	9.214 226 2601	0.730 690 2050	6.732 744 8750
9	1.423 311 8124	10.582 795 3105	0.702 586 7356	7.435 331 6105
10	1.480 244 2849	12.006 107 1230	0.675 564 1688	8.110 895 7794
11	1.539 454 0563	13.486 351 4079	0.649 580 9316	8.760 476 7109
12	1.601 032 2186	15.025 805 4642	0.624 597 0496	9.385 073 7605
13	1.665 073 5073	16.626 837 6828	0.600 574 0861	9.985 647 8466
14	1.731 676 4476	18.291 911 1901	0.577 475 0828	10.563 122 9295
15	1.800 943 5055	20.023 587 6377	0.555 264 5027	11.118 387 4322
16	1.872 981 2457	21.824 531 1432	0.533 908 1757	11.652 295 6079
17	1.947 900 4956	23.697 512 3889	0.513 373 2459	12.165 668 8537
18	2.025 816 5154	25.645 412 8845	0.493 628 1210	12.659 296 9747
19	2.106 849 1760	27.671 229 3998	0.474 642 4240	13.133 939 3988
20	2.191 123 1430	29.778 078 5758	0.456 386 9462	13.590 326 3450
21	2.278 768 0688	31.969 201 7189	0.438 833 6021	14.029 159 9471
22	2.369 918 7915	34.247 969 7876	0.421 955 3867	14.451 115 3337
23	2.464 715 5432	36.617 888 5791	0.405 726 3333	14.856 841 6671
24	2.563 304 1649	39.082 604 1223	0.390 121 4743	15.246 963 1414
25	2.665 836 3315	41.645 908 2872	0.375 116 8023	15.622 079 9437
26	2.772 469 7847	44.311 744 6187	0.360 689 2329	15.982 769 1766
27	2.883 368 5761	47.084 214 4034	0.346 816 5701	16.329 585 7467
28	2.998 703 3192	49.967 582 9796	0.333 477 4713	16.663 063 2180
29	3.118 651 4519	52.966 286 2987	0.320 651 4147	16.983 714 6327
30	3.243 397 5100	56.084 937 7507	0.308 318 6680	17.292 033 3007
31	3.373 133 4104	59.328 335 2607	0.296 460 2577	17.588 493 5583
32	3.508 058 7468	62.701 468 6711	0.285 057 9401	17.873 551 4984
33	3.648 381 0967	66.209 527 4180	0.274 094 1731	18.147 645 6715
34	3.794 316 3406	69.857 908 5147	0.263 552 0896	18.411 197 7611
35	3.946 088 9942	73.652 224 8553	0.253 415 4707	18.664 613 2318
36	4.103 932 5540	77.598 313 8495	0.243 668 7219	18.908 281 9537
37	4.268 089 8561	81.702 246 4035	0.234 296 8479	19.142 578 8016
38	4.438 813 4504	85.970 336 2596	0.225 285 4307	19.367 864 2323
39	4.616 365 9884	90.409 149 7100	0.216 620 6064	19.584 484 8388
40	4.801 020 6279	95.025 515 6984	0.208 289 0447	19.792 773 8834
41	4.993 061 4531	99.826 536 3264	0.200 277 9276	19.993 051 8110
42	5.192 783 9112	104.819 597 7794	0.192 574 9303	20.185 626 7413
43	5.400 495 2676	110.012 381 6906	0.185 168 2023	20.370 794 9436
44	5.616 515 0783	115.412 876 9582	0.178 046 3483	20.548 841 2919
45	5.841 175 6815	121.029 392 0365	0.171 198 4118	20.720 039 7038
46	6.074 822 7087	126.870 567 7180	0.164 613 8575	20.884 653 5613
47	6.317 815 6171	132.945 390 4267	0.158 282 5553	21.042 936 1166
48	6.570 528 2418	139.263 206 0438	0.152 194 7647	21.195 130 8814
49	6.833 349 3714	145.833 734 2855	0.146 341 1199	21.341 472 0013
50	7.106 683 3463	152.667 083 6570	0.140 712 6153	21.482 184 6167
51	7.390 950 6801	159.773 767 0032	0.135 300 5917	21.617 485 2083
52	7.686 588 7073	167.164 717 6834	0.130 096 7228	21.747 581 9311
53	7.994 052 2556	174.851 306 3907	0.125 093 0027	21.872 674 9337
54	8.313 814 3459	182.845 358 6463	0.120 281 7333	21.992 956 6671
55	8.646 366 9197	191.159 172 9922	0.115 655 5128	22.108 612 1799
56	8.992 221 5965	199.805 539 9119	0.111 207 2239	22.219 819 4037
57	9.351 910 4603	208.797 761 5083	0.106 930 0229	22.326 749 4267
58	9.725 986 8787	218.149 671 9687	0.102 817 3297	22.429 566 7564
59	10.115 026 3539	227.875 658 8474	0.098 862 8171	22.528 429 5735
60	10.519 627 4081	237.990 685 2013	0.095 060 4010	22.623 489 9745

Table 2 Compound Amounts and Values for Annuity Quantities: Rate 4½%, 0.045 per period

Period	Compound Amount	Amount of Annuity	Present Value	Present Value of Future $1 Payments
1	1.045 000 0000	1.000 000 0000	0.956 937 7990	0.956 937 7990
2	1.092 025 0000	2.045 000 0000	0.915 729 9512	1.872 667 7503
3	1.141 166 1250	3.137 025 0000	0.876 296 6041	2.748 964 3543
4	1.192 518 6006	4.278 191 1250	0.838 561 3436	3.587 525 6979
5	1.246 181 9377	5.470 709 7256	0.802 451 0465	4.389 976 7444
6	1.302 260 1248	6.716 891 6633	0.767 895 7383	5.157 872 4827
7	1.360 861 8305	8.019 151 7881	0.734 828 4577	5.892 700 9404
8	1.422 100 6128	9.380 013 6186	0.703 185 1270	6.595 886 0674
9	1.486 095 1404	10.802 114 2314	0.672 904 4277	7.268 790 4951
10	1.552 969 4217	12.288 209 3718	0.643 927 6820	7.912 718 1771
11	1.622 853 0457	13.841 178 7936	0.616 198 7388	8.528 916 9159
12	1.695 881 4328	15.464 031 8393	0.589 663 8649	9.118 580 7808
13	1.772 196 0972	17.159 913 2721	0.564 271 6410	9.682 852 4218
14	1.851 944 9216	18.932 109 3693	0.539 972 8622	10.222 825 2840
15	1.935 282 4431	20.784 054 2909	0.516 720 4423	10.739 545 7263
16	2.022 370 1530	22.719 336 7340	0.494 469 3228	11.234 015 0491
17	2.113 376 8099	24.741 706 8870	0.473 176 3854	11.707 191 4346
18	2.208 478 7664	26.855 083 6970	0.452 800 3688	12.159 991 8034
19	2.307 860 3108	29.063 562 4633	0.433 301 7884	12.593 293 5918
20	2.411 714 0248	31.371 422 7742	0.414 642 8597	13.007 936 4515
21	2.520 241 1560	33.783 136 7990	0.396 787 4255	13.404 723 8770
22	2.633 652 0080	36.303 377 9550	0.379 700 8857	13.784 424 7627
23	2.752 166 3483	38.937 029 9629	0.363 350 1298	14.147 774 8925
24	2.876 013 8340	41.689 196 3113	0.347 703 4735	14.495 478 3660
25	3.005 434 4565	44.565 210 1453	0.332 730 5967	14.828 208 9627
26	3.140 679 0071	47.570 644 6018	0.318 402 4849	15.146 611 4476
27	3.282 009 5624	50.711 323 6089	0.304 691 3731	15.451 302 8206
28	3.429 699 9927	53.993 333 1713	0.291 570 6919	15.742 873 5126
29	3.584 036 4924	57.423 033 1640	0.279 015 0162	16.021 888 5288
30	3.745 318 1345	61.007 069 6564	0.267 000 0155	16.288 888 5443
31	3.913 857 4506	64.752 387 7909	0.255 502 4072	16.544 390 9515
32	4.089 981 0359	68.666 245 2415	0.244 499 9112	16.788 890 8627
33	4.274 030 1825	72.756 226 2774	0.233 971 2069	17.022 862 0695
34	4.466 361 5407	77.030 256 4599	0.223 895 8917	17.246 757 9613
35	4.667 347 8100	81.496 618 0005	0.214 254 4419	17.461 012 4031
36	4.877 378 4615	86.163 965 8106	0.205 028 1740	17.666 040 5772
37	5.096 860 4922	91.041 344 2720	0.196 199 2096	17.862 239 7868
38	5.326 219 2144	96.138 204 7643	0.187 750 4398	18.049 990 2266
39	5.565 899 0790	101.464 423 9787	0.179 665 4926	18.229 655 7192
40	5.816 364 5376	107.030 323 0577	0.171 928 7011	18.401 584 4203
41	6.078 100 9418	112.846 687 5953	0.164 525 0728	18.566 109 4931
42	6.351 615 4842	118.924 788 5371	0.157 440 2611	18.723 549 7542
43	6.637 438 1810	125.276 404 0213	0.150 660 5369	18.874 210 2911
44	6.936 122 8991	131.913 842 2022	0.144 172 7626	19.018 383 0536
45	7.248 248 4296	138.849 965 1013	0.137 964 3661	19.156 347 4198
46	7.574 419 6089	146.098 213 5309	0.132 023 3169	19.288 370 7366
47	7.915 268 4913	153.672 633 1398	0.126 338 1023	19.414 708 8389
48	8.271 455 5734	161.587 901 6311	0.120 897 7055	19.535 606 5444
49	8.643 671 0742	169.859 357 2045	0.115 691 5842	19.651 298 1286
50	9.032 636 2725	178.503 028 2787	0.110 709 6500	19.762 007 7785
51	9.439 104 9048	187.535 664 5512	0.105 942 2488	19.867 950 0273
52	9.863 864 6255	196.974 769 4560	0.101 380 1424	19.969 330 1697
53	10.307 738 5337	206.838 634 0815	0.097 014 4903	20.066 344 6600
54	10.771 586 7677	217.146 372 6152	0.092 836 8328	20.159 181 4928
55	11.256 308 1722	227.917 959 3829	0.088 839 0745	20.248 020 5673
56	11.762 842 0400	239.174 267 5551	0.085 013 4684	20.333 034 0357
57	12.292 169 9318	250.937 109 5951	0.081 352 6013	20.414 386 6370
58	12.845 317 5787	263.229 279 5269	0.077 849 3793	20.492 236 0163
59	13.423 356 8698	276.074 597 1056	0.074 497 0137	20.566 733 0299
60	14.027 407 9289	289.497 953 9753	0.071 289 0083	20.638 022 0382

Table 2 Compound Amounts and Values for Annuity Quantities: Rate 5%, 0.05 per period

Period	Compound Amount	Amount of Annuity	Present Value	Present Value of Future $1 Payments
1	1.050 000 0000	1.000 000 0000	0.952 380 9524	0.952 380 9524
2	1.102 500 0000	2.050 000 0000	0.907 029 4785	1.859 410 4308
3	1.157 625 0000	3.152 500 0000	0.863 837 5985	2.723 248 0294
4	1.215 506 2500	4.310 125 0000	0.822 702 4748	3.545 950 5042
5	1.276 281 5625	5.525 631 2500	0.783 526 1665	4.329 476 6706
6	1.340 095 6406	6.801 912 8125	0.746 215 3966	5.075 692 0673
7	1.407 100 4227	8.142 008 4531	0.710 681 3301	5.786 373 3974
8	1.477 455 4438	9.549 108 8758	0.676 839 3620	6.463 212 7594
9	1.551 328 2160	11.026 564 3196	0.644 608 9162	7.107 821 6756
10	1.628 894 6268	12.577 892 5355	0.613 913 2535	7.721 734 9292
11	1.710 339 3581	14.206 787 1623	0.584 679 2891	8.306 414 2183
12	1.795 856 3260	15.917 126 5204	0.556 837 4182	8.863 251 6364
13	1.885 649 1423	17.712 982 8465	0.530 321 3506	9.393 572 9871
14	1.979 931 5994	19.598 631 9888	0.505 067 9530	9.898 640 9401
15	2.078 928 1794	21.578 563 5882	0.481 017 0981	10.379 658 0382
16	2.182 874 5884	23.657 491 7676	0.458 111 5220	10.837 769 5602
17	2.292 018 3178	25.840 366 3560	0.436 296 6876	11.274 066 2478
18	2.406 619 2337	28.132 384 6738	0.415 520 6549	11.689 586 9027
19	2.526 950 1954	30.539 003 9075	0.395 733 9570	12.085 320 8597
20	2.653 297 7051	33.065 954 1029	0.376 889 4829	12.462 210 3425
21	2.785 962 5904	35.719 251 8080	0.358 942 3646	12.821 152 7072
22	2.925 260 7199	38.505 214 3984	0.341 849 8711	13.163 002 5783
23	3.071 523 7559	41.430 475 1184	0.325 571 3058	13.488 573 8841
24	3.225 099 9437	44.501 998 8743	0.310 067 9103	13.798 641 7943
25	3.386 354 9409	47.727 098 8180	0.295 302 7717	14.093 944 5660
26	3.555 672 6879	51.113 453 7589	0.281 240 7350	14.375 185 3010
27	3.733 456 3223	54.669 126 4468	0.267 848 3190	14.643 033 6200
28	3.920 129 1385	58.402 582 7692	0.255 093 6371	14.898 127 2571
29	4.116 135 5954	62.322 711 9076	0.242 946 3211	15.141 073 5782
30	4.321 942 3752	66.438 847 5030	0.231 377 4487	15.372 451 0269
31	4.538 039 4939	70.760 789 8782	0.220 359 4749	15.592 810 5018
32	4.764 941 4686	75.298 829 3721	0.209 866 1666	15.802 676 6684
33	5.003 188 5420	80.063 770 8407	0.199 872 5396	16.002 549 2080
34	5.253 347 9691	85.066 959 3827	0.190 354 7996	16.192 904 0076
35	5.516 015 3676	90.320 307 3518	0.181 290 2854	16.374 194 2929
36	5.791 816 1360	95.836 322 7194	0.172 657 4146	16.546 851 7076
37	6.081 406 9428	101.628 138 8554	0.164 435 6330	16.711 287 3405
38	6.385 477 2899	107.709 545 7982	0.156 605 3647	16.867 892 7053
39	6.704 751 1544	114.095 023 0881	0.149 147 9664	17.017 040 6717
40	7.039 988 7121	120.799 774 2425	0.142 045 6823	17.159 086 3540
41	7.391 988 1477	127.839 762 9546	0.135 281 6022	17.294 367 9562
42	7.761 587 5551	135.231 751 1023	0.128 839 6211	17.423 207 5773
43	8.149 666 9329	142.993 338 6575	0.122 704 4011	17.545 911 9784
44	8.557 150 2795	151.143 005 5903	0.116 861 3344	17.662 773 3128
45	8.985 007 7935	159.700 155 8699	0.111 296 5089	17.774 069 8217
46	9.434 258 1832	168.685 163 6633	0.105 996 6752	17.880 066 4968
47	9.905 971 0923	178.119 421 8465	0.100 949 2144	17.981 015 7113
48	10.401 269 6469	188.025 392 9388	0.096 142 1090	18.077 157 8203
49	10.921 333 1293	198.426 662 5858	0.091 563 9133	18.168 721 7336
50	11.467 399 7858	209.347 995 7151	0.087 203 7270	18.255 925 4606
51	12.040 769 7750	220.815 395 5008	0.083 051 1685	18.338 976 6291
52	12.642 808 2638	232.856 165 2759	0.079 096 3510	18.418 072 9801
53	13.274 948 6770	245.498 973 5397	0.075 329 8581	18.493 402 8382
54	13.938 696 1108	258.773 922 2166	0.071 742 7220	18.565 145 5602
55	14.635 630 9164	272.712 618 3275	0.068 326 4019	18.633 471 9621
56	15.367 412 4622	287.348 249 2439	0.065 072 7637	18.698 544 7258
57	16.135 783 0853	302.715 661 7060	0.061 974 0607	18.760 518 7865
58	16.942 572 2396	318.851 444 7913	0.059 022 9149	18.819 541 7014
59	17.789 700 8515	335.794 017 0309	0.056 212 2999	18.875 754 0013
60	18.679 185 8941	353.583 717 8825	0.053 535 5237	18.929 289 5251

Table 2 Compound Amounts and Values for Annuity Quantities: Rate 6%, 0.06 per period

Period	Compound Amount	Amount of Annuity	Present Value	Present Value of Future $1 Payments
1	1.060 000 0000	1.000 000 0000	0.943 396 2264	0.943 396 2264
2	1.123 600 0000	2.060 000 0000	0.889 996 4400	1.833 392 6664
3	1.191 016 0000	3.183 600 0000	0.839 619 2830	2.673 011 9495
4	1.262 476 9600	4.374 616 0000	0.792 093 6632	3.465 105 6127
5	1.338 225 5776	5.637 092 9600	0.747 258 1729	4.212 363 7856
6	1.418 519 1123	6.975 318 5376	0.704 960 5404	4.917 324 3260
7	1.503 630 2590	8.393 837 6499	0.665 057 1136	5.582 381 4396
8	1.593 848 0745	9.897 467 9088	0.627 412 3713	6.209 793 8110
9	1.689 478 9590	11.491 315 9834	0.591 898 4635	6.801 692 2745
10	1.790 847 6965	13.180 794 9424	0.558 394 7769	7.360 087 0514
11	1.898 298 5583	14.971 642 6389	0.526 787 5254	7.886 874 5768
12	2.012 196 4718	16.869 941 1973	0.496 969 3636	8.383 843 9404
13	2.132 928 2601	18.882 137 6691	0.468 839 0222	8.852 682 9626
14	2.260 903 9558	21.015 065 9292	0.442 300 9644	9.294 983 9270
15	2.396 558 1931	23.275 969 8850	0.417 265 0607	9.712 248 9877
16	2.540 351 6847	25.672 528 0731	0.393 646 2837	10.105 895 2715
17	2.692 772 7858	28.212 879 7628	0.371 364 4186	10.477 259 6901
18	2.854 339 1529	30.905 652 5485	0.350 343 7911	10.827 603 4812
19	3.025 599 5021	33.759 991 7015	0.330 513 0105	11.158 116 4917
20	3.207 135 4722	36.785 591 2035	0.311 804 7269	11.469 921 2186
21	3.399 563 6005	39.992 726 6758	0.294 155 4027	11.764 076 6213
22	3.603 537 4166	43.392 290 2763	0.277 505 0969	12.041 581 7182
23	3.819 749 6616	46.995 827 6929	0.261 797 2612	12.303 378 9794
24	4.048 934 6413	50.815 577 3545	0.246 978 5483	12.550 357 5278
25	4.291 870 7197	54.864 511 9957	0.232 998 6305	12.783 356 1583
26	4.549 382 9629	59.156 382 7155	0.219 810 0288	13.003 166 1870
27	4.822 345 9407	63.705 765 6784	0.207 367 9517	13.210 534 1387
28	5.111 686 6971	68.528 111 6191	0.195 630 1431	13.406 164 2818
29	5.418 387 8990	73.639 798 3162	0.184 556 7388	13.590 721 0206
30	5.743 491 1729	79.058 186 2152	0.174 110 1309	13.764 831 1515
31	6.088 100 6433	84.801 677 3881	0.164 254 8405	13.929 085 9920
32	6.453 386 6819	90.889 778 0314	0.154 957 3967	14.084 043 3887
33	6.840 589 8828	97.343 164 7133	0.146 186 2233	14.230 229 6119
34	7.251 025 2758	104.183 754 5961	0.137 911 5314	14.368 141 1433
35	7.686 086 7923	111.434 779 8719	0.130 105 2183	14.498 246 3616
36	8.147 251 9999	119.120 866 6642	0.122 740 7720	14.620 987 1336
37	8.636 087 1198	127.268 118 6640	0.115 793 1811	14.736 780 3147
38	9.154 252 3470	135.904 205 7839	0.109 238 8501	14.846 019 1648
39	9.703 507 4879	145.058 458 1309	0.103 055 5190	14.949 074 6838
40	10.285 717 9371	154.761 965 6188	0.097 222 1877	15.046 296 8715
41	10.902 861 0134	165.047 683 5559	0.091 719 0450	15.138 015 9165
42	11.557 032 6742	175.950 544 5692	0.086 527 4010	15.224 543 3175
43	12.250 454 6346	187.507 577 2434	0.081 629 6235	15.306 172 9410
44	12.985 481 9127	199.758 031 8780	0.077 009 0788	15.383 182 0198
45	13.764 610 8274	212.743 513 7907	0.072 650 0743	15.455 832 0942
46	14.590 487 4771	226.508 124 6181	0.068 537 8060	15.524 369 9002
47	15.465 916 7257	241.098 612 0952	0.064 658 3075	15.589 028 2077
48	16.393 871 7293	256.564 528 8209	0.060 998 4033	15.650 026 6110
49	17.377 504 0330	272.958 400 5502	0.057 545 6635	15.707 572 2746
50	18.420 154 2750	290.335 904 5832	0.054 288 3618	15.761 860 6364
51	19.525 363 5315	308.756 058 8582	0.051 215 4357	15.813 076 0721
52	20.696 885 3434	328.281 422 3897	0.048 316 4488	15.861 392 5208
53	21.938 698 4640	348.978 307 7331	0.045 581 5554	15.906 974 0762
54	23.255 020 3718	370.917 006 1970	0.043 001 4674	15.949 975 5436
55	24.650 321 5941	394.172 026 5689	0.040 567 4221	15.990 542 9657
56	26.129 340 8898	418.822 348 1630	0.038 271 1529	16.028 814 1186
57	27.697 101 3432	444.951 689 0528	0.036 104 8612	16.064 918 9798
58	29.358 927 4238	472.648 790 3959	0.034 061 1898	16.098 980 1696
59	31.120 463 0692	502.007 717 8197	0.032 133 1979	16.131 113 3676
60	32.987 690 8533	533.128 180 8889	0.030 314 3377	16.161 427 7052

Table 2 Compound Amounts and Values for Annuity Quantities: Rate 7%, 0.07 per period

Period	Compound Amount	Amount of Annuity	Present Value	Present Value of Future $1 Payments
1	1.070 000 0000	1.000 000 0000	0.934 579 4393	0.934 579 4393
2	1.144 900 0000	2.070 000 0000	0.873 438 7283	1.808 018 1675
3	1.225 043 0000	3.214 900 0000	0.816 297 8769	2.624 316 0444
4	1.310 796 0100	4.439 943 0000	0.762 895 2120	3.387 211 2565
5	1.402 551 7307	5.750 739 0100	0.712 986 1795	4.100 197 4359
6	1.500 730 3518	7.153 290 7407	0.666 342 2238	4.766 539 6598
7	1.605 781 4765	8.654 021 0925	0.622 749 7419	5.389 289 4016
8	1.718 186 1798	10.259 802 5690	0.582 009 1046	5.971 298 5062
9	1.838 459 2124	11.977 988 7489	0.543 933 7426	6.515 232 2488
10	1.967 151 3573	13.816 447 9613	0.508 349 2921	7.023 581 5409
11	2.104 851 9523	15.783 599 3186	0.475 092 7964	7.498 674 3373
12	2.252 191 5890	17.888 451 2709	0.444 011 9592	7.942 686 2966
13	2.409 845 0002	20.140 642 8598	0.414 964 4479	8.357 650 7444
14	2.578 534 1502	22.550 487 8600	0.387 817 2410	8.745 467 9855
15	2.759 031 5407	25.129 022 0102	0.362 446 0196	9.107 914 0051
16	2.952 163 7486	27.888 053 5509	0.338 734 5978	9.446 648 6029
17	3.158 815 2110	30.840 217 2995	0.316 574 3905	9.763 222 9934
18	3.379 932 2757	33.999 032 5105	0.295 863 9163	10.059 086 9097
19	3.616 527 5350	37.378 964 7862	0.276 508 3330	10.335 595 2427
20	3.869 684 4625	40.995 492 3212	0.258 419 0028	10.594 014 2455
21	4.140 562 3749	44.865 176 7837	0.241 513 0867	10.835 527 3323
22	4.430 401 7411	49.005 739 1586	0.225 713 1652	11.061 240 4974
23	4.740 529 8630	53.436 140 8997	0.210 946 8833	11.272 187 3808
24	5.072 366 9534	58.176 670 7627	0.197 146 6199	11.469 334 0007
25	5.427 432 6401	63.249 037 7160	0.184 249 1775	11.653 583 1783
26	5.807 352 9249	68.676 470 3562	0.172 195 4930	11.825 778 6713
27	6.213 867 6297	74.483 823 2811	0.160 930 3673	11.986 709 0386
28	6.648 838 3638	80.697 690 9108	0.150 402 2124	12.137 111 2510
29	7.114 257 0492	87.346 529 2745	0.140 562 8154	12.277 674 0664
30	7.612 255 0427	94.460 786 3237	0.131 367 1172	12.409 041 1835
31	8.145 112 8956	102.073 041 3664	0.122 773 0067	12.531 814 1902
32	8.715 270 7983	110.218 154 2621	0.114 741 1277	12.646 555 3179
33	9.325 339 7542	118.933 425 0604	0.107 234 6988	12.753 790 0168
34	9.978 113 5370	128.258 764 8146	0.100 219 3447	12.854 009 3615
35	10.676 581 4846	138.236 878 3516	0.093 662 9390	12.947 672 3004
36	11.423 942 1885	148.913 459 8363	0.087 535 4570	13.035 207 7574
37	12.223 618 1417	160.337 402 0248	0.081 808 8383	13.117 016 5957
38	13.079 271 4117	172.561 020 1665	0.076 456 8582	13.193 473 4539
39	13.994 820 4105	185.640 291 5782	0.071 455 0077	13.264 928 4616
40	14.974 457 8392	199.635 111 9887	0.066 780 3810	13.331 708 8426
41	16.022 669 8880	214.609 569 8279	0.062 411 5710	13.394 120 4137
42	17.144 256 7801	230.632 239 7158	0.058 328 5711	13.452 448 9847
43	18.344 354 7547	247.776 496 4959	0.054 512 6832	13.506 961 6680
44	19.628 459 5875	266.120 851 2507	0.050 946 4329	13.557 908 1009
45	21.002 451 7587	285.749 310 8382	0.047 613 4887	13.605 521 5896
46	22.472 623 3818	306.751 762 5969	0.044 498 5876	13.650 020 1772
47	24.045 707 0185	329.224 385 9787	0.041 587 4650	13.691 607 6423
48	25.728 906 5098	353.270 092 9972	0.038 866 7898	13.730 474 4320
49	27.529 929 9655	378.998 999 5070	0.036 324 1026	13.766 798 5346
50	29.457 025 0631	406.528 929 4724	0.033 947 7594	13.800 746 2940
51	31.519 016 8175	435.985 954 5355	0.031 726 8780	13.832 473 1720
52	33.725 347 9947	467.504 971 3530	0.029 651 2878	13.862 124 4598
53	36.086 122 3543	501.230 319 3477	0.027 711 4839	13.889 835 9437
54	38.612 150 9191	537.316 441 7021	0.025 898 5831	13.915 734 5269
55	41.315 001 4835	575.928 592 6212	0.024 204 2833	13.939 938 8102
56	44.207 051 5873	617.243 594 1047	0.022 620 8255	13.962 559 6357
57	47.301 545 1984	661.450 645 6920	0.021 140 9584	13.983 700 5941
58	50.612 653 3623	708.752 190 8905	0.019 757 9051	14.003 458 4991
59	54.155 539 0977	759.364 844 2528	0.018 465 3318	14.021 923 8310
60	57.946 426 8345	813.520 383 3505	0.017 257 3195	14.039 181 1504

Table 2 Compound Amounts and Values for Annuity Quantities: Rate 8%, 0.08 per period

Period	Compound Amount	Amount of Annuity	Present Value	Present Value of Future $1 Payments
1	1.080 000 0000	1.000 000 0000	0.925 925 9259	0.925 925 9259
2	1.166 400 0000	2.080 000 0000	0.857 338 8203	1.783 264 7462
3	1.259 712 0000	3.246 400 0000	0.793 832 2410	2.577 096 9872
4	1.360 488 9600	4.506 112 0000	0.735 029 8528	3.312 126 8400
5	1.469 328 0768	5.866 600 9600	0.680 583 1970	3.992 710 0371
6	1.586 874 3229	7.335 929 0368	0.630 169 6269	4.622 879 6640
7	1.713 824 2688	8.922 803 3597	0.583 490 3953	5.206 370 0592
8	1.850 930 2103	10.636 627 6285	0.540 268 8845	5.746 638 9237
9	1.999 004 6271	12.487 557 8388	0.500 248 9671	6.246 887 9109
10	2.158 924 9973	14.486 562 4659	0.463 193 4881	6.710 081 3989
11	2.331 638 9971	16.645 487 4632	0.428 882 8593	7.138 964 2583
12	2.518 170 1168	18.977 126 4602	0.397 113 7586	7.536 078 0169
13	2.719 623 7262	21.495 296 5771	0.367 697 9247	7.903 775 9416
14	2.937 193 6243	24.214 920 3032	0.340 461 0414	8.244 236 9830
15	3.172 169 1142	27.152 113 9275	0.315 241 7050	8.559 478 6879
16	3.425 942 6433	30.324 283 0417	0.291 890 4676	8.851 369 1555
17	3.700 018 0548	33.750 225 6850	0.270 268 9514	9.121 638 1069
18	3.996 019 4992	37.450 243 7398	0.250 249 0291	9.371 887 1360
19	4.315 701 0591	41.446 263 2390	0.231 712 0640	9.603 599 2000
20	4.660 957 1438	45.761 964 2981	0.214 548 2074	9.818 147 4074
21	5.033 833 7154	50.422 921 4420	0.198 655 7476	10.016 803 1550
22	5.436 540 4126	55.456 755 1573	0.183 940 5070	10.200 743 6621
23	5.871 463 6456	60.893 295 5699	0.170 315 2843	10.371 058 9464
24	6.341 180 7372	66.764 759 2155	0.157 699 3373	10.528 758 2837
25	6.848 475 1962	73.105 939 9527	0.146 017 9049	10.674 776 1886
26	7.396 353 2119	79.954 415 1490	0.135 201 7638	10.809 977 9524
27	7.988 061 4689	87.350 768 3609	0.125 186 8183	10.935 164 7707
28	8.627 106 3864	95.338 829 8297	0.115 913 7207	11.051 078 4914
29	9.317 274 8973	103.965 936 2161	0.107 327 5192	11.158 406 0106
30	10.062 656 8891	113.283 211 1134	0.099 377 3325	11.257 783 3431
31	10.867 669 4402	123.345 868 0025	0.092 016 0487	11.349 799 3918
32	11.737 082 9954	134.213 537 4427	0.085 200 0451	11.434 999 4368
33	12.676 049 6350	145.950 620 4381	0.078 888 9306	11.513 888 3674
34	13.690 133 6059	158.626 670 0732	0.073 045 3061	11.586 933 6736
35	14.785 344 2943	172.316 803 6790	0.067 634 5427	11.654 568 2163
36	15.968 171 8379	187.102 147 9733	0.062 624 5766	11.717 192 7928
37	17.245 625 5849	203.070 319 8112	0.057 985 7190	11.775 178 5119
38	18.625 275 6317	220.315 945 3961	0.053 690 4806	11.828 868 9925
39	20.115 297 6822	238.941 221 0278	0.049 713 4080	11.878 582 4004
40	21.724 521 4968	259.056 518 7100	0.046 030 9333	11.924 613 3337
41	23.462 483 2165	280.781 040 2068	0.042 621 2345	11.967 234 5683
42	25.339 481 8739	304.243 523 4233	0.039 464 1061	12.006 698 6743
43	27.366 640 4238	329.583 005 2972	0.036 540 8389	12.043 239 5133
44	29.555 971 6577	356.949 645 7210	0.033 834 1101	12.077 073 6234
45	31.920 449 3903	386.505 617 3787	0.031 327 8797	12.108 401 5032
46	34.474 085 3415	418.426 066 7690	0.029 007 2961	12.137 408 7992
47	37.232 012 1688	452.900 152 1105	0.026 858 6075	12.164 267 4067
48	40.210 573 1423	490.132 164 2793	0.024 869 0810	12.189 136 4877
49	43.427 418 9937	530.342 737 4217	0.023 026 9268	12.212 163 4145
50	46.901 612 5132	573.770 156 4154	0.021 321 2286	12.233 484 6431
51	50.653 741 5143	620.671 768 9286	0.019 741 8783	12.253 226 5214
52	54.706 040 8354	671.325 510 4429	0.018 279 5169	12.271 506 0383
53	59.082 524 1023	726.031 551 2783	0.016 925 4786	12.288 431 5169
54	63.809 126 0304	785.114 075 3806	0.015 671 7395	12.304 103 2564
55	68.913 856 1129	848.923 201 4111	0.014 510 8699	12.318 614 1263
56	74.426 964 6019	917.837 057 5239	0.013 435 9906	12.332 050 1170
57	80.381 121 7701	992.264 022 1259	0.012 440 7321	12.344 490 8490
58	86.811 611 5117	1072.645 143 8959	0.011 519 1964	12.356 010 0454
59	93.756 540 4326	1159.456 755 4076	0.010 665 9226	12.366 675 9680
60	101.257 063 6672	1253.213 295 8402	0.009 875 8542	12.376 551 8222

Table 2 Compound Amounts and Values for Annuity Quantities: Rate 9%, 0.09 per period

Period	Compound Amount	Amount of Annuity	Present Value	Present Value of Future $1 Payments
1	1.090 000 0000	1.000 000 0000	0.917 431 1927	0.917 431 1927
2	1.188 100 0000	2.090 000 0000	0.841 679 9933	1.759 111 1859
3	1.295 029 0000	3.278 100 0000	0.772 183 4801	2.531 294 6660
4	1.411 581 6100	4.573 129 0000	0.708 425 2111	3.239 719 8771
5	1.538 623 9549	5.984 710 6100	0.649 931 3863	3.889 651 2634
6	1.677 100 1108	7.523 334 5649	0.596 267 3269	4.485 918 5902
7	1.828 039 1208	9.200 434 6757	0.547 034 2448	5.032 952 8351
8	1.992 562 6417	11.028 473 7966	0.501 866 2797	5.534 819 1147
9	2.171 893 2794	13.021 036 4382	0.460 427 7795	5.995 246 8943
10	2.367 363 6746	15.192 929 7177	0.422 410 8069	6.417 657 7012
11	2.580 426 4053	17.560 293 3923	0.387 532 8504	6.805 190 5515
12	2.812 664 7818	20.140 719 7976	0.355 534 7251	7.160 725 2766
13	3.065 804 6121	22.953 384 5794	0.326 178 6469	7.486 903 9235
14	3.341 727 0272	26.019 189 1915	0.299 246 4650	7.786 150 3885
15	3.642 482 4597	29.360 916 2188	0.274 538 0413	8.060 688 4299
16	3.970 305 8811	33.003 398 6784	0.251 869 7627	8.312 558 1925
17	4.327 633 4104	36.973 704 5595	0.231 073 1768	8.543 631 3693
18	4.717 120 4173	41.301 337 9699	0.211 993 7402	8.755 625 1094
19	5.141 661 2548	46.018 458 3871	0.194 489 6699	8.950 114 7793
20	5.604 410 7678	51.160 119 6420	0.178 430 8898	9.128 545 6691
21	6.108 807 7369	56.764 530 4098	0.163 698 0640	9.292 243 7331
22	6.658 600 4332	62.873 338 1466	0.150 181 7101	9.442 425 4432
23	7.257 874 4722	69.531 938 5798	0.137 781 3854	9.580 206 8286
24	7.911 083 1747	76.789 813 0520	0.126 404 9408	9.706 611 7694
25	8.623 080 6604	84.700 896 2267	0.115 967 8356	9.822 579 6049
26	9.399 157 9198	93.323 976 8871	0.106 392 5097	9.928 972 1146
27	10.245 082 1326	102.723 134 8069	0.097 607 8070	10.026 579 9217
28	11.167 139 5246	112.968 216 9396	0.089 548 4468	10.116 128 3685
29	12.172 182 0818	124.135 356 4641	0.082 154 5384	10.198 282 9069
30	13.267 678 4691	136.307 538 5459	0.075 371 1361	10.273 654 0430
31	14.461 769 5314	149.575 217 0150	0.069 147 8313	10.342 801 8743
32	15.763 328 7892	164.036 986 5464	0.063 438 3773	10.406 240 2517
33	17.182 028 3802	179.800 315 3356	0.058 200 3462	10.464 440 5979
34	18.728 410 9344	196.982 343 7158	0.053 394 8130	10.517 835 4109
35	20.413 967 9185	215.710 754 6502	0.048 986 0670	10.566 821 4779
36	22.251 225 0312	236.124 722 5687	0.044 941 3459	10.611 762 8237
37	24.253 835 2840	258.375 947 5999	0.041 230 5925	10.652 993 4163
38	26.436 680 4595	282.629 782 8839	0.037 826 2317	10.690 819 6480
39	28.815 981 7009	309.066 463 3434	0.034 702 9648	10.725 522 6128
40	31.409 420 0540	337.882 445 0443	0.031 837 5824	10.757 360 1952
41	34.236 267 8588	369.291 865 0983	0.029 208 7912	10.787 568 9865
42	37.317 531 9661	403.528 132 9572	0.026 797 0562	10.813 366 0426
43	40.676 109 8431	440.845 664 9233	0.024 584 4552	10.837 950 4978
44	44.336 959 7290	481.521 774 7664	0.022 554 5461	10.860 505 0439
45	48.327 286 1046	525.858 734 4954	0.020 692 2441	10.881 197 2880
46	52.676 741 8540	574.186 020 6000	0.018 983 7102	10.900 180 9981
47	57.417 648 6209	626.862 762 4540	0.017 416 2479	10.917 597 2460
48	62.585 236 9967	684.280 411 0748	0.015 978 2090	10.933 575 4550
49	68.217 908 3264	746.865 648 0716	0.014 658 9074	10.948 234 3624
50	74.357 520 0758	815.083 556 3980	0.013 448 5389	10.961 682 9013
51	81.049 696 8826	889.441 076 4738	0.012 338 1091	10.974 021 0104
52	88.344 169 6021	970.490 773 3565	0.011 319 3661	10.985 340 3765
53	96.295 144 8663	1058.834 942 9585	0.010 384 7396	10.995 725 1160
54	104.961 707 9042	1155.130 087 8248	0.009 527 2840	11.005 252 4000
55	114.408 261 6156	1260.091 795 7290	0.008 740 6275	11.013 993 0276
56	124.705 005 1610	1374.500 057 3447	0.008 018 9243	11.022 011 9519
57	135.928 455 6255	1499.205 062 5057	0.007 356 8113	11.029 368 7632
58	148.162 016 6318	1635.133 518 1312	0.006 749 3682	11.036 118 1314
59	161.496 598 1287	1783.295 534 7630	0.006 192 0809	11.042 310 2123
60	176.031 291 9602	1944.792 132 8917	0.005 680 8082	11.047 991 0204

Table 3 Area Under Standard Normal Curve

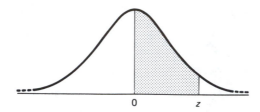

z	0.00	0.01	0.02	0.03	0.04	0.05	0.06	0.07	0.08	0.09
					Second Decimal Place in z					
0.0	0.0000	0.0040	0.0080	0.0120	0.0160	0.0199	0.0239	0.0279	0.0319	0.0359
0.1	0.0398	0.0438	0.0478	0.0517	0.0557	0.0596	0.0636	0.0675	0.0714	0.0753
0.2	0.0793	0.0832	0.0871	0.0910	0.0948	0.0987	0.1026	0.1064	0.1103	0.1141
0.3	0.1179	0.1217	0.1255	0.1293	0.1331	0.1368	0.1406	0.1443	0.1480	0.1517
0.4	0.1554	0.1591	0.1628	0.1664	0.1700	0.1736	0.1772	0.1808	0.1844	0.1879
0.5	0.1915	0.1950	0.1985	0.2019	0.2054	0.2088	0.2123	0.2157	0.2190	0.2224
0.6	0.2257	0.2291	0.2324	0.2357	0.2389	0.2422	0.2454	0.2486	0.2517	0.2549
0.7	0.2580	0.2611	0.2642	0.2673	0.2704	0.2734	0.2764	0.2794	0.2823	0.2852
0.8	0.2881	0.2910	0.2939	0.2967	0.2995	0.3023	0.3051	0.3078	0.3106	0.3133
0.9	0.3159	0.3186	0.3212	0.3238	0.3264	0.3289	0.3315	0.3340	0.3365	0.3389
1.0	0.3413	0.3438	0.3461	0.3485	0.3508	0.3531	0.3554	0.3577	0.3599	0.3621
1.1	0.3643	0.3665	0.3686	0.3708	0.3729	0.3749	0.3770	0.3790	0.3810	0.3830
1.2	0.3849	0.3869	0.3888	0.3907	0.3925	0.3944	0.3962	0.3980	0.3997	0.4015
1.3	0.4032	0.4049	0.4066	0.4082	0.4099	0.4115	0.4131	0.4147	0.4162	0.4177
1.4	0.4192	0.4207	0.4222	0.4236	0.4251	0.4265	0.4279	0.4292	0.4306	0.4319
1.5	0.4332	0.4345	0.4357	0.4370	0.4382	0.4394	0.4406	0.4418	0.4429	0.4441
1.6	0.4452	0.4463	0.4474	0.4484	0.4495	0.4505	0.4515	0.4525	0.4535	0.4545
1.7	0.4554	0.4564	0.4573	0.4582	0.4591	0.4599	0.4608	0.4616	0.4625	0.4633
1.8	0.4641	0.4649	0.4656	0.4664	0.4671	0.4678	0.4686	0.4693	0.4699	0.4706
1.9	0.4713	0.4719	0.4726	0.4732	0.4738	0.4744	0.4750	0.4756	0.4761	0.4767
2.0	0.4772	0.4778	0.4783	0.4788	0.4793	0.4798	0.4803	0.4808	0.4812	0.4817
2.1	0.4821	0.4826	0.4830	0.4834	0.4838	0.4842	0.4846	0.4850	0.4854	0.4857
2.2	0.4861	0.4864	0.4868	0.4871	0.4875	0.4878	0.4881	0.4884	0.4887	0.4890
2.3	0.4893	0.4896	0.4898	0.4901	0.4904	0.4906	0.4909	0.4911	0.4913	0.4916
2.4	0.4918	0.4920	0.4922	0.4925	0.4927	0.4929	0.4931	0.4932	0.4934	0.4936
2.5	0.4938	0.4940	0.4941	0.4943	0.4945	0.4946	0.4948	0.4949	0.4951	0.4952
2.6	0.4953	0.4955	0.4956	0.4957	0.4959	0.4960	0.4961	0.4962	0.4963	0.4964
2.7	0.4965	0.4966	0.4967	0.4968	0.4969	0.4970	0.4971	0.4972	0.4973	0.4974
2.8	0.4974	0.4975	0.4976	0.4977	0.4977	0.4978	0.4979	0.4979	0.4980	0.4981
2.9	0.4981	0.4982	0.4982	0.4983	0.4984	0.4984	0.4985	0.4985	0.4986	0.4986
3.0	0.4987	0.4987	0.4987	0.4988	0.4988	0.4989	0.4989	0.4989	0.4990	0.4990
3.1	0.4990	0.4991	0.4991	0.4991	0.4992	0.4992	0.4992	0.4992	0.4993	0.4993
3.2	0.4993	0.4993	0.4994	0.4994	0.4994	0.4994	0.4994	0.4995	0.4995	0.4995
3.3	0.4995	0.4995	0.4995	0.4996	0.4996	0.4996	0.4996	0.4996	0.4996	0.4997
3.4	0.4997	0.4997	0.4997	0.4997	0.4997	0.4997	0.4997	0.4997	0.4997	0.4998
3.5	0.4998									
4.0	0.49997									
4.5	0.499997									
5.0	0.4999997									

INDEX

Accelerated cost recovery system, 241
  modified, 241
Addition, 7–9
Add-on interest, 204
Amortization, 204, 230
  balance, 214, 446
Amount
  compound, 142
  due, simple interest, 61
Analysis
  horizontal, 111
  input-output, 482
  vertical, 111
Annuity, 170–89
  deferred, 186–87, 189, 198
  due, 184–86, 188, 198
  forborne, 187–88, 189, 198
  ordinary, 171, 198
  present value, 178, 198
  sinking funds, 219–21, 230
Arithmetic mean, 323, 358
Arithmetic sequence, 424, 450
Array, 310, 357
Assessed value, 104
Assets, 108
Assignment problem, 528–32
Automobile insurance, 284–88
Average inventory, 262

Balance sheet, 108
Bank discount, 69–73
  maturity value, 69
  proceeds, 69, 73
Banker's rule, 65
Bar graph, 349, 350
Base, 34, 48, 60, 69, 128

Bodily injury liability insurance, 284
Bonds, 223–28, 230, 235
  current yield, 224
  debenture, 224
  discount, 224
  mortgage, 224
  municipal, 224
  par value, 224
  premium, 224
Book value, 240, 269
Broken line graph, 383, 415
Brokers, commission, 97
Business ratios, 108

Cancellation of insurance, 281
Capitalized cost, 266, 270–71
Cash discounts 80, 128
Cash value (life insurance), 296
Central tendency, 322–29
  arithmetic mean, 323
  mean for grouped data, 324
  median, 325
  mode, 325
Chain discount, 78
Circle graph, 351
Classmark, 312, 357
Coefficient of correlation, 409, 415
Cofactor, 466
Coinsurance clause, 280
Column matrix, 458
Commission, 97, 128
  graduated, 97
  straight line, 97
Compound amount, 134, 165
Compound interest, 134–39
Comprehensive insurance, 287

Consumer Price Index, 159–61
Coordinate axes, 368
Cost, 86
    markup based on, 87
    net, 80
Cost recovery, 240, 245
Cross products, 27
Current yield, 224

Debenture bond, 224
Declining balance method, 243
Deferred annuity, 186–89
Depletion, 245
Depreciation, 240–54
    declining balance, 243, 270
    MACRS, 241, 269
    straight line, 242, 270
    sum of digits, 244, 270
Deviation
    average, 332
    mean, 330
    standard, 332–34, 358
Difference equation, 445, 451
Difference (subtraction), 9
Digits, 42, 244
Discount
    bank, 69
    bond, 224, 227
    cash, 80, 128
    chain, 78
    single equivalent, 78
    trade, 76, 128
Dispersion, measures of
    average or mean deviation, 330
    mean deviation for grouped data, 331
    range, 329
    standard deviation, 332
Distributive property, 14–17, 20
Dividend, 291
Double indemnity, 295
Dual problem, 517–19
Due date for cash discount, 80

Effective rate, 151, 165
    amortized, 205, 235
Endowment life insurance, 291
Equal matrices, 456
Equations, 18–23
    difference 446–47, 451
    percent, 48
    ratio and proportion, 25
    rules for solving, 20–21
    of value, 154–55

Exact interest, 63
Exact time, 63
Expenses, operating, 86
Exponents, 38–39
Extremes, 26

Face value of bond, 224
Factor, 10, 14, 16, 17
FICA tax, 99, 128
Fire insurance, 278–81
First in first out, 262
Forborne annuity, 187–89
    polygon, 314, 358
    relative, 313, 357
Frequency distribution
    polygon, 314–16
    table, 310–313, 357

Geometric sequence, 430, 450
Graduated commissions, 97
Graphs
    bar, 349, 350
    broken line, 383, 415
    inequalities, 496–98
    line, 348, 368–72
    pie, 351, 358
    step, 384–85, 415
    time series, 347, 359
Gross National Product, 163
Gross proceeds, 86

Histograms, 313, 358
Horizontal analysis, 111

Identity matrix, 457
Income statement, 108
Inequalities, 496
    linear, 496–98
Inflation rate, 162
Input-output analysis, 482
Insurance
    fire, 278–81
    life, 290–301
        endowment, 291, 304
        limited payment, 291, 304
        ordinary, 291, 304
        term, 290, 304
    motor vehicle, 284–88
        collision, 287, 304
        comprehensive, 287, 304
        liability, 284, 304
        no fault, 288

Interest
  add-on, 204
  compound, 134–39
  exact, 63
  ordinary, 63
  simple, 60–65
Interest adjusted net cost, 297
Interest computation method
  add-on, 204–205, 235
  amortized, 208–209, 235
  level, 206–207, 235
  Rule of 78, 206–207, 235
Inventory, 260–64
  average cost, 262, 270
  FIFO, 262, 270
  LIFO, 263, 270
  perpetual, 260
  turnover, 261, 270
Inverse, 9
  matrix, 464

Last in first out, 263
Less or decrease in percents, 52
Level interest computation, 206–207
Liabilities, 108
Liability insurance, 284
Life insurance, 290–301
Line
  best fit, 407–10
  horizontal, 415
  slant, 415
  vertical, 415
List price, 77

MACRS depreciation method, 241
Markdown, 92–94, 128
Markup, 86–92, 128
Matrix
  arithmetic, 456–62
  cofactor, 466
  column, 458
  equal, 456
  identity, 457
  inverse, 464
  minor, 465
  row, 458
  square, 457
  transpose, 458
  zero, 457
Maturity value, 61, 69, 73, 128
Maximum value, 502, 512
Mean, 323, 358

Means, 26
Median, 325, 358
Mills, 105
Minimum value, 502, 516
Minor, 465
Mode, 325, 358
More or increase in percent, 52
Mortgage bond, 224
Motor vehicle insurance, 284–88
Municipal bond, 224

Net price, 77
Net profit, 86
Net sales, 114
No-fault insurance, 288
Normal curve, 338–40, 358–59

Order of operations, 2–6
Ordinary annuity, 171
Ordinary interest, 63
Ordinary time, 64
Origin, 368
Outstanding balance
  add-on interest, 211
  amortized, 214–15
  level, 212
  Rule of 78, 212–13
Overhead, 254

Percent, 31–36, 48–56
  less, 52–54
  more, 52–54
Percentage, 34, 48, 60, 69, 128
Percentile ranking, 342
Pivot, 509, 512
Polygon, 314–16
Premium, 224, 227
Present value, 69, 128, 142, 165
  annuity, 178, 198
Principal, 60, 128
Proceeds, 73
  gross, 97
Profit
  gross, 86
  net, 86
Promissory note, 72
Property tax, 104–106
Proportion, 26, 124–26

Quadrants, 368

Range, 311, 329, 358

Rate, 35
    annual, 60, 69
    compound, 146–48
    effective, 151
    inflation, 162
    single equivalent, 78–79
Rate of change
    constant, 381
    zero, 381
Ratio, 25, 121
    test, 509, 512
Raw data, 310
Recursive sequence, 435
Roots, 39–40
Row matrix, 458
Rule of 78, 206–207

Sales
    gross, 114
    net, 114
    tax, 102–104
Selling price, 86–88, 128
Sequences, 424–35
    arithmetic, 424, 450
    geometric, 430, 450
    recursive, 435, 450
Series, 439–42
    arithmetic, 440
    geometric, 441
Sigma notation, 439, 451
Signed numbers, 7–13
Significant digits, 42–44
Simplex method, 508–12

Single equivalent discount rate, 78–79
Sinking funds, 219–21, 230, 235
Slope, 391–97, 415
Square matrix, 457
Standard deviation, 332–34, 358
Standard score, 341, 359
Step graph, 384–85
Straight line
    commission, 87
    depreciation, 242
Sum of digits
    depreciation, 244
    payment calculation, 212

Taxes
    FICA, 99, 128
    property, 104–106, 128
    sales, 102–104, 128
Term of discount, 73
Terms, 14, 16
Time series graph, 347, 359
Trade discount, 76, 128
Transportation problem, 522–28
Transpose of matrix, 458
Turnover, 261

U.S. Rule, 65

Value of annuity, 198
Vertical analysis, 111

Zero matrix, 457